LEARNING TO LIVE TOGETHER

LEARNING TO LIVE TOGETHER

*Preventing Hatred and Violence
in Child and Adolescent Development*

DAVID A. HAMBURG, M.D.

BEATRIX A. HAMBURG, M.D.

OXFORD
UNIVERSITY PRESS

2004

OXFORD
UNIVERSITY PRESS

Oxford   New York

Auckland   Bangkok   Buenos Aires   Cape Town   Chennai
Dar es Salaam   Delhi   Hong Kong   Istanbul   Karachi   Kolkata
Kuala Lumpur   Madrid   Melbourne   Mexico City   Mumbai   Nairobi
São Paulo   Shanghai   Taipei   Tokyo   Toronto

Copyright © 2004 by Oxford University Press, Inc.

Published by Oxford University Press, Inc.
198 Madison Avenue, New York, New York 10016

www.oup.com

Oxford is a registered trademark of Oxford University Press

Library of Congress Cataloging-in-Publication Data
Hamburg, David A., 1925–
Learning to live together : preventing hatred and violence in child and
adolescent development / David A. Hamburg, Beatrix A. Hamburg.
p. cm.
Includes bibliographical references.
ISBN 0-19-515779-6
1. Child development—United States.   2. Socialization—United States.
3. Multicultural education—United States.   4. Conflict management—United States.
I. Hamburg, Beatrix A.   II. Title.
LB1117.H36 2004
155.4'18—dc21   2003009005

1 3 5 7 9 8 6 4 2

Printed in the United States of America
on acid-free paper

To our son, Eric, and our daughter, Peggy,
who are the embodiment of our goals of empathy, kindness,
and fundamental human decency.

And to our grandchildren, Rachel, Evan, and David,
whose wonderful qualities deserve a more humane, democratic, and prosocial world
than the one they have inherited. We hope this book will provide
a socially useful step in that direction.

PREFACE

The centuries of history and millennia of prehistory indicate the profound and pervasive nature of human slaughter. From small societies to vast nations, from one era to another, we see humans' inhumanity and cruelty to each other. Indeed, the threat to human survival does not come from predators or dangerous forces of nature, but from other humans. We have reached a point where these very bad habits cannot be allowed to continue. The same intellectual and problem-solving capacities that have made human adaptation possible in the face of adverse circumstances over millions of years must be brought to focus on the prevention of mass violence: international wars, civil wars, and terrorist wars. Recent research and world experience show that the prevention of deadly conflict is both necessary and feasible. The time to begin to gain control of this great problem is now. We can develop the unused potential for prosocial behavior. Even if we start this year, it will take decades or generations to overcome the bloody legacy of our ancient and recent bad habits. It will take a massive, worldwide effort—involving leaders in many sectors of society—with a powerful stimulus from young people, today's students, as they mature and take on increasing responsibility.

One crucial and fundamental requirement is a change in our attitudes and behavior toward other groups. Throughout history, and still today, much of intergroup relations has a flat-earth orientation. For millennia, there was unquestioned belief that the earth was flat—a very plausible idea. But now we know that the earth is not flat. So, too, we have long assumed that groups other than our own (e.g., family, religious, ethnic, political, national, or whatever) are likely to be hostile, dangerous, and even evil. This had led to ubiquitous in-group and out-group invidious distinctions—a kind of "us versus them" stance for survival. In the modern world, this belief system will not work anymore. It will, in fact, lead to catastrophe on an ever-growing scale. Surely we had enough of this in Nazi Germany, Stalinist Russia, Rwanda, and many other places. The time has come to stop it. The most basic way of moving in a better direction—beyond the flat-earth perception of other groups—is through education. For new normative beliefs and behaviors, we must incorporate education at every level—from that of pre-school children to that of political leaders—and through many modalities: schools, universities, religious institutions, community organizations, the public health system, and all manner of media.

In this book, we trace the development of prosocial behavior through the years of growth and development into adulthood. Such formidable learning involves decent concern for others; readiness and ability to cooperate for mutual benefit; and helping, sharing, and respecting others while maintaining integrity as an individual, with basic self-respect and lifelong inclinations to expand horizons. In the contemporary, highly interdependent world, we must extend prosocial behavior on the widest scale possible in the world's population. For the individual, this means going from the nuclear family to the extended family, to the community, to the nation-state, to other related nation-states, to global contact that, in principle, involves all of humanity. This is an exceedingly difficult task for a species that evolved in small groups over millions of years, so that most people had no opportunity to experience the wide world until the twentieth century—and much of that experience occurred in the context of two world wars. Yet the abundant opportunities for bridging previously isolated groups and even for seeing the world in its entirety are fascinating and full of promise beyond prior imagination.

Research on prosocial behavior and ingenious, successful efforts to educate for conflict resolution have occurred mainly within single cultures and indeed can be considered in-group situations. Yet education for conflict resolution can relate to other groups and cultures, beyond the setting of any one study, even those previously strange and faraway. The deepest challenge is to find ways of enhancing prosocial behavior and learn mutual accommodation with previously adversarial groups. This is the essence of peace education. Somehow we must develop prosocial attitudes and behavior that confer decent consideration on others as well as ourselves—and grant the capacity to function cooperatively with other groups even when we have historically seen them as dangerous others. So, education for conflict resolution within one culture, especially one as large and diverse as the United States, can pave the way for peace education on a worldwide basis of constructive intergoup relations, no easy task and indeed an authentic novelty in all of human experience. Yet what task could be more vital in an unprecedented era of intimate global interdependence laden with amplifiers for hateful messages and lethal weapons?

Increasingly, scientific research must help us understand what makes us so dangerous and how we can moderate the risks. So we have tried hard, in this book, to draw together the strongest organizing principles, best evidence, and most useful practices for educating ourselves about this utterly crucial problem. In a sense, we are all children when it comes to this badly neglected subject. Thus, we address the book to children of all ages, in the hope that people in many parts of the world will be stimulated to reflect on these problems, to generate better ideas, and to do whatever they can to settle disputes without hatred and to move toward a world in which disputes do not rise to the level of killing.

We especially pay respectful tribute to children and youth, from infancy through adolescence, as they discover the world, step by step, from the crib to the whole round earth. The attitudes they develop, the knowledge and skills they acquire, the constructive problem solving they learn in relation to other people—all this is fascinating, valuable, and in the long run crucial to human survival. They can apply their growing talents, high ideals, energy, creativity, and fundamental decency to the shaping of a much better world.

We have deliberately selected a rather wide sample of promising lines of inquiry and innovation from several countries. We truly regret that we could not sample the entire world, but we have tried to convey the flavor of international interests and the universal significance of these efforts. In the final chapter, we draw together the main observations of the entire book. In the aggregate, there is a strong basis for hope.

There is no room for complacency here. Even in the established democracies, there is much need to strengthen education for conflict resolution, violence prevention, and peace with justice. The problem is harder in autocratic regimes in which powerful elites control education in rigid and often bigoted ways. The problem is hardest of all in dictatorships. Yet the worldwide spread of concern for human rights, fundamental freedoms, fairness in human relations, and democratic processes gives great opportunity—especially with the advent of new information technologies that offer the possibility of gradually opening up closed societies, giving more and more people a chance to speak for their own basic human needs and to make friendships across cultural boundaries. We consider these possibilities and suggest ways to promote them. We strongly urge governments and societies everywhere to give children the education and vision to pursue the ideals of our common humanity.

ACKNOWLEDGMENTS

First and foremost: Rosalind A. Rosenberg, our Research Associate in this enterprise, has earned special and distinctive praise for her intellectual curiosity, dedicated and utterly responsible efforts from start to finish, excellent judgment, creative eye, and collegial encouragement.

In previous books, we have gone into considerable detail to identify the ways in which individuals, organizations, and institutions have helped us throughout our lives, through affection, support, encouragement, stimulation, guidance, insight, corrective feedback, generosity of spirit, and precious friendship. We feel very lucky in these shaping and inspiring experiences, and we appreciate deeply their meaning and enduring significance.

We reject the implied attitude of some people, which is "What have you done for me lately?" We regard good prior experiences—starting with the template for decent human relationships and unceasing intellectual curiosity in the earliest years of life— as utterly crucial for whatever contributions we have been able to make. In this book, we will be more concise but not negligent in identifying some of the crucial influences that helped us along the way.

Let us start with our parents. Very luckily for us, they were utterly devoted, helpful, guiding, supporting, and encouraging to us throughout their lives. Year by year, they exemplified responsible, caring behavior for us and for others; the ethical centrality in religious belief; the value of hard work and lifelong learning, personal adaptability, earning a sense of worth, and the powerful merit of being kind to others. They saw—and experienced personally—the world's injustice and urged us to work to diminish injustice and to do what we could, however modestly, to make the world better. We have absorbed these basic precepts as best we could and have tried hard to convey them to our children and grandchildren—hence the dedication of this book to them. In a way, this is a credo book—it contains values and concepts that we deeply believe to be central to better human existence and actions we consider of great practical importance to make this happen. Over decades, we read, thought, collected materials, and worked on the problems considered in this book, and we seek now to draw together our extended experience in a way that may be useful to many others who are inclined to share our philosophy.

Beyond the centrality of our families, we owe much to many devoted and wise teachers—all too many are lost to us in the antiquity of our early experiences, like the science teacher and debate coach and student newspaper instructor, and all who did so much to get us launched.

In our college, university, and medical school years, we were inspired by our personal association with remarkable teachers and mentors such as Tracy Sonneborn, Fritz Redlich, Roy Grinker, Gerhart Piers, Helen McLean, Katie Dodd, and Eleanor Roosevelt.

In the domain of education in the context of child and adolescent development, we are deeply indebted to many teachers, friends, patients, and collaborators: Lawrence Aber, Mary Ainsworth, Dorothea Almond, Eliott Aronson, Jeannette Aspden, Paul Baltes, Albert Bandura, Patricia Barchas, Therese Benedek, John Bowlby, John Brademas, Lewis Branscomb, George Coelho, Donald Cohen, Elizabeth Cohen, Michael Cohen, Michael Cole, James Comer, Thomas Cook, William Dement, Sanford Dornbusch, Kenneth Dodge, Leon Eisenberg, Erik Erikson, Cleo Eulau, Walter Goldschmidt, Patricia Graham, Jeanne Brooks Gunn, Stuart Hauser, David Hornbeck, Klaus Jacobs, Richard Jessor, Judith Jones, Jerome Kagan, Sharon Lynn Kagan, Michele Kipke, Arthur Kleinman, Anneliese Korner, Ellen Lagemann, Gerald Lesser, Seymour Levine, Sol Levine, Iris Litt, Eleanor Maccoby, Shirley Malcom, Jules Masserman, Kathleen Merikangis, Elena Nightingale, Dolores Parron, Ann Petersen, Deborah Phillips, Jane Quinn, Julius Richmond, Judy Rosenblith, Allan Rosenfield, Joan Schine, David Shaw, Albert Siegel, Robert Slavin, Albert Solnit, Marshall Smith, Vivien Stewart, Ruby Takanishi, George Tarjian, Desmond Tutu, Robert White, Elie Wiesel, Torsten Wiesel, William Julius Wilson, and Edward Zigler.

In the field of conflict resolution, especially as it relates to child and adolescent development, emphasizing biological as well as psychosocial perspectives, we are deeply indebted to many, and again, can only name a few: Huda Akil, Gabriel Almond, Kenneth Arrow, Sidney Axelrad, Jack Barchas, Patrick Bateson, Frank Beach, Peter Bing, Robert Blackwill, Derek Bok, Sissela Bok, Esther Brimmer, William Bunney, Roland Ciaranello, Gordon Craig, Kenneth Davis, Morton Deutsch, Irven Devore, Larry Diamond, Anke Ehrhardt, Susan Eisenhower, Glen Elliott, Leslie Gelb, Alexander George, Avram Goldstein, Jane Goodall, Mikhail Gorbachev, Melanie Greenberg, Eric Hamburg, Margaret Hamburg, Harry Harlow, Robert Hinde, Richard Holbrooke, John Holdren, David Holloway, Irving Janis, Bruce Jentleson, Herant Katchadourian, Donald Kennedy, Jane Lancaster, Robert Lande, Noel Lateef, Joshua Lederberg, Marguerite Lederberg, Thomas Leney, Flora MacDonald, William Mason, Neal Miller, Martha Minow, Olara Otunnu, Ana Cutter Patel, Connie Peck, Deborah Prothrow-Stith, Anne Pusey, Condoleezza Rice, Frederick Robbins, Lee Ross, Barnett Rubin, Scott Sagan, Roald Sagdeev, Jonas Salk, Anita Sharma, Barbara Smuts, John D. Steinbruner, Fritz Stern, John Stremlau, Shirley Strum, Steven Suomi, Daniel Tosteson, Jessica Tuchman Matthews, Desmond Tutu, Amos Tversky, Sherwood Washburn, Stanley Watson, Elie Wiesel, Richard Wrangham, and William Zartman.

We have also, and increasingly, in the course of our careers, considered the contents of this book in the context of public policy and public service. For this, we are especially indebted to some remarkable leaders: Bruce Alberts, Duane Alexander, Graham Allison, Ragnar Ängeby, Kofi Annan, Richard Atkinson, Zoë Baird, Susan Berresford, Douglas Beureuter, Coit Blacker, Barry Bloom, Boutros Boutros-Ghali, John Brademas, Arne Olav Brundtland, Gro Harlem Brundtland, McGeorge Bundy, Joseph Califano, Albert Carnesale, Ashton Carter, Jimmy Carter, Rosalynn Carter, Lawton Chiles, Warren Christopher, Dick Clark, Hillary Rodham Clinton, William J. Clinton, Eugene Cota-Robles, Michael Doyle, Sidney Drell, Michael Dukakis, Virendra Dayal, Marian Wright Edelman, Peter Edelman, Jan Eliasson, Gareth Evans, John Evans, Mathea Falco, Harvey Fineberg, Ellen Futter, John Gardner, Alexander George, William Golden, M. R. C. Greenwood, Lee Hamilton, James Hunt, Jr., Steven Hyman, Nancy Johnson, Lewis Judd, Sahabzada Yaqub-Kahn, Karl Kaiser, Tapio Kanninen, Nancy Kassebaum, Thomas Kean, Edward Kennedy, Richard Lugar, Jane Holl Lute, Max Makagiansar, Michael Mandelbaum, Ray Marshall, Donald McHenry, Kathryn McLearn, Robert McNamara, Connie Morella, William Nash, Sam Nunn, Joseph Nye, Sadako Ogata, Herbert Okun, Hisashi Owada, David Owen, Connie Peck, Nancy Pelosi, William Perry, Kieran Prendergast, Eliot Richardson, Richard Riley, Dennis Ross, Robert Rubin, John Ruggie, Paul Sarbanes, Brent Scowcroft, Adele Simmons, Alan Simpson, Gillian Sorensen, Theodore Sorensen, Peter Tarnoff, Billie Tisch, Danilo Türk, Desmond Tutu, Brian Urquhart, Cyrus Vance, Melanne Verveer, James Watkins, Herman Wells, John Whitehead, and Shirley Williams.

From an administrative and intellectual standpoint, we are highly appreciative of the support and encouragement of the Carnegie Corporation, especially board chairs Warren Christopher, Helene Kaplan, Thomas Kean, Newton Minow, and John Taylor; President Vartan Gregorian; superb staff members Deana Arsenian, Barbara Finberg, Jean Grisi, Anthony Jackson, Susan King, Dorothy Knapp, Michael Levine, Geraldine Mannion, Fritz Moser, Pat Nicholas, David Robinson, Avery Russell, Robert Seman, Vivien Stewart, Astrid Tuminez, Jane Wales, and others—too many to list here.

At the William T. Grant Foundation, many were helpful, including Dale Blyth, Ronald Feldman, Martha Minow, Robert Patterson, Richard Price, Marcia Renwanz, Henry Riecken, Lonnie Sherrod, Rivington Winant. We have also appreciated our very special relationship with the William T. Grant scholars.

Likewise, in recent years, we have had extraordinary encouragement and stimulation in the setting of Weill Cornell Medical College, especially from Jack Barchas, chairman of the Department of Psychiatry, his staff members Annlouise Goodermuth and Mary Ferguson, and many faculty members. In addition, our immediate staff collaborators at Carnegie and Cornell over the years have been invaluable: Susan Smith, Jeanne D'Onofrio, Trisha Lester, Irene Germaine, Mary Lou Sandwick, Natasha Davids, and Ekua Annan. The singular contributions of our wonderful colleagues Rosalind A. Rosenberg and Stacy Dorgan made this book possible. On certain parts of the manuscript, we have had special help from Zoë Baird, Jack Barchas, Barbara Smuts, Vivien Stewart, and David Ekbladh.

At the Mount Sinai Medical Center, we received much help from Kenneth Davis, Dorothy Emam, Kurt Hirschhorn, Nathan Kase, Frederick Klingenstein, Jeff Newcorn, John Rowe, Arthur Rubenstein, Lawrence Smith, and Marvin Stein.

In our endnotes and in the bibliography, we refer explicitly to many highly significant contributors in research and innovation, and they clearly deserve our deep gratitude, even though many of them are not personally known to us. We wish that we knew them and trust that they will continue to contribute and that their influence will widen over the years ahead.

Our editor, Joan Bossert, has been simply superb from start to finish. On first hearing of the possibility of such a book, she gave us great encouragement and stimulation. Throughout the process of writing the book, her comments and suggestions were consistently thoughtful, constructive, and wise. We are deeply grateful.

Finally—and for us, most important—is the help we have been able to give each other. We met at Yale Medical School in 1948 and promptly formed a mutual aid and admiration society of the highest order. We soon found that we shared the basic values of common humanity exemplified in this book—and that we shared interests in education, health, human development, social justice, and peaceful living. Over the subsequent years, we shared an exceedingly wide variety of experiences in many fields and many places—including the suffering and recovery of our patients; the horrors of inhumanity and courage exemplified in World War II and the Holocaust; and the near-annihilation of humanity during the cold war and ultimately its resolution. All of this gave us and many others a powerful stimulus to find ways of doing better for humanity—through research, education, patient care, and public service.

For this opportunity of extraordinary collaboration for over 50 years, we are forever grateful and hope that what we have written here reflects the remarkable opportunities we have had. Above all, we hope that these observations and suggestions will stimulate the generations of our children and our grandchildren to continue to take seriously the great, perennial problems of human injustice, hatred, and violence—and to develop better ideas and actions to transcend the horrors of the human past. There is so much in the human spirit of attachment, affection, kindness, understanding, and fairness that someday this should truly be possible.

CONTENTS

LEARNING TO LIVE TOGETHER

PEACE

Everyone works for peace, but never gets it.
Because to acquire the gift of peace,
You must find the peace within yourself
And spread it to a friend, who will spread it to a friend
Until there is a web of peace that covers the world.
Then in every corner where there had been anger and hate
There will be love and peace.

Rachel Ann Hamburg Brown
Age 8
April 13, 2002

1

Growing Up in the Twenty-First Century

HOW WE BECAME THE WAY WE ARE

During the twentieth century, within only a moment of evolutionary time, human ingenuity has produced an unprecedented vast increase in the destructive power of the human species. It is now possible to inflict immense damage on almost all countries everywhere and pose the threat of annihilation of the entire world. Shortly, there will be no part of the earth so remote that a committed group cannot do immense damage to itself and others far away. The events of September 11, 2001, in New York, Washington, D.C., and Pennsylvania have made this clear.

Like it or not, conflicts have become everyone's business. The idea that countries and people should be free to conduct their quarrels on their own terms, no matter how deadly, is outmoded in the nuclear age and in a global world where local hostilities can rapidly become international ones with devastating consequences. Similarly, the notion that tyrants are free to commit atrocities on their own peoples is becoming obsolete, albeit with plenty of resistance.

Today, the human species is engaged in an increasingly dangerous proliferation of lethal weaponry, including nuclear, biological, and chemical weapons of mass destruction, as well as the worldwide, wall-to-wall spread of deadly small arms. At the same time, in all parts of the world, we also see evidence of abundant prejudice, hatred, and threats of mass violence. Sadly, the historical record is full of every sort of slaughter based on invidious distinctions of religion, ethnicity, nationality, and other perceived

3

group differences. This record confirms a part of our unique human heritage, one that we will address in more depth in the pages to follow as we seek to learn lessons from our past and search to find ways of overcoming human predispositions to violence in a technological and global era.

In a contemporary world full of hatred and violence, widespread knowledge and understanding of deadly conflicts past and present, as well as paths to conflict resolution and prevention of deadly conflict, are an urgent agenda. Such an agenda deserves major educational efforts—not only in schools and universities, but also in community organizations, religious institutions, the media, and the public health system. Education, broadly defined, has a great responsibility to provide basic understanding and insight as well as applied knowledge about implementing preventive interventions. Educational efforts addressed to young children, graduate students, and everyone in between—and not least to the adult leaders of powerful sectors and governments—have a vital role to play. Indeed, the likelihood of living a decent, full life includes dealing with the profound dangers of deadly conflict as peoples of the world are drawn together in unprecedented ways.

Historically, education everywhere has to some degree been ethnocentric—and all too often flagrantly prejudicial. If we humans are ever to live together amicably, it will be a drastic change from past practices and will only be achieved by using the unique learning capacities that made the human species so successful in evolution. Yet today's education in most of the world has little to say on the subject. Indeed, education almost everywhere retains ethnocentric orientations, for example, depreciating adjacent nations, ancient enemies, or culturally specified scapegoats.

As a practical matter, there is a powerful and growing need to develop effective education that gives our children a solid basis of knowledge about conflict resolution, violence prevention, peace with justice, and mutual accommodation—in short, decent human relationships from family to community to humanity on a worldwide basis. But if it is so desirable, why has this kind of educational program not been put in place? Are there formidable obstacles that block the path? If so, can understanding help to address them in ways that go beyond all previous efforts?

Let us now consider some of the baggage we humans carry from our ancient and recent past. If we are to adapt to the current reality, full of great potential but also exceedingly dangerous, it may help to consider how we came to be the way we are so that we can put some of the baggage down and move ahead on a peaceful path.

In the latest phase of human evolution—since the industrial revolution and mainly in the twentieth century—we humans have thrust ourselves headlong into a world of enormous complexity, characterized not only by unprecedented rates of change, technical and social transformation, urbanization, and brilliant new scientific horizons, but also by sophisticated weaponry of destructive power beyond any of our ancestors' imaginations. In this world transformed, for better and worse, suddenly much that we have learned and the adaptations used in the millions of years of human evolution no longer apply. This power is rich in promise. Most important, we must come to master the pervasive tendency toward violence in our species.[1]

Several million years ago, our ancestors lived in small, intimate groups with only the simplest tools to help them adapt for survival. They had to cope with profound dangers, threats to their food and water supply, predators, competitors, variable climate, and many other vicissitudes of nature that were far beyond their control. They had to rely not only on their wits and tools but above all on their solidarity, cooperation, joint action, and mutual support in the face of nature's hard blows. Even so, their vulnerability was great and their casualties were heavy. At the time when agriculture was invented about 10,000 years ago, there were probably more baboons on earth than people. So as recently as that (in evolutionary terms), human life was very precarious. Agriculture, as it came to be gradually implemented worldwide in the past few thousand years, succeeded in diminishing that vulnerability. But the most drastic change in the long history of our species—essentially the acceleration of technical advances and their application to human problems of adaptation—occurred only about two centuries ago, with the onset of the industrial revolution.

What a change a century can make! Human initiative has transformed the world in the twentieth century. An ordinary citizen in any of the technically advanced countries has opportunities and protections not available to kings in earlier centuries. In recent decades, science has been institutionalized on a vast scale for the first time, and the acquisition of deep knowledge of the structure of matter and life and the nature of the universe, the human environment, and even ourselves has accelerated sharply. Scientific advances have set the stage for the unprecedented technological innovations in computers, telecommunications, biotechnology—and, of course, weaponry. The potential benefits of modern technology for improving human civilization are profound in every sphere, touching on our food supply, water, health, communication, transportation, energy, and human understanding.

The transformations in science and technology could mean the virtual elimination of human impoverishment in the next several decades. For this to happen, however, human beings will have to reckon with their own nature, particularly the tendencies toward prejudice, ethnocentrism, and violent aggression. Technology, as we know so well, can increase suffering as well as relieve it. And those who have technical skills and advanced knowledge have gained power. They are able, if they wish, to turn their power against fellow humans who are weak, vulnerable, or perceived to be menacing to them. The temptation to use power in this way has proved almost irresistible.

Of great importance is the need to recognize the ubiquitous human tendency toward egocentrism and ethnocentrism.[2] We find it easy to put ourselves at the center of the universe, attaching a strong positive value to ourselves and our group while attaching a negative value to many other people and their groups. It is prudent to assume that human beings are all, to some extent, egocentric and ethnocentric. But these tendencies, under certain conditions, can lead to violent conflict.

Centuries ago, it was common for military conquerors to put captives to the sword or to reduce them to slavery. In the latter part of the nineteenth century, it was widely believed that our species had achieved a sufficiently civilized status to make such horrors impossible. Yet the world since then has seen the near-extermination of the Australian aborigines and the North American Indians. The twentieth century had scarcely begun when, under cover of World War I, Armenians living under the Turkish yoke suffered massacres and deportations that destroyed over 1.5 million men, women, and children and scattered the survivors from their ancient homeland to the far corners of the globe. The century was four decades old when the leaders of a nation that had been considered highly civilized initiated a systematic destruction of the Jews in German-controlled lands, at the cost of six million lives. The world learned, and is continuing to learn, how great the horrors can be when supposedly civilized nations set about destroying hated and devalued people.[3]

The Holocaust vividly demonstrated the human capacity to do immense harm when such was "justified" by explanations that appealed to the most disturbed emotions. As has so often happened in human history, an out-group was viewed as the cause of virtually all social ills and personal frustrations, and the destruction of the powerless was made palatable to the populace and the powerful. But now there was more. The Nazis brought to their gruesome tasks a level of sophistication in modern organization and technology that exceeded prior attempts at mass destruction. The world has moved since the 1940s to still more complex levels of organization and technology. Unfortunately, there is little to suggest that we have learned how to avoid the use of these tools for mass destruction. Yet tools and strategies of great promise to prevent deadly conflict are available. Governments, intergovernmental organizations, and nongovernmental organizations are beginning to use these tools and strategies to overcome our legacy of destructiveness. We will have more to say about the promise of this approach in later chapters.

To threaten, injure, or kill innocent bystanders in a circumstance of political, religious, or ideological conflict is an ancient form of human behavior. But in the twenty-first century, such behavior is abetted by an array of technologies that dwarf all previous efforts. From the employment of instant worldwide-televised threats to diverse miniaturized weapons of devastation, the old terrorism is rapidly becoming transformed.

Small-scale terrorist episodes may not seem to present a formidable capability to wreak havoc. But they do, as recently witnessed by the September 11, 2001, attacks. If terrorism continues to spread, aided by more powerful weapons and more publicity, such attacks have the potential eventually not only of injuring a great many innocent victims but also of arousing repressive responses by powerful governments in democratic societies as well as totalitarian ones. Moreover, terrorism tends to trigger long-term cycles of retaliation and escalation. Killing can become a way of life, and hatred an organizing principle for communities. But that path offers no authentic prospect of a decent future.

The human propensities toward prejudice, ethnocentrism, and violence have other manifestations. Skin color has long provided a lightning rod for prejudice. The Industrial Revolution occurred in the northern hemisphere—a fact that was to have profound repercussions over the ensuing two centuries. Light-skinned people in Europe developed powerful weapons and tools before dark-skinned people elsewhere. From that time to the present, there has been a tendency for light-skinned people not only to become more technically advanced and affluent, but also to depreciate, exploit, and even subjugate their dark-skinned brethren. This has been one of the most serious problems in the modern world, a root cause of human impoverishment and revenge motives.

Another manifestation is the grotesque and pervasive violation of human rights, often involving overt mental and physical torture.[4] The tragic fact is that a large percentage of the world's people live in nations that condone or foster the violation of human rights. We are becoming accustomed to this violation. What is today's shock becomes tomorrow's routine—the banality of evil indeed. Even members of the most humanitarian professions may be seductively drawn into this habitual, harmful behavior.[5]

These observations are not meant to be alarmist, but rather to provide an antidote to complacency and a stimulus to educators, scientists, scholars, policymakers, and all who care about the future of humanity. We must now learn how to marshal the forces of human knowledge, organization, and technology that have been developing over the past century to improve communication and understanding, to foster social justice, and to resolve conflicts fairly.

It is extremely important that the tendency to generate intergroup conflicts—once perhaps adaptive but now exceedingly dangerous—be widely understood. Reluctantly, we had better recognize that the human species is a potentially violent animal organized into potentially violent societies. For practical purposes, it is unwise to follow the widespread, traditional practice of attributing malevolence primarily or solely to other groups. Rather, it is useful to make the assumption that our own group as well as others has malevolent tendencies along with benevolent ones.

Even though distinctions between in-groups and out-groups are ubiquitous in human societies, easy to learn and hard to forget, and to some extent are a legacy of our evolutionary and historical experience in which such distinctions were related to survival, there is certainly the possibility that we can learn to minimize such harsh distinctions in the future. The conditions for survival are in some respects quite different than they were when these orientations evolved. In human development, we must now find a basis for fundamental human identification across a diversity of cultures in the face of manifest differences: We are indeed a single, interdependent, worldwide species. That is one of the central facts for modern education.

Can we do better? Can we modify our attitudes and orientations so that we practice greater tolerance and mutual accommodation at home and in the world? How can human beings learn more constructive orientations toward those outside their own groups while maintaining the values of primary group allegiance and security? We will examine research that shows how this might be done.[6]

The more insight we have, the more we can take our biological heritage into account. Can we understand how to compensate for our inherited biological and social vulnerabilities? Can we draw on inherited strengths in working out new solutions and coping with truly unprecedented circumstances?

THE POTENTIAL OF EDUCATION

The potential of education for diminishing prejudice and ethnocentrism and for reducing intergroup conflict is powerful. Education, broadly speaking, can convey everywhere a clear image of a single species—a huge family including many cousins, more similar than different, searching for a decent life. In all our diversity and inherent readiness to learn prejudice, we must somehow find mutual accommodations. This is a basic theme of human existence, now involving higher stakes than ever before.

Humanity must try, as never before, to enlarge our social identifications in light of common human characteristics and shared goals. We must find a basis for fundamental human identification across a diversity of cultures in the face of manifest conflict. To speak this truth, however, is not to have assimilated it as a psychological reality. The task of grasping it is daunting. But we can no longer afford to avoid it.

Each person can do something useful to address these issues, first as individuals and second by working in organizations or institutions that should be addressing this problem: schools, colleges, and universities; corporations; units of government; community organizations; churches; unions; professional and scientific societies; and foundations, among others. Each of us can ask questions of practical importance: How can my organization or institution be strengthened to cope with prejudice, ethnocentrism, and hatred in a high-risk world? What can I do personally and professionally to make a difference? We model behavior for our children, shape their attitudes and beliefs, and put them in the hands of caretakers who also influence their relations with other human groups. So it is essential to understand as much as we can about the development of prosocial behavior that involves mutual accommodation with others. We pursue this task throughout the book.

The global epidemic of intergroup conflict, with all its explosive mixture of ethnic, religious, and national strivings, is badly in need of illumination. People everywhere need to understand why we behave as we do, what dangerous legacy we carry with us, and what we can do about it to convert fear to hope. Indeed, there is an almost unimaginable basis for hope if we can create constructive, democratic, judicious uses of the advances in science and technology that are becoming available as never before. What follows in this book is an effort to formulate some possibilities for a better future by making use of many different educational vehicles for learning to live together amicably.

In the next chapter, we consider our evolutionary heritage in order to understand the baggage we carry with us—some of it from our ancient past. If we are to educate our children to carry on decent human relations to resolve conflict, prevent violence, and find just peace—we must face the obstacles that stand in our way so that we can find rational means of overcoming them. Old attitudes and beliefs will have to be modified to fit contemporary circumstances so that we do not disastrously repeat and expand the tragedies of the past.

Fortunately, at the outset of the new century, an explicit moral concern and an intellectual ferment about these matters are emerging. In subsequent chapters, we will give examples of ways in which education in all its forms can be strengthened to support decent human relations and peaceful problem-solving. We have chosen promising lines of inquiry and innovation, based to the extent possible on research and on carefully observed good practices. These concepts, data, and practices show the way toward a better future.

Despite the immense and ultimate significance of the problems of prejudice, ethnocentrism, and conflict, these subjects are still pretty low on the world's agenda—in education and science, in the media, in the business community, in places of worship, and in governments. The powerful sectors of society almost everywhere tend to be complacent about such matters and to see them as someone else's problems. Avoidance and denial tend to substitute for careful scrutiny; authority substitutes for evidence; blaming substitutes for problem-solving. The capacity for wishful thinking in these matters is enormous, as is the capacity for self-justification. But now is the time to face the issue head on.

It is certainly not beyond human ingenuity to move this subject to a higher place on the world's agenda. Strong organizations covering wide sectors of science, technology, and education can take an increasingly active role in coping with this critical issue. Scientists and educators, through their most dynamic organizations, can use their formidable influence to strengthen research and education on constructive child development, on ways to minimize the growth of prejudice and ethnocentrism, and on ways to acquire skills of conflict resolution. Attitudes, emotions, beliefs, and political ideologies from our past often hinder such efforts to enhance our understanding and even impede the utilization of scientific knowledge when it is available, but our motivation for survival is strong, our problem-solving capacities are great, and the time is not yet too late.

PREJUDICE AND CONFLICT RESOLUTION
IN CHILDHOOD AND ADOLESCENCE

How do we acquire orientations of ethnocentrism, prejudice, dogmatism, and a susceptibility to violent solutions?[7] Are there ways to foster more constructive orientations as we gain better understanding of the factors governing the development of behavior? The nature of parental care, experience with siblings and with peers, exposure to hatred and violence in schools and mass media, the cumulative effect of frustrating conditions, and previous experience in situations involving aggression are all important factors in shaping these destructive behaviors. So, also (in some countries), are official propaganda and the religious cultivation of stereotypes.

Prejudice—or the prejudgment of persons or situations—is to some degree a universal phenomenon. It is based in part on inherent processes of cognitive development. A child begins to order his or her environment by means of the developing capacity to form categories. This process allows for rapid evaluation of the child's environment to determine what is familiar and unfamiliar, so that the child can make a prompt response to changing situations.

But no one is born prejudiced against other people. Modeling, learning, and socialization build on the basic tendency to categorize and evaluate people, groups, and situations. Prejudice is a response to the social environment. It reflects the individual's psychological needs, including the need for group affiliation and for adherence to cultural and subcultural norms. There is a fundamentally similar process by which affiliation to the in-group and prejudice against the out-group are formed, whether the prejudice involves ethnicity, class, sex, religion, or nationality. The extent of prejudice can be affected by home, school, and community factors as well as by the opportunities to gain familiarity with other groups under constructive circumstances. We will have much more to say about this later.

Living with recurrent major frustrations is conducive to the formation of strong prejudices and an orientation toward harmful ethnocentrism. Frustrations—disappointments, obstacles, disruptions of deep attachment—are inevitable in human life, and social conditions may ease or aggravate both the sources of such frustration and the opportunities for coping with those that occur. In general, major frustrations of basic needs tend to elicit aggressive responses, such as irritability, a readiness to blame others, a mood to strike out at putative obstacles, and a proneness to identify vulnerable scapegoats against whom some sort of retaliation can be mounted.

What frustrations are most powerful in eliciting severe aggressiveness? One is frustration of self-esteem or the sense of personal worth. In human history, where one has had to have a place in the organized group in order to survive, respect from others has become essential to the sense of self-esteem, and behavior directed toward the establishment and maintenance of self-esteem, dignity, and self-worth has great cross-cultural generality. These are fundamental attributes of humanity.

Frustrations in crucial interpersonal relations are also of great importance in fostering individual aggression. The primary relationships within the group have been highly significant in the evolution of our species and have much to do with development of a sense of security in early life and a strong base from which exploration of the personal environment can proceed.

Closely related is frustration of one's sense of belonging to the larger group beyond the intimate few—a group with which one closely identifies and which makes an important contribution to one's self-esteem, whether that entity is a subculture, an ethnic group, a nation, a tribe, a political entity, or an occupational unit. These frustrations of deep needs significantly raise the probability of aggressive behavior.

But such threats may also elicit nonhateful, nonviolent forms of coping and usually do. Hostile responses are not the only way to cope with recurrent frustrations. A serious frustration may lead to passivity, aggression, or, more positively, to assertive behavior, personal initiative, vigorous and persistent efforts toward problem solving that may be aggressive in some sense but not hateful or destructive. Social conditions can clear this pathway. Such nondestructive, persistent efforts at problem solving may be more difficult, complicated, and tedious in the short run, but they are much more rewarding in the long run and perhaps even essential for our survival as a species.

The modern world for all its opportunities, benefits, and promises for a brighter future is full of circumstances that build major frustrations into childhood and adolescence. What will give a young person a sense of personal worth that will prevent destructive solutions to problems?

One illustrative problem area is male adolescence. For many thousands of years, self-esteem in young males was probably based to a considerable extent on competence in hunting and warlike activities. In the future, however, alternatives to warlike activities as sources of youthful self-esteem must be found. It is essential to reduce the susceptibility of young males to hatred and violence by providing them with opportunities for engrossing activity, taking the initiative, and building knowledge and skills that lead to solid accomplishments and reliable human relationships.

But there are serious obstacles to the development of such alternatives in contemporary society. Although constructive and socially valued work offers a vital source of self-esteem and a sense of belonging, in many countries, economic conditions combined with an assortment of ethnic and religious prejudices and overpopulation have produced high unemployment among youth, especially among members of depreciated minority groups. In addition, the increase of technological and social complexity in recent times has led to a prolongation of youth. Youth is now a long period following puberty when one is biologically but not yet socially mature. This situation leaves many young people feeling uncertain, confused, and largely incompetent. These are psychological conditions that predispose them to hostility and to the search for a person or group to blame. It is not difficult to see how such circumstances can increase the susceptibility of youth to in-group and out-group stereotypes, especially when they are stimulated by charismatic, hateful leaders.

The behavioral sciences have made a useful start in delineating the strategies of coping and problem solving in the emotionally charged relationships involving young people, their crucial intimate few, and highly valued groups. There appear to be several fundamental orientations that contemporary institutions—the family, the schools, religious institutions, the culture at large—would do well to encourage in the young in the search for ways to avert the ravages of hatred and violence.

A first step is to provide conditions for the development of early self-esteem. A second is to provide conditions for intimate and enduring interpersonal relationships that are based on mutual benefits. A third is to establish clear guidelines for behavior. (In earlier times the guidelines for behavior were much clearer than they are now in most societies, particularly in traditional societies, which are undergoing a transition to modern society.) A fourth is to teach the young to internalize norms of behavior that restrain violence and provide them with strategies that foster preference for, and knowledge of, other modes of coping and problem solving. (Early security in itself is important, but not sufficient.) A fifth is to develop in the young an image of the future, incorporating goals, expectations, and a sense of purpose or mission that offers hope that nonhateful, nonviolent means for achieving valued ends can in fact be effective. A sixth, along with respect for oneself and one's own group, is to encourage in the young interest in and respect for other groups. In later chapters, we explain how these positive conditions for child and adolescent development can be nurtured.

There is a growing research literature on the effectiveness of various school- and community-based efforts to overcome prejudice. Education in all its forms, from family to schools to mass media, can present the facts of a pluralistic, crowded, and interdependent world as a fascinating place, not one that is strange and hateful.

The media, especially television, are of special importance in this regard. Evidence shows that children and adolescents learn much about other groups by watching television. Unfortunately, much of what they learn is about violence. Later, we briefly review the formidable evidence relating televised violence to the propensity of children to behave violently in play and probably in real life as well. Violence is vividly presented on television and in the movies as an effective way of solving problems: The source of difficulty is removed in a way that may be attractive because it evokes bravery or boldness or skill.

Nevertheless, some research that we consider later suggests that television need not be a school for violence. Television can portray human diversity sympathetically while highlighting shared human experience. The constructive use of this powerful tool to promote compassionate understanding, nonviolent problem solving, and decent intergroup relations needs to be pursued. It will not in itself be adequate to overcome inclinations toward hatred and violence, but it can help.

THE PERSPECTIVE OF THIS BOOK

Fundamentally, the problem is learning how to live together at all levels—in the family, in the community, among diverse groups in a country, and among nations. This calls for very widespread understanding of human relations, sources of stress, and ways of coping at every level.

The central fact is the nature of the human condition: We are a single, worldwide, highly interdependent species, now driven more closely together than ever before by the forces of technological and economic globalization. We need to understand why some of our old habits are much more dangerous than before and why mutual accommodation is essential for survival.

In principle, all individuals of every nation need to have a chance of attaining decent opportunities that include a quality of life compatible with human dignity and arrangements in each country that protect human rights, respect pluralism, avoid oppression, and give children and youth a decent start.

To the extent that many countries cannot yet do this, the international community should reach out in friendship to help (1) put out fires when they are just starting and (2) build capacity to meet basic human needs and cope with their own problems in nonviolent ways. The international community needs attitudes, insights, institutions, and resources to implement a farsighted, proactive approach of assistance, cooperation, and education for countries in bad shape. Many will welcome such an approach—even if ambivalently.

The most fundamental aspiration is that all of us concerned with hatred and violence, especially in relation to war and peace, come to think preventively. We need to be aware of what is possible now, but we also need to push the limits of present knowledge and skill and to develop new research and innovations, concepts, and techniques. Organizations and institutions must come to use this information and experience to

strengthen our capacities for preventing deadly conflict, to learn to live together amicably in search of shared benefits across our common humanity.

It is time to take seriously the Constitution of the United Nations Educational, Scientific, and Cultural Organization in the aftermath of World War II: "That since wars
begin in the minds of men, it is in the minds of men that the defenses of peace must be
constructed."[8] It was written in the aftermath of the carnage of World War II and the
Holocaust, but the words apply to the furious wars of today. Yet today's education in
most of the world has little to say on the subject. Worse still, education almost everywhere has ethnocentric orientations. How can human beings learn more constructive
orientations toward those outside one's group while maintaining the values of primary
group allegiance and identity? These are matters that we try to clarify in this book.

The aim of the book is to enhance understanding of the great danger and important sources of animosity between human groups, examining the violent experience of
our species in evolutionary and historical perspective; to recognize some of the psychological obstacles to peaceful relations between groups; and to focus on developmental processes by which it should be possible to diminish orientations of ethnocentrism, prejudice, and hatred. Almost all of the book is devoted to promising lines of
inquiry and innovation that will help children and adolescents develop humane and
nonviolent behaviors. We draw heavily on research and carefully observed best practices to suggest ways in which children and youth can grow up in decent and constructive ways. We hope the book will be of interest to scholars and to the education community. At the same time, it deals with a subject of such compelling and timely significance
that we have tried to reach beyond specialists in a meaningful way for a well-educated
and socially concerned public. Our greatest aspiration is to stimulate readers in many
countries to think hard about these serious problems, to seize the opportunities, and to
generate better ideas that can help all of our children everywhere.

2

Child Development, the Human Group, and Survival

THE PRIMATE HERITAGE:
STUDIES IN THE NATURAL HABITAT

In the past several decades, the study of the behavior of nonhuman primates—monkeys and apes—has made rapid progress. We can learn from the dimly perceived past when our ancestors confronted the problems of survival without the sophisticated technological aids so inextricably linked to human adaptation in recent times. Our past is inaccessible to direct study. But by careful observation of our closest living relatives, monkeys and apes, we can begin to understand the nonhuman primate heritage from which our ancient ancestors took a long route over millions of years toward humanity.[1]

Nonhuman primates live in groups that are held together by strong and enduring bonds between individuals. These bonds may be reflected in a variety of ways: relationships between adult males and females, between adults of the same sex, between juveniles, and between adult males or females and their young. Altogether, in their natural habitats they have a rich social life. Compared with most other mammals, primates have fewer young at a time. Rather than litters, all Old World monkeys and apes have only one offspring at a time, and they give each one a great deal of attention. The young have longer periods of immaturity than other mammals, including prolonged nutritional dependence on the mother. A corollary of the prolonged physical immaturity and nutritional dependence of the primate infant is a longer and more intense mother-infant relationship and a longer period of tutelage and learning the customs and survival skills of the group.

In all higher primates except humans, infants cling reflexively to their mothers from birth, and mother-infant contact is maintained virtually all of the time until the much older infant develops the ability to keep up with the mother on its own. Nursing occurs in many short bouts around the clock; in early infancy, it is initiated and terminated by the infant, an easy process, because the infant is always clinging to the mother's body, anyway. This combination of clinging, carrying, continuous contact, and frequent nursing is characteristic of all higher nonhuman primates. Safely in contact with the mother, the infant begins to learn about the wider social world—first by observation alone; later, when the infant is independently mobile, much of this learning occurs in the context of play, not only with peers but also with older siblings and even with adults. Play in early life appears to be both enjoyable and instructive; indeed, it is necessary for full development.

Field studies have shown the adaptive significance of observational learning in a social context. This is reflected in the following recurrent sequence: (1) close observation of one animal by another, (2) imitation by the observing animal of the behavior of the observed animal, and (3) the later practice of the observed behavior, particularly in the playgroup, in the case of young animals. In circumstances of food getting, mating, and infant care, there is clear evidence of an observation-imitation-practice sequence. Infants show these sequences, commonly in their relations with older animals, from whom they evidently learn a great deal early in life. Experimental research has shown that the observing monkey is able to learn from errors of the observed animal as well as from successes. An individual can learn from the consequences of another's actions. Similar considerations apply to baboons; they are the largest and most complex of all monkeys. We will soon see how these experiences make the primate group so crucial for survival.

Both field and experimental observations indicate that fear draws the primate mother and infant together with much intensity. The infant often clings to the mother's hair or nipple in a frightening situation. When they are apart, the infant's fear scream is potent in bringing mother to infant. It appears to elicit intense distress in the mother. In a frightening situation, the infant goes to the mother, or the mother goes to the infant, or both. Evidently, the mother's fear is as significant as the infant's fear in bringing them together. These adaptive responses to danger reflect the intimate nature of the mother-infant unit.

Stephen Suomi, from his extensive primate research, observes that basic emotions help the individual to adapt by enhancing immediate survival and long-term fitness.[2] The world (often a dangerous place filled with predators and competitors) has the potential to inflict great harm, even to kill. An individual without fear and related vigilant readiness would be unlikely to survive for very long. Conversely, if an individual is overcome by fear, paralysis might ensue and limit the ability to interact effectively with the environment. So it is vital for human and nonhuman primates to be able to *regulate* the fear response. It is necessary to learn how to inhibit the expression of fear in situations that actually pose little threat. It is important also for the individual to engage effectively in aggressive action if family or friends are being threatened. Survival hinges on these abilities. Excessive violence, however, has a powerfully negative influence. It can destroy cohesive links that keep a group together over time and over generations. It is vital that group members learn to discern which forms of social stimuli are actually threatening and therefore warrant an aggressive response, and which ones do not.[3]

The early learning of what is dangerous in a particular environment is situation-specific in primates. They can learn fear responses to different objects and different circumstances in different environments. Once established, these fear commitments and avoidance responses tend to be stable and long-lasting. There is a large body of experimental research with a variety of mammals showing the difficulty of extinguishing these avoidance responses. Such responses learned in fear can be attached to a variety of objects early in life and tend to endure throughout the life span. There are comparable responses to individuals or groups. But what happens when there are rapid environmental changes during the life span of the individual? Under these conditions, are persistent fear responses likely to become maladaptive? Clinical experience makes it clear that intensely fearful responses learned early in life—for example, in child abuse—may hinder opportunities to respond sympathetically to new people or new experiences in adolescence or adulthood. So, too, early and intense learning of fearful, prejudicial orientation toward another group may be hard to shed later in life. This is a potentially serious problem that deserves further investigation in humans.

As complex organisms have evolved over millions of years, learned behavior has become an exceedingly effective way of meeting adaptive tasks that contribute crucially to individual and group survival. These tasks include finding food and water, avoiding predators, achieving fertile copulation, caring for the young and preparing the young to cope effectively with the specific requirements of a given environment. Learning in early life plays a crucial role in adaptation.

The role of behavior in adaptation is a function not only of individuals, but also of *groups*. Recent studies of nonhuman primates and of hunting-and-gathering human societies in their natural habitats suggest that group living has conferred a significant functional advantage on the more highly developed primates. The *advantages of social organization* have included protection against predators and competitors, meeting nutritional requirements, protection against harsh climates, dealing with injuries, facilitating reproduction, and preparing the young to meet the requirements and utilize the opportunities of a particular environment. These societies provide intimate, enduring relationships with mutual assistance in difficult circumstances as well as clear guidelines for individual behavior, highly relevant to survival requirements in a particular environment. All of this highlights the importance of group membership in the adaptation of our ancient ancestors.[4]

Throughout the evolution of the human species, fundamental interpersonal attachments have been formed early in life through readily available social support networks, provided mostly by kin but also by others in the familiar proximity of a small society. This enduring property of human relationships is of great importance for contemporary life.

These facts give us an evolutionary perspective on human attachment. Such behavior must have emerged over millions of years of human evolution, because infants who formed close attachments to their mothers and whose mothers reciprocated were much more likely to survive to pass on their genes to future generations than were infants who did not. Most likely, as suggested by the primate field studies, attached infants were less likely to be caught by predators, to get lost, to suffer from severe exposure, and to be injured by other members of their own species. The attached child expresses distress and reestablishes contact on separation through crying when hungry or in fear, and by shivering and seeking the mother when cold. At older ages, attached individuals share food, form coalitions to protect each other and cooperate in many activities, and give comfort and support to distressed members. These responses are an integral part of the adaptive repertoire of human behavior, and they are highly relevant to today's adaptation.

THE PRIMATE HERITAGE IN EARLY SOCIAL LEARNING: EXPERIMENTAL STUDIES

Laboratory experiments with nonhuman primates in various conditions of development provide a window on the formation of interindividual relationships and, by clear implication, their significance for group membership, survival, and reproduction—the essence of biological adaptation. Most of the experiments have been done with the rhesus macaque, the most commonly employed monkey in laboratory experiments.[5] These monkeys have also been studied extensively in their natural habitats, so it is possible to make informative comparisons. In the field studies of nonhuman primates under natural conditions, one of the most striking and consistent observations has been the extraordinary richness and diversity of interindividual contact during the years of growth and development. Laboratory investigations with primate species have provided a stark and informative contrast. In these investigations, primates have been reared experimentally in socially inadequate environments that contrast dramatically with the socially rich environment of the natural habitat. The most dramatic comparison is provided by the social isolation experiments. These studies originated through a wish to prevent tuberculosis in the animals by their isolation and led to surprising behavioral responses. (These highly informative studies probably could not be conducted today because of ethically restrictive guidelines on primate experimentation.) The behavioral effects of raising a rhesus monkey until early adolescence in total social isolation have proven devastating. The effects include gross disruption of interindividual contact, especially withdrawal and avoidance of contact; crouching for long periods with very little orientation toward the environment; a variety of self-oriented behavior patterns, including persistent thumb sucking, self-clasping, stereotyped rocking, and self-punitive behavior such as self-biting, particularly when another individual approaches. The effects of partial social isolation are similar, though less profound and somewhat more reversible. Some similar effects are still being observed in human babies reared in social deprivation in orphanages.

The monkey reared in full social isolation does show some curiosity in the earliest months of life, exploring its limited environment with some vigor. But with the emergence of developmentally programmed hardwired fear responses between 60 and 80 days of age, the isolation-reared monkey becomes disturbed. It cannot turn to a mother or even to a peer for attachment and comfort. So it stops its exploratory activity and develops stereotypical patterns of behavior at this age, minimizing input from the environment, shutting out novel stimulation to the maximum extent feasible. When the developmentally programmed aggressive responses appear between 7 and 8 months of age, the isolated monkey is in a difficult position, having no experience of social interaction—no prior relationships through which to express these tendencies in play. When it is finally put into a situation with other monkeys, it is highly aggressive, often in bizarre ways. It directs aggressive behavior not only to other animals but also toward itself. It is not discriminating in choices of targets to attack, even including dominant adult males, who then are severely punitive. The social learning so crucial to adaptation has been seriously impaired by early isolation.[6]

Evidently, isolated monkeys have no basis for knowing how to respond to others, no learned patterns of social interaction, and no secure base. When they reach sexual maturity, their behavior is highly abnormal. Although they appear to be sexually aroused, their behavior is very disoriented. Here again, the social learning necessary to acquire effective patterns of sexual behavior is lacking, and the result is a gross abnormality in ability to mate. In natural habitats they would not reproduce. Some females reared in isolation have been impregnated by artificial insemination, and they show maternal behavior that is highly abnormal; for instance, they are often abusive toward their infants—a behavior rarely seen in the natural habitat. This is especially true for first-borns. Later infants may be treated better; it appears that these mothers can learn. Altogether, rearing monkeys in social isolation has an extremely severe, debilitating effect on the most fundamental dimensions of adaptive behavior throughout the life course. This finding highlights the great importance of early attachment, of gradual social learning, of the extent to which adaptation in the natural habitat depends on the rich variety of social interactions that are always present there.

Experimenters have attempted to reverse the social deficit produced by isolation rearing. This has proved very difficult to do. A great variety of social and pharmacological interventions have been tried with little effect. However, after years of such experimentation (which revealed the profound and enduring character of the deficits induced by social isolation rearing), some reasonable means of amelioration were discovered. Monkeys reared in isolation could regain considerable function by contact with gentle, normal animals, provided that this was carried out in a very simple, gradual, nonthreatening way. The slow buildup of physical contact with a supportive, normal monkey, preferably younger than the monkey reared in isolation, without any threat of aggression or complex demands in play, could start a process in which the formerly isolated monkey could learn social interactions without being overwhelmed by emotional distress.

Isolation-rearing studies, similar to those done with rhesus monkeys, have been done with chimpanzees—the closest biological relative to humans. Chimpanzees were raised in total isolation for 3 years. In the natural habitat, a chimpanzee is normally weaned at about 4 years and is mature at 10 to 12 years. In the isolation chamber, the chimpanzees developed abnormal behavior such as rocking, swaying, thumb sucking, eye poking, and head banging. These abnormal behaviors persisted when the animals were removed from isolation. The isolation-reared chimpanzees avoided social contact with other chimpanzees, including sexual contact. Efforts to modify the abnormal behavior by placing the isolation-reared chimpanzees with mother chimpanzees or by giving them tranquilizers or stimulants showed no major effects.

In a related study, chimpanzees isolated for 3 years were placed in pairs or in groups with chimpanzees who had grown up under natural conditions. When the exposure to social stimulation was increased very gradually, some of the previously isolated males were then able to learn to copulate. These results are similar to those obtained in research on therapy for isolation-reared monkeys. This work, done with our closest primate relatives, is striking in its resemblance to human cases of drastic neglect.[7]

Thus in both rhesus monkeys and chimpanzees, a modicum of adequacy in social behavior can later be acquired by a previously isolated individual, but the task is very difficult. The process of development proceeds smoothly and effectively only when an adequate social environment is present in the early years of life.

Experiments with rhesus monkeys show that infants learn aggressive behavior very early in their lives during the process of weaning. It is a powerful stimulus for an infant monkey to bite the mother in order to obtain her nipple. To curb such infant behavior, a mother will often bite back or swat her young. Even harsher reactions occur when young monkeys try similar behavior on another adult—especially if the adult is socially dominant over the mother. When faced with punishment from adults, young monkeys learn to inhibit this type of aggressive behavior.

Aggression in normal development also takes the form of rough-and-tumble play among peers, which primarily includes hair pulling, chasing, inhibited biting, and wrestling. Seldom does it escalate to the point of injury. However, if it does, an adult usually intervenes or one of the participants backs down. Socialization hinges on this type of behavior. For example, rhesus monkey infants that are raised in laboratories with no regular access to peers during their earlier months of life will mature into individuals whose aggressive behavior is excessive and maladaptive.[8]

Altogether, this line of inquiry (comparing the behavior of nonhuman primates in laboratory experiments with their behavior in natural habitats) provides a revealing window on the profound importance of social learning during the first phase of life. In evolution, the mother's role has been crucial, but other individuals also have an important role in the mixture of support and stimulation that normally fosters healthy development. Thus, the primate group is crucial in the adaptation of monkeys and apes—and is clearly so in humans, also. Throughout human evolution, social relationships have provided the fundamental basis for human adaptation. Full membership in one's primary group was virtually a requirement for survival. This fact emphasizes the vital significance of belonging to a valued group in contemporary life.

THE PRIMATE HERITAGE IN DEVELOPMENT
OF AGGRESSIVE BEHAVIOR

Patterns of threat, attack, and submission shared by a variety of other primates are similar to some of the aggressive and submissive patterns observed in humans.[9] These similarities are impressive in chimpanzees, who raise their arms in threat; hit, punch, and pound with the arms and kick with the legs in attack; brandish and throw objects to intimidate opponents; scream when frightened; crouch and whimper to express submission; and reach out to touch, pat, or embrace to reassure an uneasy subordinate.[10] There are also similarities between the *contexts* in which threat and attack behavior occurs in nonhuman primates and humans.[11] Monkeys and apes are particularly likely to engage in such behavior in several situations, such as when competing for scarce or valuable resources that promote survival and reproductive success (for example, to obtain food), and for males to gain access to fertile females. Aggressive behavior is also observed in competition for high status within the group, when severe aggression is particularly likely during periods of unstable dominance relationships. We see aggressive behavior when protecting close friends or relatives and particularly infants from threat or attack by other group members; in response to threat or attack by higher-ranking animals—in this case redirection of aggression toward subordinates is common; toward strangers trying to enter the group and toward members of other groups, particularly when the groups are in competition for access to mates, territory, or high-quality, clumped foods; following the recent occurrence of other attacks; in defending against potential predators; and in association with a presumably painful injury. In some species, lower-ranking individuals may be attacked when they refuse to cooperate with the goals of higher-ranking animals—for example, female chimpanzees who resist a male's attempts to mate.

Thus, the contexts in which aggression occurs most frequently are those in which an aggressive response seems likely to promote an individual's survival and reproductive success by increasing access to resources, protecting relatives, or defending relatives or friends with whom the aggressor has affiliative bonds that promote cooperative efforts to achieve mutually beneficial goals. Similarly, submissive patterns of behavior that often serve to inhibit attack can be viewed as adaptive responses by subordinates who would lose more through aggressive competition than they could gain. A dominance hierarchy in which members defer to higher-ranking individuals greatly reduces overall aggression in the group.

Primate observations suggest that a cognitive, emotional, and behavioral distinction between familiar individuals and strangers is learned early and easily in monkeys reared in social groups. This distinction underlies some of the aggressive behavior of wild monkeys and apes. Aggression toward strangers occurs in two situations: when a single individual attempts to enter a new group, and when two stranger groups meet. Let us briefly consider each situation in turn.

In most nonhuman primates, members of one sex typically transfer from the familiar birth group into another group, as strangers, during adolescence. Usually males are the mobile sex, but in a few species (for example, chimpanzees) females transfer, and in a small number of species (for example, gorillas), both males and females may leave to join other groups.[12] Pusey and Packer conducted years of field research on chimpanzees and found extensive evidence of hostility to strangers who tried to immigrate.[13] In their pioneering work, they noted that chimpanzees are one of the few species in which females transfer to another group. They observed that resident females behave aggressively toward immigrant females, threatening, chasing, and attacking them.[14] The new females seek protection from the adult males, who welcome them if they are sexually receptive.

Strangers introduced to groups of captive monkeys are frequently severely attacked, mauled, and even killed, often in severe group attacks. These observations indicate that group members will kill a newcomer who is forced into proximity with no means of escape. Such extremes of violence are less common in the wild; an immigrant can choose the timing and method of approach to another group.

The second situation in which relative strangers meet is during encounters between groups. In many species, intergroup encounters are rare because groups avoid one another, often with the aid of loud calls that broadcast their locations. In other species, groups may meet routinely, feed, travel, or rest near one another without aggression, and then move apart. Yet chimpanzees, our closest biological relatives, exhibit the most sophisticated forms of intergroup violence observed in wild nonhuman primates.[15] This aggression has much that foreshadows human in-group and out-group distinctions.

Chimpanzee males are organized into distinct communities that occupy ranges, and they defend these ranges against males from other communities. When males from different communities come into contact, violent fighting may occur and individuals are sometimes severely injured. Females and infants are not immune to violent aggression by males from other communities.[16] Several studies have found the systematic patrolling of community boundaries by groups of males who behave in distinctively antagonistic ways in such encounters.[17] Males from a given community attempt to defend the community range when they hear or encounter males from other communities, and they actively seek such encounters during regular forays.

Males of one community regularly gather to engage in such patrols. Moving silently and stealthily, in contrast to their normal noisy habits, these males move toward one edge of their range, frequently stopping to climb trees and peer into the distance, evidently looking and listening for signs of strange chimpanzees. If the males locate other chimpanzees, and if the party of strangers is outnumbered, the patrolling males move forward with extreme caution until they are just a few yards from the chimpanzees of the other community. At this point, they charge, hair fully erect and vocalizing loudly in a cohesive display of aggressive intent. If the others do not manage to escape, they may be brutally attacked. Border patrols and intense aggression by males from different communities have been observed at both Gombe and another research site in the Mahale Mountains, suggesting that such violence may be characteristic of at least the East African populations of chimpanzees.[18]

What is the function of such intercommunity aggression? Some investigators have suggested that, by defending community range boundaries, a group of males achieves access to a greater number of females and other resources.[19] The main difference between male territorial systems in other mammals and in chimpanzees is that the larger chimpanzee territory is established and defended by groups of males cooperating with one another, whereas in other species single males defend areas from all other males. This is consistent with other evidence from research on higher primates suggesting that the evolution of cooperative behavior is related to the evolution of aggressive behavior in primates.[20]

In a recent major review and analysis, Richard W. Wrangham, one of the leading scientists in this field, considers many species and ecological conditions in the evolution of coalitionary killing. His key point is the following:

> Warfare has traditionally been considered unique to humans. It has, therefore, often been explained as deriving from features that are unique to humans, such as the possession of weapons or the adoption of a patriarchal ideology. Mounting evidence suggests, however, that coalitional killing of adults in neighboring groups also occurs regularly in other species, including wolves and chimpanzees. This implies that selection can favor components of intergroup aggression important to human warfare, including lethal raiding. . . . Two conditions are proposed to be both necessary and sufficient to account for coalitional killing of neighbors: (1) a state of intergroup hostility; (2) sufficient imbalances of power between parties that one party can attack the other with impunity. Under these conditions, it is suggested, selection favors the tendency to hunt and kill rivals when the costs are sufficiently low. . . . Current evidence supports the hypothesis that selection has favored a hunt-and-kill propensity in chimpanzees and humans, and that coalitional killing has a long history in the evolution of both species.[21]

The systematic, organized, brutal, and male-dominated attacks of chimpanzees are the closest phenomenon to human warfare observed in any nonhuman primate— though a very long way from contemporary war. Even so, when the chimpanzee evidence is considered along with the responses observed with strangers in a variety of nonhuman primate species, it appears likely that the human tendency to react with fear and hostility to relative strangers—as well as the related tendency to make in-group and out-group distinctions—has roots in the prehuman past. Human capacities for aggressive behavior and tendencies to respond aggressively in particular situations are partially the result of natural selection operating during the evolutionary past of our species. And such legacies need to be taken into account in understanding how our species functions in the vastly different circumstances of today. Emotional response tendencies that may have been highly adaptive under ancient circumstances may become maladaptive when environmental conditions change drastically, as they have in the most recent phase of human evolution.[22] This may well be some of the baggage we carry with us that we must cope with in learning to live together. There is ample evidence that these tendencies toward aggressive behavior can be shaped constructively by learning over the years of growth and development. War is not inevitable. Genocide is not inevitable. But we must be aware of our dangerous baggage from the past, in both our biology and in the socially transmitted cultures of many human societies, if we are to overcome the dangers.

A CLOSER LOOK AT THE FIRST RELATIONSHIPS

The process of forming a secure attachment in the first year of life, if it goes well, permits the human infant to explore actively from the base of safety established by the mother or other principal caregiver. This exploration in turn facilitates cognitive development and is a positive factor in forming friendly relations with peers. Here we see the interaction of biological, cognitive, social, and emotional factors in development.

The quality of these early events is extremely important. Infants with insecure attachments can recover later if the environmental conditions improve. Nevertheless, the opportunity for a richness of cognitive and social development is greater for the young child who has formed a secure attachment in the first year of life. A loving, joyful, nurturing, stimulating relationship with the mother or another central caregiver sets the young child on the path toward healthy development and realization of full potential.

Between the ages of 8 and 12 months, the child begins crawling and then walking. In the context of a secure attachment, the parental responses are likely to be facilitative—providing encouragement, pleasure, and protection when necessary. This is soon followed by the time, between about 12 and 14 months of age, when the child's language explorations take off and, in turn, elicit responses from the caregivers. If the attachment has formed well, these responses are likely to be characterized by talking and reading to the child as well as by playing games together. Though not all fun and games, these experiences on the whole tend to elicit shared pleasure, thereby strengthening the bond of attachment even more deeply—and they provide cognitive stimulation that is a fundamental underpinning for later curiosity and problem-solving ability.

The extent of such cognitive and verbal stimulation during the first few years of life appears to be a crucial factor in the nature and scope of the child's cognitive development. The small child's relentless energy, unpredictable behavior, and special periods of stress—such as the major transition between about 18 months and 2 years of age (the terrible twos) toward greater independence and some negative behavior—make for continuing demands on the parents and may well strain family relationships. These are the particular times when parental mutual support, or concomitant outside support, may make a crucial difference in whether or not the parent-child relationship takes a downturn. Intimate and dependable support in times of stress is a fundamental factor in child rearing. It is worth emphasizing the extent to which the maternal role is usually spread among many people, especially the father, maternal kin, other mothers, older offspring, and grandparents. Babies are often passed from one affectionate adult to another. In favorable socioeconomic settings, sick, tired, or stressed mothers have many others to turn to for assistance, and the baby learns to love and trust other members of its group of friends and relations.[23]

One window into the essential nature of human social development is through research on the effect of social deprivation as we have foreseen in considering monkeys and apes. What conditions of early experience are essential for normal social development? Studies in poorly staffed or developmentally insensitive residential institutions have provided natural experiments. In essence, the findings of such studies indicate that later human relationships fare badly if there is no close consistent relationship with at least one caregiver, or at least if there is no regular, dependable interaction with one specific adult throughout the course of the first year of life. These findings are extended in a dramatic way by looking at children who have been in conditions of extreme neglect or isolation during their early years.

The attachments so characteristic of nonhuman primate societies are further developed in human societies. Once the monkey or ape infant is weaned, it forages for itself. Even in the sophisticated chimpanzee, food sharing between adults is minimal, although males share some meat with all group members, not just immediate family. In humans, the situation is more complex. Adults provide food for their offspring into or even beyond adolescence. Food sharing between adults is crucial to subsistence in all traditional human societies. Although cooperation is important for nonhuman primates, it is rudimentary compared to cooperation in all human societies, even the simplest. The sharing of subsistence technology; organized communal efforts to find, harvest, or hunt food; cooperative building of shelters; caring for infirm or aged group members; division of labor; pooling of resources; trade; and so many other *cooperative* ventures constitute human achievements barely foreshadowed in our nonhuman primate relatives.[24] We link the survival and reproduction of the individual to cooperative action in the valued group far more richly than is possible in any nonhuman society. Human biology and learned traditions evolved over millennia in a world of small, mainly stable, face-to-face groups in which people were linked by a strong support network with ties of kinship and lifelong familiarity. Today's world is very different, often more lonely, and chiefly a product of the vast, drastic changes of the past century or two.

Although small-scale, traditional societies around the world have adapted in many ways to different ecological settings, their societies share certain essential features.[25] Traditional societies typically possess clear and shared guidelines for behavior. These guidelines were probably useful in their past for coping with adaptive tasks under predictable circumstances that did not change much for long periods of time. In contrast, the recent transformations wrought by technological advances bring continuing and often rapid change. The traditional guidelines for human development covered basic categories of experience: human relationships, relations between people and their environment, and ways to cope with problems and take advantage of opportunities bearing directly on survival and reproduction. They were mostly learned early in life, shaped by powerful rewards and punishments, and invested with strong emotions supported by shared and highly valued social norms. Among other things, they can show children how to cope with difficult situations without violence.

Such early learning of cultural norms in small-scale societies usually establishes lifelong commitments to traditional ways of life—as if to say, Follow these admonitions and you will be accepted in the group. These commitments are reinforced by the experience that self-respect and close human relationships are intimately linked with behaviors conforming to norms that are believed to have worked well for very long periods. A sense of personal worth is predicated on one's sense of belonging to a valued group. A sense of belonging, in turn, depends on the ability to undertake the traditional tasks of that society with skill, the ability to engage in social interactions in ways that are mutually supportive, and the personally meaningful experience of participation in group rituals marking shared experiences of deep emotional significance. All of these traditional activities are experienced in the context of a small, face-to-face group that provides the security of familiarity, support in times of stress, and enduring attachments through the life cycle. These are powerful attributes in the light of human vulnerability to environmental vicissitudes—disease, attack, climatic jeopardy, and much else. The enduring group still offers guidance, protection, and satisfaction; indeed, life itself. A key question for the human future is how to extend the small psychological group to a vastly larger and more diverse world community.

OUR ANCIENT LEGACY IN GROWING UP HUMAN

Human societies evolved slowly over vast periods of time in ways that fostered healthy, adaptive development during childhood and adolescence—the essence of survival. For most of human history, small, stable communities provided enduring, intimate relationships from birth, with many opportunities for children to acquire traditional adult skills and roles gradually through observation, imitation, and practice.

But adaptation has been very difficult in the face of major historical changes that have greatly transformed the conditions of human development—the shift from hunter-gatherer societies to horticultural societies and permanent settlements, the rise of agriculture and large cities, the industrial revolution, and most recently the information age. Now we have come to a time in history when much more is possible than ever before. We have developed science and technology far beyond the dreams of our ancestors. This has made possible the emergence of modern societies very different from those of the past. As a by-product of these developments—an authentic paradox of success—we have inadvertently made the process of growing up more complicated than ever before. There is now so much to be learned and relearned, there are so many changes in a lifetime, that preparation for adult life is inherently complex and difficult. The pace of technological and social change is now so rapid that the adult experience of contemporary children will differ substantially from that of their parents. We have largely moved from small villages to large urban cities, and now we are seeing the emergence of megacities all over the world.

This transformation threatens some important conditions for healthy development, such as social support and the learning of life skills to meet practical requirements of contemporary circumstances. Larger, more mobile, more heterogeneous and impersonal communities; smaller families in technically advanced societies; and rapidly changing family roles make social support less readily available than in the past. Drastic technological and social changes, more complex knowledge required for adult roles, and more segregation of children and adolescents from adults make the acquisition of life skills more difficult. These problems affect all strata of society but are most severe for children growing up in poverty.

Consider the evolution of human societies and families, and the special skills necessary for survival and reproduction. How are these skills acquired during individual development? Human development, even more than that of the nonhuman primates, is characterized by a long period of childhood and greatly extended adolescence. As we have seen, secure attachment formed in the first year of life permits the infant to explore from a base of safety. This exploration in turn facilitates cognitive development and friendly relations with peers. Children learn through observation, imitation, and practice, often in the form of play.[26] Play involves many components of adult behavior—but without immediate functional consequences. During play, children learn dominance relationships, communication skills, the regulation of aggressive behavior, and a variety of social skills. Such elements are, for example, embedded in a simple game of tag.[27]

Much of the significance of the extended period of human development centers on the opportunity to learn about the environment—its physical, biological, and social features. A great deal of learning and skill development goes on during this relatively large part of the life span between infancy and adulthood. Overwhelmingly, this time is spent in relation to other people, and they offer a lot—attachment, protection, modeling, feedback, guidance, encouragement, and support. The social interactions of juvenile and adolescent nonhuman primates, as well as humans, serve to prepare them for the requirements of adult life. They acquire resources and develop social bonds. Monkeys and apes develop patterns of behavior that continue throughout adult life—particularly grooming, infant handling, aggressive behavior, alliance formation, and sexual behavior. So there is continuity involving the gradual acquisition of knowledge and skills pertinent to survival and reproduction throughout the life span. This developmental theme foreshadows later human evolution.

Whereas nonhuman primate societies anticipate features of human societies, human societies have become far more complex than those of our ancient ancestors. And yet, human societies are generally—though not always—adaptive in their structure and function. What is most special about species that live in societies is their *capacity for cooperation*. They interact with one another to their mutual benefit, and these patterns of interaction must be learned. There are many types of cooperative activities—reproduction, care of the young, acquisition of food and water, defense against predators, protection in intergroup aggression, and others. Thus, to support survival and reproduction, individuals must learn many cooperative rules. Over the course of human evolution, complicated cooperative and aggressive behavior patterns have emerged.

Our ancestors lived for millennia in hunting and gathering societies—long after they had acquired fully human biological characteristics. A few such societies still remain in our world today. These hunting and gathering societies are characterized by the small size of their communities—commonly between 20 and 50 people. And children growing up in these societies show many characteristics similar to those of nonhuman primates such as chimpanzees.

Children learn a great deal through play and especially through observing and imitating adults. At an early age, boys join the men in their regular activities and girls join the women, and in this way both genders gradually prepare for adulthood. Parents, older siblings, and other adults dedicate a great deal of attention to the child, much of it shaping the attitudes and skills believed to be essential for survival. So children and adolescents participate extensively in the group as age and circumstances permit. They learn the skills necessary to sustain life.

Family relationships provide a powerful organizing principle throughout human evolution. Even in the nonhuman primates, kinship is an important determinant of social interaction and mutual support. In effect, the family in one form or another has been the main place for education, economic activity, and social relationships throughout human history. Although other relationships are also important, none have quite the significance of those embedded in family and kin.

Until the industrial revolution, child rearing was consistent with that of earlier eras. Children were nurtured by parents and other kin; they learned adult roles through direct observation and practice; social support networks were readily available and primarily kin-based; and children learned early the traditional guidelines for behavior. However, with the industrial revolution, the rate of innovation in Western Europe took off, creating a profound transformation with economic, political, social, and psychological ramifications that continue to the present day and have spread through much of the world.

Although some elements of change were present earlier, the transformation has been far more extensive in the past two centuries than ever before. These changes are seen in many ways in industrialized societies and information-based economies and include the smaller size of nuclear families, the high incidence of divorce, the drastically changing roles of women, the emergence of a youth culture, and the need to learn more complex information and skills. Much of this is stressful and requires learning new coping skills or upgrading old ones.

Across the entire span of human evolution, the period since the industrial revolution is a brief moment. But the technological, economic, and social changes in this instant of evolutionary history probably are more far-reaching than all of the previous changes in human evolution put together. And the effects of these transformations on the conditions of child and adolescent development are not the least of the changes. The ancient human organism grows up now in a very new habitat.

No aspect of family life has changed more strikingly than the role of adolescents. The transition from childhood to adulthood through most of human history was steady, gradual, and cumulative. Children were given tasks from an early age that bore some discernable resemblance to the responsibilities they would assume as adults. These tasks increased in scope and complexity as the children grew older. By the time they reached adolescence, they were largely familiar with what would be required of them and what their opportunities would be as adults. With some confirmation by a rite of passage, they arrived rather crisply at a point of adult status, or nearly so. The biological changes of puberty that produced adult physiques were tightly linked to the learning and mastering of adult roles in the early societies.

In a variety of ways, growing children and young adolescents have had less and less opportunity for participation in the adult world as industrialization has proceeded. It is less clear how to be useful and earn respect. The time between childhood and adulthood has become longer and has emerged as a distinctive status in its own right. The requirements, risks, and opportunities of this period are now highly ambiguous for many adolescents.[28] Modern youth have adult physiques and biology but few concomitant social roles of responsible contribution to the group.

In the face of these transformations and their profound effects on families, one of the basic issues for human survival is how to meet the crucial requirements for healthy child and adolescent development—how to cope with imminent danger, how to make a living, how to live effectively with a diversity of other people, how to meet one's personal needs and reconcile them with those of a valued group, how to participate in the society in ways that ensure the well-being of oneself and one's family, and how to relate to strangers. A great deal of complex learning over long periods of time is being undertaken throughout the course of childhood and adolescence in human societies to meet these fundamental needs. The task was relatively simple in small, stable societies. Although modern developments have provided immense opportunities, they have also made the situation more complex, development more prolonged, and long-term outcomes more obscure. In fact, there is less continuity between the behavior of childhood-adolescence and adulthood than ever before.

IMPACT OF TECHNOLOGICAL CHANGES
ON HUMAN GROUPS

Technological advances have opened new opportunities, changed lifestyles, and disrupted traditional patterns. Disruptive factors involve increased geographical mobility, including massive migrations; the crowding of strangers in vast societies; conflicts in values; the emergence of very complex, largely unprecedented circumstances; the immense heterogeneity of the modern world; and the decline of opportunities to practice traditional subsistence activities, leaving millions jobless and often lacking basic essentials. These factors disrupt long-term bonds, force individuals to compete with strangers for scarce and valuable resources, and confront people with all sorts of unfamiliar outlooks and behaviors that often are very difficult to reconcile with their own. These circumstances can be very stimulating and creative, but they also are often associated with impersonal and even harsh human relationships. When small, familiar groups are replaced by large, shifting collections of relative strangers, then suspicion, fear, and hostility are likely to ensue. A sense of mutual responsibility is often replaced by a narrow pursuit of self-protection. Bobbi Low, at the University of Michigan, did an interesting analysis of cross-cultural data showing that parents teach children to trust others in small-scale societies but to distrust others when societies are above a certain size.[29]

So social support networks have been fundamental in human life for millennia. They still bear directly on basic human needs. But they are jeopardized in many different ways by formidable pressures and disruptions associated with the modern transformations we have experienced as a species. They can no longer be taken for granted. Under contemporary circumstances, we have to improvise a great deal to protect, strengthen, or even create social support networks to meet central human needs. In this book, we emphasize the importance of the human group for psychological well-being. The other side of the coin, however, must also be confronted—group membership makes us susceptible to hatred and violence, the ubiquitous in-group and out-group distinctions that are so often invidious and stereotypical.

We inherit through genes and customs a strong need for belonging in a primary group, and under certain conditions, membership in a primary group may render us hostile to other groups. This is a dilemma we humans must solve if we are ever to minimize the immense dangers of intergroup conflict in a hypermodern world. Can we find ways to extend our supportive identity to the wide world beyond our individual primary groups? Can we continue to draw powerful sustenance from our primary groups without seriously deprecating, let alone dehumanizing, other (perhaps strange and frightening) groups? Much of this book seeks to answer such questions. In the next chapter, we turn to ethnic, religious, and nationalist factors, because these have provided in many ways and many places a powerful sense of belonging to a valued group that can even be essential for survival—yet also exceedingly dangerous when groups of different ethnicity, religion, or nationality are set against each other, especially by political demagogues or religious fanatics. This is one of the most critical predicaments of contemporary life, especially, in view of the twentieth century's brutality in these matters. Can we do better in the twenty-first?

3

Ethnic, Religious, and Nationalist Factors in Human Conflict

AN EVOLUTIONARY AND HISTORICAL PERSPECTIVE

Contemporary education must try hard to understand where we as a species came from and how our ancient heritage and recent historical transformation contribute to our current tendencies toward hatred and violence. If we are to overcome or control these destructive tendencies, we must grasp the powerful currents that make the task at once difficult and essential.

Development of our ancestors took place in the context of small, face-to-face groups that provided the security of familiarity, support in times of stress, shared coping strategies, and enduring attachments that sustained hope and adaptation for a lifetime. Reciprocity was crucial in relationships, both within and between groups. Disapproval in the form of reduced sharing, social isolation, and the threat of rejection from one's group were powerful sanctions that reinforced conformity to group norms. Indeed, the importance of sharing within the primary group was strongly conveyed to children from infancy onward.

These basic facts of small-scale, traditional life have been enduring and powerful from earliest mankind to the present day. They apply to the hunting and gathering societies in which our ancient ancestors spent several million years, to the extended families of agricultural village societies, and to the primary groups of the homogeneous neighborhoods in preindustrial towns of the past that foreshadowed modern industrial and postindustrial societies. Our ancient ancestors' world began to change drastically with the onset of agriculture 10,000 years ago. The existing evidence clearly shows that—once humans developed agriculture, settled in larger population groups, accumulated goods, and came to rely on designated areas for growing food and grazing animals—a widespread intergroup hostility became common, and at times, severe. Patterns of intergroup violence in preindustrial societies have been confirmed and described in detail by anthropologists and historians.

Whatever the evolutionary background and its biological legacy, the historical record clarifies that aggressive behavior between individuals and between groups has been a prominent feature of human experience for at least several thousand years. Everywhere in the world, aggression toward others has been facilitated by a pervasive human tendency toward harsh dichotomizing between the positively valued *we* and the negatively valued *they*. Such behavior has been easily learned, practiced in childhood play, encouraged by custom, and rewarded by most human societies.

The distinctions between in-groups and out-groups are often made in ways that are highly susceptible to interpretations that justify violence. Political, social, economic, and pseudoscientific ideologies have all been utilized in support of these hostile attitudes. Group differences have been categorized in many ways: by religion, race, language, region, tribe, nation, and political entity. Such invidious distinctions are often associated with deeply felt beliefs about superiority, a sense of jeopardy to group survival, or justification by supernatural powers. These hurtful, destructive, and enduring beliefs are an ancient part of the human legacy and are more dangerous now than ever before.

During the past few decades, valuable insights that augment the historical findings have come from research on the psychology of intergroup behavior. Social psychologists as well as anthropologists and sociologists have investigated the human inclination to distinguish between in-groups and out-groups. In both field studies and experimental research, the flow of evidence is impressive. A human being is readily able to learn in-group identification and favoritism, to develop strong preferences for his or her own group, to discriminate against other groups, to accept favorable evaluations of the products and performances of the in-group, and to adopt unfavorable characterizations of other groups that go far beyond the objective evidence or the requirements of the situation. This biased behavior is true not only in long-standing group commitments, but also in experimental situations in which only a brief orientation is given to distinguish a newly formed group. It is difficult for participants to avoid invidious interpretations of the distinctions, even when the experimenter tries to do so.

MUZAFER SHERIF—A CLASSIC BOYS' SUMMER CAMP EXPERIMENT

Nearly 40 years ago, renowned social psychologist Muzafer Sherif conducted a creative experiment involving two groups of boys at a summer camp.[1] When the youngsters arrived at the summer camp, the researchers began by actually creating a hostile atmosphere among the children in order to set up the proper conditions for conducting the experiment. Sherif divided the group in half. One group was called the Eagles and the other, the Rattlers. Then a series of athletic competitions between the two groups was arranged. This created a sense of cohesiveness within each group and strong feelings of rivalry between groups.

Once these polarized intergroup feelings were manifested, the researchers built on and intensified them by creating situations in which one group would be treated preferentially (as the in-group) and the other would be treated unfairly (as an out-group). In one example, a camp party was held, and the Eagles were invited slightly earlier than the Rattlers. The refreshments served varied in quality. Some of the food was fresh and tempting, whereas other food was stale and unappetizing. As one would expect, the group of boys who arrived early made a quick move to the more appealing spread, leaving the latecomers with the unappealing fare. Once the Rattlers realized that the Eagles had taken advantage of them, name-calling between the two groups ensued, and before long, a food fight and an all-out riot broke out.

In subsequent days, the researchers attempted to reverse the ill feelings between the groups by eliminating competitive games and by treating both groups equally well. But it did no good. In fact, the hostility grew. Even in benign situations in which the boys gathered to watch movies, trouble was often on the verge of breaking out.

Ultimately, the researchers worked out a solution for reducing the bad feelings. They did this by combining the two groups in situations in which they had to work together cooperatively to accomplish goals that were strongly valued by both groups. There was no other way to achieve what they both wanted. In one instance, the boys were on a camping trip when the camp truck broke down. The truck could only be started if it was pushed and pulled up the hill, which required the participation of every single boy, regardless of group affiliation. After the researchers arranged several incidents like this one, the boys began to feel better about each other and hostile feelings were reduced. Indeed, enduring positive feelings emerged with this ingenious experiment.

What we learn from Sherif's experiment is how easily hostility can form and become deeply entrenched between groups, and how unfairness can exacerbate intergroup animosity. We also learned that this negativity could be overcome by facilitating essential intergroup collaboration. Clearly, it is vital that schools use this knowledge and provide a structure in which students can reach valued common goals through collaboration in a climate of mutuality and belonging to an extended group. The same principles apply to pluralistic organizations and communities. We consider this in detail later.

Overall, it is easy to stimulate a strong sense of "my people"—the in-group. For our earliest ancestors, this inherited, easily learned response had adaptive functions in human evolution over a very long period. Now our modern cities and global world are enormously more complex than the small groups and small villages in which our evolutionary selection of traits occurred. The responses of our ancient ancestors no longer suffice as adaptations to the new global, information age. Invidious distinctions can readily be exacerbated by political demagogues. As we saw so vividly in the twentieth century, such exacerbation can have disastrous consequences.

Attachments, group loyalty, and warfare have ultimately been linked through millennia of human history. We risk our lives and inflict great damage in the service of devotion to valued groups (most recently, nation-states). Yet, there is no continuing need to assume that membership in a valued, supportive group must also include hateful, let alone lethal, behavior toward others. On the contrary, given the unique human capacity for adaptation through social learning and intellectual problem solving, it is reasonable to assume that we can indeed learn new ways to live together.

This chapter explores the way the human groups have reacted to the massive technological, economic, and social changes of recent times. It shows how basic human attributes as well as certain environmental factors promote nationalistic, religious, and ethnic animosity that sometimes lead to deadly conflict. It is a matter of great practical significance for the world of the twenty-first century to understand far more widely than we now do how a specific group in a society becomes targeted as a very dangerous enemy and thus subject to severe persecution and even to mass killing. Large-scale, highly organized killings have much in common; the conditions under which such behavior tends to occur, and the justifications surrounding it, can help us understand human cruelty. In the case of genocide, a society attacks a targeted group in it that is perceived or defined as an internal enemy. This is not to say that the human species is lacking in positive, affiliative, supportive attributes—kindness, generosity, love, altruism, and the like. But these positive attributes have a flip side; too often, they are tightly linked to very different ones of a highly negative and destructive character, and both are influential in determining behavioral patterns. We have more to say on this topic in Chapter 5, which discusses the development of prosocial behavior.

THE HUMAN GROUP IN AN ERA OF
DRASTIC TRANSFORMATION

Individual human beings feel the need for a sense of self-worth and a sense of belonging, both of which can best be brought to fulfillment in a valued group. The group may be a family, a religious entity, a political party, a youth gang, a cultural group, a scientific or professional organization—but one way or another, it is a universal prerequisite for human security, dignity, and distinctive identity. The fulfillment of such needs cannot be taken for granted in the large-scale human societies that have emerged so recently in the course of human history. Despite the fact that we have far more knowledge and technical competence than was ever possible before, there is, for many people, a sense of loss or even threat in the impersonal, remote, and complex character of many contemporary societies. In vast impersonal cities, individuals often feel isolated or, at times, virtually abandoned: "the lonely crowd."[2] As the world becomes functionally larger and more difficult to comprehend, many individuals react by seeking and joining supportive groups that can give meaning to life. Although this can be very constructive, the group often turns out to be an entity that provides security but is also susceptible to ethnocentric prejudice and hostility toward other groups.

As people have moved across the earth, they have always fervently sought to maintain social support networks similar in basic functions to the small societies in which our species evolved. Such social support systems facilitate the development of coping strategies and buffer stressful experiences, helping people maintain self-esteem, make a living, keep distress within tolerable limits in bad times, foster and preserve human relationships, meet requirements of new situations, and prepare for the future. The erosion of such groups generates apprehension. Very often, new groups are sought in anger born of repeated frustration. The solidarity found in the new group may be channeled toward expression of anger toward another group.[3]

Now we live in a time of growing global interdependence and concomitant social changes. These have included much contact between people from highly diverse backgrounds, differing in almost every conceivable dimension, yet thrown together in daily living and job contexts by technological and economic changes. Air transportation, television, and the Internet are perhaps the most vivid agents of this change, but there are many others as well.

In technologically advanced societies, especially those characterized by high geographic mobility, the influence of the family has markedly diminished, with loss of the richness of and frequency of relations among its members. Mass media have a greater influence than ever before, with powerful, mixed messages that bypass the family with a cacophony of new values. This modernization poses especially formidable problems in developing countries, where the shift from old to new ways has been greatly compressed in time, almost as if several centuries had been traversed in a single lifetime. Modernization weakens traditional cultures and attenuates their historic socializing, orienting, and supportive functions.

The magnitude and rate of these changes cause disorientation and make it hard to know what to believe, how to cope, and how to prepare for a better future. Any great advance has side effects, which are complex and challenging—and our institutions have had relatively little time to adapt to drastic change. Rapid technological and social change involves unforeseen dislocations that are often threatening in their erosion of traditional guidelines for behavior. What behavior will be adaptive now? What guidelines make sense? There is an inclination to overcome the troubling aspects of these changes by clinging to small, familiar groups or by seeking vulnerable, out-group targets that can be blamed for any frustrations.

This same pattern of responses also occurs when unforeseen, abrupt events radically change the social and political landscape. The resulting perplexity, insecurity, and anxiety can readily lead to a surge of nationalism.[4] An abrupt decline in the power of the central nation-state, such as that which occurred during the 1990s in the former Soviet Union, throws life into deep uncertainty. The previous compact between ethnic groups and the central government is now in doubt. That condition, together with general uncertainty about guidelines for behavior and the status of authority (and exacerbated by deteriorating economic conditions), provides the context for a surge of claims for autonomy, independence, or retribution. Such a surge can be profoundly accelerated by leaders who have personal and political axes to grind.[5]

The responses to modernization are important in understanding nationalism, especially the intense psychological effects of the rapid increase to vast scale, technical complexity, and awesome economic interdependence on a worldwide basis. Because the world transformation involves much uncertainty, insecurity, and inequity, there are widespread, smoldering frustrations, which may be transformed into virulent prejudices against minority populations, foreign populations, or infidels. Ethnocentric and nationalistic politicians as well as religious fanatics have long understood the human tendency to seek someone to blame under circumstances of intensely felt frustration. This is a point we must emphasize because of its heightened danger in contemporary circumstances.[6] It can poison education and child development.

EMERGENCE OF NATIONALISM

Nationalism is a political ideology that combines the emotional nation with the functional state. The state is administrative, and the nation is emotive—providing a sense of belonging to its members. Ultimately, nationalism is about identity. National identity is only one of many identities: occupational, religious, ethnic, linguistic, territorial, class, and gender, among others. However, in the modern world, national identity has emerged as the most fundamental of these various identities. Loyalty to the nation is seen as basic to social solidarity. The source of national identity is generally conceived as being located in a distinctive group of people who bear sovereignty. This sovereign entity is meant to be the central object of loyalty and the basis for a strong sense of belonging to a valued group. Thus, the concept of a nation is an organizing principle for a distinctive status and a sense of worth.[7]

When the term *nation* first came into widespread use in sixteenth-century England, it applied to an elite.[8] After a while, in a great transformation of meaning, the term came to be applied to an entire people. Part of this transformation involved a psychological shift in which the entire population took on attributes of an elite. Thus, a sovereign people implied high status, well worth efforts to belong.

Nation fundamentally means a people that share common attributes. It often refers directly to the people born in a particular geographic area. Typically, the people of this area were at one time closely linked by a common language, shared religious traditions, and other cultural similarities. However, the common attributes that define a nation are often myths built on imagined history. These myths include common ancestry, common language, traditions, territorial possessions, and so on. They are powerful not because they are true, but because people believe in them intensely. This intensity of belief is what makes nationalism so effective in mobilizing people to act.

The historical roots of nationalism fundamentally reflect the human propensity toward aggression and violence. To a powerful extent, the nationalist traditions and the nation-states have been shaped by the invasions of the past. Over time, through common historical circumstances and political measures, nation-states emerged. These nation-states are usually multinational in terms of language, religion, and ethnic backgrounds. People from a number of different geographic origins come together—sometimes on a voluntary basis, sometimes on a forced basis—to live in an emerging nation-state where they are subjected to a shared political authority. When religion, language, and ethnic characteristics go together, it is relatively easy to establish a nation-state. But when people with diverse ethnicities, religions, and languages must live together as a new nation-state, the risks of suspicion, hatred, and violence can arise. And yet, examples throughout the world show that such people also can live together amicably. A prime example is U.S. civic nationalism, as well as that of Switzerland and even India—one of the world's most complex cases. But such amity is never easy. The United States endured an exceedingly bloody civil war. The nation of Switzerland took 700 years to consolidate. Although India struggles with serious problems (especially the conflict in Kashmir, which is largely an international conflict), most of India's vast, diverse population lives in peace and growing prosperity.

The world has seen enormous difficulty with nationalism in contemporary times. Though the problems of nationalism are global, let us focus on Europe for the moment—especially because it is often mistakenly assumed that European states are ethnically almost homogeneous, and because it has had such a powerful shaping influence on the modern world. Europe has had a vast number of ethnicities over the centuries, hundreds in the Balkans alone. Typically, each set of people has a highly prized ethnic myth: that this group's members are an ancient people and that they exist as cohesive entities or once did. These myths often support claims to coherence as a people, even to autonomy. They hold out the vision of return to an idyllic life together. There is a general tendency to idealize the group and its history and underscore its desire for respectful treatment, at a minimum; often, the desire is for a very special status. What we now loosely call nationalism is not a constant property of a group of people. Rather, it waxes and wanes, depending in substantial part on how people view their ability to obtain a state of their own and whether that would, in fact, be helpful to their goals and values.

For most of recorded history—a short fragment of human evolution—thousands of peoples having distinctive identities have somehow found a way to live together, often mixed within a particular nation-state. These states usually favored some peoples over others but ordinarily did not try to homogenize the entire population or to eliminate altogether its distinctive attributes, which provided a sense of worth to a particular people in the state. But a dramatic change occurred late in the eighteenth century when nationalism became a powerful force in Europe. There were two different aspects to this nationalism. One of these was *state-led nationalism* in which rulers vigorously pursued a specific national interest while demanding that the entire citizenry behave according to shared purposes for the nation as a whole, even at the expense of prior loyalties having to do with distinctive ethnicity. The other form of nationalism was a *state-seeking nationalism* in which some particular people claimed a distinctive political status to match their psychological identity or even set out to obtain a separate state of their own. Could both forms of nationalism come together in demanding that the state has a homogeneous population with a distinctive psychological identity and political interests? If so, entities that combine both forms would elicit strong loyalty to the mother state.[9]

A great number of states have existed since the onset of agriculture; yet the conjunction of these powerful forces has been rare. It is mainly in the last two centuries that these two forms of nationalism have gathered great strength and moved to the center of international relations. But even during the past two centuries, coinciding with the onset of the industrial revolution, only a small fraction of the world's distinctive groups—religious, linguistic, or cultural—have formed their own states. The larger states such as Britain, Germany, France, and Italy all were inhabited by heterogeneous groupings—a fact not widely understood. Yet their rulers typically made larger demands on these inhabitants in the name of the nation as a whole. The nation-states undertook to homogenize their populations to some extent, and to build social norms with unifying shared commitments. Nonetheless, nation-states still had some oppressed cultural minorities who often sought the overthrow of state power in order to establish their own states or at least a considerable degree of autonomy.

As technology and organization became more complex, new opportunities for conquests emerged, old rivalries became intensified, and the institution of war was strengthened. In the face of greater sophistication, the demands and putative benefits for nationhood were greater. Seeking such benefits, aggressive leaders brought pressure to homogenize diverse populations in the nation-state to mobilize large-scale efforts and conduct a truly population-based war with large standing military forces—far beyond the scale of prior mercenaries. But such efforts to homogenize had a powerful effect on disadvantaged minorities and bred intense resentment. So there occurred a series of unintended but important consequences—an extended struggle in which rulers had to bargain with their populations to strengthen loyalty, an expansion of definitions of citizenship, the growth of ideas of popular sovereignty, various kinds of representative institutions, and central state bureaucracies.

With these changes came an increased central control, mainly to support large military forces. Nation-states went beyond anything they had done before to create national educational systems, to impose national languages, and to organize all kinds of propagandistic activities to promote identification with the nation-state. Such changes could powerfully affect child rearing. Pressures were put on families and educational institutions (including religious ones) to adhere to these beliefs.

There were practical advantages to this approach, and a tendency toward homogeneity throughout the nation-state was manifest in Europe during this time. The process of central control was often reinforced by formulation of an alien enemy. This might be another nation-state, but commonly it was some internal alien. Anti-Semitism was prevalent.[10] In many ways this state-led nationalism was effective, yet it also stimulated state-seeking nationalism in reaction. In any case, considerable pressure was put on children through their families, schools, and youth organizations to conform to the norms of the nation-state.

The unified nation-states of Western Europe and North America are in many cases products of earlier separations followed in due course by extensive cooperation. Over several centuries, a fission process occurred in Scandinavia in which Sweden became independent of Denmark and then Norway became independent of Sweden and so on. Yet in due course, a high degree of Scandinavian cooperation evolved among these separate countries. So, too, centuries of sovereignty for large nations in Western Europe, associated with great difficulty, eventually led in the post–World War II period to the remarkable cooperation of the European community. It is important to note that a considerable period of sovereign statehood was accompanied by the evolution of democratic government. This progression facilitated adequate representation of minorities so that they could have their rights protected and express the main features of their cultural life freely. These trends reached their peaks in the second half of the twentieth century, after the bitter lessons of World War II and the dictatorships of Hitler and Stalin.

State-led nationalism gave legitimacy to a dangerous concept of precise correspondence between a people and a state. This provided great advantages to any group that could control its own state, yet minorities were often repressed. Other dangerous conditions included the situation of cultural minorities within one state adjacent to the same cultural group constituting a majority in a neighboring state, intolerance by the principal power of a nation-state toward distinctive cultural entities, and forced assimilation of minorities. Thus, state pressure for homogeneity and assimilation tended to precipitate resistance that could lead to demands for autonomy or even independence—and sometimes civil war.

In the middle of the twentieth century, especially after World War II, there occurred a worldwide spread of secular nationalism, rooted in the idea that people owed allegiance to their nations because of shared citizenship and the idea that the state was legitimate because it had popular, not religious, sanction. Secular nationalism attracted both emerging elites and weak minorities in the newly decolonized countries. To the elites, it provided an ideology that justified their position and allowed them to create power bases from which they could vault into positions of leadership ahead of traditional and religious leaders. To minorities, secular nationalism was a means toward equal participation in a public life that would not be completely dominated by the majority religious or ethnic community. Carriers of secular nationalism in the postcolonial period came primarily from the urban educated elite, not the religious sector. These proponents of secular identity wanted to promote the separation of religion and politics and, at the same time, replace traditional religious faith with faith in a secular culture.

Yet secular nationalism serves some of the functions of religion. Structurally, it includes doctrine, myth, ethics, ritual, experience, and social organization. Functionally, nationalism resembles religion by providing an overarching framework of moral order that commands strong loyalty from those who subscribe to it. Moreover, both secular nationalism and religion carry immense power to give moral sanction to martyrdom and violence. Children seeking acceptance are subject to this power. They are brought up in the nexus of a primary group but are often subjected to different pressures from secondary groups. Thus we see the shaping of adolescent beliefs and emotions toward extreme behavior, such as suicide bombing. Political leaders, especially if ruthless and charismatic, can stimulate hypernationalism with intense fervor: positive for one's own nation, negative toward others. These attitudes and beliefs are transmitted to children and youth through their families and also through the mass media.

ETHNIC NATIONALISM AND VIOLENCE

As the twentieth century drew to a close, there was a powerful current of hostile separatism based on nationalistic orientations that are fundamentally ethnocentric in character and highly prejudicial to out-groups. In the post–World War II era of rapid and confusing transition, there was a growing tendency toward separatist nationalism, not only in direct reaction to recent colonial and totalitarian rule, but also in the democracies of Western Europe—witness the Basques in Spain, the Catalans, the Corsicans, the people of the Swiss Jura, the people of Southern Tyrol, the Flemish, the Bretons, the Welsh, and the Scots. In Eastern Europe, such separatist nationalism has been mainly a reaction against dictatorship. In Western Europe, it appears to be partially a reaction against the swift pace of European integration.

Some of the causal factors in separatism are evident. One set of these is psychological. Every individual in the in-group derives a distinctive identity from identifying with the group, and this identity has a positive evaluation. It supports an individual's sense of worth and provides a reassuring sense of belonging to a highly valued entity. There are clear implications of status that is high, and indeed of superiority at least to some other peoples, perhaps even to all. This orientation provides ready justification for depreciatory and harmful behavior toward other groups, which is conveyed by adults, media, and governments and shapes the behavior of children and youth.

Economic aspects of the problem are also important. Belonging to a distinctive group with putative high status may well provide (or may be perceived to provide in the future) economic opportunities of a special kind. It may involve clear economic interests or a wishful view of economic preference. It may involve tangible control of important assets. Under harsh economic circumstances, particularly in the face of ongoing deterioration, the sense of belonging to a valued group may have direct survival connotations. This is probably why the sense of belonging became so important during evolution in the first place: *One must belong to survive.*

There are often also political and military connotations of an ethnocentric commitment. Power may well flow from this commitment and may involve aggressively acting against others, taking what might be available, and lording it over other groups. Moreover, this aspect may readily include revenge motives or the opportunity to redress insults that go back centuries—as evidenced in the Balkans during the twentieth century.

All of this has much to do with the warfare of recent years, sometimes euphemistically referred to as low-intensity conflict but nevertheless quite deadly and increasingly so. These conflicts—based variously on ethnic, nationalist, or religious distinctions—are often intended to redraw boundaries, to destroy existing nations, to reestablish parochial identities. War, including terrorism, becomes not so much an instrument of policy as an indication of a distinctive identity and an expression of solidarity. Hatred and violence may become organizing principles in themselves that do not necessarily go away for a long time, even after a valued goal is achieved.

There is a linkage between ethnocentric nationalism and hateful, violent behavior.

Nationalism remains a very powerful basis of cultural, political, and psychological identity, and its range grew throughout the world in the 1990s. There is historical evidence revealing the differential propensity of nationalisms for aggressive behavior. The mere fact of national identity does not automatically lead to violence. But for *ethnic* nationalisms, the line between in-groups and out-groups tends to be very strong. Some ethnic groups see their nations almost as separate species. In such extreme groups, foreigners are scarcely human, and there is no moral imperative to treat them in the way you would your own people. They are made into demons and therefore are vulnerable to inhuman treatment on a basis that appears to be justified. The evil other-group is assumed to be harboring malevolent intentions toward your own group. They are ready to strike against your innocent nation when the time is ripe. You must be poised for self-defense—and often the threshold of self-defense is low. These are the ethnic groups most susceptible to violence under stress. Such intense ethnic nationalism is a kind of closed society from the point of view of its members. This stands in contrast with *civic* nationalism, which is present in a more or less open society in which people may voluntarily become members—in which the pride of patriotism need not imply hatred toward others.

Ethnic entrepreneurs often intensify a heightened sense of ethnic identity and invidious distinctions between other groups in the population. These most commonly are politicians or military leaders. Such people very often have a strong self-interest. They may have personal self-aggrandizing motives such as the need to prove their strong leadership, the need to be heads of their states, or motivations for economic gains. Such leaders proclaim—and their activated followers tend to make strong assertions about—their suitability for taking control over autonomous states under several conditions: (1) when they feel likely to be harshly subordinated to another ethnic group in the face of intense competition or claims for separate statehood; (2) when the nation-state jeopardizes their distinctive identity or their shared access to economic and social advantages; and (3) when they see a major opportunity to enhance power, status, and assets, especially if they believe the opportunity is transient and must be seized promptly.

Even in rather intense ethnic nationalism, there is considerable variability in the tendency toward large-scale violence. Not many of these have been as harsh and murderous as Nazi Germany or Stalinist Russia. Though the leaders and elites typically believe that it is their duty to assert the inherent superiority of their own ethnocentric view, they vary a good deal in how systematically and how hatefully they carry out such a program. There are often islands of tolerance in the midst of ethnocentric dominance. Moreover, a harsh ethnocentric orientation may change for the better with surprising rapidity, as seen in Germany after World War II. Ethnic groups are not unchanging entities that lie dormant for centuries and then come to life when the time is ripe. Although distinct and often feeling tension toward neighboring groups, they live together peacefully for long durations. How is this possible? When does it break down? How can perceptions of improving opportunities and current satisfactions in a multiethnic nation-state help to foster positive intergroup relations? This is discussed in later chapters.

RELIGION, CONFLICT, AND MASS VIOLENCE

The continuing, accelerating technological and socioeconomic changes of the contemporary world transformation are exceedingly stimulating and hopeful in their promise for prosperity and peace, yet simultaneously difficult and in some ways even dangerous and alarming to many people across a variety of societies. The quest for smaller and simpler communities has been revived in earnest. One aspect of this has been an intensification of religious fundamentalism, sometimes carried to the point of fanatical behavior. Nowhere is this more evident than in the worldwide resurgence of a sector in each of the world's major religions that reacts to resist such bewildering change with all its complexity, ambiguity, and deep uncertainty. Such religious movements offer simple, dogmatic answers to life's basic questions, including life after death. Often, though not necessarily, they go beyond a stabilizing, comforting position to one of harsh intolerance of other religions or other groups altogether. Such intolerance can be translated by charismatic leaders into fanatical behavior, hostile zealotry, even some kind of holy war commitment. This is most vivid now in the Islamic fanatical haters of modernity, the United States, the West, Jews, and infidels. These Islamic fanatics are the main purveyors of catastrophic terrorism. But hateful zealots from other religions are also active in today's international arena.

To proponents of intense religious commitments in the non-Western world, religious revival is the answer to the ills of modern societies that they blame on a perceived failure of secular states. Such religious nationalists are often individuals with both religious and political interests. They do not necessarily reject secular politics, but they reject the notion that what constitutes a nation and legitimates the state is a rational compact that unites everyone in a geographical region through common laws and political processes.[11]

In this book, we give examples of a variety of religions, including Judaism, Christianity, Hinduism, and Islam, in which there are indications of intensely parochial attitudes, angry orientations toward other groups, and harsh intolerance—that is, prejudicial, ethnocentric outlooks. This form of emotionally charged religious intolerance is reminiscent of the era of the Crusades, with its commitment to battle to the death for souls and a ready justification for atrocities.

The rhetoric of religious nationalists in developing countries is rife with anticolonial and anti-Western feelings. Some declare that Western secular identity erodes traditional religious constructs of state and society, causes moral decline, and leads to betrayal of the most sacred principles. In extreme terms, they demonize the West and blame all their ills on its satanic representatives. They also are drawn to the fallen-angel syndrome: What they see through the global mass media is interpreted as the secular state's dismal failure to fulfill its promises of political freedom, economic prosperity, and social justice. In response, they propose a religious nationalism, with the promise of a better future, that cannot easily fail because it is based on transcendental goals and will be harder to gauge than the more materialistic hopes of secular nationalists. This response need not be violent, and religious nationalism is quite heterogeneous. The serious problem arises where it turns to violence as a way of life.

Any kind of holy war tends to provide a strong sense of community with mutually supportive solidarity in the group, but concomitantly it generates parochialism, hostile exclusion, and facile justification of mass violence. It typically involves strict obedience to a hierarchy, fanaticism of beliefs, and a loss of creative problem-solving opportunities. Under these conditions, it is exceedingly difficult to establish a stable, progressive democracy. Efforts toward democratic reform involving such fanatical fervor tend to end up in anarchy, repression, persecution, and new forms of despotism. The holy war is one of the most difficult and dangerous problems facing the international community.

Is there a special relationship between religion and violence that predisposes it to ferocity? Violent images are plentiful in religion, and religious rhetoric is often warlike, depicting Manichaean struggles between good and evil, between the sacred and profane. Moreover, religion has a great capacity to provide justification for violence, stripping it of horror and rendering it acceptable because it is imbued with deep spiritual meaning.

Religious traditions are filled with martial metaphors and the language of warfare and sacrifice. Sometimes battles in religious texts (e.g., the Bible, Hindu epics, and the Buddhist Mahavamsa) depict not so much a struggle between categories of good and evil as cosmic conflict between insiders and outsiders, us versus them, the known against the unknown. Note the Muslim notion of jihad or holy war, or Protestant exhortations to wage war against the forces of evil. Books like the Hebrew Old Testament or Hindu Ramayana and Mahabharata are also full of military intrigue, brutality, and bloody crusades.

If religious images are meant to express violent orientations in a controlled and ritualized way, how do they get translated into real acts of savagery? One reason is that religious leaders sometimes adopt the rhetoric and images of cosmic war to rally their followers to action. Such a leader may promote the image that the religious group is besieged from all sides by rather vague but very powerful cosmic foes. Furthermore, the struggle for political and social issues may be characterized as an apocalyptic battle between good and evil. This is true of the rhetoric of Sikh nationalists in India, Christian supporters of the Sandinista revolution in Nicaragua, Buddhist militants in Sri Lanka, Muslim fundamentalists in Iran, the Taliban in Afghanistan, and right-wing Jewish activists in Israel.

Religion is a powerful political tool, partially because it can legitimate and encourage violence. Although virtually all religions preach peace and nonviolence, it is their ability to sanction violence that gives them special political power. Hence, many political activists, especially nonlegal entities, use it to achieve their worldly ends. The Sikhs in India, for example, knew that they could achieve most of their demands— greater political representation and more equitable agricultural prices—within the processes of India's political system. However, they had one demand that did not have wide support at the outset and needed all the legitimation it could get: the demand for a separate state of Khalistan. It was at this juncture that Sikh political activists used religion to transform a political issue into a religious crusade that has since produced severe violence. By defining political targets as religious enemies, militants are able to sanction their killing. They justify their violence on supernatural grounds. Because they do not have the approval of officially recognized governments, they resort to a higher source—religious justification—to legitimize their actions.

Religious violence is also attractive to many because it may empower people who traditionally have not had power in society. This is true, for instance, of Muslim functionaries in Iran, Islamic groups that won elections in Algeria in 1991 and 1992, and lower-caste Sikhs in India. By breaking the state's monopoly on sanctioned killing, religious violence may appropriate power to depreciated people.

Minorities have four serious reasons to worry about religious nationalism: (1) It can readily lead to a monopolized glorification of the symbols and culture of the majority religion, (2) it can cause the government to render preferential treatment to members of the majority community, (3) it can require minorities to adhere to religious laws that they do not respect, and (4) at worst, it can lead to the systematic destruction of minority cultures and even of minority peoples.

It is important to note that religious nationalism is not entirely closed to pluralistic tolerance. In fact, some movements have shown openness to a diversity of members and might implement tolerant rule if empowered to do so. Religious nationalism can strengthen positive identity while also favoring the political organization of the nation-state. In such cases, it attempts to reconcile traditional religion and modern politics.

Altogether, religious nationalism is more varied and flexible than these movements appear on the surface. If the technically advanced democracies were to demonize this ideology and its adherents, a new cold war might occur. Many religious nationalists themselves decry those tendencies of their ideology that the democracies find particularly worrisome: the inclination toward dictatorship and propensity for hatred of others. The basic warning signal is harsh intolerance of other groups. Effective opposition to these tendencies may be found in the religious communities themselves, but the United Nations and other international entities, as well as religious leaders, could play a moderating role in preventing the excesses of religious nationalism, seeking ways to help such societies protect human rights and foster tolerance for different sectors of the human community.

THE ORIGINS OF GENOCIDE

The expulsion of an undesirable population from a given territory—due to religious or ethnic discrimination; political, strategic, or ideological considerations; or a combination of these—has been practiced throughout human history. In fact, such practices intensified in the late nineteenth and twentieth centuries. Recent events in what was formerly Yugoslavia are a repetition of processes that nearly all other parts of Europe have undergone in efforts to create ethnically distinct territories. Children and adolescents are typically caught up in such horrors, both as victims and perpetrators.

As early as the eighth century B.C., Assyria made forced resettlement of conquered populations a state policy. In the Middle Ages, ethnic cleansing was applied primarily for religious reasons. Medieval Christianity punished nonbelievers via expulsion and massacre. Such religious cleansing targeted Jews, who formed a sizable minority in many areas. Jews were expelled in peak periods of atrocity: from England (1290), France (1306), Hungary (1349–60), Austria (1491), Lithuania (1445), Cracow (the capital of what is now Poland; 1494), and Spain (1492). By 1530, the Confession of Augsburg enthroned religious homogeneity as the basis of political order, thereby giving impetus to further cleansings.

The first major instance of cleansing for ethnic rather than religious reasons occurred in England in the 1640s and 1650s. The target then was the Irish, a group seen by the English government as a potential ally of Catholic France and Spain and, therefore, a strategic threat. In the United States in the early 1800s and later, the white population applied its own brand of ethnic cleansing vis-à-vis the indigenous Native American population. So it was, too, with the aborigines in Australia.

The nineteenth century marked the first time that the complete destruction of an ethnic group became the goal of a state. In Turkey in the late 1890s, Turks and Kurds unleashed a war on Armenian villages. This effort culminated in the devastation of 1915, when 1.5 million Armenians were killed. This number represented more than half of the Armenian population and about 90 percent of their ethnic territory at the time. By the middle of the twentieth century, ethnic cleansing reached its height with the Nazis' Final Solution campaign against the Jews. Deportation, expulsion, and massacre led to the death of about six million European Jews and several hundred thousand other people in target groups.

It is curious and troubling that education has seriously neglected the fact that the destruction of human groups has a very long history, and the importance of understanding the conditions that favor such destruction. Often such destruction is carried out in the name of one god or another—theological or secular religions will do—and religious wars have sometimes been extremely brutal. In the twentieth century, tragically, we had not moved beyond such slaughter. Given the horrors of World War II and the associated Holocaust, it would have been plausible to suppose that a worldwide revulsion toward mass violence would occur and that the second half of the twentieth century would be free of such disasters. But that was not the case. Many millions of people were killed in their own countries. Prominent among these countries were Cambodia, Indonesia, Burundi, Nigeria, Paraguay, the Sudan, Uganda, Yugoslavia, and Rwanda. Totalitarian governments have tended to follow Hitler's example as well as Stalin's, killing not only individuals, but also whole groups who are perceived as actual or potential enemies. How is it possible that such atrocious behavior should be so prevalent in a world that is in so many ways technically advanced and putatively civilized? Understanding such considerations can contribute to preventing such slaughter in the future and therefore should become an integral part of education.

Under exceedingly harsh, disappointing, frustrating, and even humiliating conditions, the strong tendency in human behavior is to protect oneself and one's immediate family in survival terms; to protect the psychological self, a sense of worth as a person, a sense of still belonging to a valued group; to try to make the terrible contemporary circumstances comprehensible or meaningful; and to find some framework in which to explain what is happening and how it might get better. It has been all too easy throughout the long history of humanity to turn toward scapegoats, toward readily available targets, to devalue certain specified out-groups perceived as dangerous or as responsible for the current difficulty—and in the process to join groups and adopt ideologies that justify harming those who are seen as the cause of the problems. Such frustrated and angry groups often stimulate the motivation to be aggressive toward out-groups and diminish inhibitions against harming the chosen scapegoats.

If the society has strongly depreciated a particular group within it over a long period of time, if the society has an intensely obedient respect for authority, and if it has beliefs about the superiority of certain mainstream in-groups, then the conditions are ripe for hitting hard against the target group. Typically, this does not happen all at once; rather, there is a gradual progression of events. A kind of habituation occurs in which small harmful acts come to seem familiar and acceptable, especially if there is no strong response from opponents or outsiders who might be expected to object. The larger harmful actions may then go forward, especially as justifications become more elaborate and well-known in the society. Indeed, a fairly comprehensive ideology tends to evolve that explains the whole problem and justifies the extensive harm being done to the target group. All too often, members of society who are not directly affected do very little to help the targets or uphold standards of common decency. Their passivity in the face of danger to others, and the tacit acquiescence of outside groups—including nearby nations—makes it easier for the damage to expand. On the other hand, active opposition by strong internal groups or by outside nations can raise concerns about retaliation or stir the moral values latent in the society.[12]

These considerations that apply to mass slaughter in a society also have considerable applicability to the origins of war, which is the other principal form of group violence. Exceedingly difficult conditions of daily life in the context of an authoritarian or totalitarian regime with aggressive leadership and a well-established external target may coincide to make the initiation of war an attractive option.

So, very difficult conditions of life occurring in the context of a rigid, authoritarian culture are dangerous. Such conditions threaten not only the security but also the sense of worth of the people involved. Then, powerful self-protective impulses are mobilized to protect the pride and the safety of the valued group, which means so much to one's survival. There is likely to be an intensification of emphasis on traditional values and the mobilization of historic myths having to do with glory, honor, and revenge.

Under harsh conditions, it is very difficult to find a useful, hopeful course of action. One of the simplest ways to respond is to turn against others, especially those who have some prior negative identification. Here we encounter the familiar, invidious distinctions between in-group and out-group. History shows the remarkable capacity of the human species to find reasons to devalue members of an out-group, to blame suffering on them, to see them as the source of evil. It is then a relatively small step to justify violence toward them. In the process, members of the in-group tend to be drawn together—their own solidarity and mutual support feel very good. They are also reassured that they are better than the out-group; their self-esteem is thus raised in a satisfying way. All of this may contribute to visions of a better society, as if to say, "When we get rid of those terrible people who have brought this on us, we will enter a glorious new era."

Most societies have reasonably strong constraints against killing others. So a process is needed by which these inhibitions can be overcome. The process tends to be gradual, until some fatal threshold has been passed. Often leaders assume responsibility in the name of a higher calling, and various ways are found to diminish any sense of personal accountability among the public. This includes some denial of reality, such as the very few people in Nazi Germany who allowed themselves to be aware of the slaughter that was going on in the concentration camps. The ideology is presented in such attractive ways that killing even comes to be seen as right, necessary, and worthy. New group norms may well evolve; institutions may be modified or created to serve the purpose of slaughter. Some individuals are well suited by personality to play a leading role. They may select themselves and come forward. For example, many members of the early Gestapo in Nazi Germany had long histories of violence, and the new social code was entirely congenial for them. Part of the process involves ways of providing justification to bystanders for their own passivity. They, too, must devalue the targets in some way.

Most cultures have some characteristics that make group violence possible or even easy under certain circumstances. If a concept of superiority is widely accepted in a culture, with the notion that it is natural for some to exert strong dominance over others, then violence is easier. Harsh economic conditions also facilitate hatred and violence. Nationalism tends to become intense when an attitude of cultural superiority combines with a strain of self-doubt, particularly when something has happened that exacerbates the doubt and therefore the motivation to reassert superiority. Such a circumstance may well arise from a severe economic downturn or from the humiliation of a lost war. These were the circumstances in which Hitler came to power.

Cultures that have undertaken mass killing tend to be ones in which there is a very strong obedience to authority—typically ingrained from early childhood onward. Thus, a habit develops of following leaders without question, and inflammatory leaders may cross the threshold of large-scale violence with their followers in hot pursuit. Such cultures give short shrift to pluralism. A monolithic set of beliefs prevails, and strong authority enforces uniformity. These conditions existed in Germany in the 1920s and 1930s.

Predisposing conditions to the Nazi Holocaust included (1) an authoritarian culture, (2) deeply embedded prejudice and ethnocentric orientations, and (3) very difficult life conditions. Similar observations could be made about the early Soviet Union after World War I. There the fanatical ideology championed by Stalin primarily identified the wealthy and powerful from the previous regime as the enemy, more than the Jews or other ethnic groups who were nevertheless secondary targets for abuse. The ideology justified violence in the name of social justice, looking to a better world that would be created by carrying out ruthless slaughter of those who were putatively standing in the way. So, both in Germany and in the Soviet Union, millions perished in the name of some higher good that provided justification for pervasive hatred and organized killing. In these cases, the ideology is nurtured in childhood and strengthened in adolescence, especially among those who are perceived by the regime as potential leaders. It is important to note that the international community played a very weak role in opposing such killing. There was much denial of reality among decent people in this failure to intervene, but there was also an underlying assumption that the violence would be restricted to these other countries far away. That turned out to be a false assumption, as such assumptions must increasingly be false in the highly interdependent, hypercommunicative world of the twenty-first century.

Hitler and Stalin were unusual examples of leadership. Even though the cultural characteristics that shape the lives of the followers are exceedingly important, and the immediate context of exacerbating circumstances is very important, too, a great deal of emphasis needs to be put on leadership characteristics. Among the leaders competing for top positions in postwar Germany and the postwar Soviet Union during the 1920s were different kinds of people, with different outcomes being conceivable. The ability of demagogic leaders to foster a climate of hatred is a crucial part of the social context that permits mass slaughter. Their ability to implement genocidal programs is enhanced in the violence-drenched circumstances of war and revolution.[13] So the international community must find ways to recognize and thwart such leaders at an early stage in their inflammatory behavior, and to strengthen the hand of moderate leaders.[14]

CONCLUSION

The transformed modern world in which we live—with all its rapidity of technological change, pressures of media and Internet in the information age, and unforeseen dislocations—pulls people toward strongly supportive groups; and these in turn (particularly with charismatic, inflammatory leadership) may easily become harsh, separatist, and depreciatory toward others. A deadly combination of predisposing cultural characteristics and severe social stress, plus distinctively hateful, fanatical leadership, can lead to mass killing, even genocide. Such conditions occur again and again. The seductive justifications for hideous atrocities can be provided, as they were by Hitler, Stalin, Pol Pot, and Milosevic. Indeed, they can be spread more efficiently and vividly now by advanced telecommunications than ever before. Deteriorating economic conditions, erosion of social norms, or mass migration may readily exacerbate such intergroup tensions. Hateful attitudes may be directed toward depreciated outsiders or toward minorities in one's own country—or both.

To diminish the likelihood of disasters, it is important to identify elements of government, social structure, institutions, leadership, and prevalent attitudes that can be used to reduce hatred and violence—to enhance orientations of caring, concern, social responsibility, and mutual aid within and between groups. We have done this in a recent book.[15] It is important that such efforts include education and other socializing factors during the years of growth and development, so that young people are prepared to learn to live together in peaceful societies. A large part of this is educating people for constructive resolution of life's ongoing conflicts through families, schools, universities, community organizations, religious institutions, and the media. Such education must include an understanding of human groups in war and peace. This is a fundamental challenge for the century that has just begun. We have more to say about the long-term value of this approach in Chapter 16. In most of this book, we provide examples of ingenious efforts being made in various countries to understand and detoxify the hateful approaches that have so often contaminated education.

4

Teaching Hatred

We turn now to egregious examples of ways that education can be used to instill hatred, with the help of authoritarian states and fanatical leaders (either theological or secular) who shape children's lives. There have been vivid examples of this throughout the twentieth century. The twenty-first century starts with the dramatic case of some Islamic fundamentalist schools that follow in this tradition of molding the lives of children for careers of hatred and violence. We describe these examples to provide a sharp contrast to the remainder of this book. Our fundamental aspiration is to inspire educators and leaders to embrace the important alternative role of education in fostering prosocial, empathic, and cooperative behavior—with insight into the destructive forces of human experience—that can provide the basis for a peaceful world in the long run. To be effective, we must address the obstacles to education in constructing such programs. Children can be brought up to hate, to condone killing, and even to participate in killing. That experiment has been done repeatedly. In the rest of this book, let us look briefly at examples of this destructive educational experience and then at the other side of the coin—learning to live together peacefully.

A VIVID HISTORICAL EXAMPLE FROM HITLER'S GERMANY

The human capacity to shape child and adolescent development toward a pervasive culture of hatred and violence was vividly demonstrated by the Nazi experience. The historian Klaus Fischer writes on youth and education, and women and the family, in his book *Nazi Germany—A New History*.[1] We begin with the origin of youth groups as a countercultural protest and move to the creation of the Hitler Youth movement and ways in which it exploited these relatively innocent youthful protests. Nazi education, its philosophy, and the creation of elite schools are described in terms of their attempt to shape the minds and bodies of boys toward devotion to the Führer and toward their future as Nazi leaders. Teachers, as well, were indoctrinated and obligated to behave in a prescribed manner toward the same end. The family, particularly the woman's role in it, was seen as the social underpinning of society. The Nazi glorification of motherhood and the family was a means of creating more children to serve Hitler and the Nazi regime.

German Youth Movements

One of the most important goals of National Socialism was to ready German youth for action. Following Germany's industrial revolution, youth (especially in the middle class) organized themselves into youth groups in opposition to the "Philistine mores and values of their elders and the materialistic imperatives spawned by modern industrial civilization."[2] Two forms of youth groups emerged from these largely escapist youthful protests. The first form involved activities like hiking trips, folk singing around campfires, sharing interests, and rites used to build bonds, including gender bonding and cultivating the myths of German heritage. These were ways of evading the constraints of middle-class existence and achieving solidarity. The second form was an escape of youth from the modern world into a Utopian fantasy that could somehow become a model for the future. After World War I, new martial youth groups were formed—for example, Bündische Jugend (Bündi Youth)—that elevated the role of the soldier and promoted the notion of self-sacrifice for the good of one's country.[3] The Nazis made clever use of these youthful protests to further their own agenda.

During the time that Hitler seized power in 1933, the Hitler Youth organization comprised about 108,000 members. By the end of that year, under the leadership of Baldur von Schirach, most German youth movements in the Third Reich had been merged by force into the Nazi Party's one Hitler Youth. Schirach, in 1936, succeeded in separating this organization from the Ministry of the Interior and transformed it into an authority that reported directly to Hitler. It became law on December 1, 1936, that all young German boys and girls (aged 10 to 18) would be educated not only at home and in school but also in the Hitler Youth to ensure that their physical, moral, and intellectual orientation was consistent with the ideals of National Socialism to promote servitude to the state. The law also stated that the Reich leader (a high-ranking official with massive power in a particular area within the Nazi Party) was the one appointed to educate young Germans in the Hitler Youth.[4] Participation became mandatory in a second law that was issued on March 25, 1939.

In 1939, Hitler Youth membership rose to nearly 8.9 million. It was structured in two main branches, one for boys and one for girls. There were two subdivisions in each of these branches: One subdivision addressed children from ages 10 to 14 and the other subdivision addressed youth from ages 15 to 18. All young people had to be registered by a parent or guardian; parents or guardians who did not register their children faced fines or imprisonment.

The Hitler Youth motto was "Führer, command—we follow!"[5] The motive behind this movement was to indoctrinate youth in the mind-set of Hitler. Young people were caught up in their own idealism. A fundamental notion was that youth should be led by youth, but given that these youth leaders were already indoctrinated and were representatives of the Nazi state, there was little focus on individual growth and no real freedom of expression. Rather, the aim was to inspire devotion to "an aggressive party spirit."[6] Toward that end, the activities took on a military tone, with marching, military-style games; songs about ideology; and intonation of passwords and common phrases (for example, "Heil Hitler" and "Hitler is Germany and Germany is Hitler").[7] Gone were the days of innocent casual outings and Utopian fantasies.

Nazi Education

The aim of Nazi education was to produce a new individual—one who was strong, a "self-conscious racial type who was proud of country and loyal to the führer."[8] The existing authoritarian school structure was fine and did not need to be altered. However, a widespread firing of individual teachers occurred at every level. First to go were teachers who were ideologically opposed—especially the Jews. The remaining teachers were forced to join the National Socialist Teachers' League, which monitored the behavior of teachers throughout Germany. The Teachers' League was responsible for indoctrinating teachers in mandatory 8- to 14-day courses held at special camps throughout Germany. Its focus was on the duties of German teachers under National Socialism. The school system was rigidly centralized, and the secondary schools were divided into three broad models with emphasis in science, modern languages, and the classics. The spirit of the new system was realized in the universities as well, through the League of German Students. A marked degradation in teaching occurred in the middle of 1933, because many outstanding Jewish teachers were eliminated due to mandatory screening. In 1935, the Nazi Party, wherever possible, assigned a new Nazi rector (headmaster), who then appointed politically obedient deans. These deans in turn appointed obedient department heads. Once world-renowned for its excellent teaching staffs, German universities suffered a tragic decline in quality. But the regime was proud of its anti-intellectualism. The Nazis did not seek independent thinking and creative problem solving, nor were they concerned with constructive relations with other students. They were concerned with anti-Semitism, hateful orientations, utter loyalty to the dictator, and the superiority of pure Germans.

Nazi Philosophy

Analytical ways of thinking were immediately suspect because they led to open-mindedness, skepticism, and tolerance.[9] The goal of Nazi education was to produce young Germans who thought along strong racist lines and were prepared for highly aggressive behavior. Educating the will rather than the mind became the primary consideration. This "wholesome racial type" was to simply use knowledge as a means to ends presented by Hitler. Any display of cleverness or initiative was discouraged. In Hitler's *Mein Kampf*, his beliefs about mass education and mass obedience are clear: "The folkish state . . . has to direct its entire education primarily not at pumping in mere knowledge, but at the breeding of absolutely healthy bodies. Of secondary importance is the training of mental abilities. But here again first of all the development of the character, especially the promotion of willpower and determination, connected with education for joyfully assuming responsibility, and only as the last thing, scientific schooling."[10]

Hitler believed that intellectuals were treacherous because he perceived them as able to destroy group cohesion and faith. He thought it was better for the community to have a physically fit person with joyful determination and strong moral character (by his odd definition) than it was to have a weakling who was bright and clever. In fact, he wished to eliminate weakness and train youth to conquer their fear of death and to be obedient followers. So, sports and indoctrination were dual supports of the Nazi world. It followed that teachers were not simply instructors, but soldiers who served the aims of National Socialism.

Above all, the new Nazi superman was to be strong physically. Sports that promoted aggression, such as cross-country running, soccer, and boxing, were added to the list of activities because they were intended to foster the spirit of attack. If a student performed poorly in sports, it was grounds for dismissal.

Nazis also had their hand in the way academic subjects were taught. For example, history was distorted to fit the Nazi model. Texts were changed to favor war stories. War imagery in textbooks was combined with stories of rabbits, robins, and flowers. Whenever feasible, pictures or stories of Hitler were used to stir up enthusiasm for the Nazi cause. Boys and girls were to be instructed in the need for and the nature of racial purity.

A dual tracking system was also set into place. One track was for ordinary Germans and the other was for future Nazi leaders. Hitler's theory for his youthful aggressors was to ready them for their daring tasks by first taking them from their parents while they were still very young. His theory consisted of six steps: (1) Hitler Youth induction and then a prescribed chain of maturation through the other incremental steps, (2) labor service, (3) army service, (4) marriage, (5) further political instruction in a high, elite academy of the Nazi Party, and (6) finally, complete absorption in a party university. Hitler's plan, presented in a speech in December 1938, was aimed at what amounted to enslavement for life. Because of his mercurial nature, this plan was never fully realized, but three elite schools did emerge. Different Nazi leaders were responsible for the creation of the National Political Institutes of Education (Napolas), the Adolf Hitler schools, and the Castles of Order (Ordensburgen).

NAPOLAS   Education minister Bernhard Rust officially presented the Napolas idea to Hitler for his birthday on April 20, 1933. Thirty-nine schools were created over a 10-year period. In 1936, these schools were run by Himmler's Schutzstaffel, or Protective Squads (SS). The primary mission was to train political soldiers destined to become future government leaders. Therefore, it emphasized political indoctrination and physical training. Besides a clear focus along strict military lines in the daily routine of drills, communal activities, and reveille, Napolas students were assigned tasks with the general German population. For approximately 6 to 8 weeks, they helped farmers to harvest crops and toiled along with factory workers. These students—on the road to becoming the future elite—were to familiarize themselves with the needs of ordinary Germans. It was a distorted exercise, because Napolas turned out to be a system of schooling that produced arrogant, partially educated technicians who thought of themselves as leaders. Theoretically, these schools were open to all German boys, but in practice, party district chiefs handpicked these young people. The cadets were selected for their intellectual ability and their physical fitness, but also for their racial purity. Romanticized activities such as nightly campfires and ceremonies celebrating manhood were rituals to instill in these youngsters the institute's motto, "Believe, Obey, Fight."[11]

ADOLF HITLER SCHOOLS   Four years later, on April 20, 1937, the Führer received a second birthday gift. A joint project by Robert Ley and Baldur von Schirach, the system of Adolf Hitler Schools functioned as an alternative to the regular German education system. Its mission was to groom future party leaders and Hitler Youth leaders. By 1942, only 11 such schools existed. Students were trained in sociopolitical subjects and early military training, similar to that of the Napolas.

ORDENSBURGEN   Education in the third type of school, the Ordensburgen, was to have been a capstone experience in political indoctrination. The students were to have gone through the Hitler Youth program, to have received Adolf Hitler School diplomas, and to have performed labor service and army duty. (A grand plan by Nazi philosopher Alfred Rosenberg for further indoctrination of the best students at a party university never happened.) Pomerania (Crössinee), Upper Bavaria (Sonthofen), and the Eifel (Vogelsang) were the three locations of operating these enormous Castles of Order. They were designed to accommodate 1,000 cadets each. Requirements for entrance were minimal. They were to be "sound fellows" (Ley's phrase) aged 25 to 30 and experienced in the Nazi Party.[12] Training, however, only prepared them for clerical or midlevel careers, not for real leadership positions. Outsiders made fun of the limited abilities of these graduates and labeled them "golden pheasants" (for their gold uniforms and limited mental abilities).

The Napolas were the most successful Nazi schools due to their traditional German military approach that appealed to upper-class parents because of the emphasis on elitism. Overall, the Nazi education efforts were riddled with distortions. Nevertheless, they were able to miseducate and misuse an entire generation of youth. In the short run, many young people felt strong under the Third Reich's indoctrination, but on the whole they were twisted and constrained in their development by this system that was fundamentally antagonistic to human dignity and intellectual curiosity. The emphasis on domination, depreciation of other peoples, strength training for aggressive aims, and preparation to hate and kill—all of this reminds us of the dangers of education in dictatorships, putting children into a destructive trajectory for a lifetime.

Women and the Family

Nazis presented a false glorification of the traditional, clean-cut German family in which Aryan parents lovingly sheltered and protected their children. Nazi art also evoked such images. But this was a ruse. What the Nazis mainly wanted from German women was for them to produce as many children as possible to serve the regime's hateful values. This aim was promoted in several ways: by curtailing women's access to economic opportunities and roles outside the home, by making abortion a crime, and by offering couples monetary incentives to encourage reproduction (for example, marriage loans, child subsidies, and generous family allowances).

Yearly, on August 12 (the birthday of Hitler's mother), the Honors Cross was awarded to the most fertile mothers. Gold was given to a mother with more than eight children, silver to a mother of more than six, and bronze to a mother of five children.

Destructive motives were behind this false aggrandizement and pious attitude toward the family. Nazis understood that the main acculturation process took place in the family unit. In this totalitarian state, the aim was to fashion the family unit as an extension of state policy. The Nazi image of a woman was traditional—she was a homemaker and a mother. So women stayed at home to raise their large families. The wife of the Nazi propaganda chief, Magda Goebbels, was tall, blond, and attractive—the quintessential woman of the Third Reich. The propaganda chief likened a woman to a female bird who makes herself beautiful for her mate in order to hatch eggs for him. In exchange, the male bird would provide food and protection for her. The female bird, however, must not preen herself too much; that was considered decadent. Instead, natural beauty was highlighted. Nazis would often compare the simple beauty of Aryan women with the heavily made-up women of Western democracies who were considered to be conniving and irresponsible.

The smokescreen of praise for womanhood attempted to hide the fact that Nazi men were stultifying female development by maintaining this stereotypical view of them. Hitler's view of women was a condescending one that was shared by most Nazi leaders. Women were likened to pets: naive, unintelligent, cuddly creatures.[13] He believed women should be used for one purpose—to contribute eternally to society by bringing up healthy, obedient children. As a result, women were essentially cut off from the legal, medical, and teaching professions, among other constraints. Declared illogical, women were also excluded from jury duty.

German mothers were encouraged to support the aggressive drive of men and to use their immense influence on their sons for the same purpose. Six ideas in particular helped to shape the aggressive and authoritarian characteristics of men:

1. Males were considered to be culturally more valuable than females.
2. The father's place was that of a king in the family. It was his right, and he was expected to rule and have unconditional family obedience.
3. German women were expected to be homemakers and to bear children.
4. German women were expected to maintain immaculately clean houses and to rule in that small domain with a very firm hand.

5. Marriage roles were split: Men were the breadwinners, and women, the homemakers.
6. Raising children was also stratified. Boys were raised to compete aggressively in the world, and girls were conditioned for homemaking.

In the face of intense social pressure, German women actively fostered the desired qualities in their children. Just like men, women were swayed by Nazi propaganda. Large numbers of women voted for Hitler; they supported him enthusiastically. The fact that they did points to a high degree of self-deception about their own well-being and the dangers of the Nazi lifestyle for their children.[14]

In the short run, the Hitler Youth organization met its goals of shaping obedient, prejudiced, hyperaggressive men and women who enthusiastically supported the Nazi enterprise. Yet the Nazi attempt at educating for hate was ultimately unsuccessful. Fortunately, the Nazi defeat in World War II gave this experiment only a 12-year life. Thus it was unable to destroy the European cultural heritage that had been built over many hundreds of years. In any event, its effects were steadily overcome during and after the postwar occupation by democracies, leading to a transformation of West Germany into a vibrant democracy over several decades of intensive reconstruction. After World War II, with much help and pressure from the United States, the people of West Germany undertook the painful process of reexamining the Nazi experience. Although many Germans were resistant to the international Nuremberg trials of Nazi leaders, these were followed in the 1960s by many trials in German courts that had a strong impact on German opinion. The new democratic leaders not only pursued justice in the courts, but also embarked on a broad process of educating the public about Nazi atrocities.[15] About a million children were taken on visits to concentration camps, and a thousand books on the Holocaust were published in Germany. The 1978 U.S. television series *Holocaust* (directed by Marvin Chomsky) was shown on German television. In classrooms and public memorial services and in vivid gestures of regret by some political leaders, the horrors of the past were recognized and bitter lessons learned. A dramatic symbol of this process occurred when German Chancellor Willy Brandt went down on his knees at the death camp and this gesture of atonement was widely reported.

Shortly after World War II the U.S. occupation forces, oriented toward the formidable task of building a German democracy, early undertook to move the educational system in this direction and worked intensively with educational and political leaders to do so.[16] This stands in marked contrast with East Germany, where the neo-Stalinist regime under control of the Soviet Union kept the authoritarian mode in a position of primacy. Its propaganda directed all blame for the Nazi era onto West Germany. The official mantle of antifascism was draped on the Soviet bloc. When East Germany finally became free at the end of the Soviet Union, it had to begin facing the fact of its active participation in two destructive dictatorships over six decades. This difficult task is still under way. In any event, the contrast between West and East Germany in the post–World War II period illustrates the human capacity to move from dictatorship to democracy with education at all levels—from schools to leaders of powerful sectors—playing an important role in the process of transformation. Perhaps some encouragement can be taken from this fact as we examine current examples of hate education, particularly in the Middle East, in the rest of this chapter.

EDUCATION FOR HATE:
CURRENT EXAMPLES RELATED TO TERRORISM

In a *New York Times* article about a month following the tragic attacks on the World Trade Center and the Pentagon on September 11, 2001, Rick Bragg describes a set of schools that shape the minds and hearts of youth in Pakistan, instilling in them distrust and hatred of the United States.[17] These youth are taught that the United States is a society of Christians and Jews whose goal is to annihilate Islam.

The *madrasa* is a kind of seminary that breeds holy warriors in Pakistan. The word translates to "university of all righteous knowledge." There is some debate as to the number of madrasas. Anywhere from 4,000 to 10,000 have been reported in Pakistan. According to Bragg's article, some 750,000 young people in nearly 7,500 madrasas learn to recite and obey Islamic law through a rigid and distorted interpretation of the Koran, which includes the duty of all Muslims to rise up in jihad, or holy war, against the infidels. They would die defending Islam and its hero, Osama bin Laden.

In March 2003, *Foreign Policy* magazine published an article entitled "The Terrorist Notebooks." Here we find chilling evidence of the type of training provided by terrorist schools of Central Asia in the mid-1990s. With the goal of religious purification, these young men are taught to hate, to distinguish between true believers and nonbelievers, and to turn against former allies with destructive weapons that they learn to create out of common, everyday items.[18] Education in the madrasas is narrow. Most teach very little if any science, math, languages, or any history beyond what is found in the Koran. The schools engender devotion from children of the poorest classes, who would go hungry if it were not for the schools' providing for their basic needs for food, clothing, and shelter.

Support of madrasas often comes from other Islamic states such as Saudi Arabia. Children's minds are honed to prepare them mentally for jihad. There is no actual training with weapons, though it is not difficult to imagine this addition, at least as an organized extracurricular activity, in this context of a hate-drenched atmosphere. But they are taught about the injustices, cruelty, and closed-mindedness of Americans. Teachers claim that Americans kill innocent people and that because the Koran forbids the killing of women, children, elders, and cattle, the students can only fight back under authority of a holy war. Jews are to blame for the attacks on the World Trade Center and the Pentagon. The events of September 11, 2001, are viewed as a plot by Israel to bring the world into war. Students are told that Muslims might be briefly discredited but that when the truth finally comes out, it will ultimately destroy the Jews. This message flows from the madrasas through its students, moving into the shops and to the people on the streets.

The outside world is largely closed off to students. There are no televisions, magazines, or newspapers available except those deemed acceptable by the elders. But the students do not seem to mind, because they believe that the elders will tell them what they need to know, and the Truth comes only from the madrasas' teachers, who claim that the attacks on the United States were the wrath of God. They claim it was Allah who put the idea into the minds of the Jews to fly the planes into the World Trade Center towers and the Pentagon.

So here we have a vivid, current example of education for hate. Though this shaping of young minds toward hatred and violence seems to achieve its own goals in the short run, the long-term prospects for these children are poor in terms of any humane or democratic values, as well as with reference to any income-earning skills; and these children are predisposed to inflict great damage on others.

Darul Uloom Haqqania—One of Pakistan's Largest Madrasas

Because the outside world is just beginning to learn about these schools, we must initially rely on high-quality journalists for information concerning them. In a *New York Times* article, Thomas L. Friedman reported on Peshwar, Pakistan, and its largest madrasa, with 2,800 resident students.[19] The madrasa, Darul Uloom Haqqania, is now famous because the Taliban leader Mullah Muhammed Omar once attended it, as did many other Taliban figures. Although Omar never graduated, he received an honorary degree because he left to perform jihad and to create a fundamentalist Islamic government.

There has been a phenomenal growth of madrasas in Pakistan over the past quarter century because the secular state education system gradually fell apart. In 1978, according to Friedman, there were 3,000 madrasas, and in the year 2001, there were 39,000. These madrasas provide room and board, education, and clothing for thousands of Pakistani boys, who are freed from a life of living on the streets.

In Darul Uloom Haqqania, for example, the curriculum is almost completely religious, with its focus on rote learning of the Koran and teachings of the Prophet Muhammad. Students hope that one day they may become mullahs, or spiritual leaders. The Mogul emperor Aurangzeb Alamgir, who died in 1707, designed the curriculum used today. Virtually no modern secular textbooks are used. Only one library shelf at the Darul Uloom Haqqania is dedicated to science books, and the books found there were mostly written in the 1920s. A sign on the classroom wall indicates that this room was a gift of the kingdom of Saudi Arabia. A famous Koranic verse, beautifully chanted by an 8-year-old boy, conveys the message, "The faithful shall enter paradise and the unbelievers shall be condemned to eternal hellfire."[20]

Historically, madrasas have served as a base for Islamic scholars who became the leaders of the Taliban movement in Afghanistan, and for their fighters prior to and during the U.S.-led military campaign in 2002. The government of Pakistan finally ended its support for the Taliban late in 2001 in response to U.S. pressure. Until then, madrasas operated with virtually no regulation. The government claimed not to notice incoming foreign students and the role that such students played in militant activities in Afghanistan and in Kashmir—the location of a territorial dispute with India.[21] The responsibility of rebuilding the schools after the war against the Taliban (so that modernity, Islam, and pluralism may be joined) falls on the citizens of Pakistan, but international cooperation can help.

Hate Media in Rwanda and Palestine

We now provide a vivid example of education for hatred utilizing radio rather than schools. The vehicle is a means to the end of inciting to violence. *New York Times* writer Marlise Simons asked, in an article published in the *International Herald Tribune*, "Can freedom of speech degenerate into genocide?" or "Can journalism kill?"[22] The prosecutors of the UN war crimes tribunal for Rwanda answered yes.

From October 2000 until March 2002, three journalists—two founding directors of the Rwandan radio station, Radio Mille Collines, and a former publisher and editor of the newspaper, *Kangura*—were on trial for their participation in the 1994 slaughter of the Tutsi. In addition to the men's being accused of genocide and incitement to genocide through use of their radio broadcasts and newspaper articles, this trial also brought into focus the larger issue of the media's role in the killing of more than 800,000 people in Rwanda.

The prosecutors in this "media trial" argued that the accused were part of a plan to use their media outlets to spread ethnic hatred and to persuade people to kill their enemies—the Tutsi and the moderate Hutu. The result was a demonization of the Tutsi, largely through use of the media. Radio Mille Collines, nicknamed Radio Hate, was the primary mouthpiece of the extremist Hutu power movement. It initially addressed the Tutsi opponents with such vitriolic messages as, "You cockroaches must know you are made of flesh. We won't let you kill, we will kill you."[23] Then, once the massacres began, prosecutors at the trial stated that broadcasts "goaded Hutu militia groups to 'go to work' and kept inciting people with messages like 'the graves are not yet full.'"

Defendants felt that these indictments were a gross mockery and harmful, whereas prosecutors maintained that their case was actually about criminal conspiracy, not about freedom or excesses of the press, and that both Radio Mille Collines and the newspaper *Kangura* were as responsible for the plan to kill the Tutsi as the extremist militias were. Because Rwandans have little exposure to television, the radio is an extremely powerful tool of public education in hatred and violence and a source of direct logistical aid to the military.

Throughout the 100-day slaughter, Radio Mille Collines actually steered the militia and called direct hits. The station broadcast names and addresses of targeted individuals, as well as the vehicle license numbers and hiding places of refugees. FM radios were at each of the thousands of roadblocks set up in Rwanda. One police investigator said in court that, in his prison interviews, "Many people told us they had killed because the radio had told them to kill."[24]

A hit song by Hutu pop star Simon Bikindi illustrates the extent of genocidal propaganda broadcast throughout Rwanda. This famous number, called "I Hate These Hutus," was a song of "good neighborliness":[25]

I hate these Hutus, these arrogant Hutus, braggarts, who scorn other Hutus, dear comrades. . . .

I hate these Hutus, these de-Hutuized Hutus, who have disowned their identity, dear comrades.

I hate these Hutus, these Hutus who march blindly, like imbeciles, this species of naïve Hutus who are manipulated, and who tear themselves up, joining in a war whose cause they ignore.

I detest these Hutus who are brought to kill, to kill, I swear to you, and who kill the Hutus, dear comrades.

If I hate them, so much the better . . .

The long struggle between Israel and the Palestinians is a political and military one, urgently in need of serious and sustained peacemaking akin to that initiated and conducted by President Jimmy Carter in the first peace talks at Camp David, which led to peace between Israel and Egypt. Carter rightly received the 2002 Nobel Peace Prize for this accomplishment, joining Anwar Sadat and Menachem Begin, who were honored earlier.

Education can help or hinder the peace program. Through television, radio, newspapers, mosques, summer camps, political rallies, and official statements, Yasir Arafat and his lieutenants have for years conducted their hate education campaign. Palestinians have been taught by indoctrination to hate and to murder while sacrificing their own lives. The Committee for Accuracy in Middle East Reporting in America (CAMERA) has urged the media to cover accurately the Palestinian Authority's role in inciting the Palestinian people toward brutal and terrorist behavior toward Israel and the Jewish people.[26] CAMERA published a memo to the media in the *New York Times* that includes a photo of a young girl pictured on a television screen with the caption reading, "About my life as a suicide warrior."[27] This example of Arafat's version of children's television from 1998 shows a young child singing about her role in jihad and about being a voice of "the exalted martyr"—an inspiration to her in the quest to become a suicide warrior. Another photograph from CAMERA's *New York Times* memo depicts the Passover terrorist attack in Netanya on March 27, 2002, in which 28 people were killed and 130 wounded.

CAMERA urges the media to ask some hard questions. For example, why do Palestinians abuse children and teenagers by teaching them to favor death and killing over life? Why have the inflammatory speeches by members of the Palestinian Authority been allowed to continue—fostering only bloodshed? A major source of Palestinian terrorism is education for hate. Yet there are moderate, problem-solving Palestinians. They need international help.

Can the media educate for peace? Whereas inflammatory Palestinian media constituted a vivid case in 2002, many others around the world are also deadly. Education for hate is an all-too-pervasive part of human experience. And the media provide exceptional vividness and immediacy to the hate messages. The fundamentally distorting nature of such education and its destructive effects deserve much more attention than they are receiving at present. Education reform in many countries, even when excellent in other respects (for example, in mathematics, science, and technology), is usually weak in this domain. Thus we see that media as well as schools can powerfully educate and shape negative attitudes that are conducive to mass violence when mobilized by a murderous leader.

MIDDLE EAST MEDIA RESEARCH INSTITUTE

The Middle East Media Research Institute (MEMRI) was created in 1998 with a goal of reporting on the Middle East policy of the United States. A pioneer in this effort, MEMRI carefully translates and disseminates print and broadcast news sources in the Middle East to audiences in the United States and Europe. Communication between the Middle East and the West is facilitated through MEMRI's use of well-timed translations of Hebrew, Farsi, and Arabic. MEMRI offers a unique analysis and a rich resource of trends in politics, ideology, culture, and religion in the Middle East. With its main office in Washington, D.C., this nonprofit organization also has branches in Berlin, London, and Jerusalem. MEMRI's research is translated into eight languages—English, German, Hebrew, Italian, French, Spanish, Turkish, and Russian.[28]

MEMRI has recently established a Jihad and Terrorism Studies Project to monitor militant Islamic groups that educate and preach about hatred in mosques, schools, and the media. The project was established in response to the reality of militant Islamic terrorist organizations that operate in the United States. Its focus is on individuals and radical Islamist organizations, sermons and religious rulings and reactions to attacks on the United States and abroad. Goetz Nordbruch prepared a series of MEMRI reports on recently updated Palestinian textbooks for first- and sixth-grade students.[29] Although nominally improved, these textbooks still present biased, ethnocentric, and often damaging messages.

In September 2000, the Palestinian Authority began its new curriculum at the Curriculum Development Center in Ramallah. This change in curriculum is now aimed at helping to prepare Palestinians to reclaim totally their rights as citizens on their territory. Jerusalem would become the capital of this independent state. These new textbooks portray a reconstruction of Palestinian identity, and the principles of Palestinian society. They also show the relationship between Islam, Christianity, and Judaism in Palestine.

The Palestinian Authority's Minister of Education states the ultimate goal of education is to prepare the individual for the successful performance of his duties. An individual's identity is intimately linked to his societal obligations. And society is described as an extension of the family. The cooperative family ideal is based on the father as the authoritative figure. Women are still portrayed as subservient to men, with social responsibilities dictated by the Koran. Children's rights are defined almost entirely in terms of access to Islamic education, which supersedes a parent's prerogative to choose schooling or otherwise shape pathways of the child's development. Although individual freedoms are mentioned as important to the society's development, the primary goal is national freedom, which is thoroughly discussed in the textbooks. The concept of martyrdom is condoned in an educational unit on "The Honorable Martyr," about a contemporary of the Prophet Muhammad who gave his life for Islam. Textbooks encourage student participation activities of the Palestinian Intifada (resistance movement). Numerous references to children as martyrs are made in presentations of the resistance movement against Israeli occupation.

The main theme of these textbooks is to instill pride for the nation, to support values of an independent Palestinian state, to avoid colonial greed, to take a stand against reactionary elements, and to teach an appreciation of the importance of Arab unity. Slogans such as "Jerusalem is ours" appear in these books. Even maps of the region avoid any reference to Israel. Jews are stereotyped throughout the texts in negative ways. Adding fuel to the fire are references to passages in the Koran and the Bible that are deprecatory toward Jews. Here as elsewhere, (too often in the history of education), efforts to improve textbooks in the direction of historical accuracy, social tolerance, and learning to live together have failed under the pressure of traditional prejudices and hateful political leadership.

EDUCATION REFORM FOR THE NEXT MUSLIM GENERATION

There are stirrings of movement in the Islamic world toward modern education, including decent human relations. For example, in an op-ed piece for the *New York Times* in 2002, Mohamed Charfi discussed ways that the next Muslim generation might be reached through education reform.[30] Charfi, the former president of the Tunisian Human Rights League and Tunisia's minister of education from 1989 to 1994, is also the author of the 1998 book *Islam et liberté: Le malentendu historique*, about liberty and the religious aspects of Islam.

Following the September 11, 2001, terrorist attacks on the United States, both India and Pakistan are now reforming their educational systems. The traditional Muslim religious schools (the madrasas), which schooled Osama bin Laden in Saudi Arabia, are now being severely criticized by the West, particularly the United States. In a recent meeting between President Bush and Pakistan President Pervez Musharraf, education was a prominent subject of discussion.

Major changes toward modernization were begun in Muslim countries in the nineteenth century. There was a power shift from religious councils and tribunals to parliaments and secular courts. Punishment for religious defection and the use of corporal punishment became less prevalent. However, the population—from state officials and the elite to members of the general public—was resistant to these fragile transitions. The change in the educational approach was particularly tenuous. Efforts were made to teach foreign languages and scientific subjects, but religion, history, philosophy, and civics were taught in the old traditional manner. For example, Muslim law was taught as being sacred, and unquestioned acceptance was demanded. The early centuries of Islam's expansion following the death of Muhammad were idealized as being like "heaven on earth."

These teachings have had adverse effects on Muslim youth, partly because of the discrepancy between what they are being taught in school and their personal experiences in a secular world. Too often, they are left unprepared to live in a changing world. For instance, many Muslim children are still indoctrinated in the ancient ideology of a triumphant Muslim Empire, a viewpoint that maintains that all non-Muslims are wrong; the goal is to bring Islam's light to the world. However, children in Tunisia actually experience their government as making honest efforts to live peacefully with non-Muslim countries. Small and tenuous steps may become larger and stronger.

Saudi Arabia, although officially an ally of the United States, has been one of the largest supporters of Islamic fundamentalism through its financing of schools that follow a rigid and aggressive doctrine. Radical Islam in Pakistan and Afghanistan has been considerably strengthened by Saudi Arabia's sponsorship of madrasas. The attitudes and beliefs expressed via the September 2001 terrorist attacks reflected this kind of schooling.

Tunisia gives reason for hope that democratic education reform is possible. There have been major efforts in Tunisia to modernize its educational system since 1989. For example, religious programs and textbooks highlight the important work of late medieval thinkers such as Averroes and Avicenna. New readings of the Koran have been developed by scholars and have "given Islam a content that allows for discussion of sexual equality, human rights and the development of democracy."[31] The upper grades' science curriculum offers Darwinian theory and big bang theories about the origin of the universe.

The goal is for young Tunisians to grow up to value individual liberty and openness to others through a more secular approach to education. These reforms, in combination with others begun in the late 1950s by President Habib Bourguiba which focused on emancipation of women and universal education, could result in an educational system prepared to help create a modern society. Unfortunately, the political structure is not yet aligned with educational reforms. Police presence is everywhere, and the press and judiciary are run by the state. Although fundamentalism is not mainstream, there is a chance that it could expand if it is used as a weapon of last resort by the angry and frustrated. Perhaps President Musharraf of Pakistan will learn from the Tunisian example and other experiences and create schools that have the capacity to foster open-minded individuals suited to a pluralistic, interdependent world. Muslim countries must begin to reengage the rest of the world in a new and constructive way. Education reform is central to this effort.

MOVING EDUCATION BEYOND NATIONALISTIC AND ETHNOCENTRIC GOALS

Given the serious problems of the Arab countries, it is heartening to see an unprecedented UN-sponsored report prepared by Arab scholars for Arab readers that makes the case for the necessity and feasibility of democratic development in Arab countries. This remarkable report includes a significant section on education reform—in effect, the basis for better societies in the future. We consider this report in Chapter 16, on peace education.[32]

Much education in Muslim countries, as elsewhere, maintains ethnocentric and prejudicial orientations. To a greater or lesser degree, this is a worldwide problem. It is not only exceedingly dangerous with respect to hatred and violence, but also with regard to preparing students to adapt to the economic and social opportunities of the modern world.

In a world so full of hatred and violence, past and present, human conflict and its resolution are subjects that deserve major educational efforts—not only in schools and universities, but also in community organizations, religious institutions, and the media. Yet today's education in most of the world has little to say on the subject. Indeed, education almost everywhere retains ethnocentric and prejudicial orientations, and in some places, these orientations take on overriding significance. As we have seen in many places over many generations, it is possible to shape youngsters in hateful ways, prepared for large-scale killing even at the expense of their own lives. Education for hatred is a harsh reality of history, amplified now by immensely enhanced capacities for destruction. Surely there is no attractive future for humanity in this direction—indeed, perhaps no future at all.

Educational institutions from early childhood to graduate education have a vitally important role to play in the human future, more so than ever before as the peoples of the world are drawn together in unprecedented ways. If we are ever to live together amicably, it will be a drastic change from past practices that can only be achieved by using the unique learning capacities that made the human species so successful during the course of its evolution. How can human beings learn more constructive orientations toward those outside their own groups while maintaining the values of primary group allegiance and security? We will examine research that shows how this might be done.

5

Development of
Prosocial Behavior

ORIENTATION TO PROSOCIAL BEHAVIOR

The next several chapters follow a developmental sequence of examining opportunities for learning peaceful human relationships in programs appropriate for children at different stages of growth and development. The focus on *prosocial behavior* is broadly applicable to the basic orientation of this book. The primary focus of this chapter is on the role of prosocial behavior in the earliest years of life.

Nancy Eisenberg and Paul Mussen of the University of California at Berkeley provide a major analytical examination of what is known about prosocial behavior—its development and the underlying mechanisms at work.[1] This body of research examines how children are socialized to behave prosocially—what are the personal attributes and capabilities involved, and what are the impacts of the social environment that inhibit or facilitate expressions of *generosity, helping,* and *comforting*?

There are fundamental questions on this topic; much has been learned, but many questions await future research to clarify significant issues. Why are some individuals predisposed toward prosocial conduct, whereas others are not? How does genetic makeup predispose one to behave compassionately? What are the specific interactions of children of differing ages, gender, and past experiences with major socialization agents such as parents, teachers, schools, siblings, peers, cultural and religious institutions, and the mass media? What are the cultural values that foster or reduce prosocial behavior? The other major variability has to do with differences within an individual's responses to the current context—the fact that everyone's behavior varies from time to time, according to the situation. The research evidence confirms the malleability of behavior across all ages and indicates ample opportunity for the learning of prosocial behavior and its modifiability over the course of development. So, ways can be found for teachers, parents, and others to contribute toward shaping individual prosocial behavior and thereby, in the aggregate, to promote and sustain a more constructive society.

Eisenberg and Mussen distinguish between prosocial behavior and altruism:

- *Prosocial behavior* is defined as voluntary action that is intended to *help* another individual or a group. Although voluntary in nature, prosocial actions may be performed for a variety of reasons—for reward, approval, sense of duty, or because of genuine sympathy.
- *Altruism* is one particular type of prosocial behavior stemming from intrinsic motivation (i.e., concern, sympathy, values, self-rewards), not from personal gain. In practice, these two forms of behavior are often considered together as prosocial.

In addition to endorsing the broad definition of *prosocial behavior*, we expand it further. Indeed, *prosocial behavior*, in our view, essentially refers to decent consideration for others as well as oneself. It involves sensitivity to the feelings of others and satisfaction in functioning cooperatively with others specifically. It does not involve a deprecation of self or a lack of assertiveness. Nor does it condone hatred by others. Prosocial behavior, as development proceeds, fosters nonviolent problem solving in resolution of the ubiquitous differences that arise between people.

EARLY DEVELOPMENT OF PROSOCIAL BEHAVIOR

It is useful to focus on prosocial *acts*, which are distinguished from the *learning* of prosocial behavior. A child must be able to perceive another's needs, correctly interpret them, and then understand that the other person can in fact be helped, before the child can *act* according to internalized or learned norms. Taken together, these responses indicate the *empathy* of the individual. Because of the critical importance of empathy, we begin our discussion of prosocial behavior with the origins and development of empathy. If these prerequisites are not met, or if the child is ignorant of how to help another person, it is unlikely that the child will help. Prosocial norms are generally accepted by children but will only sometimes guide their behavior. So internalization of norms is necessary but not sufficient to produce prosocial behavior.

Early in life, children tend to internalize the accepted expectations of the culture. This internalization is mainly done through *social learning*, which includes imitation of others and identification with key figures such as parents and teachers. In this way, according to Eisenberg and Mussen, many children learn two prosocial norms: (1) the norm of *reciprocity*—in which an individual returns the favor of help from another, and (2) the norm of *social responsibility*—especially helping others who are vulnerable and in need of help. By the age of 8 or 9 years, most children have learned the norm of social responsibility. They can even explain these norms and expectations to their peers. Yet this does not mean that knowing prosocial norms necessarily translates into consistent prosocial behaviors.

For example, someone may have learned to respond in a particular prosocial manner but may only do so under certain circumstances. In a case where a child knows that he or she should assist another child who is being attacked by a bully, he or she may choose not to respond because of the perceived danger involved (i.e., especially if the aggressor is big and strong, and the would-be helper might risk becoming a victim also). Therefore, additional considerations influence whether the norm will be activated, and these are pertinent to the teaching of prosocial behavior—for example, teaching skills and strategies to help others person without the helper endangering himself or herself.

ORIGINS AND DEVELOPMENT OF EMPATHY

Empathy is defined as a *shared emotional response* between an observer and the person observed, and it is contingent on cognitive factors involving an appraisal of the situation. Empathy may be expressed as putting oneself in the shoes of another person.

Some research has suggested that empathy may moderate aggressive behavior and foster prosocial behavior. Regrettably, empathy has been underresearched in the fields of child and social psychology and social biology. In fact, some well-known, highly regarded social psychology and child development textbooks over the past 15 to 20 years have had very little to say on either empathy or prosocial behavior. We identify this dearth of textbook information to underscore the need for further research in these important fields of study.

It is reasonable to question why so little attention has been paid to the prosocial aspects of psychology. Professors E. Mavis Hetherington and Ross D. Parke offer insight.[2] Until the 1970s, the focus of psychologists and others had been on the causes and consequences of antisocial behaviors. Psychoanalytic theory, with its foundation in clinical examination of the darker sides of troubled patients, emphasized this focus. As a result, we know more about aggression than we do about positive social behaviors. However, since the late 1970s, the study of prosocial behavior has been strengthened.

Later in this chapter, we present some of the basic and empirical research, careful estimates, and practical classroom interventions that have already been established and provide effective means toward nurturing prosocial tendencies in children and youth. Although much more research is needed, promising tools are now available to parents and educators in their efforts to acknowledge the seed of empathy that, when nurtured, can grow into prosocial and altruistic behavior. We now look at the role of emotions in constraining aggressive behavior.

Carolyn Zahn-Waxler of the National Institute of Mental Health reviewed recent research on infants, children, and adolescents that measures emotions such as jealousy, empathy, embarrassment, and sympathy.[3] She concluded that the development and expression of these emotions at younger ages is linked to the child's appreciation of standards set by others. Of particular significance to empathy *training* is an understanding of the moral emotions, especially guilt. To understand cruelty and violence, we must understand how emotions such as guilt can mitigate antisocial behavior.[4]

Empathy appears to have a biological basis and probably played a role in the evolution of mammals and their family way of life—for example, when one animal in a group alerts others to danger, they immediately follow suit.[5] Human infants have been shown to respond to the cries of other children, which implies a deep-seated human capacity for concern for others.[6] And the moral emotions of empathy, sympathy, and guilt seem to grow with age. Studies have shown that a child's concern and caring behaviors deepen as time goes on. Girls typically show more emotional concern in these tests than boys. It is nurturing by adults and the direct teaching and modeling of altruism that have resulted in the most pervasive and persistent expressions of sympathetic behavior in school-aged children. Studies of socialization involving 1- to 2-year-old children yield an interesting finding: When these children are given a firm, clear explanation of the consequences of their actions with regard to other people, they are, years later, more caring and altruistic in their dealings with others. These empathetic responses, if reinforced over the years, may well decrease aggression in the long run.

Walter G. Stephan and Krystina Finlay explored the possibility that empathy can reduce the psychological distance between prejudiced people and their targets of hostility, thereby improving intergroup relationships.[7] What they found was that more favorable attitudes toward out-group members occurred when facilitators explicitly encouraged participants to awaken their empathic responses. Prosocial behavior can be fostered when participants are given specific empathy training. For example, role-taking exercises reduce the level of bias by employing both cognitive and emotional empathy. For example, the Feshbach and Feshbach empathy training study showed that prosocial behaviors increased following empathy training.[8] They emphasized that training empathy skills to encourage prosocial behavior is especially effective when the training efforts are maintained and reinforced.[9]

We will describe several classroom interventions designed to foster the development and expression of empathy. These methods may in fact counteract some negative parental and family influences and help to promote compassionate understanding among youth, both within and outside the school setting.

Intergroup relations programs that successfully use empathy are found in the cooperative learning environment of the "jigsaw classroom," in conflict resolution programs (where individuals are encouraged to take roles), in multicultural education settings (where cognitive empathy gives insights into norms and behaviors of out-groups), and in intergroup dialogue programs (designed to encourage thoughtful reflection on the challenge of taking the perspective of members from other groups). We have more to say about this in Chapter 8 (on cooperative learning) and in Chapter 10 (on education for conflict resolution).

Thus, research shows that empathy has various beneficial results on behavior, whereas a lack of empathy has negative effects. It is well established that empathic concern leads to helping others.[10] In a standard example, people were given the task of reading about the plight of others. In the first case, they were encouraged to empathize with the individuals; the instructions given to the second group were biased to dull their empathic responses. Readers were then given the opportunity to assist a person in need. Readers in the first case offered more help to the person in need than the readers in the second scenario. The increase in helping was evidently due to the arousal of compassion and related emotions.[11] In another study, students were asked to read scenarios involving people who were suffering and then to express attitudes toward the groups of which the people were members.[12] The results showed that readers given instruction that promoted empathy had more favorable attitudes toward the groups than did the readers who were instructed in ways that minimized their empathy. Some research showed that these attitude changes lasted for a period of 2 weeks, indicating that empathy-related changes can endure for a while after only a brief experience with empathy training. Further studies are needed to establish how lasting such effects could be following a longer, intensive course of training and the value of repeated exposures to empathy training over the entire course of schooling. The enhanced and enduring impacts of longer exposure, or periodic reinforcement, seems altogether reasonable to us.

In a related study using a racial group as the focus, African American freshman students wrote essays (in first person) that depicted their everyday experiences of acts of discrimination.[13] Along with these acts of discrimination, they also included incidents in which they were falsely accused of wrongdoing and their resultant feelings of anger, hurt, resentment, and hostility. An experimental group of white students were asked to try to imagine how each writer feels. These students reported experiencing more parallel empathic emotions than the students from the control group who were not given an orientation conducive to empathy.

Various training programs have increased levels of empathy. In three separate empathy-training programs—for social work students, for rape awareness, and for medical students dealing with elderly patients—each group showed an increase in empathy. This finding has practical significance in that empathy can be learned and applied in consequential real-life situations.

RESEARCH ON PROSOCIAL BEHAVIOR: CHANGING FOCUS

The focus of research has changed with changing times. Some decades ago, in the wake of the atrocities of World War II and the Holocaust, there were deep concerns about how to improve the human condition by reducing aggressive behavior, violent delinquency, and prejudice. (This orientation is certainly not obsolete.) Empirical research done as a result of these concerns focused on understanding hateful action, and on providing ways of reducing antisocial behaviors. For example, we know that harsh parental rejection and an aggressive family atmosphere are major contributors to antisocial behaviors in children and youth.[14] Additionally, a strong body of knowledge exists on the development of intergroup tensions and ways to defuse or prevent them. We consider this extensively in other chapters dealing with intergroup contact.

This focus on antisocial behaviors faded from view for a while and has only recently had a resurgence. Instead, since the 1970s, interest in the development of prosocial behavior has gradually increased, partly because of society's increased awareness of the injustices suffered over many years by women, ethnic and religious minorities, and the disabled. Additionally, the tragedy of the Vietnam War led to broader concern with humane values. So, in this milieu, behavioral scientists addressed more of their efforts on understanding how humane values and socially responsible actions may be enhanced.[15]

A dramatic event triggered intense interest in *helping* behavior—the 1964 fatal public stabbing of Kitty Genovese in Queens, New York City. Despite numerous witnesses to the murder, no help was summoned; police were called only after the woman was dead. Social psychologists, as a result of this tragedy, began looking at the *situational* influences on an individual's motivation to intervene or help. For the next 20 years, most *social psychological* studies on helping behavior focused on the role of situational factors.

The conditions of social learning and early cognitive processes were the foci of *developmental psychologists* studying the development of prosocial behavior in children.[16] In essence, social learning was the main orientation of that research.[17] So, social and developmental psychologists found a convergence of their approaches to the understanding of prosocial behavior. Subsequently, further research from diverse perspectives came together to provide deeper insights. There is a growing evidence base for helping heterogeneous groups within societies to teach their children effective, culturally relevant techniques for strengthening their prosocial inclinations and actions across the crucially formative years of development in childhood and adolescence. Indeed, the future convergence of sophisticated developmental and social psychology research on such questions offers much promise for education in the broadest sense.

Prosocial Behavior in Child Development

Even among the very young, children between 12 and 18 months of age will exhibit sharing behavior such as holding up an object or offering it to an adult. This is often done without prompting and represents a milestone in the child's development. Such behavior contradicts the commonly held belief that very young children are essentially egocentric and shows them instead as becoming responsive, contributing members of social life.[18]

A progression of prosocial behavior is seen in children 10 months to 2 years of age. It grows from an awareness of another's distress to attempts at help—through verbal advice or physical intervention.[19] Parental encouragement can positively influence the sense of altruism that begins to emerge as early as age 2.

On the basis of a recent meta-analysis, Eisenberg and Fabes found that, as children mature, they are more likely to engage in helping behaviors. Perhaps this is due to their increasing ability to understand subtle indications that a person is distressed.[20] Experiments in both laboratory and natural settings reveal that young children (age 4) were better able to understand and respond to explicit as opposed to more subtle cues of distress. Seven-year-old children were more able to understand and respond to more subtle cues.

Genetic and environmental factors interact to determine both prosocial behavior and prosocial reasoning (thinking about and judging prosocial issues). There is a continuing fascination with trying to unravel the enigma of the relative importance of genetic inheritance and environmental influences on human behavior. The scientific field of behavior genetics has a long history that started at the end of the nineteenth century and continues with an exciting future based on recent remarkable advances in neuroscience, genetics, and the behavioral sciences.[21]

The initial phase of human behavior genetics research was initiated in England. Studies examined the similarities and variations in the traits and behaviors among genetically interesting biological populations: identical twins, fraternal twins, siblings, close family members, and unrelated persons who were raised in the same or differing environments. There was an emphasis on twins who were adopted early and reared apart as compared with twins reared in the same environment. This line of research was very productive and still persists after 100 years. Over this span of time, increasingly sophisticated research designs continue to confirm clear and substantial genetic contribution to behavior. Currently, it is generally agreed that genetic influence probably accounts for 30 to 70 percent of behavior, depending on the behaviors studied. Although varying in strength of contribution, genetic effects on human emotions and actions are significant.[22] Genetic influences on individual differences in prosocial behavior have been demonstrated. Study of twins show that identical twins are found to be more alike in prosocial behavior than fraternal twins.[23]

In the second phase of behavior genetics, some research using family genetic studies persists along with a large number of study designs that have responded to the increasing knowledge of DNA sequences. This latter research relies on an effort to identify DNA sequence variations to locate candidate genes that could link to behavioral attributes or mental disorders using techniques of association and linkage analyses. Earlier, much of this work presumed a one-gene-one-behavior relationship. So far, the research findings have not tended to support this single-gene hypothesis.[24]

The third and newest research focus holds great promise for the future. It recognizes the complexity of the interplay of the influences within and between three major systems. Their roles are studied in terms of the functional changes of brain sites and circuits as mediators of the gene expression in response to environmental stimuli. For the first time, with the modern technologies available, scientists are able to design rigorous research that addresses the interactions among complex variables. It is increasingly apparent that more than one gene is involved in influencing most behavioral responses. In a given individual, this gene expression network responds in variable ways depending on the nature of the current environmental situation and the related impact of past experience. Such complex research depends on the multidisciplinary teamwork and remarkable advances in behavioral sciences, genomic research, and the technologies of noninvasive neuroimaging of the functioning brain. This research is illuminating and much has been learned, although the promise is great—it is still at an early stage.

Because this remarkable new phase of research is so recent (though we expect significant contributions in the next decade), we will concentrate on the environmental influences that help to determine prosocial behavior. Major influences are parental behavior—both teaching and modeling, customs of the culture, and the media (especially television programming).[25]

These environmental influences make a clear difference in the prosocial behavior of children. In Rosenhan's now classic 1972 study, he shows that civil rights activists came from families that valued altruistic and humanitarian causes highly.[26]

Parents typically serve as indirect teachers and models of prosocial behavior. The manner in which a mother tends to her child is closely related to how a child will react to distress in others. Parents who reason with their child and who provide warmth and caring are more likely to have altruistic children. A study in the Netherlands by Dekovic and Janssens revealed that children whose parents demonstrated warmth and support, had high expectations, and gave guidance and positive reinforcement were rated higher on more prosocial behavior, when judged by teachers and by their peers.[27] A particularly useful technique involves a combination of parental modeling of prosocial behavior along with providing opportunities for children to perform these actions. Typically, parents can make these opportunities available by assigning children necessary household tasks such as cleaning, errands, and setting the table.[28]

Several studies have shown that television can be an effective model of prosocial behavior. For instance, children who watched *Mister Rogers' Neighborhood* (a children's program devoted to understanding the feelings of others, trying to help, and expressing concern) learned about prosocial behavior and were able to apply that knowledge to other situations with peers. These children learned more about the general rules of prosocial behavior than children who watched television with neutral content.[29] We will have much more to say on the topic of media (particularly television) as an educational system in Chapter 13.

Family Influences on Prosocial Behavior

Review of studies involving different methods and various populations reflects consistency in the patterns of the family contexts that bring about or stand in the way of the development of empathy. Children who were physically abused by their parents show notably less empathy than children of nonabusive parents.[30] This consistent finding strongly suggests a causal link between physical abuse and the absence of empathy. This failure to develop empathy is hardly a surprise, yet it is a vivid reminder of the array of damaging effects of human cruelty—from individual to family to society as a whole.

How do children acquire prosocial norms and how early are these acquired? They arise in the context of secure attachment to a nurturing adult model who provides responsive caregiving by either a cohesive family or a reliable extended social support network. The social norms that are established in early childhood are (1) taking turns, (2) sharing with others, (3) cooperating, especially in learning and problem solving, and (4) helping others, in response to visible distress. These norms, though established on a simple basis in the first few years of life, open the way to much more complex and beneficial human relationships that have significance throughout the life span. These norms are readily practiced because they tend to earn respect, provide gratification, and amplify the effectiveness of anything the individual could do alone. To minimize interindividual and intergroup hostility in childhood, educational programs need to take account of the importance and usefulness of factors that influence the development of attachment and prosocial behavior.

The pioneers of research on prosocial behavior, Marian Radke-Yarrow and Carolyn Zahn-Waxler, in a valuable overview of research on this topic, defined prosocial behavior as helping rather than hurting or neglecting, respecting as opposed to denigrating, and being psychologically supportive and protective rather than dominating or exploitative.[31] Such tendencies appear surprisingly early in life. Newborns, who make distress cries in response to the cries of other infants, are showing signs of empathy even at this very early stage of life. Children in their second and third years show emotional distress and take positive actions when in the presence of suffering and distress of others.[32] We will have more to say on these matters later in this chapter when we consider the relationship between empathy and aggression.

How important is the family in promoting or retarding these tendencies? Unfortunately, less research attention has been devoted to the development of prosocial than to the development of antisocial behaviors. In addition, research that does deal with prosocial behaviors has too rarely taken a developmental approach. Nevertheless, useful information is available.

There is evidence that family settings in which the requirements and expectations incorporate prosocial behavior do in fact shape such behavior. For example, children who are responsible for tasks helpful to family maintenance, especially caring for younger siblings, are generally more altruistic than children who do not have such tasks. A pattern of parental responsiveness, high expectations, firmness, and warm emotion tends to foster a sense of social responsibility in children. Such children are inclined to behave prosocially in relation to the needs of others.[33] Both direct family observations and experimental studies have examined the effects of a *model* on later prosocial or antisocial behavior. In the experimental studies, an adult model, behaving as a parent often does, demonstrates a prosocial act such as sharing toys, coins, or candy that have been won in a game. The sharing is with someone else who is said to be in need though not present in the experimental situation. The adult plays the game and models the sharing before leaving the child to play. Similar designs are used in studies of honesty where the procedures involve a game with rules in which an adult model either cheats or adheres to the rules. Although the contact is brief—and therefore a much less powerful influence than a parent's enduring relationship would be—the model's action is nevertheless salient because it occurs in a controlled experimental setting.[34] The results are clear. Children exposed to such models, when compared with similar children in control groups, tend to show the behavior manifested by the models—whether it is honesty, generosity, helping, or rescuing behavior. There is also evidence from naturalistic studies of toddlers' prosocial actions that *delayed* imitation by children of their mothers' ways of comforting and helping occur spontaneously in children's efforts to help others. Indeed, the imitations often involve exact reproductions of the mother's behavior. Given the child's pervasive exposure to the parents, the potential for observational learning in this sphere as in others is very great.[35]

Many laboratory and clinical studies of social learning indicate that certain factors enhance the impact of a model for the child: the adult's power, the adult's perceived competence, and the adult's long-term nurturance of the child.[36] All of this puts securely attached children in a strong position to adopt salient patterns of behavior through observational learning from their parents and other family members. The combination of early attachment plus abundant modeling over the years of growth and development leads to prosocial behavior that becomes firmly established. Prosocial behavior is particularly significant because of its powerful adaptive qualities—it is likely to open up new opportunities for the growing child, strengthen additional human relationships on the basis of mutual respect, and thereby contribute to the building of a sense of personal worth.

Young children's caring and prosocial responses have also been studied in relation to their mothers' mental health. Their responses were observed in both experimental and naturalistic settings. Results showed that attachment alone, children's problems alone, and maternal diagnoses alone were not strong predictors of deficits in caring behavior. The highest frequencies of caring were from children with the more severely depressed mothers. Girls were significantly more caring than boys. These surprising findings underscore the importance of studying interacting influences on the underlying processes in the development of children's caring responses.[37]

School and Teacher Influences on Prosocial Behavior

Early childhood educators in child care settings, by modeling desired behavior and by rewarding children's prosocial statements and actions, can develop and strengthen prosocial actions. Also in the course of teaching, there is often explicit instruction about helping, as well as stories about helping others. It would be valuable to have more systematic investigation and inventory of teacher modeling strategies in naturalistic classrooms because their effects are potentially strong. These strategies should become an integral part of the training of early childhood teachers.

Since the 1970s, both European and U.S. interest in prosocial education in schools has been growing, leading to broadened developmental research and the creation of many experimental training programs designed to promote prosocial tendencies. Let us briefly introduce several highly promising lines of inquiry and innovation.

Peer Influences on Prosocial Behavior

Although parents and other caregivers are the primary sources of a child's early socialization, as a child matures, other influences such as peers, school, and the media come into play through diverse channels.[38] Society's norms and expectations are learned through example, rewards and punishments, modeling, direct contact, and explicit instruction. Since the middle of the 1980s, research has been conducted on the influence of these socializing agents.

As we have seen, children learn to behave by certain social standards beginning with those of their parents and family and then by those of their peers. Peers offer a unique viewpoint—the perspective of equals. They affect the development of a child in many of the same ways as parents, namely through modeling behavior, social comparison, reinforcement of behaviors, and frequent opportunities for social learning.

Peers are highly salient influences and have the capacity to reinforce certain behaviors over others by paying special attention. For example, when adults coach a child's peers to reinforce helping behaviors over more negative or aggressive ones (i.e., by acknowledging helpful behaviors and ignoring negative ones), then the child's behavior changes significantly.[39] As the child matures, such influence increases.[40] For example, a 4-year-old will share, praise, and attend to his peers more often than will a 3-year-old.

By observation alone, peers will learn much from each other by witnessing a variety of responses. In the school setting, for example, they might learn which teachers are more punitive or who is the class bully. Through imitation, new social skills are learned, especially via modeling by the presumed lead member of the group.[41] Children will also tend to copy the behavior of older and more powerful peers.[42]

Peers and Aggression versus Prosocial Behavior

Much research shows that peers influence the behavior of children both positively and negatively. Aggressive behavior can be reinforced and is often imitated.[43] On the positive side, studies of withdrawn nursery-aged children show marked social improvement after children are exposed to televised models of peer interaction.[44] Also, children intensely afraid of dogs actually petted the animals after observing peer models playing with dogs.[45]

Another study involved withdrawn children. Each child was paired with another in play sessions. They both became more sociable and helping. They also participated in cooperative play. These one-on-one sessions may have provided experiences not usually found in classroom settings and may have contributed to increased prosocial behavior among the relatively isolated children.[46]

One observational study showed that approximately one-third of preschool children respond positively to the prosocial actions of their peers, whether it is spontaneous prosocial action or in response to a request, by reacting with smiles, approval, and continuation of play.[47] Experimental studies show most clearly the potential of peer reinforcement for elevating the level of children's prosocial behavior. For example, when children were encouraged to report instances of friendly behavior during sharing time in the classroom, there was more cooperative play and fewer acts of aggression.

Modeling behavior is a major means of influencing peer behavior, whether it is in real life or on television (especially if there is follow-up discussion of televised events by responsible adults with the children).[48] Children imitate helping behaviors of their peers and unfortunately also imitate less desirable qualities such as selfishness. Thus, . parental efforts to foster ongoing contacts of their children with constructive peers are important. Further research is warranted on the effectiveness of frequent contact with models of prosocial behavior as well as the usefulness of peer as opposed to adult models. It is also important to examine the effects of friendship, acts of imitation, and effects of familiar situations and people on children's prosocial behavior.[49] Of course, these are not mutually exclusive. In an ideal world, they would provide joint reinforcement for prosocial behavior; and this does in fact happen in subcultures that are strongly oriented toward fairness and thoughtful consideration of others as well as self.

Peers primarily influence helping behavior by modeling, but elementary schools can have significant influence through empathy training and cooperative learning techniques. Effects of such systemic interventions have been assessed in a longitudinal field-experimental study.[50] Each program, when compared with control groups, showed that children had an increase in helping behavior and reduction in hostile tension. Such techniques can be effectively integrated into the school curriculum. Indeed, positive effects were noted beyond the classroom.

AGGRESSION: FAMILY AND NONFAMILY INFLUENCES

Earlier, we discussed the idea that aggressive tendencies were probably inherited from our ancient past. But now let us highlight the family's role in training the child to behave aggressively.

The family provides the first social environment for the child. If the basic attachment is highly insecure or disorganized, there is an appreciable risk that aggressive behavior will develop by age 5 to 7.[51] Other research suggests that the combination of insecure attachment with other risk factors is likely to result in a child's developing problems related to aggression.[52]

Sometimes parents consciously and directly encourage children to behave aggressively (for example, telling a boy, "Fight for yourself" or "Act like a man"). More powerfully, parental modeling of *actions* gives the child indications of acceptable behavior. Children will tend to imitate their adult caregivers for better or for worse. Methods of controlling children can contribute to a child's aggressive behavior. Two factors contribute to creating a hostile and aggressive child: highly unpredictable physical punishment from parents and a parent-child relationship that lacks genuine warmth and caring or is, at worst, harsh and rejecting.[53]

The Patterson Social Learning Center in Eugene, Oregon, is a world-renowned research institution devoted to understanding the basis of aggressive behavior. Since the 1970s, this institution has been involved in research on the developmental pathways of children that lead them toward delinquent behavior, and it has developed useful ways of treating aggressive children and families.[54]

Consistency is found in research showing that the greater the empathy, the less the aggression, particularly for boys. Boys 6 to 8 years of age measuring high in aggression were low in empathy.[55] This finding is confirmed in studies of older boys utilizing a range of measures of empathy and aggression. Generally, the emotional aspect of empathy can serve to regulate aggression. Predictably, children who possess more empathy manifest less aggressive behavior. The child who responds empathically to a troubled peer is motivated to channel his or her own feelings of distress by responding in a helpful and altruistic manner to that child.

In short, empathy and prosocial behavior are clearly related to each other, but they are not inexorably linked. Nevertheless, empathy is a vital ingredient in the development of helpful behavior, and it is associated with relatively low levels of aggressive behavior.

PROGRAMS FOR TEACHING EMPATHY AND
RESPONSIBLE CONFLICT RESOLUTION

A longitudinal study was done in three schools in a middle-class suburb of the San Francisco Bay area of California. Subjects of the study were children from kindergarten through fourth grade; the control group, taken from three equivalent schools in the area, did not use the program. The goal was to strengthen children's prosocial orientation, defined as "an attitude of concern for others, commitment to the values of fairness and social responsibility, and the ability and inclination to act on these values in everyday life."[56] The program's five core components are (1) cooperative activities, (2) developmental discipline, (3) promoting social understanding (4) modeling and highlighting prosocial values, and (5) helping activities.

The assessment of outcomes was done by frequent and extensive classroom and playground observation and in structured small group work. The results were impressive. The children in the intervention program showed more prosocial behavior (i.e., were more supportive of each other, were more spontaneously helpful and cooperative, and were more concerned about others) than those in the control group classes. Additionally, the program children tended to resolve conflict in less aggressive ways, with more compromise, planning, and attention to the needs of the various individuals engaged in the conflict. They also exhibited more democratic values.

Effects of this sort clearly went beyond the classroom, and these children did well academically. The success of this experimental work shows that schools and teachers can make a difference in raising children's prosocial behavior and constructive values. Most of the techniques used can feasibly be incorporated into existing curricula; therefore administrators and teachers have an excellent opportunity to use them in the course of their everyday school activities.

Norma D. Feshbach of the University of California at Los Angeles undertook a major program of research on training to enhance empathy.[57] Although empathy is difficult to measure, researchers and educators have observed that it plays an important part in tempering aggressive behavior and fostering prosocial responses. According to Feshbach, empathy reactions are comprised of three component parts:[58]

1. An ability to interpret emotional cues in others
2. The cognitive skill of taking on the viewpoint and role of another
3. Emotional responsiveness, or the ability to experience the emotions that are the same as or very comparable to another

As we observed, an infant cries in response to hearing another infant's distress cry. This evidently is a genetically based fundamental empathic response. However, as the child develops, empathetic responsiveness becomes increasingly complex and purposeful. Moreover, children differ in their degree of empathic responsiveness to a common stimulus.

The Feshbach empathy-training program was a follow-up to earlier reports that showed the inverse relationship between empathy and aggression in elementary-school-aged children and the evidence (albeit weaker) of positive connections between empathy and prosocial behavior. The goals of this program for elementary school age children were to "help regulate aggressive behavior; to promote positive, prosocial behavior; and to develop exercises and strategies that could be used by a regular teacher in the classrooms of children between the ages of 7 and 11."[59] Thus, the innovation was aimed to link research and social action—rigorously and effectively.

Designed for third- and fourth-grade students, the Feshbach program offers a variety of classroom activities in which students are encouraged to recognize and distinguish the feelings of others, to take constructive roles, and to be emotionally responsive. Investigators observed a group of six children over a 10-week period, comparing those who participated in the empathy training with two control groups; one group did not participate in any special activities, and other other engaged in academic problem solving. Teachers, peers, and the children themselves rated aggressive and prosocial behaviors. Social understanding and role-taking skills were also rated.

Results showed that those involved in empathy training had an increase in prosocial behavior and showed an improvement in self-concept and social understanding. Neither control group showed these positive outcomes. Empathy training was effective for children who were average in aggression, as well as those who were highly aggressive.[60] Recent studies have confirmed these findings, but the amount of research is still less than the problems warrant. Empathy training programs can be useful in reducing aggression and promoting prosocial behavior. They have much potential to promote intergroup cooperation and understanding. The teacher can integrate empathy training skills and techniques into regular classroom lessons.

Therefore, it is worth looking more closely at this groundbreaking program. It consisted of 30 hours of training exercises and activities developed and designed to be used in small groups of four to six children. Children were engaged in a variety of activities such as games, story-telling, written exercises, and group discussions, with activities typically lasting between 20 and 30 minutes. In addition, more active tasks such as acting out words, phrases, and stories were included. Activities to help children identify and discriminate the emotions of another person included identifying feelings shown in photographs of facial expressions, listening to tape recordings of emotional discussions, and watching videotapes of pantomimes of emotional situations. Children also participated in role-playing exercises to help them assume the perspective of another person. These games and activities increased in complexity during the training period.

Early in the program, children were challenged to imagine different visual perspectives, such as seeing the world from the point of view of a small creature like a cat. Preferences of others were considered through imagining what type of birthday present would be suitable for each family member. Adopting the point of view of a character in a story also helped children to experience another person's perspective. As the training progressed, students role-played a part in a scene, then switched roles and played the part of a different character. In yet another activity, children watched video-tapes of their enactment to enhance understanding of themselves in a particular situation.

A control group participated in a program using a format similar to the empathy-training program but oriented toward another purpose. Also, a 30-hour training program focused on improving the students' problem-solving abilities in a nonsocial atmosphere without any empathy component. The empathy training studies were conducted with children from 8 to 10 years of age, but explorations have shown that, with minor modifications, these exercises can also be used with children 6 to 11.

In the Los Angeles Unified School District, children who participated in empathy training showed a marked change for the better in dimensions of aggression and prosocial behavior. Additionally, these children conveyed more positive self-concepts than the children from either the problem-solving control group or the children who received no training. Thus, empathy training was considered by teachers to be valuable in positively affecting prosocial behaviors of cooperation, helping, and generosity. Merely removing children from the classroom to participate in other activities was insufficient to affect prosocial behavior. Rather, it was specific training involving identification of emotions, role-playing, and emotional expressiveness—all related to the empathic process—that led to positive helping behaviors and positive self-evaluation.

Feshbach suggested that this elementary-school training model may provide a guide for the enhancement of empathy in other contexts in which we wish to reduce aggression and foster positive social feelings and interactions. For example, perspective- and role-taking exercises might involve taking the perspective of other ethnic and national groups. Evidence suggests that the greater the degree of perceived similarity between two individuals, the greater the degree of empathy. Hence, highlighting commonalities between individuals in a potential conflict may be a useful strategy. Children can learn that it is useful to keep in mind our common humanity as we move across various settings and interact with those who, though different in some way, are basically very much like ourselves.

Intergroup Relations Programs That Incorporate Empathy

Even though there is broad use of empathy in intergroup relations programs, few have actually measured empathy as a mediating or outcome variable. The jigsaw classroom (discussed in Chapter 8) is an exception. This and other methods of cooperative learning bring together children from various racial and ethnic groups to work together on academic problems. This interdependent and cooperative work leads students to take on roles of others and see the world from different perspectives.[61] In Feshbach's studies and in others, empathy scores are higher after only 8 weeks of cooperative jigsaw group study. The improvement in intergroup relations that occurs is attributed in part to empathy.[62] This is one of many examples of convergence among techniques in this field.

In conflict resolution programs designed to foster mutual understanding between opposing groups, instead of presenting the conflict in a win/lose context, it is offered as a problem that needs to be solved. Individuals are encouraged to take roles so that they can see the perspective of the other more clearly, with the goal of improved intergroup relations through changed perceptions and unique ideas for resolving disputes.[63] Indeed, recent experience in this field during the 1990s increasingly suggests the general value of this approach in conflict resolution.[64] The main goal of multicultural education at its best is the improvement of intergroup relations without loss of a sense of common humanity.[65] Information about the students' racial, ethnic, and cultural backgrounds are presented in an historical context from the perspective of each group.[66] Although not explicit, it appears that cognitive empathy is being employed when students are engaged in various exercises designed to give them insights into the other groups' norms and behaviors. Just a few studies exist that show the effects of multicultural education. But in two such studies, racial attitudes became more positive; social distance between African Americans and white students decreased.[67]

For people who are highly disposed toward empathy, simply reading about or listening to out-group members describing their experiences creates empathy for that group. But empathy can be made stronger if it is explicitly encouraged or explicitly taught.[68] Both dispositional and situational factors can enhance empathy for outgroups. It is helpful when empathy is accompanied by showing respect, and empathy training can make effective use of this orientation. Though research in this field is still at an early stage, the indications are promising that empathy training can be a useful method of diminishing prejudice and ethnocentrism in childhood.

SIGNIFICANT FINDINGS AND SOME IMPLICATIONS

Nancy Eisenberg and Paul Mussen have reviewed hundreds of studies and summarized their findings about what helps or hinders the development and expression of prosocial behavior.[69] There is no single determinant of prosocial behavior that has an influence in all situations. Complex interactions of factors influence the development of prosocial behavior. The conclusions presented here about the behavior of children in general (as opposed to the behavior of any individual) are supported by the available evidence.

Families and Prosocial Children

Active, sociable, competent, and *self-confident* are adjectives describing qualities of prosocial children. Such children also excel in their ability to take the roles of others, to make moral judgments, and to be sympathetic. Parents of these children tend to be nurturing and to consistently model prosocial behavior. They also discuss with their children the effects of such behavior on others; they discipline carefully and expect their children to behave responsibly toward others.

Children are most likely to show helping behavior in situations in which their spirits are high, they are proficient or successful, and when they feel that they will not be too overburdened or injured. It is also more likely that a child will assist another if the person being helped is liked or loved, if he or she has previously assisted the recipient, and if the recipient is appealing.

Parents, teachers, and religious educators should be consistent role models of sharing, helping, and comforting behaviors. They should hold positive expectations for children, should engage children in conversations about benefits of prosocial actions, and should ask them to empathize with others. Prosocial classroom activities engage children and involve role-playing and other activities that promote feelings of sympathy and support their prosocial tendencies. It is particularly important to include activities that promote meaningful cooperation among children to achieve valued goals.[70] Parents and teachers should press for responsible television programming that exposes young children to more altruistic behavior and to less violence and aggression. Organized efforts to put pressure on broadcasters and advertisers have shown some promise but have rarely been sustained over years. Media literacy programs in schools and community organizations also have promise for heightening the sophistication and selectivity of youthful viewers.[71]

Frontiers of Research

Eisenberg and Mussen discuss four areas that deserve deeper research to clarify their role in prosocial behavior: biology, training programs, nonfamilial socializers, and significant altruists.

Biology.   Preliminary evidence points to new understanding of the interplay of environmental and genetic factors that influence individual differences in prosocial behavior and sympathetic responses to others. The dramatic advances now occurring in molecular genetics should have applicability in identifying children who have genetic predisposition to traits that could impair empathy and/or enhance aggression. Preventive interventions are for the future, but the new knowledge will provide opportunities in the long run to compensate for vulnerabilities in both biological and environmental characteristics.

Training programs.   There have been successful training programs that enhance children's prosocial behavior. Typically, many potentially effective procedures have been implemented simultaneously, making it impossible to know how much each component contributes to the effect. So research designs to separate the independent effects of the various components are needed, as well as designs to evaluate whether or not value is added when programs are more comprehensive and multifactorial. Also, testing should be done in field settings as well as in the laboratory, to enhance the likelihood of successful application of laboratory findings to real-world situations.

Nonfamilial socializers.   Although there is some information on how the family and outside influences determine the prosocial actions of children, very little is known about their *joint* influence. Can some extrafamilial, prosocial influences bolster prosocial parental efforts? This is surely a possibility. The role of institutions may require systematic changes. We know, for example, that school structure—particularly democratic orientations including establishment of evidence-based empathy, tolerance, and proso-cial behavior training programs as an integral part of the K through 12 curriculum—could change school climate and also promote prosocial values and behaviors beyond that school.[72] Could school emphasis on student cooperation in academic and ex-tracurricular activities strongly influence prosocial development? What about the ef-fects of churches, clubs, and athletic leagues? In principle, their combined potential is likely to be important.

Significant altruists. Erik Erikson's psychoanalytic and social psychological analyses of the life and work of Mahatma Gandhi and Martin Luther are powerful examples of studies done on exemplars of humanitarian traits.[73] How far can hypotheses generated by such evocative studies be tested and applied to developmental situations involving many people?

Another potentially useful approach is the intensive study of living people who are heavily involved in humanitarian endeavors. In a study of people who rescued Jews from the Nazis during World War II, Samuel and Pearl Oliner (1988) provided a valu-able example of such work. Their analyses showed several reasons why the rescuer was motivated to act. One stemmed from an internal sense of altruism. Another was a re-sult of guilt feelings. And a third came from a feeling of commitment to the community or to a religious institution. Such study of altruists gives us insight into the whole per-son in the context of his or her environment, both personal and situational, which is useful in determining motivation and behavior.[74]

WIDENING CIRCLES OF PROSOCIAL BEHAVIOR

The concept of prosocial behavior is inherently (and desirably) broad. This chapter—though focusing on the early years of childhood—represents the foundation for top-ics that recur in greater detail in subsequent chapters. Perhaps this is so because prosocial behavior is shaped in widening circles through the years of growth and de-velopment into adulthood. We are, after all, considering the highest levels of humane behavior and values: decent concern for others, readiness and ability to cooperate for mutual benefit, helping, sharing, and respecting others—while maintaining integrity as an individual with basic self-respect and lifelong inclinations to learning and ex-panding one's horizons.

The widening circles of learning prosocial behavior become increasingly complex from the early years onward and involve (1) the nuclear family, (2) the extended fam-ily, (3) the community (neighborhood, school, community organizations, religious and other affinity groups), (4) the nation-state (or region within it), (5) other related nation-states (for example, geographically adjacent nations, or nations with a commu-nity of values such as democracies), and (6) global contacts (direct or indirect, involv-ing in principle an interconnected world evolving toward a global village). So the full development of prosocial behavior is a long, fascinating, often difficult, sometimes tor-tuous process that, in the aggregate, is of utmost importance for the human experience.

Operationally, this behavior requires healthy, vigorous, inquiring, learning, constructive growth and development that facilitates a gradual widening of these circles throughout childhood and adolescence, which should include (1) sympathetic understanding of diversity; (2) habits of give-and-take, reciprocity, and a pervasive sense of fairness; (3) learning skills of solving problems without violence—with special attention to constructive resolution of interpersonal and intergroup problems; and (4) learning about and respecting different peoples and their various traditions.

Until now, this important research agenda on prosocial behavior has occurred mainly within a single culture and indeed can be applied to in-group situations. We must consider how it relates—or could be widened to relate—to other groups and other cultures. In the orientation of this book, a fundamental challenge is to find ways of enhancing prosocial behavior much more broadly across traditional and even adversarial barriers.

6

Violence Prevention in the Context of Child and Adolescent Development

TWO COMPLEMENTARY APPROACHES

What conditions favor good results in child and adolescent development? What can shift the odds away from dismal outcomes such as youth violence? How can our children grow up healthy and vigorous, inquiring and problem solving, decent and constructive?

We approach such questions in two ways, using

1. a basic generic comprehensive developmental sequence that provides antidotes to shattered and distorted lives—lives that are conducive to youth violence and other pathologies, or
2. a specific set of targeted interventions that can help to prevent youth violence and enhance personal ability to deal with conflict in nonviolent ways.

Both of these approaches need to be considered in a multifaceted way, taking into account the pivotal institutions that powerfully shape child and adolescent development: family, community, media, health, and education systems. This chapter focuses mainly on possibilities for averting youth violence by fostering healthy, constructive, prosocial development throughout childhood and adolescence, but we also have some remarks about interventions targeted specifically to preventing youth violence.

CONDITIONS FOR FOSTERING HEALTHY DEVELOPMENT

A poor start in life can leave an enduring legacy of impairment, and the high costs may show up in various systems—health, education, and juvenile justice. We call these impairments by many names: disease, disability, delinquency, ignorance, incompetence, hatred, and violence. By whatever name, such outcomes entail severe economic and social penalties for the entire society as well as suffering for the damaged persons. During their earliest years of growth and development, children require dependable attachment to parents or other adult caregivers; they need protection, guidance, stimulation, nurturance, and tutelage in skills to cope with adversity. Infants, in particular, need caregivers who promote attachment and thereby instill the fundamentals of trust and decent human relationships throughout the child's life. Young adolescents, too, have a special need to connect with people who can guide their momentous transition to adulthood with sensitivity and understanding.

In an ideal world, all children would grow up in intact, cohesive, nuclear families, dependable in good times and bad. They would flourish in richly faceted parent-child relationships, each having at least one parent who is consistently nurturing, loving, teaching, and coping and who derives satisfaction from parenting. They would inhabit a reasonably predictable adult environment that fosters gradual preparation for adult life. They would have supportive, extended family members who are available to lend a hand and serve as positive role models. Each child would be part of a supportive community—some larger group beyond the family that is helpful, whether that group took the form of a neighborhood, religious, ethnic, or political group. Conditions such as these greatly enhance the odds that a young person will pursue lifelong learning, acquire constructive skills, maintain good health, and develop valued human attributes, including prosocial rather than hateful or violent behavior. Such a web of support provides a tangible basis for envisioning an attractive future and for taking advantage of opportunities.

In our modern world, approximating such optimal conditions for child development is a formidable task for the parents or other caregivers in any family. For single parents struggling alone, the challenge is exceedingly difficult. Child raising takes much time and care and demands that the adult should protect and guide the child, experiment to find good ways of coping, and learn from experience. Above all, it is an enduring commitment—one that is fundamentally rewarding, if often frustrating.

The institutions beyond the family that have the greatest influence on child and adolescent development are the schools, community organizations (including religious ones), health institutions, and the media. What are the essential requirements for healthy development that most families meet with the support of these pivotal institutions?

In the scientific and professional communities, an important consensus emerged in the latter part of the twentieth century on ways that parents and others can cooperate in coping with the developmental needs of children and young adolescents. Evidence is accumulating that a range of preventive interventions can set a trajectory toward healthy, constructive adulthood.[1] Beginning with early and comprehensive prenatal care, these measures include

- well-baby medical care, with an emphasis on disease prevention and health promotion;
- home visits by child service professionals, especially in homes with very young children;
- parental education to strengthen parenting competence and build close parent-child relationships;
- parent support networks that provide mutual aid in fostering good health and learning opportunities for children and parents;
- child care of high quality outside the home, especially in day care centers;
- early childhood education that combines parental involvement with disease prevention and the stimulation of cognitive as well as social skills;
- stimulating elementary school and middle grade education that is developmentally appropriate at the critical time of puberty, fosters careful decision making when adolescents in transition are making fateful choices, and encourages good health practices as well as decent human relations; and
- high school education that provides specific learning and experience in conflict-resolution skills in school, at home, and in the community.

Altogether, such opportunities have strong potential to prevent damage of many kinds, as reflected in indices of well-being in the areas of health, education, and criminal justice.

FOSTERING HEALTHY DEVELOPMENT
IN THE EARLIEST YEARS

Prenatal Care

Prenatal care has the powerful capacity to prevent physical impairment, including brain damage that can lead to so many tragic outcomes.[2] In addition to medical care of the mother and the developing fetus, an essential component of good-quality prenatal care is education of the parents. Prenatal education makes use of the distinctive motivation of the pregnant mother as well as the young father to strengthen their knowledge and skill in caring for themselves and their prospective baby. In combination with social support services, unemployed parents can be linked to job training and formal schooling that will substantially improve prospects for a stable, decent future for the young family.

Especially in poor communities, young parents need a dependable person who can provide social support for health promotion and parenting education through the months of pregnancy and beyond. This can be organized in a systematic intervention—for example, drawing on reliable women from the community who have relevant experiences in child rearing. When provided with a modicum of training and supervision, these mentors can give personal support and practical guidance to poor young mothers.

Child Care

As child rearing moves beyond the home, the quality of outside care becomes crucial. The vast majority of responsible parents are eager to ensure care that facilitates their children's healthy development. The crucial factors in quality of child care are the behaviors of the caregiver and the range of supportive services. A good description of high-quality child care follows.

> What do we mean by child care? It is not just *day care*, given the growing numbers of children who require supervision while their parents work nontraditional and shifting hours. It is also not just *care*. Beneficial outcomes for children in child care are associated with settings that provide both nurturance and support for early learning and language development. Accordingly, previous distinctions between "early education" or "preschool" and "day care" have unraveled. In fact, child care may be seen as providing a number of services, including the provision of nurturance and learning opportunities for children, preparation for school, support for working parents and reduction of poverty, respite care in child welfare cases, and access to supplemental services such as vision and hearing screening, developmental testing, feeding programs, and even parent support and literacy programs.[3]

Just as parents want a competent doctor to foster their child's health, so do they desire a capable caregiver who can understand and meet their child's developmental needs. In practice, this is often difficult to achieve, even for affluent parents.

The United States lags behind Europe in this respect. With the recent surge in demand for child care, those trying to provide it have eagerly sought to develop qualified, competent caregivers. But even though many child care providers have the best of intentions, this field is characterized by low pay, low respect, minimal training, minimal supervision, and extremely variable quality. Although most child care workers try very hard to do a good job, pay is extremely low. Many of them cannot afford to stay in their positions very long, and this instability of the workforce, in itself, puts a child's development in jeopardy. Especially for young children, dependable long-term caretaker relationships and attachments are crucial. Unfortunately, staff turnover is all too common. Quality child care, a high priority, can be provided to virtually all children. This has been demonstrated by the European accomplishments of this goal since the middle the twentieth century.

In 1994, the Carnegie Corporation task force report *Starting Points* spelled out the importance of four basic approaches in meeting the needs of the youngest children: preparation for responsible parenthood, preventive health care, high quality and ready availability of early child care (e.g., through cooperative networks, professional training, and more public support), and strong community supports for families.[4] The report suggests ways of mobilizing communities to support children. The achievement of intersectoral cooperation toward the well-being of children is difficult but not impossible. Agents of change include family-child resource centers, and federal, state, and local councils for children that include educational institutions, relevant professions, business, and local media. Together they can assess specific needs, formulate ways of meeting them, and seek ways to integrate services—for example, by linking educational, health, and social services in community schools.

EARLY ADOLESCENCE: A TIME OF OPPORTUNITY AND RISK

Early adolescence is one of the most striking developmental experiences in the entire human life span. This major transition means leaving childhood, undergoing the drastic biological changes of puberty, leaving childhood behind, and being aware of moving closer to the distant goal of adulthood. This critical biological and social transition coincides very often with the abrupt transition to the larger and more complex junior high school. How do our children learn to make the great transition? What help do they need in making it? Who can best provide such help? Why do so many casualties arise that diminish the chances for a healthy, constructive, productive adult life?

Early adolescence (10 to 14 years of age) is a time of profound biological transformation and social transition characterized by exploratory behavior, much of it adaptive and expected for this age group. But when the problems during this transitional period include extremes such as substance abuse and violence (especially if these behaviors become habitual), there can be lifelong consequences. Many dangerous patterns, in fact, commonly emerge during these years. Initially, adolescents explore these new possibilities tentatively, with the experimentation that is typical of this age group. Therefore, before damaging behavior is firmly established, there is a unique opportunity to prevent lifelong casualties. Yet this phase of life has been neglected in health care, education, and community environments.

The Carnegie Council on Adolescent Development, formed in 1986, illuminated this neglected but fateful phase of life. It published a range of studies on different aspects of adolescence, recommending constructive developmental paths. Its concluding report 10 years later drew together evidence from many studies and field experiments on fostering adolescent health, education, and constructive human relations.[5] It described practical measures that can usefully and feasibly be taken to prevent the personal misery and adoption of damaging behaviors that will have adult consequences.

The problems adolescents face are occurring across all sectors of the youth population; no part of the society is exempt from the casualties—witness the Columbine tragedy and other school massacres occurring in affluent communities. Among the more disquieting signs is the emergence in younger adolescents of very high-risk behaviors that were once associated with older groups: early smoking, early alcohol use, early sex, early alienation from school, even early involvement with deadly weapons.

What does it take to become a healthy, problem-solving, constructive adult? A young adolescent on an effective developmental path must

- find a valued place in a constructive group;
- learn how to form close, durable human relationships;
- earn a sense of worth as a person;
- achieve a reliable basis for making informed choices;

- express constructive curiosity and exploratory behavior;
- find ways of being useful to others;
- have reason to believe in a promising future with real opportunities;
- cultivate the inquiring and problem-solving habits of the mind necessary for lifelong learning and adaptability;
- learn to respect democratic values and responsible citizenship; and
- build a healthy lifestyle.

The work of the Carnegie Council consistently addressed ways in which these requirements can be met by a conjunction of frontline institutions that powerfully shape adolescent development, for better and worse. These begin with the family but include schools, the health sector, community organizations, and the media. The Council's recommendations for each of these institutions are not utopian or hypothetical. Working models can be observed in some communities. Useful lessons have been learned from the interventions that have been rigorously evaluated. National youth organizations are especially well positioned to expand their scope of activities to include young adolescents. They have extensive resources, good staffing, and outreach into all neighborhoods, including the urban disadvantaged communities. Boys and Girls Clubs,[6] 4-H Clubs,[7] Girls Incorporated,[8] the Junior League,[9] and the Foster Grandparent program[10] are good examples of such national groups that have mounted and evaluated programs for young adolescents. At the national level, the U.S. Department of the Interior has compiled data on national urban recreation available for youth.[11] Many grassroots youth-serving community organizations also provide out-of-school supportive programs for young adolescents that fill vital needs. A study of such organizations for young adolescents in inner-city neighborhoods was carried out at the University of Chicago Chapin Hall Center for Children with encouraging results.[12] The main challenge is to expand these programs to meet the nation's needs.

Preventive Interventions for Early Adolescence

The public policy response to adolescence has usually been problem-specific, often overlooking the basic underlying needs of adolescents under contemporary conditions. Most adolescent problem behaviors occur together, as clusters, and there are common causes. To meet the essential requirements for healthy adolescent development, we must help adolescents to acquire the protective factors of constructive knowledge and skills, inquiring habits of mind, dependable human relationships, a reliable basis for earning respect, a sense of belonging in a valued group, and ways of being useful to others.

Constructive interventions in early adolescence include the following:

1. Reforming middle schools to create small communities for learning in which stable, close relationships with adults and peers allow for intellectual and personal growth. These arrangements foster sustained individual attention to each student.[13]
2. Creating school environments that promote healthy lifestyles, with partic-

ular emphasis on a life sciences curriculum that includes prevention of high-risk behavior; for example, the new Stanford Human Biology curriculum—interactive, dynamic, fascinating, authoritative, and specifically oriented to young adolescents. (Because of its innovative character and strong potential, we will consider this particular program further.)

3. Training in life skills, including decision making, conflict resolution, and nonviolent problem solving.[14]

4. Strengthening social support mechanisms for adolescents by reengaging families with their children's schools and, when necessary, providing mentors to supplement the family.[15]

5. Creating safe after-school havens in community-based organizations can offset the risks of being alone or on the street. At the same time, they offer the opportunity to enrich the assets of youth in terms of artistic, academic, and sports achievements. In these ways they help to curtail or prevent major problem behaviors such as substance abuse, unwise sexual choices, or violence.[16]

6. Providing a perception of opportunity and of value to the community for adolescents by engaging them in academically-supervised community service and work-study programs.

7. Making health care services and counseling available in adolescent-friendly and accessible locations, including school-based or school-linked adolescent health centers.[17] The links between positive mental health and school success have been proven. These school centers should include mental health services with special attention to depression and recurrent anger.[18]

As children experience puberty and emerge into an era in which they often feel compelled to quickly become adults, they in effect ask, "How shall I use my body?" Any responsible education system must answer that basic question with a substantial life sciences curriculum that provides accurate information about their bodies, including the effects of various high-risk behavior patterns. But information alone is not enough.

Life skills training can become a vital part of education in schools and community organizations, so that adolescents can learn how to make informed, deliberate, and constructive decisions—rather than ignorant, impulsive, and destructive ones. Such training can also enhance their interpersonal skills, their ways of relating decently to others, and their ability to learn from experiences. Such training provides strategies and skills for coping with the prevalent life stresses and peer pressures of adolescence. In the adolescent field, there is great interest and involvement in the designing, implementing, and rigorous evaluation of prevention programs to address the full range of adolescent behaviors. Well-studied prevention programs include those to prevent smoking,[19] substance abuse,[20] teenage pregnancy,[21] AIDS,[22] and suicide.[23] A number of these programs have emphasized the importance of positive peer involvement and peer counseling.[24] Programs targeted to violence prevention are discussed in detail in a later chapter, but we need to introduce the subject here.

PREVENTING YOUTH VIOLENCE

In our lifetime, youth fights and conflicts in urban poverty settings have gone from fists to knives to pistols to semiautomatic weapons. Sadly, powerful guns are readily available to these youth. For many adolescent males, fighting is valued as showing strength and manhood. If we continue down this destructive path, fully automatic weapons could soon become the weapons of choice—with a capacity for slaughter beyond reason and imagination. Surely there is a better way.

In the United States, nearly 1 million adolescents between the ages of 12 and 19 are victims of violent crimes each year. These are, by far, the highest rates in modern, industrialized nations. The violence problem is serious. Evidence is emerging on ways to prevent adolescent violence. It is known that to be effective, prevention requires a comprehensive approach that addresses both individual and social factors. Optimally, programs build on generic approaches that meet essential requirements for healthy adolescent development through developmentally appropriate schools, supportive families, and youth-oriented community organizations. In addition, specific interventions that target youth violence can enhance adolescents' motivation and ability to deal with conflict in nonviolent ways. Policy changes, such as implementing stronger measures to restrict the availability of guns, are urgently needed, especially in light of the growing propensity of juveniles to use highly lethal weapons.

As episodes of school violence have proliferated, schools have increasingly adopted mandatory curricula for violence prevention. One promising strategy for preventing youth violence is the teaching of conflict-resolution skills as part of health education or social studies in elementary and middle schools. Most of these programs also include measures to create a positive, supportive school climate and eliminate school bullying—physical or verbal. Research indicates that conflict-resolution programs can reduce violence. Best results are achieved if conflict-resolution training is embedded in long-term, comprehensive programs to address multiple risk factors—that taken together create environments that offer little except violence. Serious, in-depth conflict-resolution training over extended periods is increasingly important in neighborhoods saturated with media and street violence. Supervised practice of conflict-resolution skills play an important role. We have more to say about this in Chapter 10, which discusses education for conflict resolution.

Assertiveness, taught as a social skill, helps young people learn how to resist unwanted pressures and intimidation, develop anger management skills, and resolve conflicts nonviolently. Students also learn how to make sound decisions about the use of weapons and to take advantage of constructive opportunities for friendship, recreation, and paid work or community service activities. Adolescent violence is as much a public health concern as other behavior-related health problems. Adolescents' propensity for exploration of new possibilities offers an opportunity to develop alternatives to violent responses. With the goal of reducing fights, assaults, and intentional injuries among adolescents, violence-prevention programs train service providers in diverse community settings in a special curriculum, translate this curriculum into concrete services for adolescents, and enlist the support of the community in preventing youth violence. The four principal components of such programs are curriculum development, community-based prevention education, enhancement and integration of clinical treatment services, and media awareness campaigns. Violence-prevention efforts of such a systematic and comprehensive design are recent. Needed rigorous evaluation is under way. At their best, such programs offer ways to provide positive alternatives to the violent behavior and promote healthy adolescent development that changes trajectories and gives the underpinnings for constructive, productive, adult lives.

Violence-prevention programs are trying to reach as many community settings as possible, including multiservice centers, recreation facilities, housing developments, police and courts, churches, neighborhood health centers, and schools. Also, there is typically a referral network for specialized health, education, and social services. Community campaigns may produce television and radio public service announcements that attract adolescents to valuable opportunities and reinforce awareness of opportunities and alternative paths. These issues of youth violence are discussed more fully in a later chapter.

EDUCATION FOR HEALTH

The AIDS epidemic has vividly brought into focus the critical nature of relations between personal behavior and health and the role of education in disease prevention.[25] A worldwide educational effort to curb the spread of HIV infection is promoted by public health professionals. There is exceptional timeliness and significance in the middle grades (early adolescence) for such preventive educational efforts. AIDS education, important as it is, constitutes only one part of a farther-reaching need and opportunity at this special time of life—to focus on education in human biology, including personal behaviors that bear upon health. The heaviest burden of illness in the technically advanced countries today is related to individual behavior, especially the long-term patterns of behavior often referred to as "lifestyles." These include health-damaging behaviors such as cigarette smoking, drinking alcohol, drug abuse, eating too many calories and too much fat, and inactivity.[26] For behavior changes that strongly affect health (for example, in eating, smoking, and exercise habits), evidence from several large studies indicates that those with more education tend to practice more healthy behaviors than those who have less education. Education matters!

A DEVELOPMENTAL PERSPECTIVE ON
HEALTH AND BEHAVIOR

What we do early in life lays the foundation for the rest of our lives. The early years can provide the basis for a long, healthy life span. Early preventive intervention tends to be exceptionally cost effective. Health and education are closely linked in the development of vigorous, skillful, adaptable young people. Programs in health and education guided by research in biomedical and behavioral sciences can prevent much of the damage to children and adolescents that results from their ignorance.

The onset of adolescence is a critical period of biological and psychological change for the individual. The dramatic bodily changes of puberty is one of the most far-reaching biological upheavals in the life span. For many, it involves drastic changes in the social environment as well: the transition from elementary to secondary school and the shift of status from childhood to adulthood. These years (from age 10 to 15) are highly formative for health-relevant behavior patterns such as the smoking of cigarettes, use of alcohol or other drugs, driving of automobiles and motorcycles, food intake and exercise, and effects of sexual relationships that include the risk of pregnancies and sexually transmitted diseases, and certainly not least, serious violence. Pubertal adolescents are deeply focused on learning about their bodies. Before health-damaging patterns are firmly established, there is a crucial opportunity for preventive intervention.

Adolescents are highly exposed to sexuality, alcohol and other drugs, smoking, motor vehicles, weapons, and a variety of other temptations to engage in health-damaging behaviors. Although their use may appear to young people to be casual, recreational, or tension relieving, their effects endanger the users and others. The experience of industrialized nations suggests that rapid social changes, the breakdown of family supports, and prolongation of adolescence are associated with an increase in behavior-related problems such as substance abuse, school-age pregnancy, educational failure, and violence. The opportunities for prevention rest heavily on finding constructive ways to meet the basic aspirations of adolescent development in a new social context.

It is possible to provide teenagers with the basis for making wise decisions about the use of their own bodies or about how to plan a constructive future. It is possible to build social support networks in every community for stimulating interest, hope, and skills among people to pursue education and protect their health. One of the most important tasks that preventive efforts face is convincing these young people that they are indeed vulnerable, while not raising their fear in destructive ways that may lead to denial or rebellion. In assessing potential consequences, adolescents also appear more likely to focus on immediate rather than long-term effects of their behaviors.

HUMAN BIOLOGY: TOWARD A BROADER AND MORE USEFUL VIEW OF THE LIFE SCIENCES

The life sciences, by stimulating children's interest in understanding nature, can also lead the way to a deeper study of other scientific disciplines such as chemistry and physics, as well as the behavioral and social sciences that deal with matters of deep human concern.

An important goal in understanding human biology is to permit better solutions to biological aspects of social problems, such as environmental hazards, with less strife and more informed public participation. Knowledge of human biology is particularly important in making health related decisions such as whether or not to use alcohol, cigarettes, or drugs. It is also important in understanding what constitutes a healthy diet and a healthy amount of exercise, in addition to facilitating decisions on when to seek health care. Thus, education for health is a potentially powerful component of education in the life sciences.

In "HUMBIO: Stanford University's Human Biology Curriculum for the Middle Grades," published in *Preparing Adolescents for the Twenty-First Century,* H. Craig Heller and Mary L. Kiely describe Stanford University's human biology initiative for the middle grades and the ways in which the curriculum engages young adolescents' attention and is of relevance to their lives.[27] It uses topics of great interest to adolescents—such as sexuality and reproduction or the effects of drugs on the nervous system—to capture their attention, teach them about themselves, identify high-risk behaviors, and show how they can affect their health. The choice of topics and an activity-based approach serve to attract the students' attention while also helping to develop adolescents' problem-solving skills—skills that can be applied to real-life situations and help promote good health practices. The program's results were evaluated by teachers across disciplines throughout the United States, and constructive criticism was used to develop the final 22-module curriculum.

The HUMBIO curriculum is comprised of units intended for three weeks of class work (though some of the units may be extended) in the life and behavioral sciences, with opportunities to include health, social, and environmental issues in the lessons. Activity-based coursework not only maintains the students' attention but also fosters group work, which helps to satisfy another of the program's goals: to engage their interest and actively involve minorities and females in science, where they are notably underrepresented. HUMBIO took differing levels of English-language ability and academic achievement into consideration in the development of the program. The resulting curriculum creates a "positive interdependence" within the groups of students. It incorporates social and ethical questions into the study of science and technology, illustrating to students the interconnectedness of science and everyday life. Although this curriculum does not emphasize violence prevention, it provides a strong platform of biological and public health knowledge on which to build such education.

SCHOOLS AS HEALTH-PROMOTING ENVIRONMENTS

The Carnegie Council on Adolescent Development's concluding report, *Great Transitions,* highlights the important role of middle grade schools in nurturing adolescent health through curriculum, school policy, and the presentation of behavior conducive to good health. Through these means, "schools can encourage students to form good health habits and recognize that education and health are mutually reinforcing."[28] Ways to create such an environment include (1) teaching proper nutrition in the classroom and providing nutritious foods in the cafeteria, (2) creating smoke-free environments and discouraging student and staff smoking, (3) educating students about the ill effects of alcohol and illicit drugs, (4) providing ample opportunities for exercise apart from varsity sports, and (5) emphasizing personal safety and violence prevention including explicit warnings about drug dealing and carrying weapons.

The Council's report also details how the life sciences curriculum, life skills training, and social support programs are crucial to advancing good health in early adolescence:[29]

1. *Life sciences curriculum:* This curriculum uses the curiosity of early adolescents, who are themselves in the midst of visible bodily change, to teach adolescent development within the study of human biology. From here, curriculum can address the study of behavior, critical choices, and the impact of high-risk behavior throughout an individual's life.

2. *Life skills training:* Though largely derived from life sciences curriculum, this training is insufficient without developed decision-making or interpersonal skills. Instruction, practice, and role-playing are useful in developing these skills, whereas highlighting developmentally relevant negative effects of detrimental behaviors on peer popularity, including nicotine-stained fingers and bad breath, can further discourage such behavior. "Having these skills can help students resist pressure from peers or from the media to engage in high-risk behaviors, increase their self control, acquire ways to reduce stress and anxiety without engaging in dangerous activity, learn how to make friends if they are isolated, and learn how to avoid violence but also assert themselves effectively."[30]

3. *Social support programs:* Research has shown the effectiveness of these programs in nurturing health and education for adolescents and their families. Schools and community and health care organizations can work together to reinforce shared values and goals to meet this end.

Combined, these three elements effectively foster healthy adolescent development, and consequently are of relevance to the prevention of serious health problems.

COMMUNITY SUPPORTS IN EARLY ADOLESCENCE
AND ALTERNATIVES TO VIOLENCE

High-risk youth in impoverished communities urgently need social support networks and life skills training. Both can be provided in schools and school-related health centers as well as in community organizations, including church-related youth activities and sports programs.[31] They work best by building enduring relationships with responsible, caring adults and constructive peers. Such an approach offers alternatives to violent groups by providing a sense of belonging, a source of enjoyable activity, a perception of opportunity, mentoring, and a chance to prepare for social roles that earn respect. Efforts to build such social support networks have been growing in recent years.

A variety of organizations and institutions can provide supplements or surrogates for parents, older siblings, and an extended family. Across the country, there are many examples of such interventions. Some are based in churches, such as the initiatives of the Congress of National Black Churches; some are based in community organizations like the Boys and Girls Clubs. Others such as Campus Compact involve youth service and are based in colleges and universities, still others are based in minority organizations. Businesses can also build constructive social support networks that attract disadvantaged or alienated youth. These networks can foster opportunities for young people to improve their health, their education, and their capacity to be accepted by the mainstream society. They offer adolescents healthy alternatives to substance abuse and violent gang membership.

Communities must provide attractive, safe, growth-promoting settings for young adolescents during the out-of-school hours—times of high risk when working parents are often not available to supervise their children.[32] Community organizations are expanding their reach by providing attractive and enjoyable opportunities for youth; offering more activities that convey information about life chances, careers, and places beyond the neighborhood; and engaging youth in community service and other constructive activities that foster education and health. Such programs have had to learn how to attract and retain the young adolescents. Unlike schools, where attendance is compulsory, in community settings the youngsters can attend if they wish. Good programs attract a dedicated and loyal clientele of adolescents.

In 1992, the Carnegie Council on Adolescent Development published a report, directed by Jane Quinn, on youth development and community programs called *A Matter of Time*. A distinguished and diverse 26-member task force, led by James Comer and Wilma Tisch, formulated the study, which resulted (10 years later) in several promising outcomes. The following excerpts from *A Matter of Time* provide a fundamental overview of the content of the report:

> By any standards, America's young adolescents have a great deal of discretionary time. Much of it is unstructured, unsupervised, and unproductive for the young person. Only 60 percent of adolescents' waking hours are committed to such essentials as school, homework, eating, chores, or paid employment, while fully 40 percent are discretionary.
>
> Many young adolescents spend much of that time alone. The 1988 National Education Longitudinal Study, which surveyed a nationally representative sample of some 25,000 eighth graders, found that approximately 27 percent of the respondents regularly spent two or more hours at home alone after school. Eighth graders from families in the lowest socioeconomic group were more likely to report that they were home alone for more than 3 hours, while those in the highest income group were least likely to be unsupervised for that amount of time.
>
> Young adolescents do not want to be left to their own devices. In national surveys and focus groups, America's youth have given voice to a serious longing. They want more regular contact with adults who care about and respect them, more opportunities to contribute to their communities, protection from the hazards of drugs, violence, and gangs, and greater access to constructive and attractive alternatives to the loneliness that so many now experience. . . .
>
> Community-based youth programs can provide enriching and rewarding expe-

riences for young adolescents, and many do: Their young members socialize with their peers and adults and learn to set and achieve goals, compete fairly, win gracefully, recover from defeat, and resolve disputes peaceably. They acquire life skills: the ability to communicate, make decisions, solve problems, make plans, and set goals for education and careers. They put their school-learned knowledge to use, for example, by working as an intern in a museum. In these activities and others, they prepare themselves for adulthood by interacting with and learning from responsible, caring adults and their peers. . . .

Most troubling, many existing programs tend to serve young people from more advantaged families. They do not reach millions of young adolescents who live in low-income urban and rural areas. Some programs reach young people for only 1 or 2 hours a week, far less time than it takes to give sustained support to those who can most benefit. Fully 29 percent of young adolescents are not reached by these programs at all.[33]

Overall, the research and experience in this field indicates that the most effective programs do the following things:

- Tailor their program content and processes to the needs and interests of young adolescents.
- Recognize, value, and respond to the diverse backgrounds and experience of young adolescents.
- Extend their reach to underserved adolescents.
- Actively compete for the time and attention of young adolescents.
- Strengthen the quality and diversity of their adult leadership.
- Reach out to families, schools, and a wide range of community partners in youth development.
- Enhance the role of young adolescents as resources in their community.
- Serve as vigorous advocates for and with youth.
- Specify and evaluate their programs' outcomes.
- Establish strong organizational structures, including energetic and committed board leadership.[34]

A consensus set of policy recommendations for generating community supports through local, state, and national action has emerged. Funders of all types—private and public, national and local—should work in partnership with youth development organizations and with one another to identify and address the pressing needs of youth in communities across the country. Local, state, and federal policies should be coordinated, focused on increasing support for basic youth development services, and targeted to areas of greatest need.

Jane Quinn, now of the Children's Aid Society in New York City, has written about recent and encouraging findings surrounding the ideas generated from *A Matter of Time* and summarizing the positive outcomes in youth development since the publication of that earlier report.[35]

Increased public understanding.   Several polls, including those backed by Public Agenda and the Charles Stewart Mott Foundation, suggest that a large majority of people agree that the nonschool hours have the potential for risk and for opportunity for young people. Children and youth therefore must be offered support during this vulnerable interval to prevent adverse behaviors and to maximize opportunities for growth through health-promoting services in the community.

Increased research attention.   A research committee of the National Research Council (NRC), National Academy of Sciences, critically examined recent studies in this field and published its analysis in *Community Programs to Promote Youth Development.*[36] It clarifies and documents the progress that has been made over the last decade. This report examines the evidence base for program design and the essentials of implementation and makes recommendations for practice, policy, and research.[37] The NRC report is entirely consistent with *A Matter of Time* and serves to update it. The report identifies distinctive features of positive developmental settings that are likely to be helpful in achieving the goals set out in this chapter. Key features cited include providing physical and psychological safety; assuring an age-appropriate structure providing constructive guidelines for behavior; supporting interpersonal relationships; offering opportunities for a sense of belonging to a valued group; exposing positive social norms; supporting efficacy in youth service and recognizing contributions made by youth; building tangible skills that provide a basis for future opportunities; and integrating the efforts of family, school, and community so as to maximize the chances of beneficial impact on youth development.[38]

Farsighted public policies.   Both the philosophy and the approach to youth development have strong presences in public policy at state and federal levels. For instance, federal agencies (e.g., Department of Agriculture, Education, Health and Human Services) now make use of the language and practices of youth development in positive and meaningful ways in their programs. Also, many states now utilize a structure of youth development in similar terms.

Increased public and private funding.   The 21st Century Community Learning Centers program is the largest public funding source to use this approach. Between 1997 and 2002, their program expanded from $1 million to $1 billion. YouthBuild USA designed a highly effective program for older teenagers and won federal support to expand it to the national level. Local state governments and private foundations have placed dollars into programs for youth that are partially assisted by groups such as the Coalition of Community of Foundations for Youth and the Youth Development Funders Network.

Improved quality and number of programs.   The number and quality of programs over the last 10 years have improved because of various professional development opportunities, which include staff training. These efforts have been led by organizations such as New York's Youth Development Institute and San Francisco's Community Networks for Youth Development.[39]

OVERVIEW

We can make many constructive responses to the casualties of early life. Some interventions are well documented and can be readily adopted with much benefit. Others are promising, but much more research is needed. We can make substantial progress by deepening our understanding of human development, by fostering public understanding of our children's urgent needs and opportunities, and by strengthening our scientific and professional commitment to tackle these problems over a wide spectrum of constructive approaches.

In the long run, the vitality of any society and its prospects for the future depend on the quality of its people—on their knowledge and skill, health and vigor, and the decency of their human relations. Preventing children from experiencing damaged lives would therefore have powerfully beneficial social and economic impacts, including a more effective workforce, higher productivity, lower health costs, lower prison costs, and so much relief of human distress. Youth violence is the tip of an iceberg. Tragic as it is, it should give us a powerful stimulus to enhance the life chances of all children, including those who suffer personal misery and lost opportunities in quiet pain and sometimes violent eruptions that can do irrevocable damage.

7

Contact, Intergroup Relations, and Opportunities for Education

WHEN IS CONTACT HELPFUL?

If groups are strange to each other and therefore fearful or hostile, why not bring them together so they can get to know each other and become friendly? This plausible approach is more complicated than it looks at first glance. Under what conditions will intergroup contact be helpful? Can it sometimes be harmful? A variety of field and laboratory experiments support the hypothesis that intergroup *competition* tends to strengthen social relations *within* each group and to disrupt relations *between* the groups. If the experiments are arranged in a way that deliberately fosters competition between the groups, these effects are heightened. But even in the absence of such direct instruction or arrangement, potent factors favor interpersonal attraction or mutual attachment within a group: frequency of social interaction, proximity to each other, familiarity, and similarity of attitudes and values. Almost any sort of interaction within a group tends to promote in-group favoritism. Actually, it seems rather difficult to avoid this effect even if one tries to do so.

Humans are highly susceptible to invidious in-group/out-group distinctions. Extensive experimental work strongly confirms the rich variety of observations from fieldwork in many cultures over extended times and in a variety of societies. This does indeed seem to be a profound and pervasive human characteristic—one of great practical significance throughout history. We will return to this theme and examples throughout the book.

Findings of this sort have led some psychologists to formulate a principle of social identity, which emphasizes the powerful effects of social categorization in its own right. Such categorization seems to highlight an important aspect of the individual self-concept (and self-esteem) based on group membership. Such membership has, from the evolutionary and historical record, been an important feature in human survival over the millennia. In contemporary people—at least, in those who participate in psychological experiments—the cognitive delineation into an in-group and out-group, even without invidious attributions, tends to set in motion a process by which there is an accentuation of similarities within groups and differences between groups. It seems very convenient, easy, and somehow natural for people to deal with these via simple schemas or stereotypes. It is as if we readily abstract what we view as the essential features of our own group that distinguishes it from other groups, and in so doing we distinguish ourselves from a lot of other people. This sort of cognitive distinction is readily learned and almost inextricably linked with self-evaluation, typically favorable to oneself and one's own group—and more or less unfavorable to other groups. Similarities and differences may have a factual core, but they readily become value-laden and fall prey to simplistic and prejudicial exaggerations.

Such in-group/out-group distinctions are ubiquitous in human societies—easy to learn and hard to forget. But even so, there is certainly the possibility that we humans can learn to minimize invidious in-group/out-group distinctions. We will have to try much more than humankind has ever tried before to transform intergroup relations more and more into intragroup relations. To some extent, we will have to broaden our social identifications in light of shared characteristics and superordinate goals across all boundaries and countries. In short, if we could come to think of ourselves in a fundamental sense as a single, interdependent, meaningfully attached, worldwide species, we would be much better off than we are now. That is in fact what we are. Can we find a basis for common human identification across a diversity of cultures, even conflicting ones? Can we see underlying shared interests even in the face of substantial manifest conflict? These are among the most crucial questions of our time.

The importance of overlapping group memberships in the modern world may help us forge global cooperation. The role of group membership in social cooperation—or its failure—is one we need to understand more deeply, both in its fundamental properties and in its myriad possibilities in the world of large-scale international contact that has so recently emerged. People who belong to groups that cut across ethnic or national lines may serve a bridging function across cultural barriers. We see this, for instance, in strong positive bonds in the international scientific community. To build such bridges, we will need many people who elicit a high level of respect and have some leadership functions in their communities. Little in our history as a species prepares us for inclusive identifications across spatial and cultural gulfs. Yet we can hardly afford to neglect serious exploration of this possibility.

CONFLICT RESOLUTION THROUGH PERSONAL
CONTACT AND COOPERATION

One source of insight into these matters comes from decades of research in social psychology and related fields on racial prejudice in the United States and ways to reduce such prejudice. Research of this kind shows that proximity can play a positive role under favorable circumstances. Contact and proximity encourage interaction between people of different backgrounds as they learn to live together, and often they come to like each other more than they did before.

In this context, a great deal of work has been done on desegregation in the United States by pioneering investigators such as Morton Deutsch of Columbia University. In a classic study, Deutsch examined two New York City public housing units undergoing desegregation.[1] In one, families were assigned apartments at random without regard to race. In another, blacks and whites were assigned to separate buildings. A subsequent survey showed that those in the desegregated housing were much more likely to favor interracial living than were those in the other arrangement. The experience of human contact had diminished negative stereotypes.[2]

But research on school desegregation has yielded varying results. Clearly the problem is complicated, and desegregation alone does not produce strong results. So what then are the conditions under which desegregation does in fact reduce prejudice between groups? Putting together a great deal of laboratory and field research, it appears that the quantitative *amount* of contact between racial groups does *not* have a high degree of relevance to the outcome. As we have noted, much depends on whether the contact occurs under favorable conditions. If the conditions involve an aura of suspicion, if they are highly competitive, if they are not supported by (or are even undermined by) relevant authorities, or if they occur on the basis of very unequal status, then they are not likely to be helpful, whatever the amount of contact. Indeed, such unfavorable conditions can exacerbate old tensions and can reinforce stereotypes.

On the other hand, there is a strong effect of *friendly* contact in the context of *equal status*, especially if such contact is *supported by relevant authorities*, is embedded in *cooperative activity*, and is fostered by a *mutual aid ethic*. Under these conditions, the more contact, the better. Such contact is associated with improved attitudes between previously suspicious or hostile groups as well as changes of patterns of interaction between them in constructive ways.

Research in military settings shows that bringing people of different backgrounds, previously suspicious of each other, into equal status contact under circumstances in which they are highly interdependent can also have positive effects. In this instance they are helping each other, they are fighting a common enemy, they are working toward a shared objective. Similarly, circumstances of cooperative learning in elementary and secondary education are conducive to the improvement of intergroup relations, but highly competitive, extremely individualistic circumstances in the classroom are more likely to have a negative effect. We will have more to say about this later.

SUPERORDINATE GOALS AND COOPERATIVE BEHAVIOR

Superordinate goals have the potentially powerful effect of unifying disparate groups in search of some common aspiration that can only be obtained by their cooperation. In Chapter 3, we described the classic experiments of Muzafer Sherif in a summer camp for adolescent boys. For decades, Sherif's studies provided the most vivid examples of this case. A shared goal that can only be achieved by cooperative effort overrides the hostile differences that people bring to the situation. In Sherif's classic experiments, he readily made strangers into enemies with isolation and competition, but when he introduced powerful superordinate goals, he was able to transform enemies into friends.[3]

These experiments have been fundamentally replicated since then in work with large numbers of business executives in many different groups.[4] So the effect is certainly not limited to children and youth. Indeed, the findings have been extended in ways that indicate the beneficial effects of working cooperatively under conditions that lead people to formulate a new, inclusive group that goes beyond the subgroups with which they entered the situation. Such effects are particularly strong when there are tangibly successful outcomes of cooperation—for example, clear rewards from cooperative learning. In the successful case of cooperation, previously suspicious groups come to have a new appreciation of each other. Overall, this work can be joined with other evidence to indicate that prejudice tends to be reduced when there is equal status contact between groups in the pursuit of common goals and shared efficacy in reaching those goals.

As a matter of fact, this evidence is consistent with a great deal of human experience showing ways in which families are drawn together by common efforts in sharing housework or recreation, ways in which solidarity at the community level is enhanced by shared efforts in community building or in sports. Indeed, individual, family, small group, and community experiences of many kinds suggest that equal status contact in behalf of a shared goal with manifest efficacy tends to draw people together across prior barriers and to strengthen their positive commitment to each other. Can the same kind of process occur in the context of larger intergroup relations? Understanding and respect can be fostered across cultural barriers by serious collaborative efforts in science and technology and in business. What about joint efforts to overcome the serious global problems of food, water, health, and the environment? The world is one in which friendly personal contacts on an equal status basis and cooperative ventures can occur more readily than ever before, despite all the cultural barriers that have so long separated peoples. A great opportunity and challenge now is to identify superordinate goals and organize cooperative efforts to meet them. One good place to start is *education* at every level. Marilyn B. Brewer, a distinguished scholar in this field, discusses motivations for maintaining in-group boundaries and the implications of in-group boundary protection for intergroup relations, conflict, and conflict prevention.[5] Can in-group love be separated from out-group hate? If so, how? Brewer cites a chapter ("Ingroup Formation") in Gordon W. Allport's classic work, *The Nature of Prejudice*, in which Allport proposed that in-groups are "psychologically primary"—that familiarity and preferences of in-groups come before the development of attitudes toward out-groups.[6] Therefore, this preferential positivity toward in-groups does not necessarily mean that negative or hostile feelings must be held toward out-groups.

Brewer also believes that the root of identification and attachment to in-groups is independent of intergroup conflict. She considers the prevailing conditions under which attachment and loyalty to in-groups may become linked with out-group hate, and the implications of this relationship for reducing prejudice and preventing conflict. If there is a gap between in-group love and out-group hate, this would provide an opening for education to diminish the risks of violence.

Although there are many situations in which in-group positivity and out-group negativity are linked, there is evidence of space between the two in some circumstances. It is unnecessary to have hostile intent toward out-groups to stimulate allegiance to in-groups. In 1976, Brewer and Campbell conducted a study of the reciprocal attitudes among 30 ethnic groups in East Africa.[7] Results across all 30 groups showed a positive evaluation of the in-group over all out-groups when factors such as trustworthiness, obedience, friendliness, and honesty were considered. However, there was virtually no relationship between in-group preference and out-group distancing. Studies from 1971 and 1992 show a willingness to benefit the in-group along with a reluctance to harm out-groups.[8] Allport clarified the possibility of building on the notion of "concentric loyalties"—where there is compatibility between loyalties of larger groups (for example, nation, humankind) and of subgroups (for example, family, profession, religion).[9] The needs of the in-group and out-group are seen as compatible if these groups are subsumed by the superordinate group. Out-groups can be perceived in a variety of ways not necessarily hostile. Let us put it simply: "We have our ways and they have their ways."[10]

Every group can attain constructive uniqueness by valuing different things. If an in-group surpasses an out-group in aspects of vital importance to the in-group's identity, then it can accept the superiority of an out-group in areas of less importance to the in-group.[11] However, there is competition over the search for positive distinctiveness when there are shared common values. How to be different in a good way? How to carve out a distinct ecological niche in identity terms?

Because the identities of individuals in a more complex social structure include attachments to various groups (such as religious, occupational, residential), they are more apt to be fellow in-group members in one category and out-group members in another. In this case, the individual does not rely so heavily on any single identity. This in turn makes it easier to accept out-groups and thereby diminishes the risk of serious conflict. Such observations have been independently made by various social scientists.[12] Indeed, Lipset, a leading scholar of democracy, believes that such conditions are vital to stable democracies.[13]

One of the most extensive efforts to apply the intergroup contact hypothesis to education occurred in Israel. A paper by Yehuda Amir, growing out of this interest, soon became a classic of social psychology.[14] We draw on Amir's paper in the following few pages because of its significance. The paper was inspired by a meeting between psychologists and policymakers of the Israel Ministry of Education and Culture who were dealing with the restructuring of Israel's educational system. They addressed the issue of ethnic relations and the opportunity for intergroup contact among children and youth. The policy in place at the time was for children to attend the schools closest to their homes, which meant that they would be in contact only with members of the same socioeconomic and ethnic backgrounds. There were broadly two classes, the lower class (consisting mostly of immigrants from African and Asian countries) and the higher class (composed of groups from Europe and America). The planned educational reorganization took these divisions into consideration and aimed at providing opportunities for intergroup contact across class lines. The assumption was that this contact would enable children to know each other better, thereby reducing ethnic prejudice and intergroup tension.

Amir evaluated studies of the effect of intergroup contact on the changing of attitudes and ethnic relations. He also evaluated the assumption that intergroup contact tends to produce better intergroup attitudes and relations. Amir considered the effect of contact on intergroup relations in several dimensions that reflect the state of research in the field. His findings are consistent with many others in this field of inquiry. They can be generalized beyond the borders of Israel and used as a stimulus elsewhere for research on the uses of intergroup contact for education.

Generally, most studies have shown that the effect of contact is positive, but it is necessary to clarify the conditions most likely to produce good effects. Social psychologists generally agree that, when speaking about contact, one needs to consider the type of contact involved, because *contact* per se is an ambiguous and therefore an inadequate term.[15]

Is Opportunity for Contact Enough?

Careful studies of intergroup contacts give mixed results. Clearly, opportunity alone does not produce improvement in intergroup relations. It may be a necessary condition, but it is surely not sufficient. The nature of the contact is important. Let us now look at the main factors in the nature of the contact that have a strong bearing on outcomes.

The Importance of Equal Status

In the late 1940s and early 1950s, works by Allport and by Allport and Kramer provided leading ideas in the field of contact theory.[16] Allport showed that prejudice could be reduced by contact if it is founded on "*equal status contact* between majority and minority groups in the *pursuit of common goals*" (emphasis added).[17] It is likely that the effect of contact on attitudes will increase with the support of institutions of society. Also, several studies have shown that friendly contact between members of a majority group and high-status individuals of a minority group can reduce prejudice toward the whole minority group. To summarize many studies, in essence, equal status contact will most likely produce positive attitude changes, provided that there is equivalence of status and acceptance by social groups that are mutually respected—and especially when the contact is supported by relevant authority. Amir followed these concepts in his research on Israeli schools. Elsewhere in this book, we note conditions that interfere with such positive effects—for example, harsh competition and lack of support from relevant au-thorities.[18]

Cooperation and Competition

Sherif maintained that merely bringing together hostile groups in a contact situation was not sufficient to foster cooperation across group lines.[19] Rather, they should have or should be given superordinate goals that can be attained only by their cooperation. In fact, cooperation is greater in situations in which both groups are given highly at-tractive superordinate goals. When the contact between groups is to the disadvantage of one of them, this may actually intensify intergroup conflict.

In Israel, a prevailing policy was to establish new settlements with mixed ethnic pop-ulations. The assumption was that this would enhance intergroup relations and create a united and homogeneous nation. To the contrary, often this policy produced tension and conflict and in due course was abolished. The reasons for the failure are not entirely clear, but unequal status seems to have been a major factor. Striking differences in cultural norms and attitudes produced a threatening situation, minimizing the chance of estab-lishing superordinate goals. In any event, superordinate goals were not formulated.

In summary, the evidence points to the fact that cooperative and competitive fac-tors may be significant and even decisive in situations of intergroup contact. Coopera-tive factors seem to further intergroup relations, and competitive factors generally hin-der them.

Closeness of Contact

To produce change in attitudes between ethnic groups, it takes casual communication between them, though casual communication may provide a useful starting point. Nei-ther does regularity of contact encourage positive interethnic relations. It may even in-crease prejudice if the surrounding conditions are unfavorable.

Intergroup contact may produce different types of relationships, ranging from ca-sual and superficial to deep ego-involving intimacy. Casual intergroup contact has lit-tle or no effect on basic attitudinal change, whereas intimate contact tends to produce the most positive changes. Intimacy creates a nonstereotypical view of the out-group member, thereby allowing the person to perceive the other as an individual who shares many similarities and can be understood in human terms.

SUMMARY OF RESEARCH FINDINGS

The following are some recurrent findings presented by Amir that have grown from re-search in this field of research on contact between ethnic groups.[20]

Contact produces changes in attitude that may be positive or negative de-pending on the conditions under which contact occurs.

The *intensity* of an attitude toward another group is important—for example, strengthening a weak preexisting positive attitude toward another group may produce constructive behavior change. Behavior change is often limited to a specific circumstance (for example, work situations).

Favorable conditions that reduce prejudice include the following contact situations: (1) when groups have equal status, (2) when majority group members are in contact with high-status individuals within a minority group, (3) when contact is supported by authority or social climate, (4) when contact is intimate rather than casual, (5) when contact is pleasant or rewarding, (6) when there are highly valued common or superordinate goals that can be achieved only by cooperating.

Unfavorable conditions that heighten prejudice include contact situations that (1) are competitive; (2) are unpleasant, forced, or filled with tension; (3) when the reputation of one group is lowered; (4) when group members are frustrated or led to seek a scapegoat; (5) when a group's based on ethnicity are offensive to the other; (6) when the minority group is deeply depreciated in relation to the majority group.

These concepts could be usefully adopted and evaluated in education and elsewhere to diminish intergroup hostility and minimize prejudice in child development. Further research is necessary to enhance the efficacy of policies and practices based on contact theory, but the promise of this approach is clear.

PROMOTING POSITIVE INTERGROUP RELATIONS IN SCHOOLS

We have sketched the extensive body of research on intergroup contact, with special attention to the conditions that tend to diminish intergroup hostility. Can these favorable conditions for positive intergroup relations be widely applied to schools? After all, this is the primary locale for most children and youth for many hours every day, week in and week out, for most of each year. The potential for shaping prosocial attitudes and behavior during these meaningful hours is formidable. Could schools be organized from beginning to end in ways that are favorable to forming decent human relationships? Could classroom and extracurricular activities, in the natural course of events, minimize prejudice and hateful attitudes? In this chapter and several others to come, we explore attractive possibilities in this domain.

Janet Ward Schofield, a leading scholar in this field, has applied this approach to American schools.[21] She emphasizes that improving intergroup relations between children and youth from different racial and ethnic backgrounds is vital because serious problems still exist in intergroup relations, and because minority-group members are becoming an increasingly large part of the U.S. population—now more diverse than ever before. Because residential segregation is so pervasive in U.S. society, children frequently have their first contacts with people from different racial or ethnic backgrounds in school. Therefore, Schofield focuses on an exploration of policies and practices favorable to improving intergroup relations in school settings. The following sections summarize her review of strategies that attempt to foster positive relations and inhibit negative relations in situations where intergroup isolation or tensions exist but there have not been major conflicts. This is analogous to primary prevention of disease in public health.

Limitations in What We Know about Intergroup Relations

A large amount of what is known about intergroup relations in school settings stems from research in the late 1970s and early 1980s. This research has some limitations: (1) It is mostly correlational in nature although some is experimental; (2) the work is mostly a decade or two old and focuses largely on improving relations between whites and African Americans; multiethnic/racial situations are more common today and are beginning to be researched; and (3) the work does not adequately reflect the generational changes in intergroup attitudes and behavior that have occurred in the past 10 to 20 years. The latter time period has had surprisingly little research that focused directly on strategies to improve intergroup relations among children. The most notable exception is cooperative learning. Part of our intention with this book is to stimulate research on these problems.

Finding the Right Approach to Improving Intergroup Relations in Schools

First, it is vital to examine the current state of relations between the groups in question. There is a difference between hostile tension and overt conflicts. Second, some approaches emphasize ongoing structural features of a school setting, whereas others are circumscribed human relations programs. Third, aiming to reduce negative intergroup attitudes and behaviors and intending to increase positive intergroup attitudes and behaviors are not necessarily the same.

A Common Barrier to Improved Intergroup Relations

It is feasible that a school could have a diverse ethnic and racial makeup and still the individuals from different groups could have practically no contact with members of groups outside their own. Resegregation of dissimilar groups occurs under certain conditions. First, common educational practices such as categorization on the basis of standardized tests can inadvertently lead to resegregation. Second, students often resegregate themselves in free choice situations such as eating in the school cafeteria or choosing playmates. There is nothing intrinsically wrong with students who share certain interests and backgrounds associating with each other, but when these groupings arise from fear of rejection or resentment, they do not help to overcome barriers between groups or improve intergroup relations. Moreover, the extent of group isolation is important. Building high psychological walls is not likely to help.

There are some policies that can be implemented to prevent resegregation and to undercut children's tendency to stay in racially homogeneous groups out of fear or stigma. Teachers can assign seats in a way that fosters interracial contact (such as alphabetical order), and then they can occasionally change the assigned seats. There can be conscious planning to encourage minority and majority group students to participate jointly in extracurricular activities.

Conditions Conducive to Improving Intergroup Relations

There is a difference between desegregation and real integration. Real integration involves the creation of a setting that is favorable to the development of positive relations between members of different groups. Putting children together is not enough. Gordon Allport's 1954 contact hypothesis is the most influential. Now we focus on conditions conducive to positive outcomes in schools. There are three aspects particularly important to such contact situations: equal status for members of all groups, an emphasis on cooperative more than competitive activities, and explicit support for the contact by authority figures. How do these general principles apply to the school situation?

EQUAL STATUS   If equal status is not created for groups, existing stereotypes and beliefs of superiority or inferiority of the groups involved are likely to endure. Finding methods to prevent unequal status in the school is difficult, but a set of studies suggests that multiethnic curricula have a positive impact on intergroup relations when the program components are reasonably complex and of significant duration.[22] On the other hand, tracking of students in separate categories and classes can create and perpetuate unequal status.

COOPERATIVE INTERDEPENDENCE   Cooperation, rather than competition, is important because the results of competition often support stereotypes, unwarranted devaluation of other groups' achievements, and sharp hostility. Theory and research point toward the value of cooperation in achieving a shared goal that cannot be accomplished without the contribution of members of all groups, such as the production of a school play, team sports, or class committees. These cooperative activities must be carefully structured so they do not reinforce traditional stratified modes of interaction between majority and minority group members. Educators must ensure that all groups contribute to the final product, instead of assuming that a putatively cooperative group automatically means that all children will be motivated or permitted to contribute.

Although U.S. schools have traditionally stressed competition, this orientation is not unchangeable. With the arrival of self-paced instructional approaches and research on mastery learning, there is increasing acceptance of the observation that children can benefit by working at their own pace. Also, more educational scholars in recent years have emphasized the importance of teaching children how to work cooperatively to achieve a joint end product—a sensible trend, because productivity in the contemporary economy increasingly involves working in groups.

How does cooperation lead to positive effects on intergroup relations? The precise dynamics are not clear, but there are some components worth considering. The first factor is that cooperative activities create a crosscutting social identity. The fact that students from different ethnic backgrounds now share something with members of an out-group and simultaneously differ on some dimension from the in-group can diminish out-group bias. This suggests that finding ways to develop and highlight shared social-category memberships for youths of different racial and ethnic backgrounds would be constructive.

The personalization of out-group members is another factor that may explain the positive results of cooperative activities. Developing a personal relationship with members of another group and seeing them with their own personality traits, skills, and experiences may lead to the discovery of similarities between the self and the out-group. Stereotypes may weaken once the member of the out-group behaves in a manner that contradicts the initial stereotype. In addition, an ongoing experience with several members of the out-group might undercut the tendency to see out-group members as relatively similar to each other, whereas in-group members are seen as more diverse.

Moreover, cooperative interaction can create emotionally positive environments. This is especially true once the goal has been accomplished. Some experimental work shows that successful cooperation increases intergroup attraction, whereas cooperation that leads to failure decreases liking for the out-group members. The subject of cooperative learning has emerged with such significance that we devote a chapter to it.

SUPPORT OF AUTHORITIES   Authorities who support cooperation are crucial in creating positive changes in intergroup attitudes. In U.S. school settings, the leadership and supportive role of the principal is vital. The principal can serve an enabling function by making choices that facilitate positive intergroup relations, such as encouraging teachers to adopt cooperative learning techniques. The principal can also set a model of behavior for both teachers and students and can serve a sensitizing function by placing positive intergroup relations as a high priority for the school. Finally, the principal can play a sanctioning role (positively and negatively) by rewarding prosocial practices and behaviors, discouraging negative ones, and clearly expressing an expectation of respect for others' rights and dignity.

Teachers are also vital authority figures with the power to foster or inhibit positive relations in the school setting. They can serve some of the same enabling, modeling, sensitizing, and sanctioning roles as principals. One important way that teachers and principals can encourage the development of intergroup relations is the acknowledgment that individuals in a desegregated school may misunderstand each other's motives or intentions due to cultural differences, or just uncertainty and fear. Encouraging students to relate to each other as individuals rather than stereotypes can become a part of the school climate in the basic work of students.

Parents are significant authority figures, so it is crucial that educators find methods to encourage parents to involve their children in diverse settings and encourage intergroup contact. Parents can be involved in creating school and communitywide multiethnic committees that serve educational or youth development functions. The mixture of people addressing a shared task of high significance such as educational success can be helpful.

Some parents, teachers, and principals involved with racially or ethnically diverse settings believe that a color-blind perspective is the fairest way to handle intergroup relations. A color-blind approach can lessen potential racial or ethnic conflict in the short term by not emphasizing the importance of race and by encouraging equal application of rules to all students. It can also lessen possible discomfort by strongly asserting that race does not matter.

Although this approach is appealing in some ways, it misrepresents the reality in a way that could inadvertently encourage discrimination against minority group members. To try to ignore group membership, as if no one notices race or ethnicity, may lead to policies that are detrimental to minorities; it could readily lead to policies that result in resegregation. The color-blind perspective may also lead to curricula that do not adequately reflect the perspectives and contributions of minority and majority group members. Yet there is a necessary balance here. Constantly reminding students of their group membership and heightening its salience can be harmful. The most constructive approach is to encourage students to approach each other as *individuals*—in the context of policies that foster mutually respectful interaction between groups.

Program Design for Reducing Prejudice

This section delineates principles for designing and administering effective strategies for improving intergroup relations and reducing discrimination. The design principles—created under the auspices of Common Destiny Alliance (CODA)—are meant as guidelines for those selecting or developing strategies. Strategies do not need to incorporate every tenet in order to be effective. On the other hand, weak implementation will undermine even the best-designed strategy.

In a scholarly, multiauthored book on this topic, W. D. Hawley and his colleagues assert that racial and ethnic discrimination can best be eliminated by understanding the sources of prejudice and discrimination.[23] This information can be used to develop and implement well-grounded strategies for changing beliefs and behavior and to alter the institutions and structures within which people function.

There are many different approaches to improving intergroup relations: instructional methods, curricula, extracurricular activities, workshops, and simulations. The CODA panel believes the principles outlined below will enhance the effectiveness of each method.

- "Strategies should address both institutional and individual sources of prejudice and discrimination in the contexts and situations in which the participants in the program or activity learn, work, and live."[24] It is often futile to try to change individuals without dealing with contextual influences. Real or imagined power differences must be dealt with, because they are often at the heart of intergroup tensions.
- "Strategies should seek to influence the behavior of individuals, including their motivation and capability to influence others, and should not be limited to efforts to increase knowledge and awareness."[25] If strategies do not

specifically include lessons about how to *use* new awareness and knowledge, they will probably not change relationships. Because prejudice and discrimination are strongly socially influenced, we must address the social environment to alter such behavior.

- "Strategies should deal with the dispositions and behavior of all racial and ethnic groups involved."[26] Where racial and ethnic diversity exists, diversity offers an opportunity for learning and comparison that can aid in avoiding oversimplification or stereotyping.

- "Strategies should include participants who reflect the racial, ethnic, and linguistic diversity of the social context and should be structured in such a way as to ensure cooperative, equal-status roles for persons from different groups."[27] All participants should be given the opportunity to help design such strategies to foster useful and valued contributions from everyone, to the extent possible.

- "Strategies should have the support and participation of those with authority and power in any given setting."[28] When those in positions of authority are too busy to participate in intergroup relations programs, the impact of the program will be undermined unless the leaders' record on discrimination is clear.

- "Strategies should involve children at an early age, and new entrants to organizations should be continually encouraged and reinforced."[29] However, early intervention is not enough. Lessons learned at an early age may not stick, but they make later related lessons easier to teach and learn. Improving intergroup relations is a challenge that requires ongoing work. There is no magic bullet, no single injection of tolerance that will do the job for a lifetime. Steady attention to these high-priority tasks is required for the long term.

- "Strategies should be part of a continuing set of learning activities that are valued and incorporated throughout the school, college, or other organization."[30] Strategies to ameliorate intergroup prejudice should not be just highly focused activities; efforts should be made to ensure that positive intergroup relations are aspired to throughout the organization.

- "Strategies should examine similarities and differences across and within ethnic groups, including differences related to social class, gender, and language."[31] Beliefs and values *shared* across racial and ethnic lines should be underscored. Making the other seem less exotic or strange can advance positive interactions and avoid stereotyping.

- "Strategies should recognize the value of bicultural and multicultural identities of individuals and groups, as well as the difficulties confronted by those who live in two or more cultures."[32] Strategies that require people to identify with only one racial or ethnic group unintentionally express a lack of respect for people with bicultural and multicultural identities.

- "Strategies should expose the inaccuracies of myths that sustain stereotypes and prejudices."[33] Examples of such myths include assumptions about the proportion of black males who commit violent crimes or the rates of alcohol and drug abuse among Latinos and African Americans. Confronting such myths undermines the justifications for prejudice.

- "Strategies should include careful and thorough preparation of those who will implement the learning activities and provide opportunities for adapting methods to the particular setting."[34] Preparation is particularly important if the strategy is focusing on the sources of conflict. Additionally, those responsible for implementing a strategy will convey their indifference if they are not visibly committed.

- "Strategies should be based on thorough analyses of the learning needs of participants and on continuing evaluation of outcomes, especially effects on behavior."[35] Often strategies fail to invest adequately in diagnosing the problems that are particular to the setting involved. Evaluation is vital to program improvement, and follow-up studies of individuals and organizational change are needed, even if the studies only involve low-cost self-reports of changes in behavior and policies.

- "Strategies should recognize that lessons related to prejudice and its consequences, for any particular racial or ethnic group, might not transfer to other races or groups."[36] Lessons focused on relationships between any given two groups may not affect the prejudices being held against the people of a third group. Yet lessons can be learned that may usefully be adapted with suitable changes to other intergroup settings. The basic orientations of respect for individuality, breakdown of stereotypes, and seeking bases for mutual respect should be applied to the full range of diversity that exists in a given school.

Thus, we see that basic research on intergoup contact has substantial, intrinsic interest; and it can be usefully applied in educational settings as diverse as the schools of Israel and the United States. Indeed, similar work is under way in many countries and it is plausible that this approach will (with suitable adaptations) be useful on a worldwide basis.

In another context, intergroup dialogue programs, as they have recently developed, fulfill many of the predictions of contact theory. Typically, groups are comprised of between 10 and 20 participants, with programs conducted in university and community settings on a basis of equal status. Run by supportive facilitators, topics such as the participants' experience with stereotyping, prejudice, and discrimination are discussed. The dialogues are designed to encourage introspection and to take the perspective of members of other groups.

In the following chapters, we look at schools from multiple perspectives, but they are linked in the sense that all are concerned with ways in which schools can help to prevent violence—ranging from issues at the interindividual level to small intergroup relations and broader issues of war and peace.

8

Cooperative Learning

U.S. society is becoming increasingly multicultural. With the proliferation of enclaves of arriving immigrants, it follows that conflict will often be defined along ethnic lines. Unfortunately, a legacy of prejudice, sometimes even hatred, has been passed on to some youth by parents, grandparents, and their ethnic communities. Although in general acts of intolerance in the United States are at a more subtle level than that of 20 years ago, currently there are more obvious expressions of violent discrimination and prejudicial behavior in schools.[1] The wide spectrum of U.S. diversity is also experienced in the public school setting, with the racial and ethnic mix far greater than it was even 10 years ago. Similar circumstances now exist in many countries, because immigration and refugee movements have increased in a globalized, turbulent world. The challenges this presents for educators are great. Schools must seek to create safe environments for students to reach out across racial and ethnic borders and begin to empathize with members of other groups. One of the educators' responses to this challenge has been the development of cooperative learning techniques.

In cooperative learning programs, the traditional classroom of one teacher and many students is reorganized into heterogeneous ability groups of four or five students who work together to learn a particular subject matter. Cooperative learning is also an excellent example of contact theory, as previously discussed in Chapter 7, and the relationship is elaborated later in this chapter. Cooperative learning has grown steadily since the early 1970s. These efforts stem partly from a desire to find alternatives to the usual lecture mode and to involve students actively in the learning process. In part, cooperative learning builds on the recognized benefits of peer tutoring. Cooperative learning can offset the negative impacts of traditional individual competitiveness for grades, approval, and achievement in which there are inevitable and (after a while) predictable winners and losers. Moreover, cooperative learning can instill appreciation for student diversity and belief in the value of mutual aid. Teachers utilize cooperative methods in small groups in a variety of ways, seeking to strengthen students' motivation to learn as well as providing individual help for students in the quest for content learning such as mathematics. They also seek to develop skills that lead to high productivity in joint problem solving.

Small group teaching is a more comprehensive cooperative learning program that is very effective in promoting prosocial behavior among children. An experiment in Israeli classrooms—in lower-socioeconomic-level schools—restructured their classes into a "group of groups." The classroom functions as a "peer society organized into subunits" and each unit works on a certain aspect of a broad learning task. Mutual help and support are fostered within each subunit.[2]

Compared with students in the control group, students in the cooperative learning situation achieved more in academic tasks and received higher scores in tests of thinking and creativity. Most important, there was a reduction in conflict and an increase in helping behavior. These findings support the notion that experiences in school can improve the prosocial behavior of elementary school-aged children.[3]

Dozens of reports of well-designed studies in secondary schools have involved systematic comparisons of cooperative versus standard methods. More than two-thirds of these comparisons favored a cooperative learning method. Indeed, as classroom experience has accumulated and research evidence has grown, the overall success rate has steadily become more impressive in recent years.[4]

Research has demonstrated that student achievement is at least as high and often higher in cooperative learning activities than in traditional classroom activities. At the same time, cooperative learning methods enhance positive interpersonal relations, motivation to learn, and self-esteem. These benefits hold at all age levels in middle grade schools and high schools, for all subject areas, and for a wide range of tasks.

The research shows that, as interaction among the children increases, their learning gains also increase. Key to this is that children use each other as resources, understand that it is their right and duty to get and give help, and are able to show classmates how to do an assignment without doing it for them. One practice is for the children to ask others what they think and then make an individual decision, taking into account these different views.

One of the leaders in this field is Professor Robert Slavin of Johns Hopkins University. He is also the creator of a remarkable large-scale educational innovation for young children called "Success for All." Research has shown the value of this comprehensive program, and cooperative learning is prominent among many elements in it.

In a 1999 review paper, Slavin and Cooper offered a summary of research showing improved intergroup relations and an increase in academic achievement when a variety of cooperative learning interventions (based on Allport's 1954 contact theory) were applied.[5] As we have noted, Allport's theory holds that when students from diverse backgrounds have a chance to work together on equal footing, they form friendships and find it difficult to hold prejudices against the others.[6] Cooperative learning not only helps students to acquire academic knowledge and skill, but also helps them to cross group boundaries to form new intergroup friendships and a new group culture.

NEGATIVE INTERGROUP RELATIONS IN THE SCHOOL CONTEXT

Despite the efforts of policymakers, educators, and researchers, children from diverse backgrounds in many countries still have limited contact with each other, thus sustaining conditions that foster entrenchment of hostile stereotypes and intergroup tension.[7] So, rather than being taught to enjoy diversity, many children are implicitly being taught that it is acceptable to respond to diversity with intolerance, which sets the stage for prejudice in adulthood.[8]

COOPERATIVE LEARNING METHODS

Overall, cooperative learning is one of the most effective and widely used educational strategies to defuse friction and enhance learning in increasingly diverse classrooms.[9] Students are put into mixed groups in terms of academic achievement, ethnicity, race, gender, and language proficiency. They work together, typically in small groups, to complete a challenging task or to solve a problem. These learning activities are designed to promote academic success for all students through discussion, learning from each other, and encouraging each other to excel. Recent research has confirmed earlier findings showing that not only do students improve their academic performance, but their intergroup relationships improve as well.[10] Through positive social interactions in a diverse student body, there is opportunity to build "cross-ethnic friendships and to reduce racial stereotyping, discrimination, and prejudice."[11]

This method attempts to reduce competition among students; in fact, student rewards depend on the performance of everyone in the group.[12] In some situations a group is awarded points based on the average performance of each person. This gives incentives to stronger members of the group to bring up the level of those who do less well by tutoring their peers and by heightening their academic motivation with support and encouragement. The teacher may delegate some authority to the students, with appropriate preparation, so that they assume the responsibility for managing the group and for learning.[13] Instructional methods put the students in an equal-status situation—giving each a chance to contribute substantially to the team. Group work and cooperative learning are different methods.[14] Cooperative learning is mainly concerned with each student achieving academic success.[15]

COOPERATIVE LEARNING: A VARIETY OF STRATEGIES

Slavin and Cooper outlined seven strategies have been well researched and illustrate the principles of contact theory as applied in cooperative learning programs for students.[16] Additionally, implementation of these methods is straightforward. They do require modest additional resources from the school, and there is a premium on teacher preparation to manage the process adequately.

1. Student Teams–Achievement Divisions (STAD)

This is a strategy for assigning group rewards for individual achievement.[17] Here is an example from Robert Slavin's 1979 study: The group is comprised of 4 to 5 seventh- and eighth-grade students of mixed gender and ethnicity with a mix of high-, average-, and low-performing students. They meet twice weekly for 40 minutes for 10 weeks and receive instruction, then discuss and learn English language arts material. Test preparation involves team members helping each other with the material. However, the students answer the questions individually.

Rewards are generally divided into three categories: *individual* for individual achievement, *group* for group achievement, and *group* for individual achievement. In the STAD method there is a group reward that is based on the individual progress of each student.

Outcomes of field experiments show that more cross-racial friendships develop in these groups than in control groups. One study by Slavin showed that close to four times more children in these groups than in the control group named friends from another race.[18]

2. Teams-Games-Tournaments (TGT)

This technique is very similar to STAD, except that quizzes and the improvement score system used in STAD are replaced by a system of academic game tournaments. Teams of students compete with other student teams that share the same past performance level, in an attempt to raise their team scores.[19]

Results of four studies of seventh- to twelfth-grade students in desegregated schools showed that, in three out of four cases, students involved in TGT classes gained significantly more friends from outside their own racial groups than did control students.[20] Similarly, Kagan and his colleagues found positive results as well on friendship choices among African American, Mexican American, and Anglo students.[21]

3. Team-Assisted Individualization (TAI)

This is a combined strategy using STAD and TGT relative to cooperative teams, with the addition of individualized instruction. Elementary school students, grouped in four- to five-member teams, work on self-instructional mathematics at their own levels and rates. Students are responsible for all checking, management, routing, and assisting one another with problems. Each week, every student in a team must attain mastery of a predetermined number of units in order for the team to be awarded a certificate.[22]

Studies of intergroup relations show positive effects on cross-racial nominations on two sociometric scales: "Who are your friends in this class?" and "Whom would you rather not sit at a table with?" Additionally, these students made far fewer cross-racial ratings as *not nice* and *not smart* than did the control group.[23]

4. Jigsaw Teaching

In the original jigsaw technique, students are assigned to six-member heterogeneous teams (we go into detail on this in chapter 10). Each person is given a unique set of information in which the student becomes proficient to discuss in his or her "expert group." He or she then returns to the original team to teach the specific information to teammates. A quiz is given and individual grades are assigned.[24]

Jigsaw II modifies this original jigsaw model and relates more closely to the student team learning format.[25] In four- to five-member teams, students read a story or a chapter, and each person is given a topic on which to become an "expert." The topics are discussed in expert groups, then each member teaches the topic to students in the original team. Quiz scores are added to form team scores, and as with STAD, teams are recognized in a school newsletter. In a study of a Jigsaw II intervention, substantially more cross-ethnic friendships were present than in the control classes.[26]

5. Johnson Method

This learning method, developed by David Johnson and Roger Johnson, is closest to a pure cooperative model. A small heterogeneous group completes a common worksheet and then is praised and rewarded as a group.[27] Outcomes of two studies show greater friendship across racial lines in the cooperative setting as opposed to an individualized method that did not allow for student interaction.[28]

6. Group Investigation

Developed in Israel, the group investigation method involves organizing the classroom into small groups (two to six members), with each group choosing subtopics from a unit of study. These subtopics are further broken down into individual tasks. The students in each group then carry out the necessary activities involved to prepare a group report. Each group communicates its findings to the class and is judged on the quality of its report.[29]

Findings from a study done in Israeli junior high schools showed that children (Jews of Middle Eastern backgrounds compared with Jews of European backgrounds) who participated in group investigation and in STAD had far more positive cross-ethnic attitudes than did students in traditional classroom settings.[30]

7. The Weigel, Wiser, and Cook Method

This work was done in a triethnic classroom setting of Mexican American, African American, and Anglo students and is one of the largest and longest studies of cooperative learning.[31] Multiethnic teams engaged in a variety of activities in several subjects, and they won prizes based on team performance. The clearest positive effects were seen on Anglo students' attitudes toward Mexican Americans. Additionally, teachers reported fewer incidents of intergroup conflict.

Although the effects of cooperative learning were not totally consistent, 16 of 19 studies showed that students from different ethnic backgrounds experienced an improved appearance of friendship when contact was made under these cooperative conditions. Attitude improvements, revealed in several studies, were found mostly among white students toward their minority peers.[32]

An important finding is that student achievement increased, particularly in the cases of STAD, TGT, and TAI, where cooperative goals and tasks are combined with a high degree of individual accountability. The group investigation method fits this pattern as well. So, both intergroup relations and student achievement are enhanced. This combination strengthens the acceptability of this approach in communities with high academic aspirations.

FOCUS ON CROSS-RACIAL FRIENDSHIPS

Intuitively, it seems that the effects of only a few weeks of cooperative learning would not be enough to establish the trust and respect needed to build strong interracial friendships. However, several analyses point to positive cross-race peer relations— whether at the level of weak or strong friendship choices.[33] These findings show that students transcend cultural norms to form meaningful relationships. This does not mean that they ignore or eliminate their differences, but rather that they understand them through a different cultural model. The collaborative work used in solving complex problems or completing tasks that hold great meaning involves broadening the cultural framework, and it is not simply a matter of children's liking each other or having positive feelings for each other.

The research literature shows that cooperative learning increases friendliness and trust. Children are more willing to work together, and there are fewer stars and isolated students. There is an increase in prosocial behavior and a decrease in competitiveness. Value systems are changed, and cooperative modes are more likely to be chosen over competitive ones when the choice exists. But high-grade cooperative learning cannot occur without serious teacher training to master these techniques. The teachers' mastery and commitment are essential to the success of these programs.

MYTHS AND CONCERNS OF TEACHERS AND PARENTS

Parents and teachers are sometimes initially resistant to cooperative learning because of four common concerns, although interest in this method has been rapidly growing. One concern is that cooperative learning does not prepare children for the highly competitive adult world. Although it is true that competition is an important element of adult activities, it is also true that the ability to cooperate with others is central to such adult venues as marriage, family, community, and the workplace in the modern technical economy—and indeed to a peaceful world. Cooperative learning does not advocate the elimination of competition; rather, it seeks to balance competition with a healthy and much-needed dose of cooperation.

A second concern is that working in heterogeneous cooperative learning groups might penalize high achievers. Research shows, however, that high achievers learn at least as much in cooperatively structured classrooms as they do in traditional ones. Furthermore, cooperative learning does not advocate that fast learners do their work at exactly the same pace as their slower colleagues.

A third concern about cooperative learning is that it results in unfair grading. This might have some truth if teachers use only group grading, but this is not necessary; teachers can use individual grading at any time.

Fourth, some believe that cooperative learning encourages lazy students at the expense of good students. This is not true, because individual accountability is expected of all students; in addition, working in groups often stimulates poorly motivated or reclusive students to become active participants.

CONCLUSION

In our view, there are several aspects of cooperative learning that have practical importance. Children learn to work together; everyone contributes in some way; everyone is good at something; everyone learns to appreciate diversity; a meshing of different skills in a division of labor takes place; and a mutual aid ethic is encouraged. And most important, youngsters engaged in cooperative learning have gratifying firsthand experiences, learning that working together constructively allows all members of the group to be winners and that cooperation with other people increases rewards. Taken together, these are valuable lessons for future work as well as family and community relationships.

Cooperative learning strategies are the most extensively studied methods used to improve relationships among students of different ethnicities. Research demonstrates that the effects of cooperative learning on intergroup relations are strong and lasting and may lead to close cross-ethnic friendships. Additional research is needed to clarify the full effects of cooperative learning on actual intergroup behavior outside school, the long-term effects of cooperative learning, and the critical components of cooperative learning. But it is clear that all cooperative learning methods have had some demonstrable positive effects on intergroup relations.[34] So this is an approach that deserves wider application and support of ongoing research that can further enhance the efficacy of the best techniques. These promising lines of inquiry and innovation provide a tangible basis for hope that academic achievement and prosocial development can be jointly fostered during middle childhood and adolescence.

9

A Framework for Understanding
and Addressing School Violence

AN ECOLOGICAL, LIFE COURSE DEVELOPMENTAL
APPROACH TO YOUTH VIOLENCE

The increased violence in American schools over the past decade has stimulated serious scholarship to determine the major factors underlying such violence and to develop school-based strategies for preventing it. One of the most comprehensive and systematic efforts to make sense of this body of research was presented in a book edited by Delbert S. Elliot, Beatrix A. Hamburg, and Kirk R. Williams in 1998.[1] In this book scholars from the fields of social ecology, child and adolescent development, criminology, psychiatry, sociology, educational psychology, and public health presented relevant new perspectives, methodology, and data from their diverse fields. The authors developed an *ecological, life course, developmental approach*. The ultimate goal was to integrate diverse bodies of knowledge into a comprehensive approach to designing new basic research as well as rigorous program evaluation methods.

Five themes emerged within this approach. These are summarized as follows:

1. The interconnectedness of family, peer group, school, and neighborhood influences
2. The dynamic interaction between the individual and social contexts in influencing developmental patterns

3. Collaboration and comprehensiveness as requirements for effective prevention programs
4. The need for a public health approach to violence prevention
5. Rigorous implementation of evidence-based programs and strategies for preventing violence

The Interconnectedness of Family, Peer Group, School, and Neighborhood

This theme speaks to the ecological nature of the approach, which relates not only to the interrelationships among individuals within society but also to the connectedness and interplay across larger spheres of influence such as schools, neighborhoods, workplaces, and other social institutions. An important factor in youth violence is that as a result of a cascade of major social changes in family, labor force participation, and neighborhood cohesiveness, the family, and neighborhood social institutions once responsible for youth development have been undermined. This has shifted more responsibility to the schools to fill the gap. Since 1960, urbanization, changed roles of women, and powerful media impacts has converged in a troubling mix.

For both married couple families and single parent households, the *parental* labor force participation has sharply increased. In 1985, 63 percent of all children in the United States had working mothers. By 1998, 71 percent of all school age children ages 6 to 18 had working mothers.[2] Whether married or single, most mothers with school-aged children are working mothers. Many of these caring, concerned mothers now have latchkey children who have no adult care or supervision in the nonschool hours. Tragically, too many of today's youth grow up in unhealthy environments of neglect or violence. They lack the caring, discipline, and positive role models needed for competence in academic, social, and personal pursuits. By default, many schools now need to take into account the powerful impacts of deteriorating communities on educational processes as well as on the health and socioemotional well-being of their students.

The ecological, life course development approach emphasizes that no school is an island. Aggression in the home environment carries over into the school. Violence in movies, TV, and video games helps to cultivate a taste for violence in some children. Factors *outside* the school environment create risks of children's becoming victims of firearm violence both at school and in their home neighborhoods. Community violence shows up in school classrooms and hallways as well as in the neighborhood. Typically, deteriorated, disorganized, violent neighborhoods are almost totally lacking in safe havens or positive resources. In fact, local neighborhood crime rates and measures of community disorganization are the strongest predictors of school violence.

A developmental approach to reducing youth violence in and around schools is central to a comprehensive preventive strategy that pays attention to the many social contexts in which youth live and function. Programs must be part of a larger family and community violence-prevention system. An approach that involves family, community, and the school itself is the most hopeful strategy for reducing school violence. "School-based" programs must be redefined to include family and community. Also, after-school programs must include comprehensive community-wide efforts, linking the schools closely with community organizations that provide recreation, social services, and development enhancing activities for youth.

The Dynamic Interaction Between the Individual and Social Contexts in Influencing Developmental Patterns

Social contexts clearly influence the thoughts, feelings, and behavior of people. The same person behaves very differently in church, or at a rock concert, or in a hostile confrontation. In turn, individuals can and often choose to influence their social climate or their social settings. For example, hostile youths can be influential in setting the classroom or school climate. Through their words and actions they can disrupt task-oriented constructive learning in a classroom. When their verbal provocations are reciprocated, an escalation of conflict can progress into actual physical violence. Other youngsters can change the school climate by consistent bullying or other intimidations throughout the entire school building, such as pushing in the hallway, threats in the bathroom, or skirmishes during recess. In a number of schools, these minor, out-of-classroom violent behaviors are ignored by the school personnel.

At other times, usually out of school, violence-prone youth seek out like-minded friends to engage in aggressive behaviors together. This voluntary selection of antisocial contexts and behaviors serves to greatly augment and sustain their experiences with conflict and violence and thus extend their repertoire of such behaviors. These contexts also tend to produce heightened perceptions and sensitivity to potentially disrespectful, provocative attitudes and behaviors of others. Accidental touching or misunderstood facial expression can set off explosive responses at times.

These patterns of interaction between the individual and the social context can result in a self-perpetuating set of antisocial perceptions, attitudes, and behaviors that produce a specific and predictable pattern of antisocial behavior. Over the course of development, these behaviors can become further entrenched when such persons learn to find gratification and to meet normal adolescent developmental needs for recognition, respect, and a sense of efficacy by using their learned negative behaviors.

Aggressive behaviors may serve to resolve disputes and meet personal needs but in a destructive way. Aggression may become a way to develop and maintain dominance in their social hierarchies. The high status achieved is often used to gain materially and to abuse power. Based on these kinds of insights, the newer school-based conflict resolution and violence reduction programs now have goals of creating and sustaining positive school environments that greatly enhance the likelihood that the social climate and school context will have prosocial experiences and role models, life skills training, and opportunities for gratification and self-esteem in nonviolent ways. Specific interventions are described throughout this book.

Collaboration as a Requirement for Effective Prevention Efforts

To prevent youth violence, collaboration is needed between adults involved in public and private sectors that have an impact on youth. Every institution of society is affected by youth violence. Work at the local, state, and national levels should be done collaboratively. There must be comprehensive evaluation and dissemination of promising programs, especially those with proven results. Schools and local communities must combine evidence-based efforts in program planning for youth. Institutions need to examine closely the traditional concepts and practices that may impede collaboration. Agencies should provide training and experience in interdisciplinary, cross-agency activities on a systematic basis. Teachers are frontline persons who can see early warning signals in their students. Teachers need a dependable backup system that includes a range of mental health professionals and social services as well as community youth agencies as collaborating and referral resources. In fact, among those endorsing the ecological, life course, developmental approach, there is consensus that there is a need to redefine school as an inclusive term that includes the parents, neighborhood, and community resources.

The Need for a Public Health Approach to Violence Prevention

This is one of the most important themes of the ecological, life course developmental approach. The prevalence and lethality of violence against children and youth has sharply increased since 1960, while overall death rates during the same period have dropped. By 1996, all injuries including homicide and suicide were the leading causes of death. They accounted for 52 percent of deaths to children ages 5 to 14 and for 80 percent of deaths to youth ages 15 to 19. In 1998, although other age groups showed substantial declines, 80 percent of all deaths among youth ages 15 to 19 were due to injuries that included homicide and suicide.[3]

This alarmingly high and preventable source of death in children and youth is clearly a public health issue. The primary focus of public health research and practice is on prevention. Approaching violence as a public health problem brings new concepts, tools, and analytic techniques for program design and evaluation to addressing problems of youth violence.

Historically, major killer diseases have been greatly reduced or eliminated by public health measures. Despite all of the remarkable advances in medicine over the past century in the development of powerful antibiotics and sophisticated biotechnology, it is still the case that more lives have been saved by public health measures than by all of the biomedical discoveries. This powerful public health model is only beginning to be applied to violence as a public health problem. It seems likely that this is because youth violence has traditionally been viewed as an issue for the criminal justice system. The criminal justice system focuses on punishment and blame. The public health approach emphasizes prevention, early detection of those at risk, and effective programs. The key elements of the public health approach are the following:

- The public health perspective provides a multidisciplinary scientific approach to the problem of violence leading to effective prevention that can be validated through research.
- Looking at violence through the public health lens allows it to be viewed as a population problem, not just the problem of an isolated individual.
- Helpful steps can be formulated on the basis of risk factors identified through research and tracked by public health surveillance.

Programs and Strategies for Preventing Violence

Recommendations for dealing with the youth violence problem are organized around three strategies: (1) systemic changes for schools, (2) programs for individual youth, and (3) public policy positions. The primary goal is to support healthy youth development within social contexts that range from the intimate and personal to the more distant surroundings.

Systemic changes for schools are of primary importance. Clearly, next to the family, schools provide the most highly significant and potentially life-changing experiences in the lives of children and youth. As such, they have great potential for good or harm. School shootings provide a tip-of-the-iceberg warning of the larger unrecognized group of youngsters who experience deep unhappiness that predisposes them to violence. Unwittingly, many schools (across the range of socioeconomic settings) have permitted social climates of intolerance and disrespect that cause alienation and misery for many students on a regular basis. Other students bring with them to school the distress of neglect or abuse in their home lives, or they bring with them the effects of residing in truly dangerous neighborhoods. Flagrant school violence is no longer unique to the United States. Youth violence has mobilized efforts in other countries to implement systemic changes that will create school climates of support, tolerance, and early recognition and treatment of serious emotional problems in some students.

Enlightened school superintendents, principals, and teachers are in a unique position to set standards and adopt and enforce practices that create school and classroom climates that are understanding and supportive, with high personal and academic expectations for all students. From top to bottom, such schools also teach, exemplify, and assure respect, tolerance, and civil behavior for all members of the school community. At the classroom levels, such attitudes and behaviors are explicitly taught and modeled in violence prevention programs. Teachers are trained to understand the principles of conflict resolution and to adapt them personally as well as helping their students use them consistently across contexts and on a daily basis.

Schools also can assure that the norms of prosocial behaviors are consistently observed and practices of nonviolence in patient, persistent, and explicit ways are incrementally taught and enforced across grades as the child progresses. Schools can be open after school hours for special constructive activities such as safe recreation, homework help, arts, and music. With help, school-linked programs can be developed to identify and help traumatized children. These achievable goals require strong guidance from the school administration as well as support of parents and community agencies. Schools, in collaboration with community agencies, can help their students to receive needed services not readily accessed by high-risk families.

Given the increasing lethality of violence against children and youth, it is also important to focus some interventions on weapons-related issues in addition to the non-weapons-related interpersonal disputes. Role-playing and theater games led by facilitators can guide youth through the various stages of violent behavior, including the roles of bystanders. Students are typically unaware of the importance of bystander behaviors. With bystander encouragement, taunting, or direct calls to show who is more macho, a verbal exchange can escalate into a nasty fight or major injury if weapons become involved. Conversely, bystanders who advise an adversary to ignore the comments, or advise just walking away, and so on, can dissipate tension and avert conflict. These can be enacted in role-plays. These modalities can teach the practice of nonviolent problem solving. The combination of prosocial education in early childhood and constructive family support has been shown to prevent dangerous aggressive behavior.[4] We cite many promising violence prevention and youth development programs in this book. A recent publication from the National Research Council is helpful in providing further insight into these programs.[5]

For poor inner-city teenagers, after-school activities must provide an opportunity to enhance status, peer approval, and independence and a basis for hope by establishing opportunities for physical, interpersonal, intellectual, and social accomplishments. Although effective programs all share core elements, recommendations for prevention should be adapted to be responsive to differing cultures and communities. Programs must be created with sensitivity and understanding in order to meet the needs of diverse populations. Clearly, success involves "buy-in"—a collaborative engagement of stakeholders representing the pivotal institutions that strongly influence youth development.

The interdisciplinary, integrated framework of an ecological, life course, and developmental approach to understanding and addressing school violence represents a significant influence on the field. This comprehensive conceptual model of school violence has been useful for research scientists, practitioners and policy makers.

The example of Morton Deutsch's framework for teaching conflict resolution in the schools is presented here as an example of a major contribution to the conceptual base for teaching conflict resolution in the schools. His pioneering programs anticipated many of the newer research findings. In turn, his efforts created new knowledge that has advanced the field and encouraged significant work in the area of peer mediation as exemplified in the peer mediation programs also described in this chapter.

TEACHING CONFLICT RESOLUTION IN THE SCHOOLS

Professor Morton Deutsch of Columbia University, a distinguished scholar in conflict resolution over several decades, identifies families and schools as the two most important institutions that influence children's predispositions to love and to hate.[6] In groundbreaking work, he outlined a program that schools can use to promote attitudes, values, and knowledge that will help children develop constructive rather than destructive relations throughout their lif course. This program includes (1) cooperative learning, (2) conflict-resolution training, (3) constructive use of controversy in teaching, and (4) creation of dispute resolution centers.

Deutsch provides a framework for teaching conflict resolution in the schools. In his view, constructive conflict resolution is characterized by cooperation, good communication, recognition of fundamental similarity in beliefs and values among all group members, acceptance by each of the other's legitimacy, problem-centered negotiations, mutual trust and confidence, and information sharing. Destructive conflicts, in contrast, are characterized by harsh competition, poor communication, coercive tactics, suspicion, emphasis on basic differences in values, an orientation to increasing power differences, challenges to the legitimacy of other parties, and personal insecurity and need to fix blame. Based on a survey of conflict-resolution programs in U.S. schools, Deutsch suggests that, though progress is being made, some programs are not yet sufficiently informed by systematic research and well-founded theory.[7] Students need a serious evidence-based curriculum with repeated opportunities to learn and practice cooperative conflict-resolution skills. Deutsch sets out the following key concepts that are useful for this purpose:

1. *Know the type of conflict you are involved in.* Deutsch emphasizes cooperative problem solving, which entails finding a solution that opposing parties can mutually accept a win-win strategy. In cases where aspirations cannot be equally realized, parties can devise mutually acceptable fair procedures for deciding on the outcome and also on conditions to ensure peaceful relations after an outcome is reached. Finally, tactics for cooperative conflict resolution generally involve joint fact-finding and research, along with reasoned persuasion.

2. *Become aware of the causes and consequences of violence and of alternatives to violence.* A realistic understanding of the amount of violence in society and the deadly consequences of such violence is needed. Violence begets violence. There are healthy and unhealthy ways to express anger. Nonviolent alternatives for dealing with conflict are available and do work.

3. *Face conflict rather than avoid it.* Avoiding conflict through denial or submission with pseudoagreeable responses can cause tension, irritability, and persistence of the problem. It is best to face conflict honestly, albeit with sensitivity. There will be some instances when the conflict will disappear shortly, is inherently unresolvable, or is a win-lose conflict where an adverse outcome is predictable.

4. *Respect yourself and your interests, and respect others and their interests.* Respecting yourself and your interests helps in assessing the proportions of a conflict accurately for seeking constructive responses. Respecting others' interests helps avoid coercion, power competition, deprecation, and deception that can escalate conflict and cause violence. (Indeed, the development of attitudes of mutual respect is of fundamental importance in human adaptation.)

5. *Be alert to the natural tendencies to bias, misperceptions, misjudgments, and stereotyped thinking that usually characterize all parties involved in conflict.* Conflict resolution requires parties to avoid taking starkly contrasting perspectives, demonizing the adversary, and prematurely narrowing the decision, time frame, or the options for problem solving. Both parties must also avoid the fundamental attribution error, whereby one party tends to attribute the other side's aggression to innate personality while blaming his or her own aggressive tendencies on the situational causes—thereby avoiding personal responsibility.

6. *Avoid ethnocentrism, and understand and accept the reality of cultural differences.* Some cultural misunderstandings cannot be helped, but they should be used as learning opportunities rather than reasons for estrangement. Discussions that provide greater knowledge about the history, customs, and contributions of other cultures is not only interesting but can change attitudes.

7. *In communicating with others, listen attentively and speak so as to be understood.* Clear communication is critical to conflict resolution. Skills should be developed for effective listening, including repeating and paraphrasing what the other says to assure accurate understanding. It is also helpful to think of reversed roles in order to develop empathy for the other side's perspective.

8. *Distinguish clearly between interests and positions.* The stated positions taken by each party are not likely to be the same as the underlying interests beneath them. Positions may be opposed when unspoken, underlying interests are not usually recognized. Often, interests refer to basic human needs. Orienting in that way fosters the search for areas of common ground.

9. *Define the conflicting interests of yourself and the other as mutual problems to be solved cooperatively.* It is important not to personalize conflicting interests but rather to define them as types of defined issues or conflicts with a focus and perhaps to deal with the easier issues first. In cases where the conflict cannot be solved to mutual satisfaction, the parties should agree on fair procedures to determine the outcome. Help might be sought from neutral third parties.

10. *Explore your interests and the other's interests to identify the common and compatible interests that you share.* If distrust impedes your ability to explore each other's interests openly, it might be useful to invite a trusted *third party* to participate as facilitator, mediator, or conciliator. Keep in mind the fundamental human attributes that we all share. (This sense of common humanity can have pervasive significance in a globalized world.)

11. *Develop skills for dealing with difficult interpersonal tensions so that you do not become helpless when confronted by those who are more powerful, who do not want to use constructive conflict resolution, or who use dirty tricks.* Three approaches are useful. First, recognize that you usually have the op-

tion of getting out of unpleasant or unequal relationships and situations. Second, explicitly tell the other person what is being done that affects you and why—that is, hold up a mirror in as friendly a context as possible, reflecting the behavior of the other. Third, avoid reciprocating the other's unacceptable behavior and avoid attacking him or her personally for negative acts—criticize the specific *behavior* but not the person.

12. *Become aware of unhelpful responses to conflict.* It is important to learn that extreme reactions to conflict can be avoided. Extreme reactions usually occur along six dimensions: (a) becoming excessively involved in conflict versus avoiding or diminishing conflict; (b) being overly hard or unyielding versus being overly soft and accommodating; (c) taking a rigid stance versus using loose, informal arrangements; (d) repressing emotion and preferring a purely intellectual approach versus high emotional intensity, and (e) compulsively revealing all of your thoughts and feelings versus selectively concealing them.

13. *Throughout the conflict, remain a moral person who is caring and just and who regards others as members of your moral community who deserve care and justice.* As much as possible, try to see the situation from the other person's situation and circumstances. Keep in mind the shared humanity of the adversary, especially under stress.

CONSTRUCTIVE USE OF CONTROVERSY IN SCHOOLS

Controversy, if put into a cooperative context, can help promote academic learning and conflict-resolution skills. For example, in dealing with a controversial topic, teachers can assign students to groups of four, dividing each group into two pairs. Initially using a modified debate format, each pair is assigned a different position on the controversy to defend. However, all four are subsequently required to arrive at a reasoned consensus and submit a report on which *all* arguments will be evaluated. Teachers instruct students to be critical; to focus on making the best possible decision, not on winning; to encourage everyone to participate; to listen carefully to all ideas, even when they disagree; to restate what someone has said if it was unclear; to bring out ideas and facts that support both sides and strive to synthesize them in a way that makes sense; to try to understand both sides of the issue; and to be willing to change their minds if the evidence warrants it. It should be understood that all of this does not mean that any difference will be split down the middle. It does mean that different perspectives will be carefully considered. This approach has come to be embodied in the techniques of cooperative learning.

In a groundbreaking paper prepared for a 1993 Carnegie Conference on education for conflict resolution, Peter Coleman and Morton Deutsch summarized findings from research done by a group from Columbia University in a New York City school.[8] The International Center for Cooperation and Conflict Resolution at Teachers College completed an extensive study in an inner-city alternative high school with a conflict-resolution program. The data revealed that as students improved in managing their conflicts, they experienced increased social support and less victimization from others. This improvement in their human relations led to increased self-esteem and also to a decrease in feelings of anxiety and depression, along with a heightened sense of positive well-being. The students' higher self-esteem was associated with a greater sense of personal control over their destiny. This constellation of positive responses, together with an enhancement of critical thinking ability, contributed to higher academic performance.

SCHOOL MEDIATION PROGRAMS

In the 1990s, many colleges and universities undertook mediation programs intended to provide a neutral third party to help adversaries sort out their differences and seek mutual accommodation. In recent years, this movement spread rapidly to elementary and secondary schools. Peer mediation was introduced at these school levels. Students were given training in the principles of conflict resolution and were supervised in practice mediation as part of the training. A growing body of educators considers conflict-resolution and mediation training to be successful. Many programs involve training students to be these third parties seeking conflict resolution. Evaluations of student mediation programs show that the student disputants felt that their grievances were understood and that the process was fair, reporting that they were generally satisfied with the mediation outcomes. Studies of peer mediators show that they also benefit from the training and that their self-esteem is strengthened. Parents have also reported positive effects of conflict-resolution and mediation training. They placed the most emphasis on the positive changes they observed in their children at home.

Parents of the students have benefited from conflict-resolution programs in other ways too. In one study, parents involved in disputes with the school were more satisfied with conflict mediation after the school personnel had been trained in conflict-resolution skills than they had been earlier. Independent observers of the parent-school mediation rated the conflict-resolution performance of the participants as more effective. The general tendency was improvement in the school climate.

Coleman and Deutsch conducted an experience survey based on interviews with a select group of expert mediators in the New York area who had served as mediators of interethnic conflicts in educational settings. Follow-up interviews were done with disputants who had been involved in the mediations and were willing to waive their right to confidentiality. These interviews clarified the scope of mediator activities, which included establishing a working alliance with the parties, improving the climate between them, addressing the issues, applying pressure for settlement, and assuring implementation of the agreement.

Van Slyck and Stern argue that the general orientation of dispute resolution along with the specifics involved in mediation are compatible with needed conditions for optimal resolution of the developmental tasks of adolescence.[9] Skills involved in active problem solving of this sort also encourage prosocial skills that can be used in other settings encountered over a lifetime.[10]

Altogether, the limited research so far available in this new field of mediation in the schools suggests that school mediation programs have positive effects in reducing violence as well as in enhancing the self-esteem and social skills of the mediator. Thus, students learn conflict resolution in practice as well as in concept. We have much more to say about this in the next chapter, because mediation is the "fastest growing type of conflict-resolution program being implemented in American schools."[11] At its best, school-based dispute resolution offers a much-needed constructive alternative to suspension and expulsion.

CONCLUSION

Currently, most schools in the United States are mandated to have some form of conflict-resolution and/or violence-prevention program. With this widespread demand for violence-prevention programs, there has been explosive growth in the marketing of programs and curricula to school districts. These programs are of varying quality and often are not subjected to rigorous evaluation.

The emergence of consensus on a core framework that serves to anchor programs in evidence-based concepts, goals, methods, and curricula content represents an important advance. Most of the rest of this book gives details on the most promising recent programs to prevent or minimize youth violence. These programs cover the full spectrum of developmental periods from early childhood through the end of adolescence.

10

Education for
Conflict Resolution

*From Public Concern to
Research to Practice*

GROWING PUBLIC INTEREST IN
CONFLICT-RESOLUTION PROGRAMS

Public interest in education for conflict resolution has increased in response to the violence of recent years. Serious articles now appear in newspapers and magazines, reporting research that might explain the background and meaning of the surge in youth violence. This widening concern suggests the real possibility of building a public constituency for education on conflict resolution and related questions.[1] Probing educational policy issues are also being raised in the media. For example, Alina Tugend asked the question, "Do conflict-resolution programs really deliver on their promises to reduce school violence and teach conflict resolution?" in her November 2001 article in the "Education Life" supplement to the *New York Times*. She examined the existing conflict-resolution program of Public School 217 in the Ditmas Park section of Brooklyn in the aftermath of the September 11 terrorist-induced tragedies.[2] She also looked at other conflict-resolution programs nationwide, along with studies that assess their effectiveness. Based on these data, she concludes that overly aggressive and hateful behavior among students can often be reduced, but she noted that to be effective, lessons must be frequent. Brief exposure to one or two presentations of conflict-resolution techniques will do nothing toward improving behavior. In cases of peer mediation, the greatest beneficiaries are the student mediators themselves. Disadvantaged minority students have unique needs that require specific attention. For these students, there are significant differences between the culture at school and the culture in their own homes and communities. These differences can give rise to disputes or overt aggression.

The *New York Times* article goes on to describe the student interest in understanding the events of September 11 and some responses by teachers. For example, the teachers at Brooklyn's Public School 217 were looking for ways to explain the tragic attacks to their students. They began by using a simple lesson from their existing conflict-resolution program. Because children were almost exclusively focused on the U.S. desire to retaliate, teachers, drawing on the conflict-resolution program, were able to give the students a basis of understanding conflict on an international scale and a framework in which they could identify and articulate their feelings related to conflict. They also offered grief and trauma counseling.

These articles by Alina Tugend represent very useful, timely, responsible, in-depth reporting that does a great deal to highlight and clarify complex and troubling issues for the general public. However, there are other resources beyond media articles for fostering public understanding. Scholars in the fields of social relations and conflict resolution have responded to the importance of providing the public with authoritative, comprehensive, and readily understandable information. This chapter discusses several such reports. We briefly summarize research on the concepts, scientific studies, and rigorous program evaluations that are foundations for state-of-the-art conflict-resolution programs.

Because of the deep public concern about school violence and other evidence of more pervasive youth aggression, most public schools in the United States are now mandated or strongly encouraged to provide some kind of conflict-resolution program to their students. As discussed in chapter 9, a large and diverse array of violence-prevention programs have been heavily marketed to the schools across the country. Not only has their quality been uneven, but some have actually been found to be counterproductive.[3] As a result, schools are beginning to recognize the importance of solid data to use in selecting evidence-based, effective curricula for their students. Based on the current research, it is now possible to give educators scientific knowledge, guidelines, and criteria for selecting and implementing effective conflict-resolution programs for all grade levels in their schools and make it possible to translate research into evidence-based programs and practices.

As a field, psychology (with its subspecialties in cognition, social psychology, developmental psychology, and educational psychology, and aspects of behavior genetics) has been at the forefront of research on aggression, violence, and conflict resolution. This knowledge base is fundamental to providing the concepts and empirical data that constitute the field of aggression and conflict resolution in both research and practice. A diverse group of psychologists with concerns about youth violence felt that it would be important to review this rich body of work on youth antisocial behavior and to present the scientific findings in a form that would be readily accessible to the general public as well as to policymakers and practitioners. To achieve this goal, the American Psychological Association (APA) convened a commission on violence and youth. The APA appointed a diverse group of leading psychologists as commissioners and charged the commission with five tasks:

1. To articulate the state of psychological knowledge related to violence and youth;
2. To define existing practical problems and how psychological knowledge can be applied to resolve or constructively intervene in these problems;
3. To describe effective intervention models;
4. To recommend promising direction for public policy, research, and program development; and
5. To recommend APA policies, projects, or programs that will constructively influence research, practice, and education on these issues.[4]

The report of this commission was published in 1994 in a volume entitled *Reason to Hope: A Psychosocial Perspective on Violence and Youth*.[5] This title was chosen to reflect the commissioners' collective hopeful outlook after reviewing the data. Hope was based on their conviction that—despite the complex interplay of biological, psychological, and sociocultural factors—aggressive, hateful behavior is learned, and therefore it can be unlearned or modified. Most important, the review of research found that it is possible, in systematic ways, to educate children and to provide conditions that foster prosocial, empathic, and collaborative behaviors that can be maintained over the course of development. The commission emphasizes that most violence is not random, unpredictable, or uncontrollable.

Another important conclusion highlighted by the commission was the significance of the multifactorial nature of the development of hateful, violent attitudes, and behaviors. Despite some myths or beliefs, no single factor has been pinpointed as the cause of aggression. Therefore, preventive and remedial programs work best when they are comprehensive and integrate salient multiple components into the intervention.

The volume focuses on six areas: the causes of violence, the experience of violence across ethnic groups, vulnerable populations in relation to violence, broad societal influences on violence, prevention and intervention issues, and research and policy needs. The work of the commission was augmented by reviews of specialized topics by nonmember experts. The commission also maintained regular contact with an international group of about 150 psychology professionals, the "cadre of experts."

The chapters on preventive and treatment interventions have been of particular interest to us. In the course of this scholarly review of studies of youth and violence over the past 50 years, the commission also charted a history of the evolution of the field.

At the midpoint of the twentieth century, youth violence was still chiefly recognized in terms of delinquency and the juvenile justice system or conduct disorder and the mental health system. *Delinquency* is a legal term that may be defined and adjudicated with varying standards in different jurisdictions. At midcentury, the psychiatric diagnosis of conduct disorder linked violence and aggression with emotional disturbance and psychiatric disorder but was not precise in its characterizations or diagnosis. The overlap between delinquency and conduct disorder was murky. Under these circumstances of ill-defined, inconsistent definitions, it was not possible to clearly delineate the nature and scope of the problem.

Historically (and very prominently, in the 1950s), the research on interpersonal violence, including youth violence and delinquency, was carried out by criminologists. Their pioneering studies were largely based on arrest reports and court and detention data. These data have some advantages for tracking local crime trends, but also many limitations. As noted, the problems of varying legal definitions and adjudication practices do not lend themselves to rigorous scientific studies of antecedents and outcomes. Furthermore, these data were cross-sectional and reflected observations made at a discrete point in time, with little attention to antecedents or longer-term outcomes. Because of this earlier focus on the criminal system, the interventions proposed were also programs for youth punishment or reform of schools within the justice system.

Research methods for the psychiatric study of conduct disorders were, for the most part, descriptive and limited, often to single case reports. Psychiatric interventions were largely ineffective. It should be noted that at the same time, there was also a burgeoning field in academia that focused on normal child development and received little attention from those concerned with youth violence and antisocial behavior. However, the productive database from normal child and adolescent development literature later proved to be very valuable.

About a decade later, in the 1960s, there was a growing influence of the public health perspective in clinical medicine. Prevention is at the core of the public health model. The public health methodology (a) emphasizes surveillance of the general population; (b) monitors the locations, incidence, and prevalence of health events; (c) recognizes personal and environmental factors that put specific sectors of the population at risk; (d) designs and evaluates preventive interventions; (e) disseminates information; and (f) provides services at the community level. The public health model specifies three levels of intervention: primary (universal) programs in which total populations receive the intervention (e.g., vaccination of all children against specified childhood diseases), secondary (selective) interventions for populations with risk factors but not yet ill, and tertiary (indicated) treatment for those populations who have diagnosable disorders and require specialized services.

In the 1970s, when personal social behaviors began to be recognized as significant health risks—for example, smoking, alcohol consumption, and substance abuse—the public health concepts and methods were widely applied to them. However, it should be noted that youth violence was not generally viewed as a public health problem until the 1990s.

When community surveillance was carried out in the 1970s and 1980s using youth self-reports of aggressive and antisocial behavior, prevalence rates were found to be extremely high. Among youth 13 to 18 years old, 35 percent admitted to assault, 45 percent to property damage, 60 percent to engaging in more than one kind of antisocial behavior (e.g., aggression, substance abuse, vandalism, or arson).[6] These unexpected and disquieting research results broadened the almost exclusive focus on psychiatric treatment or criminal interventions for severely aggressive or violence adolescents to considerations of programs that were much more widely targeted to include the general population of children. The youth survey results also raised new research issues about the need to look at younger children and preadolescents for early signs that might foreshadow subsequent serious adolescent aggression or violence. In addition, there was a new focus on research efforts to identify risk factors in the past and present lives of those adolescents who manifested aggressive, antisocial behaviors. The influence of the public health model represents a clear example of how a strong conceptual base and appropriate research methodology can lead to evidence-based programs and practices. It also shows how scientific progress always raises new questions which, when studied, will not only inform practice but also define further research agendas.

Another theoretical construct that has had major impact on the design of interventions for antisocial youth is the problem behavior model.[7] On the basis of earlier surveillance-oriented research, scientists found that adolescent problem behaviors such as aggression, alcohol abuse, smoking, and illegal drug use, early and unprotected sexual activity, poor school achievement, or dropout often occur together as a package. The theory states that these clustered behaviors are linked by the fact that all of them have similar underlying antecedents. They also meet similar psychological needs for the individuals, because the behaviors are usually experienced as rewarding. Some of these needs are normal adolescent developmental needs such as gaining peer acceptance, experimentation with risky behaviors, experimenting with adopting adult behaviors, and seeking autonomy from parents. Prior to the recognition of these packages of adolescent problem behaviors, most interventions to influence normative or at-risk youth were categorical and each targeted only a single problem behavior. There were anti-smoking programs, drug abuse prevention programs, reduction of teenage pregnancy programs, and so on. The problem behavior model led to a shift from the categorical and single problem approach toward comprehensive programs that addressed the underlying antecedents of clusters of problem behaviors. Newer interventions gave students a tool kit of basic skills: emotional self-regulation, anger management, social competence, critical thinking, decision making, and problem solving. They also provided a clear and cogent information base regarding personal and health risks, along with guidelines for respectful positive interpersonal behaviors.

The rich body of psychological research on normal development of children and youth has made important contributions to clarifying the pathways to both normative and aberrant outcomes over the life course. Also, in those developmental contexts, the definition of aggressive and antisocial behavior expanded beyond traditional legal and psychiatric definitions to include a broad array of identifiable aggressive and antisocial behaviors across the full range of all children and youth.

In the newer definition, the core elements of intentional aggression in interpersonal interaction and the explicit intention to harm are retained. Harm or distress categories are expanded to include nonassaultive physical behaviors such as pushing, unwanted touching of all kinds, and grabbing or damaging personal property. Nonverbal aggression includes grimaces, finger signs, and mimicking of behavior. Verbal aggression includes ridicule, taunts, insults, unkind comments about appearance, varying levels of verbal intimidation from innuendo to threats and bullying, and use of ethnic slurs or other derogatory comments about cultural differences. Among girls, it may include malicious gossip or revealing secrets. For both genders, exclusion from clubs or cliques and other forms of hostile or demeaning rejection may be included. Often, relatively minor behaviors can become significant when they are frequent or serve as the opening move in an escalation of anger and hostility that, depending on the context, can result in an outburst of assaultive violence or smoldering cumulative resentment. Important contextual factors include the behavior of bystander peers who may act either to discourage or to encourage the confrontation. The school climate regarding rules of behavior and discipline, the cultural norms of the students, regarding aggression reflect attitudes, values, and behaviors of the family, school, community, and neighborhood are critical social environmental factors that determine the likelihood of hostile, aggressive responses.

The understanding of the importance of contextual variables in shaping the development of behavior patterns and the expression of behavioral responses at a given time in a given place have resulted from rigorous research and have been refined using the theoretical model of the social-ecological perspective. This model was initially proposed and elaborated by the child development psychologist, Urie Bronfenbrenner, who was deeply influenced by insights from sociology. His seminal volume, published in 1979, has had a major impact on the understanding of youth antisocial behavior and has influenced the design of preventive and treatment interventions.[8] The social ecological perspective is both specific and integrative. It suggests that behavior of an individual is the result of the interplay of personal attributes in a particular social context. These personal attributes include biological traits, temperament, and impact of personal past experiences that, taken together, determine stable predispositions for emotional and behavioral responses to others. Individuals develop "scripts" that determine a stable tendency to attribute motives either benign or hostile (attribution bias) and to facilitate typical or habitual behavior patterns of approach or response in interpersonal contacts.

Bronfenbrenner's socioecological model proposes that individual developmental change results from the interactions of a person at a central core with three concentric social contexts that surround the core. The person in the central core is the embodiment of the genetic inheritance that determines the individual set of biologic attributes for that person over the life span. The three concentric circles of social contexts are:

Circle 1. Immediate Environment
Circle 2. Social and Economic Context
Circle 3. Cultural Context

The central core and three circles of context mutually influence each other. The salience and power of the influence of each social context is linked to the developmental stage of the individual. For example, although the family is always an important aspect of the Immediate Environment context throughout life, the influence is of critical importance for infancy and early childhood, but the influence is diluted over time and in adolescence, peer influence may outweigh family influence for some individuals.

Bronfenbrenner's socioecological model delineates three major social contexts to be considered. The *immediate environment* is the social context of home and family, with attention to the family as a system for learning social relationships, patterns of behavior, and problem-solving strategies. The family system includes *parents* (at times single parent), siblings, grandparents, close family members, and regular child caretakers carrying out parental functions. For older children, peers and *schools* are the *immediate environments*. The *social and economic context* includes the home, the community and their respective resources and characteristics. Notable community variables are employment level, average income, violence level, and community assets and resources. The negative impacts of joblessness, poor housing, high crime level, poor schools, and poor health care have been extensively studied. The *cultural context*—the larger society and cultural milieu—provides a set of rules, values, and expectations that constitute the norms of the dominant culture. The combined impacts of the social-ecological contexts on children is a process called socialization. For some children, there are differences, even clashes, between the dominant culture of a society and the values of their own subculture. When this occurs, significant stress and maladaption to one or both may occur. This social-ecological perspective has broadened and deepened the knowledge of the multilevel, multicausal pathways of normal development that can lead to violence and antisocial behavior. The advances in this line of research have greatly contributed to new insights for designing and evaluating multicomponent programs to prevent or reduce antisocial behavior. There is also a heightened appreciation of the value of cultural sensitivity. The influence of all three social contexts on each other is linked to developmental stage. The research based on this model has increasingly shown that individuals at all stages are highly responsive to their social contexts. Deeper understanding of the nature of responsiveness to context thus becomes the foundation for developing preventive and remedial interventions for children and youth.

Surveillance and related rigorous epidemiological studies reveal that there is a consistent finding of significant across-group disparity in the prevalence and risk of the development of antisocial and aggressive behavior and related injury or death from violence. The populations at high risk are disadvantaged minorities, abused and neglected children, and children who are shunned or taunted by their peers. Although ethnicity, in and of itself, is not considered a causal or risk factor for antisocial behavior, the data show that ethnic minorities are much more likely to be exposed to the mix of numerous adverse developmental experiences that arise from poverty, related joblessness of family, inadequate housing, and deteriorated neighborhoods with few, if any, safe havens. Urban poverty environments are likely to also be violent and unstable. Such neighborhoods also tend to have family disorganization, negative parenting, inadequate schools, harmful adult role models, and few supportive community resources or opportunities. For ethnic minorities, there is often stress related to racial stereotyping. The specifics of the subculture vary across ethnic groups; nonetheless, many of the features of marginalization and poverty are similar across disadvantaged minority ethnic groups.[9] There is continuing research on interactions in the social environment of disadvantaged minorities, with the goal of better understanding the mechanisms of high levels of adverse impacts. The reduction of adverse health disparities experienced by minorities is a national goal set forth by the Department of Health and Human Services in *Healthy People 2000*, which addresses the critical importance of school and community involvement. This is addressed in the section on reduction of violent and abusive behavior. Priority objective 7.16 states, "Increase to at least 50 percent the proportion of elementary and secondary schools that teach nonviolent conflict resolution skills, preferably as a part of quality school health education."[10] Priority Objective 7.17 states, "Extend coordinated, comprehensive violence prevention programs to at least 80 percent of local jurisdictions with populations over 100,000."[11]

Perhaps the single most important contribution of the field of child development has been the elaboration of powerful insights and organizing principles of the developmental perspective. This perspective documents and explains the typical sequence of normative changes and reorganizations of behavior that characterize the growth of children and adolescents from birth to adulthood. There is a predictable pattern of orderly, directional, and cumulative developmental progression. The sequence of developmental change is very stable. At the same time, the timing of these events of the developmental stages are not absolutes. Rather, they exhibit a range in the timing and details of the developmental changes. For all stages there are early and later bloomers. This individual variation in the experiencing of normative developmental changes, interacting with individual experience, is ultimately the basis of the individuality of each person. However, the basic developmental tasks for any given developmental stage are specific and universal, even though the timing of emergence of various abilities is typically expressed as an average age range. In general, there is continuity across developmental stages, and predictability for much of the individual variation. Recognition that basic developmental tasks, needs, and capabilities are linked to developmental stages gives guidelines for developmental appropriateness in designing and implementing programs across the various stages of growth. When programs are not developmentally appropriate, they are likely to be ineffective. Also, the developmental perspective has provided an important rationale for longitudinal research and evaluation of continuity of interventions over time. In addition to studies that evaluate immediate effects, it is therefore important to monitor an earlier intervention for long-term favorable or unfavorable outcomes in a later developmental stage.

Over the past 20 years, youth violence and antisocial behavior have notably increased.[12] Youth violence has spread far beyond minority and disadvantaged populations. The recent series of school shootings called attention to serious youth violence problems in rural and affluent suburban areas. Surveillance studies also revealed trends toward increasingly younger ages of initiation into antisocial behavior. Greater involvement of girls in aggressive behavior was also noted. These disturbing trends and realization of the universality of the issues of antisocial behaviors among children and youth resulted in a national consensus for mounting a major public health antiviolence program in the schools, with a focus on universal violence-prevention curricula across all grades.

It is clear that the knowledge and insights gained from basic research in the behavioral sciences, particularly psychology, have undergirded the design and content of school-based prevention and early intervention programs. The multidisciplinary and integrative approaches have provided a model for the implementation of comprehensive multicomponent programs. Basic research into areas of prosocial behavior and conflict resolution is very active. We can look forward to continuing advances in this field.

EVALUATION OF SCHOOL-BASED VIOLENCE-PREVENTION AND CONFLICT-RESOLUTION PROGRAMS

Along with the proliferation of school-based violence-prevention and conflict-resolution programs over the past two decades, the vital importance of rigorous assessment of their effectiveness has become widely recognized. It is important for those mounting the programs to measure their success in attaining the desired goals. It is important for policymakers and funders to learn whether or not their money is wisely spent. Evaluation is important for increasing knowledge of how and why programs work or how they can be improved. Rigorous scientific evaluation is *applied research*. It studies the effectiveness of evidence-based programs when moved beyond the laboratory into natural settings. Applied research works hand in hand with basic behavioral research. Basic research undergirds the design and content areas of programs and specifies the goals and measurement of outcomes to determine effectiveness. In essence, applied research tests the theoretical models of basic research that offer the best evidence base for successful intervention programs on a large scale.

In turn, the results of this model testing confirm or reject hypotheses and suggest new basic research directions to be pursued. Persons mounting the programs in schools or other natural settings learn about barriers to implementation or aspects of the programs that are effective for some students but not others—for example, age, ethnic, or gender differences in responsiveness. They may also learn much more about the realities of the amount of teacher time required or other real costs of the program. They may also discover unintended positive or negative outcomes.

There is now consensus on high and specified standards for rigorous evaluation. The gold standard is a controlled clinical trial in which children participating in the intervention program are compared with a control (nonintervention) group of carefully matched children. For many practical and ethical reasons, this standard is often not attainable for school-based research, and careful quasi-experimental designs with no control group are more typical. The fidelity of implementation of the program model is given great attention. No matter how excellent the design of a program, it cannot be effective unless implemented as specified. Implementation includes factors such as the actual amount of time and material resources required by teachers and program leaders as compared with the amounts allocated by school administrators, and adherence to standards for exposure, such as the number of sessions actually taught, duration of the intervention, extent of follow up, and reinforcement sessions over the course of schooling. There is consensus concerning rigorous methodological standards for statistical analytic strategies.

EVALUATION OF U.S. DEPARTMENT OF JUSTICE–SUPPORTED PROGRAMS TO PREVENT YOUTH VIOLENCE

In 1996, the U.S. Congress required Attorney General Janet Reno to provide a comprehensive evaluation of the effectiveness of intervention programs supported by the Department of Justice to assist states, local law enforcement, and communities in preventing violence and crime. Congress called for the evaluation to give special emphasis to "factors that relate to juvenile crime and the effects of these programs on youth violence, including risk factors in community, schools and family environments that contribute to juvenile violence."[13] This mandate provided an opportunity for experts to carry out a rigorous national study of school-based programs for the prevention of youth violence and antisocial behavior. The Department of Justice under Reno manifested strong interest in prevention of youth violence during her entire term of office (8 years).

Congress required that the evaluation be conducted as an independent, outside evaluation that included review of the relevant scientific literature and specified that rigorous, scientifically recognized evaluation standards and methodology be employed. Independent experts carried out the project at the University of Maryland. The published report is entitled *Preventing Crime: What Works, What Doesn't, What's Promising.*[14]

The independent experts studying school-based crime prevention selected (nationwide) 149 high-quality peer-reviewed programs for evaluation. It was rare to find serious violent crime as a measured outcome for school-based programs. Less serious or unspecified crime was measured in 25 programs. The outcomes measured by most programs were antisocial or aggressive behaviors and involvement in problem behaviors such as alcohol, tobacco, or drug use. For children and adolescents, these problem behaviors are illegal. These programs also measured the presence of risk or protective factors. It should be noted that a substantial investment in prevention programs for these normative populations by the Department of Justice represents a dramatic shift of emphasis and policy from the 1950s, when incarceration and legal control of youth offenders and delinquents was the major focus of the Department of Justice. This shift to emphasis on prevention of violence and conflict-resolution programs in public school classrooms appears to reflect the new perspectives based on scientific knowledge regarding antecedents, ongoing influences, and pathways to the adoption of antisocial behaviors. The experts strongly made the case for the unique suitability of schools as the locus of prevention programs. They highlighted the mandated regular school attendance for at least 10 crucial developmental years of childhood and adolescence. Recent research in neuroscience and cognition confirm the importance of experience in early childhood brain and behavior development.[15] Some kindergarteners arrive at school with socioemotional and cognitive school readiness that is a firm base for effective learning and continuing progress on favorable developmental pathways. For other young children, there are significant gaps in school readiness and/or the presence of significant risk factors. Those children are highly likely to exhibit both learning difficulties and behavior problems in elementary school. School-based programs can detect and address such problems. The critical developmental transitions of adolescence can be addressed in school-based interventions. School experience in later childhood and adolescence is also of importance because youngsters are making critical life choices that will determine adult outcomes.

The very important roles of classroom climate and school environment are now understood. The school is a major aspect of a child's world and has a critical independent role in shaping self-image, attitudes, and behaviors, as well as defining norms and values across the developmental stages. The school is seen as the interface between the family and the broader context of neighborhood, community, and general society. Research has confirmed that schools in poor, disorganized, and heavily minority urban communities have higher percentages of troubled students. Such schools are most in need of prevention and intervention programs. All of these considerations, as outcomes, were also evaluated by the reviewers, even though they are not included in the narrowly defined legal outcomes mandated by Congress.

PROGRAM EVALUATION RESULTS

The 149 programs reviewed cover all grade levels—kindergarten, elementary school, junior high school, and high school. Programs were classified into two major categories: (1) individual change strategies and (2) strategies to change school environment, both classroom and schoolwide. Each of the major categories was evaluated using nine subcategories. These nine subcategories are:

INDIVIDUAL CHANGE STRATEGIES

Instructing Students: Involves life skills training in recognizing and avoiding risky or potentially harmful behaviors; giving a relevant factual knowledge base and teaching tolerance and respect for others.

Behavior Modification and Teaching Thinking Strategies: Involves using cognitive-behavioral strategies, learning through role-play, and learning assertiveness in refusal behaviors to resist peer pressures.

Peer Programs: Involves using peer counseling, peer mediation, and programs using peer leaders.

Other Counseling and Mentoring: Involves individual counseling by a trained professional, case management, and mentoring by a layperson in informal interactions.

Providing (community based) Recreational, Enrichment and Leisure Activities: Involves after-school and weekend programs, community service activities, and drop-in recreation centers.

CLASSROOM AND SCHOOLWIDE CHANGE STRATEGIES

Building School Capacity: Involves administrative and management changes to include parents, teachers, and school staff in making decisions and setting goals.

Setting Norms for Behavior: Involves establishing and enforcing norms and rules for appropriate behavior.

Managing Classes: Involves adhering to instructional methods to increase student cooperation and engagement in learning techniques such as cooperative learning and experiential learning.

Regrouping Students: Involves structural changes to reduce class size, introduce a more heterogeneous mix of students, create "schools within a school," and increase flexibility in scheduling.

It is often not possible to classify a given school program by category, because most school-based prevention programs contain a mix of activities. In the 149 programs reviewed, 94 percent contained multiple components. About 40 percent had components in four or more of the subcategories. The four categories with the highest representation were *instructing students*, 78 percent; *managing classrooms*, 66 percent; *thinking strategies*, 49 percent; and *setting norms for behavior*, 33 percent.

The reviewers welcome the multicomponent mix within the programs. They suggest that in designing programs, the particular mix of components should also reflect related school program goals, for example, the recognition that individual-oriented conflict-resolution programs are not likely to be effective in reducing antisocial behaviors when presented in the classroom if there is a schoolwide environment that typically ignores fighting, threatening, or insulting behavior.

METHODOLOGY OF REVIEW PROCESS

A library search located all peer-reviewed published studies of school-based prevention programs. This yielded a total of 149 programs. Multicomponent programs were assigned to the major category that was most prominent. Programs were coded for methodological rigor and effect size of outcomes. In general, the preventive school-based programs to achieve the desired outcomes for normative populations were found to be notably more successful than the remedial programs to change delinquent or serious violent behavior.

In reality, most school-based programs are *administered* at either the classroom or total school level, or both. Ideally, the evaluations of school-based interventions should also be analyzed at the classroom or school levels when they are administered at those levels. However, they are usually *analyzed* at the individual student level. This happens because, for practical reasons of access and cost, it is almost impossible to mount studies with a sufficiently large number of classrooms or schools to achieve the required statistical analytic power. Unfortunately, in this methodology statistical errors are introduced that systematically cause a reduction in the effect sizes for classrooms and schools when the individual student observations are clustered and analyzed. This is a technical factor that reduces apparent effect size for interventions, and not one that is truly related to program impact. This problem can only be remedied by increased funding that is sufficient to mount programs in large enough numbers of schools to meet standards that assure that appropriate statistical measures can be applied.

Fidelity of implementation is important to the efficacy of programs. Analyses showed that when identical school-based programs are not implemented faithfully for whatever reasons, the identical program is less effective or not effective at all.[16] Further research is needed to increase understanding of the conditions and strategies required to implement programs in real-world school settings in ways that their full potential can be realized.

What Works?

According to the Department of Justice report, strategies for which at least two different studies have found positive effects on measures of problem behavior, for crime and delinquency and for substance abuse and for which the preponderance of evidence is positive are as follows:

1. Crime and delinquency (antisocial behavior):
   a. Building school capacity to initiate and sustain innovation.
   b. Setting and communicating norms about behaviors—by establishing school rules, improving the consistency of their enforcement (particularly when they emphasize positive reinforcement of appropriate behavior), or communicating norms through school-wide campaigns (e.g., antibullying campaigns) or ceremonies.
   c. Implementing instructional strategies for students that focus on a range of social competency skills (e.g., developing self-control, stress-management, responsible decision-making, social problem solving, and communication skills) and that are delivered over a long period of time to continually reinforce skills.
2. Substance use:
   a. Setting and communicating norms about behaviors.
   b. Implementing comprehensive instructional programs that focus on a range of social competency skills (e.g., developing self-control, stress-management, responsible decision-making, social problem-solving, and communication skills) and delivering programs over a long period of time to continually reinforce skills.
   c. Behavior modification strategies and programs that teach thinking skills, role play, and assertiveness techniques to high-risk youths.

What Does Not Work?

The following are strategies for which at least two different studies have found no positive effects on measures of problem behavior and for which the preponderance of evidence is not positive.

- Counseling students as an exclusive strategy, particularly in a peer-group context, does not reduce delinquency or substance use.
- Offering youths alternative activities such as recreation and community service activities in the absence of more potent prevention programming does not reduce substance use. This conclusion is based on reviews of broadly defined alternative activities in school and community settings. Effects of these programs on other forms of delinquency are not known.

- Instructional programs focusing on information dissemination, fear arousal, moral appeal, and affective education are also ineffective for reducing substance use.

Specific recommendations for strengthening programs include the following:

1. Increased congressional appropriations for school-based prevention activities. Office of Justice Programs (OJP) funding for school-based crime prevention is meager compared with OJP expenditures in other domains within OJP and compared with expenditures by other agencies on school-based prevention. Total expenditures on school-based prevention are less than $25 million per year,[17] compared with $1.4 billion for extra police programs and $617 million for prison construction. This limited investment in school-based crime prevention, in light of its promise as demonstrated in this chapter, represents a lost opportunity for preventing crime.
2. Support for multiyear prevention efforts (e.g., programs that span the elementary school years, the middle school years, and the high school years rather than single-year programs).
3. Support for multicomponent prevention efforts that include both school-wide environmental-change and individual change strategies.
   a. Programs aimed at building school capacity to initiate and sustain innovation.
   b. Programs aimed at clarifying and communicating norms about behaviors.
   c. Comprehensive instructional programs that focus on a range of social competency skills (e.g., developing self-control, stress-management, responsible decision-making, social problem-solving, and communication skills) and that are delivered over a long period of time to continually reinforce skills.
   d. Behavior modification programs teaching new behavioral skills, and programs that teach thinking skills to high-risk youths.
4. Reducing funding for program categories known to be ineffective (e.g., counseling students for delinquency prevention; alternative activities such as recreation and community service activities in the absence of more potent prevention programming for drug prevention; and instructional drug prevention programs focusing on information dissemination, fear arousal, moral appeal, and affective education). (Affective education involves teaching a person to recognize and express accurately their own emotions as well as identify accurately another's emotions.)
5. Support activities to disseminate information about school-based strategies to practitioners and to local- and state-level program managers and policymakers to enable them to discriminate between the effective and ineffective programs.

Additional recommendations for evaluation and research needed to improve the effectiveness of school-based prevention include

1. requiring (and providing substantial financial investment for) rigorous evaluation of the long-term multicomponent models recommended here, insisting that studies of the effectiveness of strategies aimed at altering school and classroom environments be conducted using schools or classrooms as the unit of analysis, and testing the generalizability of effects across different types of communities.
2. supporting replication studies of the promising strategies just identified in the summary section.
3. supporting basic research theory-building and testing efforts, which seek to clarify the causal models relating school experiences and delinquency.
4. supporting research to investigate school conditions conducive to high-quality implementation of prevention programs.
5. supporting the development and rigorous testing, especially in urban areas, of strategies designed specifically to improve the level of implementation of prevention programs.

The congressionally mandated review of government-sponsored school-based youth violence programs offered an unusual opportunity for providing a nationwide report card on violence-prevention and intervention programs from kindergarten to the end of high school. After a thorough search for high quality published and peer-reviewed programs, as we noted, 149 were selected for detailed evaluation. At the end of this process, the reviewers concluded that school-based programs are generally effective. However, they did note that some of the same programs had differential results. Youths who were already identified as delinquent or with criminal records required much more intensive and specialized remedial efforts beyond the typical school-based programs. Reviewers also found that overall results for programs for the normative students could vary even when identical programs were used, depending on the fidelity of implementation. The technical problems of statistical analysis that reduce effect size were also noted.

Areas of discrepancy should all be addressed by both basic and applied research. If this is done, the outlook for continued advances in school-based program efficacy is good. The significant conclusion and message to Congress was that schools have great potential for mounting programs that can be effective in reducing aggression and violence among children and youth. Schools are excellent sites for initiating appropriate programs in the early school years and then provide continuity and reinforcement with school programs over the developmental span of childhood and adolescence. The study also noted the additional advantage of easy access to parents as collaborators in the comprehensive violence-prevention interventions.

So far, this chapter has described three significant institutional responses to the public's need for clarification of the causes of the increase in youth violence and explanations of efforts to address the problem. First, there was a detailed description of well-researched newspaper articles, as exemplified by the one published in the *New York Times*. Second was the initiative taken by the American Psychological Association (APA) to recruit outstanding scientists to carry out a comprehensive, major analytic review of the basic and applied scientific research findings. This report was intended for the general public, public policymakers, and practitioners. Third was the congressionally mandated independent study of the effectiveness of government-sponsored antiviolence-prevention or early intervention programs.

A RECENT META-ANALYSIS ON SCHOOL-BASED VIOLENCE-PREVENTION PROGRAMS

The most recent and extensive meta-analysis of school-based violence-prevention programs was published in August 2002. It is a systematic review of secondary prevention trials dealing with overt violence among high-risk children in elementary, middle, and high schools.

This meta-analysis of 28 studies of programs is unique in its focus on randomized clinical controlled trials of secondary violence-prevention programs.[18] All studies took place in the United States and Canada and involved children and youths from elementary through high school age who were recognized as exhibiting aggressive behavior or being at high risk for it. They were assigned randomly to either a violence-prevention program or a comparison group that was not exposed to any violence-prevention program. Many of the studies measured the impact shortly following completion of the program and again a year later. The programs were taken from the 1970s through 1990s and included a variety of approaches:

1. Individual or group anger management training
2. Think Aloud program (a program on self-control)
3. Therapeutic mentoring
4. PATHS (Promoting Alternative Thinking Strategies) curriculum
5. Empathy training
6. Peer mediation
7. Social skills training

Data from this meta-analysis comes from many large and small studies in a number of schools. Usually, program analysis looks only at the effect of one program in one school, which may not necessarily translate to other situations where curriculum, teachers, and school environment are different.

Two central criteria were used to measure a program's effectiveness: (1) reduction in aggressive behavior (measured by standardized tests and actual fights or bullying events) and (2) the number of school and agency actions in response to aggressive behavior (e.g., student suspensions, detentions, and youth court assignments).

Several valuable insights were gained in this rigorous analysis:

1. Not all programs worked, and those that did were not necessarily effective for all students.

2. School-based programs aimed at the most aggressive children were apparently the most successful.

3. Programs that involved girls alone and girls and boys together were both effective. Girls may actually reap the most benefit from these programs.

4. The most effective programs were those that trained children in combined self-control and anger management skills, and programs that improved overall interpersonal skills.

5. Aggressive behavior decreased almost equally for elementary and high school students. But older students (from mixed groups of boys and girls) benefited most, as shown by a decrease in actions (by either school or agency) taken in response to aggressive behavior.

Overall, school-based violence-prevention programs show indications of reducing violent and aggressive behavior in already aggressive children. It should be noted that some of the studies included were done in the 1970s and 1980s; more recent programs are probably more effective. These initial results deserve to be confirmed by comparable analysis of updated, large, and high-quality studies—more differentiated and nuanced than those presently available.

A COHERENT SET OF INTERVENTIONS TO REDUCE VIOLENCE AND FOSTER PROSOCIAL BEHAVIOR IN HIGH SCHOOLS

Within the scientific community, there are also personal responses to the public concerns about youth violence. One very respected social psychologist is Elliott Aronson of the University of California at Santa Cruz. Aronson wrote a highly readable, volume that gives the research background for understanding the issues and presents a model for using this knowledge to develop intervention strategies. His significant effort is summarized here.

School killings have stimulated the scientific community to address youth violence. The Columbine High School tragedy of April 1999 occurred, not in a poor urban high school setting as one might assume, but rather in the affluent suburban community of Littleton, Colorado. Two adolescent boys shot and killed a teacher and fellow students before turning their guns on themselves. In total, 15 people were killed and nearly two dozen others seriously wounded.

Following this (the worst school massacre in the history of the United States), Professor Aronson set himself the task of writing about ways to teach empathy and compassion in the schools in order to contribute to the public dialogue on the subject of school violence. Aronson has over 40 years' experience as a social psychologist, including extensive work in the schools teaching students skills for behaving with compassion and empathy toward one another. Aronson's book, *Nobody Left to Hate*, offers a clear analysis of interventions that address the serious problem of school violence. But it also clearly summarizes major lines of research that bear on education for conflict resolution, in or out of school.[19] It is a useful model of authoritative scholarship expressed in nontechnical language for public understanding.

Aronson suggests that analyzing violence in schools should involve examination not only of the psychological makeup of the individual, but also of the *social environment* in which the individual is immersed. Because humans are deeply social beings, we are highly influenced by the way others treat us and by our social surroundings. The behavior of the two boys responsible for the Columbine shootings was pathological, but they also acted out their murderous plan in response to a high school environment that left them feeling excluded and rejected. Clearly, an important interaction exists between personality and the environment. Studies have shown that otherwise normal people will behave abnormally depending on the situation.[20]

The overall rate of violent crime in U.S. schools has actually decreased over the past 10 years. In contrast, the ironic and sober reality is that instances of *multiple victims* being killed at or near schools have *increased* drastically in the past few years. For example, eight accounts of multiple shootings of students by their peers occurred in less than 2 years in suburban and rural areas and none in the inner city.[21] As a result, many students now fear going to school because of worry over possible violent attacks by their classmates. In each instance of recent mass violence, there is a single common element. Adolescent boys committed all of the murders. So the question is what are the factors present in these adolescent males that are absent among adolescent females of the same age? A biological factor is testosterone—a hormone known to be linked to aggression. By taking on the role of a macho male, many adolescent males feel better about themselves and enjoy more peer approval. This is evidenced in taking on dares and challenges in fights, assuming an aggressive attitude, and by taking pride in gun ownership. The combination of gun possession and eagerness to prove themselves by physical aggression is a deadly combination. Girls are much more likely to use interpersonal and verbal aggression in their expressions of anger and hostility.

As tragic episodes have shown, adults can also become quite unhappy and overly stressed in their jobs when the environment breeds daily harsh competition, their work is undervalued, coworkers express joy when mistakes are made, and harsh distinctions are drawn between the in-group and the out-group. Unfortunately, this is precisely the social climate of many high schools. Students in such schools regularly experience a hostile environment in which they are taunted, excluded, and lonely. As a result, self-esteem drops, along with academic performance. These are some of the reasons for high rates of anxiety and depression among youth.

Aronson seeks to create school environments for children and youth by defining conditions that will not only educate students, but will also foster their emotional and interpersonal well-being and social skills. These various aspects of behavior go hand in hand in promoting success in school. In fact, such an education has clear implications for today's marketplace, where employers value individuals who are able to work harmoniously with a variety of coworkers, to work as team members, to take initiative, to assume responsibility, and to communicate well.

Relevant to our theme, we look at Aronson's way of teaching compassion in schools by examining two scientific experiments, two categories of intervention, and a jigsaw classroom structure created by Aronson with his graduate students 30 years ago to help ease a highly unstable situation in an Austin, Texas, city school that had recently been desegregated. In response to current public concern, these techniques have spread widely in recent years, mostly supported by careful research.

Experiments and Studies

LEE ROSS'S QUIZ SHOW EXPERIMENT   Lee Ross (a highly respected social psychologist at Stanford University) and his associates skillfully designed an experiment set up in the format of a quiz show.[22] Three participants were involved: a questioner, a contestant, and an observer. From the beginning, a coin was tossed to randomly determine who would be the questioner and who would be the contestant. The questioner's job was to come up with difficult questions and the contestant's role was to answer the questions. The observer watched the quiz show and then was asked to rate the overall intelligence and general knowledge of the questioner and the contestant.

Results showed that observers reported the overall intelligence and knowledge of the questioners to be higher than that of the contestants. Essentially, they succumbed to the temptation of attributing what they observed to personal qualities of the questioner and the contestant rather than to situational constraints. If one looks closely at the setup, one finds the questioners in a position of advantage—they could compose questions based on particular esoteric knowledge that they happened to have, whereas contestants were at the mercy of answering questions for which they were unprepared. They were bound to answer a few questions incorrectly. All participants, including observers, were aware of the random assignment of roles, yet observers did not consider the differentials of power within the situation itself when making their ratings.

What this experiment and many others like it show is that when trying to account for an individual's behavior in a complex situation, most people attribute the behavior mainly or solely to individual characteristics. The fact that people rarely take the context into account is of great importance to social psychologists, because it has significant influence on ways in which human beings relate to each other.

DAN OLWEUS: A STUDY OF AGGRESSION AND BULLYING AMONG NORWEGIAN SCHOOLCHILDREN   In a government-sponsored survey of all of Norway's 90,000 schoolchildren, Dan Olweus found that bullying was a widespread and serious problem.[23] Some schools reported that 17 percent of their students were continuously victimized by bullies. In addition, parents and teachers were only remotely aware of these incidents, and when they were aware, rarely did they attempt to help the harassed students. To them, such victimization was taken as an unpleasant, but not dangerous, fact of life that was assumed to be inevitable. Nonetheless, the facts were disturbing, and the ignorance, secrecy, and denial were seen as major contributors to the perpetuation of the problem. In response to the findings, the government of Norway sponsored a three-stage campaign led by Olweus with the goals of heightening awareness and motivation, developing strategies to deal with bullying and victimization, and improving the social climate in schools to reduce or prevent the development of a culture of bullying and victimization. Educating all concerned was the first priority. The significance of the problem was explained to citizens in communitywide meetings. The need to eradicate the behavior was emphasized. Parents were given written information that detailed their role in addressing the problem. Teachers participated in training on ways of identifying and handling bullying. Students watched videotapes geared to elicit empathy and sympathy for victims of the bullies.

The second phase focused on in-school interventions involving students, teachers, and administration. Class discussions took place on functional ways to prevent bullying and to reach out to socially isolated and lonely children. Teachers instituted cooperative learning groups. They also adopted a zero tolerance stance and responded quickly to early signs of bullying such as derogatory name-calling and other aggressive behavior. School principals took on the responsibility of making sure that public areas such as lunchrooms, restrooms, and playgrounds were well supervised with heightened vigilance for bullying and prompt action to eliminate the unwanted behavior.

Finally, the third tier of intervention was used if earlier preventive measures failed. Bullies were given counseling and intensive therapy, along with their parents. Sometimes the offending student was placed in another classroom. Victims were also counseled and tutored to help develop their social and academic abilities.

In less than 2 years, this campaign helped to reduce bullying by 50 percent. Significant improvement was found at every grade level. Olweus concluded from these positive results that it was no longer legitimate for students, parents, or school personnel to use the excuse of lack of awareness to avoid taking responsible actions against bullying problems. These difficult situations can only be addressed satisfactorily if adults assume responsibility for the health and well-being of their children and set conditions that result in a shift of norms for all concerned regarding the problem behavior.

Classroom Interventions

NORMA FESHBACH: TEACHING EMPATHY   We described this 30-hour empathy-training program for elementary children in Chapter 5 ("Development of Prosocial Behavior"). We summarize it here because it illustrates Aronson's coherent package of prosocial, antiviolence interventions—a response to growing public concern. This program is extremely successful in teaching children to recognize, relate to, and adopt the perspective and feelings of another person. The children are challenged to think deeply about questions such as "What birthday present would make each member of your family happiest?" These youngsters also listen to stories and retell them from the point of view of a different character. The children also learn to identify their own feelings. They are videotaped and then watch the tapes and analyze the way they looked and sounded as they expressed their feelings.

It may appear that such a program is unrelated to academic achievement. But such programs actually promote a kind of cognitive flexibility that is taught in adult corporate creativity workshops. Norma Feshbach has reported on the positive correlation between high empathetic ability and high academic achievement. Participants in empathy-training programs develop better self-esteem, greater generosity, less aggressive behavior, and more positive attitudes than nonparticipants.

And most important, Feshbach showed that empathy can be taught. She also designed curriculum materials on the history of immigration to the United States, for high school teachers. The goal of this curriculum is for students to gain an understanding and appreciation of the perspectives of different immigrant groups, to empathize with them, and to feel the pain associated with prejudice that so many of these groups suffered.

THE JIGSAW CLASSROOM   In Chapter 8 ("Cooperative Learning"), we discussed several classroom interventions, including the jigsaw strategy. But we go into greater detail here to describe its method and the reasons for its success in fostering compassion, empathy, and academic achievement.[24]

The jigsaw strategy is a carefully structured classroom method of cooperative learning. This has been the core reason for its success since 1971, when it was first introduced into an Austin, Texas, school classroom. Just as a jigsaw puzzle requires each piece to complete the picture, each student is a vital part of the jigsaw classroom. The full understanding and production of the final class product can only be realized by each student's essential contribution.

The structure works in the following way. Imagine a classroom history project in which the task is to research and learn about World War II. To complete the project, the class is divided into small groups of five students. The teacher then chooses five topics of study. Each student in the group is assigned the responsibility to learn about one of the project topics. For example, in one group, Kate learns about Hitler's rise to power, Joe covers concentration camps, Liz researches the role of Great Britain, Sam analyzes the Soviet Union's role, and Jennifer handles the development of the atom bomb.

Across the groups, students who were assigned the same topic meet together to form an expert group. It is here that they are given the opportunity to check facts, exchange ideas, and rehearse their presentations before returning to their original heterogeneous groups where they report on their topic as part of the group. This technique is especially helpful to students who might have difficulty organizing their assigned material. After students educate their home groups on their individual specialties, they are tested on what they have learned as a group from fellow students on World War II.

There are numerous benefits from the jigsaw classroom. It is a very efficient way of learning the material. Listening, active engagement, and empathy are fostered because each group member is an essential player in the academic task. To reach their common goal, students must pool information and cooperate as a team, and group and individual goals are inexorably linked. In this cooperation by design, students value each other as useful contributors to learning the material.

Thus, we see that Aronson drew on extensive research to reduce the violence-promoting atmosphere of the school—seeking to enhance public understanding and social action. Several areas come into focus in educating for compassion, empathy, and nonviolent problem solving. Students deserve a dependable and nurturing environment in which to learn. Schools can offer such a place, provided that adults—parents, teachers, and administrators understand the benefits and are willing to become actively involved in children's healthy development and take into account the effects of the social environment on behavior.

We have seen how the intersection of personality and environment shapes behavior. If a troubled adolescent is placed in a school environment where he or she is regularly taunted and bullied and where adults turn a blind eye to his or her misery, then adverse outcomes are likely, especially the suffering of depression that sometimes leads to suicide and occasionally even to multiple killings. We have noted that adolescent boys, in particular, are at risk of being pushed to the brink of serious violence. So special attention must be paid to their needs during this significant time of development.

Serious concerns about youth violence are not unique to the U.S. Increasingly, the prevalence of major youth violence is comparable in advanced nations. The reports of the extent of bullying in Norway and the traumatic consequences for the victims were a surprising revelation and a wake-up call. School shootings in Erfurt, Germany, and in Banja Luka, Bosnia-Herzegovina, serve as impetus to examine this tragic problem from a global perspective. Cultural boundaries continue to blur. The U.S. pop culture is international reality; omnipresent media have profound positive and negative influences. Children worldwide have increasing access to the World Wide Web, and violent American movies are highly popular with youth and are favored over those of their own countries. School-based conflict-resolution and violence-prevention programs rely on teaching empathy, sharpening skills in recognizing feelings of self and other, learning communication skills, and creating cooperative learning environments as key curricular elements, not only in the United States but worldwide. It does not mean that assertiveness and competition are eliminated from students' experience. In fact, healthy competition often inspires greatness, whether it occurs in building a better instrument, developing gifted athletes, or inspiring creative scientists. But *excessive and harsh* competition, especially in the classroom, creates a dichotomous atmosphere of winners and losers—a breeding ground for feelings of isolation and unhappiness. This is where the jigsaw strategy offers a particularly useful model for building cooperation, trust, empathy and compassion, which also leads to improved academic achievement. Thus, it is possible to formulate a coherent strategy to shape environments for children in which they can learn, develop intellectual curiosities, work well with other people, and prepare for their future roles as healthy, effective, and responsible members of society.

IMPLICATIONS FOR CONFLICT-RESOLUTION EDUCATION FROM RESEARCH ON RISK AND PROTECTIVE FACTORS

Research on social development indirectly supports the value of conflict-resolution education, especially for at-risk youth. To improve strategies for preventing violent and other antisocial behavior, it is important to understand what factors increase the risk that adolescents will develop those behaviors. David Hawkins and Richard Catalano, distinguished researchers at the University of Washington, identified a variety of specific risk factors for which research is consistent in predicting youth delinquency or other antisocial behavior. In summary, factors such as poor parenting, adverse or abusive experience in the family, negative school climate, community violence, extensive violent media exposure, and impoverished, chaotic homes combine to form the major risk factors:

- Alienation and lack of bonding to family, school, and community
- Early, persistent antisocial behavior
- Family history of high-risk behavior
- Poor family management practices
- Exposure to media portrayals of violence
- Family conflict
- Economic and social deprivation
- School failure
- Lack of commitment to education
- Association with delinquent peers
- Community disorganization (little sense of community, high crime, low surveillance, easy availability of drugs, easy availability of firearms, etc.).[25]

Although the presence of these risk factors does not make certain the development of violent or other antisocial behavior, their presence does represent an increased probability of such behavior occurring. They are warning signs calling for early intervention. Many interventions have been studied in recent years that foster child and adolescent development characterized by good health, active learning, and decent human relations. Significant ways of improving health, education, and the social environment of children and youth have been documented.[26] These go beyond the scope of this book, but they provide a very important context for the efforts to improve human relationships in ways that diminish hatred and violence. They are discussed briefly in chapter 6.

Research also shows that *some* children exposed to multiple risk factors manage to avoid damage and behavior problems later, even though they are exposed to the same kinds of risks as children who do develop serious behavior problems. These children are *resilient*, benefiting from protective factors in development. They usually have the following characteristics:

1. Responsiveness to others
2. Conceptual and intellectual flexibility
3. Caring for others
4. Good communication skills
5. Sense of humor
6. Ability to apply abstract thinking
7. Engagement in reflective thought
8. Critical reasoning skills
9. Development of alternative solutions in frustrating situations
10. Positive sense of independence
11. Emerging feelings of efficacy

12. High self-esteem
13. Impulse control
14. Planning and goal setting
15. Belief in the future

Hawkins and Catalano found that *bonding* (the feeling of being connected to others) is the *overarching protective factor* in the development of such healthy behaviors.

Research on resilience by other behavioral scientists has reached similar conclusions. Even in the face of serious adversity, one solid *attachment* and one *reliable interpersonal relationship* can go a long way toward facilitating constructive coping. Hawkins and Catalano suggest that three protective processes are necessary for developing strong bonds: opportunities, skills, and recognition.[27] These can be built into effective educational programming. In developing conflict-resolution curricula, schools can create environments that support the development of resilient characteristics in children by

1. resolving conflicts in principled ways that promote and preserve relationships, thereby facilitating the bonding that is essential to the development of resilience. From the start of the conflict-resolution encounter, the issue is put in the context of sustaining a mutually rewarding long-term relationship—or at least of keeping that option open.
2. conveying to youth that they have the power to control their own behavior by making choices that satisfy their needs while taking into account the needs of others.
3. giving students the opportunity to resolve their conflicts peacefully. A conflict-resolution education program sends to involved youth a powerful enabling message of trust and perceived capability.

The following chapter describes in detail a sampling of the exemplary school-based programs that hold great promise for preparing and guiding young persons in pathways to prosocial, respectful, and empathic behaviors.

11

Exemplary Programs of
Conflict-Resolution Education

As more has been learned about the antecedents of youth violence and the core elements of effective prevention programs, there has been growing interest in development of multicomponent programs with a sharp focus on conflict-resolution education. This trend has been fueled not only by the nationwide school shootings, which are dramatic and frightening though actually quite rare, but by two other considerations as well. There is a realization that disruptive behavior in the classroom is highly prevalent and that it takes a great toll in terms of both student distress and major erosions of classroom teaching time. Changing demographics have introduced far greater diversity in the schools, and new challenges are confronted with the mix of cultures.

Richard Bodine and Donna Crawford of the National Center for Conflict Resolution Education provide a major review and analysis of current and recent specific efforts to educate for conflict resolution in U.S. schools.[1] They present key research findings from the emergent field of conflict-resolution education and include an overview of relevant contributions from the literature on risk factors and resilience in youth development. Based on these data, they have developed a comprehensive four-part program of conflict resolution education. In doing so, they delineated four curricula segments for conflict-resolution education that are independent but also interrelated. These are the *process curriculum*, the *mediation program*, the *Peaceable Classroom*, and the *Peaceable School*. The four curricula segments represent a nested set of components, each of which can be used independently, but when taken together, as intended, for each additional component added there are increasingly positive results with maximal efficacy and long-term impact when the full program is mounted. When the full program is implemented, it has direct impacts on students, teachers, other school personnel, and parents. Although there are gains with partial implementation, achievement of the full potential of the program depends on the successful implementation of all segments. When possible, there should be continuity of training across grades, usually in the form of short courses, informal follow-up opportunities, or curriculum development. Shared key themes are central to all four segments, and all apply equally to children and adults. These key themes are (a) awareness of biases, (b) learning the skill of good listening, (c) learning the skill of constructive response, and (d) making conscious commitments to mutually beneficial, win-win solutions. Methods used are developmentally appropriate to each age group. The development of these skills leads to greater self-esteem and willingness to engage in constructive, proactive ways with other people. Conflict-resolution skills are transferable from one situation to another. They can be implemented in one-on-one situations such as peer mediation and can have a broader impact such as improving the school environment and, in turn, the community at large. There is a strong commitment to the principle that conflict-resolution education should be given to all students, not just those with disruptive behaviors.

THE PROCESS CURRICULUM

This introductory segment of the conflict-resolution education program devotes considerable specific instructional time to teaching a three-unit curriculum of *foundational abilities*, *problem-solving principles*, and *structured processes* of conflict resolution. This is an independent course curriculum, with regular lesson plans. Using methods appropriate to the developmental stage, it is integral to the full program and introduces the students to the core concepts of the entire four-part program.

Foundational Abilities and Values

In order to emphasize the fundamental importance of certain values and skills as the basic underpinnings of all segments of the full four-part program, Bodine and Crawford have chosen Foundational Abilities and Values as their descriptive term. In this unit, the focus is on the values of fairness, trust, justice, and nonviolence. This focus leads to the specific teaching of compassion and empathy, respect for self and others, and the celebration of diversity. Students also discover that controversy may also serve as an opportunity for them to develop critical thinking, improve academic performance, and grow as a person.

Problem-Solving Principles

Problem-solving principles (principled negotiation elements), as described in the work of Fisher, Ury, and Patton (1991), formed the conceptual framework for the program elements in this unit.[2] The curriculum content for teaching problem-solving principles builds on the foundational values and abilities taught in the initial unit. The focus in this subsequent unit is on the more specialized personal attitudes and skills that are critical to successful interpersonal transactions and core elements of principled negotiations. The personal skills emphasized are communication skills, including how to listen effectively and how to give clear messages to others. Emotional self-regulation, with special attention to anger management, is also taught.

The curricular elements of principled negotiation present a sequential approach to defining the issues and learning strategies for successful dispute resolution. After an initial statement of the problem, students are taught to:

- Share differing perspectives regarding the problem and sort out the differences
- Separate the people from the problem and deal with each separately
- Focus as objectively as possible on core *interests*, not purely personal or political *positions* (e.g., Be sure that your best interests are being served by the positions taken)

This curricular content is presented both didactically and in training exercises. The final phase of the curriculum focuses on more technical aspects of creating options, evaluating options, using objective criteria, and reaching a resolution of the dispute that is mutually acceptable and well understood.

Structured Process Curriculum

The structured process unit of the curriculum builds on the two preceding units and presents an overarching framework for conflict resolution processes. Three forms of conflict resolution are delineated. Negotiation is the process in which two individuals or parties work together to resolve the disputed issue. Mediation is the format in which the disputing parties work in concert with a neutral third party, the mediator, in resolving the dispute. Consensus decision-making occurs when multiple parties to a conflict resolve a dispute with or without the participation of a mediator.

In this curriculum, the structured process elements for resolving conflict are refined and more specific. Teachers and administrators learn that conflict resolution education can be a major component of an effective classroom or school management system.

THE MEDIATION PROGRAM

The focus of this program is the training of selected school-based individuals (adults and students) in the principles of conflict resolution and mediation processes to provide neutral third-party facilitation services to help those in conflict reach a resolution. In schools, the role of mediator can often be fulfilled by *trained students*. They can help resolve disputes between peers, such as those involving jealousies, rumors, misunderstandings, bullying, harassment, threats or fights, personal property, and damaged friendships. Additionally, students and adults may serve together as comediators to resolve disputes between students and teachers that might involve personality clashes, issues of respect, unacceptable behavior, perception of unfairness, and other conflicts that undermine student-teacher relationships. Mediation is a process in which the mediator (or comediators) serves as a neutral process facilitator to help disputants negotiate an agreement. The mediator creates and maintains an environment that fosters *mutual problem solving*, not recrimination. During the mediation, a six-step problem-solving structured process taught in the structural process curriculum is the framework used for dispute resolution. Its core elements are summarized as follows:

1. Set the stage by establishing ground rules for problem solving
2. Gather perspectives by listening to each disputant's point of view
3. Identify interests contributing to the conflict
4. Create options that respectfully address the interests of both disputants
5. Evaluate these options according to objective criteria
6. Generate an agreement that involves genuine mutual accommodation and a win-win outcome

The school mediation program may lead to positive outcomes such as a reduction in the number of detentions, suspensions, or expulsions. It can also reduce the time teachers and administrators spend dealing with conflicts between students. In addition, the school climate is likely to improve, because the school mediation program provides both students and faculty with an alternative forum for problem solving and reduces the violence potential of long-simmering, unresolved disputes and grievances. Students perceive peer mediation as a way to think through and talk out problems without fear of an authoritative adult harshly judging their behavior, thoughts, or feelings. The self-empowering aspects of the process appeal to youth and foster self-esteem and self-discipline in the process.

EVALUATION OF MEDIATION PROGRAMS

Robin Hall, of Charles Sturt University, provides an overview of peer mediation studies with a focus on how peer mediation relates to learning conflict management.[3] Although the literature offers different definitions of mediation, Hall's focus is on "a process in which a third party (the mediator) manages the negotiations of the disputing parties to enable them to reach an acceptable solution to their dispute."[4] Primarily, it is concerned with interpersonal conflict within the schools. Several important characteristics of the mediator include the ability (1) to facilitate rather than arbitrate, (2) to maintain a neutral position, (3) to provide guidance during the negotiation of agreements, and (4) to help conflicting parties control their own destinies by taking responsible action. Through constructive handling of conflicts, relationships between students can be enhanced. Peer mediation is a way for students to learn these skills. And often these skills can be transferred to family relations and other social situations.[5]

Positive effects are seen on both mediators and the disputants, but it is especially striking among mediators themselves. Self-esteem grows along with problem solving ability. This is most true in situations in which student mediators help to train other students. There is an additional indirect benefit. Children who previously performed poorly academically improve after peer mediation training. Mediators become more confident and capable in making decisions about their lives.[6] There is also growth toward responsible citizenship.[7]

When selecting student mediators, care must be taken not to choose only the best-behaved or most intellectually superior students. Instead, even though the selection process may produce tension, teachers should seek a broad range of students in terms of gender, ethnicity, age, language, and special education requirements. The number of mediators should be large enough to ensure an adequate pool of students to handle all the disputes without infringing on academic responsibilities. To effectively conduct such programs, as with other educational innovations, it is essential to prepare teachers adequately: to stimulate their interest, clarify the value of the program to the students, show how it can reduce the discipline role of teachers, and help them understand negotiating procedures.[8] Depending on characteristics of the disputes, programs will differ accordingly. They are usually of short duration with the goal of forging an agreement between disputants. Students are given the opportunity to tell their stories; they are helped to clarify issues and understand feelings of other participants, and then to reach a solution. Although most programs focus on disagreements between students, some disputes may also be between students and teachers. For these disputes, adults need to be recruited as mediators. Sometimes there is a dearth of conflict incidents to be mediated. This becomes the main reason that mediators leave the service. Often this result may be viewed as a paradox of success of the program.

The content of disputes may be organized in terms of physical aggression, verbal arguments, gossip, name-calling, and other harassments. Also, gender differences are notable. Boys, although more involved in school disputes, do not utilize peer mediation as often as do girls. Perhaps a reason for this stems from the perception that mediation is more appropriate for verbal conflict, which typically involves females, than the more physical disputes typical among males. However, it is interesting to note that both boys and girls demonstrated similar strategies for managing conflict and produced essentially the same resolutions after they were trained in mediation.[9]

Evaluation of peer mediation programs deserves further attention and research, because only a small number of evaluations meet the requirements of quasi-experimental design. Some studies are found to be weak because of an overdependence on self-report measures as the primary data. The focus has been on attitudes and short-term behavior outcomes, neglecting long-term aspects of the duration of effects such as which outcomes fade away, stay the same, or improve. Also, establishing the effects of programs is made more difficult when the nature and duration of goals are not clearly specified from the start. Even with these difficulties, a recent burst of data is being accumulated.[10] Discipline problems are found to be drastically reduced in self-reports after the introduction of mediation services.[11] Mediation success rates are reported to approach 90 percent. Most studies report only the *occurrence* of an agreement. It is interesting to note that the school environment is usually improved, and this may have independent educational benefits. Anecdotal evidence from violence-prevention programs suggests that positive changes in school climate often occur. Teachers can benefit through their understanding of conflict, acquisition of new teaching skills, and sensitivity to students' needs have been reported. These observations are important and deserve to be followed up in light of the burdens placed on teachers by conflict-laden atmospheres.

In any event, further systematic research is badly needed to clarify not only the nature and scope of success, but also the conditions under which success is most likely to be achieved, especially for the long term. Some examples of current programs are given below.

Program for Young Negotiators (PYN)

This program was founded in 1993 as an adaptation of the Harvard Negotiation Project and was piloted in the Boston area that same year. It also uses principles formulated by Roger Fisher and William Ury in *Getting to Yes*; this approach has been found to be widely useful in a variety of disputes.[12] The concepts have been adapted and improved by students, teachers, and PYN staff in order to make them developmentally appropriate as well as enjoyable for primary and secondary school students.

Hundreds of teachers and thousands of students have now been trained in the Boston area. PYN has also spread to California, New York, and Toronto. The program teaches people how to achieve their goals without violence. It also helps students to envision scenarios in which both sides of a conflict can be satisfied with a positive outcome and both are able to achieve their essential goals. Four primary components of the program are teacher training with parent and community involvement, negotiation curricula in schools, follow-up opportunities, and ongoing curriculum development and innovation.

Street Law, Inc.

This program helps teens understand how crime affects them, their families, friends, and communities. It also involves them in service focused on making their communities safer. It has produced two conflict-resolution education curricula. *We Can Work It Out!—Problem Solving Through Mediation* and *The Conflict Zoo. We Can Work It Out!*, for elementary schools. These curricula use a step-by-step design to teach the skills of *personal* conflict management and the process guidelines of *mediation* to prepare students to assist others in disputes. For secondary schools, it follows the same format except that the terminology used and the scenarios created are appropriate for the older age group. *The Conflict Zoo* is a curriculum for the third and fourth grades designed to teach the building blocks of conflict resolution and the concepts of justice and fairness. Street Law programs can be used separately or integrated into existing curricula and programs.

Illinois Institute for Dispute Resolution

This is a statewide professional development program on conflict resolution in schools. Six developmental phases are used, as described in the program guide, *Peer Mediation: Conflict Resolution in Schools:*[13]

1. Develop a program team and a commitment to the program.
2. Design and plan the program.
3. Select and train mediators.
4. Educate a critical mass of the school population.
5. Develop and execute a promotional campaign.
6. Operate and maintain the program.

In general, peers have considerable credibility with each other, since they share many experiences, interests, orientations, and values.

Basic training (12 to 15 hours) is involved in this student mediation program. Students are challenged to understand the conflict and its sources and to learn responses to it. They are taught communication skills, the role of the mediator, and the mediation process. Advanced training, also 12 to 15 hours, includes a more complex set of skills such as becoming aware of the role of social diversity and bias, learning nuanced communication, uncovering hidden interests, dealing with anger, caucusing, negotiating, and group problem solving. The program builds the conflict-resolution skills of both adults and students and offers opportunities for everyone in the school community to use conflict-resolution processes in their daily lives. It also contributes to an improved school climate by exemplifying the fact that personal problems, ongoing conflicts, and recurrent grievances can be handled constructively without violence.

THE PEACEABLE CLASSROOM

The name "The Peaceable Classroom" originated as part 3 of the four-part model for the conflict resolution education program in the schools designed by Bodine and Crawford.[14] This approach is a *whole-classroom* methodology that includes salient aspects of the foundational abilities, the problem solving and principles, and the structured processes of conflict resolution described at the beginning of this chapter. They are integrated with conflict-resolution education and incorporated into the core subjects of the curriculum and into classroom management strategies as part of the daily lives of the students. Peaceable Classrooms can be initiated by teachers. They are the building blocks for achieving the Peaceable School, part 4 of the total comprehensive conflict-education program. Teachers learn to create classroom environments that support conflict resolution and prosocial behavior and incorporate conflict-resolution strategies and skills into their daily lesson plans. William Kreidler, an early advocate of the Peaceable Classroom, approaches the classroom as a caring and mutually respectful community in which five qualities are present: cooperation, communication, emotional expression, appreciation for diversity, and conflict resolution.[15] Both teachers and students are trained in key aspects of the process curriculum and mediation programs if they have not undergone this training at an earlier time.

Combined cooperative learning and the constructive academic controversy methods, developed by David Johnson and Roger Johnson, are also used extensively by teachers in Peaceable Classrooms.[16] Cooperative learning, as we have noted, involves students' working in small groups to accomplish shared learning goals. They are to learn the assigned material and to ensure that all other group members also learn it. Academic controversy exists in a cooperative learning group when one student's ideas, information, conclusions, theories, or opinions are in conflict with those of another and the two seek to reach an agreement. Controversies are resolved by engaging in deliberate constructive discourse using conflict-resolution skills—optimally with patient and deliberate teacher guidance. Examples of application and adaptation of elements of the Peaceable Classroom are given below.

Cooperative Learning Center, University of Minnesota

Teaching Students to Be Peacemakers is a 12-year school program that began in the mid-1960s at the University of Minnesota. The students learn increasingly sophisticated negotiation and mediation procedures, and educators and students alike are trained in resolving conflicts constructively. Building positive relationships among disputants and reaching negotiated agreements are major emphases of the program.

Thousands of preschool, primary, intermediate, middle school, high school, and college faculty members and administrators have been trained to implement the program throughout North America and countries in Europe, the Middle East, Africa, Asia, and Central and South America. These decades of experience with this systematic program have given the opportunity for nearly worldwide use. Overall, students and teachers usually find it a rewarding experience. There are four parts to this program: creating a cooperative environment; teaching peacemaking; implementing the program in practical ways; and upgrading of peacemaking skills over extended time.

Educators for Social Responsibility

Educators for Social Responsibility (ESR) is a well-respected nonprofit organization in Cambridge, Massachusetts. It is recognized for promoting children's ethical and social development through its national leadership in conflict resolution, violence prevention, intergroup relations, and character education. The primary mission is to help young people develop the convictions and skills to shape a safe, sustainable, and just world. The on-site training prepares educators to teach conflict resolution, communication, and intergroup relations. ESR has also distributed over 35,000 educational resources to support Peaceable Classrooms across the United States.

Workshops, curricula, and ongoing support help educators develop instructional and management practices that foster skills in the six interrelated areas of cooperation, caring communication, appreciation of diversity, expression of feelings, responsible decision making, and conflict resolution. Interviews with teachers who have created Peaceable Classrooms at four different developmental levels are useful to teachers who are new to this approach. The program notes that far greater meaningful changes occur when a group of teachers that are actively engaged in creating and maintaining Peaceable Classrooms combine efforts with other school personnel, parents, and community-based conflict-resolution enterprises.

Children's Creative Response to Conflict

Children's Creative Response to Conflict (CCRC) grew from the Quaker Project on Community Conflict in New York City and is generally identified as a pioneer organization in the field of conflict resolution in schools. The program was first used in some New York City schools in 1972.

The four original themes of CCRC were cooperation, communication, affirmation, and conflict resolution. Subthemes have emerged from these, including problem solving, mediation, and bias awareness. The CCRC program developed a workshop format that was adopted by a number of other conflict-resolution programs. Training programs provide adults with a variety of teaching activities to use with youth in developing these themes.

As an organization with a long history of conflict resolution in the schools, CCRC has evolved with research advances in the field. The activities are well tested and useful for creating Peaceable Classrooms. CCRC's current goals include changing the school or community culture by establishing a critical mass of teachers and community members who practice creative conflict resolution, modeling the skills of active listening, and seeking solutions that are fair to everyone. The aim is to integrate conflict resolution and bias awareness into the curriculum and everyday lives of students, parents, staff, and community members.

In summary, it is impressive that various (overlapping) Peaceable Classroom approaches have been developed and refined over several decades. Their feasibility is clear and their social value tangible—though some are not as well evaluated as we would wish. Their use is spreading widely across national boundaries. This is an important area in which support for research on fidelity of implementation, manualized curricula, and systematic evaluation involving a large number of schools are required to reach valid and reliable conclusions should be a priority.

THE PEACEABLE SCHOOL

This is a comprehensive whole-school methodology that builds on the Peaceable Classroom approach of the Bodine-Crawford conflict-resolution education program discussed at the beginning of the chapter. The Peaceable School approach incorporates the other three approaches. It expands those trained to include librarians, teachers, counselors, students, principals, and parents. Peaceable school climates reflect caring, honesty, cooperation, and appreciation of diversity. They incorporate cooperative learning environments, direct instruction and practice of conflict-resolution skills and processes, noncoercive school and classroom management systems, and integration of conflict-resolution concepts and abilities into the curriculum. The most important challenge of an educator in the Peaceable School is to relate consistently and noncoercively to each learner, with attentive individual responses.

To transform the school into a Peaceable School, all aspects of the school community need to cooperate and address specific elements. There are multiple points of entry to becoming a Peaceable School. These steps range from training adults in conflict resolution to building cooperative contexts for classroom learning to providing peer mediation training. However, these points should not be incorporated in an arbitrary sequence. Instead, they should be adopted according to the specific needs, abilities, and interests of the school. Examples of differing pathways are (1) a major redesigning of all school activities in light of conflict-resolution theory to the maximal extent possible and (2) adopting a gradual approach that maintains an evaluation process for monitoring movement toward becoming a Peaceable School and learning from experience.

Regardless of method, systemic change in a school never comes easily. Very often, policies and practices inherent in the operation of schools provide powerful contradictory messages that obstruct the shift to schoolwide peaceful resolution of conflicts. Unless the school personnel and functioning of the system consistently support desired behavioral expectations for the individuals in the system, the contradictory messages are likely to work against achieving change. Two overarching areas of transformation are (1) reducing the degree of harsh competition tolerated or fostered in the system and (2) enforcing the style and consistency in which rules or behavioral expectations are carried out. The goal of the Peaceable School approach is to create a positive schoolwide climate with a discipline program that focuses on clear, fair rules and norms of acceptable behavior, consistently enforced, that enable students and school personnel to regulate and control their own behavior in a framework of mutual respect with others throughout the school. Educators must construct an orderly, productive system accomplished through cooperation in a dependable climate of respectful, constructive behavior. Likewise, students must be provided with constructive alternatives in ways to behave—rather than harsh or punitive responses to stress or anger in their school experiences. Building constructive community and parent relationships with mutuality of goals is also an important ingredient in creating a successful Peaceable School.

Resolving Conflict Creatively Program

The Resolving Conflict Creatively Program (RCCP) is a Peaceable School program. It is a comprehensive K-through-12 approach to conflict resolution and intercultural understanding, aiming to reduce violence by promoting caring and cooperative schools and communities. RCCP began in 1985 as a collaboration of the New York City Board of Education and the ESR's New York City chapter. By 1993, the model was being replicated across the nation, and it now operates in school systems in 8 of the 50 states. This program focuses on reaching young people through the adults who relate to them daily at home, in school, and in their communities. The program incorporates the following components: introductory interpersonal and conflict-resolution skills, training, and staff development; substantive curriculum; peer mediation; and administrator and parent involvement. RCCP develops an ongoing, long-term commitment with the school district. Conflict resolution and understanding diversity are upheld as basic to youth education, not as add-ons.

Community Board Program

The Community Board Program is a nonprofit conflict resolution organization that provides free dispute resolution services to every neighborhood in San Francisco. Since its inception in 1976, the central goal has been to infuse their dispute resolution programs with the values and concepts of conflict resolution and to put mechanisms in place to implement them.

Parent involvement is an integral part of this whole-school approach. Partnerships between school-based mediation programs and their community-based counterparts serve to strengthen and benefit both programs. The Community Board Program and the San Francisco Unified School District have developed a very strong relationship through the years and have put the following strategies into place: sharing mediators; cross-referral system; parent-child mediation; training youths as trainers; and youth clubs and youth councils. The program's staff and volunteers make a sustained effort to reach out to youth-serving organizations and schools to alert students as to how they may refer disputes to this program for practical help.

INTERNATIONAL PROGRAMS

There is global interest in teaching tolerance. Programs have arisen in several of the countries that are involved in serious violent conflicts. There is an increasing impetus to teach tolerance and attempt to overcome harsh, hateful stereotypes. A preventive approach is being taken, and programs have been created to develop understanding, empathy, and tolerance of those differing ethnic or religious backgrounds.

William Ury provides a useful example of teaching tolerance in the City Montessori School in Lucknow, India.[17] Here Sikh, Hindu, and Muslim students from kindergarten through 12th grades are inspired by the teachings of Mahatma Gandhi, which are embedded with values of religious and cultural tolerance. Some classroom activities include collaborative problem solving and teachers demonstrate the importance of showing consideration and respect for others by rewarding students for such behavior. Parents and grandparents contribute to the curriculum design, and the school encourages them to reinforce the principles of toleration and cooperation at home. Indeed, teaching tolerance is about respecting the core humanity in each person.

In various countries, including the U.S., people are increasingly teaching about tolerance and challenging stereotypes. Some exemplary education-for-tolerance programs can be found in the following school systems:

- The Department of Education in Northern Ireland, using its program called Education for Mutual Understanding (to ensure learning of traditions, history and culture of the Protestant and Catholic communities)
- Israel's "School for Peace" at Neve Shalom/Wahat al-Salaam, a Jewish-Arab community in Israel (encounter workshops and summer camps for over 16,000 Arab and Jewish children)
- Boston public schools, where children learn about perspective taking and empathy and then write their personal stories and read them aloud in class
- On request in many locations across the United States, Teaching Tolerance, a project of the Southern Poverty Law Center, assists K-through-12 teachers and other educators in helping to promote respect for differences

RESEARCH FINDINGS ON WHAT WORKS

It is clear that all of these program efforts reflect high ideals, dedication, and serious work. There is an intellectual and moral ferment in many cities, states, and nations to find effective ways of educating for conflict resolution. In their early, highly innovative, groundbreaking years, these programs usually involved careful observation of promising developments but little evaluative research. We now turn to an instance in which systematic research has been applied to such programs and the useful lessons learned.

Evaluation of Teaching Students to Be Peacemakers Program

David Johnson and Roger Johnson have conducted 11 field research studies examining the effectiveness of the "Teaching Students to Be Peacemakers" program.[18] The research is significant because this particular program has provided the foundation for many school programs of conflict resolution that are in operation today. The students involved in the studies were from kindergarten through 10th grades, from inner city and suburban school districts in the United States and Canada. The rigorously controlled field-experimental studies addressed nine questions:

1. How often do conflicts among students occur, and what are the most commonly occurring conflicts?
2. Before training, what strategies did students use to manage their conflicts?
3. Was the peacemaker training successful in teaching students the negotiation and mediation procedures?
4. Could students effectively apply the negotiation and mediation procedures to conflicts?
5. Do students transfer the negotiation and mediation procedures to non-classroom and nonschool situations?
6. When given the option, would students engage in "winners and losers" tactics or use problem-solving negotiations?
7. Does the peacemaker training increase students' academic achievement?

8. Does the peacemaker training result in fewer discipline problems that have to be managed by the teacher and the administration?
9. Does the peacemaker training result in more positive attitudes toward managing conflict?

The conflicts that were most frequently reported were put-downs and teasing, playground conflicts, access or possession conflicts, physical aggression and fights, academic work conflicts, and friction in turn taking. The frequency of student-student conflicts that teachers had to manage dropped 80 percent after the training, and the number of conflicts referred to the principal was reduced to nearly zero. This research also supports the importance of teaching an integrative negotiation strategy: All untrained students used the win-lose strategy, and trained students primarily used a win-win integrative negotiation strategy in which both parties clearly benefited.

CONFLICT-RESOLUTION EDUCATION: ASSESSMENT HIGHLIGHTS FROM THE FIELD

Ten highlights of other research from the field are noted in a review by Bodine and Crawford:[19]

1. The Ohio School Conflict Management Demonstration Project was conducted in 17 schools between 1990 and 1993. Research showed that most students improved their attitudes toward conflict, increased their understanding of nonviolent problem solving methods, and enhanced their communication skills.
2. The Clark County Social Service School Mediation Program in Nevada reported for the 1992–1993 school year that the amount of conflict among students in the two participating elementary schools was markedly reduced and that the existence of the program helped prevent fights among students.
3. Evaluation of a mediation program in a suburban Chicago high school indicated positive results. Research shows that mediation helped to reduce instances of interpersonal conflicts. Also, most disputants and student mediators felt satisfied with every aspect of the mediation process.
4. Evaluation of the impact of the RCCP in four multiracial, multiethnic school districts in New York City showed that, in response to a survey, 84 percent of teachers reported positive changes in classroom climate.
5. Project S.M.A.R.T. (School Mediators' Alternative Resolution Team), ongoing in six New York City high schools, reported that suspensions for fighting dropped markedly in five high schools during the first year of operation. In two schools, the number of suspensions was reduced by over 40 percent; in three schools, suspensions dropped by over 60 percent.

6. An evaluation report for the New Mexico Center for Dispute Resolution Mediation in Schools program indicates that teachers in program schools witnessed less violence and hurtful behavior among students, whereas teachers in nonprogram schools reported more violence.

7. Early findings from the Harvard Graduate School of Education on the impact of the Program for Negotiators suggest that the majority of students participating in it are learning and using the basic messages taught by the program.

8. In 1991, the Peace Education Foundation (PEF) Conflict Resolution and Peer Mediation programs were initiated throughout Dade County (Florida) Region II public schools. Results from student surveys indicated that those who received training were more willing to respond to conflict situations with nonthreatening and nonviolent actions. Postintervention surveys showed significant attitude change among students toward conflict after learning the PEF model.

9. The Mediation Project of the Public Justice Department of St. Mary's University of San Antonio, Texas, has provided conflict-resolution training for middle and high schools through a school-university-community project. Early studies have shown significant decreases in disciplinary problems and student violence on school campuses.

10. Through the Lawyers Adopt-a-School Program of the American Bar Association, lawyers have successfully adopted several schools in Montgomery County, Maryland. After one year of operation, the program reported markedly reduced fighting and suspensions. As a result of the program's success, it is being replicated in sites across the country.

To date, research on the efficacy of conflict-resolution education is very encouraging. However, evidence of success of both Peaceable Classroom and process curriculum approaches is difficult to separate from general research into effective classrooms, because conflict resolution elements are either integrated into other curricula or offered as a part of the total classroom curriculum. So it is important for research and evaluation to continue in order to specify the essential elements that either alone or in combination are the active ingredients in the success of conflict resolution programs in varying contexts.

CONCLUSION

In the past decade, there has been a worldwide surge in student mediation programs, including in New Zealand, Australia, the United States, Canada, and the United Kingdom. There have been few published systematic evaluations, and some have been criticized for weaknesses in methodology. Yet the preliminary assessment of the peer mediation experiences is positive. There is growing evidence of educational value to the mediator, a high success rate of mediation, and reduction of disciplinary events in the

schools. These observations are sufficiently encouraging that further innovation and research are well justified. Learning to manage conflicts effectively without violence in
school provides a microcosm of similar issues in the world beyond the school. Hopes
are raised that divisive in-group and out-group hostility can be transcended in other
contexts.

The educational programs reviewed in this chapter are mainly oriented to helping individuals learn nonviolent modes of problem solving and how to meet basic human needs without becoming mired in bitter frustration. Valuable as this is, it does not
focus much specific attention on coping with larger patterns of prejudicial intergroup
dissension or learning about the thorny issues of war and peace. We will turn shortly
to these global problems and ways of approaching education that can encourage peaceful human relations across the broader cultural, national, and adversarial boundaries.

12

Community Service

Preparation for Socially Responsible Adulthood

BACKGROUND

There is a growing trend in education that has considerable potential for fostering constructive, unselfish behavior during adolescence: community service. Supervised community service, when started in early adolescence, can play a critical role in the shaping of responsible, caring, altruistic behavior. Service programs can be organized effectively by schools, by community organizations, and by religious institutions.

How we help others is crucial. We must not convey superiority over others. We must impart a sense of the mutuality of being full members of the community and sharing a common fate as human beings in a world that sometimes is insensitive and at times even cruel.[1]

In 1989, a Carnegie report on the middle grades, *Turning Points,* stated an important insight. Early adolescence offers a superb developmental opportunity to learn values, skills, and a sense of social responsibility important for citizenship in democracies. Every middle grade school should include youth service—supervised activity helping others in the community, ideally, in collaboration with schools—in their core instructional programs for the middle grades.[2]

Turning Points 2000, a follow-up book to the 1989 landmark report, *Turning Points,* provides an in-depth examination of how to improve education for the middle grades and gives practical guidance to practitioners wishing to implement the *Turning Points* model.[3] The research base has grown over the past 10 years, and this chapter reflects the findings of the research. It also bridges the gap between research and practice by presenting theory in practical and understandable terms. Specific to our theme of service learning, *Turning Points 2000* provides a sound argument for integrating the community into the curriculum.

SERVICE LEARNING

Mutual respect and understanding, a sense of belonging, and pride in making valued contributions to others are the essence of school and community collaboration. The Early Adolescent Helper Program (EAHP), a pioneering project initiated by the City University of New York in 1982 and led by Joan Schine, brings school personnel, community-agency staff, and the middle grade school Helpers together. An effort was clearly made to integrate the school curricula with youth in community service programs. Between 1982 and 1989, almost 700 students in 17 New York City middle and junior high schools were involved in the Early Adolescent Helper Program. In addition, school systems of Bridgeport, Connecticut, and Phoenix, Arizona, have adopted this program. These school-community program initiatives have had ground-breaking significance and launched the field of service learning.[4]

Early Adolescent Helpers are trained and assigned to work in organizations in the community that are safe and supervised by adults. These after-school placements include such organizations as Head Start and senior citizen centers. Students are given ample, systemic training prior to their community service. Their training includes seminars to help them build a knowledge base, skills, communication, and social competence. There are serious discussion and writing tasks to emphasize reflection on the community experience. Helpers also learn to take personal responsibility in daily life and to maintain appropriate dress and behavior while on assignment. Seminars also encourage young people to discuss feelings about their newfound experience of finding that they can inspire trust in others by their actions along with taking responsibility, for example, not to let others down who have come to depend on their help.

Helpers learn to listen and to trust and be trusted. They value getting to know teachers outside the classroom setting and meeting new nonparent mentoring adults in the community. They also highly value being treated as co-staff, feeling that they are contributing something valuable, and being acknowledged for their efforts and judgments. Adults report that students behave responsibly and professionally. They attend to their work dependably and with seriousness of purpose. In addition, adults note positive changes in attitudes, values, and prosocial behavior of the students.

Based on evidence of the array of positive impacts, the Carnegie Council on Adolescent Development's Task Force on Education of Young Adolescents stated in *Turning Points* that community youth service should be part of the core curriculum of middle grade education.[5] The Task Force cites Boy Scouts, Boys and Girls Clubs, Camp Fire USA, and 4-H Clubs as just a few examples of national youth organizations that give youth service an important place in their programs. These groups participate in the Youth for America program (sponsored by the Colgate-Palmolive Corporation) that gives awards to local affiliates of these organizations in recognition of their outstanding youth service.

David Hornbeck (1999), then superintendent of Philadelphia's public schools and chair of the task force that earlier produced *Turning Points*, made efforts to integrate excellent service learning into the shared common practices of all 259 public schools in Philadelphia. The school board adopted service learning as an important element of the district's promotion and graduation standards for students in elementary through high school. Project-based requirements involved the student in real-world problem solving to meet genuine community needs, and projects were tied to the academic curriculum. Comments from teachers were very encouraging. They found that when their students became actively involved in the community, they became intellectually engaged and felt personally strengthened. Teachers themselves reported feeling creative, enthusiastic, and even inspired about the work.

We saw a marked increase in service learning during the 1990s. In the early years of the twenty-first century, about 38 percent of all middle grade schools in the United States have active programs.[6] In a 1999 study of more than 1,000 sixth- through eighth-grade students by the Search Institute, it was found that when students engage in service for 31 hours or more per year, are given ample time for reflection, and hold the belief that service learning inspires interest in other academic classes, overall positive effects are achieved.[7] For example, their sense of duty to others improved along with the feeling that what they did could make a difference in another's life. To some degree, their motivation for pursuit of good grades improved (although this is not a central goal of most service learning). As a result of their opportunities for socially useful decision making and with recognition from adults, students felt more capable and valued at school.

PEER-LED PROGRAMS

Peer leadership is effective in both education and health-oriented service programs, provided that teachers and other adults appropriately supervise the peer leaders.[8] Research has shown that constructive peers can more readily reach troubled youth than can adults. Evidence shows that peer-led programs with appropriate adult backup and support can effectively reduce risky behaviors such as smoking, drug abuse, angry outbursts, and engaging in unprotected sex. They can help other students to identify and practice healthful activities. In the context of community service, we see youth leading other youth in caring activities where they help other, typically younger adolescents through tutoring, counseling, mediation, or working in day care centers or nursing homes. Typically, in peer counseling, peer tutoring, and peer mediation, the peer helpers derive measurable benefit, as do those they are helping. Again, caring adults must provide students with adequate training and supervision for this to be successful. Solid peer groups are especially helpful when stressful events occur.

AT-RISK YOUTH

It is a widely held belief that community service has special value for disadvantaged minority youth.[9] By making solid social contributions, broadening their experience beyond the inner city, and developing useful skills for future employment, these young people build greater self-efficacy and hope. It is important that service is not seen as imposed tasks or viewed in a demeaning or punitive way; rather, it should be seen as a courageous, socially valued contribution.

Campus Compact is a national higher education organization comprised of over 800 college and university presidents with a network of 28 state offices and a National Center for Community Colleges. Founded in 1985 by the presidents of Brown, Georgetown, and Stanford universities and the president of the Education Commission of the States, Campus Compact works toward bringing about public service opportunities for college and university students and integrating service experiences with undergraduate studies. The ultimate goal of Campus Compact is to help mobilize the United States to become a country of active and responsible citizens who fully promote the welfare of the democracy.[10] In January 1999, a grant of $3 million from the Pew Charitable Trusts was made to encourage civic engagement on college campuses nationwide.[11] Although rigorous research is needed to determine the nature and scope of Campus Compact's efficacy in helping at-risk youth, indications over a dozen years are clearly encouraging. Key to its success is the dependable, caring, and regular contact between disadvantaged youths and older mentors when both take the task seriously and form a solid relationship.

Another promising program, based on the highly respected Civilian Conservation Corps of the 1930s, is the Urban Youth Corps. These at-risk youth provide vital tasks by working toward rebuilding or revitalizing very poor communities. Again, outcomes have generally been positive, but additional quantitative research is required to determine more specifically the effects of these programs on at-risk students.

WHY YOUTH SERVICE?

In a major study, James Youniss and Miranda Yates find that community service is a way to encourage youths to experience themselves as moral agents, because it places them in real-life situations of personal need and social inequality.[12] It gives youths the opportunity to make a critical connection of self with society and to take part in making history. Although Youniss and Yates do not view service as a panacea for ridding society of its problems, they find service to be a powerful developmental opportunity that builds on the strengths of young people and their desire to participate constructively in society.

In a Long Island and Ontario study of 1,200 high school students, youth service was performed by one-third of the students on a regular basis through youth organizations (Boy Scouts, Girls Club, 4H), sports associations, formal charities (Heart Fund and Cancer Society), and local organizations (churches, schools, hospitals, and residential care settings for the elderly). The part-time work and the service experiences of youth provide regular, meaningful contact with adults and offer them opportunities to see themselves as members of community organizations and to identify with the aspirations and values of the community.

Despite common widespread barriers of age, class, race, and culture that can keep youth from full participation in society, evidence shows that when they are given the chance to engage in community service activities, they usually do so with enthusiasm and a high degree of commitment.[13] Because of the novelty and potential of service learning as an integral part of education, we reiterate that service programs can provide youth with the opportunity of being taken seriously as contributing members of society who engage in effective, needed, and desirable actions to solve problems. It helps youth to develop an industrious sense of efficacy, self-respect, and being valued members of the community, and this constructive orientation can be transferred to other situations.[14] These are powerful assets for adolescent development in constructive directions.

TEN IDEAS FOR THE DESIGN AND IMPLEMENTATION OF COMMUNITY SERVICE

Youniss and Yates present 10 ideas for educators, program operators, and policymakers to help them design and implement service-learning programs.[15] These recommendations are drawn from their case study of the St. Francis school-based service program and are supported by their review of empirical literature on adolescent service programs. Particular emphasis is placed on the form of service activity, the supporting curriculum, and the people with whom young people serve. Although the St. Francis data come from a school-based program, the concepts can be adapted to community-based organizations.

In addition, the authors elaborate on several standards set by the Corporation for National and Community Service and the Alliance for Service-Learning in Education Reform, which state that service activities should (1) address actual needs and that service programs should expand connectedness with the community; (2) make the mission and goals of service clearly understood to participants and staff; and (3) give youth the opportunity for reflection following their participation.[16]

Youniss and Yates also make salient pivotal ideas particular to the St. Francis program: (1) emphasize working as a group, (2) recognize the diversity and unique experiences of each participant, and (3) view service as having an important influence in the context of history and tradition.[17]

Meaningful Activity

Each St. Francis student was required to perform 20 hours of community service at a soup kitchen. Although the amount of time invested was relatively short, many students offered surprising reports 10 years later, which stated that their experience was transformational and helped to shape not only their high school identities but their present characters as well.

To make service meaningful in shaping the individual's identity, it must provide an examined experience. The young people involved need to reflect on and record their opportunities to make decisions, identify and assess their personal values, absorb appropriate criticism, and take credit for work well done. This reflection and self-evaluation component is a core aspect of the service program. Other central activities of the St. Francis students' experience include discussion with peers and adults. These discussions were considered valuable opportunities for reflection on preconceived notions about the homeless and the daily life reality of people in urgent need of help.

Students said that the homeless persons they met motivated them. They realized that their contributions were vital; the homeless needed their services, not their pity. The students benefited by such meaningful activity in several ways. Social needs were addressed; students were challenged in their ability to organize and work responsibly within routines and to set procedures; they were encouraged to engage in dialogue and useful social interaction with a diverse group of people extending beyond their prior range of experience.

Emphasis on Helping Others

The unique benefit of service is that it helps students to understand the interconnection of their lives with the lives of others.[18] The key emphasis is to encourage caring attitudes and enhance commitments to create a more just society. These opportunities foster a sense of being a part of a process larger than themselves.

Integrating Service into Educational Principles

Since 1980, there have been widespread calls for service opportunities for youth. Some advocates have suggested that there be a mandatory number of hours to be fulfilled as a requirement for high school graduation.[19] But how do we bring this aspiration to educationally meaningful fulfillment?

St. Francis integrated service into the school's educational guiding principles, as described in the school's mission statement. This was communicated to students in concrete ways through special events and yearlong visual reminders that emphasized the school's commitment to serving homeless people. At times, there was disagreement between students and faculty about this ideology. So questioning, discussion, and debate at all levels were actively encouraged and acted on.

Michelle Fine (1991) believes that service can be understood as part of the general mission of public education.[20] Her central point is to allow youth to have the experience of viewing social problems as modifiable, and to place students in active positions as participants in the process of change. She values the growing knowledge among students that flows back and forth between school and community.

Thus, service should be connected to the defining goals of the sponsoring institution (whether it is a school or community organization), it should be a part of the daily practices of the organization, and free discussion about the guiding principles should take place. Taken together, these experiences help adolescents move positively toward adulthood and responsible citizenship.

Group and Individual Action

St. Francis students were defined not only by their individual characteristics but also by their identification with a valued group, their school, teachers, and peers acting together in a mission to ameliorate injustice. Research shows the importance of group awareness, and that being a part of a group actually intensifies both short- and long-term commitment, even after the group disperses.[21] These notions run counter to some educators' belief that youth should be given a choice of service activities based on their needs and personality traits.[22]

Junior students in the St. Francis program perceived themselves as part of a tradition at the school and viewed their participation as a rite of passage. Alumni described their soup kitchen experience and the social justice course as defining experiences in their lives.

Opportunities for Reflection

Studies show that academic and reflective opportunities are valuable in supporting service.[23] Youth who participate in service should be prepared for the work, be debriefed, and then be given the opportunity to reflect on their experience. Essays, personal journals, and peer discussion groups provide strong educational support for students.

Service Organizers as Models and Integrators

In the St. Francis school, the passionate and dedicated work of two teachers, in the classroom and at the homeless shelter, served to motivate and unify the students. By living their ideals and becoming increasingly involved in the school community and service program, these educators not only had an impact on their students while in school, but also years later. In fact, alumni reported judging themselves against the criteria set in their high schools, regardless of whether they agreed with the teachers' articulated positions. These exemplary teachers remained available to their students and were authentic models of lifetime commitment to service.

Site Supervisors as Models

When service organizers are locating sites for their students, serious consideration should be given to the site supervisors. Their insight into social problems and into the ways in which they try to solve them is valuable information for students. Often, these dedicated resource people are underappreciated and underutilized; yet students tend to respond well to their guidance. At St. Francis, the service organizer actively engaged the site supervisors throughout the year through regular phone conversations and visits.

Another benefit of student interaction with site staff members involved students' critical thinking skills. For example, they were asked to report, through discussion and essays, perceptions of how two groups of staff members treated the homeless individuals. Treatment varied greatly between the two groups, largely due to their socioeconomic backgrounds and personal experiences. Although students were critical when the homeless were treated disrespectfully, they generally did not favor one group over the other. Instead, they described specific organizational practices and individual actions that they approved of and disapproved of in each group.

Students in the St. Francis program benefited from working with adults in the program who treated them respectfully, who were actively involved and interested, and who honestly shared their own experiences of service, including difficulties and ways of coping with them.

Acknowledging Participants' Diversity

Diversity (among participants, service organizers, site staff, and recipients) can be uncomfortable for students. This problem needs to be acknowledged and can be used as a focal point for education. Students may need support in coping with novel diversity.

Class, race, and gender were obvious influences in the service experience at St. Francis. For example, in the soup kitchen line, some students encountered their own friends and relatives, whereas others (from racial minorities) saw overrepresentation of their own races. In discussion groups, students tried to relate their own experiences of being prejudged or discriminated against in trying to understand the situations of the homeless. Gender issues were raised in two situations: When male students served food and perceived this activity to be female work, and when homeless middle-aged males flirted with female students. In one instance, a female student gave her phone number to a man and subsequently learned that he had previously attacked two women at a homeless shelter. The student was so distressed by the situation that she stayed home from school for a week. Service can be stressful, and students need support in coping with problems that arise.

Discussion groups were formed to consider how to address issues that arise between students and the people they serve and to practice guidance, such as how students might respond to a diner's request for a phone number. Ultimately, the St. Francis data show that ignoring issues of race, class, and gender is counterproductive. Organizers need to anticipate and address these issues directly and help to turn uncomfortable situations into learning opportunities without glossing over difficulties. After all, coping with stressful experiences is a fundamental part of personal development in moving toward adulthood.

Sense of Being a Part of History

As we have seen, one way that young people enrich their identities is through service, especially when it connects to society and to larger historical processes. Participation in the civil rights movement or the Peace Corps are examples of youth investing in service that they believe is helping to make history. However, most service is much less dramatic and may even seem trivial at times. So it is helpful to view community service in a larger social context of peace and justice approached step by step through daily constructive ideas and activities.

Three characteristics found in the St. Francis program help to promote a sense of historical significance. These are embedded in a particular religious tradition. In other settings, other traditions are applied to service.

- The course curriculum emphasized that students' actions were part of a historical Catholic perspective. Students were told that by applying the theologies of Karl Rahner and Pierre Teilhard de Chardin, they were part of an evolutionary process that was moving humanity closer to God.
- Much of the course content focused on moral exemplars in the United States. One teacher offered as a recent model the Reverend Dr. Martin Luther King, Jr., describing the impact of this leader on his own life and thereby encouraging his students to enter into a tradition of moral activism.
- An 18-year tradition of St. Francis students' working with the same soup kitchen gave these juniors a palpable experience of taking part in the school's own historical process and enduring values.

Responsibility

When students are active members in the community, a sense of responsibility is fostered, countering claims that adolescents are disdainful of the responsibilities of citizenship. Personal and social responsibilities were stressed through class work, group discussion, and essays. Students did not blindly accept the teacher's interpretation of social problems. They actively struggled with their understanding in discussion and essays. A recurrent theme is the search for ways to take social action on the moral dilemmas of poverty and injustice.

Youniss and Yates concluded that several concepts are important for youth identity development and are geared toward helping service programs motivate adolescents to become prosocial members of society. They emphasized that the following points should be seriously considered in any service program:

- Provision of opportunities to meet real social needs
- Consistency with the originating guidelines of the sponsoring organization
- Presentation of opportunities for youth to engage in serious reflection in both private and public contexts
- Selection and recruitment of program organizers and site supervisors suitable to become important adult role models and mentors
- Recognition of and thoughtful response to social diversity
- Promotion of a sense of historical significance and social accountability

A NEW AUTHORITATIVE SURVEY

For over a decade, the distinguished W. K. Kellogg Foundation has supported service learning as the key vehicle for its commitment to find ways of engaging youth in learning and becoming actively engaged community citizens. In 1998, the foundation established a major program entitled Learning in Deed: Making a Difference through Service-Learning.

In addition, in 2000, the Kellogg Foundation engaged the National Commission on Service-Learning (a part of its 1998 program) to document the status of service learning throughout the United States. The National Commission on Service-Learning was chaired by former Senator (and pioneering astronaut) John Glenn. The 18 members represented the leadership in fields of education, government, business, media, entertainment, youth service agencies, and concerned citizens. The National Commission was also cosponsored by the John Glenn Institute for Public Service and Public Policy at the Ohio State University.

The National Commission on Service-Learning (2002) provided an ethically based overview of rationale, accomplishments, and prospects in this field. It emphasized that service learning combines meaningful community service with classroom, curriculum-based learning. Service-learning opportunities are extensive. Study sites for service learning include kindergarten, elementary through high school, higher education classrooms, and community-based organizations.

In January 2002, the Commission published its final report, *Learning In Deed: The Power of Service-Learning for American Schools*. The report was aimed at policymakers, educators, and leaders in the community who are aware of the promise of service learning and want to understand more.

In this report, the Commission challenged the United States to ensure that all children—from primary through secondary grades—have the opportunity to participate in high-quality service learning as part of their formal public school education.[24] The National Commission proposed that service learning is a powerful method of engaging students in learning by offering an opportunity for young people to experience learning in a real-life context that links classroom experience with the outside world. It also builds on students' desire to become active citizens while engaging them intellectually. In the process, youth are preparing for personal and career development.[25]

Senator Glenn summarized service learning in the following ancient saying: "I hear, I forget. I see, I remember. I do, I understand."[26] In addition, he stated his belief that service learning provides a critical fourth *R*—responsibility—in addition to the traditional three *R*s of education. The major recommendation is to promote service learning as a universal public school experience.

The commission emphasizes several important reasons for implementing service learning in public education. It promotes students' academic achievement while simultaneously fostering civic participation, it improves students' social skills, and it helps to prepare youth for entering the workforce. Service learning enhances a sense of competency and promotes active engagement in improving the conditions of life. In addition, the relationship between schools and community improves along with the overall school climate.

For two decades, political leaders and policymakers nationwide have intensively sought favorable conditions for creating excellent learning practices in U.S. public schools as part of a major national reform effort. Even with high academic standards, assessment, and accountability, these steps are ineffective unless students are inspired and highly motivated to learn. White Knoll Middle School is an example of such emotional and intellectual engagement, which we discuss in the next section on the growth of service learning.

Studies show that schools involved in service learning have a more cohesive student-teacher relationship. A deeper connection to the school exists among students, whereas teachers report having more substantive conversations about teaching and learning and the best conditions under which learning occurs.[27]

Community and school connections are also strengthened through service learning. Members of the community who are directly involved with students have an altered and more positive view of young people. They begin to see them as responsible contributors and valuable resources. Another important gain is for the direct beneficiaries of service. A study showed that on "average, participants produced service valued at four times the program costs."[28]

In summary, service learning is effective in re-engaging students in academic life by giving them the responsibility for their own learning and helping them to become more interested in school activities. The standards-based reform movement is strengthened in a real-life context for learning. Students' realize that what they are learning in school has practical applications. The public purpose of education is promoted by readying students for active citizenship. Service learning builds on the existing willingness of students to become involved in their communities. Finally, it provides personal and career development. Service learning is intrinsically worthwhile and addresses some of the vital issues of our time.

The Growth of Service Learning

Community leaders, parents, school district superintendents, teachers, and students have long been among the advocates for service learning. These local level representatives are the primary agents who drive the activity.

During the past half century, service learning has broadened in U.S. schools. In the past 10 years, federal government funding has become a catalyst for this growth. In 1990, the federal government passed its first legislation to create a federal commission to award grants to states, schools, and community organizations to develop and implement service learning. In 1993, the National and Community Service Trust Act expanded this national role and gave funds to each state to bring service learning into the schools. Also, funds come from many states and school districts that are geared toward service-learning development and implementation in grades K through 12.

As recently as 2000, the Corporation for National Service's Department of Service-

Learning gave more than $20 million to support local service learning through its program Learn and Serve America. Other funders include the W. K. Kellogg Foundation, the Corporation for National Service, the Carnegie Corporation of New York, Dewitt Wallace–Reader's Digest Fund, the Ford Foundation, Ewing Marion Kauffman Foundation, Charles Stewart Mott Foundation, and Surdna Foundation.[29]

Currently, schools in all 50 states offer some service learning. A 1999 survey by the National Center for Education Statistics showed that 32 percent of all public schools had organized a service-learning program as part of their curriculum, which includes almost half of all high schools. Examples of service learning opportunities range from fourth-grade elementary students' creation of alphabet books for preschoolers to high school foreign language students' creating English vocabulary books to aid a growing population of Spanish-speaking citizens in the community. Other examples include science projects of middle school students who analyze the community water supply for pollutants and then write letters to local government officials informing them of the findings and suggesting remedial actions.[30]

A Post–September 11 Example of Service Learning

The tragic events of September 11, 2001, have inspired rich service learning experiences. The following is a remarkable example, one of many expressions of youths' concern for serious problems and their desire to be actively involved in finding solutions.

The September 11, 2001, terrorist attacks on New York City inspired students at White Knoll Middle School in West Columbia, South Carolina, to try to help a city in need. As part of their class lessons, they learned that in 1867 a New York City fire company had sent a fire wagon to firefighters in Columbia to replace equipment lost in the Civil War. A local museum had records of this gift and with it a pledge from a former Confederate soldier that the capital city of South Carolina would reciprocate if a similar tragedy were to strike New York.

Students of White Knoll decided to make good on this promise and began an effort to raise $354,000, which they successfully achieved only 2 months after the start of their campaign. This project helped to deepen the students' experience of civics, history, communications, and responsible action. This example illustrates how the service-learning approach joins community service with academic study and helps students to become responsible, caring citizens while strengthening the community bonds with the larger needs of the nation.

The ambitious goal of making service learning a universal experience for all young people in public school is outlined in four major recommendations of the National Commission on Service-Learning:[31]

1. *Reclaim the public purpose of education.* The public school mission of giving students the knowledge and skills to succeed in life and in work must be reaffirmed and felt daily in the lives of students and teachers. This can be encouraged by creating a dialogue about service learning as a strategy to promote the purpose of public education. Second, the definition of stu-

dent achievement must be expanded to include the work of students in the community. Third, cooperation must exist between schools that foster citizenship education and service learning—a kind of institutional peer learning.

2. *Increase policy, program, and financial supports for service learning in K-through-12 education.* Both school districts and states need to develop policies, programs, and financial supports—unique to their local needs—to insure high-quality service learning experiences in elementary school through high school. Service learning should be embedded into the regular activities of the school. Funds must go towards research and documentation of service learning outcomes in order to improve the practice in light of ongoing experience.

3. *Develop a comprehensive system of professional development regarding service learning.* A comprehensive system of ongoing professional development needs to be created among schools of education, education organizations, and government agencies. This system would allow teachers to form stronger linkages between their curriculum knowledge and service learning. It could be accomplished by ensuring that all preservice and accreditation programs for teachers and administrators include a service learning component. Ongoing professional development in service learning must be provided for teachers at all levels of proficiency and experience. This should include the creation of multimedia professional development, including additional Web-based teacher resources.

4. *Provide meaningful leadership roles for youth in all aspects of service learning.* Those who believe in the usefulness of service learning must first encourage adults to grant students a modicum of actual authority and responsibility in the development of service-learning projects. Second, youth must be given meaningful roles and allowed to participate in decisions at every level of development. Third, the national network of youth leaders should be expanded and supported. Fourth, youth must be given ample opportunities for reward and recognition for their real contributions to meeting community needs.

Why Promote Service Learning in Public Schools?

Studies have shown that a large percentage of students are not fully engaged in their classroom studies. Many are bored in school and have a tendency to disengage from civic activities such as voting, keeping abreast of current events, or taking an interest in the political life of the community. However, a striking and positive paradox exists. Primary and secondary school students' free time is increasingly being occupied with volunteer activities.[32] Clearly, a gap exists between students' after-school spirit of volunteerism and what actually takes place in the classroom. This is where service learning enters to address students' academic needs while retaining democratic values of contributing in a substantial way to the community. In the course of such efforts, there is an important opportunity of worldwide significance: the opportunity to get acquainted with people from diverse social backgrounds in an empathic way that moves beyond stereotypes to real people sharing a common humanity.

Although systematic research is still developing, much reliable evidence indicates the positive impact of service learning on students, schools, and communities. When service learning is explicitly linked to curriculum, students are more inclined to complete their homework. Many also show an increase in test scores and grade-point averages. School attendance increases and dropout rates decrease in association with service learning. When compared with peers who have not been engaged in service learning, students actively involved show more understanding of community needs; their understanding of politics and morality is more sophisticated; and their skills in communication and career development increase as they develop positive attitudes about work.

EVALUATION

Shirley Sagawa writes about 10 years of youth service in *The Forgotten Half Revisited*—following up on the pioneering report of the W. T. Grant Foundation.[33] The last decade has seen a development of youth service opportunities in a variety of contexts: school-based programs, community-based programs, college-based service, full-time youth service, and other specialized programs such as Youth Service and Conservation Corps and YouthBuild. Sagawa details objectives, target audiences, successes and shortcomings of each, as well as lessons learned.

Sagawa makes a strong case for service to be a part of every child's experience, describing research showing that youth service has a positive impact on character building, values formation, and academic performance. Unlike the 1980s, the United States now has a well-developed national youth service infrastructure. The public currently sees the value of youth service as a response to the challenges that young people face and the importance of its integration into learning at each level of school curriculum.

For service to become a reality for every child, Sagawa lists several commitments that must be made:

1. All funders, such as foundations, must reconsider their approaches to youth development, civic engagement, and service delivery in order to determine how youth service advances these goals.
2. Youth-serving organizations and institutions must learn how to engage young people in community service activities.
3. Educational institutions must connect service to learning in the early grades.
4. Communities should create new youth service opportunities targeted at youth in middle grades.

Sagawa suggests that these commitments can be accomplished with a relatively small financial investment and argues that primary funding should be for more than a brief pilot trial; rather, it should be enough to provide predictability and stability and for the program to be positioned to attract supplementary funding. Finally, she suggests that research and evaluation efforts are needed, especially in assessing the impacts of community service on youth at risk over a range of outcomes. Indeed, a high level of professionalism in the area of youth service is needed. Achieving this goal can be done in a way that also fosters opportunities for young people to take leadership roles responsibly, with appropriate training and supervision.

CONCLUSION

We have sampled several programs that have put youth to work in community service. Taken together, they indicate that such experiences, if well constructed in a fully educational context, can have beneficial influences in a time of developmental turbulence—and may even have a lifelong impact. In some respects, community service draws together major strands of development that we have considered earlier: the enhancement of empathy; growth of prosocial behavior; learning in cooperative modes; fostering the resolution of conflict without violence; reaching beyond the self in ways that overcome selfish, greedy orientations; and creating a sense of belonging in a valued group that is characterized by a sense of fairness and mutual aid. These are formidable assets for healthy, constructive development.

13

Media as an Educational System

Can the Media Help?

MOVIES: A POWERFUL EDUCATION
FOR BETTER AND WORSE

The media, even in democratic societies, have been faulted for glorifying violence, especially in the entertainment industry. And we have seen how the harsh use of hateful propaganda through the media, by nationalist and sectarian leaders, can inflame conflicts in many parts of the world.

The international community can support media that portray accurate information on current events, show constructive relations between different groups, and report instances in which violence has been prevented. Foundations, commissions, and universities can work with broadcasters to help provide responsible, insightful coverage of serious conflicts. For example, through constructive interactions with the Carnegie Commission on Preventing Deadly Conflict, CNN International moved to balance coverage of violence and strategies for peaceful conflict resolution. Social action for prosocial media may become an effective function of nongovernmental organizations, similar to their achievements in human rights.

Research findings have established a causal link between children's television viewing and their subsequent behavior in the United States and a variety of other countries (e.g., Australia, Finland, Israel, the Netherlands, Poland). Both aggressive and prosocial behaviors can be evoked, depending on the content of programs. There is no reason to assume that the impact of movies is substantially different. As early as age 2, children imitate behaviors (including violent behaviors) seen on television, and the effects may last into their teen years. Must violent content predominate forever? How can the media help to prevent deadly conflicts in the future?

The proliferation of media in all forms constitutes an important aspect of globalization. Films, television, print, radio, and the Internet have immense power to reach people with powerful messages, for better and worse.[1] At present, the United States is largely responsible for the output of film and television content seen by people worldwide. But advances in technology are making it increasingly feasible for media to be produced in all parts of the world—all too often with messages of hate, and they may become even more dangerous than the excessive violence in U.S. television and movies.

Films have great, unused potential for encouraging peace and for nonviolent problem solving. They entertain, educate, and constitute a widely shared experience. With the advent of videocassette players and recorders and cable TV, movies now can be seen many times, years after they are first made. At their best, movies and television can portray tender, loving human relations, and considerate accommodation of one group by another in a sense of fairness and mutual benefit.

Films have the potential to teach important lessons about the prevention of deadly conflicts. A good example is the 2001 commercial film *Thirteen Days,*[2] about the Cuban missile crisis. It is a popular film that combines entertainment and education. It provides dramatic entertainment—looking into the abyss of nuclear war—that also has educational value in preventing the deadliest of all conflicts. It conveys its messages with strong emotional impact that enhances the likelihood of their being remembered. What are these messages?

1. The nature of the threat: the possibility of millions of people being killed through escalation of conflict to Berlin and even to a general nuclear war.
2. The personal relation of these losses to families and deep attachments, which makes the message more emotionally meaningful as actors portray their serious concerns over their own families.
3. The critical issues of leadership: Decision making is used to prevent catastrophe, illuminating factors that help leaders make rational, problem-solving decisions, including
   a. getting a broad base of information pertinent to the threat.
   b. analyzing this information carefully from many perspectives, taking into account the reliability and biases of different sources.
   c. constituting and using an advisory group manifesting high competence and freedom of expression in the group, with an emphasis on getting the facts straight and formulating policy options objectively on the basis of these facts.
   d. considering carefully multiple options for mutual accommodation with the opponent.
   e. not jumping to conclusions or violent actions before these steps have been taken.
4. The crucial importance of civilian control over the military—a funda-

mental element of democratic societies—while making thoughtful use of the knowledge and experience of military professionals.

5. Flexibility and creativity in considering various ways of meeting the needs of each adversary, including an emphasis on win-win strategies and helping an adversary off a dangerous limb without losing face or suffering humiliation. This may involve the use of Track 2 diplomacy—an informal process of listening to intentions of adversaries in order to find a solution to conflict. This back channel of communication works in parallel with official channels.

6. Putting the danger in a larger context with a humane worldview. The film ends with an excerpt from President Kennedy's American University speech of June 1963, emphasizing our common humanity and mortality, seeking to learn from the near-global catastrophe of the Cuban Missile Crisis—and reaching out to the adversary to consider ways of permanently reducing the nuclear danger. We quote a part of this great speech in our Epilogue.

Movies cannot become a substitute for history texts and classes, but they can be a valuable stimulus to historical curiosity and inquiry. They can also reach a very broad audience, stimulate interest in the lessons of history, and prompt people to do further reading on their own. In this example, the focus is on settling exceedingly dangerous disputes without war. Dealing thoughtfully with this vital subject could, in the future, contribute significantly to education in this field. As technology permits the cost of movie making to decrease, filmmakers in poor countries (often war torn) may contribute. It is important to bear in mind that a major segment of movie audiences consists of adolescents.

By lowering the costs and making films accessible on the Internet as well as in theaters and on TV, digital video may change the economics of film production and the relationship between producers and consumers. In the future, as digital video technology becomes cheaper, filmmaking will likely become more widely accessible in all countries. This, in turn, will offer more opportunities for children to see life in different cultures, to grasp the diversity of human societies, and to acquire an authentic worldview. Already, documentaries like the recent *Behind the Veil* (about the plight of Afghan women) have been filmed with small digital cameras and shown on international cable television. This gives, for example, unique insight to girls in Europe, North America, and Japan into the problems of female repression. It is now possible for anyone who owns a personal computer and a digital video camera to make movies and distribute them over the Internet. As the Internet merges with television, any kind of film will be readily available on demand to anyone at minimal cost. Consumers can search by subject matter for what they want and order it for instant viewing. Movie theaters will continue to exist, but they may become more like stage theaters, for specialized audiences.[3] This will provide important opportunities for organizations concerned with human rights, democracy, and just peace. The technological advances will greatly enrich the range of opportunities for children to grasp other cultures, different ways of life, and the underlying common humanity of meeting basic needs for adaptation.

THE INFLUENCE OF TELEVISION

A former member of the Federal Communications Commission stated, "All television is educational television. The only question is, what is it teaching?"[4] A wide variety of studies show that violence on television has a causal effect on aggressive behavior of children and adolescents—with long-term effects. After 22 years, young people who had frequently viewed violent television in childhood were still very aggressive and more likely to be convicted of serious crimes than those who had less exposure to television violence as children.[5] Such studies have accumulated over the years, including comprehensive reports by the U.S. surgeon general. An illuminating new report deserves attention.[6] The good news is that television also has the capability of influencing the behavior of children in a positive direction, as shown in experimental studies in both laboratory and natural settings. We present the evidence and potential of prosocial television in this chapter.

Growing Up with Television

We need not repeat here the extensive evidence that has linked TV viewing of violent content with aggressive behavior in children and adolescents. There is a rich research literature on this subject.[7] Television programming has a clear impact on the behavior of both young and older children, and prosocial programming elicits prosocial behavior. Most influential, in schools, is a combination of television programming, actual role-playing of behavior shown on TV, and verbal labeling. The results are applicable in other settings. However, long-term effects of television on prosocial behavior need more attention.

Concerns about television's effects and the effects of television violence date back to 1946, when television first became a household item. The U.S. surgeon general wrote in 1972, "Televised violence, indeed, does have an adverse effect on certain members of our society."[8] Throughout the years, similar conclusions have been reached by such highly respected professional organizations as the American Psychological Association (APA) and the American Academy of Pediatrics. The American Psychiatric Association concluded recently that "the data point overwhelmingly to a causal connection between media violence and aggressive behavior in some children."[9] Despite agreement among experts that violence in the media contributes to actual real-world violence, the message has not been fully assimilated by the public. This is partly due to news reports that downplay the evidence for these effects. This diluted treatment by the news media has served to perpetuate the debate about the effects of television violence and aggression. It can be likened to the cigarette smoking/cancer debate that went on much longer than necessary, given the scientific community's awareness that lung cancer and some other cancers were caused by smoking.[10]

Rather than only relying on a single method for evaluating the effects of media on aggression, researchers now use a triangulation strategy to examine the problem. The rationale is that using different methodological approaches produces a clearer picture than using just one method. Four approaches have been used to investigate the hypothesis that exposure to media violence increases aggression. Each one shows a positive connection:

1. Laboratory experiments yield a slightly larger effect than the other types of studies.
2. Field experiments show causal effects in naturalistic settings.
3. Cross-sectional studies show a positive link between violence in the media and different kinds of aggression in the real world (e.g., assault).
4. Longitudinal studies show long-term, substantial effects of early exposure to media violence on the incidence of acts of aggression later in life. Recent evidence also indicates that violent video games produce a similar effect on aggression.[11]

Overall, the effects of media violence on society are clear. Children exposed to violent television are prone to acts of aggression in real-world situations. Holding social class constant does not alter the relationship between TV viewing of violence and aggression. It is true, however, that lower parental education and socioeconomic status are associated with more aggression in children, more TV viewing and more viewing of violence, greater belief by both children and parents in the realism of television violence, and greater identification with television characters. In general, the relationship between television violence or prosocial behavior and subsequent viewer behavior holds in a variety of countries. Cross-national research includes Australia, Finland, Israel, the Netherlands, Poland, and the United States.[12]

What is the process by which TV viewing influences children's behavior? One element is *arousal*. In the area of aggression, researchers focus on the heightened state of tension, with a physiological component, that results from observing high-action sequences. Another important element is *observational learning* as children see their favorite characters solve problems in either an aggressive or a cooperative way. The more frequently the child rehearses the sequence by continued viewing, the more likely it is to be remembered and reenacted. Finally, by consistently observing either aggressive or prosocial behavior, the child comes to believe that these are expected, appropriate ways of behaving.

Research shows that television need not be a forum for violence. Rather, it can be used to teach positive intergroup relations. Educators, psychologists, policymakers, and parents can promote constructive uses of the media to portray human diversity in positive ways, and to teach skills that are vital to children's social development. Some of these efforts are known as media literacy.[13]

Sesame Street, an example of highly effective and positive use of children's television, began airing in the United States in 1969. It is now seen in more than 140 countries. It depicts constructive, respectful, and enjoyable situations of social tolerance, which help young children learn such behavior. In fact, research shows that children who see examples of cross-group friendships are more likely to form such friendships than children who have not seen them.[14] Because of *Sesame Street*'s groundbreaking, worldwide role, we explore it in some detail later in this chapter.

Another example of constructive programming is seen in the 1995 initiative of the Carnegie Corporation of New York and the Voice of America then led by Geoffrey Cowan. This Conflict Resolution Project introduced to television audiences worldwide the principles and practices of conflict resolution. Journalists produced stories that involved efforts of local citizens to resolve their disputes, improve relations between groups, and promote peace efforts.

A comparable effort was seen in BBC (British Broadcasting Corporation) Radio's educational series on democracy for Russian audiences shortly after the cold war ended. Ted Koppel, of ABC's (American Broadcasting Corporation's) *Nightline*, also produced programs on U.S.–Soviet relations during the cold war, on Israeli-Palestinian relations with regard to peace in the Middle East, and on South Africa during apartheid. These programs depicted rational, civil discourse among adversaries and highlighted possibilities for fair settlements.

The development of independent media has played a major role in the democratization of postcommunist states, albeit with resistance on the part of some governments. Research shows that international support positively affects the norms and practices of postcommunist media by assisting them in becoming more professional and believable and helping them to join the international media community.[15]

Television and Violence: How Viewing Habits in Adolescence and Adulthood Affect Aggressive Behavior

Edward Donnerstein has studied effects of viewing violence on television under various conditions.[16] The 1993 final report of the American Psychological Association's Commission on Violence and Youth (*Violence and Youth*)[17] shows how effects of watching television violence can be moderated. Parents and educators play a large role by teaching children to watch television violence with a critical eye, and helping them to distinguish between fact and fiction in portrayals of violence. Unrealistic behaviors, such as violence without negative consequences, can also be made salient. A particularly effective approach to teaching young people nonviolent conflict resolution is through adults' expressions of disapproval of violence as a solution to problems, and their subsequent presentation of peaceful alternatives. These are elements of teaching media literacy.

Results of a recent study published in *Science*, the journal of the American Association for the Advancement of Science, show additional links between television viewing and violence.[18] Columbia University's Jeffrey G. Johnson and collaborators in the New York State Psychiatric Institute reported on a student spanning 17 years, of a group of children from approximately 700 families in two northern New York counties.

This community-based longitudinal investigation examines whether television viewing in adolescence and early adulthood is associated with increased likelihood of aggressive behavior. In order to measure adequately this association, it was necessary to examine TV viewing and aggressive behavior repeatedly during adolescence and adulthood, and determine also the environmental and personal characteristics that could underlie this association.[19]

The report is unique for several reasons. First, it deals with adolescent and young adult populations, whereas most research of this kind has been conducted on children. Second, it links watching television in general (as opposed to just watching television with violent content) to violent behavior. And third, the report shows an increased likelihood for adolescents and young adults to commit aggressive acts later in life if, as adolescents, they watched more than 3 hours of television per week.[20] Still, these findings are correlational, not experimental, meaning the cause and effect relationship is not proven. But the findings are strongly suggestive.

This community-based longitudinal study involving 707 families was begun when the children were 1 to 10 years of age. In this 17-year study, families (91 percent white and 54 percent Catholic) were asked about their television viewing habits. Several assessments were made of the children's violent behavior. Detailed questionnaires were completed by a random group of youngsters (in the year 2000) in which they answered questions about a wide range of violent behavior. Scientists also had at their disposal reports from New York State and the Federal Bureau of Investigation, regarding arrests and charges for adult criminal behavior.[21]

These interviews were conducted at regular intervals. The years and average ages of the individuals were as follows:[22]

Year of Interview	Average Age
1975	5.8
1983	13.8
1985–1986	16.2
1991–1993	22.1
2000	30

Time spent watching television was associated with subsequent aggressive behavior whether or not a history of aggressive behavior existed in the individual. Although aggressive individuals may spend somewhat more time watching TV than do other individuals, this tendency does not explain the prevalent association between TV viewing and aggressive behavior.[23]

This longitudinal study is important for several reasons:

1. It is the first published longitudinal study indicating that exposure to television in adolescence and early adulthood leads to aggression in later years. This indicates that it is not just young children who are uniquely affected by violence in the media. So, it adds to existing research that links childhood television viewing habits to aggression and violence in adulthood.
2. The large sample size (of just over 700 families) and the length of time that the individuals were followed (17 years) allowed for a meaningful test of television exposure on aggressive behavior (such as assault and robbery).
3. Investigators were able to rule out many alternative explanations for aggressive behavior (for example, childhood neglect, family income, neighborhood violence, parental education, and psychiatric disorders) by statistically controlling for these important childhood factors.

Although the research literature shows that many factors in development influence aggressive behavior, there is little remaining doubt that many people are affected by media violence and that interventions such as media literacy for adolescents as well as children may help to reduce the rate of violence in today's society.[24] This research enhances our motivation to find ways of diminishing exposure to violence in childhood and adolescence, to enhance media literacy as part of education, and to provide much more prosocial programming like *Sesame Street*—not only for young children but for adolescents.

Can TV Be Used to Teach Prosocial Behavior?

Nancy Eisenberg and Paul Mussen of the University of California at Berkeley cite a pioneering 1973 study by L. K. Friedrich and A. H. Stein of children aged 3 to 5 showed that, regardless of the economic class, prosocial television elicited prosocial behavior. Over a 4-week period, children were divided into three groups: The first group watched aggressive cartoon programs (*Batman, Superman*), the second group watched prosocial programs (*Mr. Roger's Neighborhood*), and the third group watched programs with neutral content, neither aggressive nor prosocial. The positive effects seen in the children who watched the prosocial programs could still be observed 2 weeks after the experiment ended.[25] To enhance the beneficial effects of prosocial television programming, researchers have found that it should be combined with other experiences such as role-playing (of enacted events on the program) and verbal labeling (discussion of television show events and identification of feelings and behaviors of the characters).[26] In another study involving kindergarten-aged children, children were assigned to one of the following combinations:

1. Prosocial television and role-playing
2. Prosocial television and verbal labeling
3. Prosocial television and verbal labeling and role-playing
4. Prosocial television and irrelevant activity
5. Neutral television and irrelevant activity

The investigators tested the children on their learning of the program content, the generalization of the learning to other situations, and actual helping behavior. The hypothesis was upheld: Prosocial programs had positive effects. Tests of generalization showed that children exposed to prosocial television programming made more prosocial responses that those who saw the neutral programs. However, there were no gains in helping behavior as a result of simply watching prosocial television. But helping behavior was significantly enhanced by a combination of prosocial TV and role-playing. The tendency of girls to assist others was increased by verbal labeling and role-playing. Yet boys' helping behavior was not increased by verbal labeling. The results of these investigations suggest the applicability of experimental techniques to naturalistic settings.

Repeated exposure to prosocial television among preschool-aged children showed that both genders became more cooperative than children exposed to episodes of the same television series that lacked prosocial content. In the same study, children who participated in role-taking activities but were not exposed to either prosocial or neutral television had an increase in helping behavior that went beyond those of children who were only exposed to the programming. Still, it is established that there are positive influences of exposure to prosocial programs, and these effects can be generalized to other situations (beyond situations portrayed on television).[27] The conclusion is that preschool children are positively affected by prosocial television, but these influences are less powerful than the effects of specially designed school programs, training in empathetic role-taking, or the combination of prosocial television, role-playing, and verbal labeling. Prosocial television can be a supportive element to other training when attempting to influence the tendencies of children toward prosocial behavior.[28]

Older children respond in similar fashion in both experimental laboratory and natural settings. The results showed that those older children who were exposed to programs showing constructive behavior were more apt to behave in a prosocial or helping manner. These were mostly brief TV exposures. What are the effects of prolonged viewing of prosocial TV (such as regular viewing of the *Sesame Street* series) over months or years by younger children? It seems that such effects would be stronger. But opportunities to collect such data in the real world are all too sparse. Yet the day may come when this will change for the better.

Eisenberg and Mussen believe that older children, at a more advanced cognitive developmental stage, probably pay closer attention and can make more generalizations from what they have observed.[29] They may be able to remember and use these generalizations when called to perceive others' needs and to act cooperatively. There is potential value in combining prosocial television with other constructive experiences to increase children's helpful orientations and actions.

There are now multiple video technologies that offer tangible promise for education, with more to come. In principle, education from the early years onward can utilize multiple media, taking into account the distinctive strengths and limitations of each medium—television, videocassettes, video games, computers, and books. One method of instruction is not necessarily the best for teaching every subject. Television is good for presenting physical transformations and spatial relations as well as vividly portraying actions. But print is stronger in presenting the thoughts of a person. Video games are better than television in giving a child a sense of what it is like to make a discovery—though many of these are far too violent. The videocassette recorder (VCR), which has spread so widely for entertainment purposes, also has much potential for education. Unlike on-air television, the VCR can be stopped to analyze a specific scene; a teacher can rewind to an earlier scene to clarify a thematic connection; portions can be viewed in slow motion for close inspection—for example, to consider interpersonal or intergroup relations. In short, many opportunities arise from systematic, explicit consideration of television and related technologies for educational use—and using these to expand the child's view of the world in developmentally appropriate ways. In the next chapter, we consider the strengths and limitations of the Internet in this context.

Evidence of Beneficial Effects of Television

There is research evidence that television need not be a school for violence but can indeed by used in a way that reduces intergroup hostility. We need to consider carefully the constructive use of this powerful tool to promote compassionate understanding, nonviolent problem solving, and decent intergroup relations. Television can portray human diversity while highlighting shared human experiences—including the common humanity of our adversaries, even in times of stress. But so far, we have had only glimpses of its potential for reducing intergroup conflict.

There is growing scientific evidence of the educational capacity of television in a variety of contexts. The research is encouraging, even though it has only been a few decades since behavioral scientists began intensive efforts to study the potential advantages of using television in education. There are several key findings:[30]

1. Television can teach a wide range of skills and behaviors that are important for the intellectual and interpersonal development of children. For example, *Sesame Street* teaches various skills needed by children, especially children from poor communities, to enter the early grades comfortably. *The Electric Company* helps children who are failing to learn to read in the early grades; the program facilitates reading skills that help such students keep up and also tends to increase their self-esteem—a process that has general significance for later learning.

2. Television can stimulate interest in what children need to learn. For example, *3-2-1 Contact* stimulates curiosity about scientific inquiry and problem solving in the upper elementary school grades. Such stimulation can be especially useful for girls and minority children who have historically been turned off to science and math by teachers and other authority figures who have held low expectations of these youngsters' academic success.

3. Television can both entertain and educate simultaneously. This is vividly illustrated by *Sesame Street*; we will look at that experience shortly.

4. The involvement of parents, older siblings, or teachers in the young child's television viewing increases substantially the child's learning. Discussing with a child what has been observed can reinforce and shape the direction of learning.

5. Television can open the eyes of children to the world around them. It can stimulate interest in other cultures and respect for human diversity.

6. Research shows a variety of countries using television in education effectively. In Asia and Latin America as well as Europe, many nations have much educational programming on the air. In some of them, mothers and teachers are systematically involved in sharing these experiences—and the educational benefits are impressive.

Mexico has had remarkable success in using the soap opera format to encourage family planning and literacy. For instance, a government instruction project in which people with reading skills taught others how to read with material prepared for the purpose attracted 99,000 people before television was used to spread the word. However, when a soap opera appeared on Mexican television featuring a story about people forming a reading self-instruction group, there was a sharp increase of interest. While the TV series was on the air, 840,000 Mexicans enrolled in the national self-instruction project. The next year, 400,000 people took part in the project. A similar televised format fostered societywide family planning in addressing the nation's burgeoning population growth. This, too, elicited widespread interest.

SESAME STREET: A UNIQUE EDUCATIONAL PROGRAM   Professor Gerald Lesser of Harvard University summarized features of *Sesame Street* that are of interest in this context. The series originated in the United States but now appears in 140 other countries. Each program is fitted to the language, culture, and traditions of a particular nation. The atmosphere of respect for differences permeates all of *Sesame Street*'s many versions.

Research from many countries is encouraging. For example, the Canadian version of *Sesame Street* shows many sympathetic instances of English- and French-speaking children playing together. Research from Canada clearly shows that both English- and French-speaking children who see these examples of cross-group friendships are more likely to actually form such friendship than Canadian children who do not see them. The same is true for Dutch, Moroccan, Turkish, and Surinamese children who see *Sesamstraat* in Holland. The findings suggest that appealing and constructive examples of social tolerance help young children to learn such behavior.

The creators of *Sesame Street* defined specific educational goals to emphasize in the series, which was designed to open children's minds to the value of differences among people and to

1. show children a variety of alternative ways to resolve conflicts without resorting to violence.
2. teach children to take another person's point of view, socially or emotionally.
3. teach children how to listen.
4. show children examples of cooperation: sharing, reciprocity, negotiation, compromise, taking turns.
5. show children constructive ways to enter social groups and constructive steps to overcome feelings of exclusion.
6. focus on self-esteem—a sense of identity and personal worth based partly on respect earned through competence and including persistent coping in the face of frustration.

Recent research permits us to look closely at this pioneering and virtually unique program.[31] *Sesame Street* began in 1969 as an experiment in children's educational television and continues in this vein to the present day. The merging of broadcaster and researcher is a remarkable feature of this highly innovative program. *Sesame Street* was the first series based on such collaboration to systematically teach a curriculum to young children (with special attention to low-income and minority families). The driving force was "to foster intellectual and cultural development in preschoolers" and help them to become ready for school.[32] The close, ongoing collaboration of content experts, television producers, and educational researchers made it a reality. *Sesame Street* also made possible systematic studies on the impact of educational television for children.

Two kinds of evaluative research, formative and summative, helped to guide and assess the value of *Sesame Street* in the areas of school readiness and social development in both domestic and foreign programming. The following summarizes a recent synthesis of research on the impact of *Sesame Street* on preschool children, especially considering data of longitudinal studies.

Several landmark studies show *Sesame Street's* influence on children's performance in literacy, mathematics, and other academic subjects. There is particular emphasis on longitudinal studies that examine the effect of preschool viewing on later school performance and academic skills. These studies give less attention to interpersonal and social aspects and focus on cognitive features.

Early research on the impact of *Sesame Street* showed that children who watched it regularly made significant improvement in a variety of cognitive skills. The Educational Testing Service (ETS) conducted two studies in 1970 and in 1971.[33] The first study tested nearly 1,000 children aged 3 to 5 from diverse geographical and ethnic backgrounds, most of whom were from disadvantaged backgrounds. For 6 months, these children were either encouraged or not encouraged to watch *Sesame Street*. Before and after exposure, the children were tested on their knowledge of the alphabet, names of body parts, knowledge of relational terms, and skills that involved sorting and classification. Children who did the most viewing had the greatest gains in their pre- and post-test scores. The more a topic was emphasized (for example, letters), the greater the effect.

The second ETS study was divided into two sections: The first part repeated the earlier study and used newly revised programs with an expanded educational curriculum. This test confirmed the earlier results. The second part of the study examined about one-quarter of the children from the initial study, half of whom had begun school in the interim. They were tested on verbal readiness, quantitative readiness, attitude toward school, and relationship with peers. Results showed that teachers rated frequent *Sesame Street* viewers as being better prepared for school than those who did no or little viewing.

Cook and his colleagues argued that their own research showed that it was not the viewing of *Sesame Street* alone that produced the positive effects, but a combination of viewing and adult involvement.[34] Research that followed confirmed that parents who watch television with their children have an effect on their learning.[35] However, in the reanalysis of ETS results by Cook and colleagues, it was found that parental involvement had an effect but the ETS results still remained statistically significant, which showed that *Sesame Street* had made a significant contribution in its own right, as well as by mobilizing parents.

Three recent studies on the impact of *Sesame Street* showed outcomes similar to those of the earlier studies.

Wright and Huston (1995).   This 3-year longitudinal study, which tracked approximately 250 low-socioeconomic-status children beginning at either age 2 or age 4, considered the viewing of all television, including *Sesame Street*, and other non-television-related activities (e.g., reading, music, video games).[36] Results indicated that preschoolers who watched educational television, particularly *Sesame Street*, spent more of their time engaged in reading and other educational activities. They also scored higher than their peers on age-appropriate standardized achievement tests in letter and word knowledge, mathematics skills, vocabulary size, and school readiness. Bogatz and Ball (1971) also found long-term effects. Teachers rated these *Sesame Street* viewers as well-adjusted to school.[37]

Zill, Davies, and Daly (1994).   Using data in a national survey of parents of approximately 10,000 children, this correlational study found that preschool *Sesame Street* viewers were more likely to recognize the alphabet and to tell connected stories when they pretended to read, and in the course of doing so recognized letters of the alphabet. The strongest effects were in low-income families.[38] Also, on entering the first and second grades, these children were more likely to be reading independently and less likely to need remedial instruction. No causal relationship between watching *Sesame Street* and these various educational outcomes can be definitively stated, because the data are correlational. However, they are consistent with the results from the Wright and Huston study.

Anderson, Huston, Wright, and Collins (1998).   A recontact study examined nearly 600 high school students who either watched or did not watch *Sesame Street* as preschoolers.[39] Results indicated that those high school students who did watch *Sesame Street* as preschoolers had higher grades in mathematics, science, and English. Boys who watched *Sesame Street* 5 days per week as preschoolers benefited more than boys who had not watched it as preschoolers. Girls showed similar positive gains, though slightly less than boys. Also, teenage boys and girls who had viewed *Sesame Street* in preschool were more frequent users of books, exhibited higher academic self-esteem, and placed more value on academic performance.

Research shows that the overall positive impact of *Sesame Street* occurred immediately, once the child entered school, and continued over the years—perhaps influencing a young person's love of learning as far as high school. In the context of this book, an important line of research has to do with effects on social behavior. Since the beginning, *Sesame Street* has kept its emphasis on fostering both social and academic skills. This orientation to social interactions and social units has been continued and expanded in recent research.[40] Leading educators and psychologists were consulted in the creation of several broad categories for programming:

- Affective: to include emotions, pride, and self-esteem
- Social interactions: to include friendship, conflict resolution, cooperation, sharing, turn taking, entering social groups
- Human relations: to include diversity, differing perspectives, different cultures (e.g., African, Indian, Asian, and Latino Americans, Spanish language, children with disabilities)

A study done in the mid-1970s examined children's modeling social behavior after exposure to a *Sesame Street* series.[41] These 3- and 4-year-old children were given pre- and post-tests on their level of cooperation. The outcome revealed a greater degree of cooperative behavior among viewers than nonviewers. However, test situations were similar to those found in the *Sesame Street* programs, and results did not generalize to prosocial behavior during free play.

Other studies conducted in the 1970s found similar results—that children exhibited prosocial behavior specifically related to the *Sesame Street* segment viewed, but that the same behavior did not transfer to situations of free play.[42] However, aggressive behavior in children was reduced during free play on the same day that they viewed a 30-minute videotape of prosocial segments.[43] The recent experiments of I. E. Zielinska and B. Chambers, conducted in eight day care centers, showed that the central effect of viewing prosocial segments of *Sesame Street* was an increase in prosocial play activities, whether or not viewing was followed by related activities or discussion.[44] Also, in support of Bankart and Anderson's 1979 study, those same viewers who subsequently engaged in cooperative follow-up activities showed the lowest rates of antisocial behavior during free play.[45]

Six specific topics relating to social issues were dealt with, usually in one episode each. Experts in relevant fields guided the development of each episode, followed by (smaller scale) research to follow up on the material understood by preschool children. Death, love, marriage, pregnancy, race relations, and divorce were the included topics. Children showed an increased understanding in each area. Of particular interest was the area of race relations, where parental approval of intergroup friendships was found to be very influential.

Indicators are clear that *Sesame Street* exerts a positive influence on children's social behavior. Because it is difficult to measure social behavior precisely, findings are not as uniform as those in the areas of literacy or school readiness. But this remarkable program and the extensive research on its follow-up give reason for hope that television can indeed make a positive contribution to human relations.

SESAME STREET AROUND THE WORLD   Shortly after *Sesame Street*'s first broadcast in the United States, in November 1969, producers from Mexico, Canada, Brazil, and Germany separately approached Children's Television Workshop (CTW) because they saw the value of *Sesame Street* and wanted to bring similar programs to their countries' children—ones that would address their specific educational requirements. The producers devised a flexible production plan that would address these needs, and it is used to this day to create international *Sesame Street* productions. The result is that the programming is essentially the same as in the United States, but programs are set in contexts that address the local values, cultural attributes, and educational priorities of each country. Major adaptations have been devised in several countries, among them Brazil, China, Germany, Norway, Mexico, Poland, Russia, and Spain.[46]

The coproduction process involves two stages in each country. First, feasibility and the need for the production are determined. Then the production team gathers a group of local educational specialists from various fields (e.g., child development, child language, cultural studies, sociology, music, cognitive development, and literacy) to discuss educational priorities and to develop a plan.

Although common elements of the curricula include numeracy, literacy, and perceptual skills, each country has its unique aspects. For example, China incorporates aesthetics into a section of the curriculum; the joint Israeli-Palestinian program teaches children about mutual respect (we will address this in greater detail in the following section). And the series in Russia prepares Russian young people for life in a new free society. The series is thus capable of addressing both broad curricular areas and specific educational needs of the world's diverse regions.

Just as in the domestic version of *Sesame Street*, both formative and summative research is conducted on the impact of *Sesame Street* coproductions. Formative research has looked at a wide range of topics. For example, children view segments or entire episodes, and their reactions to studio sets and characters are considered. Researchers note children's viewing behavior and attention as well as their comprehension. Production teams use these results to refine individual segments and gather more general information about future productions.

Summative evaluations have also broadened the understanding of *Sesame Street*'s value. Studies have examined the scope and the appeal of the program. In a Netherlands study, ratings, parent and teacher interviews, and observations of children's attention were used to determine the degree to which *Sesamstraat*'s first season reached Dutch and Belgian audiences.[47] It was found that over 50 percent of all children between the ages of 3 and 6 had some access to the program, and it was a program most frequently mentioned by parents when asked to name their child's three favorite programs. Dutch teachers, however, suggested that the pacing of the program was too fast. Several recommendations grew from this study that related to pacing, the quality of characters' voices, the way objectives and educational goals were presented, appropriateness of the series for the target audience, and the schedule of broadcasts.

Another summative study done in the early 1970s in Mexico was one of the earliest and most comprehensive. It was a controlled experimental study of over 200 children.[48] Children who had viewed *Plaza Sésamo* regularly performed better than their nonviewing peers on tests of general knowledge, numbers, letters, and word skills. Similar findings were shown nearly 20 years later in studies done in Turkey and again in two cities in Mexico, with additional gains in areas of ecology, nutrition, and hygiene in the Mexico City group.[49]

In Russia, the program's impact was evaluated in an area beyond the broadcast region. Children viewed videotaped versions of each of the 65 episodes and were compared with children who viewed animated Russian fairy tales. After 6 months of watching *Ulitsa Sezam*, viewers had more quickly developed basic numeracy and literacy skills, along with some social gains, compared with their nonviewing peers.[50]

To summarize, the strongest findings historically and cross-culturally are in areas of literacy and numeracy. Also, some of the studies focus primarily on academic rather than social skills because of the difficulty in quantifying social skills. Although the findings in social development are generally positive, they are uneven, and this signifies the need for improvement of research design and measures in the social domain.

Overall, significant effects in the United States and in other countries have been found on children's *academic skills* and *social behavior* as a result of exposure to *Sesame Street*. Several points of particular interest deserve attention.

1. It is remarkable that television, particularly *Sesame Street*, can be effective in encouraging a wide range of academic and social skills among young children.
2. Research has shown that effects last in the range of 1 to 12 years.
3. International and domestic programming support the effectiveness of the coproduction model in consistency of effects. Targeted audiences are successfully reached and positively influenced primarily because of the cultural relevance of each particular coproduction.
4. From a historical perspective, it is interesting that the same types of effects found in the early 1970s are true in the 1990s. *Sesame Street* has continued to evolve. It has constantly been updated to change with the times, reflecting best practices in education.

Educational television can be developed in ways that reduce intergroup hostility in different cultures, as research on *Sesame Street* has demonstrated. The world has only scratched the surface in the constructive use of this powerful tool to promote understanding among different cultures and to convey nonviolent ways of coping with life's frustrations. One such effort, developed under exceedingly difficult conditions, is described next.

Israeli-Palestinian Sesame Street.   *Rechov Sumsum* (*sumsum* is the Hebrew word for *sesame*) is the Israeli coproduction of *Sesame Street*, which began broadcasting in 1983. It consisted of nearly 200 half-hour programs aimed at a target audience of Israeli Jewish and Arab preschool children. During the Gulf War, with the permission of CTW, the characters from *Rechov Sumsum* were seen daily—often for hours at a time—to help comfort frightened children. Three years later, in 1986, a study was conducted on 120 5- and 6-year-old preschool Jewish children who watched series segments that focused on social tolerance (with primarily Arab characters). The majority of these children, from lower- to middle-income Tel Aviv neighborhoods, reacted positively and displayed tolerance toward the characters who spoke languages other than Hebrew. It was an experiment done in a natural setting.

In 1994, when the peace process between Israelis and Palestinians was under way, CTW and the Ministry of Education's Israel Educational Television planned a coproduction and broadcast 65 new episodes of *Rechov Sumsum*. These new episodes focused on Israeli-Palestinian understanding, respect, and tolerance. Also, new curricula in Hebrew and Arabic were developed to help Israeli and Palestinian children learn about each other's cultures.

CTW assisted in identifying and training young Palestinian producers and writers, with the goal of having the project evolve into a full Israeli-Palestinian coproduction. On April 1, 1998, the first program of Israeli-Palestinian *Sesame Street* was broadcast in

Israel and to parts of the Palestinian Autonomous Region. Segments were produced by both Israelis and Palestinians and spoken in both Arabic and Hebrew. Simultaneously, the Palestinian version of the program premiered on Palestinian Educational TV.[51] This Israeli-Palestinian *Sesame Street*, called the *Kids for Peace Project*, lasted for just over one year, with generally positive results. It was aimed at children aged 3 to 7. The *Sesame Street Kids for Peace Project* is a sophisticated television production that can appeal to young children across adversarial boundaries and contribute to long-term relations between groups. Although they recognize that deep-seated animosities and inflammatory political leadership can, in the short term, overwhelm the positive attitudes shaped by such television programming, the producers believe that their model is useful elsewhere, especially in regions where chronic violence has not become the norm.

At the time of this writing (late 2003), the peace process has broken down. Daily violence occurs, some of it quite serious, and international efforts to foster conflict resolution are minimal. In this exceedingly hostile context, such a program cannot thrive. But it may come back to life again if the peace process resumes in a serious, sustained way. In any event, the creative lessons learned from this experience may be adapted to other hot spots in the world where the depth of hostility is not so severe.

Another Encouraging Exploration

Evidence shows that children and adolescents learn much about other groups by watching television. Unfortunately, much of what they learn is about violence. Violence is vividly presented as an effective way of solving problems: The source of difficulty is removed in a way that may be attractive because it evokes bravery or boldness or skill. Adverse consequences of such actions, however, are often left out. But this is not the whole story. Television can portray human diversity sympathetically while highlighting shared human experience. The constructive use of this powerful tool to promote compassionate understanding, nonviolent problem solving, and decent intergroup relations needs to be pursued. It will not in itself be adequate to overcome inclinations toward hatred and violence, but it can help if used wisely.

In the 1980s and 1990s, the Carnegie Corporation made grants to examine the role of the media as a major socializing force for adolescents in our society. The Hollywood office of the Center for Population Options, for example, brought expert information about adolescent sexuality and pregnancy to the attention of Hollywood writers, directors, and producers. The Children's Defense Fund and the National Urban League used posters and public service announcements on radio and television to promote responsible sexual behavior among adolescents.

A major weakness of both commercial and public broadcasting is the lack of programs geared specifically to the developmental needs and concerns of young adolescents. Evidence of this is the fact that, although the Public Broadcasting system reaches some 70 percent of preschoolers, fewer than 20 percent of 12-year-olds ever watch public television. On commercial television, adolescents watch adult programs. The Carnegie Council on Adolescent Development identified programs geared to 10- to 15-year-olds as one of the greatest needs in this field.

Fortunately, in 1986, *Degrassi Junior High* appeared as a series specifically geared toward adolescents. It grew out of the Emmy and Prix Jeunesse award-winning program, *The Kids of Degrassi Street. Degrassi Junior High* is a Canadian-American coproduction by Linda Schuyler, a Canadian producer, and Kate Taylor of television station WGBH in Boston. Both are former junior high school teachers. *Degrassi Junior High* is a weekly dramatic series set in an unnamed North American city with a diverse ethnic composition. It presents people that young teenagers can identify with, people who are dealing with very real issues that teenagers confront: problems with self-image, peer pressure, friendship, sexuality, family relationships, alcohol, drugs, dating, stereotypes, and leadership. By using drama and humor, *Degrassi Junior High* strives to create popular entertainment that will also help young teenagers appreciate the wide variety of choices available in personally important situations.

The series began broadcasting on public television in 1986 and continued through 1989, with a total of 42 half-hour episodes.[52] Reruns continue to be broadcast throughout the world.[53] It received considerable acclaim from critics and from school and youth-serving organizations. The research on adolescents' reactions to *Degrassi Junior High* indicated that they found it exceptionally appealing, that the program was highly effective in presenting the choices and pressures that face young teenagers, and that the programs did indeed stimulate in-depth discussion of the issues and of alternative ways of approaching problems. When the series aired in Canada, it reached a quarter of the adolescent audience 12 to 17 years of age. *Degrassi Junior High* received a 4 percent share of the television viewing audience, which essentially translates to several million viewers per show. This is a relatively high rating, especially given that the U.S. Public Broadcasting System invested minimally in promotion of this initial series.[54]

A major public education effort was mounted to encourage the use of the *Degrassi Junior High* series in discussion groups in schools and youth-serving organizations. Some 25,000 copies of the *Degrassi Junior High Discussion and Activity Guide* were distributed to educators, health workers, and youth organization leaders. In addition, a 16-page tabloid designed for student viewers was published by the *Philadelphia Inquirer* and used as a supplement in 10 other newspapers.[55]

A second series of *Degrassi Junior High* programs explored generic issues of adolescence (relationships with peers, maturing ideas of self, emerging sexuality, and so on), incorporating audience feedback from the first series. It also incorporated some new themes, including pressure to succeed and not to succeed in school, money and values, first jobs, and parents remarrying.

The *Degrassi* programs clearly showed the educational value of using serious programming to encourage constructive adolescent development. It is a model worth emulating. But funding for work of such high quality is scarce. Foundations, governments, and commercial broadcasters would surely do well to support such programs that include dilemmas of personal aggression, intergroup relations, and nonviolent ways of resolving personal and social problems. The struggle for such prosocial television is not yet over.

CONCLUSION

It would be valuable to create an international educational telecommunications delivery system that combines in a coherent way various promising technologies. In principle, for example, it would be possible to establish an International Educational Telecommunications Corporation as an independent entity to design, build, and maintain a modern educational telecommunications system that effectively links educational organizations in many nations to sources of creative audiovisual learning materials. There could be an active pool of material over a wide range of content and format generated for a variety of purposes—mainly those of peace and democracy.

Administration might be provided by a reliable nongovernmental organization drawing on a mix of government and private funds from many nations. An international commission of impeccable standing could employ the highest standards. In managing this enterprise, venture capital could be obtained for creative programming and careful selection of the best available material from the world's storehouse.

Of all the technological advances of the twentieth century, the emerging telecommunications revolution is one of the most important for the future of our species. This technology provides worldwide, instantaneous, comprehensible networks with vast resources of information and high emotional impact. It can link different groups, different cultures, indeed the entire planet, as never before. That is why we have gone into considerable detail in this chapter to describe and document a number of positive, prosocial examples. They are still all too rare, but these pathbreaking examples suggest what might be accomplished if major efforts can be mobilized in the next few decades on a worldwide basis. We devote the next chapter to information technology's potential to aid in efforts to educate for peace.

14

Information Technology

Its Potential to Educate for Peace

THE INTERNET'S PROMISE FOR EDUCATION

In this chapter, we are mainly interested in ways that use of the Internet can promote helpful, legitimate, and practical support to teachers, students, and others interested in education for peace, conflict resolution, and violence prevention. The World Wide Web, a powerful global network, has immense capacity to influence people (especially children) that can be compared to the influence of television. Research that has been done on television viewing shows that it can have positive and negative effects on behavior beginning in early childhood. It does not affect everyone in the same way—variables such as age, socioeconomic status, and identification with television characters all play significant roles in how content affects a child. The Internet and other interactive media are similar to television by way of underlying factors (such as observational learning, attitudes, and arousal) that influence behavior.

Over the past several decades, some of the most profound changes in the way we live have come from the revolution in information technology (IT). A wide range of technologies has not only made it easier to communicate but also to send and utilize information. These devices have not stayed in the province of institutions or specialists but have found their way into common use. From cell phones and personal digital assistants to computers (just to touch on some of the most common of these technologies), they have changed the way ordinary people interact and behave. Their effects have been profound, as reflected in the speed with which these technologies have evolved and insinuated themselves into everyday life.

Perhaps the most important of these technologies is the personal computer (PC). In itself, the rise of the PC was a dramatic event, allowing more people to apply the capabilities of the computer to small business, personal activity, and schoolwork. But in the past decade, other information technologies that utilize the PC, the most important of which are the World Wide Web and electronic mail (e-mail), have appeared and promise further large-scale uses.

An indication of the speed with which these systems of communication have grafted themselves onto everyday life (particularly in the technically advanced countries) is the exponential increase of one of the most basic of these services, e-mail. The number of electronic mailboxes jumped by 84 percent during 1999, to over 570 million. At that time, the total number of e-mail messages sent was estimated to be in the range of 4 trillion, and it is certainly far higher today. The Internet (a term in general use as synonymous with the World Wide Web, as it will be used here) is also growing rapidly. Its capacity to carry information doubles every 100 days, and in just a single day the Web may increase by 3.2 million new Web pages. The number of total daily hits (a *hit* being defined as one individual viewing one Web page) on Web sites was estimated to be around one billion in late 1999.[1]

Not only have these technologies evolved with astonishing speed, their domestication for common use has been rapid as well. Some idea of how quickly this has happened is given by a few comparisons. It took 46 years from its initial availability for 30 percent of all U.S. homes to receive electricity; 38 years passed before 30 percent of all U.S. homes had a telephone; and television took 17 years to reach 30 percent of all U.S. households. The Internet found its way into 30 percent of all U.S. homes within 7 years.[2] And in addition to all the homes that now have Internet connections, many more people who do not have Internet access at home can regularly access it at work, school, a public library, or other public places. All these figures are increasing rapidly, as everyday experience shows. So the acceleration has been historically dramatic, if not unique. But for what purpose? Can Internet access help to make the world more peaceful, just, and prosperous? If so, how? Where do children fit in?

What is clear is that these technologies are changing how we live, work, and interact. Although many dot-com businesses did not live up to the hype of their boosters during the "Internet bubble" of the late 1990s, the Web has had considerable effect on how we shop and do business. As a form of personal communication, the Web and e-mail have changed the way individuals interact with one another. E-mail alone has shifted the manner in which people keep in touch and reach out to others.[3] Insight into the speed with which the technology has become an integral part of everyday life is given by its rapid inclusion in dating rituals.[4] More revealing of e-mail's ability to help people make emotional connections are its uses in times of crisis. After the September 11, 2001, attacks on the United States, nearly 100 million U.S. citizens sent or received what have been termed *I Care Mail*. Researchers at UCLA found that the medium was not just being used as a means to get or exchange information but also to show emotional support or concern for others.[5]

These computer-based technologies are extremely flexible. They can transmit huge amounts of a variety of data (not merely text but audio and video, too) easily. They also hold the potential to be far more interactive than earlier communication technologies such as radio and television. It is hardly surprising then that one of the areas in which they hold some of their greatest potential is education.

How a technology is actually employed is not something that can be dictated or readily foreseen. The Web itself is an unforeseen variation of a program that started with very different aims. In 1969, the U.S. Department of Defense began a confidential study to test techniques that would enable computer networks to remain intact, by forcefully diverting messages, in the event of military attack. The Internet grew from this government project, and by 1972 it had become known to the public. It grew from a small network of four laboratories between California and Utah, to include approximately 50 universities and research organizations with defense contracts. In 1973, the first connections were made internationally. In the mid-1990s, the Internet was taken over by the private sector and was driven by the increased popularity of personal computers and the World Wide Web.[6]

The World Wide Web, a network to use the Internet, was introduced in 1991 and greatly expanded by 1993.[7] The Web is essentially a huge electronic library, comprised of text, multimedia documents, and network services, from which one can easily retrieve information through intuitive searches. It makes use of hypertext technology and a graphical interface to retrieve data contained in documents that are specially formatted and may be located in the same computer or be distributed across an international network. With a simple click on the computer's pointing device (mouse) on a hyperlink, users may travel across sites that are linked together.

The creation of such a flexible, interactive, and global system has had rapid and significant impacts on daily life. And no group has the potential to be more profoundly effected by IT than children. Children in more developed countries (particularly Western Europe, Japan, and North America) grow up surrounded by media, a category that includes TV, radio, recorded music (CDs and tapes), printed matter, and video games, as well as the Web and e-mail. Currently, the dominant media force in the lives of children remains television—seemingly an old medium, but recall that it only became widely available in the 1950s. The average U.S. child watches about 2 hours and 45 minutes of TV per day, whereas recreational use of the computer and Internet use, combined, come to about a half hour. Yet, when children are asked what they would choose if they could have access to only one form of media, the largest single group (33 percent) chose the Internet as their solitary portal on the world—which shows that many children already have an appreciation of the versatility of the medium.[8] Internet use among children is growing quickly. Like much about the Internet and other information technologies, the research is thin, although it is growing through the thoughtful work of the Markle, Pew, and Kaiser Foundations and the UCLA Center for Communication Policy. (All of these organizations are studying how these technologies are changing our lives and may do so even more in future years.) So far, there has been very little research on the use of information technology to foster prosocial development. Thus the crucial topics of this book have been neglected—but this need not continue.

Research concerning the effects of IT on behavior is at an early stage. Even so, these investigations have shown important differences in the use of media by children of different ages, income, ethnic backgrounds, and gender. Gender, in particular, has been shown to affect children's use of computers. On any given day, 42 percent of boys and 41 percent of girls use a computer, although boys spend significantly more time (20 minutes) at the computer. Much of that time is spent by boys in playing video games, something girls do not do nearly as much.[9]

Beyond these breakdowns by group, there has been interesting initial research into the effects that new media could have on children's behavior. Many of these are related to broader social changes that are the results of the rapid domestication of the Internet. Recent studies have shown that Internet access is steadily increasing. By 2001, some 72.3 percent of all Americans were online, compared with 66.9 percent in 2000. Among those people who use the Web regularly, the average amount of television watched has declined. This is true of children as well. A UCLA report has shown that nearly one-quarter of children who go online watch less television than before they started using the Internet. Largely, adults do not see use of this technology as dramatically influencing children's schoolwork or social interaction.[10]

Although Web use by children has been seen as potentially isolating, some studies indicate that Internet use can also be a means for children to interact with those who share similar interests and could be an important means for social development. Preliminary research on children from ages 4 to 10 has shown that exposure to exceedingly violent video games has increased short-term aggressive behavior, attitudes, and thoughts (although the long-term effects have not yet been clarified). Video games can also serve as a common ground for children to interact, providing them a shared interest as well as the ability to compare notes about how to play the game. Socializing, particularly by boys, is often primed by this sort of media use.[11]

These new studies on the use of computers, Web sites, video games, and other media illustrate that their use is less important than what these media contain. The actual content of the video games, for example, is far more significant than the fact that a child plays video games.[12] The same is broadly true of the Web. Our concern should not necessarily be that children are spending more time using the Web; instead, we should ask what sorts of ideas and attitudes they are being exposed to through the Web sites they view. What sorts of contacts do they make with others? Could they cross cultural and national boundaries in constructive ways?

It is doubtful that any of the Internet's creators in 1969 could have predicted the meteoric rise of the Web, let alone the coming of eBay or Amazon.com. Neither could they have seen the role the Internet might play in educating a child to be caring, respectful, and considerate of others. Nor could they have seen a darker side to the Web. Groups preaching hate can use the Web for intolerance just as easily as those wishing to foster harmony. Because the content of the media children are exposed to matters so much, the use of the Internet by groups who have harshly negative agendas as a tool for their distinctive brand of education is a cause for serious concern.

One problem with the Internet is that its Web sites are highly volatile. They come and go. For example, an excellent educational Web site may disappear because the sponsors lose funding or lack sustained interest or move on to other positions. Sometimes such a Web site may be saved by shifting it to another institutional sponsorship. For our purposes, the fact that a highly informative, prosocial Web site has existed for a while gives encouragement. If it can be done once, it can be done again later and perhaps better by those who stand on the shoulders of their predecessors.

CONCERNS ABOUT THE INTERNET

In recent years, few developments have generated as much discussion of their potential to alter societies everywhere than the World Wide Web. In the 1990s, various boosters and commentators spoke of the Internet as a revolutionary force. Although it has had profound effects on the way many people live and work, some claims for the technology were overly grand. As the technology has settled into more regular use, there is a greater appreciation of the limits and even the threats this new technology can pose.

There is a growing understanding that the Web is not something that liberates information from geography. The Web is not a cloud of ether but data that must be stored somewhere on expensive equipment that requires a great deal of electric power. The origination point of the data being transferred matters, because downloading materials from a server closer to your computer will affect download speed and reliability. The expense of maintaining the large server computers that send data over the Internet also has physical aspects. Increasingly, companies and institutions are trusting the material that they post on the Web to companies that run large "server farms." Companies rent storage space for their data on these farms. This is more cost-effective for many firms than providing their own storage space, but it also means that information on the Internet, in some respects, is becoming more susceptible to concentration of power.[13] There is also increasing control over the means of delivering that data. A handful of companies like AOL Time Warner and AT&T have strengthened their control over the broadband cable lines so necessary to deliver the growing volume of information coursing through the Internet. This, along with Microsoft's domination of computer operating systems and the software most people use to navigate the Internet, means greater concentration of power and less competition.[14]

The increasing concentration of control over this technology in the hands of a few groups has led to calls for programs to secure the public interest in the new IT environment. Newton Minow and Lawrence Grossman, who have long and distinguished careers in media, have proposed an Internet equivalent of the public interest spectrum, akin to public radio and public television. Public use of resources that can have educational, cultural, or other civic benefits go well back into U.S. history. Minow and Grossman point to the Northwest Ordinance of 1787 that set aside land for the support of public schools, the Merrill Act of 1862 that set aside land for 100 land-grant colleges, and the GI Bill of Rights in 1944 as valuable precedents. Nor is public use of communication technologies limited to the United States. Commentators on Minow and Grossman's proposal have noted the creation of the British Broadcasting Corporation in 1927 as a kindred attempt to use communications as a public trust, and its continuing worldwide social value.[15]

How a public interest spectrum in such a new media environment might operate remains an open question. However, the rapid shifts in control of some of the key technologies makes it an issue that must be confronted to make sure that the benefits of such powerful and versatile information technologies can be employed in a manner that benefits the broadest collection of people possible. Such shifts are a further reminder that this new technology has not only sparked a whole set of new applications but important policy issues. These will be ongoing questions because, as some commentators have noted, we are only in an early phase of comprehending and guiding the effects of a "communications revolution."[16]

Added to concerns about the *content* of the Internet, there is also worry over the *use* of the technology to cause physical harm. Until recently, U.S. government experts were not aware of the technical skills of members of Al Qaeda, or of the full extent to which a terrorist group could use cyberspace to cause damage, such as disabling or controlling dams, electrical power, and communications as well as for international planning of terrorist attacks. Hope for an abatement of risk comes from the positive use of technology to anticipate and head off such attacks.[17]

Some have suggested that the speed and freedom with which the Web moves information could challenge the rule of authoritarian regimes. This has certainly happened in some cases and has much potential for democratization, but repressive regimes have also learned to contain and even benefit from the technology for their autocratic purposes. A recent study by the Carnegie Endowment for International Peace examines how the authoritarian governments of Cuba and China have responded to the challenge of the Internet. In both countries, there has been a great deal of restriction of access to the Web as a means to limit its effects on the population. Moreover, the Web is also a tool for these regimes to cultivate support. In Cuba, the government allows e-mail and Internet access to individuals and organizations, but only those who have shown their loyalty, while China maintains a national firewall. It is also a mechanism for extending state legitimacy: Cuba uses the Internet to support the diffusion of information and services within its strained public health infrastructure, and China used it to modernize bureaucracy, spread the official voice, and improve the economy. Although this has some positive impact for the people of Cuba, it also solidifies the place of the autocratic government. In both countries, the Web is a powerful and relatively cheap means of getting the government's propaganda line out to its people and a global audience.[18]

The new information technologies should also be viewed with an understanding of the diversity of their impacts. The communication media discussed here are universal in their use but particular in their local applications. Peoples of similar levels of affluence and even culture will employ IT differently. Finns, for example, are much more "wired" and prone to use the Internet and related technologies more often and differently than their counterparts in other areas of Europe. Much attention in this chapter is on the United States, yet cultural differences abound. Although the U.S. experience overlaps and reflects the experiences of other peoples, it is necessarily distinctive in some respects.[19]

These tempered views of the effects of the Internet show that it is not an unequivocally positive force and that its use and reception within cultures is highly variable. We have learned that the information superhighway is a multidirectional street, and that it has off-ramps that can lead users into some nasty neighborhoods. This is not to dismiss its powerful actual and potential effects in education and other fields, but to remind us that we have to deal with the bad that the Web brings, even as we try to harness it for democracy and peace.

This nuanced view of the Web includes concerns about its impact on children. There is real danger from hate Web sites, which often include calls to violence. Although the trend toward monopolies over Web content is alarming, so is the ease with which the basic hate site can be a one-person, low-cost show. The equipment and maintenance costs for publishing online, as well as the expertise for doing so, are low when compared with print publishing, especially considering that one Web site can satisfy a worldwide readership. What's more, the anonymous nature of Web use enables individuals to drop their identities and social inhibitions to exchange views that they would typically avoid for fear or shame of recrimination. The Web may have the potential to create communities, but in a "place" where people are transformed into identity-less "users," the Web can also succeed in stripping away their humanity. In these instances, the educational potential of the Web can be turned into a means to foster hostile attitudes, invidious distinctions, and even outright hatred in those who do not know better. This is a real, present danger and an issue we should consider as we also explore the Internet's potential to foster positive relationships.

Hate Web Sites

The influence of hate groups is becoming more widespread as societies rapidly become more heterogeneous and as these groups find their way onto the Internet—targeting their attention to young people. Clearly, counteractive education, based on accurate information, is essential in diminishing the dangerous effects of these groups. There are encouraging examples of such counteracting education, but they are still modest in relation to the need.

In the year 2000, the *Intelligence Report* published by the Southern Poverty Law Center (SPLC) examined the Internet's role in creating an atmosphere of intolerance and looked at possible legal remedies to address the problem.[20] Don Black, a former Ku Klux Klansman (who had previously served a prison term for plotting to invade a small Caribbean country) was responsible for the first hate Web site's being posted in March 1995. The SPLC categorizes such Web pages as those linked to Klan, neo-Nazi, skinhead, Christian Identity, Black Separatist, and "Other" hate groups. The *Intelligence Report* in spring, 2002 revealed a significant increase in such Web sites from 1999 to 2001, a increase that correlated with the 12 percent increase in hate groups in the United States that year.[21] The report also details the growing connection between extremists around the world, including neo-Nazi groups and Middle Eastern fundamentalists. Though neo-Nazis have traditionally despised Arabs and Muslims, they have found some common enemies with Muslim extremist groups: the United States, Jews, and ethnic diversity.[22]

Middle- and upper-class youths with easy access to computers are the unfortunate primary targets of hate Web sites. This medium encourages the sharing of anti-Semitic or racist views that under normal circumstances would be discouraged as socially unacceptable. Legislative bodies and courts have tried to tackle the problems posed by hate speech in several ways. Arizona, for example, passed a law in 1999 mandating that public schools and libraries use filtering software. In December 2000, the U.S. Congress under President William J. Clinton enacted the Children's Internet Protection Act. The law requires public schools and libraries that receive federal funding for technology to adopt Internet monitoring policies and install filtering software—thus blocking material harmful to children. The requirement mandating filtering software was declared unconstitutional by an appellate court in Philadelphia in May 2002, but the Supreme Court reversed this decision in June 2003.[23] Despite these measures, however, Congress has been unable to require Internet service providers to offer such software to customers free of charge or at cost (although some offer filtering options and parental controls nonetheless). And they have failed to make it a criminal offense to teach or demonstrate how to make bombs and other destructive devices on the Internet. Besides stating the obvious issue of prohibiting free speech, libraries have countered that while blocking dangerous material on the Internet, filtering software may also block credible sources of information about offensive topics. These might include scholarly publications and information provided by constructive organizations, even if the information provides a preventive or corrective point of view. Yet it is not obvious why instructions on making weapons of mass destruction should be readily available. The pros and cons of filtering software are being debated and are so far unresolved.

These efforts have typically come up against constitutional guarantees of free speech in the United States. The question of how the First Amendment guarantees of free speech apply in cyberspace is ongoing, with the shape of the law yet to be established. The U.S. Supreme Court ruled that the Internet more resembles print media than broadcast media for First Amendment purposes. However, as boundaries continue to be tested, more legislative initiatives can be expected. The law prohibits shouting "Fire!" in a crowded theater (unless a fire is actually occurring). What is the equivalent constraint here?

In the United States print is generally considered to be a freer medium than nonprint media, with no prior censorship allowed and much freedom to communicate almost anything except criminal threats or narrowly defined obscenities. In the case of the broadcast media, laws have reflected the people's interest in regulating radio and television because of the limited number of available airwave frequencies and the invasive nature (e.g., individuals could unintentionally come across unexpected or offensive material very easily).

The Internet is strongly backed by judicial protection of free speech. It is seen as a vast democratic forum. In June 1997, the U.S. Supreme Court voted seven to two to invalidate portions of the Communications Decency Act and rejected the government's argument that the Internet should be as highly regulated as the broadcast media. The court's reasoning was that the Internet is not invasive because people rarely encounter material on the Internet by accident, and a warning usually precedes this type of objectionable material. In reality, it seems that anyone who uses the Internet regularly does receive offensive spam e-mails or will at some point be unwittingly led to an obscene Web page. Nevertheless, the Internet was awarded the court's strongest protection of free speech. This gives users access to sites that advocate the overthrow of the government, denigrate racial minorities, and show how to make or use lethal weapons—and gives the same access to children. Only when advocacy is an impetus for lawless action—or is an actual threat—is it punishable. Whether threats come by phone, mail, or e-mail, they are punishable by law. In 1996, a former student at the University of California at Irvine, 19-year-old Richard Machado, sent e-mail messages to 67 Asian students threatening to kill each of them. After the initial mistrial, he was convicted of two misdemeanor counts and sentenced to one year in prison.[24]

In a 1999 lawsuit in a federal court in Oregon, the court ruled on an Internet case that may indicate the start of a broader interpretation of what constitutes a threat. The suit was filed by Planned Parenthood against 12 abortion opponents for helping to create "wanted" posters featuring doctors known to perform abortions and an Internet site called the "Nuremberg Files." This site featured a list containing the names of 225 doctors, including some of their home addresses, phone numbers, car descriptions, and license plate numbers—details that would definitely help someone who wanted to kill such a doctor. Since 1993, seven doctors who were known to perform abortions have been killed. When each death occurred, a line was drawn through that individual's name on the Web site; if a doctor was wounded but not killed, his or her name appeared in gray. Although the Web site did not specifically advocate murder, it was linked to a letter from a convicted doctor-killer describing the joy he felt in killing his victim.

The concept behind the lawsuit was that "publicizing names of doctors violated federal law that was meant to protect people's access to abortion facilities. The defense called it free speech."[25] The federal judge asked the jury to determine if the alleged threats were true threats. The jury determined that they were actual threats, and on February 2, 1999, the plaintiffs were awarded $107.9 million. Additionally, Presiding Judge Robert E. Jones said that the wanted posters and the Web site were "blatant and illegal communication of true threats to kill."[26] He also ordered the defendants to stop publishing wanted posters and contributing information to the Nuremberg Files Web site.

All in all, there is an intellectual and legal ferment about proper use of the Internet, consistent with constructive social purposes. Dangerous elements are still protected and may well have inflammatory effects on troubled youth.

Global Threats

Adolescents may readily tap into vivid hate material. *U.S. News and World Report* published an article in September 2000 describing the Internet's role in creating a Web of violent and well-funded racists.[27] Until 1980, white supremacists in the United States were largely local Ku Klux Klansmen and neo-Nazis with little connection to people or events overseas. Now, however, the Internet has enabled such individuals to become part of an era of globalization. Web sites and e-mail make it readily possible to connect disparate cultures and share destructive information globally. The United State's First Amendment is being manipulated for such purposes. Neo-Nazi and other hate groups can host Web sites in the United States that would be illegal elsewhere. American racist Gary Lauck, popularly called the "Farm Belt Führer,"[28] shipped racist literature to Germany for 20 years. He was arrested during a visit to Europe and served four years in prison. But now the Internet allows him to rest easy in America and distribute Nazi media published in multiple languages to readers throughout the world.[29] The Web makes these interconnections for intolerance much easier to forge and maintain.

U.S. Web services reportedly contain most of the rapidly proliferating German neo-Nazi Web sites, many of which are illegal under German law. A particularly shocking example of gross misuse of the Internet was found in 1999 when a U.S.–based Web page posted a $7,500 reward (in German) for the murder of a young left-wing activist, listing his home address, job, and phone number.[30] All of this is available to children, who are learning to use the Internet at earlier and earlier ages. These items are of special interest to many adolescent boys.

The Internet provides an electronic connection between the world's most active neo-Nazi groups, such as the Hammerskin Nation (known for their violence and presence in Australia, New Zealand, Europe, and North America), the Ku Klux Klan (which has now gone abroad and established chapters in Great Britain and Australia, with speaking engagements scheduled in Germany), and the World Church of the Creator (with chapters in Australia, Belgium, Canada, France, and Sweden). This shows the international nature of hate-oriented communities that may well lead to international cooperation in fanatical violence. Many other examples could be given on the basis of present Internet content linking hate groups in different countries. But this is sufficient to indicate the real dangers, especially for impact on susceptible adolescents groping for a sense of worth and belonging—and feeling a sense of international solidarity by identifying with hate groups.

The United States' own National Alliance, with its 300-acre Virginia compound, is a white supremacist group labeled by the Anti-Defamation League (ADL) as the largest and most dangerous in the nation. The National Alliance has completely adopted use of the Web, offering materials online in five European languages. The worldwide commerce of hate that the Web can enable is an international problem.

The Internet has facilitated a consistent ideology and a common culture for hate-oriented, extremist, and violent groups. The gravity of this problem deserves the utmost attention of organizations and institutions concerned with peace and decent human relations. One such organization that is actively involved in using the Internet to resolve conflicts is the William and Flora Hewlett Foundation, which funds the Conflict Resolution Information Source (http://www.crinfo.org), a project directed by the Conflict Research Consortium. The site brings together over 13,000 conflict-resolution resources and more than 20,000 Web links that include current news and information on strategies for finding positive solutions to difficult problems. These strategies may address specific problems, such as postgenocidal reconstruction in Rwanda and Burundi, and also broader issues in the field, such as the use of communication behavior in conflict negotiation.[31]

The European Union, a strong organization of Western democracies, has been a powerful force in tackling hate speech online. As reported by Safer Internet Exchange (http://www.saferinternet.org), an organization set up by the European Union (EU) to counteract illegal and racist Internet content, the final report of the European Commission Directorate General Information Society workshop in June 2001 addressed the issue of racism on the Internet. Safer Internet Exchange prefaced its discussion on policy in Europe by pointing out that the U.S. Constitution protects the publishing of hateful racist material on the Internet in the United States, with the United States being more permissive than European countries in this respect. The workshop proposed options for protecting children from dangerous material on the Internet. Among the suggestions made were these: Internet Service Providers should be required to provide filtering technology, awareness programs should be developed to teach both parents and children about the risks online, and Internet material should be regulated to the extent possible by parents and the state.

Report of the California Governor's Advisory Panel on Hate Groups

In August 1999, Governor Gray Davis of California announced the formation of a panel to seriously examine existing and potential laws relating to California's operating hate groups.[32] This announcement followed the tragic murder of a Filipino postal worker, Joseph Ileto, and a shooting at a Jewish community day care center in Southern California.[33] The following month, a nine-member advisory panel (cochaired by former U.S. Secretary of State Warren Christopher and former California Governor George Deukmejian) reviewed existing laws that relate to possible criminal or civil liabilities of hate groups. In addition, they considered laws and other measures that might minimize the violence-promoting influence of these groups, within constitutional boundaries.

The panel's report covered several areas: (1) existing legislation in California; (2) law enforcement; (3) education; (4) the Internet; and (5) community, public interest, and society groups. The statements on uses of the Internet are of particular interest to us here.

With all of its positive aspects, the Internet has also made it possible for hate groups to reach an unprecedented number of people with their well-crafted but inaccurate statements. The unfortunate truth is that many people, including young students, are unaware of the need to question the accuracy of what they see on their computer screens. One particularly striking example found in the California report was of a student who wrote a research paper on the Holocaust with information completely taken from the Internet (specifically, from a white supremacist Web site). Although the paper was extremely well written, the student received a failing grade because his thesis was that the Holocaust never took place. Because of such vivid and disturbing abuses of the Internet, the industry has sometimes indicated a willingness to consider voluntary self-monitoring. However, no agreement exists about how this should be accomplished or even if it should be done at all. This discord directly impairs attempts to find a solution to online hate groups, and it will most likely increase the pressure on legislators to intervene directly as abuses increase.

Because of the ease of initiating contact, the appearance of credibility, and the ability to disseminate assertions broadly and cheaply, hate groups make wide use of the Internet. The Simon Wiesenthal Center monitors hate-related Web sites; it has at various times included the following categories:

- Messages oriented to influencing youth
- Hate music online
- Religious extremism and separatism
- Holocaust denial and revisionism
- Hate groups and promotion of extremism
- Bomb making and mayhem

The abundance of material on such sites, much of it oriented to children and adolescents, points to the need for continuous monitoring. The California report noted that the Internet industry responded to this need for monitoring Web activity in several ways:

1. *Acceptable use policies:* Most Internet service provider contracts have acceptable use policies as part of their documents. They are particularly effective if account violators are dealt with quickly and appropriately, such as removing the offending content or terminating the user's contract.
2. *Cooperation with law enforcement:* Microsoft employs four experts in law enforcement and investigative techniques. Together with a staff of 20, they assist law enforcement agencies in determining when and where such activities have taken place and helping to apprehend the suspects. Microsoft responds to about 1,000 requests per year, according to the 2000 California report.
3. *Filters:* These are effective especially when attempting to minimize the impact of hate messages on young people. They are regularly updated by the filtering service and can be easily customized to suit the customer's needs. Such filters as Net Nanny, Disk Tracy, MoM, and SurfWatch can be freely used on private computers. The risk that filters pose is that legitimate communications may also be impeded; but these consideration do not justify education for hate and incitement to violence.

The California report encourages the Internet industry to undertake stronger self-regulation in order to "provide a commercially successful and societally acceptable mode of communication."[34] Just as with other technology that preceded it, the Internet, as it develops, will receive public pressure to promote prosocial behavior or at least monitor the incitement to violence. The hope is that industry leaders and other participants will seriously consider the safety and welfare of the public along with constitutional concerns of free speech and association—not to speak of their self-serving preoccupation with freedom from external constraints. The Report of the Governor's Advisory Panel considered governmental legislation and regulation but stated that it preferred to be cautious about such constraints at the time of its release.[35]

As we have seen, the Internet can have impact on a global scale with an ease and flexibility nearly unmatched by other technologies. This ubiquitous means of communication can be harnessed for nefarious as well as noble aims. Just as authoritarian regimes have long used movies as propaganda tools and as extremists used radio to spur violence in Rwanda, other groups can and do use the Internet to create or deepen the invidious distinctions that are so often at the root of human conflict. This does not mean that unpopular viewpoints should be banned or strict censorship practiced, but sustained vigilance is necessary concerning what sort of information can be accessed by children through the Internet. We should be aware of the hateful and violent potentials of the Web even as we explore its great promise to support positive, prosocial efforts in education. Industry, universities, and democratic governments have vital and distinct roles in addressing the serious problem of hatred and violence promoted too often by the expanding information technology. These institutions must strive to foster the judicious use of information technology for constructive, educational purposes.

USING THE WEB TO COUNTER HATE

Nongovernmental organizations have provided leadership in using IT to keep track of groups that espouse hate. The SPLC, the Simon Wiesenthal Center, and the ADL keep a sharp eye on hate groups' activities, a watch that includes awareness of their Web activities. These organizations then use their own Web sites to counter or expose the dangerous messages put out by hate groups. Yet these groups are not simply reacting to those with negative messages but are promoting education for tolerance on its own merits, oriented not so much to the haters as to the large portion of the public who are *not* preoccupied with negative feelings about other groups or target scapegoats.

At ADL's Web site (http://www.adl.org), one can find information on a wide range of topics focused on the fight against bigotry and prejudice. Among the many links provided are pages on anti-Semitism, combating hate, education to promote tolerance and understanding, and the use of the Internet. The education page provides guidance for parents on ways to speak to children about hatred, prejudice, and violence. The work of the World of Difference Institute is also described here. The Internet link provides a guide to hate on the Internet and the promotion of hatred online. ADL also offers its Internet HateFilter—a tool for parents to help them make intelligent judgments about whether or not to expose their children to hateful ideas—free of charge. More than blocking hate sites, the HateFilter offers users the opportunity to link to an ADL Web site to learn about hate's causes and effects.

Current ADL campaigns are promoted online as well. For example, ADL and Barnes and Noble launched a Close the Book on Hate campaign in the fall of 2000. It was specifically designed to provide children, their parents, and caregivers with tools to help fight racism, anti-Semitism, and other forms of bigotry and discrimination. The book *Hate Hurts*[36] was at the heart of the campaign. The book gives guidance on how to answer hard questions frequently asked by youth, and also guidance to caregivers on ways to comfort children who have been victims of hate and how to deal with individuals and groups who exhibit intolerance.

The ADL provides parents, teachers, students, and community leaders with a host of materials to combat prejudice, hatred, and bigotry. The assumption is that no one is born prejudiced—it is something that is learned and it can also be unlearned. ADL strives to teach the value of diversity through its catalog of books, videos, curriculum guides, posters, magazines, and other materials, including online information.

A collaboration between ADL and WCVN-TV in Boston, A World of Difference Institute was initiated in 1985 as a campaign to overcome prejudice, promote democratic ideals, and strengthen pluralism. It is a national effort involving 29 cities throughout the United States and may come to attract others. Schools, universities, corporations, and community and law enforcement agencies in the United States and abroad use its diversity education programs. These programs are practical and experiential; they give participants skills to live and work successfully in a diverse environment. Prejudice and discrimination are challenged and positive intergroup relations fostered.

Stop the Hate, an antibias and antihate crime training program begun in 1996 by A World of Difference Institute, was created in response to a request for proposals from the U.S. Department of Education, which was looking for intervention strategies under the Safe and Drug-Free School Program. The Stop the Hate proposal took the shape of a one-year pilot program for high schools in need of antiviolence and antibias intervention. Four U.S. cities successfully implemented this training program for school administrators, teachers, students, parents, and members of the community. Elementary and middle schools feeding into these high schools also became involved in the program.

The Los Angeles Regional office was awarded a grant from the Times Mirror Foundation to replicate the Stop the Hate pilot project at Culver City High School in Culver City, California. The school was selected because of its demonstrated commitment to diversity and community involvement. The program began in early 1999 with workshops, parent meetings, peer training, and collaborations with other complementary programs. By the end of the year, a peer trainer was asked to attend and speak at a town hall meeting on hate behavior and hate crimes, which was intended to provide a forum for California students, educators, and legislators to talk in person about hate crime prevention.

Because of Culver City High School's success and the success of the four pilot sites under the U.S. Department of Education grant, ADL staff gave a presentation on the Stop the Hate program to several leaders in California government. The presentation was built around the recommendations of the Governor's Advisory Panel on Hate Crimes—the distinguished panel headed by former U.S. Secretary of State Warren Christopher. A budget item was recommended to offer Stop the Hate throughout the state of California. Beginning in fall 2000, three new schools undertook this program through funding from foundations and corporations. Though this experience was far from definitive, it was an interesting example of ingenuity and dedication in efforts to diminish prejudice and hatred.

The SPLC has some of the best-developed resources for education in tolerance. It has long supported education as an extension of its legal and advocacy efforts. In 1991, it started its Teaching Tolerance program, which has since developed a Web component (http://www.splcenter.org/teachingtolerance/tt-index.html). This has been joined by a Web site recently established by the SPLC that is devoted to the creation of "a national community committed to human rights" (http://www.tolerance.org/). Both use the Web as a mechanism to deliver materials that can support a curriculum for tolerance education.

Of course, such efforts are unlikely to reach the ingrained haters, but positive progress can have an effect on the large silent majority of decent people who are not seeking scapegoats and are genuinely interested in humane attitudes and constructive relationships. Positive information can deepen their understanding and strengthen their resistance to hateful messages whenever they are encountered.

The Web and Education at All Levels

International interest in these matters is reflected in a coinitiative of the United Nations Educational, Scientific, and Cultural Organization (UNESCO) and the Academy for Educational Development (AED), *Technologies for Education: Potential, Parameters and Prospects*, which confronts worldwide challenges brought about by rapid change in the twenty-first century. The book addresses how information and communication technologies (ICT) can be used effectively in dealing with the challenges of the world's globalizing environment and the implications these challenges have for education. Educational initiatives are seen as a vital means toward reaching the International Development Goals adopted by the United Nations General Assembly in September 2000: "The goals are set in terms of reducing poverty, improving health and education, and protecting the environment."[37]

The report of the Digital Opportunity Initiative (a joint effort of the Markle Foundation, Accenture, and the United Nations Development Programme), published in July 2001, cites IT's role in the social and economic progress of developing nations. The report not only emphasizes the beneficial nature of IT for socioeconomic development projects in health, education, and economic growth, it outlines how developing countries can use technologies to achieve sustainable results.[38] UNESCO and AED have corroborated these findings. They have explained how the use and understanding of ICTs are imperative to participation in a rapidly changing world market, tackling the fluctuating challenges of social development, delivering higher levels of education (including continuing education in keeping with technological advancements), and meeting the ongoing need for new skills in the global marketplace.[39]

UNESCO and AED have explained how information and communication technologies can satisfy education's most far-reaching needs: Technology can (1) deliver secondary and tertiary education, as well as skill training; (2) instill problem-solving and critical thinking skills, (3) ensure that everyone can be educated; (4) make education possible at any time, throughout people's lives; (5) make education possible anywhere on the globe, no matter how far removed from major population centers; and (6) empower teachers who may be working in adverse circumstances. To take advantage of these benefits, we must be prepared to see and understand ICTs' potentials.[40] We need to "think differently and radically. The education model developed for the Industrial Age cannot achieve educational empowerment effectively in the Information Age."[41]

From efficient, far-reaching delivery of content to improved quality and educational management to flexible, on-demand, lifelong learning opportunities, the rewards of ICTs in education can be great, though care must be taken with their implementation. Technologies must be thoroughly understood to be effectively implemented, and educational concepts and practice must be up to the task, as must the implementers and infrastructure. Finally, practical issues concerning the maintenance of devices that transmit content and the training of personnel should be considered early on in the process and are essential to the success of ICTs in education.[42] This upbeat assessment, rich as it is in promise for future education, does not deal substantially with the paucity of content on education for conflict resolution and for peaceful accommodations. This gap is as true in the new as in the old technologies of education. Given the violent turbulence in today's world, this is a glaring deficiency that must soon be corrected.

The work of the SPLC illustrates how the Web is regularly being used in education for social tolerance. Universities in the United States and Europe have been on the leading edge of Web use in education. They were fundamental, particularly in the United States, to the creation and evolution of the technology, and therefore the technology moved more easily into the operations of institutions where it initially appeared. The speed with which the Internet and related technologies became indispensable in higher education in the 1990s is a function of the usefulness of such technology in education. Its promise for education on human conflict and violence prevention has yet to be fulfilled.

Other Educational Uses of the Internet

Web support is now commonplace in higher education. Much of this is administrative, because schools and programs put important information from their missions and requirements for applications on their Web sites. But there is also an increasing amount of high-quality scholarly work accessible through the Web. Not only are library catalogs online, but also scholarly materials are available internationally at all times of the day to those with Web access. JSTOR, "the scholarly journal archive" (see http://www.js-tor.org), is a prime example of this. Funded by the Andrew Mellon Foundation, JSTOR provides the contents of many prominent scholarly journals in the humanities and social sciences, from each journal's inception to the present. Publication of some of the journals began in the nineteenth century. JSTOR is only one of a number of collections of electronic journals across almost all disciplines, which, taken together, provide unprecedented access to materials that previously were simply not available to students and scholars in many places around the world.

This has considerable potential for allowing those in poor countries to gain access to materials and information that would otherwise not have been available. Medicine, in particular, has been quick to adopt IT. The Internet and other computer-based technologies are now regularly used for distance education in many fields and in many countries. This is in addition to other types of data gathering, information sharing, disease tracking, and even online diagnosing that are used in the actual practice of medicine. There is an obstacle in the fact that many of these online databases and services charge high subscription fees or require expensive equipment. However, many programs have rightly adopted the means to lower or waive these fees for those groups and organizations that could not otherwise bear this cost.[43] This is a critical issue for developing countries that must be addressed internally while such countries also press for technical cooperation and financial aid from rich countries and international organizations (both public and private).

Professors commonly post syllabi and course requirements for their classes. But information technology is used for much more than just bureaucratic tasks in higher education. The Internet is now regularly used for direct pedagogical purposes. Materials are often circulated via e-mail or posted on Web-based bulletin boards before class to prime classroom discussion. Students may be able to get their course reading materials in electronic format. There may also be video or audio components accessible on a course Web site that can be used to flesh out or illustrate a point made in a lecture. These are only a few ways the Internet is used in higher education. Nevertheless, they illustrate the flexibility and usefulness of the Web. Its ability to be adapted to a number of different tasks is a widely appreciated and utilized asset in the diverse world of education. Yet there are many complaints about the quality of educational material available. As usual, the hardware tends to run ahead of the quality of the software—that is, the content of educational opportunity. Likewise, a focus on technological tools rather than on actual education has been blamed for the failure of the costly virtual universities that were created in the mid-1990s. These ventures had been seen as moneymaking opportunities and a solution to the anticipated increase in college enrollment. However, business models incorrectly estimated the costs of development, and universities—in their failure to focus on the connection between teaching practices and technology—did not effectively communicate the concepts of Web learning to prospective students.[44]

It is now almost impossible to discuss new university programs without considering the role the Web will play in any innovative effort. When the University for Peace (UPEACE; http://www.upeace.org) recently gathered a group of experts from the academic world, government, and nongovernmental organizations to further the institution's program of revamping and broadening its international curricula in peace studies and conflict resolution, the use of the Web was a fundamental issue. UPEACE's goal is to create a program that will serve as a focal point for excellent global scholarship in a wide variety of fields that clarify issues surrounding peace and provide a means for people around the world to utilize this expertise. As a means of forging these links, the Internet is an indispensable resource to reach those who might not otherwise be able to participate. The Web is seen not only as a means for supporting networks of scholars with clearinghouses of information but also as a way to support UPEACE's primary focus, working with students and scholars in the developing world. By using Web components to support extension courses and other academic activities, the university can increase its ability to reach out to these groups considerably.[45]

There are nevertheless difficulties in using the Internet. The first is cost. Another is the transitory nature of information available. Web sites that hold valuable information change their Web addresses or simply disappear. It is sometimes hard just to keep up with the changes in existing sites.[46] Another problem comes from its vastness. For instance, when one types *peace education* into a search engine, thousands of links appear on the screen. So, how does one begin to sift through the storehouse of information? To effectively navigate the vastness of cyberspace, guides are needed to verify legitimacy of resource material. This is where the notion of a Web site clearinghouse comes in— a useful beginning as one attempts to sort through extensive information.

One serious effort in peace and conflict studies is the Initiative on Conflict Resolution and Ethnicity (INCORE; http://www.incore.ulst.ac.uk). INCORE is a joint effort by the University of Ulster and the United Nations University based in Tokyo to undertake research and policy studies on the resolution of ethnic, political, and religious conflicts. Largely, its focus is on international questions, but it is also a repository of policy evaluation materials and a collection of documents that provides information on contemporary conflicts and peacemaking efforts. In addition, it provides a wide-ranging selection of links to other related Web sites. The guiding principle of this site is to be an optimal entry point into the World Wide Web for scholars, practitioners, or students of international affairs. The home page offers options for the user to access on-line books and journals, conference papers, working papers, and publications from institutes, universities, and commissions. It is regularly updated, making available information that would otherwise be very difficult to find. Links are also provided to other sites and institutions. There are a number of other sites that provide clearinghouse services that are the work of universities, research institutes, and other institutions. These services are helpful in guiding those interested in education for peace as they seek to examine the mass of material available and make sense of it.

Many groups also use the Internet and e-mail effectively in building networks of scholars, practitioners, and administrators who are interested in similar issues. Web sites remain an essentially passive medium in terms of outreach to users—individuals must seek out and then come to a site on their own. A more active way to communicate information (e.g., curricula and other educational tools) and data to scholars or other interested parties is addressed by e-mail listservers. When users subscribe to a listserver, they receive information by simply logging onto their e-mail. Communications for a Sustainable Future (CSF) at the University of Colorado at Boulder hosts the PEACE listserver. It is part of a larger project integrating the discussion group with a peace studies and peace research database (which includes conflict resolution). This is a virtual peace studies library called PEACE and CONFLICT on the World Wide Web. The Peace Education Commission (PEC) listserver is a worldwide electronic forum to discuss teaching strategies and research related to education for peace. PEC is a branch of the International Peace Research Association. Both PEACE and PEC are excellent examples of informative listservers.

Outside the universities, a number of independent and state-based programs use the Web to support their work and to foster conflict resolution in the schools at all levels. Conflict Resolution Education Network (CREnet) was one of the largest national organizations pushing for conflict resolution to be an integral part of school curriculum. It used its Web site to support innovation in this field and has since merged with the Academy of Family Mediators and the Society of Professionals in Dispute Resolution to form the Association for Conflict Resolution (http://www.acresolution.org). The Colorado School Mediation Center (http://www.csmp.org) and the Ohio Commission on Dispute Resolution and Conflict Management (http://www.state.oh.us/cdr/) also use their Web sites to facilitate their programs. The Peace and Justice Studies Association (PJSA; http://www.peacejusticestudies.org/index.php), an organization created by the Consortium on Peace Research, Education and Development (COPRED) and the Peace Studies Association (PSA), is a community of educators, activists, and researchers working toward finding alternatives to violence and war. Membership has grown to hundreds of institutional and individual members. COPRED is now a hub for many university degree programs in peace and nonviolence studies worldwide, and it works to strengthen programs and networks in the public schools.

Beyond constructing networks, educational organizations also use IT to provide curricular support for primary and secondary programs engaged in peace and conflict-resolution education. Workable Peace (http://www.workablepeace.org) is a good example of such activity. This group (based in Cambridge, Massachusetts) supports conflict-resolution programs in a number of high schools around the United States. Workable Peace uses its Web site to support the implementation of conflict-resolution programs that have already been set up, where school staff and other participants have been trained in face-to-face sessions. The Web site is a buttress to these programs, providing easy access to curricula and other materials so that teachers and students can implement conflict-resolution programs. A key part of this three-pronged curriculum, central to the Workable Peace project, are role-playing exercises, in which students take on the roles of historical and contemporary figures in situations of intergroup conflict. Workable Peace makes use of its Web site to distribute materials (e.g., role descriptions, timelines, maps, and other documents) to students and others involved in the project around the country.

The United Nation's Global Teaching and Learning Project creates material for teacher training as well as for primary, intermediate, and secondary school instruction and activities. Its online teaching component, Cyberschoolbus (http://wwwo.un.org/cyberschoolbus/), provides a curriculum and resources to teachers for integrating peace education and the study of human rights, poverty, and world studies into the classroom. Cyberschoolbus projects bring together diverse student groups and teachers from around the world to learn about and take part in efforts that seek solutions to major problems, such as land-mined schoolyards, deficiences in world health, and other international problems. While assisting in teaching students about world affairs, the Cyberschoolbus projects create opportunities for students to be active in changing the world and give them a voice in world issues.[47]

There are also a number of other relevant sites, though all are not specifically devoted to peace education, that use the global nature of the Web to support a worldwide view in education. The Thomas J. Watson Jr. Institute for International Studies at Brown University hosts the Choices program (http://www.choices.edu). The project not only provides curriculum materials for teachers that are accessible through its Web site but also supports teacher-training workshops and materials for community programs to engage individuals with public and foreign policy issues. The Peace Corps (http://www.peacecorps.gov) also has created a Web site that holds resources useful to teachers and students that provide a window on different peoples and cultures across the globe. UNICEF has undertaken a similar effort with its Voices of Youth page (http://www.unicef.org/voy/), which allows students and teachers to learn about and discuss global issues that affect their lives.

Outside schools, the Web has also found an important place in reinforcing other educational media. Children's television programming like *Sesame Street* and its newer cousin, *Between the Lions* (both of which were originally funded by the Carnegie Corporation of New York) have demonstrated the ability of TV to serve as a means for prosocial educational development of children. The Web plays little role in the actual episodes of these shows but it does allow greater educational depth. *Between the Lions*, for example, uses its Web site (http://pbskids.org/lions/) to enhance its focus on improving children's reading skills. The site provides stories, games (some of which are printable to allow children to write on, color, and otherwise interact with the material), audio, and video clips that help reinforce themes raised in the program itself. It also provides materials to guide parents in helping their children learn to read. There are segments available on reading with children, visiting the library, and using the computer. There are also guides for kindergarten teachers to improve literacy. These efforts point the way for similar uses in other areas of education. In the context of this book, we are especially hopeful about uses in teaching constructive patterns of human relationships at all levels, from family and community to ethnic, religious, and international. Enough has been done to show the feasibility of this approach.

A great deal of educational software is available for use both at school and at home, although there are many complaints from educators that much of this has so far been of low quality. Over time, this situation may well improve. During the 1990s, the President's Committee of Advisors on Science and Technology (White House) devoted major attention to this problem and stimulated grant making by various government agencies, which led to promising innovations in education that made use of advanced technology. The President's Committee emphasized that the technology, important as it is, remains a means to the end of acquiring knowledge and problem-solving skills.

A review of the children's interactive media environment conducted by the Markle Foundation in April 2002 identified and analyzed the trends, dynamics, and parties involved in the industry. The results, published in *An Environmental Scan of Children's Interactive Media from 2000 to 2002*,[48] could be of use in discovering new, positive ways of using interactive and software technologies for children.

For all the creativity that has been shown in putting the Web and connected technologies to work for education, the impact of the Internet on the public schools in the United States and most other countries has been modest. Work is needed on teacher knowledge and computer accessibility. Here, as elsewhere, teachers are crucial. Often teachers have limited understanding of technology, are undertrained, have severe time constraints, and are limited by school budgets. New York State provides a useful example of such problems. Various incentives have been used in New York State in recent years to educate teachers in the use of computers and to bring them up to date on the latest technology.[49] However, these skills are hardly useful to students if there is little or no access to computers in the classroom. This problem is greatly exacerbated in developing countries.

In a November 2000 article of *New York Teacher* (a newspaper for the statewide union of New York State United Teachers), Richard Miller, vice president for the middle and junior high schools at the United Federation of Teachers in New York City, commented on helping teachers to reach higher standards for their students, "Many of the materials and professional development opportunities don't reach the teachers."[50] The State Education Department (SED) only provides curriculum resource guides, sample tests, and model lessons through the Internet. Miller went on to say, "Most schools are not wired and don't have access, or don't have the printing capability."[51] Similarly, a Staten Island teacher complained that teachers had not received lessons because they were available only on an SED Web site. "You think my school has access to the Internet? Not even our secretaries can get online."[52] A first-grade teacher from the Bronx, Luis F. Rivera, in an opinion column in *New York Teacher*, wrote about classrooms being overcrowded and teachers and students being overwhelmed.[53] From his 7 years' teaching experience, he recognized that children can learn when taught under the proper conditions and when nurtured by their families, schools, and communities. As a teacher, he felt that he was unable to offer children a quality education because of limited resources and wondered why nurturing children is not considered the highest priority. This poignant refrain occurs in many educational contexts, not only technology. The centrality of teachers remains a cardinal fact of successful education and its adaptation to new opportunities.

Considering these larger problems, the Web is certainly not a magic cure-all for the problems faced by education. Simply providing more computers and Internet access will not solve the larger problems that face the educational system unless they are part of more comprehensive efforts, based to the extent possible on educational research and on content of great significance for human adaptation—not only to teach children how to make a living but to learn how to live together amicably.

CONCLUSION

Discussion of the Web recently has been overheated. Much rhetoric in the 1990s about the revolutions it was to bring to business, education, and society at large seem premature and overblown, only a few years later. There is a digital divide. Many people, even in prosperous Western Europe and North America, do not have regular access to the Internet or even own a computer. Those who do often do not have the latest technology that allows full exploitation of the Web. For example, many people who have Internet access may have slow modems, meaning that video files and detailed graphics of some Web sites take a long time to load onto a computer or are simply not accessible.

What's more, the digital divide is not just socioeconomic but also generational, with the result that parents are often unaware of the risks the Internet poses for their children and are unable to help their children use it for sound educational purposes. This issue will be exacerbated as new technologies that allow Internet access through mobile devices come into common use and parents have less opportunity to monitor their child's Internet use. Furthermore, for those not accustomed to the established norms and visual cues of the Web, it can be daunting to navigate. There is so much material available that it is easy to get lost—bogged down in irrelevant information that Web searches turn up—even if you know what you are looking for. Even well-informed advocates see the current state of the Web as awkward.[54] More troubling for the long-term use of the Web as a tool for education is the transient nature of information on it. In preparing this chapter, we noted that several promising Web sites dealing with the education of children appeared and then just as quickly disappeared. This is a commonplace occurrence. As more established institutions (such as universities and financially well-supported schools) establish Web components for their educational efforts, these sites are more likely to become valuable sources of information. In any event, the volatility of Web sites is a problem that must be addressed.

There is no doubt that the Internet has great potential for education; yet we have seen that its role is not always positive. Hate groups have seen this educational potential and use the Web to disseminate their own messages that prey on young users. There is an ongoing need to combat this harshly divisive use of technology. We should realize, as groups like the ADL and SPLC have shown, that the Web itself is one of the most effective ways to combat hate on the Web. Furthermore, those interested in fostering peaceful, equitable human relations should take advantage of the Internet to support educational efforts in many ways. There are applications at all levels from preschool teaching to advanced scholarship. The creative efforts in education generally have considerable promise in education for peace and fairness specifically. Because of the flexibility of the technology and, most important, the creativity of the people who employ it, its use will grow. The challenge is to make its use timely, informative, affordable, and constructive for education, especially in the vital domain of nurturing decent human relationships, overcoming intergroup animosity, and fostering prosocial development.

We extend special gratitude to Zoë Baird, President of the Markle Foundation, and her excellent staff for all their helpful contributions toward this chapter.

15

International Education

A Global Outlook

WHY LOOK ABROAD?

The world is rapidly moving toward greater interdependency and globalization, driven by technological advances, economic opportunities, and intellectual curiosity. There is more movement across national boundaries than ever before: of people, money, information, ideas, images, and much more. We are embedded among billions of people, mostly strangers, yet we need them and they need us: to make a living; to travel; to cope with widespread problems like infectious diseases and terrorism; to secure the safety of our food, water, and environment; and to protect us physically.

So now we humans in virtually every country must of necessity find decent ways to interact with strangers, move beyond stereotypes, and to the extent possible turn strangers into familiar people, even turn potential adversaries into friends. Yet this is a task that goes far beyond the prior experience of humanity. Yes, we have done some of this before, but much less than we will have to do as a practical matter in the twenty-first century. In our ancient past, this would have been exceedingly difficult. Among monkeys and apes, a very powerful instigator for harmful aggression is the crowding of strangers in the presence of valued resources.[1] Probably the same was true for our early human ancestors over many millennia. Now we have to learn how to transcend ancient suspicions and biases, learn how to live together with people who are initially strange and perhaps implicitly threatening. To do so, we must widen the horizons of education from childhood onward and learn—in a reasonable sampling process—about other peoples, cultures, ideas, preferences, ways of life. In this process, strangeness can be converted to familiarity, suspicion to fascination. That is why international education bears not only on economic well-being in a world of technoeconomic globalization, but it also bears on the vital issues of war and peace.

TERRORISM AS A STIMULUS FOR INTERNATIONAL EDUCATION

Americans have typically focused their attention on domestic concerns rather than looking abroad. But this mindset is no longer viable. As the world community continues to become evermore interconnected, U.S. citizens will need to look beyond their shores with an attitude of curiosity and open-mindedness. The same need exists in many nations throughout the world. And this extends to our children.

A recent article in the *Christian Science Monitor* emphasized the need to improve and expand the current K-through-12 curriculum to include study of the Middle East.[2] Educational organizations within the United States are rapidly moving to accommodate the demand from educators for more information on the Middle East since the tragic terrorist attacks of September 11, 2001. Educators, students, and many citizens are discovering that they need to improve their knowledge and understanding about this dangerous area of the world.

The Los Angeles–based Constitutional Rights Foundation (CRF) for 40 years has specialized in creating a civil-education curriculum. Since September 11, 2001, it has addressed this issue aggressively. There has been a prompt response from curriculum developers to write more on the Middle East to help teachers structure new classroom lessons. The demand among teachers has been great. For example, the CRF Web site witnessed an increase in demand for materials of 500 to 600 percent in the weeks following the terrorist attacks. Textbook publishers, too, are responding by including last-minute changes to update materials currently in press.

Educators, although glad to see this surge of interest in the Middle East, find that it sadly illuminates the past U.S. tendency to focus on domestic or crisis concerns, and highlights its failures to teach the richness of world history. At present, most schools offer little if anything in the way of Middle Eastern studies, with the exception of some affluent schools that teach at least a modicum of information about the world beyond the borders of the United States.

By contrast, an example of forward-looking instruction is demonstrated in the teaching of a recently retired high school teacher from Williamstown, Vermont, who, well before September 11, made it a point to teach about the Middle East and Central Asia in a course, "Conflict in the Twentieth Century." As a former military man with 15 years' experience abroad working in counterterrorism, this teacher felt that his students should feel comfortable with maps of the Middle East region as well as the Islamic religion's contemporary culture. Following the terrorist attacks, former students contacted him to express their gratitude. He had given them a framework to understand the events of that terrible day.

Since 1995, the American Textbook Council has urged textbook publishers and educators to increase and improve the coverage of world history, including the world's religions. Yet little response occurred. Although there has been much talk of global education, the curriculum in this respect is substandard, though most states require at least a modicum of instruction on comparative world religion. In California, perhaps the most pluralistic of all U.S. states now, 3 years of world history is required—2 years more than in most other states.

The tragedies of international terrorism can serve a useful, albeit inadvertent, purpose if they stimulate the public and educators to a serious, in-depth interest in international education—but not limited to areas of terrorism. Whereas we here focus on the United States, this need is apparent in many other countries.

EDUCATION FOR INTERNATIONAL UNDERSTANDING AND GLOBAL COMPETENCE: AN INTRODUCTION

In January 2000, the Carnegie Corporation of New York convened a meeting to discuss strengthening U.S. understanding of the world through education. Representatives from educational associations, organizations, agencies, and foundations debated several key questions:

1. Are schools, colleges and universities preparing their students to function effectively in a global society in which time and space no longer insulate the nations, peoples, and markets of the world?
2. Do U.S. citizens understand enough of the world beyond our national borders to evaluate information about international and global issues to make sound judgments about them?
3. Is education in the United States preparing Americans for sustained involvement in a highly interdependent world?[3]

During the cold war, the federal government and major foundations committed large resources to studying international relations, foreign languages, and economic development. Given this divided world, the dynamics of international relations needed to be understood in addition to knowledge about the societies, politics, and economics of international rivals, allies, and nations coming out of colonialism. Centers for international and areas studies were established, in part, for this purpose.

When the cold war receded, issues that went beyond national borders and politics survived but with a different emphasis. There was now concern about the health of the global environment and globalization of markets. People within and across national boundaries intensified affiliations based on their own cultural identities, especially ethnic and religious, often conducive to hostility and bloodshed. Yet the rapidly changing world was not adequately addressed in most classrooms around the globe, even in the face of massive killing and repression occurring in such diverse places as Yugoslavia, Rwanda, Afghanistan, and Congo during the 1990s.

Teachers with a Global Perspective and Resources to Help Them

Most teachers are not adequately prepared to teach global studies. But those who are motivated to do so and who have the proper skills often find their efforts blocked because of the many external demands on course content. Yet actions can be taken to integrate global perspectives, even within the current restraints:

- Increase the opportunity for teachers to travel; emphasize immersion in other cultures and societies—even for brief periods—to help bring the outside world back into the classroom.
- Provide intercultural experiences at home.
- Use the Internet to give students insight into other cultures. Although it is less than ideal, using the Internet as a virtual exchange is an accessible alternative to travel. Technically, the richness of input from Internet resources is likely to increase in the years immediately ahead. Research is needed to clarify potential uses for international education.

Four resources available for global education were highlighted at the Carnegie meeting. Motivated teachers may take advantage of the following:

1. The American Forum for Global Education has published over 200 books on curriculum; it offers preservice and in-service workshops for teachers.
2. The National Endowment for the Humanities offers summer seminars and institutes. In the year 2000, nearly one-half of the offerings had a focus on another country or offered a global viewpoint.
3. The National Peace Corps Association sponsors Global TeachNet, a network of professional development for K-through-12 teachers who are fostering a global perspective in their U.S. classrooms. Small incentive grants are offered to teachers who provide documentation on successful global education curricula. In addition, they are posted on the Global TeachNet Web site. "Adaptor" grants are given to teachers who wish to adapt a curriculum to their particular classroom needs.
4. The World Bank Institute created Internet connectivity and training in the use of technology for the classrooms in 15 countries in Africa, Latin America, Eastern Europe, and the Middle East. The service is called World Links for Development. If sustained for the long-term, this could provide a powerful resource for intercultural understanding.

It is not enough to have resources available, important as that first step is. How are the resources to be *used*? Innovations and interventions have only limited impact unless there is a *sustained* effort and *incentives for teachers* that will allow them to integrate resources such as new content and technology into their classrooms.

Several approaches for sustained improvement were offered in the Carnegie conference:

- Standards and assessments should be developed that include *global* perspectives. This would create a demand for integrating them into the curriculum in order to meet the standards. Assessment results could then be used to focus on the need to develop specific additional resources and strategies for global learning.
- A concentration of multiple resources throughout school districts in curriculum and instruction is likely to elicit long-term change. One example is the National Geographic Society's renewed effort to teach geography and to cover topics such as weapons of mass destruction and the worldwide emergence of megacities.
- The business community is a potential source of support. Business needs a workforce skilled and knowledgeable about global issues, able to adapt to changing world conditions. Similarly, community leaders and state governors are concerned about building capacities to participate effectively in the changing global economy—for example, to attract foreign investment.
- The accessibility and power of new information technologies make them desirable tools to use for this purpose; ongoing research is necessary to make effective use of technology for education, and especially for international education.

Schools, Colleges, and Universities Can Work Collectively for Change

The Carnegie meeting participants agreed on the necessity of links between (a) higher education institutions and (b) elementary and secondary schools. This is an essential factor in improving global education. As we shall see, it is also vital for peace education. Fortunately, the priorities of higher education institutions are now moving in this direction. This commitment is certainly necessary for training teachers to be knowledgeable about global issues. Enthusiastic teacher participation is necessary here as in other educational innovations.

Foreign language study is worthy of attention at all levels of education. In order to understand the rest of the world, competency in another language is exceedingly helpful—especially when communicating with the majority of the world's population that has only basic education and limited or no access to modern communications. Language facility helps to gain a modicum of understanding of the history and culture of other peoples. Besides economic utility, this can help to diminish ethnocentrism. Contrary to students' high interest in learning another language, colleges and universities across the United States continue to reduce their foreign language requirements.

From Outlook to Action

What are informative indicators of internationalization in higher education? For example, do area studies, courses on global environmental change, strong foreign language departments, or the presence of foreign students and the availability of study abroad indicate that a college or university is achieving useful internationalization? It is plausible that they do so. The American Council on Education (ACE) has done a study in the year 2000 that provides some interesting findings. Two surveys, conducted by the ACE, were designed to inform higher education institutions of the importance that Americans place on opportunities to learn about international subjects.[4] The ACE used telephone sampling of approximately 1,000 Americans 18 years of age and older, and a telephone sampling of 500 college-bound high school seniors.

The results, prior to the terrorism of September 11, 2001, already showed a public keenly interested in learning about international issues and languages, and a university and college system that has not been adequately responsive. Highlights from the surveys are categorized by international experience, international attitudes, and international knowledge.

Most Americans have traveled outside the United States, mostly close to home or to countries of the West. The most significant factor to predict travel abroad was education. Nearly twice the number of college graduates traveled abroad, as compared to individuals who had not finished high school. Nearly half of the respondents indicated a fair or somewhat proficient grasp of another language, and about one-quarter felt they were fluent in another language. A similar survey done in 1988 showed that 58 percent of the respondents reported either a fair or fluent command of another language.

Sixty-four percent of the national sample followed international news, a figure substantially lower than that given for those who were interested in local news (89 percent) and national news (82 percent). Results also indicated that an interest in international affairs in the news correlated with travel experience abroad. College graduates, when compared with students without college degrees, showed more interest in international news events.

Most respondents believed that globalization is an important factor in their daily lives, report being increasingly informed about many international issues, and express sustained interest in events outside the United States. A vast majority felt that the United States should be involved in international affairs—a jump of almost 15 percent from just 5 years earlier. Half the respondents believed that international concerns would have a somewhat or very important impact on their careers in 10 years. Almost 90 percent felt that it would be important to the professional careers of future generations.

More than 85 percent of the national respondents believed that foreign language knowledge is important (a much higher percentage than was found in a Gallup Poll conducted 20 years ago). In addition, they thought that knowing a foreign language would help them find better jobs. This same percentage of the respondents said that the availability of foreign language classes would be a factor in choosing a college or university. Approximately three-quarters of those surveyed believed that foreign language training should be a high school requirement and that it should be required in higher education institutions. Students wanted colleges and universities to require general courses on international topics and felt it important to study or participate in internships abroad during their educational careers.

The results of these two surveys strongly support a growing public interest in events beyond U.S. borders even before September 11, 2001, and the belief that international skills and knowledge are increasingly important in today's globalized world.

There is a strong consensus that colleges and universities should provide all students with an opportunity for international education. This includes foreign language study, opportunities to study abroad, and courses with an international dimension. There is very little evidence of old-style isolationism or xenophobia.

Thus, a solid foundation for international education exists in public attitudes, beliefs, and preferences. It remains for educational institutions to translate this outlook into action. But they cannot do so without adequate funding for this purpose. Over the past 10 years, federal funding has dropped for post secondary international studies (e.g., education and cultural exchanges, language, and faculty research).[5] The exceptions are: the National Security Educational Program (NSEP), which began in 1994, but then was cut significantly in 1995. The U.S. Department of Higher Education Act (HEA)—Title VI Programs and the Department of Education Fulbright–Hays Programs have been funded since 1990. President Clinton's "Memorandum on International Education Policy" of April 2000 calls for a dynamic change and commitment to colleges and university-level internationalization efforts. State funding for international education has also declined, with few exceptions. Foundation priorities have not been favorable to international education. So, a major requirement is an increase in public and private support for international education. This will make it possible for educational institutions to respond to the need.

Despite weak funding, much useful work continues. Area studies still exist illuminating geographic and cultural features of selected other countries. They have traditionally been the core of research, graduate education, and undergraduate teaching about the rest of the world. Much government and foundation support was granted after World War II to area studies centers to help develop U.S. expertise in areas of cold war competition. Clearly this now needs reassessment and reinvigoration beyond cold war considerations. We must ensure that knowledge and understanding of particular geographic areas is supported by serious study of culture, language, and history. Finding fresh ways of thinking about area studies is needed to take into account the rapidly changing forces of interdependence now underway. And any particular area must be seen in the context of a wider world.

Academic study abroad, for credit, has increased in recent years, but terrorism may have a chilling effect on the future. Students wish to prepare for careers in which they are likely to have opportunities to work overseas. However, even with this increase, fewer than 10 percent of undergraduate students at 4-year higher education institutions actually study abroad. The largest number of students comes from research universities. The impact of foreign study is dependent on students' preparation, the extent to which they are immersed in the host culture, and opportunities to build on these experiences upon return to the home campus.

Not only does internationalization occur when students study overseas, but also with the presence of foreign students and teachers on campus. With the increased presence of foreign students on U.S. campuses and the decline in U.S. students studying abroad (a drop from 40 to 30 percent since 1982), U.S. institutions can take more advantage of these foreign students and scholars to enrich campus and community life.

Business schools have also responded to economic globalization by providing graduate and undergraduate level education. But it is doubtful whether international education has truly been integrated into business education. Yet there will be growing incentives to do so in the global economy, and some leading schools of business are moving in this direction.

An Action Plan

The Carnegie conference participants recommended that international and global perspectives be an integral part of education from kindergarten through graduate school. But how can schools, colleges, and universities respond to this need? Several strategic opportunities were proposed.

First, *integrate international and global perspectives into the curriculum in a substantive way*. These perspectives should be reinforced by reflecting their importance in admissions requirements for higher education. For example, students should show competence in a second language. As higher education institutions review their commitment to liberal education at the undergraduate and preprofessional levels, they should recognize the importance of increasing knowledge about the entire world and promote the necessary skills for intercultural communication.

Second, *learning by doing should be encouraged*. This involves emphasizing the importance of study abroad and making it feasible for the full range of students—including minority and low-income students—to take advantage of the opportunity. Also by encouraging *diversity in the student body*, campuses may provide additional opportunities for students to engage with people from different parts of the world.

Third, *technology* should be used to full advantage. The *Internet* is highly accessible and provides a virtual international exchange with the ability to connect classrooms around the world. Much innovation is currently happening in this area. The challenge is to ensure that these resources become integrated into the classroom for sustained impact. We said more about this prospect in Chapter 14, in our discussion of information technology.

Fourth, *teachers are central* to each of these strategic opportunities. They are the individuals responsible for bringing international perspectives into the classroom. Study abroad and other professional development experiences are key factors for teachers to bring this promise to fulfillment.

Finally, support should be given for the development of an *international education policy*. The cold war was a period when the federal government made large investments in international and area studies. The time is ripe again to make this a priority, not for war but for peace, justice, and prosperity. The Association of International Educators has proposed the development of an international education policy. To develop and implement such a policy will require real leadership in education, business, government, international organizations, and philanthropy. Each of these sectors has a natural interest in strengthening international education. But can they come together for a concerted effort on policy to implement their aspirations?

A RESOURCE FOR INTERNATIONAL
EDUCATION, K THROUGH 12

The journal *Social Education* published guidelines in 1998 for global and international studies.[6] These guidelines converge (largely independently) with the Carnegie conference consensus. The recommendations are based on the premise that students in the United States must be prepared for a world in which boundaries are increasingly diffuse and worldwide conflict continues to occur. The authors ask questions about subjects that students should learn; what skills they should master; and what attitudes they need to face large-scale global issues.

The summaries here reflect the knowledge of many scholars and educators, in an effort to help curriculum developers address international themes for kindergarten through high school. Themes fall into three broad categories:

1. Global challenges such as major violent conflicts, economic and religious belief systems, environmental and political issues, and problems of population and technology
2. Global cultures and world areas
3. Global connections: the United States and the world

Within each theme, a rationale is given for study, knowledge objectives, relevant skills for evaluating issues, and participation objectives. For our purposes, we focus only on the first theme and identify relevant categories summarized in the guidelines. The first theme is most pertinent to the central aims of this book.

To best identify major global challenges, 75 documents were studied, from the past 50 years, written about global and international education. Included in this documentation are surveys, reports, and scholarly pieces written by citizens of other countries. These scholars emphasized that change and interdependence are central to the sciences and that they deserve continuous attention through the course of any program educating students toward global literacy.

Major Global Challenges

The following categories are not exhaustive, nor are they mutually exclusive. In fact, many overlap. But they do provide a basis for examining how teaching and learning about international concerns can be improved in kindergarten through 12th grade.

CONFLICT AND ITS CONTROL: VIOLENCE, TERRORISM, WAR   This broad category encompasses several subtopics, ranging from localized conflict to international violence. Thus, international education can naturally pave the way for peace education (see Chapters 16, 17, and 18). Several topics come into focus that can be usefully explored in the classroom:

1. *Subnational conflicts*, including revolutions, assassinations, and guerilla activities, in addition to genocide and ethnic cleansing, and tribalism and secessionist movements.
2. *Weapons proliferation*, ranging from the conventional to chemical, biological, and nuclear and including arms races, which involve sales, sanctions, controls and trafficking.
3. *Terrorism*, including state-sponsored terrorism, social revolutionaries, sanctuaries, religious fundamentalists, and conflicts across borders based on irredentism or revanchism.
4. *National Security*, including force used by nations acting alone or in combination with other nations.

All of these topics naturally lead to the kind of conflict resolution and violence prevention opportunities we discuss in subsequent chapters for education for peace.

ECONOMIC SYSTEMS: INTERNATIONAL TRADE, AID, INVESTMENT   The more recent the source, the greater the focus on problems of economics and on social concerns related to technological economic transformation—reflecting growing interdependence and globalization. The aim is for students at all levels to develop gradually an understanding of ways in which international economics is not only pertinent to their job opportunities as adults but also to the world's chances of avoiding disastrous wars in their lifetimes.

1. *Comparative economic systems:* Developing nations are typically engaged in transitional and fragile economies, struggling to modernize and seeking ways out of massive poverty. Their comparison with the economies of established democracies can be intrinsically illuminating and a stimulus to the search for equitable economic growth throughout the world.
2. *International trade*: Following from the above, these matters bear heavily on opportunities for prosperity and managing conflicts without violence. Therefore, it is worthwhile to study the nature and scope of trade among various countries and the factors that influence relatively free trade on the basis of *mutual* benefit.
3. *Foreign aid:* Public opinion surveys from the late 1990s indicate that the U.S. population is largely ignorant of foreign aid. For instance, the percentage of the national budget devoted to foreign aid programs is grossly overestimated. The purposes, forms, amounts, and factors conducive to success of foreign aid deserve study. Other important topics are related to direct foreign investment with a focus on the role of multinational corporations, transnational enterprises, and regional trading blocs such as the European Union.
4. *Economic and political concerns in the developing world:* Issues such as debt crisis and relief, escape from repression, trade policies that give opportu-

nity to developing nations, and the risks (such as infectious diseases and international terrorism) of deterioration in developing countries are in urgent need of understanding. It is no longer feasible to ignore these faraway places as exotic oddities or even as virtually nonexistent. Our fate is bound up with theirs.

GLOBAL BELIEF SYSTEMS: IDEOLOGIES, RELIGIONS, PHILOSOPHIES   This category includes the study of comparative ideologies such as communism and capitalism as well as study of philosophies that are linked to a specific religion such as Confucianism, Hinduism, Daoism, and Islam. The implied goal is to build empathy for other cultures through improved understanding; and to prepare for coping with dangerous aspects of some ideologies—indeed the extreme, absolutist form of most political and religious ideologies.

HUMAN RIGHTS AND SOCIAL JUSTICE, HUMAN NEEDS AND QUALITY OF LIFE   The sources consulted by the *Social Education Journal* showed a broad range of human concerns related to quality of life issues worldwide. The more recent resources place strong emphasis on global human rights—mostly developed in the second half of the twentieth century.

1. *Gender and equity:* Equal access to justice, violations of human rights based on identities linked to race, ethnicity, political, or sexual orientation.
2. *Food and hunger:* These high-profile public concerns are expressed intensely in the media and include global food security, unequal access to food, nutritional concerns including disease related to inadequate diet, food aid, and the green revolution.
3. *Health, education, and welfare:* These broad concerns encompass serious infectious diseases (especially HIV and AIDS), substandard sanitation, use of illicit drugs, inadequate shelter, illiteracy, low standards of living, and absence of a social safety net.

PLANET MANAGEMENT: RESOURCES, ENERGY, ENVIRONMENT   Major emphasis was placed on the depletion of natural resources. This includes pollution of the environment and energy degradation. Energy source topics were particularly focused on petroleum and nuclear energy (including problems and potential uses). Also alternative energy sources such as solar power and hydropower were considered along with the need and opportunity to conserve energy. Ways to care for the environment—air, land, water, and seabed pollution, global warming, ozone depletion, toxic and nuclear wastes, and acid rain—were among the major concerns. In addition, the importance of degradation of land through erosion, deforestation, drought, and reductions in biodiversity were discussed.

INTERNATIONAL POLITICAL SYSTEMS   Many sources recommended studying political systems and ideologies that differ from the United States in order to get a sense of the world's diversity. Institutions recommended most for study were the UN and its agencies. Also, the roles of regional organizations such as NATO, Organization of American States, Organization of African Unity (changed in 2002 to African Union) were also suggested for study.

Another cluster of interest centered on the role of alliances, treaties, and negotiations. Recent sources recommended for study included "political disintegration, irredentism, secessionism, devolution of nations, separatism, and the opposing trends of regional integration and increased democratization and autonomy."[7] The study of nongovernmental organizations with their rapidly increasing role in international affairs was also recommended.

POPULATION: DEMOGRAPHIC GROWTH, PATTERNS, MOVEMENTS, TRENDS
The study of populations, especially ways of diminishing unsustainable rapid population growth, was considered to be vitally important. Many scholars feel that unless populations can be limited, specifically in very poor countries of Africa, Asia, and Latin America, then solutions to most of the other world problems will continue to go unanswered. Basic information on population growth—birth and death rates, migration, immigration, and emigration with all the changes—was one focus. Another focus centered on the practical necessity of thoughtful family planning, including contraception practices. A final category spanned various population-related issues such as aging, illegal aliens, guest workers, political asylum, refugees, and displaced persons.

HUMAN COMMONALITY AND DIVERSITY   Most sources consulted recommended that all students study this topic. In particular, studies should center on reducing prejudice, avoiding stereotypes, and eliminating discrimination to the extent possible—keeping in mind the fundamental shared characteristics of all humanity.

TECHNOCRATIC REVOLUTION: SCIENCE, TECHNOLOGY, COMMUNICATIONS
Nearly all of the recent sources consulted recommended that science, technology, and communications be studied because of the increasingly important roles they play in contemporary society. Social studies, mathematics, and science teachers can use the study of science and technology to develop cross-disciplinary analysis of contemporary world problems and unprecedented opportunities.

Altogether, these are high aspirations that will require major educational adjustments, public policy changes, and community support. The issues are so important in a rapidly transforming world that these adaptations must be undertaken. A promising new example shows how this might be done.

INTERNATIONAL EDUCATION: ASIA AS AN ENTERING WEDGE

For several reasons, it is important for Americans and Europeans to be informed about Asia. First, it is the world's largest and most diverse continent, with 60 percent of the world's population and 30 percent of the world's land mass. Second, in aggregate it constitutes the second largest economy in the world, including some of the fastest growing national economies. All this is significant for world economic well-being. Third, Asia purchases over 40 percent of U.S. exports. Fourth, the United States and Europe need cooperation with Asia on many fronts, ranging from the spread of nuclear weapons and terrorism to health problems to human rights. Fifth, Asia is unfortunately the seat of serious threats to peace and security.

Tommy Koh, former ambassador to the United States who now directs the Institute of Policy Studies in Singapore, wrote in 2001 on the *mutual* ignorance between the peoples of the United States and Asia.[8] This lack of knowledge of each other's history and cultural practices is a breeding ground for misunderstanding and trouble between these two powerful and increasingly interdependent areas of the world. Complex global activities, once held largely in the domain of the diplomatic corps, are rapidly becoming everyday experiences of business and government professionals as well as institutions of civil society such as the scientific community and the media.

The task of improving U.S. students' knowledge of Asia is daunting, but not impossible. Pedagogically, there are models and curricula of the past 15 years on which to build. There are past experiences with teacher exchanges and non-European language programs that can be helpful. Recently there has been a move toward integrating international content within parameters of the current school day and in support of higher standards. This can include a sampling of language, history, culture, and contemporary problems, including economic and security issues. Such information can be included in K-through-12 education along with reading, math, and science.

The National Commission on Asia in the Schools is a newly established entity of the Asia Society (based in New York City). It recently conducted a survey on Americans' knowledge about Asia. Results showed a disturbing ignorance among most Americans. For example, half of the adults and two-thirds of the adolescents believed that Vietnam is an island nation; two out of three Americans are ignorant of Mao Tse-tung's role as the first leader of the People's Republic of China; 80 percent of the respondents were ignorant of the fact that India is the world's largest democracy; and 25 percent of high school students did not know that the Pacific Ocean separates the United States from Asia.

There is no equivalent survey of Asian knowledge about the United States, but experienced observers like Koh estimate that they probably suffer a similar degree of ignorance about the United States. Koh points out several known misunderstandings of Asians about Americans:

- Big business or the military-industrial complex runs the United States. (A core of truth is exaggerated to make a caricature.)
- The United States is an ungodly country. (It is actually the most religious in the West.)
- Racism is rampant in the United States. (In reality, those in the United States are probably less racist than residents of many Asian and European countries. For example, President Bush's cabinet includes two Asian Americans.

Advances for minority groups in recent decades are dramatic, though there is still much to be done.)
- Americans are single-mindedly materialistic and worship the dollar. (Actually, Americans are quite philanthropic, with volunteerism being one prominent way of life.)

The differences in Asian and U.S. history and culture are another critical source of misunderstanding, so each needs to understand the other's unique cultural frameworks and historical contexts. Cultural frameworks determine the unique ways of viewing and behaving in the world. Take the example of human rights. Asians fear chaos for historical reasons, and therefore value public order and social harmony above personal freedom. This is largely due to the many tragedies caused by war, conflict, and anarchy—and by autocratic governments in some cases. By contrast, the people of the United States choose personal freedom over public order because, historically, the founders of the United States were European settlers who fled persecution and oppression. This was reinforced by subsequent waves of refugees to the United States—for example, the Jews who fled Nazi persecution and death camps. The government is seen as necessary and protective, but it should be restrained with checks and balances.

Despite their differences, Asians and Americans have important similarities and are now drawn more closely together than ever before and so must find ways to increase mutual understanding. Educating students is a vital starting point. Useful steps include encouraging more student exchanges, especially Americans studying in Asia, since so little has been done; encouraging tourism; and promoting the use of the Internet to increase understanding of cultural practices and norms. By increasing contact and obtaining more knowledge of each other, misunderstandings can be reduced, interest stimulated, and respect strengthened.

The recent work of the Asia Society provides a valuable example of efforts to expand education's horizons in our intimate, interdependent world. A major report prepared for the Asia Society gives useful guidance in ways to make education more deeply international. The Society's educational initiatives focus on improving the quality of elementary and secondary education on Asia by providing curricular materials, services, and support for educational practitioners and schools nationwide. Its broad use of state-of-the-art interactive media makes the Society a leader in this area. With the New York City office as its hub, the Society also has offices in several other cities in the United States, as well as in Australia, China, and the Philippines.

With many changes taking place worldwide and within our society, it is critical for today's children and youth to learn how to function effectively in an interconnected world. It is largely the job of elementary and high schools to lay the foundations of knowledge, curiosity, and respect for this challenging future. Global trade, commerce, national security, and health concerns as well as the increasing size of the Asian American community, link the United States with Asia now more than ever before.

In the 2001 report of the National Commission on Asia in the Schools, strong arguments are made for the need of preparing U.S. youth for an increasingly interconnected global community.[9] It emphasizes a top-down approach (leadership from a national organizations of goodwill and expertise), but also underscores the importance of individual interest, motivation, and enthusiasm of both teachers and students to make global studies in general, and Asian-related studies in particular, a reality in the United States.

Asia studies can give students broad and transferable skills, and many students are eager to learn about Asia and other parts of the world. In addition, many teachers are motivated to learn and teach about Asia. Despite these findings, U.S. schools have not made much progress regarding incorporating Asia-related content in curriculum materials, teacher preparation, language courses, textbooks, and other educational tools. Yet most Asia studies are readily integrated into existing core subjects. They can be woven into studies of geography, the sciences, the arts, and economics. Excellence in education will be defined, in the twenty-first century, by numeracy and literacy, but also by developing students' ability to interpret information in global terms and to understand other peoples. These considerations surely apply to other countries as well as the United States. Though there is much international variation, there remains a worldwide tendency to parochialism and ethnocentrism in education.

What U.S. Students Need to Know about Asia

The National Commission on Asia in the Schools established a task force to clarify the "general parameters of content and approach necessary for *global* education" (italics added).[10] The work of the task force can guide future curricular work.

The following are six key curriculum principles emphasized by the Commission:[11]

1. Study of Asia should be integrated across the curriculum at various levels and woven into the fabric of existing course content.
2. K-through-12 education should reflect current scholarship on Asia and Asian American content.
3. Balance general studies of international experience with in-depth studies of Asia.
4. Both teaching and learning should occur in the spirit of respect and empathy. Cultural stereotypes should be challenged.
5. Direct experiences of Asian cultures should occur to the extent possible through language study, travel abroad, expanded programs in the arts, media (Internet included), and student exchange programs.
6. Emphasis should be on the dynamism and interconnection of cultures throughout history. Asia should not solely be described in the context of its relationship to the West.

All students are expected to achieve understanding, skills, and attitudes through formal and informal learning about Asia. The following six fundamental skills involving intellectual knowledge constitute a high level of aspiration for which striving is worthwhile even though not all desiderata can be fully implemented. Students should

1. understand the potential influence of Asia on the United States and how U.S. decisions and actions are affected by its relationship to Asia.
2. learn about Asia's physical and cultural diversity by studying geography, languages, cultural traditions, values and beliefs.
3. become versed in global systems and current issues as they relate to Asia.
4. study the growth of major Asian civilizations, and their influence on world development.
5. become informed about the changes within our society that have come from the growth of the Asian American community and other demographic groups.
6. develop the ability to communicate well with people outside the United States in English and at least one other language.

The fundamental actions—*pertinent to all parts of the world*—are to

1. Recognize the ways in which personal involvement and active citizenship affect international problems; be able to make informed decisions about global problems.
2. Be willing to learn about people from other countries—including their culture, language, and lifestyle.
3. Become aware of cultural diversity that extends beyond the boundaries of cultural stereotypes.
4. Be able to function effectively in different cultural settings and interact with diverse populations.

Models of Excellent Teaching and Learning about Asia

The Commission's report describes 16 schools, districts, and institutions of higher education in 11 states. These represent a sampling of excellence in teaching and learning about Asia that are taking place throughout the United States and provide a basis for hope about international education altogether. When creating or evaluating an Asia-related effort within a school system, there are several key considerations. They include classroom content and methodology, crafting the art of teaching, and linkages between the classroom and the larger community. Not all of the recommendations that follow will be reflected in any given program, but they can give guidance to these initiatives.

Content within the classroom should be able to show scholarship in several areas. A student must be able to demonstrate knowledge and integration of several disciplines. Materials must be accurate and authentic; social, cultural, and historical diversity of Asia must be taught in an age- and context-appropriate manner. Teaching materials must be clear; the curriculum must be integrated with the existing curricula. And there should be ample and regular use of Asian-language material.

The methods most appropriate are in fact those that have emerged from education research in recent years. They apply to other subjects as well as to international education:

1. Critical thinking and problem solving skills are required.
2. Methods should have the potential to be transferred and replicated in other settings.
3. Evaluation and assessment must be regular and follow accepted practices.
4. Students' emotional, intellectual, and social development needs serious consideration.
5. Learning based on inquiry and interaction must be promoted along with comparative skills.
6. Various communication technologies should be utilized in order to make the information personally meaningful to students.

The art of teaching involves teacher education and commitment linked to curriculum development. Teachers must be exposed to accurate and current scholarship on Asia, both in preservice and in-service training; travel and study grant programs should be included as well as conferences, seminars, and effective training in communications technologies. Every effort should be made to inculcate a distinctive sense of mission. This is a tall order. Not all of it can be done at any one time or place. But it provides a framework and a level of aspiration that can be stimulating and helpful.

Learning that takes place in the classroom must be connected to events in the world. By partnering schools with community organizations and especially with colleges and universities, students will benefit through increased knowledge of world events and other core subjects. It has already begun to happen in science and technology. We return to this special opportunity in chapter 18, "Education for Peace: The Role of Universities."

School Models

Following are three model programs that illustrate ways in which high-quality education on Asia studies is achievable, even with limitations of time and financial resources.[12] It is encouraging to note that many U.S. schools already have in place the key elements needed to improve the study of Asia. Outreach personnel as well as national, regional, and state organizations and foundations support committed and innovative teachers in many schools. The commission calls for a national education mandate to stimulate initiatives at the local level and to encourage state support. In this way, excellent existing models can spread to schools throughout the nation. In our view, such a mandate should not be limited to Asia, but rather should cover international education broadly.

A CALIFORNIA MIDDLE SCHOOL   Here, a principal took the lead in introducing Asia studies. Nancy Girvin of Emerald Middle School in El Cajon, California, and her team of four teachers traveled to New York City to attend a 2-week summer workshop in preparation for the TeachAsia program developed by the Asia Society in 1994. It is a national network of grassroots educational collaboratives that forge partnerships between schools and local resource institutions such as universities, museums and libraries. In following up at their school, the five educators were gratified that 52 percent of the faculty attended Saturday training sessions and expressed enthusiasm about the training and its potential for international education.

The TeachAsia program also fostered curriculum development. It utilized professors at the University of California, San Diego, and San Diego State University to prepare high-quality reading materials for the teachers specifically geared to middle schools and to the existing curriculum. And the program paved the way for the possibility of partnerships with universities in San Diego—providing a special opportunity for Emerald Middle School. We have repeatedly emphasized the value of cooperative efforts of universities and high schools, not only in this field but also in others.

The teachers integrated their Asia studies into the sixth- and seventh-grade curriculum. In California, there is a mandate that China be taught in the sixth grade and that Japan be taught in the seventh grade. The sixth grade was especially changed by the TeachAsia program. For example, math teachers used the abacus to teach place values; the science class explored the Tokyo subway system to teach skills of reading a map and learning about distances; the social studies instructor worked with the Asia Society staff to develop cultural exchange boxes for use in the classroom and to exchange with other U.S. as well as Australian schools.

Three variables are vital toward success of such a program, according to Girvin. First, the school principal must make international studies a high priority on the school agenda and provide strong leadership to make it happen. Second, programs need to be woven together with state standards and assessments just as TeachAsia has done. Third, encouraging teachers' talents and interests makes the program come to life. In effect, this helps to build a constituency for international education.

A SCHOOL FOR THE TALENTED AND GIFTED IN NEW YORK CITY   Hunter College High School (HCHS) is a campus school of Hunter College that is composed of very talented and intellectually gifted students and a highly respected faculty. Although it is a public school, it does not come under the mandate of the New York City Board of Education. It must meet state requirements, but there is valuable flexibility in its curriculum.

In 1993, a Global Studies program was introduced. Beginning in the second semester of seventh-grade, students are required to take six semesters of Global Studies. The program has long had a strong focus on South Asia in addition to Japanese and Chinese sections because of personal interests of the social studies faculty. Susan Meeker, head of the social studies department, says "it is often the passion of the individual teacher that fleshes out our curriculum offerings."[13]

Although teachers use texts prepared for the Global Advanced Placement test, there is generally "little material that covers the world the way the curriculum has been set up."[14] Also, there is a problem with the quality of the materials. Meeker believes that high quality curriculum material available for South Asia is largely lacking. As a result, teachers have developed many of their own materials as best they can. Another problem in teaching Asia studies has been the cut in offerings of Asian languages. The late 1990s budget cutbacks resulted in the cancellation of Chinese language classes. Only French, Spanish, and Latin are currently offered at HCHS.

Because of increased numbers of Asian students in the school, which reflects the changing population in New York City, the faculty feels an obligation to recognize and study these cultures. Several teachers are currently developing a senior interdisciplinary course. It will have a strong Asian component and cover art, English, social studies and literature. Meeker believes the grounding that students get in their Global Studies classes will help to make this humanities core approach successful in their senior year.

A NORTH CAROLINA PUBLIC HIGH SCHOOL   Shirley Benson, a 10th-grade teacher at James Kenan High School in Warsaw, North Carolina, had long been interested in teaching her students about the world. She had the opportunity to do so when she learned about the International School-to-School Partnerships through Technology (ISPT) run by the North Carolina Center for International Understanding. When she went for computer training in the project, they linked her with a Japanese school. This was how she first introduced Japan to her world literature students.

In this rural school of about 500 students, consisting mostly of minority and economically disadvantaged students, children exhibited little knowledge about other parts of the world. Through ISPT, diverse peoples from different cultures around the globe have become real to these students through the use of e-mail and photos of students from their partner school in Japan. Information has been exchanged on topics ranging from fads to serious world problems. They cocreated—with the Hamamatsu Kita High School in Shizuoka, Japan—a shared Web site called "Threaded Discussion." Students discuss topics ranging from Tanaka poetry to the Columbine shootings in Colorado. This electronic relationship is highly useful for increasing international understanding and knowledge. Benson and her Japanese partner teacher were able to coordinate projects that advanced their required course work while they helped to enhance their students' international knowledge. It was as if they were at once team teaching across two hemispheres.

FUTURE MODEL SCHOOLS   A remarkable additional opportunity to create such schools arose in September 2003 when the Bill and Melinda Gates Foundation gave the Asia Society a 5-year grant of $7.5 million to establish America's first national network of urban secondary schools devoted to international studies.[15] The ten model schools in five cities will be designed to address the international knowledge gap—the divide between the growing importance of other world regions, languages, and cultures to the nation's economic prosperity and national security, and Americans' relative lack of international knowledge and skills.

The schools will be created by a team of area and international studies scholars and standards-based instruction and youth development experts in collaboration with local school district leaders. They will integrate intellectually rigorous international content into all the core subject areas, including history and geography, science and math, literature and arts. They will put special emphasis on world languages and creative uses of technology to link students and educators in American classrooms to those in other nations. The schools will also create partnerships with local internationally oriented businesses and cultural institutions. The new schools will use international content as a means of improving learning and achievement across all different subject areas and prepare urban youth for college attendance.

The new schools will begin operation in New York City, Los Angeles, and North Carolina during the 2004–2005 school year. Additional cities will be added in 2005. Information about the new schools, including examples of courses and a timeline, will be posted as it becomes available at *www.InternationalEd.org.*

INCREASING AWARENESS AND DISSEMINATION OF INTERNATIONAL EDU- CATION   The Goldman Sachs Foundation in collaboration with the Asia Society created an annual prize program in June 2003 to publicize and reward excellence and advancement in U.S. international education programs for students and teachers at all school levels, as well as for innovators in the field. These $25,000 awards are intended to heighten public awareness of the importance of international education and also to provide exemplary models for the dissemination of such programs nationwide. Awards will be given annually in five categories: elementary/ middle school, high school, higher education, state initiatives, and media/ technology. A distinguished jury rigorously evaluated the hundreds of eligible applications from the schools and the other categories; three finalists were chosen from each category.

A UNIQUE DISCUSSION PROGRAM ON INTERNATIONAL RELATIONS: THE FOREIGN POLICY ASSOCIATION   The Foreign Policy Association (FPA) initiated the Great Decisions Discussion Program in 1954, during the post–World War II period.[16] Under the current brilliant leadership of President Noel Lateef, the Great Decisions Discussion Program is the keystone of the FPA's expanding educational outreach activities. A network of 250,000 people— representing public schools, universities, religious groups, and civic-minded community organizations—participate annually in exchanging information and ideas on U.S. foreign policy. The FPA publishes an annual briefing book that presents expert background papers on eight timely major U.S. foreign policy issues as the core of the discussion agenda. The Foreign Policy Association also produces a teacher's guide, a video series, and bulletins that update recent developments in the chosen eight topics. The FPA Web site (www.fpa.org) provides another useful resource for informing the public about the Great Decisions program and stimulating participation in world affairs.

What Different Sectors Must Do

Research by the National Commission on Asia in the Schools reveals that citizens and educators agree on the need to strengthen teaching and learning about Asia in the schools. By the year 2010, the Commission hopes to implement its goals for every child and every teacher. To do so, it advocates a role for several sectors of society.[17]

GOVERNORS   These are leaders in education and supervisors of their states economic health and should raise public awareness of the need for better education about other areas of the world. They should also develop plans for the state to achieve this goal. They can legitimately emphasize economic and security aspects as well as the intrinsic learning value.

PARENTS AND GUARDIANS   Working as advocates, parents and guardians should communicate with teachers and parents' groups to encourage international education as an integral part of elementary and secondary education.

STATE EDUCATION DEPARTMENTS   It is the responsibility of the chief state school officers and their departments of education to make certain that their policies mirror the national priority for students to learn about Asia and the world. As a state priority, it could help to shape curriculum, assessment tools, and funding for teachers' professional development, along with acquiring resources for the classroom.

SCHOOLS AND DISTRICTS   By building on successful classroom programs—moving them into the entire school and into the district—teaching and learning about Asia could be strengthened.

PROFESSIONAL ORGANIZATIONS AND TEACHERS' UNIONS   These are primary players in the improvement of the elementary through high school education system. They can give teachers necessary tools to bridge the gap between policy mandates and the realities of the classroom. Their influence as national and regional organizations could be used to reach a wide audience.

HIGHER EDUCATION INSTITUTIONS   These institutions should commit themselves in two major ways: (1) by extending their resources and their scholars to enrich the learning experiences from elementary through high school and (2) through schools of education that would encourage future teachers to increase their knowledge about Asia and enhance their abilities to integrate international materials across subjects.

ACADEMIC ASSOCIATIONS AND INDIVIDUAL SCHOLARS   Such scholarly networks as the Association for Asian Studies and the World History Association should modify their priorities so that scholarship and teaching share an equally important emphasis and have effective links with elementary and secondary schools.

BUSINESS COMMUNITY   Companies operating internationally should help policymakers and schools to promote educational policies, standards, and content in international and Asia-related education. They can use their experienced personnel and political clout to strengthen international education.

PUBLISHERS   Those involved in publishing educational tools such as textbooks, standardized tests, videos, and trade books should involve content experts on Asia, especially scholars, in developing materials. These products should be current and accurate—reflecting serious scholarship about Asia.

THE MEDIA   Media professionals should be leaders in raising public awareness about the influence of current events involving Asia on the lives of U.S. citizens. In addition, they should report international education as a novel and important aspect of adapting to a rapidly changing world.

MUSEUMS, CULTURAL INSTITUTIONS, LIBRARIES, AND NONPROFIT OR-GANIZATIONS   These organizations with expertise on Asia, Asian American issues, and other world regions should actively advance international education by cooperating with schools and school districts.

PHILANTHROPIC ORGANIZATIONS   These organizations support mobilization efforts and assessment of best practices to improve instruction and learning about Asia and other regions in the schools. This stimulus should be at both local and national levels.

THE NATION   The president, secretary of education, secretary of state, and Congress should begin a dialogue nationally on the importance of learning about diverse cultures and world regions so that Americans can meet the challenges of the twenty-first century. The U.S. effort can benefit from experiences of international education in other countries. Indeed, the U.S. effort must not be paradoxically parochial. It should involve cooperation with educational systems in other countries and encouragement in international education on a worldwide basis—for example, as a component of aid to developing countries and as a contribution to conflict resolution.

It is important to note that these considerations apply to international education in general—whether the focus is Asia, Africa, Latin America, or Europe. The essential point is the widening of educational horizons beyond the parochial focus that currently predominates.

Implementing the Dream

In May 2002, the National Coalition on Asia and International Studies in the Schools held its first meeting in Washington, D.C.[18] The Coalition consists of 40 national and state political, educational, and corporate leaders who are addressing the knowledge gap in international studies. They believe that knowledge of the world is key to educational excellence, which benefits not only the individual but also the nation.

The Asia and International Studies in the Schools Initiative is sponsored by the Asia Society and supported by several national foundations and corporations. Future plans include state and national initiatives in addition to the development of resources for teachers and schools. States will be selected each year to participate in roundtables of state business, political, and educational leaders. The Coalition will engage both business and political leaders in order to raise their awareness of the importance of our nation's lack of knowledge about other regions of the world. This agenda will be promoted by enlisting help from key educational organizations. The Coalition will report on the most effective practices and initiatives happening in the states. By working with Ministries of Education in other countries, joint programs of mutual benefit can be created such as teacher exchange programs. Also, the Coalition plans to makes resources available by creating and promoting Web sites that include materials and lesson plans, creating networks of teachers and schools, linking classrooms between the United States and other world regions, and providing guides to best practices on vital issues.

CONCLUSION

Many of the ideas, techniques, and partnerships useful for international education can be applied to education for conflict resolution and education for peace. Especially important is the notion of integrating such information into the curriculum, because add-ons are too burdensome for most teachers. Support and guidance from the top within the schools, especially from the principal, are vital. Teachers need to become interested, competent, and valued in order to teach these subjects effectively.

Surprisingly, the work on international education so far makes little connection with conflict and violence. Ironically, *Sesame Street's* international conflict prevention programming is a notable, constructive exception. In the long run, international education is fundamentally linked to peace education. We must learn how to get along globally through understanding, communication, empathy, respect for other cultures, and nonviolent problem solving to meet basic human needs and redress grievances at an early stage.

16

Education for Peace
Concepts and Institutions

What is distinctive about education for peace? It subsumes much else that precedes it in this book, drawing especially on the basic concepts and educational processes for conflict resolution. But it goes beyond education for conflict resolution in that it addresses the crossing of adversarial *large-scale intergroup boundaries*. This includes hostility across national boundaries and hostility across ethnic, religious, or political boundaries within a nation. The first condition is conducive to international war; the second condition is conducive to civil war. The large-scale hostilities have not been so much the focus of attention in recent education as interpersonal and community education for conflict resolution. Education for peace is more complex and daunting than education for conflict resolution. But the stakes are so high, and likely to get so exceedingly dangerous in the twenty-first century, that education for peace must be addressed in serious and sustained ways—the sooner the better.

In this and the next two chapters, we try to clarify the following:

1. The essential content of education for peace, or at least the critical issues that need to be addressed
2. How to upgrade such information and concepts on a continuing, long-term basis so that education for peace can grow in strength over the decades ahead
3. How to make such content personally meaningful and widely available throughout the world

What evocative and thoughtful efforts have addressed the preceding three points? Peace education works toward giving children, adolescents, and young adults clear ideas about how to contribute to the creation of peaceful communities on both local and global scales. Starting from a low baseline, this century has seen an increased interest in peace education, but still it has not entered mainstream education. Although many schools have adopted conflict-resolution programs, they usually stop short of addressing the larger issues of war and peace. Yet there is a connection between the two. The challenge is to move beyond a narrow arena (for example, the school) to a broader view—indeed a worldwide outlook. The worldwide predilection to violence is both a serious constraint and profound challenge to peace education. So, too, is the paucity of research in this field.

Peace education gives a long-term strategy for dealing with problems of violence. The aim is for children to grow up to be citizens committed to finding alternatives to violent conflict. Such a preventive strategy offers little immediate reassurance to those concerned with local violence, including violence in and around schools. Yet, the ability to build peaceful societies is one of the world's most pressing problems. This fact constitutes a powerful stimulus to the education community to formulate curricula, materials, and school environments conducive to peaceful living. Likewise, it challenges religious institutions and community organizations as well as the media.

Essentially, we need to understand ourselves better. Human beings need not be destructive; we can learn to work cooperatively. Modern technology has made warlike behavior suicidal. In our actual struggle for survival, we must maximize the likelihood that all of humanity can legitimately be treated as potential allies. Because cooperation needs mutual confidence, major educational efforts should be made to augment prosocial behavior and to generate a sound basis for trust across cultural and national boundaries—not trust based on wishful thinking.

PEACE EDUCATION IN THE UNITED STATES, 1820–1990

Peace education in the United States has a long history.[1] In the early nineteenth century, the peace society journals in various parts of the country began to mark violence as a social ill and peace as a symbol of a civilized society. As the century wore on, there was an increasing belief (linked to ideas inspired by Darwin on evolution and progress) that, with intelligence and reason, human action could bring about a peaceful and just world. A number of prominent social thinkers and educators—the ranks of which included such luminaries as John Dewey, Horace Mann, and Jane Addams—felt that ethical principles were essential factors for a healthy citizenry and should be included in children's education. This ethical education was predicated on the belief that beneficial changes could come about by peaceful, gradual, and nonviolent means.

These hopes were severely jeopardized in the course of the twentieth century. World War I dashed many of the concepts of peace that appeared in the nineteenth century, but despite this, pacifist movements along with educational efforts gained considerable status in the wake of the war. However, they were often tarred as socialistic or communistic by critics and could be billed as un-American. This generally kept peace education from firmly establishing itself in the mainstream. So, too, did the illusion that such efforts could lead to a pacifist utopia.

After the horrendous second world war, with the superpower tensions of the cold war that held the potential for catastrophic nuclear conflict, there were redoubled efforts to reinforce peaceful behavior on the part of the United States and the Soviet Union. For example, the Nobel Prize–winning Pugwash organization, in addition to its analysis of ways to reduce the nuclear danger through arms control and efforts to influence policy, established the international Student Pugwash organization in the 1970s. To this day, Student Pugwash supports programs that encourage young people to examine the ethical impacts of technology from a global perspective and to foster peaceful international relations.

The Vietnam War was a significant moment in peace education. The anguish of the conflict led to an expanded view of the responsibilities of citizenship. Greater emphasis was placed on illuminating differing viewpoints on issues rather than simply obeying authority. The general concept of what constituted peace education itself was also broadened. Rather than just focusing on physical security, it came to include underlying problems that stimulate or exacerbate human conflict. Broader questions of inequity entered too, such as serious environmental damage and opportunities for often-oppressed women in societies across the world.

Peace education is gradually achieving a broader acceptance in the educational system. Within the universities and schools, it is not uncommon to find conflict prevention and peace education courses. Nevertheless, it can hardly be characterized as a widely established, mainstream part of education—an odd circumstance in view of the higher-than-ever and rapidly growing stakes at issue, even before the terrorist destruction of September 11, 2001.

Types of Peace Education

Since the middle of the nineteenth century, teachers have tried to educate children on the atrocities of war so that it might be avoided.[2] The horrors of modern warfare dominated peace education at the end of the nineteenth century and at the turn of the century, Maria Montessori taught young children to think for themselves to counteract the effects of fascism.[3] The 1970s peace education was a response to the Vietnam War. Nuclear threat and global devastation were themes of the 1980s. At the end of the twentieth century, peace education was, more than ever, seeking to give children positive alternatives to violence in building their own lives and contributing to their society's paths to peaceful problem solving—thinking of peace as something more than the (often transient) absence of war.

Although there is a lack of longitudinal studies about the effects of peace education in classroom settings, short-term observations are encouraging. There is an inherent plausibility in teaching pupils peaceful ways to respond to conflict—and giving them experience in practicing those skills—in order to prepare them to become peaceful adults.[4] Some research has shown cognitive changes in response to peace education.[5]

College students have exhibited a serious interest in changing their own behavior as a result of peace education.[6] Peer mediation programs have shown that students are able to learn peacekeeping skills in school and then apply their knowledge to daily living.[7] We have noted a successful program in the New York City public schools, the Resolving Conflict Creatively Program. Though it is not international, it does involve a variety of ethnic and religious groups, largely strangers to each other. This program focuses on cooperation, communications skills, responsible decision making, conflict resolution, and cultural competence. Research has shown a remarkably positive change in student behavior as a result: Teachers (71 percent) report a moderate or great decrease in physical violence in the classroom, and 66 percent noted less hostile name calling and verbal putdowns. In addition, teachers reported that they also changed—over 84 percent reported that their own listening skills improved and enhanced their understanding of conflict resolution—and that they used this increased knowledge in their personal lives.[8] Teachers in many countries are showing growing interest in peace education as a result of such positive findings and the compelling nature of the subject matter.

Different Emphases of Peace Education

A subject so complex as this, often involving highly charged emotions, naturally calls for different approaches. Many disciplines are involved, and the problems are looked at from different angles.

GLOBAL PEACE EDUCATION   This system is closely linked to international studies. It gives students an awareness and understanding of other cultures and helps young people to see themselves as compassionate global citizens by identifying with their basic humanity. Students also learn about security systems, which could eventually lead them to create new laws and institutions designed to avoid the horrors of violent conflict. Current and salient examples of such institutions are the United Nations and regional organizations such as the European Union. Global peace education would engage, for example, in teaching fundamental international law embedded in the United Nations charter as well as the UN's Universal Declaration of Human Rights.

CONFLICT-RESOLUTION PROGRAMS   This training helps children to deal with interpersonal conflicts constructively by utilizing skills of empathy, mediation, and alternative dispute resolution methods. To qualify as peace education, it must go beyond in-group boundaries.

Studies have shown that students who learn negotiation procedures in school are able to apply these skills at home and with friends. They also are more apt to seek peaceful solutions to their conflicts.[9] A study by Metis Associates of conflict-resolution programs in New York City schools showed that as a result of this training, students spoke in a more supportive manner, behaved more cooperatively, and showed more caring behavior and increased understanding of another's point of view.[10] The challenge is to extend such work to the wider sphere of international relations.

VIOLENCE-PREVENTION PROGRAMS   The goal of these programs is to create a safe school environment and reduce the violent behaviors that some children exhibit in and around school. Concern often revolves around street crime, fights, and unruly student behavior in school. Prejudice and stereotypes are examined in the context of enemy image formation. Anger management techniques are taught as a way of helping students to avoid fights. In school and community, the immediate and vivid aim is to provide these young people with alternatives to fighting.[11]

Evaluations of these programs show that they help to reduce physical acts of violence, and increase prosocial behavior.[12] By clarifying risk factors for violent behavior—family patterns, violent social settings, substance abuse, weapon availability—such education can give students insights into sources of violence as well as constructive alternatives. Here again, we have a platform for *peace* education on which future efforts can build—beyond the community to large heavily armed adversarial groups.

EDUCATION FOR DEMOCRATIC SOCIOECONOMIC DEVELOPMENT   This approach focuses on oppressive social institutions and ways of transcending the violent habits they condone. It examines hierarchies and their propensity for heavy-handed dominance. Human rights and environmental studies are included in development education. It seeks to promote the development of and participation in democratic communities.

NONVIOLENCE EDUCATION   This type of education calls on the work of great nonviolent thinkers such as Mahatma Gandhi, Martin Luther King, Jr., and Jiddu Krishnamurti, as well as religious leaders such as Desmond Tutu. It strives to conceive of a world where human beings work cooperatively toward sustaining a peaceful future. It offers solutions to problems in which both sides can win. We sketch a few examples here from recent history.

The value of nonviolent social action has been seen in several situations internationally in recent decades. One of the most powerful came in the epoch making year of 1989. That year, in East Germany, there were growing tensions as the country's citizens sought to leave the country and other Eastern Bloc nations opened their borders. The situation was dangerous since the East German government had a history of violent repression against internal dissent. Its leader, Erich Honecker, kept to this tradition and generally resisted Mikhail Gorbachev's examples of liberalization. Street protests became commonplace as Germans sought not only the right to move freely but also began to agitate for democratic reform. Leading the way in organizing these protests were a number of protestant pastors who used their churches as sanctuaries for this purpose and also used their high standing to maintain the peaceful nature of the protests even when faced with repressive government measures.

Organizers made sure that crowds maintained their composure while exerting strong social pressure, and thankfully, the security forces backed down from confrontation. People from all walks of life joined in such demonstrations.[13] The streets of various cities were soon swollen with their citizens. They remained peaceful, which not only gave the regime no legitimate cause to crush dissent but also gave the protesters and their message considerable moral authority. In the face of this swelling evidence of people power, the fierce East German regime tottered and then fell in November of 1989.

Protests of this sort hark back to the nonviolent movements of Mahatma Gandhi against colonial rule and of Martin Luther King, Jr., against racial discrimination. They show that these movements can be educative forces for social change and also for the prevention of deadly conflict.[14] Here, as in the East German and South African situations, adolescents and young adults played a vital role in the dynamic, nonviolent uprising for peace and democracy.

This approach does not always work. The violence used to sustain repressive systems can be terribly harsh. Yet in the Philippines, East Germany, Czechoslovakia, Poland, Mongolia, and most recently in Serbia, leaders and activists—and the people themselves, young and old—understood the true power of principled mass nonviolent protest. They made sure that their demonstrations remained peaceful in the face of provocation. In this way they minimized the risk of violent conflict and moved toward a better life.

A PERSPECTIVE FROM COLUMBIA UNIVERSITY

Professor Betty A. Reardon of Columbia University, whose career has been thoughtfully devoted to peace education, provides an informative review of the history and various approaches to this field.[15] Though peace education has been characterized, historically, by a trend toward multiple approaches to accomplishing common causes, Professor Reardon recognizes that it must come to be understood and accepted by mainstream society. Her assessment of the field is heavily influenced by her experience internationally; yet she naturally approaches her work from a Western orientation. She describes the history and practice of peace education, identifies common purposes and goals among its practitioners, and highlights important aspects of the field.

Defining Peace Education and Recognizing
Common Purposes among Practitioners

Whereas other fields are structured by the professional organizations and academic departments of their practitioners, peace education has very few such places devoted entirely to its development. Citizens' organizations may support its practice and professional organizations contain subgroups dedicated to networking with their colleagues; however, peace itself has only recently gained the time and resources of far-reaching organizations such as UNESCO. The birth and growth of peace education initiatives globally have often taken place independent from other programs and in a variety of disciplines. There has, therefore, been virtually no unified approach to the practice of peace education thus far, though there have been common purposes.

Most practitioners cite the construction of a humane society, on a local, national, or international scale, as their primary purpose. Their means toward attaining that goal:

"positive, mutually beneficial relationships among the members of the society."[16] Practitioners around the world recognize that public policy must result in positive environments that provide all citizens opportunity. Such is the consensus born of a universal respect for human rights that permeates nonviolent solutions to controversies.

Broad-gauged education is steadily gaining acceptance as an effective way to achieve this end, as evidenced in UNESCO's focus in the field, its Declaration and Integrated Framework of Action on Education for Peace, Human Rights, and Democracy.[17] Although comprehensive philosophically and pedagogically, this approach includes incorporation of peace education at all of the students' developmental stages. With good intentions, UNESCO's efforts in this field are so far quite limited. Education for peace may also be substantively based in various disciplines, such as international relations, political science, international law, human biology, and developmental or social psychology. The linkage of peace with human rights and democracy strikes us as important.

One approach emphasizes human rights education, an aspect of peace education originally inspired by the basic concept of human dignity. Human rights education developed standards based on the Universal Declaration of Human Rights, which was drafted and adopted under the leadership of Eleanor Roosevelt in 1948. It had a worldwide influence on human aspirations for just, humane, and equal treatment of all people. Human rights education is an important component of peace education, as it teaches respect for the common humanity of people from different cultures. The ultimate goal of alleviating prejudice supports indelibly two important principles: fair treatment for all and the ideology that people from different cultural, religious, or ethnic groups need not be feared by one's own group. Such education has been implemented in areas of the world experiencing demographic change, change that has frequently taken place as a result of conflict.

The History and Growth of Peace Education in Schools

The establishment of the International Peace Research Association in 1964 had a stimulating influence on the field as a whole. It was here that the term peace research was first coined and entered universities. Universities have been research-oriented, in that they either conduct research or offer coursework focused on peace research methodology. This research informs university peace studies curricula, though the coursework is mostly in the social sciences. Professor Reardon focuses on the ways in which peace education can be incorporated into the methodological approach to creating instructional techniques for general education—both in the middle grades and at other levels, including colleges and universities. There are potentially valuable linkages across levels. For example, universities can go beyond concerns about instructional approaches and focus on curriculum development for the middle grades. As detailed in Chapter 18, they can create curricula that engage students' attention, incorporate social and ethical questions, and are of relevance to everyday life.

Though peace education entered schools as a result of individual citizens, teachers, and community organizations, these local movements have received material and guidance from organizations such as Educators for Social Responsibility. This organization, founded by U.S. teachers, provided school- and community-based education programs to teachers. Those involved in the peace movement and associations often supported such programs. It was not until 1963 that a sharp focus on critical issues emerged following Pope John XXIII's encyclical, *Pacem in Terris* and President John F. Kennedy's great speech at American University, "Toward a Strategy of Peace," which also announced the Nuclear Test Ban Treaty.

Though it is difficult to define peace education precisely, Reardon delineates a unity of purpose among its practitioners and a growing awareness of the necessity for peace education initiatives. Citizens, organizations dedicated to peace, and some political and religious and academic leaders have increasingly advocated the protection of human rights by democratic institutions as crucial pathway to peace. This approach is stimulating peace education in the schools. The dialogue is now open not only to instructional approaches, but also to curriculum development.

CONCEPTUAL FRAMEWORKS FOR PEACE EDUCATION

Robert A. Hinde and Patrick Bateson, biologists of great distinction at the University of Cambridge, explore the goals of peace education and define it as embracing all the conditions conducive to individual fulfillment and the continued progress of the whole human species.[18] The content they propose for peace education builds on concepts in our earlier chapters dealing with education for conflict resolution within a single nation. Now we extend these ideas to international conflicts. Peace is more positive and complex than the mere absence of war, or of simply keeping the peace—which implies a situation of tension and mistrust. This comprehensive view covers many situations and many factors that influence human aggression, from two schoolboys fighting over possession of an object, to village warfare involving relatively small groups of people, to modern warfare viewed as a set of human institutions in which individuals have specific roles with attendant rights and duties. The institutions of war shape the inclinations of leaders to impose war on the country and exploit the propensities of soldiers and other citizens to cooperate and obey their superiors. We fight for those to whom we are closely attached and are obedient to aggressive leaders. Propaganda is used as a tool by leaders to foster the institutions of war, often playing on the solidarity of in-group attachments. This viewpoint suggests that two goals of peace education might be described as clarifying those individual propensities that are conducive to the institutions of war and learning how to counteract the consequences of those institutions on the behavior of individuals.

Individual Propensities

In this view, education for peace must address several objectives: (a) to raise children to be disciplined in restraint toward violence, (b) to arrange society so that human assertiveness can benefit humanity without damaging individuals, (c) guide human potentials for cooperation and prosocial behavior so that they are employed to the benefit of mankind and not set one group against another, and (d) to be concerned with humane values as well as aggressive motivations.

Hinde and Bateson also seek to inform people about how the institutions of war can have a powerful effect on their individual behavior. They emphasize stereotypes of potential enemies, along the lines of our earlier discussion of invidious distinctions between in-groups and out-groups. They pay special attention to fear of the strange or the unknown and the need for identifying with valued groups—all too often identifying with one group exclusively and devaluing others. It is important to understand how political, religious or ethnic leaders can manipulate these tendencies to promote and justify war. This occurs in many cultures and is so ubiquitous throughout history that it deserves close scrutiny. They explicitly advocate promoting knowledge of other peoples—friends and adversaries alike, on the basis of the most solid information available. Here, the basic requirements and opportunities of international education (see Chapter 15) mesh with those of peace education.

The world is composed of a multitude of cultures with their own unique value systems and special merits. At the same time, there is a *shared humanity*. For example, teaching about the global problems of air pollution and depletion of the world's resources is not only intrinsically important but also illuminates crucial *universal values* in the service of *survival*. Moreover, fundamental human biology, key attributes of human societies, and basic human needs are central to our shared humanity. Diversity must be understood and respected in this framework of shared humanity. This does not mean that all cultures must be equally valued. Although all seek ways to solve basic problems of human adaptation, some are more humane and compassionate than others; some are more democratic and protective of human rights than others.

Because the institutions of war were created over a long period of time, we need to examine ways in which our current behavior is influenced by past events, even obsolete attitudes and customs. Education for peace must show that some societies are not inclined to war and have built structures for maintaining peace based on widespread physical security, emotional well-being, and social justice. Indeed, we have learned from some nations (for example, Sweden) that a previously war-prone nation can change its orientation in fundamental ways.

History often gives war a glorified status. Another goal of education for peace is to present a multifaceted picture of war, bleeding warts and all. Also, history must not be seen as an inevitable unfolding of events. The interplay of leaders and those being led is a fundamental topic for understanding war and peace. A careful assessment of conditions that justify war is essential.

Finally, Hinde and Bateson offer a basis for hope in building and sustaining a peaceful world:

1. We now have the means to limit population at sustainable levels.
2. We understand the urgency to conserve the world's resources for future generations.

3. We see how extreme human self-absorption can contaminate the planet but also human ingenuity can find ways to reduce the dangers.
4. The threat of nuclear war has provided a historically new, essentially unprecedented, incentive to reach an understanding of worldwide problems, and the will to do so is increasing.
5. There has been a real expansion of social conscience in the democracies. For example, now governments' commonly dispatch aid to those suffering from disaster or famine half a world away. Many concrete steps that can be taken by governments, intergovernmental organizations, and nongovernmental institutions—especially the pillars of civil society—have been clarified in recent years.[19]

Human Aggressiveness and War

In a notable gathering of scientists from many fields and many countries marking the 50th anniversary of the creation of Pugwash, Robert Hinde and Lea Pulkkinen examine the issue of human aggressiveness. They ask the fundamental question: Why do humans participate in war?[20] Conflict is a natural part of human interaction—between individuals, groups within states, and in relations between states. They are concerned with factors that move conflict into violence. We summarize here their focus on socialization and education in relation to human aggressiveness and war.

AGGRESSION BETWEEN INDIVIDUALS   In studies of human twins, research shows that genetic factors affect differences in antisocial behavior, which includes aggression. This is especially true when aggressive behavior appears early in life in combination with persistent hyperactivity. However, there is no direct effect of genetic differences on overt aggression or violence. Genes determine the protein structure in our cells. Then there is a long series of developmental processes affected by factors in the environment. So, it is difficult to generalize about the relative importance of genetic and environmental factors. Gene differences could also affect some other inclination that influences the frequency of experience that could be associated with aggressiveness.[21] For example, in the case of an irritable infant, parents may treat the child in a manner conducive to the development of an aggressive temperament. Childhood aggressiveness does not necessarily lead to adult antisocial behavior, except when it is intense and linked with other symptoms such as hyperactivity and rejection by peers.[22]

In most cultures, males are more aggressive physically than females, and the incidence of violence increases with age. The peak is reached in the late teens or early 20s and then declines.[23] The extent to which hormonal factors, especially testosterone, affect these processes is under investigation.

Many studies show that life experience strongly affects the development of individual aggressiveness.[24] In cases of nuclear families in Western society, a disruption in parenting is associated strongly with subsequent aggressiveness in the child. Parenting that is disorganized or insecure, very cold, or highly permissive, or where punishment is highly inconsistent also relates to subsequent aggression in the child.[25] In 1971, Baumrind found that children whose parents are highly controlling and lacking in affection and highly permissive parents were more aggressive than those children of parents who are authoritative in a constructive way.[26] Punishing a child for behaving aggressively has complex outcomes. On one hand, the child learns that the aggressive behavior results in a negative response. On the other hand, the pain involved with punishment induces aggression in the child and shows the parent behaving aggressively, thus providing a model for future aggression. In general, the interaction of family members has an important impact on the development of aggressive behavior, so too do influences of the peer group (especially peer rejection).

The values and norms of society are significant in bringing about aggressiveness. Some cultures promote harmony within the group while encouraging aggressive behavior toward other groups. A tough image may be created in the search for self-esteem or as part of coping with harsh conditions, as was the case in frontier areas of the United States in the nineteenth century and in many modern cities.[27] Poverty is a strong force related to aggressiveness within and across societies.

Mass media reflects as well as creates social norms. Although there are consistent links between television violence and aggressive tendencies, these are not strong in a randomly selected population. However, violence in the media clearly increases aggressive tendencies in an individual who is at risk for aggressiveness for other reasons (such as inadequate parenting and violence in the family).[28] Being exposed to violence in the community can enhance aggressiveness.[29] Video games that involve active participation in simulated violence are especially strong influences on aggressive behavior. In recent years, their popularity and the intensity of their interactive violence have come to constitute a serious social problem.

Situational factors such as crowded inner cities raise emotional levels of individuals and are associated with aggressive behavior. Architectural design can perpetuate feelings of alienation. For instance, high-rise buildings, with their impersonal nature, tend to reduce feelings of community, which predispose to violence.[30]

Individual factors make aggression more likely, but it is important also to examine triggers that lead to aggressive behavior. Aggression is usually stimulated by a desire to attain or maintain a highly desired goal—especially by blockage of such desires. Frustration is an important cause of aggression, but the concept of frustration is sometimes used so broadly that its value is diminished. Other factors leading to aggression are (1) the desire for power, especially if an aggressive act will improve the status of the actor in the eyes of peers or a wider population; (2) pain and fear; and (3) the presence of weapons. There is no question that availability of weapons is an important factor in the high levels of homicide in the United States; however, of greater importance is the abundance of light weapons in many poor countries that are in fact highly destructive.

INTERGROUP AGGRESSION   Intergroup aggression spans a large, multidimensional middle ground ranging from individual aggression to interstate wars. These include gang wars, terrorism, and civil wars (sometimes based on religious or ethnic differences) common since the mid-1900s. Also, violence between groups can include violence perpetrated by an individual who identifies himself or herself as part of a group (as in many acts of terrorism), or a group act of violence toward an individual viewed as representing a group (such as in apartheid).

The nature of antagonistic groups is critical to understanding the nature of aggression between groups. It is necessary to understand the way group members see themselves and how they respond to given circumstances that lead to violence. It is important to understand human groups, as we tried to do in Chapter 2 ("Child Development, the Human Group, and Survival"). In the course of human evolution, it was important to survival and reproduction for individuals to be associated with a particular group or community. It has been argued that the advantages to be gained by dealing with a complex society are largely what drove the development of the primate brain.[31] Individuals identify themselves in two ways: first as unique individuals and second as members of a group. So, individual and social identities can be linked to group survival.[32] Reasons for defending land or resources, for example, can be seen as necessary to the survival of everyone in the group—thus providing a legitimate reason to go to war.

Members of one group tend to view members of another group as being different, and these differences are readily amplified in times of stress especially when emphasized by an antagonistic leader. By belonging to a group, one defines one's position in society. When a member of one's group achieves something highly positive, this reflects positively on all members of the group, even if other group members did nothing to contribute to the achievement. Members of a group who believe in the group's unique values and reject outside values are poised on the threshold of conflict with other groups.

In group situations, several factors contribute to violence: (1) Near anonymity defines the individual; (2) intense arousal occurs; (3) psychological support of individuals with similar perceptions may reduce the inhibitions against violence; and (4) individuals may conform to aggressive group norms and pressures. The act of sharing values gives added potency to each of these factors.

Group solidarity is encouraged by promoting the evils of the out-group and the superiority of the in-group. Perception of reality changes readily and is easily manipulated by leaders. Propaganda is especially useful when designed to encourage the belief in the superiority of the in-group.

Often perceived deprivation or suffering is linked to aggression, but this does not mean that violence is simply a reaction to relative deprivation. It is a predisposing factor that is often politically exacerbated. Escalation to violence is likely to occur when group members are highly frustrated; there are repeated failed negotiations and poor intergroup communication; the out-group is perceived as using power illegitimately, and the in-group sees itself as able to control its own destiny.[33]

Internally peaceful societies are rare, but some research is available on the Zuni of the southwestern United States, the !Kung bushmen of the Kalahari, the Arapesh of New Guinea, the Xingo of Brazik, the Semai of Malaysia, and the Buid of Mindoro. These relatively peaceful societies share several characteristics. Their value systems look unfavorably on anger, boasting, quarreling, and violence. Such characteristics as generosity, gentleness, and avoidance of conflict are embraced, as are institutions that promote conflict resolution. According to spiritual beliefs, helpful spirits defy malevolent spirits that prey on human beings. These societies are generally egalitarian and mutually supportive.[34] Lessons can be learned not only from the structure and values of such simple societies, but also from more complex ones that have undergone a transition from war-proneness to peaceful living. A remarkable example is provided by today's Scandinavian countries, among the world leaders in fostering peaceful conditions far and wide. They were among the most violent only three centuries ago—a short time in the sweep of human evolution.

National characteristics, religions, and propaganda play large roles in perpetuating the institutions of war. Traditions vary from country to country. If attacking orientations are generally given high status in the society, war obtains legitimacy for solving conflicts. Religions generally teach about peace, yet too often wars have been defined as holy wars. In these instances, religion plays a major part in perpetuating the institution of war.[35]

Official propaganda is used to enhance the belief that war is a compelling necessity to preserve national integrity or international order. It is used to convince the population that war is justified. Often prejudice is used to justify war. The motivation stems from hatreds passed down from one generation to the next and frequently leaves participants of the war with no knowledge of its original cause.[36] If war is seen as justified, then it follows that citizens must contribute to the effort so that victory may be won.

Hinde and Pulkkinen have examined how violence comes to occur at individual, group, and international levels. To find long-term solutions, they conclude that it is necessary to improve the education of future generations in all of these areas. Education should be strengthened to enhance international understanding and cooperation; establish social justice; and move towards eradicating prejudices against other groups and nations. Educational objectives should be critically reviewed in each country in relation to the fostering of positive human relations and mutual accommodation, not the fostering of hatred and violence. Education should encompass upbringing in the home, day care and school, and adult education.

Education for peace involves *a culture of peace that clearly identifies the ideals of peace and cultivates a will for peace*, which includes habits of mind that allow one to think critically about propaganda, favor tolerance and sympathy toward others, and behave with high ethical standards based on awareness of shared humanity. It is important to put old and obsolete rivalries into a new perspective and to teach tolerance explicitly. Beyond teaching, education must encompass the notion that at every level—individual, group, and international—violence is not a satisfactory solution to ubiquitous human conflicts. Individuals need to understand that violence breeds more violence; that with today's weapons, violence may readily become mutually suicidal; and that win-win solutions must be sought. It is vital that conflicting parties feel a sense of success by learning nonviolent ways of solving real problems and meeting basic human needs.

INSTITUTIONS THAT CAN PROMOTE EDUCATION FOR PEACE

In *No More Killing Fields*, we considered a variety of institutions and organizations that can be conducive to just peace in many ways.[37] Here we summarize a few that are of great long- term importance. This is only a sampling of relevant, constructive influences. But they provide a framework within which effective education for peace becomes possible.

Democratic Institutions

Education for peace must include substantial content and strong emphasis on education for democracy, because this is by far the best long-term path to peaceful living. The basic orientation of democracies encourages people to attempt to see the perspectives of others and to learn mutual accommodation from early life into adulthood.[38] Pluralism is the heart of democracy. Here the attitudes of tolerance, mutual respect, and sensitivity to and protection of human rights are valued and perpetuated. The culture itself must be supportive in order for democracy to exist. Leaders of all sectors need to accept the principles of free speech, freedom of worship, the rule of law, human rights, and other fundamental ideals such as free education for all citizens. Minorities must *not* be marginalized; their rights must be respected and maintained by the majority.

Democracy is an evolving process whereby democratic values are built by civil society through nonviolent means of conflict. What are some of the positive conditions created by democracy that can help it take hold as countries emerge from hostile, repressive regimes? First, more prosperity generally exists in democratic countries than in countries with nondemocratic governments. Second, a democratic government can provide the maximum prospect for persons to exercise the opportunity to live under laws of their own choosing. Third, there is a greater chance of exercising moral responsibility within a democracy. Fourth, human development is fostered more fully than in other feasible alternatives. Fifth, the practical and fundamental notion of human equality (albeit taking into account biological and cultural variability of human experience and attributes), which gives people equality before the law, is an effective means of resolving grievances in the absence of violent conflict. Moreover, legislative and judicial processes help to diminish patterns of discrimination and provide mechanisms for dealing with grievances. This is closely linked to the ideal of equal opportunity. The main paths for implementation are through *free public education over many years* and legal protection for civil rights. It is fundamentally important to *educate specifically for democracy*—ranging from the most fundamental principles to operational details: How do democracies actually work, and especially how do they resolve conflict without violence?

The international community can and should play a strong role in fostering democracy worldwide so that as many countries as possible can share at least a minimum standard of democratic values—especially those countries that are developing socioeconomically from poor, repressive, and belligerent conditions. There is emerging a global movement of mutually supportive democratic organizations—both governmental and nongovernmental. Ever-growing communication technologies are extending the potential for international cooperation on building democracies. *Democracy in its essence is a way of resolving ubiquitous human conflicts with a minimum of violence.*

At the earliest stages of democracy building, children and youth must understand the possibilities for nonviolent conflict resolution and the practical value that mutual accommodation holds among the different sectors of society—across all sorts of group barriers.

Human rights have been placed front and center in recent years, the significance of which is measured by the fact that nations and interest groups increasingly seek to justify their actions in human rights terms. There is extensive independent monitoring of human rights protections. Democratic institutions are the most secure protectors of human rights. These rights are increasingly recognized as having universal value in the fundamental quest for human dignity.[39] This is one of the main factors that has stimulated worldwide, visible cooperation among democratic governments.

We have shown in previous chapters how democratic principles form the necessary underpinnings for effective peace education and education for conflict resolution. In recent years, a growing worldwide interest in promoting democratic governments and institutions has begun to emerge. But what is democracy? Robert R. LaGamma, Executive Director of the Council for a Community of Democracies defines it meaningfully as "a process to allow ordinary people to act to advance their own best interests through laws and institutions. And it is a faith that ordinary people know their own best interests and do not need to be told what those interests are by leaders who interpret a reigning dogma."[40] He makes a point of distinguishing democracy as a process as opposed to a doctrine. A process allows for flexibility and interpretation. Therefore institutions and laws under a democracy can reflect the country's unique traditional practices, cultural heritage, and historical background.

Educating for peace has the best chance for success under democratic conditions, and it is heartening to see the development and acceptance of these ideals. In recent years, the full range of world democracies has joined efforts in two meetings so far to pursue a common goal of encouraging the spread of democracy, which includes civic education. The Warsaw meeting in 2000 set the stage for global democratic solidarity, followed by a similar meeting in Seoul Korea two years later, and a third meeting will be held in Chile in 2004.[41]

THE WARSAW MEETING 2000   In June 2000 Warsaw, Poland was host to a meeting of representatives from 107 countries who met to discuss international democracy issues. U.S. Secretary of State Madeleine Albright, in the Clinton Administration's final year, began this initiative with collaborators who were heads of states from several democracies. The central goal of this initiative was to encourage a cooperative spirit among democracies around the world with a joint focus on finding solutions to a range of shared problems.[42] A movement known as the Community of Democracies grew from this meeting.

Representatives from eight nations organized the Warsaw meeting: the United States, Poland, Korea, India, the Czech Republic, Chile, Mali, and Portugal. At the Warsaw meeting, high officials of foreign ministries from 107 countries deliberated on issues of international democracy. In the end, a final declaration was signed by 106 countries that pledged to do the following: Give aid to democracies that are vulnerable or in danger; form a united presence in the face of regimes under dictatorial or authoritarian rule; usefully coordinate assistance to democracy; and make effective, organized use of regional and international organizations that support democracies.

The committee hoped their declaration would be as significant as the Helsinki declaration of human rights of 1975 during the cold war. In fact, the UN Charter, the Universal Declaration of Human Rights, and UN membership were major benchmarks in the writing of the Warsaw Declaration. Each provided the foundation for developing a consensus on democracy and provided examples of developing norms and practices.

The Warsaw meeting highlights the importance of UN presence in such discussions.[43] Present at this historic Warsaw meeting was UN Secretary General Kofi Annan. In associating himself with the new coalition of democracies, Kofi Annan stated that the coalition is "dedicated to expanding the frontiers of freedom and to ensuring that, wherever democracy has taken root, it will not be reversed." Annan said also that "when the United Nations can truly call itself a community of democracies, the Charter's noble ideals . . . will have been much closer to fulfillment."[44]

SEOUL, KOREA 2002   In an International Herald Tribune article, John Richardson and Richard C. Rowson reported on the Community of Democracies ministerial conference meeting in Seoul, Korea, on November 9, 2002.[45] Linked to this conference was another meeting held concurrently—a forum comprised of representatives from more than 100 international nongovernmental organizations that proposed an initiative for "global civic education for democracy."[46] This was a unique proposition that reflects an urgency for such education, especially in the dim light of the terrorist attacks of September 11, 2001.

Teaching the fundamentals of democratic governance is not a new idea; it was a major highlight and requirement of U.S. policy during and after occupation of Germany and Japan. Now with threats to democracy by global terrorist activities, it is more important than ever to teach education for democracy, or civic education, in primary and secondary schools throughout the world. Nongovernmental organizations such as the National Endowment for Democracy, the Open Society Institute, Freedom House, the American Forum for Global Education, and the Council for a Community of Democracies all recognize the urgency of creating an initiative for global civic education; in fact, they helped to influence the Seoul conference planners to include this on their ministerial conference agenda.

Terrorism is bred in countries where governments fail to provide hope and opportunity for their people. Al Qaeda and others prey on a flawed educational system for their own dangerous and hateful purposes. Students emerging from such education cannot possibly be prepared in terms of values or basic tools to be effective citizens who would support human rights, rule of law, free and fair markets, and legitimate elections.

Regarding civic education, we can hope the result of the Seoul meeting will promote the following: (1) expanded commitment of governments to education for democracy, (2) expanded cooperation between governments for this purpose, (3) commitment of experienced countries to help others who have little experience in this field, and (4) appeal to international institutions to provide resources for education for democracy.

Schools and educational media must, whenever possible, promote civic education for democracy. The meeting at Seoul is potentially a turning point in the growth of a global movement on behalf of education for democracy.[47] Yet this is not the only path to education for democracy. Many organizations in many countries can, in their own distinctive ways, contribute to this great effort. It is time to move beyond lip service to stimulate the creativity of free peoples to educate their children and youth about the essence of democracy and how they can and indeed must actively participate to bring their own lives to fulfillment.

The established democracies have much work to do to strengthen education for democracy to fulfill its promise, to make adaptations in keeping with global interdependence, and to overcome inherent dangers such as the tendency to plutocracy—the corrosive effect of big money in politics. But the hardest problems involve the dictatorships and autocracies whose leaders tend to suppress such education. In this context, it is heartening to see an unprecedented UN-sponsored report prepared by Arab scholars for Arab readers that makes the case for the necessity and feasibility of democratic development in Arab countries. This remarkable report includes a significant section on education reform.

EDUCATIONAL REFORM IN DEVELOPMENT OF ARAB STATES   The UN sponsored a report compiled by a team of Arab scholars for the United Nations Development Programme. The most striking weakness identified in the report, underlying all the other problems, is a lack of democracy that leads to poor governance.

The report points out that political participation in the Arab region is still very limited compared to other regions—and this region is rated lower than any other for freedom of expression and accountability of government. The Arab media was described as seriously lacking in freedom. Even when civil rights are written into constitutions and laws, they are often ignored in practice. Above all, the Arab people have been hobbled by poverty of capabilities and poverty of opportunities. In addition to a lack of freedom, failures in the areas of women's opportunities must to be remedied to help the region break out of its current inertia.

Education, too, has been moving in the wrong direction. Spending levels have fallen since the mid-1990s, and school enrolment levels are not keeping up with rapid population growth. The report strongly advocates drastic upgrading of educational opportunities and quality.

"Education is a key factor in today's knowledge-intensive world. As education stimulates a critical outlook and creative skills, it simultaneously accelerates the pace of change, development and progress. Education and progress should therefore be mutually reinforcing. To help to achieve this goal, this section proposes a radical revision of education systems in Arab countries as they move into the twenty-first century."[48]

The report covers important educational topics. The areas for educational expansion and improvement include

1. Adult education
2. Preschool education

3. Education for children with special needs
4. Technical and vocational education
5. Higher education

"A powerful shake-up to improve quality is needed in the existing institutions of higher education. . . . Higher education should encompass the concept of lifelong education through various modes of continuing learning."[49]

Although these prescriptions for fundamental reform of education in Arab countries are generally constructive and forward-looking, they have essentially nothing explicit to say about education for conflict resolution and for peace—indeed, even little about mutual accommodation among various Arab peoples. Nevertheless, there is a progressive, humane tone in the report that at least implies openings for such education in the future. These are perhaps the hardest cases in the world today, and this report offers encouraging ideas that may in several decades provide valuable results.

Development Institutions

Much of the world has been poor, uneducated, and repressed for so long that the inherent dangers of these conditions have been overlooked in the more affluent parts of the world until recently. But now serious efforts to foster socioeconomic development are growing.[50] For example, the Carnegie Corporation of New York built a program on African development in the 1980s and 1990s with a three-part focus, paying special attention to South Africa during apartheid. The first was to *build democratic institutions.* The second was to *strengthen the role of women,* with special attention to *health and education.* And the third was to promote *science and technology* that would support development. All of these measures *enhance economic opportunity* and *competent governance.* They provide a basis for hope and a sense of emerging fairness. On the other hand, failures of development are conducive to mass violence, for example, civil wars.

During the 1990s, a reexamination of the world's development experience from 1950 to 2000 took place to better understand its successes and failures. A feature of this effort was to view more broadly the development process and recognize the importance of *human* development. The United Nations Development Program (UNDP) was a leader in this effort in the 1990s and provides a valuable source of analysis. The Nobel Prize winner in economic science of 1998, Amartya Sen, made a major contribution to this work. His analysis of the relevant research points to development essentially as a process of *enlarging the actual freedoms that people can utilize for meeting basic human needs* and fulfilling their potentials. Although there is worldwide economic growth and much opulence, a great number of people are still without elementary freedoms, opportunities, or minimally-adequate incomes—not to speak of the ravages of disease such as AIDS. Human development requires basic education, health care, and the ability to live in the context of *human rights*, with widespread equal opportunity and broad *political participation* in a democratic framework.

In a series of analytic papers by Joseph Stiglitz, another Nobel economist and former senior vice president of development economics and chief economist at the World

Bank, he shows that the past quarter century has experienced dramatic advances in many areas of the developing world. By investing in the health and *education* of people, economic growth is stimulated. In turn, this provides resources that can be further invested in people so they may achieve higher levels of development.

Increasing evidence points to the fact that educating girls and women is an invaluable investment in developing countries. Vast potential rests in women's contribution in the economic, intellectual, political, and social spheres. The education of women has several effects: marriage tends to be delayed past the very early teen years, and contraception is likely to be more widely used, thus easing the burden of nonsustainable population growth. Family well-being is enhanced. Borrowing and investment opportunities are improved through education, which contributes significantly to economic growth. Children raised by more informed women benefit in many ways, not least in their intellectual and problem-solving capabilities.

In our view, *knowledge, skill,* and *freedom* are the three pillars of development. And education is crucial in constructing these pillars. Altogether, democratic development is in the long run the best hope for a peaceful world. Therefore, the *processes of achieving democratic socioeconomic development through international cooperation are an essential component of peace education.*

If development is badly neglected, states fail, suffering is severe, and a human morass occurs. This is a breeding ground for pandemic diseases, disruptive and painful mass migrations, serious environmental damage, and above all, hatred, violence, and terrorism. So, major international efforts to foster constructive development are not an altruistic luxury, but rather an essential component of the quest for a just, peaceful world. *Clarification of the paths to development,* in the educational work of both rich and poor countries, *is a vital component of education for peace.*

Scientific Institutions

In virtually every corner of the world, we are faced with ubiquitous hatreds, prejudice, and threats of violent conflict. Because of its danger, complexity, and pervasiveness, this problem must become a serious issue for the global scientific community.[51] This deeply destructive tendency of humanity requires an increasingly unified and in-depth examination by researchers in the physical, biological, behavioral, and social sciences. This community of scientists can provide a crucial public service by sharing insight and new perspectives on the age-old problem of deadly conflict.

Historically, scientific inquiry in this area of aggression and conflict has been marginalized, even in many of the world's foremost educational and scientific institutions. Some useful approaches have nevertheless emerged.[52] Among these is the neurobiology of aggressive behavior, which has been explored through research into cells, circuits, and biochemistry mediating such behavior. Relative to this line of inquiry has been the role of drugs in precipitation, exacerbation, and therapy of hyperaggressive behavior. Research done on child abuse has led to increased understanding of aggression in children and youth and to influences on prosocial and antisocial development.

The behavioral sciences have recently studied many conflicts, which include studies of real-life and simulated negotiations. Inquiry has been made into ways in which past conflicts began and their subsequent resolution, and into how these relate to contemporary situations. Studies have also been made on various intergroup and international institutions and processes as they relate to large-scale conflict. Excellent historical research has emerged. This is all connected to research specifically focused on war and peace—including lessening chances of nuclear war by arms control, crisis prevention, and reducing risk of accidental or inadvertent nuclear confrontation. Improvement in relations among nuclear nations has also been studied. Many levels of conflict have been examined—from family to nations. The search for commonality of factors and basic principles in one area helps to illuminate understanding in other areas. Prejudice and ethnocentrism have been clarified by studies of intergroup relations in social psychology, anthropology, sociology, as well as evolution and history of human violence.[53] Although much more must be done, these powerful and converging lines of inquiry provide valuable insights into ways of modulating human aggressiveness and violent behavior. This can be facilitated by systematic, substantive cooperation of leading scientific institutions all over the world. A fine example is provided by the U.S. National Academy of Sciences, which (under the leadership of Bruce Alberts, its president) is linking closely with other science academies throughout the world to pursue the kinds of purposes considered here. The newly formed Inter-Academy Council is beginning to provide science-based, objective analysis of development problems such as ways of providing adequate food for Africa.

INTERNATIONAL RELATIONSHIPS IN EDUCATION FOR PEACE: COOPERATION AND TRUST

Writing in the late 1980s, the distinguished ethologist Robert Hinde identified several ways that education for peace can facilitate cooperative international relations involving trust.[54] This is a long and tortuous but essential process that has changed in some respects since the end of the cold war.

According to Hinde, education for peace can

- promote common appreciation of the terrible risks of weapons of mass destruction. The avoidance of arms races can be viewed as a *common goal* of mutual benefit.
- promote the general appreciation that alternative styles of international relations are possible, facilitated by changes in attitudes toward other groups —especially by moving away from dehumanizing adversaries.
- promote the idea in individuals that a new ethic in international relations is possible—one in which flaunting military or economic power to achieve national advantage is not condoned, nor is the passive acceptance of dictatorial, repressive regimes, nor the permission of massive inequities.
- increase familiarity with other nations, so that they are seen as *related human beings*, not as aliens or subhuman creatures.

- promote personal familiarity across national boundaries and the assumption that they too probably wish to live their lives peacefully unless there is clear evidence to the contrary.
- Promote trust in many ways. Personal relationships can help, not only among leaders but also among people at large—hence the value of people-to-people exchanges.
- Expand social conscience to reach the entire world population, thinking of all humans as significantly related to each other and in need of each other's help to solve global problems.

Cooperation, trust, and mutual commitment in interpersonal relationships and between groups are core concerns when educating children to be caring, thoughtful, and peaceful individuals. To build a learning environment that can promote such attributes, Hinde suggests several actions:

- Provide incentives so that the benefits of cooperating outweigh the disadvantages.
- Create short-term goals that can best be achieved by cooperation.
- Foster the establishment of mutually beneficial, long-term relationships, thereby creating a sense of familiarity and kinship.

Trust can be enhanced in environments that

- foster good communication (teacher/student and student/student as well as between groups).
- create long-term interests that are shared across boundaries and that are mutually beneficial.
- explore common values—including the fundamental shared humanity in a world of diversity.
- increase likelihood of mutual benefits from respectful communication and joint efforts.

When dealing specifically with groups as opposed to individuals, it is important to minimize the in-group–out-group effect. The challenge is to nurture understanding of other groups and strive toward appreciation without attempting to make "them" be like "us." Finally, improving a group's social conscience can be enhanced in many ways—for example, through study, games, art, movement/dance, and role-playing that explores ethical themes of decent human relationships.

The Case of Finland: An International View of Education for Peace

The distinguished psychologist Lea Pulkkinen has reviewed progress in education for peace in Finland.[55] She asserts, "Peace in one country is not enough for the protection of its citizens. Responsibility must be broadened across national borders."[56] She provides an overview of education for peace in Finland, covering the background of education for peace in Finland, peace education as compared to related terms, the attitudinal foundation in Finland, the legislative situation in Finland, and education for peace in practice. This provides a constructive illustration of one country's efforts to take this subject seriously. Other countries are proceeding in a variety of ways, and they can learn from each other.

Peace education since its inception in Finland has included the long-term goal of active peace between nations, groups, and individuals. The emphasis is on developing a framework for education, not on defining what traits a child should have. The aim is to foster growth toward shared responsibility, cooperative nonviolence, and international understanding through social and ethical education.

The Ministry of Welfare and Health in Finland in 1985 followed UNESCO's recommendation and defined education for peace as education "to help the individual grow into a critically thinking, empathetic person aware of his/her responsibilities, who in cooperation with other peers is capable of acting towards the creation of the conditions for peace of all nations. Education for peace means the gathering of information on the larger problems of humankind, the formation of attitudes favoring nonviolence and preparation for practical improvement of conditions for peace."[57]

Pulkkinen views the objectives of education for peace as twofold: the creation of a culture of peace and the cultivation of persons with a will for peace. First, creating a culture of peace means actively eliminating structural violence, decreasing the idealization of physical violence, fulfilling human rights, avoiding the glorification of weaponry, objectively analyzing the image of an enemy, and clarifying of ideals of peace. Second, cultivating a person with a will for peace involves several aspects of personal development: awareness of the goals of peace; an emotional life, which includes empathy for other people and nations; the will to assume an ethically high level of responsibility for one's own actions; and skills for resolving conflict. There are several settings in which education for peace is applicable in Finland: day care, home upbringing, schools, and adult education.

DAY CARE   The psychological point of departure for peace education is the recognition of the child's age and level of development. Developmentally appropriate education for peace includes the development of empathy, role-playing capability (to help in understanding other people), and cooperative skills. Materials for social education to this end have been developed. Information is provided about the children and customs of other nations. At an early stage, there must be room in a child's thoughts for children of other nations. This room is needed since emotional responses to other nations begin to develop early and adoption of this basic attitude facilitates the acquisition of later information. Parents must help by understanding the goals of education for peace. The education of day care personnel is essential; there have been obstacles such as lack of information, and negative attitudes. In the town of Espoo, near Helsinki, it was decided to educate the whole town for peace. A daylong course in peace education was given to key personnel in early education as a launching process. Espoo was subsequently divided into 10 districts; in each one, existing day care centers were helped to provide education for peace for both staff and parents. A variety of innovative efforts have been made in Finland to promote norms of peace early in life.

HOME UPBRINGING   Literature was supplied on education for peace in the home. The material emphasized, among other issues, ensuring basic security, analyzing the effects of violent entertainment, and refraining from purchasing war toys.

SCHOOLS   The action taken in schools to develop peace education moved more slowly than in day care. The Department of Public Education was slow in implementing the law but in due course moved to implementing education for international understanding and for peace. Some communities have assembled peace education materials to aid teachers. In the elementary grades, recommendations cover social and ethical education without touching the questions of war and peace. In junior high school, emphasis is taken off the historical glorification of war and shifted to peaceful development. Now, education for international understanding has achieved a more stable position in school education than has education for peace. A study of teachers in the 1980s showed that only 10 percent were active in working for peace; the majority of teachers lacked interest, because they did not feel that appropriate teaching materials were available. However, over the past 20 years, teachers have generally adopted more positive attitudes toward peace education.[58] According to Helena Kekkonen, the director and a founding member (in 1981) of the Peace Education Institute at Helsinki and a central figure in developing peace education in Finland, at the onset of the twenty-first century, 30 percent of teachers were interested in peace education. In her frequent visits to schools and teacher training colleges, she has observed that teacher trainees have a strong interest in this topic, and she noted the ease of working with schools today as compared to the past. In the 1980s, some teachers believed that education for peace was a form of political propaganda. However, that is not true today. Ms. Kekkonen and Ms. Pulkkinen have concentrated their efforts along with others to promote peace education as a general concept unrelated to party politics or political ideology—that is, focusing on the well-being of humanity everywhere.

The culture of Finland has become increasingly heterogeneous since World War II, with a recent focus on tolerance to immigrants and refugees. Finnish President Tarja Halonen actually highlighted this in her televised 2001 New Year address. There are also schools that feature tolerance as a major theme within their ethical education studies. The Peace Education Institute works in *developing countries* with immigrants and schools. It has five friendship schools in developing countries. Thus, the need for curriculum materials of high quality is highlighted. So, too, is the need for preparing teachers to provide educational leadership and the readiness to reach beyond national boundaries.

ADULT EDUCATION   Education for peace among adults, in university education and informal adult education, should advance along with that of youth and children. This is the goal of Finland's Peace Education Institute, which is supported by 14 organizations. It is a resource to stimulate lifelong education in concepts and techniques relevant to sustaining peace. It has had relations with other countries to assist in similar efforts.

Thus, a small country with intellectual vitality and high ethical standards is trying to elicit international cooperation in education that centers on intergroup and international relations. There are indications of growing interest and concern throughout the world. But there is still a very long way to go.

Education for Peace in Developing Countries

UNICEF has earned respect throughout the world for its activities on behalf of children's health, education, and well-being. It addressed these problems in a study published in the year 2000 by the UNICEF Innocenti Research Centre in Florence, Italy, entitled *The Two Faces of Education in Ethnic Conflict: Towards a Peacebuilding Education for Children.*[59] The goal of the study was to stimulate critical thinking about the ways in which formal and informal education have an impact on ethnically based conflict-ridden areas of the world. We hope that UNICEF will continue to build on its contributions in this field in the years ahead.

This UNICEF study emphasized that fundamental changes must occur in education at every level. Simply adding extra peace-education or conflict-resolution ideas or methods to an already complicated mix will not yield the desired results for peace, especially in societies riddled by ethnic strife. It is easier to add educational initiatives than to alter old ones, principally because changing old initiatives poses a threat to regional political authority. However, without convergence between political, methodological, and educational resources, there can be little if any meaningful support from these essential players toward maintaining systemic change.

As noted in Chapter 4 ("Teaching Hatred"), education can actually be a negative force that fuels potential and actual violent conflicts around the world. Even curricula that defend ideals of tolerance and egalitarianism can be overwhelmed by an intolerant and inegalitarian social climate. In matters of identity, education, and conflict, both global hemispheres are affected. Both of them divide along lines of class and/or color and are upheld by relevant authorities in political, social, and economic spheres, thus reinforcing depreciatory and hostile attitudes.

The UNICEF study revolves around four central themes, which we summarize here: (1) education's negative face, (2) the positive side of education, (3) principles for education to build peace, and (4) goals of peacebuilding education.

EDUCATION'S NEGATIVE FACE   Through education, peace can be destroyed and conflict encouraged or maintained, especially where conflicts are based on rigid identity. An unfair balance of social, economic, and political privileges can be continued by unequal distribution of education. When education is used as a weapon, a culture can be depreciated along with personal self-worth. Similarly, the discriminatory denial of education can stimulate conflict. Education can distort the meaning of historical events for political ends. Stereotypes, inequality, and inferiority are ensured by segregated education. Textbooks that do not encourage creative thinking rob children of problem-solving capacities and keep them from constructive paths of resolving conflicts and moving toward peace.

THE POSITIVE SIDE OF EDUCATION   By contrast, education can exert a powerfully decent impact. Constructive opportunities in education can reduce the risk of violent conflict. Education can promote and sustain a climate of ethnic tolerance. It can also discourage segregated patterns of intergroup thinking. It can further ideals of inclusive citizenship and avoid glorification of violence in history. Education, broadly speaking, can promote all forms of peaceful orientations and counteract oppression by the state.

PRINCIPLES FOR EDUCATION TO BUILD PEACE   The *process* of building peace is highlighted, as opposed to achieving an end product. It must be understood that educating for peace is not a quick fix; rather it must be built and measured over the long term. Local resources should be accessed more than relying on contributions from external players. Education that seeks to build peace will envision the creation of opportunities for all and avoid imposing putative solutions on depreciated groups.

GOALS OF PEACEBUILDING EDUCATION   Promoting peaceful, sustainable change agents rather than legitimizing the use of violence to address problems is central to any education focused on peacebuilding. Interethnic conflict is inherently complex, but two key issues must be examined to pursue reconciliation. First, assess the situation for possible shared values that might help communities find a common ground from which to build peace on the basis of mutual benefits. Second, encourage a spirit of joint participation rather than aggressive competition.

Talking Peace: The Unique Contribution of a Great Peacemaker

In a remarkable book for children, *Talking Peace*, President Jimmy Carter (winner of the 2002 Nobel Peace Prize), provides "a vision for the next generation."[60] It is a richly informed and accessible account of fundamental issues in war and peace, throughout history and in the contemporary world. He starts with his own historic achievements in making peace between Israel and Egypt, looking back at the Camp David process. He identifies food, shelter, and health care as foundations for peace. He covers protecting the environment: the earth, our home. As he did in his pioneering foreign policy, he emphasizes human rights, mediation, and elections. He closes by advising young people on what they can do to prevent war in the future. In our judgment, this book should be required reading, at a minimum, in schools of all the established democracies.

CONCLUSION

Educating for peace, even in developed and industrialized areas of the world, is very limited. The history of peace education dates back at least to the mid–nineteenth century, and much has been learned. With recent advances in developmental psychology and social psychology, there is a solid foundation for practical application. We have seen how research has led to practice in educating for conflict resolution and peace, not only in the classroom, but also at the community level through after-school programs for children and youth, and through adult education. However, a comprehensive infusion of these promising techniques into mainstream education is still needed—and so is further research and innovation.

Typically, it has been the industrialized democracies of the North who have had the chance to put these techniques into practice. Neighbors in the South and other developing countries can benefit from the lessons learned; these concepts can be adapted to their unique cultures. But it is a daunting task by virtue of living conditions that so often prevail in these areas of the world. Poverty, illness, lack of basic education, and threats of violent outbreaks are conditions that interfere with teaching about peace. Indeed, educating for peace sometimes seems like a luxury only available to those whose basic needs have been met. But paradoxically, it is also a necessity. It will be very hard to meet basic needs without minimizing violence. So how do we begin to create conditions conducive to teaching about peace, tolerance, and conflict resolution in developing areas of the world that could ultimately benefit greatly? We try to answer this complex question by touching on the crucial elements of democracy and development, which, when taken together, compose the foundation of any society wishing to educate for peace and achieve its profound benefits. In chapter 14 we considered how advances in information technology can facilitate this process. In chapter 18 we show how universities in worldwide cooperation can strengthen the intellectual underpinnings of the whole enterprise.

17

Putting Education
for Peace into Practice

Now let us turn our attention toward the practice of education for peace from several perspectives. We will examine some developmentally appropriate approaches to children and youth in understanding issues of war and peace, practical applications of teaching the prevention of deadly conflict and conflict resolution in schools, international relationships in education for peace, and other institutions with strong potential to promote peace education and conflict resolution.

DEVELOPMENTALLY APPROPRIATE APPROACHES TO
UNDERSTANDING WAR AND PEACE

Even first-grade children can distinguish between societal conventions, noncontroversial questions, and controversial issues. Also, they expect their teachers to teach these types of knowledge differently. They are able to recognize that others may hold opposing viewpoints different from their own.[1] With increasing age, elementary school children in democratic societies expect teachers to present different viewpoints on questions about which there is little societal consensus.[2] And teachers are expected to present different viewpoints in addition to the one that students favor.

Adolescence is the period when students markedly increase their ability to generalize the perspective of society, which is most important when discussing issues related to war, peace, and conflict. It is also a time when young people are most interested in issues related to fairness, justice, and equality. In the 1960s, Joseph Adelson, conducted a series of classic studies involving young people aged 11 to 18 from the United States, Great Britain, and West Germany.[3] Interviews were conducted about concepts of law, community, individual rights, and the public good. It was found that at the age of 14, a shift in quality of thought occurred. They could see the possibility of conflict between individual rights and public good; they could connect specific examples of rights with abstract principles; they could consider long-term consequences of specific actions on individuals and communities. Similar findings were noted in subsequent research, leading to the belief that the period of adolescence is appropriate for developing critical thinking skills.[4]

Teaching an Understanding of War and Peace through Structured Academic Controversies:
An Experimental Approach with Research and Longitudinal Experience

Patricia G. Avery (of the University of Minnesota) and David Johnson, Roger Johnson, and James Mitchell present research on ways children and adolescents understand the concepts of war and peace in the context of their development.[5] Instructional processes that motivate learning have not been researched to the same degree that the sources of knowledge have been studied (family, school, media, peers). So these authors focus on the process of instruction of *academic controversy* and *teacher scripts* relative to young people's understanding of the complex relationships of war and peace. We briefly sketch what controversy looks like in the classroom, the process of controversy, how students can benefit, and key elements for making controversy constructive.

The condition in which one's ideas, information, and theories are incompatible with another's is used to help children to understand the complex concepts of war and peace. To best illustrate the nature of academic controversy, outcomes are studied such as what controversy looks like in the classroom, the process of controversy, how students can benefit, and key elements for making controversy constructive.

Teacher scripts are defined as an expected series of events based on prior experiences. Teacher, student, and societal scripts are explored and issues raised about ways they may obstruct students' thoughtful, constructive engagement in academic controversies. In dealing with *developmental appropriateness,* research has been conducted on the ability of youth to deal with social issues, their expectations of teachers, shifts in quality of thought, and political influences. David Johnson and Roger Johnson have devoted many years to innovation and research in this field. They formulate four goals that must be attained for students to understand the complex issues of peace and war:[6]

1. It must be understood that *war, peace, cooperation, and conflict are interrelated.* Peace and war are on opposite ends of the spectrum; however, peace does not mean simply the absence of war. Rather, it is a state in which ongoing conflicts are resolved constructively with mutual benefit and without violence.
2. Daily experiences of children help them to gain constructive understanding of the nature of peace and war. Their conceptions will differ depending

on their primary experience with cooperation and conflict—whether it is mainly competitive, individualistic, or cooperative. When all parties are satisfied with the outcome, when relationships have been enhanced (or at least not harmed), and participants have learned how to improve their ability to resolve future conflict, then conflict is considered *constructive*. War and peace concepts have personal meaning when students have actual experience of cooperation and constructively managed conflicts.

3. Students need to become experienced and *reach a level of expertise* in dealing effectively with others. So, solid procedures must be taught and used frequently.[7] These procedures are thoughtful academic controversy and conflict resolution training in problem-solving negotiations and peer mediation.[8]

4. The *scripts that lay beneath teachers' traditional patterns* of behavior need to be changed to use academic controversy in a way that the classroom becomes a lively environment for clarifying the nature of war and peace, taking into account a variety of perspectives. Academic controversy engages students to participate actively in the conflicts of ordinary life and learn how to resolve them constructively. A combination of cooperative learning and structured intellectual conflict, academic controversy is here contrasted with simplistic learning and deprecatory debate.

Because the process itself teaches students critical information about conflict resolution—so germane to war and peace—the direct study of war and peace is not necessary though it is certainly germane.[9] For example, a social studies class considers issues of civil disobedience from two perspectives. Cooperative learning groups of four members divide in half. One pair works to present the best possible case for the *constructiveness* of civil disobedience within a democracy, while the other pair strives to present the best case possible for the *destructiveness* of civil disobedience within a democracy.

In the Johnson and Johnson approach, the teacher guides the students through five steps.[10] There are predictable instructional results from this process of reflective controversy:

1. Researching and preparing a position involves each pair of students becoming well acquainted with the material, determining what information is most meaningful to their argument, and then finding the best way to make their presentation. Sharing information is also encouraged between pairs that are given the same position to represent.

2. When presenting and advocating their position, students are urged to be as persuasive as possible. Each pair, in order to learn the material presented, must take notes and listen carefully.

3. While engaging in an open discussion, students refute the opposing position and rebut attacks on their own position. Informed and persuasive reasons are given to present their position. They give as many salient facts as

possible to support their viewpoint and critically evaluate the information of the opposing pair. Students are asked to keep in mind the complexity of the issues and the need to understand both sides to be able to write a good report.

4. Pairs are asked to *reverse* perspectives, with the goal of seeing the issue from both sides concurrently.

5. All four members drop their points of view in favor of *synthesis and integration* of knowledge that all parties can agree on to the extent possible. Then they complete the report, present their conclusions to the class, individually take the test (covering both sides of the issue), and finally, take steps to understand how well they worked together, and what might need improvement the next time.

The Process of Constructive Controversy

David Johnson and Roger Johnson have synthesized the work of developmental, cognitive, and organizational psychologists since the 1950s on processes by which conflict can lead to positive outcomes.[11]

- Initially, when individuals are presented with a problem or a decision to make, they tend to jump to a conclusion based on incomplete information and a personal perspective. This temporarily freezes the learning process.
- To present conclusions to others, individuals mentally rehearse, may deepen their understanding, and find persuasive reasoning strategies.
- Uncertainty about their own conclusions occurs when individuals are confronted with other people's information, experiences, and perspectives. With this perturbation, they tend to unfreeze the previous cognitive process.
- This uncertainty motivates curiosity and an active search for more information in the hope of resolving the uncertainty.
- By combining one's own cognitive viewpoint with those of others, a new conclusion is reached, which is often more distinctive and complex. At this point, the process may begin again or it may be ended by concluding that this new conclusion is valid.

HOW STUDENTS BENEFIT   Over several decades, David Johnson and Roger Johnson's systematic research has clarified the *consequences* of structured controversy.[12] When compared with purely individualistic efforts and conventional debate, this approach to controversy is likely to give the following results:

1. greater student mastery, subject matter retention, and increased ability to generalize principles

2. better quality decisions and solutions to complex problems through empathic perspective-taking and reasoned argument

3. deeper insights into the issues being discussed, and a creative synthesis of different perspectives
4. more positive attitude toward constructive uses of conflict
5. more frequent development of cognitive and moral reasoning to a higher level
6. more constructive change in attitude
7. greater exchange of expertise
8. increased accuracy in understanding the perspective of others
9. greater involvement in tasks
10. more positive relationships within the group and greater perceived peer academic support
11. higher academic self-esteem, and
12. mastery of cognitive and social skills.

These accomplishments bear not only on peace education but on personal development as well.

In addition to cognitive skills, social skills give students the tools they need to solve complex conflicts and teach them implicitly that peace is possible when skills of conflict management are mastered.[13] These skills encompass the following: an emphasis on mutuality; confirmation of others' competence even in disagreement with one's own position or reasoning; separation of personal worth from criticism of one's ideas; the need to listen seriously to others even if one disagrees; the importance of clarifying position differences and integrating various ideas; the ability to take a different perspective; the flexibility to change one's mind if evidence indicates the need to do so; the benefit of paraphrasing what another has said if it is unclear; a focus on rational problem-solving in seeking the best possible answer; and the principle of behaving toward opponents as one would have them behave toward oneself. The ways in which controversy is handled dictate whether or not it is beneficial. David Johnson and Roger Johnson give five key elements: "(1) a cooperative context, (2) heterogeneous participants, (3) relevant information distributed among participants, (4) social skills, and (5) rational argument."[14]

Academic controversy, in this mode, provides teachers with the chance to maintain a peaceful classroom, and through experience in managing various conflicts, they learn to improve their own abilities to cooperate and achieve mutual goals. Students learn ways to resolve conflict constructively and acquire skills for effective practice. They learn that peace and effective cooperation are achieved by experience with well-managed conflicts. Thus, students learn about achieving peace both in the microcosm of the classroom and the macrocosm of world affairs.

Conflictual content and instruction need to take place in an open-minded classroom setting where teachers address the complexity of sensitive issues by clarifying analytical processes, fairly considering different policy options, and sharing concerns.[15] An environment is created in which important problems are discussed in depth rather than treated superficially. The prevailing attitude is that life is complex, different views are inevitable, everyone has something to contribute, problems can be tackled in an atmosphere of mutual respect, intellectual curiosity, and a culture of fairness. In a way, this experience is a microcosm of the experience needed to resolve intergroup or international conflict.

PREVENTING DEADLY CONFLICT: PROGRAMS AND STRATEGIES

Why Teach Prevention of Deadly Conflict in Schools?

There is no content more vital in this field than the avoidance of unnecessary or unjust wars. A key goal of teaching prevention is to help build, through education, societies that are not inclined to go to war except in circumstances of unequivocal self-defense or social justice.

There is an extensive literature on just and unjust wars—on the ethical and legal criteria by which such decisions can be made.[16] The most widely accepted criteria for just war are as follows:

1. The war can be undertaken only as a last resort when all reasonable nonviolent options have failed.
2. The weapons of war must differentiate to the maximum extent possible between combatants and noncombatants.
3. The violence inflicted must be proportional to the damage imposed by the aggressor.
4. The war must have the legitimate authority of the society undertaking it.
5. The peace established after the war must be a clear improvement over the preexisting conditions.
6. The right of self-defense is explicitly recognized in international law, but there must be clear evidence of actual or imminent attack. (The clearest case in the memory of living generations is World War II, in which the aggressive dictatorships of Germany and Japan attacked innocent countries in search of world domination.)

Education for conflict resolution, peace, and violence prevention is teaching concepts and strategies so that most people can learn ways to live a decent life together in a world without war. Although very difficult to achieve, these goals are at least dimly within sight. It may well take generations before we feel the full positive impact of such instruction. It is crucial to begin by implementing proven techniques that can pave the way for future efficacy, based to the extent possible on continuing research.

The work of David Johnson and Roger Johnson and their colleagues, which we have just described, is one promising line of inquiry and innovation, and we now turn to others. We will first look at educational institutions generally and then at specific ways in which education from elementary through graduate school levels have made constructive use of empathy training, assertiveness training, and cooperative learning, as we have considered earlier, in addition to optimal contact situations. Second, we present a broad overview of the work of the Carnegie Commission on Preventing Deadly Conflict.[17] Last, we discuss curricula on the prevention of war. The Carnegie Council on Preventing Deadly Conflict collaborated with staff at Hopewell Valley Central High School in New Jersey to create a curriculum, for a course begun in 1997, on preventing deadly conflict—a requirement for all seniors. At Stanford University in California, a similar curriculum published in the year 2000 (and based partly on Hopewell's model) was created for secondary school youth in grades 10 through 12 and for students in community colleges. This work reveals the extraordinary opportunities that can come from linking higher education with elementary and secondary education.

Educational Institutions

Educational institutions from early childhood to graduate education have a vitally important role to play in the future of humanity, more so than ever before.[18] This not only has to do with the modern, global economy that requires deeper and broader education than ever before, but also with the necessity of learning to live together in this globalized, highly interdependent, culture-mixing world. Historically, as we have noted at the outset, education everywhere has to some degree been ethnocentric—and all too often flagrantly prejudicial. The time has come for schools and indeed international educational organizations to work together to provide war and peace content based on the best of the world's scholarship, not ethnocentric in intergroup relations or hateful in orientation, nor tending to glorify war. Such content can be adapted to different levels of development in keeping with the age and experience of children and youth.

Can we educate ourselves to cope with antagonistic intergroup attitudes peacefully? Is it possible for us to modify our attitudes and orientations so that we practice greater tolerance and mutual aid at home and in the world? The question is how human beings can learn more constructive orientations toward those outside one's group while maintaining the values of primary group allegiance and identity. From an examination of existing research, it seems reasonable to believe that this is possible in spite of very bad habits from our ancient past. We deal with this question in several chapters of this book because it is so central to the future of humanity.

The findings of much research have pointed to the beneficial effects of working cooperatively in schools and elsewhere under conditions that lead people to formulate a new, inclusive group, going beyond the subgroups with which they entered the situation. Such effects are particularly strong when there are tangibly successful outcomes of cooperation—for example, clear rewards from cooperative learning. This research has important implications for childrearing and education.

Education everywhere should convey an accurate portrait of the contemporary human species—a vast extended family sharing fundamental human similarities and a fragile planet. The give-and-take fostered within groups in childhood can be extended toward relations between adults and into larger units of organization, even including relations between nations. All research-based knowledge of human conflict, the diversity of our species, our common humanity, and the paths to mutual accommodation should be a part of education.

Schools can augment what parents can do—use positive discipline practices, be democratic rather than autocratic in procedure, teach the capacity for responsible decision making, foster cooperative learning procedures, and guide children in prosocial behavior outside the schools as well as in it.[19] They can illuminate the facts of human diversity and the common humanity we all share. They can convey the fascination of other cultures, making understanding and respect core attributes of their outlook on the world, including the capacity to interact effectively in the emerging world economy.

Building blocks for such an outlook involve specific ways of forming decent human relations with peers in childhood and adolescence. The Carnegie Council on Adolescent Development's Working Group on Life Skills Training (chaired by the present volume's second author, Dr. Beatrix Hamburg) provided in 1990 the factual basis and organizing principles on which life skills interventions can be based.[20] It also described a variety of exemplary programs. This work has strong, practical value in applying sound concepts to actual situations of conflict. One category of life skills is learning to be assertive. An example of assertiveness is knowing how to take advantage of opportunities—for example, how to use community resources such as health and social services or job training opportunities. Another aspect is knowing how to resist pressure or intimidation by peers and others to take drugs or carry weapons—and how to do this without isolating oneself. Yet another aspect of assertiveness is knowing how to resolve conflict in ways that make use of the full range of nonviolent opportunities that exist. Such skills can be taught not only in schools but also in community organizations and religious institutions. They can be extended to cover relations between different groups, cultures, and nations.

The Growing Emphasis on Prevention of War

Because prevention of deadly, heavily armed, intergroup conflict is fundamentally important, we now turn our attention to it. Here, for example, are major approaches to preventing war that we considered in a related book recently published.[21] They grow out of worldwide research and international meetings seeking paths to prevention.

- "The Origins of World War II and the Holocaust: Powerful Stimuli for Prevention"
- "Governments and Intergovernmental Organizations: Paralyzed Giants or Serious Players?"
- "Institutions of Civil Society: Partners for Peace"
- "Preventive Diplomacy: Early Help with Empathy and Problem Solving"
- "Democracy and Prevention: The Essence of Nonviolent Conflict Resolution"
- "Toward Competent, Decent, and Prosperous States: Updating Socioeconomic Development"
- "International Cooperation for Prevention: Emerging from the Shadows"
- "Preventing Catastrophic Terrorism: International Cooperation, Weapons of Mass Destruction, and Democratic Development"[22]

This list suggests the broad range of topics that need to be considered in understanding the possibilities for prevention of deadly conflict. It is necessarily a large subject, yet one that is of urgent necessity in which new insights are emerging all over the world. Information of this sort is beginning to be taught not only in colleges and universities, but also in secondary schools; valuable cooperating links between these different levels of education are emerging, as we shall see.

HIGH SCHOOL PROGRAMS ON PREVENTING DEADLY CONFLICT

In the following section we summarize several programs on preventing deadly conflict. First, we describe a unique international relations high school curriculum. Second, we tour an educational institution's program on nonproliferation and disarmament. Third, we look at how foundation support can help facilitate peace and conflict resolution programs between the educational, research, and scientific communities. And finally, we explore ways in which online programs enrich education and provide valuable resources on nonproliferation.

Hopewell Valley Central High School

In 1991, Governor Thomas Kean of New Jersey, a distinguished leader in education improvement, instituted many educational reforms, one of which was the establishment of a 3-year study of non-U.S.-focused social studies as a requirement for high school graduation. Hopewell Valley Regional School District established an international relations course in response to this state requirement.[23] It was designed and implemented by members of the Hopewell social studies department. The International Relations (IR) team spent summers revising, updating, and improving the course for the following year. In 1997, the IR team worked with the Carnegie Commission on Preventing Deadly Conflict to produce a curriculum unit on preventing deadly conflict. Once tested, one goal was to make this curriculum available to other high schools— first in New Jersey and then throughout the United States and possibly abroad. Upon review of the Carnegie Commission materials, they concluded that a course on preventing deadly conflict would be a valuable addition to the International Relations program, and one likely to stimulate more interest than the standard international relations units.

This 14-day unit was pilot-tested in the 12th-grade IR course in Hopewell Valley Central High School in Pennington, New Jersey, in the 1997–1998 school year. Although this is a small initiative, a major curriculum along these lines would have much potential to contribute to the healthy development of children and youth, to strengthen democratic institutions in the United States and abroad, and to prevent deadly conflict. A core belief of Carnegie Commission on Preventing Deadly Conflict was that the long-term solution to the problem of mass violence begins with education.

UNIT GOALS AND ORGANIZATION   The unit was structured with the following components:

- A detailed program of instruction for use by the teacher
- A target set of achievements for the student
- Student activities (projects, exercises, reading, worksheets, videos, etc. to support the targeted achievements)
- Assessment strategies for the objectives of the unit
- Suggested scoring or evaluation rubrics for student work
- A list of readings (both Carnegie Commission publications and other works)

Although shortened in length by several days, this unit is still taught at Hopewell with much success, according to the head of the social studies department. The faculty continue to work with Carnegie Commission on Preventing Deadly Conflict publications, especially the ones that relate to flash point problems.

DISSEMINATION   Initially, creators of this unit hoped for wide dissemination to high schools nationally and internationally, by stimulating interest in a variety of educational institutions. An important step was made in this regard in 2000.[24] The Carnegie Commission on Preventing Deadly Conflict collaborated with the Stanford University Program on International and Cross-Cultural Education (SPICE) to produce a module entitled *Preventing Deadly Conflict—Toward a World without War*. Hopewell's *Preventing Deadly Conflict* unit was used as the prototype for Stanford's module with several ideas incorporated into the text. In the next chapter, we consider this and other university initiatives in education for peace.

The Critical Issues Forum: A High School Program on Nonproliferation and Disarmament

Following a 1997 lecture at a community organization given by William C. Potter (director of the highly respected Monterey Institute's Center for Nonproliferation Studies) on the spread of weapons of mass destruction, a high school student in the audience asked why such material was not being presented in high school courses.[25] This was the seed planted for an initiative that the Center for Nonproliferation Studies (CNS) began in 1998 called the Critical Issues Forum (CIF). The Science and Technology Education Program at the Lawrence Livermore National Laboratory was a partner in creating this program for secondary schools designed to provide curricula and instructional materials on weapons of mass destruction. Students are given instruction and guidance in research methodologies, which include brainstorming, evaluation of content, synthesis of information, developing writing skills, and strategies that can be used with the Internet. The goal is to increase the awareness of nonproliferation issues and to prepare the next generation of specialists in the field. The program was based on a 1996 initiative of the Science Education Team at the Los Alamos National Laboratory. Their Critical Thinking Model is the pedagogical foundation of the CIF.

PROGRAM FORMAT   Beginning with a summer workshop, a core group of CIF teachers meet in Monterey to develop a curriculum that will be presented to students in the coming academic year. Next, a winter workshop that includes CIF teachers and CNS personnel introduces the curriculum to teachers participating in the program. Last, students and teachers from participating schools attend a conference to learn about each other's projects.[26]

Themes differ from year to year. For example, in 1998–1999 the topic was non-proliferation of nuclear weapons. In 2000–2001, chemical and biological weapons were studied (which we say more about in the next section). In 2001—2002, the focus was on Missiles and Missile Defense. In 2002–2003, the topic was Weapons of Mass Destruction in the Middle East and South Asia. CIF has steadily grown to involve more U.S. states, which in the year 2002–2003 included California, Georgia, Maryland, New Mexico, Texas, Washington State, and five schools from Russia's closed nuclear cities.[27]

A STUDY OF TOXIC TERROR   For a 10-month period during the academic year 2000–2001, students participated in the CIF that started with summer workshops for teachers at the Monterey Institute where they developed the curriculum with attention paid to particular classroom needs. Students began their spring term working with teachers and staff at CNS. As a follow-up to the Forum, students participated in a 2-day conference at which they shared the results of their investigations with other students, including Russian students and teachers and international experts in the field of nonproliferation. Students from 12 high schools in California, New Mexico, Texas, and Washington State made presentations on topics that included the toxic insecticide sarin, an introduction to terrorism, and the use of protective gear in the event of a chemical attack.[28] It is a hopeful sign that such educational efforts will increasingly become international in nature.

The scope and depth of these student projects were impressive, indicating serious inquiry into this timely subject. For example, at the conference two high school seniors from Texas presented a policy statement against the use of biological or chemical weapons in any circumstances and advocating immediate disposal of such weapons. Their analysis provided an opportunity for these students to consider deeply reasons why it is important to get rid of these exceedingly dangerous weapons. In a California technical high school, students created an online classroom to teach other high school students about the problem via the World Wide Web. The presentation made at the conference was designed to enlighten students on the urgent need at the local level for cities to plan for hazardous materials emergencies. The small Texas town of Sterling was involved in the local high school students' research project on the chemical nature, development, and effects of the chemical agents sarin and tabun. Students interviewed World War II veterans in their town and asked about their experiences with these weapons during the war. Other people in the community also regularly engaged students by questioning them about the issues. The high quality of student presentations impressed the Russian teachers at the conference. Plans for expansion of the CIF will add more U.S. and Russian schools.

Foundation Support for High School Programs on Nonproliferation Studies

The CIF program provides another useful example of partnerships created between ed-ucational, scientific, and foundation communities. The Compton Foundation, began as a Trust in 1946. Its mission was "to build the foundations for peace and to help pre-vent another world war."[29] Now headquartered in Northern California, the foundation provides funding for CIF. Founders Dorothy Danforth and Randolph P. Compton both believed in the importance of combining research and activism, scholarship and equal educational opportunities for minorities to address the world's problems. Their intent is to use information obtained from research to inform the public of the facts, en-courage discussion, and influence national policies toward improving conditions that threaten human survival. The CIF program meets these standards and was a suitable match for support by the Compton Foundation.

In July 2000, Ted Turner, media executive and philanthropist, commissioned a group of global experts to explore whether a private foundation could make a difference in reducing the threat of nuclear, biological, and chemical weapons. Based on recom-mendations from the study, Turner pledged $250 million to form the Nuclear Threat Initiative (NTI) in response to two central challenges: (a) that nuclear, biological, and chemical weapons represent the world's greatest threat, and (b) that the gap between the global threat and global response is dangerously increasing.[30] He and the distin-guished former senator Sam Nunn cochair the initiative and have built an excellent pro-fessional staff. They work together to raise public awareness, inspire worldwide coop-eration, and find ways to reduce the danger of weapons of mass destruction: nuclear, biological, and chemical.

In the fall of 2001, the Center for Nonproliferation Studies developed an online learning resource (*WMD 411*) on nuclear, chemical, and biological weapons for high school debaters.[31] The Nuclear Threat Initiative supports this program that is available on the NTI Web site (http://www.nti.org). NTI continues work with CNS on other dis-tance learning programs for high school students in the United States, Russia, and other countries. Foundations and government must recognize the importance of support-ing such efforts that typically involve long-term commitment of resources. The success of these efforts depends on sustained support because there is no quick fix or ready-made solution to the complex issues of nonproliferation.[32]

Online Educational Resources on Nonproliferation

WMD 411 and CIF, the two resources mentioned earlier, and the *Learning Resources Guide* (ERB), which we describe here, underscore the Center for Nonproliferation Stud-ies' (CNS) commitment to educate youth through current, accurate, and readily avail-able online information.

A Web page of CNS, *Learning Resources Guide* (ERG), maintains a collection of re-sources for education on nonproliferation and disarmament—crucial aspects of edu-cation for peace.[33] ERG provides an online service for students, educators, researchers, and the general public to access reliable educational material on nonproliferation and related topics. One may browse by topic and also use key words to search for information. For example, a database search for a listing of sites of organizations engaged in nonproliferation will provide the user with specific information about each organization. It includes a paragraph description of the organization; major topics (e.g., chemical and biological weapons); special features (e.g., available databases or multimedia opportunities); and the educational level that is addressed (e.g., high school or university.)

Organizations must meet a set of criteria to be included in the ERG. First, they must be sites of official organizations that are among the following six categories: government, international, educational institutions, media, research institutions, and NGOs (involved in nonproliferation, arms control, and disarmament). Second, the site needs to have accurate information about at least one of the following keyword categories: arms control; disarmament; export control; missile defense; nonproliferation; organizations; regions; treaties. Third, the sites must have information designed for or especially useful to students and educators. Fourth, sites must primarily have original material.[34] A special feature that adds value for student users is an icon (i.e., "Resources") that directs the user to information on opportunities for internships or fellowships. It is common for many organizations to offer undergraduate or graduate internships in both the summer and academic year.

ACCESSIBLE INSIGHT INTO TERRORISM AND WEAPONS OF MASS DESTRUCTION
The September 11, 2001, attacks on the World Trade Center and the Pentagon were catalysts for the creation of *Terrorism and Weapons of Mass Destruction: Resources for Students and Teachers*.[35] It answers timely questions such as If terrorists struck our town, what would happen? Will nuclear, chemical, or biological weapons be used in the next attack? What are the United States and the community of nations doing to stop terrorism? These and other questions are addressed with the purpose of giving students and teachers in high schools, community colleges, and universities solid information that may stimulate education and research in a variety of ways.

The CNS online resources demonstrate the feasibility of providing consistent, timely, and highly accurate information on topics of nonproliferation, disarmament, weapons of mass destruction, and terrorism. Other educational institutions would do well to provide similar services to the public—especially to youth—in areas of conflict resolution and peace studies.

Now we turn to a unique and highly constructive program involving youth primarily from countries of the Middle East who join in a shared camp experience designed to foster mutual respect and understanding. Participation in the Center for Coexistence in Jerusalem, follow-up conferences, and Internet correspondence are among the ways these young people can maintain and extend their relationships and broaden understanding of one another beyond their initial camp experience.

SEEDS OF PEACE

Seeds of Peace was created by the late John Wallach in response to the first World Trade Center bombing in 1993. That summer, 46 young people from Palestine, Israel, and Egypt attended the first Seeds of Peace International Camp. Located in rural Otisfield, Maine, the Seeds of Peace camp provides a safe and nurturing setting in which young people from conflict regions of the world can learn, share ideas, and explore conflict resolution strategies.[36] As empathy and compassion build between these adolescents, tendencies for misunderstanding, negative stereotyping, and violent behavior diminish.

The central focus of Seeds of Peace is to bring Arab and Israeli teenagers together before perceptions of each other are committed to mistrust and hatred. By nurturing trust, the organization aims to develop mutual and long-lasting friendships that will contribute to peace in the next generation. By seeing the face of one's neighbor—not as the enemy but instead as a potential ally and friend—the seeds of peace are sown.

There are currently over 2,000 first-year applications submitted from students in Egypt, Jordan, Palestine, Israel, Morocco, Tunisia, Qatar, Yemen and other Middle Eastern countries, as well as from Americans from the inner city of Portland, Maine. Students outside the United States are selected by their governments' Ministries of Education. Each applicant must show a proficiency in speaking English, skills in leadership, and must write an essay on his or her reasons for wanting to attend the camp. The selection process is based solely on the leadership abilities and performance of students, regardless of their social class or economic background.

Young people, most of them between the ages of 14 and 16 years, are being prepared to lead the cause against violent conflict in the next generation. The pursuit of peaceful coexistence does not end with the few short weeks of camp experience. In 1999, Seeds of Peace established the Center for Coexistence in Jerusalem to encourage these young people's commitment to pursue coexistence and to maintain and build on the relationships formed at camp. At the Center and at regional activities in other conflict areas, students engage in advanced sessions on coexistence; continue programs with adult leaders; and participate in workshops, seminars, and other community-based events; they also write and produce a magazine, *Olive Branch*, which was begun in 1996.[37]

Since 1994, the number of annual participants has grown from 50 to over 450 in the summer of 2002. The summer camp program utilizes many activities including sports, drama, music, fine arts, and modern computer classes that help to draw young people together. The program is divided into eight component parts:[38]

1. *Coexistence Program*—This is the core of Seeds of Peace Summer Program, in which participants gain enhanced understanding and compassion for "the other," delve into contentious issues, and learn meaningful and productive communication skills. Their critical reflection skills are also challenged as they explore different ways of understanding each other and the nature of the conflict.

2. *Religious services*—All participants have the opportunity to take part in Sabbath services in order to experience directly their fellow campers' tra-

ditions. The Muslim and the Jewish services are held on Friday afternoon and Friday evening respectively and the Christian services take place on Sunday morning.

3. *Delegation meetings*—Several hour-long meetings are scheduled during each session in which members of each delegation along with delegation leaders (teachers, high school principals, and other chaperones) join to speak in their own languages (normally, everyone speaks the common language of English) about negative and positive experiences of camp life.

4. *Cultural Night*—One night during each session, campers share their unique cultural heritage through exposure to traditional clothing, listening to indigenous music, and sampling new and enjoyable foods with new friends from around the world.

5. *Arts programs*—The program incorporates the visual and dramatic arts, as well as creative writing, into its daily experiences. Campers also have the opportunity to collaborate on a monumental project with the artist-in-residence. These works are displayed at the camp during the summer and then shown in galleries around the country.

6. *Group Challenge*—This is a carefully designed series of activities for the group that complements both the coexistence program and life at the camp. It is a flexible, to meet the needs of the participants as they grow through the Seeds of Peace coexistence program. Team spirit, cooperation, trust, and communication are reinforced, promoting stronger bonds between young people.

7. *Color Games*—This is the culmination of the camp experience and is a kind of Olympics competition. The camp is divided into two *multinational* teams that compete in every camp activity ranging from sports to fine arts, and even contests involving computers and cooking. Although intensely competitive, the games also foster a profound cooperative spirit in each group that goes beyond ethnic and cultural divisions. In effect, each in-group for the games involves enjoyable cooperation with traditional out-group persons.

8. *Washington, D.C.*—The entire program concludes with a trip to Washington, D.C. Campers visit the White House, the State Department, and a variety of national monuments and museums. It is a tradition for the Seeds of Peace delegates to meet with either the president or vice president, the first lady, or the secretary of state. This has a strong impact on students as they reenter the real world and see for themselves positive responses from world leaders about what they have learned and achieved. It is also heartening for these young people to hear officials express faith and trust in them to help create a more just and humane world, especially in the Middle East, Cyprus, the Balkans, and areas anywhere in the world where violent conflict exists. By the same token, President Clinton was deeply impressed by these young people and the quality of their coexistence efforts.[39]

Keeping the Connection Alive

With the help and cooperation of 10 Arab and Israeli teenage graduates of the Seeds of Peace program, an educational CD-ROM by the same name was created.[40] The purpose was to craft a tool to enable young Israeli and Palestinian students of the same age to learn about each other. In early 2001, students from two schools—the Yotveta Kibbutz School in Israel Negev and the largest Palestinian school in East Jerusalem—had the opportunity to experience the human side of their neighbors rather than the usual exposure to hatred and violence. In addition, a three-dimensional virtual tour of both Israeli and Palestinian homes was included, along with 6 hours of discussion about teenage life and opinions about the conflict. There were also tours of refugee camps, Jerusalem, and more. As Middle Eastern students make their way through the CD-ROM, they have the opportunity to reflect on their own identities, which are then uploaded on the Internet for other Middle Eastern students to see. The Internet is a valuable medium for this highly constructive communication and relationship building that bypasses the borders created by adults.[41]

Because of the current situation in the Middle East, direct physical contact among youth alumni is extremely difficult, so the program relies heavily on the use of technology and print media to stay connected. SeedsNet is a secure listserver in daily use that reaches all Seeds of Peace graduates, enabling them to communicate by e-mail. So regardless of borders or political situations, students can keep in touch with one another. Also, Seeds of Peace alumni maintains a private Web site called ClubHouse. It is a way for graduates of the program to report new developments, post stories and messages, and engage in online chats.[42] In a hostile area, passions may undermine the utility of technology. But the ingenuity, dedication, and decency reflected in these efforts offer some basis for hope in the long term.

Olive Branch, the magazine written and published by Seeds of Peace, is another venue for learning about each nation's leadership, a way to share reactions to current events, and a means for participants to stay in dialogue with each other. The Seeds of Peace network distributes the magazine to schools and youth groups. Alumni have used it as a basis for school discussions and classroom presentations. Teachers have also taken an interest in the magazine as a supplement for their classroom curriculum.[43]

INTERNATIONAL LEADERSHIP CONFERENCES   The 1998 Middle East Youth Summit (the first *Seeds of Peace* leadership conference) convened 100 Israeli and Arab graduates in Villars, Switzerland. The result was a proposed Israeli-Palestinian peace treaty—the Charter of Villars—that provided 50 pages of feasible solutions to the most difficult problems of the Middle East that are tragically still with us today. Topics addressed included Jerusalem's status, security arrangements, rights of refugees to return home, borders, water, and sovereignty.

Graduates were given the opportunity to enter into discussion with world leaders including Her Majesty Queen Noor of Jordan, Israeli Foreign Minister Shimon Peres, President Flavio Koti of Switzerland, Dr. Sáeb Erkat (chief Palestinian negotiator), and (via satellite from the White House) U.S. First Lady Hillary Rodham Clinton.[44]

The second summit was held 2 months after the catastrophic events of September 11, 2001, in New York City. "Uprooting Hatred and Terror" was the topic of discussion by a 150-member Seeds of Peace delegation representing 22 countries. They talked about the fundamental causes of terrorism and completed a 28 page Youth Charter, presented to UN Secretary-General Kofi Annan, that focused primarily on education, media, pop culture, economic differences, safety and security, religion, and principles of governing.[45] We summarize their ideas on these main topics:[46]

- *Education*—Poor education contributes to terrorism. Textbooks should be rewritten to maintain a neutral viewpoint using unbiased language and accurate factual reporting in order to block the roots of hatred, terror, and violence.
- *Media*—Must be free and independent in order to present an accurate representation of world events.
- *Pop culture*—Those who produce, market, and distribute popular culture messages are often guilty of omitting the voices of developing countries, resulting in rejection and even shame. The need of those in developing countries to defend their cultures is strong, and angry reactions may ensue.
- *Economic differences*—Because all peoples of the world are responsible for each other, it is both the duty and the privilege of world citizens to work toward prosperity for all.
- *Safety and security*—It is everyone's birthright to live in safety without fear of discrimination. Hatred—the root of violence—instills a sense of fear into communities. Once hatred infiltrates the hearts of thousands of people, the safety and security of the minority are at terrible risk of uncontrolled violent acts by the majority.
- *Religion*—The clergy comprise a powerful group that influences billions of people, especially those whose lives revolve around religious principles and teachings. It is vital for the clergy to promote ideals of respect for all social groups, promote tolerant attitudes and behaviors, and advocate for peace. Spreading constructive religious education that does not infringe on the rights and freedoms of others may help to prevent manipulation and misinterpretation.
- *Principles of governing*—Each person has the right to be represented in the government through a fair system of elections. This is key to meeting individual and group needs. Governments must strive to eradicate corruption and be true to the will of the people. Otherwise frustration and anger will follow, which are likely to lead to violence.

A third youth conference was scheduled for fall 2003, circumstances permitting, called "Breaking News, Making Headlines." The goal of this meeting was to build on understanding of root causes of violent conflict and suggest ways of reversing negative trends. Plans were to focus entirely on the media and try to answer a question meeting participants asked themselves at the November 2001 summit: How can we redirect the power of the media towards the positive aim of building a culture of peace?[47]

After a decade of earnest, thoughtful efforts, no one can say what the future will bring. Seeds of Peace has earned the respect of the international community as an attractive model for helping to resolve conflict worldwide. The program helps participants to develop empathy and prosocial behavior; learn respect for others, even if they appear different and unfamiliar; enhance communication and negotiation skills; and instill a sense of confidence and hope. These are core ingredients for learning to live together in harmony. If such a program can be created in the midst of terrible strife, others may arise elsewhere. Someday, somehow, there may be cumulative effects.

PREVENTING RECURRENCE OF MASS VIOLENCE AFTER WAR

We now turn to an important program recently developed jointly by the United Nations High Commissioner for Refugees (UNHCR) and Harvard Law School. Its goal is to prevent the recurrence of mass violence following war by aiding citizens in finding common ground so they may re-create and maintain peaceful conditions for coexistence. In subsequent sections we examine issues of human security, the role of education, conflict resolution, positive contact between groups, and human rights. Each is framed in the context of preventing the rampant violence that so often follows war. We also look at an outstanding program that helps students to develop empathy and compassion through the study of history—particularly periods of extreme suffering.

Imagine Coexistence

In the later years of the twentieth century, one of us (D.A.H.) served on the Advisory Group of the former United Nations High Commissioner for Refugees, Sadako Ogata. Mrs. Ogata served for a decade in this difficult capacity with great distinction, insight, and courage. From Bosnia and Kosovo to Rwanda and Congo, to East Timor and beyond, the United Nations High Commission for Refugees (UNHCR) had to care for many millions of forced refugees and internally displaced persons—many of whom were escapees from genocide. The carnage was horrible. It was as if all the emergency rooms and intensive care units of all the world's hospitals were concentrated in these UNHCR areas of utmost human cruelty. In coping valiantly with these crises, Mrs. Ogata formulated some basic concepts and operations that bear directly on how we humans can learn to live together decently even after catastrophic fights or persecutions.

Enabling People to Live in Security

Mrs. Ogata delivered the keynote speech at the International Symposium on Human Security in Tokyo in 2002.[48] We summarize some of her key views here because they vividly highlight grave problems that must and can be addressed by the international community as well as by adversaries. By implication, they highlight the urgent need for prevention of deadly conflict.[49] We need reconciliation *before* slaughter, and education is crucial for reconciliation. Generally, insecurity is about the human fear of suffering and dying. Conflicts and terrorism elicit this fear most strongly. UNHCR is most familiar with viewing human security in the context of "forced human displacement. [It is active in] defending asylum, helping people return home, and promoting resettlement to third countries"[50]—all in an effort to assist people in the difficult transition from insecurity to security. There can be no success without support from the world at large. Humanitarian action, with all its good intentions, is insufficient. Rather, action must address root causes.

Despite the world's immense monetary resources and breadth of opportunities, humanity has not yet found a means of preventing violent conflict and enabling people to live in peace. As a global community, we lack the political means to stop violence, which is a central cause of human insecurity. Where conflicts within nations are concerned, what means does the international community have to assure the security of a threatened population?

The first step to human security is to stop the gunfire. But for a sense of real security, Mrs. Ogata advocates a "horizon of security,"[51] which extends and broadens the short-term and tenuous effects of a cease-fire. To maintain security, the international community must become engaged and offer tangible, caring support to postconflict societies. The period directly following the end of conflict is when the international community system provides a delicate link—bridging efforts between conflict resolution and development. During the period of peace negotiations, long-term rebuilding needs to be addressed. People must be given the chance to exercise their power and influence, which is primarily accomplished through training and education.

UNHCR is a humanitarian agency that concentrates on helping people to return to their lives within their communities. Local institutions and civil society require support. Often it is national, nongovernmental organizations and groups, at the grassroots level, that provide security to states that have suffered internal violence. But food, shelter, and physical protection are not enough.

Once internal conflicts cease, refugees are then able to return to their home states, often having to coexist with the people with whom they fought. Stunning examples are found from Bosnia to Rwanda and from Liberia to East Timor. When large populations return to their homes, the two central challenges are to help people become aware of the potential for coexistence and find ways to implement this potential. As we have learned from many examples all over the world, there is great unifying power found in working together to achieve a highly valued object or opportunity—be it a water well, or a playground, or a school. Mrs. Ogata believes that the success of future reconstruction projects needs a vision of potential for coexistence and the creation of joint activities to meet important shared needs.

UNHCR is working with Harvard Law School on a program called Imagine Coexistence. In many ravaged and war torn areas of the world, courageous people—often women—have initiated projects that help to unite people in their work, play, and planning activities. The goal of Imagine Coexistence is to choose clusters of such activities and give them financial support and help to become consciously aware of the coexistence potential of their efforts. Work of this kind is underway in Bosnia and Rwanda.

Mrs. Ogata believes that an income-generating activity can be helpful at the center of such projects. For example, a small factory would receive inducements for hiring people from various ethnicities and social origins, transcending adversarial boundaries. Surrounding this income-generating activity would be related initiatives such as children's playgrounds, theater groups, sporting activities, games, and designated areas for different people to meet each other in pleasant circumstances. Peaceful coexistence requires acceptance by the diverse populations involved. This approval fosters trust, a major support for building a secure society. Transformation from insecurity to security requires joint efforts that are at once far-reaching, creative, and informative.

Coexistence Education

Professor Martha Minow, distinguished professor of law at Harvard University, writes meaningfully about education for coexistence. Indeed, her work has had a stimulating, mutually beneficial interaction with that of Sadako Ogata. Like that of the UNHCR, much of Minow's focus is on reconciliation after disastrous outbreaks of hatred and violence. Although these are vitally important approaches, our emphasis throughout this book and in two previous ones (*No More Killing Fields: Preventing Deadly Conflict* and *Today's Children*) is finding ways of preventing such outbreaks before they reach the level of mass violence. These approaches overlap, and both are necessary: that is, primary prevention and prevention of recurrence of violence are both needed.

What will it take to stop dehumanizing others to the point of slaughter? What are practical and psychological shifts that need to occur for people to work in the long term to become less prejudiced and overcome political differences? Typically the response, following violent conflicts between groups, is to turn to education, because that is where the best hope for transforming the thoughts and behaviors of future generations is likely to occur.[52]

Education is embedded into the larger project, Imagine Coexistence, where emphasis is placed on recognizing the dangers that people face when they return home after an ethnic conflict and assisting them in supporting coexistence. It also can be an integral function of humanitarian aid organizations. Intergroup distrust becomes inflamed when well-meaning outside international aid agencies overlook persistent areas of intergoup conflict. Providing blankets, police support, or economic aid is simply not enough. When UNHCR helped Bosnians and Rwandans to return home, it risked exacerbating tensions between the group that stayed and the group that returned, as well as between Muslims and Christians, Serbs and Croats. It is useful to identify and focus on ways in which *all* people can benefit, such as providing jobs, joint community centers, and housing, as well as caring for orphans.

The project's name—Imagine Coexistence—was conceived by a team of scholars, evaluators, and UNHCR staff specifically to distinguish it from deep reconciliation that takes time, to recognize what is possible in the near future, and to respect different needs of people coming out of crisis. The very act of imagining helps one to hold the idea in mind, which is a central component for achieving peace. And simply grasping the concept is an important first step in the right direction.

Imagine Coexistence, at its core, is about education. It is about exploring what is possible between groups in conflict, especially concerning ways to collaborate for mutual benefit and thereby help to build fundamental trust. Following the terror of mass violence, returning to normal is not the goal, because "normal" is what produced the conflict in the first place. A focus on young people is most important. Studies of memory show that experiences in adolescence and young adulthood form the source for very strong memories throughout the life span.

In recalling the horrors of September 11, 2001—both the causes and the aftermath—Minow asks what kind of education could lead those 19 young men to want to hijack U.S. planes and then use them as massively destructive weapons to kill thousands of civilians along with themselves, and launch a political attack on the United States. What now is the appropriate response of schools in teaching about these tragic events?

Instruction in managing anger, preventing violence, avoiding bias, and conflict resolution were intensified across the United States in response to the events of September 11. The need is clear. We must learn constructive ways of treating groups that appear to be different, whether they are residents or immigrants. Educating for coexistence is pertinent both to the United States and to other areas of the world where intergroup conflicts simmer.

Professor Minow outlines several methods for education for coexistence, each one providing a useful example and a unique judgment of the requirements to promote coexistence. Though they deal with postviolence situations, they overlap with our earlier treatment of previolence settings.

CONFLICT RESOLUTION AND COEXISTENCE   Training in conflict resolution is a primary focus in education for coexistence for young children through adolescents. In relatively peaceful contexts, training might involve mediation between peers, within communities and in wider circles of influence, as well as about how to resolve conflict without violence. In societies where fragile peace agreements are being constructed, or where people are moving from conflict situations to peace, the focus is more on peace education which attempts to raise the notion of community and resist indoctrination from harshly nationalist or ethnic sources, and build skill in students to resolve or move beyond conflicts.[53] Between 15 and 20 percent of public schools in the United States offer some type of conflict resolution training within social studies or peer mediation courses or in special programs targeted to mediation skill development. These experiences are applicable to postconflict situations like Bosnia.

INTERGROUP CONTACT   The goals of intergroup contact are distinctive; they are meant to encourage exchanges between various racial, ethnic, and religious groups to build positive experiences of cooperation where acceptance becomes mutual, stereotypes are overcome, and equality becomes the norm.[54] The United States has engaged not only in mandated programs of racial desegregation and voluntary school desegregation, but also in highly focused, less formal programs of several weeks' duration, which, for example, bring together Palestinians and Israelis, or adolescents from opposing parts of Ireland, or suburban and urban U.S. teenagers. We have earlier specified the conditions that are favorable for improvement of intergroup relations through contact.

Intergroup relations can also benefit from well-thought-out cooperative-learning work groups, which we discussed in Chapter 8. In his work as a school reformer and scholar, Robert Slavin forged studies in the mid-1980s that showed improved attitudes in students along with friendship building across groups. In Slavin's studies over many years, students in multiethnic and multiracial groups work together and are graded as a team, although individual improvement is also reflected in the group's grade.[55] Minow finds this approach promising for imagining coexistence to prevent recurrence of violence.

HUMAN RIGHTS   Model United Nations is a program that replicates the practices of the United Nations and involves nearly 200,000 U.S. students from the middle grades through college. Different from typical intergroup contact models that utilize conflict resolution, music, or community service, Model United Nations encourages students to "introduce resolutions, hold committee meetings, plan strategies and engage in negotiations."[56] In this context, youth are taught about human rights.

Reflecting the human rights movement, educational efforts make explicit the principles involving equality, liberty, institution building and practices rooted in those principles. By focusing on broad ideals, this method seeks to draw people away from specific conflicts or unjust behaviors. Both human rights documents and human rights education share "faith in the rule of law, the power of social movements, and the potential of rights language to build reciprocal respect among people."[57] There is a widely shared belief throughout the global community that a set of institutions can be created along with a shared language that will promote equality and liberty.[58]

A United Nations teaching guide, "ABC: Teaching Human Rights: Practical Activities for Primary and Secondary Schools," is available online.[59] It echoes the UN's commitment to teaching human rights. Early in the teaching guide, there appear teaching materials about conflict resolution. Later, the guide focuses the educational program on core documents in international law. There is a direct linkage from human rights instruction to preventing violent conflict between groups. We have learned the hard way that egregious, widespread human rights violations engender serious conflict and often mass violence.[60]

COMPARATIVE HISTORY AND SELF-REFLECTION   Professor Minow cites Facing History and Ourselves (FHAO) as an exemplary program that enhances students' critical thinking skills, and develops attitudes of understanding and compassion. Facing History and Ourselves, a nonprofit organization based in Brookline, Massachusetts, was founded in 1976 by Margot Stern Strom.[61] It continues to examine the root causes of racism and anti-Semitism. By investigating periods in history such as the Holocaust that are particularly devastating—in which violence, human degradation, and mass murder were committed—students are required to think about their own lives and ways in which they may act to prevent hatred and violent behavior between groups. Understanding of history is deepened along with an ability to think about root causes of atrocities such as the Holocaust. They are engaged in study about what it takes to build and maintain democratic institutions; and what is required, individually and collectively, to defuse situations in which individuals or groups are at risk of demonization.

Over a 25-year period, FHAO has succeeded partly because teachers and students are joint partners in learning. A variety of professional development activities are available to teachers, such as weekend or weeklong workshops and conferences, discussion with leading scholars on current and historical topics, and exploration of teaching techniques involving visual arts, poetry, and community service.

The curricular materials developed by FHAO combine primary historical sources, fictional works, and other readings. The sponsors have offices throughout the United States and in other countries that give pedagogical ideas to teachers and provide them access to other resources including films, guest speakers, and experience in leading discussions on difficult issues. Teachers are able to modify the material to suit their own classroom requirements. Programs have recently been developed in Eastern Europe and South Africa.

On a regular basis, FHAO engages in both self-evaluation and external evaluation. Results of external evaluation show that students participating in the program have more knowledge about history; they are better able to reason from a moral perspective; their ability to exhibit empathy and social interest is higher, along with their sense of worth. One study showed that the FHAO students were stronger than the comparison group in their interpersonal and intergroup relationships; relationship maturity was higher; they were less engaged in fighting; racist and ethnocentric attitudes were lower. Program students showed less sense of isolation because they perceive themselves as active members of a learning community involved in important work.

Overall, these various programs outlined by Minow show distinctive ways of engaging students and teachers in the realities of animosities and ways of moderating them. The UNHCR places education for coexistence high on its agenda, as do nations recovering from massive violence. Even in conflicted societies where little violence has occurred, it is still vitally important to engage in education for coexistence. Altogether, the work on Imagine Coexistence demonstrates a fruitful interplay between scholars and humanitarian aid practitioners in coping with the problems of deeply divided societies. It is worth noting that post-conflict reconciliation draws upon some of the same concepts and techniques that we have described earlier in the context of pre-conflict violence prevention.

As a final consideration in our examination of practical applications for peace education, we now turn to the powerful influence of religion. We include in our discussion religious education, autonomy of religious leaders and institutions, and human rights as being part of the identity of all human beings regardless of religious affiliation.

RELIGIOUS LEADERS AND INSTITUTIONS: THE CHALLENGE OF PEACE EDUCATION

Given the vast reach of religious institutions and the worldwide prevalence of religious education, it is sad but necessary to note the paucity of serious, substantial content and spiritual emphasis on education for peace, including its fundamental underpinnings in prosocial behavior, pervasive human fairness, democratic governance, mechanisms for early resolution of intergroup grievances, and overcoming of traditional harsh distinctions between different human groups—be they religious, ethnic, political, national or other invidious distinctions.

Yes, there is abundant rhetoric of goodwill, and often there are exhortations for peace from religious leaders. Such proclamations are useful but not sufficient. We need specific tools and strategies of preventing deadly conflict, the handles on reducing risk of mass slaughter. There are wonderful exemplars of violence prevention, such as those provided in South Africa by Archbishop Desmond Tutu and in the United States by Professor Elie Wiesel and Father Theodore Hesburgh of Notre Dame. Indeed, these remarkable spiritual leaders are truly citizens of the world and foster constructive interfaith and international dialogues even across traditionally adversarial lines. If Tutu, Wiesel, and Hesburgh can serve the cause of peace so well, then why not many others? Surely there is great opportunity in religious education for peace, specific and in-depth. Much of the content of this book could be used in religious schools as well as secular schools.

During the Civil Rights movement in the United States during the 1960s, some clergymen took an active part, even risking their lives in peaceful demonstrations that were attacked by violent segregationists. These clergymen were white as well as African American; Jewish, Protestant, and Catholic. They steadfastly pursued nonviolent problem solving and taught young people how to do so. On return to their congregations, they exemplified democratic ideals for a generation of young people in religious education—and indeed for their parents as well. Some, such as the highly respected Rabbi Sidney Axelrad of California, provided authentic inspiration in the service of mutually respectful intergroup relations and fairness throughout society. But worldwide, such examples are still rare, and they unfortunately must be balanced with religious leaders who have supported hatred as in Serbia and Croatia.

A vivid and poignant example of the problem and the opportunity is provided by an excellent book by Douglas Johnston and Cynthia Sampson on the potential uses of religious education at a high level in international relations, and especially in heading off or terminating violent conflicts. Former President Jimmy Carter concisely states the essential concepts of this valuable book in a superb introduction.[62] It is well known that wars have often been the tragic result of religious differences, both historically and in the present day. Former President Carter notes that, on the other hand, religion can also be a powerful, unifying force in conflict situations.

In 1978, Jimmy Carter's role in facilitating the Camp David peacemaking dialogue between Anwar Sadat and Menachem Begin highlights the fact that religious belief and practice can be significant influences in peacemaking efforts. Sadat and Begin were deeply religious men, as is Carter, and they worshipped separately during the course of their Camp David talks. Their religious convictions helped to form their personalities and their historical perspectives, as well as their political beliefs. Not only did the Camp David negotiation involve statesmen in discussions toward political settlement, but it also engaged men who were committed to their religious beliefs. Carter writes, "As the mediator of the talks, I am convinced that to have overlooked the importance of religion for both Sadat and Begin would have resulted in a failure to understand these two men. Such a failure could have had a pervasive and incalculable impact."[63]

Movements toward developing democracy throughout the world have also been given critical support by religious communities. The moral authority of religious leaders must be exercised toward mobilizing community efforts in the interest of peace. Laypersons, too, need to understand the important role of religion and to join their religious leaders and communities in formal and informal efforts to promote just peace. So, in confronting conflict and its peaceful resolution in today's world, it is vital to consider the positive and constructive roles of religious individuals and institutions.

These ethical and pragmatic principles provide a religious base on which a far stronger structure of religious education for peace could be built. We now turn our attention to some promising examples and useful concepts in this field.

We emphasize that education for peace is not limited to schools. Religious leaders have the capacity for teaching the ethical and pragmatic basis for tolerance in a pervasive way.[64] Their great investment in education of the young can be directed toward sympathetic understanding of other religions and nonviolent means of problem solving.

In a meeting convened by the Carnegie Commission on Preventing Deadly Conflict, religious leaders and scholars regretfully presented negative findings about religion's historical role in exacerbating hostile situations. Yet they emphasized that religious leaders have the capacity to do just the opposite. Their prominence in their communities and their legitimacy for promoting intergroup relations gives them a distinct advantage in conveying clear, constructive messages to their followers. Particularly promising is a strategy used by the World Council of Churches, in which people of many faiths engage in regular dialogue on intergroup relations. Religious leaders worldwide should encourage such interfaith dialogue at local through regional levels. The historical orientation to peace and goodwill that religious groups share could make them much more useful than they have been in preventing the spread of hatred and violence. The general rhetoric of goodwill in many religious schools cries out for translation into social action.

There are some recent examples of religious leaders helping to solve serious problems through development of democratic ideals and practices. South Africa's Archbishop Desmond Tutu was a model of courageous, nonviolent conflict resolution in the democratic struggle for freedom from apartheid. And as we have described, near the end of the cold war, churches in East Germany helped to avert mass violence while promoting freedom from dictatorial rule.

The Community of Sant'Egidio (a Catholic organization) has worked tirelessly to broker settlements of major armed conflicts in Africa, Latin America, and Europe. Their activities in the 1990s highlight ways in which religious NGOs can cultivate partnerships with secular governments and nongovernmental organizations for resolving conflicts and educating adversarial groups.[65]

Algeria is the prime example of the way the Community of Sant'Egidio provided new, positive pathways of communication between Muslim, Christian, and Jewish groups. By pushing for negotiations, which led to the signing of a 1996 Appeal for Peace by over 20,000 local political activists, after which talks were conducted by other governmental and nongovernmental organizations. Increasingly, the goal of similar NGOs is a movement toward peace that includes all religious communities and education of various sectors on concepts and techniques of mutual accommodation.

Religious leaders can benefit from the inspiring positive results of NGOs, and themselves take on efforts to promote worldwide respect for diversity and nonviolent problem solving. Their focus should be on intrafaith and interfaith meetings to examine constructive ways of dealing with intergroup hostility. They should condemn hate-promoting coreligionists, and they should strive to establish international norms of tolerance. And they should incorporate such concepts into their regular classes for children and adolescents.

In a volume prepared for the Carnegie Commission on Preventing Deadly Conflict, Professor Scott Appleby of the University of Notre Dame presents a strong argument for the positive potential of religion in preventing deadly conflict.[66] Despite the fact that limited information is available on the effects of religious education (or religious literacy) on violence prevention and peace building, Appleby offers some examples of ways that improvements might occur. Although historically religion has often instigated conflict, Appleby argues that religious peace building is taking shape among and across local communities that are immersed in violence. Fragile as it is, the promise is sufficient that testing of methods and more involvement of trained religious practitioners would be well justified.

Appleby's study considers religious literacy in the context of conflict resolution and positive peace efforts, and the role of religious education in offsetting ethnoreligious extremism. These themes are interwoven into the topics discussed in the following sections:

1. Religious Traditions: Linking the Past to the Present
2. Religious Education: A Foundation for Peace Education
3. Challenging Ethnoreligious Extremism
4. Freedom of Religious Leaders and Institutions from Repressive Control
5. Human Rights

Religious Traditions: Linking the Past to the Present

The religious past holds a wealth of knowledge in the form of laws, doctrines, moral norms, and practices, which spiritual leaders can draw on when situations arise that call for changes in religious practices—utilizing the best of prior experience—in view of emerging danger. Science and technology, for example, may shift the believer's worldview and moral decisions, justifying changes in some traditional beliefs. A practice found in all religions is the attempt to find the good in causal links between the wisdom of the past and the possibilities of the present moment.[67] For example, Catholics and Muslims who engage in the birth control debate are sometimes seeking to find such a connection. So, too, emphasizing humane and compassionate aspects of religious beliefs may diminish traditional hostility.

Religious Education: A Foundation for Peace Education

Being formed in a religious tradition constitutes internalizing teachings and precepts of theological and ethical doctrines and upholding these ideals. However, depending on the religious institution and particular leaders, there are many variations in each major religious tradition.

Religious fundamentalists present a special problem.[68] Their approaches to conflict are distinctly different from those of other religious people. Fundamentalists can be among the most violent religious extremists. Other religious believers, whose spiritual and ethical formation is oriented toward forgiveness and reconciliation, can be a significant vigorous force in the interest of peace. Under normal conditions, most religious believers favor peace over extremism and pragmatic problem solving over rigid, hostile demands on others. This provides a foundation for serious educational work oriented to the prevention of violence and preparation for other modes of coping with life's stresses. Such efforts may be facilitated by international cooperation—for example, to strengthen moderate elements in a hostile religious community by virtue of successful moderation elsewhere, a kind of peer learning.

Providing religious education to the greatest number of believers, disciples, or novices may well be the first priority of spiritual leaders. To be effective, they must draw on common symbols, ideas, values, and norms of behavior shared by the larger community and convey a sense of common humanity in the face of all religious and other diversity. Second, spiritual leaders and other valued coreligionists must invest time and energy participating in conferences and other dialogues, developing sensitive methods of addressing differences without hatred. Finally, religious authorities must collaborate with trainers, educators, and facilitators outside the religious community who are also working for mutual accommodation.

There are two important reasons for increasing peace-oriented religious literacy: (1) An uneducated population tends to fuel ethnoreligious extremism, and (2) deep commitment by peaceful religious people can transform conflict through humanitarian intervention, peacekeeping, community organizing, election monitoring, conflict mediation, and dialogue with aggrieved parties of rival ethnic or religious communities.

Religious literacy varies among religious communities, but it is the core group of dedicated, constructive believers who keep benevolent traditions alive through acts of mercy and teaching peaceful religious doctrine. Religious authorities and their religious communities must make the choice to invest in education that reinforces the values of this compassionate core. Here, as elsewhere, it is important for the international community to do whatever it can to strengthen the hand of moderate leaders who favor mutual accommodation.

In President Carter's Nobel Peace Prize lecture of 2002, he states the essence of religion's role in peace:

> The unchanging principles of life predate modern times. I worship Jesus Christ, whom we Christians consider to be the Prince of Peace. As a Jew, he taught us to cross

religious boundaries, in service and in love. He repeatedly reached out and embraced Roman conquerors, other Gentiles, and even the more despised Samaritans.

Despite theological differences, all great religions share common commitments that define our ideal secular relationships. I am convinced that Christians, Muslims, Buddhists, Hindus, Jews, and others can embrace each other in a common effort to alleviate human suffering and to espouse peace.

But the present era is a challenging and disturbing time for those whose lives are shaped by religious faith based on kindness toward each other. We have been reminded that cruel and inhuman acts can be derived from distorted theological beliefs, as suicide bombers take the lives of innocent human beings, draped falsely in the cloak of God's will. With horrible brutality, neighbors have massacred neighbors in Europe, Asia, and Africa.

In order for us human beings to commit ourselves personally to the inhumanity of war, we find it necessary first to dehumanize our opponents, which is in itself a violation of the beliefs of all religions. Once we characterize our adversaries as beyond the scope of God's mercy and grace, their lives lose all value.[69]

The Dalai Lama expresses a similar view in considering the constructive potential of Buddhism:

If we look at humanity as a whole, we are social animals. Moreover, the structures of the modern economy, education and so on, illustrate that the world has become a smaller place and that we heavily depend on one another. Under such circumstances, I think the only option is to live and work together harmoniously and keep in our minds the interest of the whole of humanity. That is the only outlook and way we must adopt for our survival.[70]

Challenging Ethnoreligious Extremism

Appleby cites the conflict in the former Yugoslavia as a complex example of ethnoreligious extremism and draws on its generalizable aspects to make his point. Although the top leaders of the various religious communities were not helpful to peacemakers such as Cyrus Vance, there were some religiously literate actors willing to challenge the manipulations of ethnonationalists on religious sensibilities of the people. Several did speak out against the violence and made efforts to promote nonviolent resistance. Some refused to join in the bloodshed; Catholics, Muslim, and Orthodox war resisters became martyrs or were imprisoned for their beliefs. As atrocities became increasingly clear, some religious leaders (Catholics and Orthodox) became awakened to their moral responsibility and repented their preoccupation with crimes of "the other" and began to recognize the suffering of those outside their own community.

Why were these attempts not more effective? Appleby gives several answers. First, attempts to thwart conflict were too few and far between—and too late. Second, when courageous figures (such as Bishop Franjo Komarica) surfaced, religious support was much less effective than it might have been because religious community support came too late and lacked organizational structures that would have linked to a wider religious population. Third, religious education to prevent violence either did not exist or was poorly conceived. Called for, but lacking, were programs designed to involve segments of the larger religious population in nonviolent resistance to religious and ethnic chauvinism. A greater level of peace-oriented religious literacy might well have counteracted the extremists' efforts to incite extreme violence against the outsider in the name of religion.[71]

Providing excellent religious education programs in conflict-laden areas, although intrinsically worthwhile, cannot by itself undermine hateful, extremist leaders. Often, inflammatory leaders are poorly trained, yet they appeal to the strong emotions of followers on quasi-religious grounds. Much depends on the susceptibility of the general population in which they are embedded. All too often, this population base is not educated in the peaceful and tolerant aspects of its own religion. This is a widespread problem. In the ethnoreligious extremism of the former Yugoslavia and some Muslim countries, and in the religious nationalism of India and Northern Ireland, one finds the religious sensibilities of the general population to be a dangerous mixture of folk religion, parts of formal religion, nationalist myth, inflammatory media, and politically constructed racial and cultural stereotypes.

Fundamentalism presents a dangerous irony, often taking root in response to a people's sense of humiliation with loss of respect for their religion by other groups. Then it is not difficult to exploit the victims of that loss. For example, Hamas recruits teenagers and forms them into a narrow version of Islam, advancing the ideological and political purposes of their leaders, condoning and encouraging violence as an integral part of religious belief.

Policymakers, diplomats, and educators—those leaders who are concerned with transforming conflict over the long term—can learn important lessons from the struggles of Northern Ireland.

- In order for the top-down political structural processes to succeed, there must be parallel cultural initiatives created to build an infrastructure of peace.
- Religious leaders (including those in community, grassroots positions) can be very effective in bringing about peace. To ensure success, people of goodwill from various faiths must implement both economic and political measures to improve the quality of life for all parties to the conflict. In societies where conflict has been perpetuated for centuries, there must be changes in the hearts and minds of the people—a difficult but not impossible task. Religious peacemakers have the role of enhancing dialogue between religious factions (e.g., Protestants and Catholics) and promoting common education along with joint economic programs: mutual understanding, mutual accommodation, and mutual benefit from cooperation. A continuum of education is crucial—from children to youth to adults.
- The "politics of forgiveness," a term coined by political scientist Paul Arthur, seeks to foster different styles of religious expression, which emphasize forgiveness and reconciliation as opposed to revenge (a singularly lethal emotion) and grievance seeking.[72] In part, this work involves religious leaders to

help convey practical wisdom about the need to heal memory and guide people in the practices of true reconciliation. It requires a rare combination of qualities sought by people of faith: a zeal for justice supported by the willingness to forgive, the ability to be patient and to show restraint when face to face with setbacks (such as a violation of a cease-fire), and the ability to sustain hope in the face of adversity—reflecting an underlying faith in shared humanity. Finally, the politics of forgiveness calls for ways to replace historical narratives of righteous revenge with new stories that portray an image of divided peoples coming together in a new pattern of active tolerance for their joint benefit. In this way, educators can demystify deeply ingrained myths promoted in religious symbols, propaganda, and textbooks. The application of this approach before mass violence has occurred is a consummation devoutly to be wished.

Freedom of Religious Leaders and Institutions from Repressive Control

An important condition determining the attitudes and behaviors of religious leaders with regard to violent conflict is the degree of autonomy that they and religious institutions benefit from within the society. At issue is their independence from control by a harsh state or repressive pressure toward hateful positions. Most important is their freedom and commitment to educate and train followers in a religious tradition with emphasis on decent human relations and nonviolent problem solving. The international community, religious and otherwise, must lend its support to fostering these conditions.

Human Rights

In 1965, the Roman Catholic Church made a breakthrough in human rights by locating it in humanity altogether, rather than in any particular religious identity. Other religions have also moved toward this consensus. This provides a most useful framework for productive dialogues between religions on the values, rights, and responsibilities of human beings in an interdependent world, as well as dialogues on human rights per se.

In this connection, it is interesting to note the code of ethics developed by the theologian Hans Küng and endorsed by a worldwide group of distinguished religious leaders. It is clearly a peace-oriented, mutually accommodative, socially tolerant code. Codes of this kind can be taught in some depth and applied to everyday life in religious education—in faith-based schools and from the pulpit and in family counseling. This universal code of ethics provides an example of positive religious education that fosters peace and human rights. Other codes are available, and differences of opinion inevitably exist, but such serious efforts to strengthen global norms of human decency should be encouraged. They can provide a basis for empathic dialogue among a variety of religions and help to detoxify old animosities.

18

Education for Peace

The Role of Universities

HOW CAN UNIVERSITIES STRENGTHEN
EDUCATION FOR PEACE?

This chapter emphasizes the potential leadership functions of universities in this field. They can (1) heighten awareness of the gravity of the problem, especially by international cooperation in sharing data; (2) conduct research with emphasis on interdisciplinary collaboration that gives deeper understanding of causes, nature and scope, amelioration, and prevention of mass violence; (3) upgrade education for peace in the universities and also extend the reach to educate the general public and leaders, including political, religious, ethnic, and military leaders—all of whom have massive responsibility for preventing catastrophes rather than inducing them; and (4) program excellent developmentally-appropriate educational materials for elementary and secondary schools, working in conjunction with teachers at each level.

In March 2001, an international group of experts from various fields met to discuss the current status of education for peace and ways to improve it. Scholars from academia, prominent UN officials, and experts from nongovernmental, governmental, and multilateral organizations considered ways in which the University for Peace (UPEACE) might be able to strengthen the field of peace education. More broadly, participants analyzed the current state of peace education internationally. All concurred that the concerns posed by human conflict in the twenty-first century must be more adequately addressed. This initial section outlines important issues raised at the conference as well as its recommendations.[1]

In opening this meeting at the United Nations, Kofi Annan, UN Secretary General, made these remarks:

> Knowledge, research, and teaching are vital in our new global environment. To achieve effective education for peace, we need to reach out to as many actors as possible to devise new approaches to challenges that are in themselves only beginning to be fully understood. . . . How do we promote the good governance needed to underpin stable and transparent societies? How do we make the unprecedented opportunities offered by science and technology work as a tool for peace? . . . Achieving decent, just, and peaceful relations among diverse human groups is an enterprise that must be constantly renewed—and education for peace is a fundamental part of that enterprise.
>
> Yet the world's record on education for peace has been weak indeed. . . . To address complex causes, we need complex, interdisciplinary solutions.
>
> That is why, in the next generation, we have a mission to stimulate large numbers of students on every continent to reflect seriously on human conflict, its causes and consequences, and ways to prevent its deadly outcome. An awareness of growing dangers in the new century might help us consider fundamental changes in our relations with groups beyond our own and accept the mutual benefit that can be gained through political accommodation, respect for diversity, and the active promotion of social justice. It might enable us at last to move beyond the ancient habits of blaming, dehumanizing, repressing, and attacking "the other side."[2]

Why Peace Education?

Countless crises of the 1990s underscored the need for across the board understanding of the issues of war and of peace; it is critical not only to understand the causes of war, but also the causes of peace. With massive prejudice, hatred, and consistent threats of mass violence looming large in today's world, we are faced with an increasing need to learn how to use the tools and strategies of prevention to avoid deadly conflict. There is serious global concern, currently, in the proliferation of all types of weapons technology and the spread of mass communication technologies to incite hatred and justify violence. Although humans have always been prone to making hateful distinctions, too often we now face catastrophic results. This is where education is called upon to provide information on the profound dangers of deadly conflict. Reliable information needs to be disseminated to all people, and new methods of coping with the issues leading up to violent conflict need to be provided.

Enduring peace has never been achieved and will be exceedingly difficult in this terribly dangerous century. Clearly, it requires a collaborative effort from virtually all sectors of society and all nations of the world. Major players include governments, nongovernmental organizations (NGOs), businesses, religious groups, universities, schools, and the media. Individuals, groups, organizations, and institutions all have the potential for making real and lasting contributions to the cause of peace, with education as the leader. It is a sobering reality that the subject of peace education, so badly needed for our future, has been profoundly neglected and sometimes distorted. Universities are particularly significant. Their faculties generate much of the reliable information on this subject and have some influence with policymakers and citizens. Today's university students will soon be the leaders who can put new knowledge to use for peace.

The State of the Field: The Emergence of Conflict Resolution and Violence Prevention

The beginning of the twenty-first century has brought renewed interest in preventing deadly conflict. As a result of the various disasters and profound dangers of the twentieth century, a new set of approaches to containing and preventing conflict has emerged. Indeed, there has been a surge of interest in prevention of mass violence. NGOs, for example, have proliferated and play a much more prominent role than before. They often arouse interest in creating peace and work in direct response to the incipient emergence of violence. Sometimes larger NGOs such as the Carter Center and the International Crisis Group join forces with smaller NGOs to clarify the causes of conflicts and may arrange mediation between hostile groups. The last time there was such an awakening of interest in prevention was in the aftermath of World War II, when the United Nations was created in a major effort to avoid another world war. The Marshall Plan and concerted efforts to foster democracy and regional economic cooperation were also products of that era.

Recently, university programs and research institutes concerned with the study of peace, conflict, and international affairs began to change their emphases to look at the new questions spurred by the turbulent 1990s. The Carnegie Commission on Preventing Deadly Conflict (CCPDC) was one strong stimulus to these institutions. From 1994 to 1999, it funded numerous studies concerned with prevention of violent conflict and held many international meetings, thus providing new challenges to academic institutions as well as new opportunities. It published its own definitive report, *Preventing Deadly Conflict*. But this intellectual ferment is a recent development.

Traditionally, there have been boundaries around the field of peace studies that persist today. Universities typically have, at best, only a few departments concerned in part with this area and often only a few courses. This is caused not only by lack of funding, too few faculty, and inappropriate teaching materials, but also because of academic priorities. This is paradoxical in light of the increased interest, internationally, among students who generally do not relish the prospect of soon becoming warriors or victims of war, snuffing out their young lives when there is so much to anticipate in a good life. Because the scope of programs is often so narrow and the opportunities so restricted, students get discouraged, which in turn sends a false signal to university administrators that these programs are unnecessary. In general, this broadly international conference at the UN found there is an urgent need to expand and upgrade university offerings in this field, especially in the critical area of preventing war.

University faculties in the developing world have the difficult problem of feeling excluded from international discussions on peace and conflict resolution. Often, they face problems of internal repression as well as a drastic lack of resources. Thus, an active outreach from the established democracies to cooperate in education and research will be essential. A number of excellent textbooks are available, and they should be more widely used in developed countries, as well as in poor countries. (See our Bibliography for a list of valuable resources.) In the latter case, international organizations will have to pay for distribution initially, as well as translation costs where necessary. It is an investment of great potential value. In addition, new technologies may before long greatly facilitate this process of making vital knowledge on war and peace available to students of all ages throughout the world. We considered some of these emerging opportunities in the chapter on information technology.

In the prior chapters on education for peace, we have touched on numerous substantive problems: causes and consequences of war, concepts and techniques of conflict resolution, and the conditions favorable to long-term peaceful relations. Universities have an important role to play in this regard by seriously addressing these fundamental problems in their research and education, including newer concepts such as human security, preventive diplomacy, structural prevention, nonproliferation, and changing norms of national sovereignty. Not only are universities able to provide undergraduate and graduate courses for their own students, but they are uniquely positioned to train the trainers through teacher education and curriculum development for kindergarten through high school. Next, we will address several examples of such linkages between universities and schools.

WHAT UNIVERSITIES CAN DO FOR ELEMENTARY AND SECONDARY SCHOOLS: MODELS FOR PEACE EDUCATION

Since universities in most of the world are strongholds of excellent scientists and scholars over a wide range of fields, they constitute a repository of knowledge and skill that is valuable for many purposes: research, higher education, patient care and public health, and community service. Yet only recently have we seen an emerging movement to make these strengths available in precollegiate education.

Mobilizing Science and Scholarship for Primary and Secondary Education

Universities can do a great deal to strengthen education at the precollegiate level. There are a growing number of examples that have clear implications for international and peace education. In the area of science education, Carnegie Corporation of New York has had successful experiences in mobilizing higher education for the benefit of primary and secondary education. These are examples of what foundations can do to forge relationships between leading scientists and scholars on the one hand and precollegiate education on the other. If it can be done in science education, then the same can be accomplished in peace education. The basic concept is to make available for elementary and secondary students the most accurate and useful information that the scientific and scholarly community can provide.

HUMAN BIOLOGY AND OTHER SCIENCE EDUCATION INITIATIVES AS MODELS
FOR PEACE EDUCATION   Stanford University's Human Biology Program (HUMBIO)
is a very successful interdisciplinary undergraduate major, now in its 33rd year, that
brings together the study of biological and behavioral sciences to provide a broad grasp
of the human organism, from molecules to functional systems to human societies and
their environments.[3] It was created in 1971, from the belief that human beings are faced
with exceedingly complex problems and opportunities that are not adequately covered
in undergraduate education. Because of this inherent complexity, a broad range of life
sciences must be covered and to some extent integrated with each other. Many reports
on education reform from the late 1980s have endorsed this interdisciplinary approach
to teaching and learning science. The work of the Carnegie Council on Adolescent Development and others have indicated that the HUMBIO curriculum is especially suited
to middle grade students, in early adolescence, as this is a time of profound and rapid
changes in their bodies and their lives—and development is one of the organizing principles of biology. Studies have also shown that student interest in science begins to
dwindle during the middle grade years as currently taught. Girls and minorities, especially, were shown to have diminishing interest (partly due to biased teaching practices
and unfair social conditioning) and to take only the minimum required courses, which
are often based on rote memorization and hold little practical application to their personal interests.

In 1987, Carnegie Corporation responded to this need by engaging Stanford's
HUMBIO to develop a 2-year curriculum for middle grade students, along with teacher
training materials.[4] Carnegie's support of the planning, design, and initial prototypes
for a new curriculum made it possible for the HUMBIO Middle Grades Life Science
Project to compete for a National Science Foundation grant, which it received in 1990.
With this substantial funding, Mary Kiely became the Director of the Middle Grades
Life Science Project and served as its Senior Academic and Research Program Officer in
HUMBIO from 1990 to1999.[5] She was greatly aided by collaboration with such distinguished members of the Stanford faculty as Craig Heller, Herant Katchadourian, and
Donald Kennedy. A lively, sophisticated, engaging curriculum was developed, field
tested, and prepared for publication. The curriculum proved to stimulate interests of
adolescents in science, and in addition, it helped them to face serious social, behavioral,
and health problems that occur during adolescence. We sketched this program earlier,
but we consider it here as a vivid example of ways in which university faculty can help
primary and secondary schools to deal with critical issues.

THE 2-YEAR CURRICULUM   The life sciences provide a central organizing principle for this early adolescent curriculum, with health playing an integral role. Young people possess a natural curiosity about changes in their own bodies and the transition
from childhood to adulthood can be built on in an engaging way. Through an increased
grasp of human biology and behavior, adolescents are better equipped to make good
choices regarding their health.

At its core, the HUMBIO curriculum includes studies of ecology; evolution and genetics; cell biology; physiology; human development (cognitive, psychological, so-cial); society and culture; and health and safety.[6] During the first year, studies revolve around adolescent development with a focus on puberty—its biological basis and the social responses to it. Next, students examine the concept of culture and the ways in which different cultures treat marriage and family. The focus of the second year is on physiology of bodily systems and ways in which behavior interacts with physiology. Health promotion and social consequences are also studied in this context. Health-damaging behavior can have lasting biological effects. But such behavior can be mini-mized by health-promoting behavior with awareness of risk factors. There is an anal-ogy here with avoiding war.

The information provided by a strong life sciences curriculum is crucial, and it can usefully be combined with training in social skills and decision making. With this added component, young people can increase their ability to control their emotions; they can increase their self-esteem and find ways to reduce anxiety and stress without engaging in dangerous practices.

The curriculum also stimulates interest in the relevance of the life sciences for pub-lic policy—for example, in health, agriculture, and the environment. This is a model for similar activities in peace education, linking universities with secondary schools.

The Harvard Children's Initiative

We include here a summary of work at another great university. Like Stanford's HUMBIO, it involves scholars from a variety of fields and relates to the surrounding community. It provides a stimulating focus for enhancing the opportunities of children and their prosocial behavior. Its founding director is Professor Martha Minow of the law faculty.

The Harvard Children's Initiative (HCI) is a university-based educational program focused on providing children and youth with opportunities for promoting mental and physical health and positive social interaction leading to a productive adulthood. This initiative has been successful in fostering meaningful collaboration between faculty and students, which is especially needed given the complex challenges currently facing to-day's youth. Such efforts are reflected in its centers, institutes, projects and groups en-gaged in children's issues—both on and off campus. In all of HCI's interdisciplinary re-search, educational endeavors, and community activities, the primary focus is on the healthy development of children and youth.

SOCIAL AND ETHICAL DEVELOPMENT   The social and ethical development of children, topics of intense interest in most of the established democracies, are reflected in schools, faith-based institutions, and mentoring programs. Unfortunately, they of-ten lack solid research to inform their efforts, and many important aspects of children's social and ethical development remain undocumented. At HCI, the focus is on gener-ating a knowledge base about the ways in which children develop socially and ethically and to bring this knowledge to programs and activities in the community and in the schools. The primary goal is to foster fundamental ethical and social skills such as taking the perspective of others, compassion, moral reasoning, and awareness of differences in culture and ethnicity.[7]

An interdisciplinary group of researchers and practitioners at HCI promotes and supervises research, encourages fellowships for students who are interested in social and ethical development studies, and creates undergraduate and graduate moral development courses. One aim is to reach beyond the campus and inform a wide variety of practitioners—teachers, after-school childcare providers, police officers, and social workers—who have daily contact and significant relationships with children. In HCI's work on social and ethical development, there are several aims: (1) understand the way children from different racial and ethnic groups and classes communicate important ethical and social abilities, (2) explore unrecognized moral strengths of at-risk children and children from diverse ethnic and cultural backgrounds, (3) help children understand and appreciate the perspective of people from other cultures and ethnic groups, especially important during this time of unease and anxiety, (4) assess the impact of a variety of schools (e.g., parochial, charter, and public schools) and after-school settings on the moral and social development of children, and examine ways that these institutions might improve their effectiveness, (5) study the impact of specific interventions including the curricula on ethical and social skills, and (6) determine the best tools of measurement to track significant changes in the social and ethical development of the child.

Research and Teaching Programs at Harvard on Children   Currently, 10 schools of Harvard University are engaged in research and teaching about children's topics. In particular, faculty members at the Harvard Graduate School of Education represent diverse interests in research and teaching about children, which include the study of adolescence, at-risk youth, child development, desegregation, diversity, family issues, international education, parenting, racial discrimination, and moral and ethical studies. Degree and training programs on children's issues are available to university students from the level of bachelor to postdoctoral to continuing/executive education. In the following sections, we describe several programs outside the university that focus on children, which are affiliated with three schools at Harvard—(1) the School of Public Health's Violence Prevention Programs, (2) Judge Baker Children's Center, affiliated with Harvard Medical School, and (3) the Graduate School of Education's Program in Afterschool Education and Research.

VIOLENCE PREVENTION PROGRAMS   Deborah Prothrow-Stith, M.D., became a faculty member of the Harvard School of Public Health in 1990. Her research, teaching, and service activities are centered on youth violence prevention at the community level. The Division of Public Health Practice, Violence Prevention Program (VPP) staff, under her direction, offer training programs for young people and adults, disseminate helpful information, and give technical support in an effort to promote safer communities.[8]

Several agencies of the federal government (including the U.S. Department of Education, the U.S. Department of Justice, and the U.S. Department of Health and Human

Services) work with VPP toward fulfilling the program's goals. A recent national train-ing initiative in violence prevention makes use of the latest distance learning technology.

A local program in the Boston area received funding from the Centers for Disease Control and Prevention to help start the Harvard Youth Violence Prevention Center (HYVPC). In October 2000, this was established through collaboration with the Har-vard Injury Control and Resource Center. Through the Division of Public Health Prac-tice at Harvard, the initiative provides training to local agencies in the community to study the community resources and create a plan to prevent neighborhood violence. The primary goal of the Center is to advance the science of violence prevention by col-laborating with community organizations. This is intended to help both researchers and the communities. It makes for more informative research and creates more effective prevention interventions. Interrelated issues addressed by the Center include injury pre-vention, community improvement and youth development. In addition, the Center provides funding for new projects in the community. Formal training is also offered to hospital residents and other physicians, leaders in the community, and State Health de-partment injury control personnel.

VPP engages in many community-based initiatives. One example is a collabora-tion with the Boston Public Schools in developing curricula with a focus on developing social skills geared to elementary school children called the Peace Zone. The curricu-lum's four units are based on important skills: (1) trying your best, (2) self control, (3) thinking and problem-solving, and (4) conflict resolution.

Last, in an effort to increase knowledge about the various national violence pre-vention programs, VPP has developed *Peace by Piece: A Violence Prevention Guide for Communities*.[9] This new guide draws on the wisdom of many effective programs from many locations in the United States. Easy to use, this how-to publication gives ordinary citizens guidance in ways of establishing their own antiviolence programs within the community. UNESCO has recently published a similar guide to best practices on a broadly international basis.[10]

Judge Baker Children's Center   The Harvard Medical School as well as the Children's Hospital of Boston and community organizations collaborate with Judge Baker Chil-dren's Center.[11] This nonprofit organization was founded in 1917 toward finding ways to improve the lives of children at risk of not fulfilling their potential through emotional and behavioral difficulties. Through its affiliation with the Harvard Medical School, the Center attracts excellent professionals in the field of developmental psychology, edu-cation, and child mental health. Its research has added to current knowledge about what constitutes healthy families. It has also trained hundreds of professionals. Its research and teaching are pertinent to understanding treatment and prevention of violent be-havior. The Center, an administratively and financially independent organization, is in-volved with community, school, and public policy initiatives. Its practices take cultural differences into account and foster mutual accommodation in a highly pluralistic society.

Program in After-School Education and Research   Five innovative programs seeking to understand good practices in after-school education and raise the quality of both in-school and after-school programming and research find their home in the Program in Afterschool Education and Research (PAER).[12]

ONGOING EVENTS   HCI sponsors ongoing events that focus on issues of children. In October 2002, 40 workshops, conferences, seminars, or lectures were offered and open to all in the community in the university and beyond. Generally, they are pertinent to the subject of this book. For example, presentations included "Casualties of Conflict: Human Rights Issues in Afghanistan," "Teacher: One High School Teacher's Transforming Impact on His Students," "What Is Your Child's Race? Race in Surveys," "Risk and Resilience: Protective Mechanisms and School-Based Prevention Programs," and, "On Human Rights: Seminar in Ethics and International Relations."[13]

A CONCLUDING WORD ON HARVARD   Harvard serves as a useful example and resource for other colleges and universities (1) by bridging the gap between university education and community outreach through offering various levels of training, (2) in teaching the next generation of teachers to be skillful in implementing the kind of initiatives described in this book, and (3) strengthening understanding and cooperation among families, professional service providers, children and youth in the surrounding communities.

Other Science and Mathematics Initiatives: Another Model
for Building Peace Education

From the mid-1980s through the 1990s, the Carnegie Corporation of New York supported mathematics and science education programs in major cities throughout the United States.[14] Philadelphia, Cleveland, Pittsburgh, San Francisco, San Antonio, and Los Angeles were among the cities chosen, because they are large cities with public school districts that serve a high percentage of minority students from low economic backgrounds, suffering from high dropout and illiteracy rates. These programs were collaborative, drawing on leadership from the scientific and business communities and community organizations working in collaboration with the schools. Of particular value were partnerships forged between universities and these newly developed math and science programs. For example, in 1984, the Science Institute of the Pittsburgh Public Schools (a program that spanned kindergarten through 12th grades), enlisted support from industry, community science centers, and universities to convene with public school teachers and administrators to discuss the state of science education in the Pittsburgh public schools. The University of Pittsburgh, Carnegie-Mellon University, and others endorsed the idea of the Science Institute and supported a comprehensive, well-designed curriculum as the basis for the Institute's work.[15]

Overall, the goals of these collaborative programs were to improve education in the public schools generally, to raise the quality of science and math education in keeping with the technological advances of the times, and reach poor children in doing so. For example, the University of Texas at San Antonio established the Science Collaborative of San Antonio in 1987 with Carnegie support.[16] This consortium of university professors, professional science educators, local private-sector scientists, and business people worked toward responding to specific deficiencies in the teaching of science in local public schools. Attention was also given to science teachers in elementary schools who lacked training, and teacher in-service programs at the middle and high school levels that rated poorly. Shortages of laboratory facilities and supplies were also addressed.

The Science Collaborative was originally organized under the direction of an ambitious community organization, Target 90/Goals for San Antonio, established in 1985. It monitored implementation and progress toward specific goals to be achieved by the year 1990. Because that mission was achieved, Target 90's public education programs, including the Science Collaborative, merged with the Alliance for Education based at the University of Texas at San Antonio. From 1987 to 1990, the Science Collaborative developed a number of programs aimed at San Antonio's 12 school districts. Their reach to students and teachers was broadly successful, and actually raised just over $1 million additional dollars from private and public sources. The cornerstone of the Science Collaborative's activities was the development and implementation of professional training for science teachers by the University of Texas Health Science Center. This program's goal was to connect with 1,500 elementary, middle, and secondary science teachers, 100,000 students, and 160 administrators over a 3- to 5-year period to improve the teaching, learning, and administering of science education through new methods.[17] San Antonio (along with San Francisco and Los Angeles) was also chosen as one of six sites participating in the American Association for the Advancement of Science (AAAS) Project 2061 to develop and test new science curricula for kindergarten through 12th grades. We go into some detail on Project 2061 in the next section.

Important in all of these collaborative efforts are ways in which they foster the overall instructional continuity from one grade to the next, maintain explicit goals for teachers and students, and foster systemwide support. This science literacy is a model for similar efforts in peace literacy. Those who have the most advanced knowledge in such fields have shown that they can work collaboratively with teachers and others in public schools to stimulate students and enrich curricula. This role of universities has great potential for the enhancement of education generally, and for peace education in particular.

Project 2061

AAAS, one of the main umbrella organizations of the scientific community, established in the mid-1980s the National Council for Science and Technology Education. Its mission was to stimulate a nationwide education reform effort that would transform education in science, mathematics, and technology from kindergarten through twelfth grades, because AAAS recognized that public schools had not adequately prepared children for a science-based and highly technological world. In fact, studies had confirmed that most adolescents were scientifically illiterate. In an ambitious, long-range effort to remedy this situation, Project 2061 was born and named for the year when Halley's comet will return. The dream was for people living in the year 2061 to have an education that not only prepared them for their current times, but also for their future.

Five panels comprised of leading individuals from a variety of backgrounds in science, technology, engineering, business, government, and education were created from the National Council to begin to address the demanding task of identifying precisely the knowledge all people should have to be able to navigate in a highly scientific and technological age. They concluded that the nation badly needed "the evidence, principles, and concepts of the biological and health sciences, the physical and engineering sciences, the social and behavioral sciences, technology, and applied mathematics."[18] A report, *Science for All Americans*, published by the Oxford University Press, grew from five reports written by these five panels and became a resource document for those interested in new opportunities in science education. Recommendations are made on the scientific knowledge, skills, and attitudes that precollegiate children should acquire. It highlights links between academic disciplines, and emphasizes thinking skills rather than memorization ability. Teachers are given guidelines for ways to present material to students. For example, a teacher may begin with questions about nature and encourage active participation among students; focus on the collection and use of evidence; give a historical context; promote clear expression; work in teams for mutual aid; understand that knowing is not distinct from discovering; and diminish the emphasis on memorization of technical language.[19]

Project 2061 has had a great influence in teacher education, in curriculum redesign, reorganization of schooling, and the creation of new educational materials (including testing and assessment). Also, linking university scientists with science teachers to create specific educational activities adds to the value of the science curricula and to the competence of teachers. From beginning to end over the years of this ambitious enterprise, scientists from universities played a major part.

Today, Project 2061's Web site offers public access to existing programs, its mission, projects, and available educational materials. For example, highlights include an online supplement to a recent public television broadcast on evolution. By accessing Project 2061's maps online, teachers, parents, and students will be able to see the different grade level topics regarding biological evolution and natural selection. Publications made available on the Project 2061 Web site include the *Atlas of Science History*, the newsletter, *2061 Today*, a booklet on current products, activities, and workshops, a new guide to improving the K-through-12 science literacy program, and results from an in-depth study of widely used algebra textbooks. Teachers can also register online for professional development programs, and access proceedings from a conference on technology education research hosted in 1999 by AAAS. Finally, portions of Project 2061's Web site are now offered in Spanish—and interesting example of the international potential of such enterprises.

The governmental National Science Foundation works in partnership with several private foundations to maintain the work of Project 2061. Support is given by Carnegie Corporation of New York, the Hewlett-Packard Company, John D. and Catherine T. MacArthur Foundation, Andrew W. Mellon Foundation, and the Pew Charitable Trusts. Thus, this broadly stimulating activity that upgrades education is made possible by collaboration of a large scientific organization, a variety of foundations, a leading publisher, a high-tech company, and many schools across a large country. There is no reason why such cooperation could not be elicited for peace education. It may take the powerful stimulus of ongoing wars and terrorism to bring this potential to fulfillment.

Just as HUMBIO can become a central organizing principle for middle grade education, so too could learning to live together peacefully become a key element for learning at every level of education, providing that lessons are developmentally appropriate. Experience has shown that such exemplary programs as HUMBIO and Project 2061 engage students in meaningful ways through academic achievement and in development of personal and social skills. Teachers also reap benefits from these programs through increased professional alliances and specific classroom support, which includes carefully tested curriculum guidelines. Practical alliances formed among government, universities, foundations, and the private sector make implementation of such ambitious projects possible. Now is certainly the time to forge such partnerships in pursuit of peace through education. The current wave of catastrophic terrorism raises a level of concern that can motivate leaders to adapt such models from science education to the critical issues of war and peace. We come now to a fascinating example.

The Stanford Example: How Universities Can Foster Peace Education in Secondary Schools

The Stanford Program on International and Cross-Cultural Education (SPICE) is part of Stanford University's Institute for International Studies (IIS), an interdisciplinary research and education center. SPICE serves as a connection between Stanford and precollegiate public schools. It collaborates with IIS faculty and researchers to clarify complex world issues that affect us all. With its outstanding track record, since its founding in 1976, SPICE makes vital issues of international security, political economy, health policy, world cultures, and environmental change accessible to students of all ages. The program produces thoughtful, thoroughly reviewed, supplementary curricula to schools—weaving proven, successful teaching strategies into each unit. They also provide user-friendly guides to teachers and give alternatives to the presentation of full units by offering individual lesson plans.

In close cooperation with IIS faculty and researchers, materials are prepared that reflect the research done at the institute and elsewhere. SPICE publishes supplementary curriculum materials on issues of international policy in their historical and cultural context. All of their materials are carefully reviewed by experts for content and pedagogy prior to publication. Classrooms are used as testing grounds for the interactive teaching strategies that utilize role-playing, small group activities, simulations, cooperative learning, and visual and performing arts activities.

Exceedingly complex, international issues concerning the environment, security, and economics, together with the study of world cultures, history, and geography are made remarkably accessible to young people from elementary grade level through college. One general lesson of the SPICE experience is that *complexity can be made comprehensible.*

SPICE also makes it convenient to access its materials through dissemination centers throughout the United States. These curricula are reasonably priced and easily obtained by phone, facsimile, U.S. mail, and electronic mail. In principle, they could come to have worldwide utility.

EXAMPLES OF SPICE PROGRAMS: CURRICULA ON PEACE, SECURITY, AND CULTURE FOR MIDDLE GRADES THROUGH COLLEGE   The following are examples of topics, related to peace, security, and the study of cultures, offered to schools by SPICE educators and researchers:

> *Peace and security*: The role of the United Nations, the anatomy of conflict, choices in international conflict.
> *Cultures*: China and the world in 2010; nationalism and identity in a European context; living in a global age; understanding the Korean peninsula; and a study of unity in diversity in Europe.

Through use of short stories, poetry, news articles, simulations, and reader's theater, students engage in these learner-centered curricula. Additionally, slide photographs, background materials, audiotapes, and suggested lesson plans are provided as aides to the teacher. Issues of culture and cooperation are geared to younger students. Cultural-related themes such as traditional Chinese celebrations, exploring roles of grandparents in Mexican society, and study of Japanese aesthetics and poetry are all student-centered. They make use of audio and videotapes, slides, and recorded music.

PREVENTING DEADLY CONFLICT: TOWARD A WORLD WITHOUT WAR   This is the prime example of a curriculum developed by SPICE to address the global concern of preventing deadly conflict.[20] We will go into some detail here because of its relevance to our central theme. It also provides an outstanding prototype for other universities who may seek to develop similar curricula for schools on the subject of violence prevention.

Preventing Deadly Conflict: Toward a World without War is based on the final report of the Carnegie Commission on Preventing Deadly Conflict (CCPDC). CCPDC was established in 1994 to "address the looming threats to world peace of intergroup violence and to advance new ideas for the prevention and resolution of deadly conflict."[21] Development of the module was funded and supported by the Carnegie Corporation of New York with the intention of making the content of the Commission's report accessible to secondary school youth.

Published in the year 2000, this module was created specifically for high school students in grades ten through twelve and students in community colleges. Typically, high school students are only marginally interested in violence that occurs in remote regions of the world. They also may assume that deadly conflict is not preventable. This curriculum module shows students proven techniques for predicting, limiting, and preventing deadly violence. In addition, it is recommended for use in subject areas of global/international studies, world history, contemporary issues, and conflict-resolution classes.

Three lessons comprise the Preventing Deadly Conflict (PDC) module. The first lesson is designed to take three class periods, whereas Lessons 2 and 3 typically require three or four class periods each. Although Lessons 2 and 3 could be separated from the module and taught as part of the general curriculum, it is recommended that the complete three-lesson module be taught as a whole.

Lesson descriptions   In the first lesson, students are asked to consider the effects of deadly conflict on different groups of people. It aims to define "deadly conflict" and answers the question of why we should be concerned about violence on a large-scale that could erupt anywhere in the world.

Some of the common causes of conflict are taught, and students learn just how much knowledge they actually have about recent armed conflicts throughout the world. Slides are used to view scenes of conflict, and the effects of violence are considered especially with regard to noncombatants. In conclusion, students discuss whether or not the United States should care about deadly conflict in other parts of the world.

Lesson two analyzes conflict. Students are given five foreign policy tools that governments might use to influence events in other countries. Creative activities such as making posters and giving presentations precede student analysis of an actual war—for example, the war in Bosnia in the autumn of 1992. In this exploration, students learn about what causes war, its destructive effects, and the main elements of actual conflicts. In addition, possible solutions are explicitly explored.

In small group activities, students work through the problem from the point of view of the United Nations or the United States. Each poses a rationale for using a specific foreign policy tool to end the strife. Then the class compares their intervention plans to the ones actually employed in Bosnia from 1993 to 1995.

In the third lesson, students learn about prevention and look into possible ways that recent conflicts could have been prevented. Working in groups, students choose a conflict area from the list of ten choices given in the lesson. Together they create a plan for preventing the conflict in that region. They work as a group to uncover root causes of the conflict and find ways of addressing these causes.

Groups present their findings to the entire class in a cooperative learning mode and give their prescription for solving the conflict. The final exercise of the module allows the students to create their own list of the most common causes of conflict and the key elements of any plan to prevent conflict.

General aspects of the module   Handouts and primary-source documents are the basic materials provided for each lesson. Overhead and slide projectors are also used to enhance lessons. The PDC module complies with the National Standards for History in its recommendation that "the student understands major sources of tension and conflict in the contemporary world and efforts that have been made to address them." In particular, students should be able to "Analyze the causes, consequences, and moral implications for the world community of mass killings and famines in such places as Cambodia, Somalia, Rwanda, and Bosnia-Herzegovina."[22]

Given that students often work together in small groups, the module makes recommendations for six student roles: Facilitator, Recorder, Timekeeper, Materials Manager, Harmonizer, and Reporter.

The role of the teacher   The teacher is given a detailed plan for covering each lesson. A set of organizing questions and an introduction to the problem precede a list of objectives that the teacher would like to see actualized by each student. The three objectives are *knowledge, attitude,* and *skill.* A detailed list of materials (for example, student handouts, slide projector, transparency, teacher information cards) precedes the detailed procedure for teaching the lesson. In addition, icons used throughout the module provide the teacher with easily identifiable symbols of the modality to be used for any given exercise, whether it is a slide presentation, a small group activity, use of a transparency, or a group presentation.

In a typical lesson, the teacher might present a slide on a particular subject of conflict. *Background information* is provided on each slide in addition to the *goal* and the *discussion topics* on which to focus.

In an example from the first lesson—"What Is Deadly Conflict?"—the teacher has *background information* that describes the subject of a slide: "A South Korean soldier on duty at the demilitarized zone (Panmunjom, South Korean side). Since soldiers here cannot carry weapons, they are experts in the martial arts. Several soldiers spend the day staring down their counterparts across the border, in effect engaging in psychological warfare." The *goal* would be to have "students think about what it would be like to have a job in which conflict is a constant preoccupation." Students seriously consider how conflict creates fear. Finally, the *discussion topics* are: "How does it feel to be afraid? What happens to one's body and mind if one is afraid over a long period of time?"[23]

The end of the module contains appendices, including a glossary of frequently used terms and a reference list categorized by lesson. To assess student achievement, teachers ask the student, at the end of the third lesson, to compose an essay about how deadly conflict can be predicted and the necessary components of a plan to prevent such conflict. In evaluating students' essays, the teacher is able to determine how much the students have learned about creating concepts from several case studies and to what extent they have drawn together the information on conflict prevention.

Student benefits   Students are given opportunities to work individually, in small groups, and with the whole class. This experiential approach engages the students' critical thinking skills and allows their creativity to be applied to real-world problems of deadly conflict. Not only do they learn to apply skills of conflict resolution to a particular geographic area of conflict, but they also learn how these same skills might transfer to their own personal interactions with peers and family. Students become aware that conflict is not intrinsically bad; it can be turned to useful clarification and deeper reconciliation. It can thus actually have beneficial results provided it does not degenerate into violence. They learn that violence is only one way of handling a dispute—as a last resort. But there are valuable alternatives and these are clarified in the course.

Dissemination   By logging onto the official Web site of Stanford University, one can readily locate information on the SPICE program and ways to obtain curriculum units.[24] Because SPICE is committed to addressing the needs of diverse classrooms, their curriculum materials are designed to effectively reach students of all backgrounds.

Some lesson plans are available online free of charge. They have been edited and modified to provide teachers with a brief introduction to the content and style of the SPICE materials. The complete list of modules is available in the SPICE catalog online. One can choose from dozens of curriculum units on Africa, Asia and the Pacific, Europe and Latin America, the global environment, and international and political economy. Materials are available through loan or purchasing centers from across the United States. Summaries of existing and developing units can be accessed as a way of previewing materials before purchase. For example, the unit we discussed in the previous section, *Preventing Deadly Conflict: Toward a World without War*, can be purchased (as of this writing) for approximately $35. If adequately supported by governments or foundations, such material could be more widely available in developing countries where need for such insight is urgent.

EMERGING EDUCATIONAL INITIATIVES ON WEAPONS OF MASS DESTRUCTION

Since the September 11, 2001, attacks on New York and Washington, D.C., the Center for Nonproliferation Studies (CNS) at the Monterey Institute has become increasingly visible because of the staff's expertise in the fight against terrorism. Proficiency in this area, including knowledge of chemical, biological, and nuclear weapons, makes this institute highly salient now. Although technical information in these areas is crucial, there is also a wider arena in which terrorism is addressed that includes proficiencies in languages other than English, cross-cultural communication skills, analytical tools, negotiation and conflict resolution, and area expertise.

CNS is the largest nongovernmental organization in the United States devoted to serious examination and training on issues of curbing the spread of weapons of mass destruction (WMD).[25] With a staff of over 60 full-time and 65 part-time faculty, this organization is unique in its focus on nonproliferation education offering a master's degree in international relations at the Monterey Institute, with a concentration on nonproliferation issues. Their three-tiered approach includes formal coursework, on-the-job training at CNS, and opportunities for participation in internships.[26] Training is provided to young faculty members and parliamentarians in Russia and China. There are 16 trainees from the foreign ministry in China. CNS publishes a peer-reviewed journal, *The Nonproliferation Review*, three times a year. International authors contribute to the discussion of a broad range of issues related to WMD, specifically on the consequences of use and ways to control their spread. Offices are located in Monterey, Washington, D.C., and Almaty, Kazakhstan. Student scholarships and internships are offered to individuals at the Institute interested in pursuing a certificate in nonproliferation studies. These internship opportunities in international organizations help to expand the career possibilities and the interest of these students.[27] The nonproliferation program is concerned with five main projects with interrelated and mutually supporting activities. Two programs listed below—the NISNP and EAUP—are of particular interest because they combine training and community building activities in their work:[28]

1. The Newly Independent States Nonproliferation Program (NISNP)
2. The Chemical and Biological Weapons Nonproliferation Program (CBWNP)
3. The Proliferation Research and Assessment Program (PRAP)
4. The East Asia Nonproliferation Program (EANP)
5. The International Organizations and Nonproliferation Program (IONP)

William C. Potter established the Center for Nonproliferation Studies in 1989. He is an institute professor and is director of CNS and of the Center for Russian Eurasian Studies, both at the Monterey Institute's Graduate School of International Policy Studies. In addition, he has for some years been a member of the United Nations Secretary-General's Advisory Board on Disarmament Matters.

Potter's teaching philosophy involves active learning on the part of the student, in which the professor principally serves as facilitator. For example, by using simulation techniques, students assume roles such as international arms control negotiators. Some have gone on to become career diplomats.

United Nations Study on Disarmament and Nonproliferation Education

In the setting of the UN, a group of expert governmental officials presented a study on disarmament and nonproliferation education to the General Assembly's First Committee (Disarmament and International Security) on October 9, 2002.[29] Secretary General Kofi Annan's Advisory Board on Disarmament Matters recommended the creation of this expert group because of concern over widespread complacency about the present dangers of nuclear weapons and the chance of a renewed arms race. They concluded that everyone's education should include a significant study of disarmament and nonproliferation because of their belief that each individual should be responsible for knowing the means by which a nation prepares to defend itself and the profound dangers involved.[30]

In a series of meetings during 2001 and 2002, this group of governmental experts also invited participation from university educators, disarmament and peace-related institutes, and NGOs with special qualifications in education and training in the field of disarmament and nonproliferation. The study group conducted a wide survey of current education and training programs, courses, and curricula in this field at all levels of education throughout the world. The survey was sent to governments, UN agencies, university educators, disarmament and peace-related institutes, and to NGOs. Thus, there is a serious, substantive effort to stimulate education in this field.

The study group had the complex task of clarifying contemporary disarmament and nonproliferation education and training that took into consideration the need to promote a culture of nonviolent resolution of disputes. It recommended ways to promote this type of education and training—be it formal or informal education—particularly education of teachers, parliamentarians, municipal and military leaders, and government officials; the group examined and reported on evolving pedagogical methods—in particular, the information and communications technology revolution. Distance learning was addressed, especially ways in which it can be useful to educators in developing countries. The report speaks to the need of the UN system's organizations to coordinate its various specializations in the field of disarmament and education. Recommendations were also made for ways of introducing nonproliferation education into situations recovering from conflict as a means of building peace.

Among the papers submitted to the UN Secretary General's Board on Disarmament Matters was one particularly relevant paper written by William C. Potter.[31] It focuses on education as the primary tool for promoting disarmament and nonproliferation. The report underscores that, to date, education has been seriously underutilized, and the UN is well positioned to put to use new information and communication technologies for pedagogical purposes. The goal would be to change the mindset of the public toward the norms and principles of disarmament, nurturing a global disarmament and nonproliferation culture. Obstacles to disarmament are ignorance and complacency, as well as the inability to find expression in most national parliaments that sadly remain uneducated and underprepared to face current dangers. Citizens everywhere exhibit a disturbing lack of awareness about these issues, but it is understandable given the dearth of opportunity to study the subject. For example, very few high schools and universities have even minimal curricula that teach disarmament or weapons proliferation and strategies for their control. Some minimal recent progress has been made in universities, however, which is reported in the July 1999 *Report of the International Association of University Presidents/UN Commission on Disarmament Education, Conflict Resolution and Peace*. But, currently, only two universities in the entire world offer a graduate concentration in the field of nonproliferation education.

Undergraduate Nonproliferation Education

The Nonproliferation Review conducted a recent survey to understand how undergraduate institutions in the United States address the topic of WMD.[32] From February to October 2002, *The Nonproliferation Review* examined undergraduate programs at 78 of the top United States institutions of higher education. They chose schools on the basis of a *U.S. News and World Report* ranking of universities and colleges from 2001. Their focus was on departments of political science, government, and international relations to determine the content and number of courses that were offered at the schools. They categorized two types of courses and ranked them accordingly. The first were specialized courses, primarily focused on WMD issues and involved 75 percent or more of course time. Second were general courses (e. g., focused on U.S. foreign policy or international security) that devoted a minimum of one week's study on issues of WMD.

The purpose was to get an overall sense of the amount of attention given to WMD, to understand course content and focus, and to review the successful approaches used by instructors to teach the subject. WMD courses were chosen for review because of a dearth of courses taught on nonproliferation—only six nonproliferation courses were actually found. A roughly equal sampling of the top national universities, public universities and liberal arts colleges (totaling 74) were examined along with four military academies. School web sites and referrals were used to identify relevant courses and professors. An online questionnaire was used to collect survey responses (more than 150 received). Supplemental data was obtained by telephone and e-mail communications (more than 125 faculty were contacted), along with course syllabi.

Results showed that 95 percent of universities and colleges offered at least one course that generally touched on WMD. Seventy-three percent of the schools sampled offered more than one course that minimally dealt with the topic. However, two-thirds of U.S. nonmilitary colleges and universities (51 out of 74 sampled) offered no courses principally devoted to WMD. Included in this group were a very highly respected public university, the University of California at Berkeley; a leading technical university, the California Institute of Technology; and eight of the best liberal arts colleges: Amherst College, Swarthmore College, Williams College, Wellesley College, Bowdoin College, Carleton College, Haverford College, and Pomona College.

Schools that offered specialized courses included 10 national universities (e.g., Harvard), nine public universities (e.g., the University of California, Los Angeles), and four liberal arts colleges (e.g., Middlebury College). One WMD course was offered at each of the four military academies. In all of the schools surveyed, there were a total of 41 specialized courses identified. Only a dozen undergraduate programs offered more than one course that specialized in WMD.

Several reasons for these findings include a lack of student interest in the topic during the 1990s; the fact that policy studies were superceded by theoretical and quantitative studies; the supposed antidefense political orientation of college and universities; and, in the case of smaller schools, a limited amount of available resources. Following the September 11 tragedies, there has been an upsurge in the demand for teaching the subject along with several new courses. But a gap in teaching WMD will unfortunately continue because of slow processes in hiring new faculty.

Overall, results of the survey showed that as the threat of weapons of mass destruction grows, instruction lags behind. Of the 74 top schools in the United States, 51 fail to offer specialized courses on WMD. There must be a major new push to train future scholars, diplomats and program managers. It is useful to note that this survey examined the top schools in the United States. One can fairly assume that the example set by these leading schools affects the behavior of other schools. What we have seen as relative inattention paid to WMD in these schools may also indicate a broader trend— oddly neglecting one of the most vital and dangerous of all subjects.

One of the primary goals of undergraduate education is to help students recognize what is truly important in the world they are entering as adults and to grasp at various levels the forces at play in shaping the world. Since September 11, especially, the United States and other countries must recognize the need for large numbers of highly trained individuals to meet short- and long-term challenges. Undergraduate education, although not the primary arena for training in this field, can nevertheless be a strong foundation for educating future diplomats, scholars, program managers and other professionals needed to address this problem. Undergraduate education can introduce students to reference points in history, to current developments, and new thinking in the field, and provide mentors who can validate the importance of this work in the future of the United States. The same is surely true in other countries. How, if at all, are they meeting the need?

Clearly, the need exists for more attention to weapons of mass destruction in undergraduate curricula and evidence shows that student interest is growing. This survey provides a point of reference for measuring progress. It is a wake-up call not only for the United States, but also for the world. No country is immune to the dangers of proliferation. All need knowledge on how to contain the danger. Models exist to ease the task of education on these problems.

A LIBERAL ARTS APPROACH TO VIOLENCE

The Harry Frank Guggenheim Foundation has for many years been largely devoted to enhance understanding through teaching about human violence.[33] Grants are made for research projects at the postdoctoral level that are directed toward social change by providing a better understanding of violence, aggression, and dominance. This foundation provides an exceptional example of ways in which philanthropy can support education for conflict resolution.

In 1969, the foundation's grant-making program in this field was launched, and since then nearly 500 research projects on violence, aggression, and dominance have been supported. Fields of study include the biological and social sciences, humanities, law, and criminology. Their grantees have produced hundreds of books, articles, and monographs written largely for an academic audience, which have contributed to our understanding of the causes and expressions of violent behavior. Teachers have drawn on this information to enrich their classroom instruction.

In the foundation's quarterly review in spring 2000, its president, James M. Hester (former president of New York University), who has provided excellent leadership in this field, emphasized the need to enhance teaching about violence.[34] He highlighted the lack of college courses focused on violence, and in light of these considerations, he explained that the Guggenheim initiative was to stimulate teaching on these ancient, disturbing, and critical human experiences. The centerpiece of the review was Professor Robert Jackall's syllabus—winner of a competition to design an undergraduate course about violence.

Few College Courses Focus on Teaching about Violence

Hester believes there are three core reasons for the lack of college courses that focus on violence. First is a problem of structure. It is very difficult to present violence in the confines of a single discipline; professors find it exceedingly challenging to design a course whose content reaches beyond the limits of their specialization. Second, it is simply not customary to accept the study of violence as part of the standard curriculum. Certainly aspects of violence have been presented in psychology, sociology, and criminology courses, but it is rare for a college or university to present violence as a substantial influence in U.S. history or Western civilization. Third, it is attractive to highlight positive aspects of U.S. history, culture, and society as found in many curricula. This is a worldwide tendency; each country enhances its self-concept. But it is foolish to minimize the study of violence if educators are seriously striving to prepare youth for responsible citizenship. The phenomena of violence are simply too dangerous to be left in a marginal place.

The Guggenheim Foundation Request for Proposals

Several years ago, the board of directors of the Guggenheim Foundation agreed to stimulate teaching about violence, based on the best available research. The first step was to look for existing comprehensive courses, and results were disappointing. An initially promising example fell short of their expectations. Although an inspiring curriculum, it lacked realistic recommendations for controlling violence. In this field, exhortation does not substitute for specific actions. So the next step involved a competition for the design of a comprehensive undergraduate course on violence. It proved extremely useful, resulting in 17 promising projects that warranted funding. The winner in the final round of competition was a syllabus submitted by Professor Robert Jackall of Williams College. It provided an exemplary guide to course development that could alternatively be used in a number of ways as study modules. Details of this worthwhile and practical example follow in the next section.

VIOLENCE—A COMPREHENSIVE UNDERGRADUATE COURSE DESIGN   This undergraduate curriculum reflects Professor Jackall's view that the study of violence is a way of looking into the cultural and intellectual understanding of the human experience.[35] He offers an introduction to the study of violence and aggression from the perspective of liberal arts, integrating the humanities with natural and social sciences. The goal is to provide students with a means of grasping the complex and grave importance of violence—something that they can draw upon as they enter adulthood.

Violence maintains such a prominent and dangerous place in human life that it deserves serious and comprehensive study. Despite human fascination with the subject, which often finds expression in the arts and literature, its comprehensive academic study has been thwarted. Due to its generally disturbing nature, the subject tends to be ignored until violence erupts and demands immediate attention and solutions, because it exerts such a powerful impact on human relationships and social order.

Jackall's syllabus is principally drawn from the social sciences (especially sociology, anthropology, political science and social psychology), scientific inquiries (regarding the primal roots of human violence), and philosophy (looking at different perspectives on violence and reflecting on the human fascination with it). These three perspectives help to promote the habits of mind necessary to understand the history of violence and to distinguish what violence means to the perpetrators and to those victimized by it. The central component of Professor Jackall's course examines various types and meanings of violence, as summarized in the following sections.

INSTITUTIONAL AND IDEOLOGICAL VIOLENCE   Some examples of this form of violence include historical warriors and the meaning of war to them, the twentieth-century

phenomenon of industrialized violence, ethnic and racial destructiveness, religiously motivated violence (e.g., from the Crusades to totalitarian cults), and political violence.

INTERPERSONAL VIOLENCE   This form of violence explores notions of honor and
the violence that comes from the meanings that humans attach to it, antagonism between males and females that can lead to domestic violence, and males' violent fantasies
and women's roles in them.

CRIMINAL VIOLENCE   This type of violence includes deep psychological disturbance (e.g., as found in Dostoyevsky's *Crime and Punishment*), occupational violence
endemic to the drug trade, wartime criminal violence, and the rationalized punishment
of criminal violence.

ORDER AND PEACE   Here the curriculum looks at the structure and culture of traditionally peaceful societies, heroic acts of individuals and groups who resist societal
oppression, efficacy of moral commitment and nonviolent disobedience, use of force
and threats of force to curtail violence, and important roles of key institutions of law
and bureaucracy in finding tolerable compromises.

This liberal arts perspective prepares students for participation in world affairs.
They become critical thinkers, poised to assess the worthiness of current and proposed
policies to remedy violence in general or in specific cases. The interdisciplinary framework also offers insights into human motivations for violence. Dr. Jackall's reading list
for the course is ambitious and geared to advanced college students. There are many
readings and perspectives from which instructors may tailor courses suited to their particular classroom needs.

The development of this curriculum and others like it may well challenge professors and leaders of educational institutions to consider incorporating violence as a focal topic in university courses. Ultimately, students should be able to discern truth from
fiction as it relates to violent behavior and to integrate this understanding into their
adult lives. Such courses can provide a basis for understanding violence, improving
public discourse on the subject, and ultimately help in violence prevention. The terrorist violence of September 11, 2001 may well stimulate many colleges and universities
to enhance their teaching and research on problems that are in the long run fundamental to achieving a peaceful world.

PREVENTION OF DEADLY CONFLICT: TEACHING AND
RESEARCH IN UNIVERSITIES ALL OVER THE WORLD

Of all of the aspects of violence that we have touched on, none has such practical significance nor is so badly neglected as the prevention of deadly conflict. This requires a conjunction of deep scholarship and careful examination of serious conflicts (especially recent ones that reflect contemporary circumstances). Only in the past few years has there
been a surge of inquiry and innovation in this field, and these advances have much prom-

ise. But they are only beginning to penetrate university education and research. A sharp upgrade here is necessary not only to inform and stimulate university students (adolescents and young adults soon coming to a maturity in which they can make a practical difference in avoiding unnecessary or unjust wars), but also to inform and stimulate their professors, who can have substantial impact on policymakers in democratic countries in the foreseeable future. Indeed, a few are already doing so. For these reasons, we now summarize two vital domains of preventing deadly conflict that can profoundly stimulate college students and their faculties: not putting Humpty Dumpty back together again after a terrible war, but finding ways to prevent war in the first place. These two central topics in prevention of mass violence are preventive diplomacy and international cooperation for democratic development. Indeed, the future of humanity in the twenty-first century may hinge crucially on the extent to which educated people everywhere truly grasp these opportunities. We must understand (widely throughout the world and fully among adolescent and adult populations) that the destructive and incitement power and stresses of living may well reach such a peak in the twenty-first century that all humanity may be destroyed. Hence, it is crucial for education to deal seriously with prevention.

Many opportunities for preventing violent conflict do exist, but they have usually been missed at enormous human, social, and economic cost. From detailed study of many cases of conflict, guidelines emerge for upgrading preventive capacities. Especially important in this transformation are specific ways in which the international community can strengthen its capability for promoting democratic governance, productive economic development, and nonviolent problem-solving in dangerous situations. There are helpful roles of national governments, intergovernmental organizations, NGOs, and the pivotal institutions of civil society, such as the scientific community. There is new evidence on preventive diplomacy and the fostering of democratic socioeconomic development. Effective prevention requires a high degree of cooperation among governments, international institutions, and NGOs. There are ways of improving this multilevel cooperation to mobilize effective leadership for prevention and to enhance public understanding—starting at the college level.

So too, students in higher education need to understand that human aggressive behavior is undertaken in the service of attachment to a valued group. Since developing and maintaining a network of close relationships has long been crucial to an individual's survival and reproductive success, it is likely that such aggressive responses would have been favored by natural selection over millions of years.[36] For many millennia, human survival depended on belonging to a group, being loyal to a group, and a readiness to defend one's group. Everywhere in the world, aggression toward other people has been facilitated by a pervasive human tendency to make harsh dichotomies between a positively valued *we* and a negatively valued *they*. Belonging to an intimate group has long been exceedingly valuable, and other groups are often viewed with suspicion. Historically, demagogues and tyrants have utilized this tendency for their own purposes, and this trend has shown little sign of abating, as we have seen recently in Yugoslavia, Central Africa, and Afghanistan. Moving beyond the ancient habits of blaming, dehumanizing, and attacking is evidently very difficult in practice but far from impossible. For millennia, we were utterly convinced that the earth was flat. So, too, we have believed in invidious in-group/out-group distinctions and harsh intergroup relations as a way of life. But the earth is not flat. And we are now all part of a single, worldwide, highly interdependent species.

Higher education must emphasize foresight based on knowledge. The international community should not wait for a crisis. Ideally, there should be ongoing programs of international help—offered by governments, intergovernmental organizations, and also by NGOs. These would build the capacity of groups to address grievances effectively without violence and establish mechanisms for sorting out conflicts peacefully before they become explosive. Fortunately, there is movement in this direction—toward using techniques of active, nonviolent problem-solving, sharing of experience across national boundaries, and bringing the world's experience to bear on different local conflicts. Tackling serious grievances as early as possible denies political demagogues and hateful fanatics a strong platform of discontent. Incitement to violence becomes more difficult.

Major new studies converge on key points of preventive diplomacy—that is, how to head off a war while tension is building. These studies send a to-whom-it-may concern message to the international community: to governments, intergovernmental organizations, NGOs of many kinds, and leaders in different sectors.[37] Some recurrent elements of the preventive diplomacy message may be stated simply, to

1. Recognize dangers early; beware of wishful thinking.
2. Get the facts straight from multiple credible sources, including history and culture of latent or emerging conflict.
3. Pool strengths, share burdens, and divide labor among entities with the capacity, salience, and motivation to be helpful.
4. Foster widespread public understanding of conflict resolution and violence prevention. This gives a basis for hope of just settlement.
5. Offer mediation early; a fair-minded third party can facilitate problem-solving by adversaries.
6. Formulate superordinate goals—that is, goals highly desirable to both adversarial groups that they can only obtain by cooperation.
7. Use economic leverage: carrots and sticks, what can be gained by peaceful settlement and lost by violence.
8. Support moderate, pragmatic local leaders, including emerging leaders, especially democratic reformers.
9. Bear in mind the pervasive need of negotiators and their constituencies for respect and dignity, help negotiators strengthen cooperation between the constituencies in their own groups, and maintain an attitude of shared humanity and possibilities for mutual accommodation.
10. Strengthen preparation for preventive diplomacy in relevant entities—for example, governments, the UN, regional organizations; strengthen dedicated units for preventive diplomacy that maintain knowledge and skill in early conflict resolution and knowledge of the region; strengthen specific training for staff, updated in light of ongoing worldwide experience; and

strengthen the roster of experts on call for leadership organizations such as the UN and democratic governments.

If guidelines of this sort are incorporated into the thinking of governments, intergovernmental organizations such as the UN, and peace-oriented NGOs, it is likely that the risk of drifting into disasters will be diminished. Students and faculty in universities can help to build a constituency for prevention, through understanding of such anticipatory guidelines.

Universities must provide understanding of democracy's crucial relation to preventing unjust and unnecessary wars. Democratic traditions evolve in ways that build ongoing mechanisms for dealing with the ubiquitous conflicts that arise in the course of human experience.[38] Democracy seeks ways to deal fairly with conflicts and to resolve them below the threshold of mass violence. This is a difficult process, there are failures, and the transition from a closed authoritarian society to a fully viable, open democratic society can be stormy—and emerging democracies need international help at such turbulent transitional times. Building worldwide democracy is the best chance for dealing justly and peacefully with the tensions of humanity.

The attitudes, beliefs, and procedures of democratic societies are useful in intergroup conflict within and beyond state borders. In government and civil society, processes of negotiation and mediation are common. There is encouragement for seeing the perspective of other people and learning mutual accommodation—starting in childhood, becoming more complex through adolescence, and attaining deeper understanding in higher education.

There are effective means for promoting democracy internationally. For new, emerging, and fragile democracies this involves technical assistance, financial aid, and social exchanges to build the requisite processes and institutions, including widespread education of citizens about the actual workings of a democracy. University exchanges of students and faculty can be helpful in this regard.

Toward these ends, the democratic community has begun to establish special funds to strengthen emerging democracies. Such funds may be administered through NGOs as well as government agencies and international multilateral organizations—depending on which circumstances offer the best prospects. Funding, technical assistance, and human solidarity must be *sustained* over a period of many years to support the complicated processes of democracy building. There is much more to it than one successful election. Recent research indicates that much can be accomplished in spite of all the obstacles.

This work is best done through international cooperation, not conquest. An important and neglected part of university education involves the economic aspects of democratic development.[39] Why are there still widely prevalent threats to survival when modern science and technology have made such powerful contributions to human well-being? What can we do to diminish the kind of vulnerability that leads to violent desperation? Many nations, especially in the Southern Hemisphere, have been late in getting access to the unprecedented opportunities now available for economic and social development. They are seeking ways to modernize in keeping with their own cultural traditions and distinctive settings. They need help in finding ways to adapt the world's experience for their own development. It is surely in the interest of countries near and far away to facilitate the development of knowledge, skill, and freedom in these countries so they can become contributing, responsible members of the international community rather than breeding grounds for social pathology, infectious diseases, and terrorist violence. To foster economic development, it is essential to enhance political participation, to provide basic education and health care, and to live in a context of respect for human rights. These circumstances are not only of value to the individual, but they contribute powerfully to economic progress of the society.

Education is crucial for development and should be a primary requirement for development. One priority is the education of females, which is badly neglected in many poor countries. It is a highly valuable investment for developing countries because it enhances women's skills, opportunities, health, and nutrition. The more educated the mothers, the less likely that their children will die, regardless of differences in family income. As we have noted, education helps delay marriage for women, partly by increasing their chances for employment, and educated women are more likely to know about and use contraceptives, thus helping to maintain population growth within sustainable limits.

Education in mathematics, science, and technology is also a priority matter. The judicious use of science and technology is a key element in development. Participation in the world economy now requires a modicum of technical competence everywhere. This must be fostered by the international cooperation of scientists and educators. A third priority in education, now badly neglected, is the subject of this book: education for conflict resolution and for peace.

Altogether, the essential ingredients for development center around knowledge, skill, and freedom. Knowledge is mainly generated by research and development; skill is mainly generated by education and training; freedom is mainly generated by democratic institutions. These crucial pathways usually require international cooperation over many years in very poor and oppressed countries. They are prime agenda items for university education and research.

The great tasks of preventive diplomacy in near-crisis situations and of long-term socioeconomic development to promote peaceful societies are formidable. Moreover, these tasks of prevention are demanding, sometimes expensive, and often dangerous. Thus, the effective pursuit of these tasks requires much cooperation across national boundaries and among various institutions and organizations

All of these promising developments occur in the context of urgent need and in light of great dangers, such as catastrophic terrorism and the threat of nuclear war (for example, in India and Pakistan). But the prevention approach has long been neglected. Therefore, universities have a great opportunity and responsibility to teach and research these crucial topics. At present, few universities, even in the most affluent countries, give systematic, comprehensive coverage of these issues in their curricula. Although a small cadre of faculty has made seminal contributions to the recent advances in this field, much more is needed.

In short, the universities should be one of the major focal points for the intellectual ferment now arising in preventing deadly conflict. To fulfill this promise, they need to give a higher priority to research and teaching in this field; to get more adequate support from governments, foundations, and other donors; and to foster interdisciplinary and international cooperation in order to get stronger data, deeper insights, and to extend education far beyond any individual campus. In the early part of the twenty-first century, university and precollegiate students as well as concerned citizens everywhere should have the opportunity to understand how conflicts can be settled promptly and fairly—and how conditions for peaceful living can be fostered on a worldwide scale.

19

Overview

Toward a Better World for Our Grandchildren

A DIFFERENT WAY OF SEEING THE PROBLEM

The growing destructive capacities of humanity make this the prime problem of the twenty-first century. How we cope with this problem will have a profound bearing on the world of our grandchildren. The twentieth century was the bloodiest ever. World War II caused at least 50 million deaths. Six million died in the Holocaust.

At Hiroshima, one bomb caused 100,000 deaths. Now thousands of such bombs (smaller and more conveniently transportable tactical bombs) are housed in Russia. Many are poorly guarded, susceptible to theft and bribery. Others may be made elsewhere. Danger increases with the number of such weapons existing in the world. Why? There is a greater chance of error, theft, and bribery—and ultimately their use in war or terrorism. Therefore, we should diminish the numbers as much as we can and secure responsible stewardship for those that remain. Moreover, there are still thousands of nuclear weapons that are far more powerful than the smaller tactical weapons.

Biological and chemical weapons are easier to make than nuclear warheads and therefore have special appeal to terrorists. Small arms and light weapons now cover the world wall-to-wall. They include highly lethal machine guns, mortars, automatic rifles, and rocket launchers. Altogether, the destructive capacity of humanity is almost beyond imagination. Moreover, there is an exciting effect of today's vast weapons on political demagogues, religious fanatics, and ethnic haters—and plenty of them exist in the world. Incitement to hatred and violence can occur with radio, TV, the Internet, and many other media. Thus, we can more powerfully incite violence, utilize more lethal weapons, and do much more damage than ever imaginable before. No group is so small or so far away as to prevent it from doing immense damage anywhere.

The time has come to move beyond complacency, fatalism, denial, and avoidance. We must urgently seek to understand and strengthen an array of institutions and organizations that have the capacity to use tools and strategies to prevent deadly conflict. The first author (D.A.H.) considered many such possibilities in his recent book, *No More Killing Fields: Preventing Deadly Conflict*. Overall, this gives humanity a greater range of possibilities than ever before for building a system for preventing war and genocide. It will not be easy. The time required will be decades and generations. But we must intensify such efforts greatly in the first decade of the twenty-first century. And this is beginning to happen.[1] Education in the broadest sense is crucial for this great mission.

Early in this book, we looked at the great danger and some sources of animosity between human groups, examining the violent experience of our species in evolutionary and historical perspectives; we reviewed some of the psychological obstacles to peaceful relations between groups; and we focused on developmental processes by which it should be possible to diminish orientations of ethnocentrism, prejudice, and hatred.

There has long been complacency all over the world about prejudice and ethnocentrism—taken for granted like the air we breathe. Yet the dangers of hateful outlooks are likely to be much greater as the twenty-first century unfolds, as we saw on September 11, 2001. Although teaching such attitudes and beliefs to children occurs all too often in so many places and has been virtually automatic—conveyed by parents, reinforced by clergy, enshrined in textbooks, and inflamed by political leaders, it has been widely ignored. All of this has been conducive to terrible harm in the past.

We are not searching for a pacifist utopia, but rather we are facing the emerging realities of our exceedingly interdependent world, which throws us humans together more extensively and dramatically than ever before—for example, via international travel, highly valued economic transactions, and large-scale immigration. Our species has a very long history of distrusting strangers, despising out-groups, fighting each other in many ways and many places, and using the most damaging technology available at the time. Today, the capacity for incitement of hatred and violence is much more powerful than ever before. Not only does radio cover the most remote areas of the world with its ready capacity to become hate radio, but also the Internet provides unprecedented opportunities to vilify out-groups and describe ways of making weapons of all kinds for their destruction.

Thus, we are coming to a situation in which ancient predispositions toward harsh attitudes and hateful beliefs acquire powers to destroy that dwarf those of our ancestors. This is the central challenge of our time. There must be many responses, involving many sectors of society and many kinds of governments, institutions, and organizations. But scholarship and practice in international relations, including war and peace issues, have gravely neglected both the crucial psychological aspects and the educational opportunities of these terrible problems.

There is a fruitful conjunction of developmental and social psychology in the context of educational research that can help us to understand such vital issues and work toward ensuring a humane, democratic, and safe course of development for all children and adolescents that can in turn affect the safety of humanity in the long run.

The mainstream efforts to modernize education largely neglect these topics even in the established democracies—not to speak of bigoted dictatorships. Nevertheless, an intellectual and moral ferment is stirring in and around education in many countries that gives us a basis for hope. Thus, there are many intriguing examples of research, educational innovations, and visionary leadership emerging in various parts of the world. It is this promise that we must seize and develop for the sake of our grandchildren. So, we have devoted most of this book to promising lines of inquiry and innovation that promote humane, democratic, and prosocial development in childhood and adolescence.

We hope the book will be interesting and credible to scholars and to the education community. At the same time, we seek to reach beyond specialists in a meaningful way to a well-educated and socially concerned segment of the public. We undertake in this final chapter a substantial summary of what we have said, and why, so that readers can readily grasp the essential concepts and lines of evidence in each chapter. Then we look ahead to what is possible on the basis of such transformation of education in various modalities—in schools and beyond.

In our violent world, proliferation of lethal weaponry, prejudice and hatred, and every kind of slaughter have become too commonplace. We must therefore look to the scientific and educational communities to generate and disseminate reliable information on these serious problems and ways to cope with them. Education must provide understanding, insight, and constructive ways of dealing with the profound dangers of deadly conflict. Human conflict and its resolution—above all, the prevention of mass violence—are a subjects that cry out for pervasive educational efforts from early childhood to elementary and secondary schools to universities, community organizations, religious institutions, business firms, and the media.

We have faced the fact that education everywhere has been ethnocentric—and all too often virulently prejudicial. If we humans can come to live together amicably in the face of great dangers, it will be a drastic change from our past that can only be achieved by using the unique learning capacities that have made our species so remarkably effective in adapting even under very adverse conditions. Most of this book shows how it can be done.

THERE IS A BASIS FOR HOPE

Human initiative has transformed the world since the Industrial Revolution. Ordinary citizens of the most technically advanced countries have opportunities and protections not available to kings in earlier centuries. In recent decades, science has been institutionalized on a vast scale for the first time, and the acquisition of deep knowledge of the structure of matter, life, the human organism, the nature of the universe, the human environment, and even our own behavior has accelerated sharply. These scientific advances have provided an unprecedented basis for technological innovation in computers, telecommunications, biotechnology—and weaponry. The potential benefits of modern technology for human well-being are profound in every sphere—touching on our food, water, health, communication, transportation, energy, and human understanding. How do we actualize this potential? Dark sides of human behavior and human societies stand in the way. But these obstacles can be understood and, sooner or later, dealt with constructively.

How can human beings learn more reasonable orientations toward those outside their own groups while maintaining the values of primary group allegiance and security? In this book, we have examined research that shows how this can be done. We can nurture constructive orientations as we gain understanding of the factors governing the development of behavior. The nature of parental care; child care; experience with siblings and with peers; exposure to hatred and violence in schools, mass media, and on the street; the cumulative effect of frustrating conditions; and previous experience in situations involving aggression are all important factors. So also, in some countries, are official propaganda, the glorification of war, and the religious cultivation of negative stereotypes.

We find it easy to put ourselves at the center of the universe, attaching a strong positive value to ourselves and our groups while attaching a negative value to many other people and their groups. Experience shows that human beings everywhere have egocentric and ethnocentric tendencies, and these tendencies, under certain conditions, can be conducive to violent conflict. In recent years, we have seen that terrorism tends to trigger long-term cycles of retaliation and escalation. Killing can become a way of life and hatred an organizing principle for communities. But that path offers no decent future, only endless suffering and failure to fulfill human potential.

It is extremely important that the human tendency to generate intergroup conflicts—once perhaps adaptive but now exceedingly dangerous—be widely understood. Reluctantly, we must recognize that the human species is a potentially violent animal organized into potentially violent societies. It no longer makes sense to follow the widespread traditional practice of attributing malevolence primarily or solely to other groups. Rather, it is prudent to adopt the stance that all groups have inherited malevolent tendencies along with benevolent ones. But there is a large difference for the outcome depending on the way these tendencies are shaped and reinforced through education at every level.

Even though in-group/out-group distinctions are ubiquitous, entrenched in human societies, and to some extent a legacy of our evolutionary and historical experience in which such distinctions were related to survival, we have the capacity to learn to minimize such harsh distinctions in the future. The conditions for survival are very different than they were when these orientations evolved long ago. We must now find a basis for fundamental human identification across a diversity of cultures in the face of manifest differences and even overt conflict. Because modern humanity is a single, interdependent, crowded, worldwide, heavily armed species, we must learn to live together, now more than ever before. This should be one of the central pillars of modern education.

The global outbreaks of intergroup conflict, with their explosive mixture of ethnic, religious, and national strivings, are badly in need of illumination. People everywhere need to understand what motivates our behavior, what a dangerous legacy we carry with us, and what we can do to convert fear to hope. Indeed, there is an almost limitless basis for hope, provided we can create constructive, democratic, judicious uses of the advances in science and technology that are becoming available as never before.

In these chapters, we have given examples of ways in which education in all of its forms can be strengthened for decent human relations and peaceful problem solving. We have chosen promising lines of research and innovation based to the extent possible on well-designed research and on carefully observed good practices. These strong concepts, data, and practices point the way toward a better future.

Prejudice—or the prejudgment of persons or situations—is to some degree a universal phenomenon. Early learning builds on our basic tendency to categorize and evaluate people, groups, and situations. Yet prejudice is mainly a response to the social environment; families, media, governments, and religious institutions are all instruments widely used for conveying negative and deprecatory stereotypes.

Frustrations in crucial human relations such as rejection by parents, bullying in school, governmental violation of human rights, and official brutality are also of great importance in heightening individual aggression as well as susceptibility to prejudice and hatred. Yet hostile responses are not the only way to cope with recurrent frustrations. Nonviolent, persistent efforts at problem solving—by individuals, groups, governments, and international organizations—may be more difficult, complicated, and tedious in the short run, but they are much more rewarding in the long run and perhaps even essential for our survival as a species.

Fundamentally, the problem is learning how to live together—at all levels—from the family to our global relations among nations. This calls for very widespread understanding of human relations, sources of stress, and ways of coping at every level of organization from the intimate to the vast impersonal. How can we provide decent life chances in every country for a quality of life compatible with human dignity, and arrangements within each country to protect human rights, respect pluralism, avoid oppression, and give children and youth a decent start?

We need to be aware of what is possible now; to push the limits of present knowledge and skill; and to develop new research and innovations, concepts, and techniques. A wide range of organizations and institutions must come to use this information and experience to strengthen our capacities for preventing deadly conflict and to learn to live together amicably in search of shared benefits across our common humanity. This book and two previous ones seek answers to these difficult crucial questions.[2]

THE HUMAN GROUP: HOW WE FOSTER ATTACHMENT AND AVOID HATRED IN OUR CHILDREN

We view child development in the context of the human group and its ancient role in survival. Though circumstances have changed drastically in modern times, the group is still vitally important and emotionally charged. How did belonging to a primary group get to be so important? Several decades of research on our closest biological relatives, monkeys and apes, have clarified the heritage from which our ancient ancestors took a long route over millions of years toward full humanity.[3]

Monkeys and apes have only one offspring at a time, and they give each one a lot of attention. They have longer periods of immaturity than other mammals, including prolonged dependence on the mother—hence an intense mother-infant relationship. Safely in contact with the mother, the infant begins to learn about the wider social world—first by observation alone. Later much of this learning occurs in the context of play, not only with peers but also with older siblings and even with adults—often play that consists of imitating patterns of behavior such as aggression that have been observed earlier. Play in early life appears to be both enjoyable and instructive; indeed, it is necessary to full development. Thus, social learning in the fundamentally protective context of the mother-infant relationship flows naturally into the adaptive functions of the small, primary, intimate human group.

These basic elements are carried over into human adaptation. Throughout the evolution of the human species, fundamental attachments have been formed early in life through readily available social support networks, provided mostly by kin but also by others in the familiar proximity of a small society. This enduring property of strong, positive human relationships is of great importance for contemporary life.

The advantages of social organization in our long evolutionary history have included protection against predators and competitors, meeting nutritional requirements, protection against harsh climates, dealing with injuries, facilitating reproduction, and preparing the young to meet the requirements and utilize the opportunities of a particular environment. All of this highlights the heritage of positive group relationships and the powerful importance of group membership in the adaptation and survival of our ancient ancestors.[4]

Among humans, the link between survival and reproductive success of individuals with their cooperative roles as members of a valued group are far richer and more complex than is possible in any nonhuman society. Human biology and repertoires of learning and traditions evolved over millennia, in a world of small, mainly stable, face-to-face groups within which people were linked by enduring ties of kinship and mutual support. Today's world is very different, chiefly a product of the vast, drastic changes of the past two centuries.

A sense of personal worth has long been predicated on one's sense of belonging to a valued group; a sense of belonging, in turn, depends on the ability to competently undertake the traditional tasks of that society, to engage in mutually supportive social interactions, and to participate in the meaningful and emotionally significant shared experience of group rituals. The enduring group offers guidance, protection, and satisfaction—even life itself. A key concern for the human future is how to extend the psychological group of human survival to a much larger world community.

In effect, the family in one form or another has been the main place for education, economic activity, and social relationships throughout human history. The education provided by the family prominently has included other groups: who to love, who to hate, how to relate to others for better and worse. Although other relationships are also important, none have quite the significance of those embedded in family and kin. In the entire span of human evolution, the period since the industrial revolution is a brief moment. But the technological, economic, and social changes in this instant of evolutionary history probably are more far-reaching than all of the previous changes in human evolution put together. Not least, these transformations have affected the conditions of child and adolescent development. The ancient human organism grows up now in a very new habitat.

In a variety of ways, growing children and young adolescents have had less and less opportunity for participation in the adult world as industrialization has proceeded and the pace of technosocial change has accelerated. It is less clear to them how to be useful and earn respect. In fact, there is less continuity between the behavior of childhood and adolescence on the one hand and adulthood on the other than ever before. Other influences beyond family control now loom large in shaping attitudes, beliefs, knowledge, and skill. And adults are predicting into a largely unknown environment of decades later as they guide their children's future.

Altogether, kin-based group membership has been utterly crucial in human evolution. But strong group membership can also make us susceptible to hatred and violence. We inherit through genes and customs a strong need for belonging in a primary group, and all too easily our primary groups may render us hostile to other groups.

The historical record clearly shows that once humans developed agriculture, settled in larger numbers, accumulated goods, and came to rely on exclusive areas for growing food and grazing animals, intergroup hostility became even more common than it had been before. Everywhere in the world, aggression toward other people has been facilitated by a pervasive human tendency toward harsh dichotomizing between positively valued *we* and negatively valued *they*.

Human beings are readily able to learn in-group favoritism or in-group bias. People are remarkably prone to form partisan distinctions between their own and other groups; to develop sociometric preferences for their own groups; to discriminate against other groups; to accept favorable evaluations of the products and performances of the in-group; and to accept unfavorable characterizations of other groups that go far beyond the objective evidence or the requirements of the situation. We learn from experiments how easily hostility can form and become deeply entrenched between groups and how unfairness can exacerbate intergroup animosity. So it is vital that schools and other child-rearing institutions provide a structure in which young people from different groups can transcend the in-group bias to reach valued common goals in an atmosphere of collaboration with a sense of belonging.

Attachments, group loyalty, and warfare are intimately linked throughout human history. We risk our lives and inflict great damage in the devoted service to a valued group, most recently the nation-state but also religious, and ethnic, and political groups. Now the human group is reacting to the massive technological, economic, and social changes of recent times. These are replete with novel opportunities but also with stressful experiences. These developments have included extraordinary contact among people from many different backgrounds differing in almost every conceivable dimension, yet thrown together primarily by technological and economic changes. Television, air transportation, and the Internet are the most vivid symbols of this change. Terms like *interdependence* and *globalization* refer to these drastic, rapid changes. Some as yet are ambiguous, and many more are yet to come.

Because the world transformation in which we are now immersed involves much uncertainty, insecurity, and inequity, there are widespread frustrations that may be transformed into virulent prejudices against minority populations, foreign populations, or infidels. Ethnocentric and nationalistic inflammatory politicians and religious fanatics have long understood the human tendency to seek someone to blame under circumstances of intensely felt frustration. This is a particularly significant point because of its heightened danger in contemporary circumstances. Part of this danger relates to the search for secure identity and clashes among identity groups. In dichotomous societies, the potential for intergroup conflict is greater than in societies with more complex, crosscutting identities.[5] Because individuals in a more complex social structure identify themselves with various groups (e.g., religious, occupational, residential), they are more likely to be fellow in-group members in one category and out-group members in another. These crosscutting intergroup linkages lessen the intensity of the individual's dependence on any one group for meeting psychological needs for inclusion. Polarization is reduced between groups and perhaps there is an increase in tolerance for out-groups in general, which helps to stabilize the society.

National identity is only one of many identities: occupational, religious, ethnic, linguistic, territorial, class, gender, and others. For most of recorded history—a short fragment of human evolution—thousands of peoples having distinctive identities have somehow lived together, often mixed within particular nation-states. But a dramatic change occurred in connection with the industrial revolution. As technology and organization became more complex, new opportunities for conquests emerged, old rivalries became intensified, and the institution of war was strengthened.

With these changes came increased central control, mainly to support large military forces. Nation-states went beyond anything they had done before to create national educational systems, to impose national languages, and to organize various propagandistic activities to promote identification with the nation-state. Such changes could powerfully affect child rearing. Thus, children were reared to accept these beliefs and emotions, including their hateful components.

Some ethnic and religious groups see their group as if it were a separate species. In such extreme groups, foreigners are scarcely human, and there is no moral imperative to treat them in the way you would your own people. To proponents of very intense religious commitments, religious revival is the answer to the ills of modern societies that they blame for all their troubles. One aspect of this has been an intensification of religious fundamentalism, sometimes carried to the point of fanatical behavior. In a variety of religions, including Islam, Judaism, Christianity, and Hinduism, there are zealous subgroups with intensely parochial attitudes, angry orientations toward other groups, and harsh intolerance—that is, prejudicial, ethnocentric outlooks.

Any kind of holy war tends to provide a strong sense of community with mutually supportive solidarity within the group, but concomitantly it generates parochialism, hostile exclusion, and facile justification of mass violence. This is one of the most difficult and dangerous problems facing the international community. Yet religious nationalism is not entirely closed to pluralistic tolerance. In fact, some movements have shown openness to a diversity of members and might implement tolerant governance if given the opportunity. This gives the international community an opening to reach out in friendship to moderate leaders and democratic reformers. With substantial help, they may over time change their societies. One crucial set of changes is the strengthening of education, fully including the education of girls and women, teaching science and technology for the modern economy, and practical understanding of nonviolent conflict resolution. These efforts must overcome powerful historical traditions that are conducive to hatred and violence, especially in the hands of inflammatory leaders. So, education for peace must overcome both psychological and social obstacles—no easy task, yet surely not impossible.

HUMAN INHUMANITY: THE STRUGGLE TO UNDERSTAND GENOCIDE

So there are, in human nature and social heritage, predispositions that can form obstacles to our desire to educate for peace, but our heritage also allows us to recognize the urgent need to adapt. The most vivid example is genocide, which is the expulsion or attempted extermination of a supposedly undesirable population from a given territory due to religious, ethnic, or political discrimination. It has been practiced throughout human history from antiquity to the present. Children and adolescents are typically caught up in such horrors, both as victims and perpetrators.

History shows the remarkable capacity of the human species to find reasons to devalue members of an out-group, to blame suffering on them, and to see them as the source of evil.[6] It is then a relatively small step to justifying violence toward them. In the process, members of the in-group tend to be drawn together—their own solidarity and mutual support feel good.

Most cultures have some characteristics that make group violence possible or even easy under certain circumstances. If a concept of superiority is widely accepted in a culture, with the notion that it is natural for some to exert strong dominance over others, then violence is easier. Harsh economic conditions also facilitate hatred and violence.

Both in Nazi Germany and in the Soviet Union, millions perished in the name of some putative higher good that provided justification for pervasive hatred and organized killing. In such cases, the ideology is nurtured in childhood and strengthened in adolescence, especially among those who are perceived by the regime as potential leaders. It is important to note that the international community has historically played a very weak role in opposing such killing. In a book relating to this subject, the first author has suggested many ways in which international cooperation could greatly diminish these terrible risks, partly by strengthening education along the lines described in the present book.[7]

To diminish the likelihood of these disasters, it is important to enhance orientations of caring, concern, social responsibility, and mutual aid within and between groups. This includes education in various modalities during the years of growth and development, so that young people are prepared to learn to live together in peaceful societies. Educating people for constructive resolution of life's ongoing conflicts through families, schools, universities, community and religious organizations, as well as media is a fundamental challenge for the century that has just begun. And its scope will have to transcend ethnic, religious, political, and national boundaries.

BRINGING UP HATEFUL CHILDREN AND VIOLENT YOUTH

One of our fundamental aspirations is to move educators to develop and widely use curricula that will influence child development so that children form prosocial, empathic, and cooperative human relationships that can ultimately provide the basis for a peaceful world. To be effective, we must address obstacles to education that do not foster constructive human relationships. We must face the fact that it is possible to educate for hate and to shape young minds toward destructive ends.

The human capacity to inspire hatred and violence in children is vividly demonstrated by the Nazi experience. Nazi education, its philosophy, and the creation of elite schools shaped the minds and bodies of boys toward devotion to the Führer and to their future as Nazi leaders. Teachers, as well, were indoctrinated and obligated to behave in a prescribed manner toward the same end. The regime was preoccupied with anti-Semitism, hateful orientations, utter loyalty to the dictator, and the superiority of "pure" Germans.

The Hitler Youth met its goals of shaping obedient, prejudiced, hyperaggressive men and women who enthusiastically supported the Nazi enterprise. Fortunately, the Nazi defeat in World War II gave this regime only a 12-year life. Its effects were steadily overcome during and after the postwar occupation by democracies—leading to a transformation of West Germany into a vibrant democracy over several decades of intensive reconstruction, a genuine source of hope for the topic of this book. But the experience of education in the Nazi period provides a dramatic, tragic example of how young lives can be shaped to embrace hatred and violence.

There are also current examples, and they are related to terrorism. An Islamic *madrasa* is a kind of seminary that breeds holy warriors in Pakistan and nearby countries. Education in such schools is narrow. Most teach very little, if any, science, mathematics, languages, or any history beyond what is found in the Koran. In the worst of these—and there are many—children's minds are honed to prepare them mentally for holy war. There is usually no actual training with weapons, though it is not difficult to imagine this addition, at least as an organized extracurricular activity, in a hate-drenched atmosphere. They are indoctrinated with the putative injustices, cruelty, and closed-mindedness of outsiders. The outside world is largely closed off to students.

This current example of education for hate shows that the capacity is very much alive. Though this shaping of young minds toward hate and violence seems to achieve its own goals in the short run, the long-term prospects for these children is poor in terms of any humane or democratic values, as well as income-earning skills, and they are predisposed to inflict great damage on others and on themselves, especially if self-destruction is viewed as religious martyrdom with eternal benefits.

This is a vivid case, one that is highly salient in 2003, and there are many others around the world with varying intensities. Education for hate is an all-too-pervasive part of human experience. And the media often provide exceptional vividness and immediacy to the hate messages. The fundamentally distorting nature of such education and its destructive effects deserve much more attention than is now the case. Education reform in many countries, even when excellent in other respects (for example, in mathematics, science, and technology), is usually weak in the domain of preparing children for decent human relations and finding (or creating) nonviolent mechanisms for addressing serious grievances.

The examples we have given of Nazi education and extremist Muslim education have much in common: to indoctrinate more than educate, to teach extreme interpretations of political and religious doctrines, to focus hatred on scapegoats, to depreciate women in many roles beyond procreation of obedient children, to control the use of textbooks and media and use them to spread messages conducive to violence as development proceeds. These examples illustrate human susceptibility to shaping child and adolescent development in very dangerous ways. Yet, there is no reason to assume that this approach must come to dominate world experience.

HOW BRINGING GROUPS TOGETHER
CAN DIMINISH HOSTILITY

We have drawn heavily on the potential of intergroup contact for helping to overcome the deadly obstacles of the past. If groups are strange to each other and therefore fearful or hostile, why not bring them together so that they can get to know each other and become friendly? This is not so easy. A variety of field and laboratory experiments indicate that intergroup competition tends to strengthen social relations within each group and to disrupt relations between the groups. Humans are highly susceptible to invidious in-group/out-group distinctions.

Such in-group/out-group distinctions are ubiquitous in human societies—easy to learn and hard to forget. They are probably, to some degree, a legacy of our evolutionary and historical experience in which these distinctions were related to group membership, a sense of belonging, human attachment, and survival itself. Yet humans can learn to minimize invidious in-group/out-group distinctions. This is one of the crucial roads we have to travel to cope with conflict in the transformed world we live in.

Research suggests the importance of overlapping group memberships in the modern world. There are myriad possibilities in the world of large-scale international contact that has so recently emerged. People who belong to groups that cut across ethnic or national or religious lines may serve a bridging function across cultural and even adversarial barriers.

How can conflict resolution occur through personal contact and how can cooperation be achieved? Much depends on whether the contact occurs under favorable conditions. All too often, they are not favorable. If the conditions involve an aura of suspicion, if they are highly competitive, if they are not supported by relevant authorities, or if they occur on the basis of very unequal status, then they are not likely to be helpful. Indeed, such unfavorable conditions can exacerbate old tensions and can reinforce stereotypes. On the other hand, there is a strong, positive effect of friendly contact in the context of equal status, especially if such contact is supported by relevant authorities, is embedded in cooperative activity, and is encouraged by a mutual aid ethic. Under these conditions, the more contact the better. Such contact is associated with improved attitudes between previously suspicious or hostile groups as well as constructive changes in patterns of interaction between them.

In this vein, circumstances of cooperative learning in elementary and secondary education are conducive to the improvement of intergroup relations; whereas a highly competitive, extremely individualistic atmosphere in the classroom is more likely to breed negative effects and hostility. Superordinate goals have the potentially powerful effect of unifying disparate groups in the search for a vital benefit that can only be obtained by their cooperation. In experimental research, strangers were made into enemies with isolation and competition but then transformed into friends when exceedingly valuable superordinate goals were introduced that could only be achieved by cooperation.[8] There are beneficial effects of working cooperatively so that people formulate a new, inclusive group that goes beyond the subgroups with which they enter a situation. Such effects are particularly strong when there are tangibly successful outcomes of cooperation. In general, prejudice tends to be reduced when there is equal status contact between groups in the pursuit of common goals and shared efficacy in reaching those goals.

Despite all the cultural barriers that have so long separated peoples, the modern world is one in which cooperative ventures and friendly personal contacts on an equal footing can occur more readily than ever before. A great opportunity now is to identify superordinate goals and organize cooperative efforts to meet them. The place to start is in education at every level.

CONTACT AS A MEANS OF IMPROVING INTERGROUP RELATIONS IN SCHOOLS

What policies and practices are favorable to improving intergroup relations in schools? There are strategies that promote positive relations and inhibit negative relations in situations where intergroup isolation and tensions exist but have not become major conflicts. This is a common situation in schools, and so such strategies provide practical opportunities.

In schools as elsewhere, we reemphasize the circumstances that make contact situations work effectively: equal status for members of all groups, an emphasis on cooperative more than competitive activities, and explicit support for the contact by authority figures. Much has been learned in recent years about how to teach children ways of working cooperatively to achieve joint goals. This has economic as well as social value, because the contemporary economy increasingly involves working in groups.

Cooperative activities help to create a broad social identity, transcending a narrow in-group. Developing a personal relationship with members of another group and seeing them with their own personality traits, skills, and experiences often leads to the discovery of similarities between oneself and out-group members.

Support by school authorities is crucial in creating positive changes in intergroup attitudes as a result of intergroup contact. Teachers are vital authority figures with the power to strengthen or inhibit positive relations in the school setting. They can serve enabling, modeling, sensitizing, and sanctioning roles, as can principals. Encouraging students to relate to each other as individuals rather than as stereotypes can become a part of the school climate. There are many different school approaches to improving intergroup relations: instructional methods, curricula, extracurricular activities, workshops, simulations, and joint ventures.

Parents are significant authority figures as well, so it is crucial that educators find methods of encouraging parents to involve their children in diverse settings and encourage intergroup contact. Parents can be involved in creating school and communitywide multiethnic or multireligious committees that serve educational or youth development functions. The mixture of people addressing a shared task of such high significance as educational success can be helpful.

Basic research on intergroup contact has substantial, intrinsic interest, and it can be usefully applied in educational settings. Indeed, similar work is underway in many countries, and it is likely that this approach will be useful on a worldwide basis, provided that cultural differences are adequately taken into account.

VIOLENCE PREVENTION AS A FUNCTION OF HEALTHY CHILD AND ADOLESCENT DEVELOPMENT

We have identified conditions that favor good results in child and adolescent development—ways in which children grow up healthy and vigorous, inquiring and problem solving, decent and constructive. We specified two kinds of helpful interventions:

1. A basic *generic* comprehensive developmental sequence that provides antidotes to shattered, distorted lives associated with neglect, abuse, or parental loss. Children who have endured such hardships are more prone to violence and other pathologies.
2. A specific set of *targeted* interventions that can provide antidotes to youth violence and enhance personal ability to deal with conflict in nonviolent ways. We emphasize preventing youth violence by fostering healthy, constructive development generically throughout childhood and adolescence, but we have also considered interventions targeted specifically to prevent youth violence. Both are valuable.

During their earliest years of growth and development, children need dependable attachment to parents or other adult caregivers; they need protection, guidance, stimulation, nurturance, and skills to cope with adversity. Infants, in particular, need caregivers who can promote attachment and thereby instill the fundamentals of decent human relationships throughout the child's life. But a good start is not enough. Healthy child development requires a sequence of experiences and opportunities, each building on the previous phase, extending through adolescence.

In an ideal world, all children would grow up in intact, cohesive nuclear families, with at least one parent who is consistently nurturing, loving, and able to enjoy child rearing, teaching, and coping. They would have supportive extended family members who are readily available. They would be part of supportive communities beyond their families. Conditions such as these greatly enhance the odds that a young person will pursue lifelong learning, acquire constructive skills, be in good health, and develop valued human attributes, including prosocial rather than hateful or violent behavior. Democratic societies should do what they can to create such favorable conditions for healthy development. But often these conditions are not available, and other strengths for child development must be mobilized, involving the institutions beyond the family that have the greatest influence on child and adolescent development. These are the schools, community organizations (including religious ones), health institutions, and child-oriented media. This set of pivotal institutions can provide guidance, stimulation, protection, encouragement, and nonviolent problem solving.

Evidence is accumulating that a range of preventive interventions can set a young person onto the path toward healthy, constructive adulthood.[9] Beginning with early and comprehensive prenatal care, these measures include well-baby medical care, with an emphasis on disease prevention and health promotion, and home visits by human service professionals, especially in homes with very young children. Important, too, are opportunities for adolescents and young adults to learn competent parental behavior, which can build close parent-child relationships. Parent support networks can provide mutual aid in promoting health and education for children and parents; child care of high quality outside the home, especially in day care centers; early childhood education that combines parental involvement with disease prevention and the stimulation of cognitive as well as social skills; and stimulating elementary and middle grade education that is developmentally appropriate, teaches fundamental skills, encourages good health practices, and decent human relations. Altogether, such opportunities have strong potential to prevent damage of many kinds, as reflected in indices of health, education, and criminal justice.

Early adolescence is one of the most striking developmental experiences in the entire life span. This transition means going beyond childhood toward the distant goal of becoming an adult. We reemphasize here several goals adolescents should reach that facilitate healthy development and ameliorate violent tendencies. Responsible, caring adults can explicitly foster movement toward these goals throughout the years of adolescence. Ideally, each adolescent should

1. find a valued place in a constructive group.
2. learn how to form close, durable human relationships.

3. earn a sense of worth as a person.
4. achieve a reliable basis for making informed choices.
5. express constructive curiosity and exploratory behavior.
6. find ways of being useful to others.
7. believe in a promising future with real opportunities.
8. cultivate inquiring and problem solving habits of mind necessary for life-long learning and adaptability.
9. learn to respect democratic values and responsible citizenship.
10. build a healthy lifestyle.

Institutions can take a variety of measures to help adolescents accomplish these goals. Here are several important examples. Institutions can

1. reform middle and high schools to create small communities for learning, establishing a sense of belonging and sustained individual attention.
2. create school environments that promote healthy lifestyles, with particular emphasis on a life sciences curriculum that includes insight into factors influencing high-risk behavior such as smoking.
3. establish training in life skills, including decision making, conflict resolution, and nonviolent problem solving.
4. construct social support mechanisms involving constructive peers as well as caring adults.
5. create safe after-school havens in community-based organizations that offer educational as well as recreational activities.
6. provide a perception of opportunity and of value to the community.
7. make health care services and counseling available in adolescent-friendly and accessible locations.

These are generic interventions that are of great importance for preventing damage to children, including the development of violent behavior. In addition, specific interventions that target youth violence can enhance adolescents' ability to deal with conflict in nonviolent ways.

One promising targeted strategy of wide applicability for preventing youth violence is the teaching of conflict-resolution skills as part of health education or social studies in elementary and middle schools as well as high schools. Research indicates that such programs can reduce violence; best results are achieved if teaching of conflict-resolution skills is embedded in long-term, comprehensive educational work on understanding human conflict. Serious, in-depth conflict-resolution training over extended periods is increasingly important in cultures saturated with violence—whether the origins are mainly political, religious, ethnic, or media-induced.

Adolescent violence is as much a public health concern as other behavior-related health problems. Violence-prevention programs train service providers in diverse community settings in a special curriculum, translate this curriculum into concrete services for adolescents, and enlist the support of the community in preventing such violence.

The four main components of such programs are curriculum development, community-based prevention education, clinical treatment services, and media campaigns.

High-risk youth in impoverished communities urgently need social support networks and life skills training. Both can be provided in schools and school-related health centers as well as in community organizations, including faith-based youth centers and sports facilities. Communities must provide attractive, safe, growth-promoting settings for young adolescents during the out-of-school hours—times of high risk when parents are often not available to supervise their children.

Overall, we can make substantial progress by deepening our understanding of human development, by increasing public understanding of our children's urgent needs and opportunities and by strengthening our scientific and professional commitment to tackle these problems over a wide spectrum of constructive approaches. The success of such efforts would not only diminish the risk of school violence and community intergroup violence, but would also diminish the susceptibility of youth to hate-promoting political demagogues and religious fanatics. Thus, the fundamental basis of violence prevention rests on substantial public understanding and support for basic ways of nurturing healthy child development, while also providing specific antidotes to violence through targeted education and constructive social support systems that contrast with those of violence-oriented gangs.

LEARNING TO LIVE TOGETHER: FROM PRESCHOOL THROUGH UNIVERSITY

We have considered obstacles to learning to live together peacefully and steps that can help to overcome these formidable obstacles. Now we turn to specific, constructive ways of fostering prosocial, cooperative, nonviolent problem solving in childhood and adolescence. This is a developmental sequence of experiences and opportunities that can promote decent, constructive behavior in relation to other people—from the simplest interactions to worldwide communication.

Development of Prosocial Behavior

Learning prosocial behavior occurs in widening circles through the years of growth and development into adulthood. Such learning involves decent concern for others; readiness and ability to cooperate for mutual benefit; and helping, sharing, and respecting others while maintaining integrity as an individual with basic self-respect and lifelong inclinations to expand horizons. Such learning becomes increasingly complex from early years onward, moving from the primary group to the wider world: (1) the nuclear family; (2) the extended family; (3) the community (neighborhood, school, community organizations, or religious or other affinity groups); (4) the nation-state (or a region within it); (5) other related nation-states (for example, geographically adjacent nations or nations with communities of values, such as democracies); and (6) global contacts (direct or indirect, involving in principle all of humanity and its environment). So the full development of prosocial behavior is a very long, fascinating, and often difficult process that is of utmost importance for the human experience. It includes sympathetic understanding of diversity; habits of give-and-take, reciprocity, and a pervasive sense of fairness; learning skills of solving problems without violence—with special attention to constructive resolution of interpersonal and intergroup problems; and learning about different peoples and their various traditions.

Research on prosocial behavior has occurred mainly within single cultures and indeed can be applied to in-group situations. Yet it can also be extended to other groups and cultures. A fundamental challenge is to find ways of enhancing prosocial behavior across traditional and even adversarial barriers.

We have presented an analytical examination of what is known about prosocial behavior—its development and the underlying mechanisms at work.[10] The main concern is how children are brought up to behave prosocially, the personal attributes and capabilities involved, and the impact of the social environment. In our view, *prosocial* behavior broadly refers to decent consideration for others as well as oneself, to the capacity of finding satisfaction in functioning cooperatively with others. Starting with the family, mutually respectful social support networks are essential for a satisfying and productive life.

Family Influences on Prosocial Behavior

Excellent research on this topic defines prosocial behavior as helping rather than hurting or neglecting, respecting as opposed to denigrating, being psychologically supportive and protective rather than dominating or exploitative.[11] Precursors appear early in life. Newborns who make distress cries in response to cries of other infants are showing early and basic signs of empathy. Children in their second and third years show emotional distress and take positive actions in the presence of distress of others. Families have many opportunities to reinforce such behavior. When they do, the consequences are clear from research. Family settings in which the requirements and expectations incorporate prosocial behavior do in fact heighten such behavior. A pattern of parental responsiveness, high expectations, firmness, and warm emotion tends to foster a sense of social responsibility in children. Such children are inclined to behave prosocially in relation to the needs of others.

In experiments, children exposed to adult models of prosocial behavior, when compared with similar children in control groups, tend to show the behavior manifested by the models, whether that behavior is honesty, generosity, or helping or rescuing behaviors. There is also evidence from naturalistic studies of toddlers' prosocial actions that delayed imitation by children of their mothers' ways of comforting and helping occur spontaneously in children's efforts to help others. The combination of early attachment (primarily to family members) and abundant modeling over the years of growth and development leads to prosocial behavior that becomes firmly established, strengthens additional human relationships beyond the family, and contributes to a sense of personal worth.

Beyond the Family

Society's norms and expectations are learned through examples, rewards and punishments, modeling, direct contacts, and explicit instructions.[12] For example, television programming has a clear impact on the behavior of both younger and older children; prosocial programming elicits prosocial behavior. Television has the capability of influencing behavior of children in a positive direction, as shown in experimental studies in both laboratory and natural settings. The largely unfulfilled potential of television and other media for teaching prosocial behavior has been widely underestimated.

Experimental studies show clearly the potential of peer reinforcement for elevating the level of children's prosocial behavior. For example, during sharing time in the classroom, where children are encouraged to report instances of friendly behavior, cooperative play increases and aggressive acts decrease. Children imitate the helping behaviors of their peers and unfortunately also imitate the less desirable attributes such as selfishness. Thus, parental efforts to strengthen ongoing contacts between their children and constructive peers are very important.

Since the 1970s, both European and U.S. interest in moral education in schools has been growing, leading to the creation of many experimental training programs designed to promote prosocial tendencies. In a variety of classroom activities, students are encouraged to recognize and distinguish the feelings of others, to take constructive roles, and to be emotionally responsive. Those involved in such training have seen an increase in prosocial behavior as well as an improvement in self-concept and social understanding.

Many programs concentrate on cooperative techniques of learning tasks that reduce competition and promote interdependence, coordination, cooperation, exchange, and helping. Such techniques encourage group participation, individual responsibility, and a tendency among children to learn and communicate necessary information. Children in these cooperative-learning groups tend to be more helpful, considerate, and cooperative than those in conventional lecture-type, competitive classes.

Longitudinal field-experimental studies have been done to strengthen children's prosocial orientation and behavior. The results show that children in such intervention programs are more supportive of each other, more spontaneously helpful and cooperative, and more concerned about others than those in the conventional classes. In addition, the program children are able to resolve conflict in less aggressive ways, with more compromise, planning, and attention to the needs of the various individuals engaged in the conflict. They also manifest more democratic values. Effects clearly go beyond the classroom, and academic achievement is not compromised. Most of the techniques used are readily incorporated into existing curricula. Therefore, administrators and teachers have an excellent opportunity to use them in the course of their everyday school activities.

Parents, teachers, and religious educators can be consistent models of sharing, helping, and comforting behaviors. Prosocial classroom activities that are enjoyable to children, such as role-playing and other activities that promote feelings of sympathy, support their prosocial tendencies. Parents and teachers can also organize to put pressure on television organizations for responsible television programming that exposes children to more altruistic behavior and to less violence and aggression. Organized efforts to influence the media have shown some promise.

Empathy training programs show that empathic responses can be enhanced by deliberate, explicit efforts to elicit them. This finding has practical significance, in that empathy can be learned and applied in consequential real-life situations. Empathy is a vital ingredient in the development of helpful behavior, and it is associated with relatively low levels of aggressive behavior. For these reasons, empathy training has been undertaken in elementary school-age children to regulate aggressive behavior, promote prosocial behavior, and develop exercises and strategies useful for regular classroom teachers of children between seven and eleven. Such innovations, like others described in these pages, link research and social action.

This elementary school training model provides a guide for the enhancement of empathy in other contexts in which we wish to reduce aggression and enhance positive social interactions. Perspective- and role-taking exercises can enhance one's ability to understand other ethnic, religious, and national groups. Evidence suggests that the greater the degree of perceived similarity between two individuals, the greater the degree of empathy. Hence, delineating similarities between individuals in a potential conflict is a helpful strategy. Time and again, we encounter the need to grasp our common humanity.

Multiple Benefits of Learning in Cooperative Settings

Many societies in a highly interdependent, globalized world are becoming increasingly multicultural. It follows that conflict will often be defined along ethnic lines. The challenges this presents for educators is great. One of the important responses to this challenge has been the development of cooperative learning techniques. These methods enhance positive interpersonal relations, motivation to learn, and self-esteem. When students from diverse backgrounds have a chance to work together productively on equal footing, they form friendships and are not inclined to hold prejudices against each other.[13] Cooperative learning not only helps students to acquire academic knowledge and skill, but also helps them to cross group boundaries to form new intergroup friendships and a new group culture. These benefits hold at all age levels that have been studied in middle grade schools and high schools, for a variety of subject areas and a wide range of tasks. Such cooperative learning is a microcosm of what the world will need in the twenty-first century.

Learning Conflict Resolution in School

Violence in schools has stimulated serious scholarship to determine the major factors underlying such violence and to develop ways of preventing it. Many countries are facing this problem. Research has highlighted some findings that have widespread application. Aggression in the home environment carries over into the school. Community violence also shows up in classrooms, hallways, and playgrounds. Factors outside the school environment create risks of becoming a victim of violence. To reduce violence in schools, prevention programs must be part of a larger prevention system, involving family and community as well as the school itself. This comprehensive view of interrelated influences is useful in education for conflict resolution and for peace education as well. Social contexts influence the thoughts, feelings, and behavior of children and youth. Thus, we must not only focus on the schools, but also on the wider setting in which young people develop.

Public health utilizes a multidisciplinary scientific approach to the problem with research on effective approaches to prevention. In this framework, recommendations for dealing with the youth violence problem are organized around three strategies: systemic changes for schools, programs for individual youth, and public policies. The goal is not just to address violence, but also to improve the quality of the lives of children.

Research over several decades identifies families and schools as the two most important institutions in democracies that influence children's predispositions to love and to hate.[14] Both are taken into account in teaching conflict resolution. Such programs include cooperative learning, conflict-resolution training, constructive use of controversy in teaching, and creation of dispute resolution centers. Students need a serious curriculum with repeated opportunities to learn and practice cooperative conflict-resolution skills.

School mediation programs are spreading rapidly. Research suggests that school mediation programs have positive effects on reducing violence and enhancing self-esteem as well as the social skills of the mediator. Thus, students learn conflict resolution in practice as well as in theory. Skills involved in active problem solving of this sort also encourage prosocial skills that can be used in other settings encountered over a lifetime.[15] What is learned in school needs to be transferred and reinforced in the home and community. School programs can actively encourage this transfer of learning.

Because humans are deeply social beings, we are highly influenced by the way others treat us and by our social surroundings. The need is to create learning environments for children and youth that will not only educate them academically but will also strengthen their emotional and interpersonal capacities. These aspects of behavior go hand in hand in promoting success in school and in today's marketplace, where employers seek individuals who are able to work harmoniously with a variety of coworkers as well as to take initiative, to take responsibility, and to communicate well.

Creating cooperative learning environments is crucial. This does not mean that competition is eliminated from students' experience. In fact, healthy competition often inspires greatness, whether the competition is in building a better instrument, developing gifted athletes, or developing creative scientists. But *excessive and harsh* competition, especially in the classroom, creates a dichotomous atmosphere of winners and losers—a breeding ground for feelings of isolation and alienation.

Learning through Community Service

There is a growing trend in education that has considerable potential for fostering constructive, unselfish behavior during adolescence: community service. This can be organized effectively not only by schools, but also by community organizations and religious institutions.

It is important that service be viewed not in a punitive way, but rather as a courageous, socially valued contribution, which goes beyond any selfish aims. There are several important reasons for implementing service learning in public education. It promotes students' academic achievement while simultaneously encouraging civic participation; social skills improve; and it helps to prepare youth for entering the workforce. Service learning enhances a sense of competency, promotes active engagement in improving the conditions of life, and establishes the role of being a valued member of a valued group. Students realize that what they are learning in school has practical applications. Learning motivation is enhanced, and school-community relations are improved. Readying students for active citizenship enhances the fundamental public purpose of education.

In some respects, community service draws together major strands of development: the growth of prosocial behavior; enhancement of empathy; learning in cooperative settings; resolving conflict without violence; reaching beyond the self in ways that overcome selfish, greedy orientations and creating a sense of belonging in a valued group that is characterized by a sense of fairness and mutual aid. These are formidable advantages in promoting healthy, constructive development. At the same time, students usually enjoy the community service, find it rewarding, and are eager participants.

Potential of Media to Reduce Prejudice and Hatred

We have emphasized that schools and universities must be augmented by other influences. Given the immensely powerful reach of the print and especially the nonprint media, their strong impact for better or worse cannot be overlooked. Sadly, the media industry is exactly that. It is a business in which profits are the prime objective, with little attention given to adverse effects. We have cherished some positive examples, *Sesame Street* for one, even though they are fewer than we would wish.

Public support is needed for media that portray accurate information on current events, show constructive relations between different groups, and report instances in which violence has been prevented. Foundations, commissions, universities, and advocacy organizations can be stimulated to work with broadcasters to help provide responsible, insightful coverage of serious conflict and ways of resolving it. In the same vein, there needs to be encouragement to portray and emphasize examples of successful prosocial activities and programs.

Television has immense latent capacity as a force for global transformation of attitudes and beliefs about different human groups. The medium is international, readily crossing boundaries. Each side in a war may be able to watch the other's television broadcasts.[16] The fascination and excitement of such dramatic programs are worldwide and deeply engrossing as beliefs and attitudes are being shaped.

A pioneering study of children ages 3 to 5 showed that, regardless of the economic class of the children studied, prosocial television elicited prosocial behavior.[17] The conclusion is that preschool children are positively affected by prosocial television and that these influences can be strengthened by specially designed school programs, training in role-taking, or the combination of prosocial television, role-playing, and verbal labeling. Prosocial television may be used as a supportive element to other training when attempting to influence the tendencies of children toward prosocial behavior.

Public television has provided excellent models. Commercial television has greatly lagged in building on such models. In principle, television can portray human diversity while highlighting shared human experiences—including the common humanity of our adversaries, even in times of stress. But so far we have had only glimpses of its potential for reducing intergroup conflict. Radio, TV, comic books, and some other media are accessible regardless of viewer literacy level, so they can reach almost everyone, everywhere—if only we make a sustained effort for engrossing, prosocial content.

Sesame Street was the first series to teach a curriculum to young children, with special attention to the needs of those in low-income and minority families. The driving force was to build intellectual and cultural development in preschoolers and help them to become ready for school.[18] The close, ongoing collaboration of child development experts, television producers, and educational researchers made the series a reality. *Sesame Street* also made possible systematic studies on the impact of educational television for children. Indicators are clear that *Sesame Street* exerts a positive influence on children's social behavior. Overall, significant effects in the United States and in other countries have been found on children's behavior in academic skills and social behavior as a result of exposure to *Sesame Street*. As research on *Sesame Street* has demonstrated, entertaining and educational television programming can be developed in ways that reduce intergroup hostility in different cultures, especially because the program now appears in well over 100 countries. The research on television and children enhances our motivation to find ways of diminishing exposure to violence in childhood and adolescence, to enhance media literacy as part of education (this helps children to distinguish fact from fantasy), to help children cope with media violence, and to provide much more prosocial programming like *Sesame Street*—not only for young children but for adolescents.

Information Technology and Education for Peace

Over the past several decades, some of the most profound changes in the way we live have come from the revolution in information technology. A wide range of technologies has made it easier not only to communicate, but also to utilize information across cultures on a worldwide basis. These materials have not stayed in the province of institutions or specialists but have found their way into common use. From cell phones and personal digital assistants to computers, they have changed the way that ordinary people interact.

In recent years, few developments have generated as much discussion of their potential to alter societies everywhere as the World Wide Web. In the 1990s, various enthusiasts predicted the rise of the Internet as a revolutionary force. Although it has had profound effects on the way many people live and work, some claims for the technology were overly grand. As the technology has settled into more regular use, there is a clearer grasp of the limitations and even the threats that this new technology can pose.

There is real danger from hate Web sites, which often include calls to violence. In these instances, the educational potential of the Web can be turned into a means of generating derogatory distinctions and even outright hatred in those who do not know better or are predisposed to hatred. This is a real, present danger and must be addressed alongside the Internet's potential to promote positive relationships. Clearly, using education as an antidote with accurate information is essential in diminishing the dangerous effects of hate groups. For every hateful lie, a bevy of truthful facts about decent human relationships must be conveyed via this and other media.

There are a number of relevant sites, though not specifically devoted to peace education, that use the global nature of the Web to support a positive worldwide view in education. A strong opportunity exists here to give children and youth a vivid and fascinating sense of their counterparts in other countries. There currently exist notable examples of interactive Internet use in classrooms that help students to learn about customs, beliefs, attitudes, and practices of other peoples. Both cultural diversity and human similarity can be better understood through such communication.

These computer-based technologies are extremely flexible. They can transmit large amounts of data easily (not merely text, but also audio and video), and they can be far more interactive than earlier communications technologies like radio and television. So they hold great potential for education and deserve vigorous exploration in education for peace.

Because of the flexibility of the technology and, most important, the creativity of the people who employ it, use of the Internet will continue to grow. The challenge is to make its use accurate, informative, affordable, and constructive for education, especially in the vital domain of decent human relationships, overcoming intergroup animosity, fostering prosocial development, and interactive communication across national and adversarial boundaries.

International Education: Seeing the Whole Wide World

The world is rapidly moving into a higher state of interdependency and globalization, driven by technological advances, economic opportunities, intellectual curiosity, and personal contacts. There is more movement across national boundaries than ever before of people, money, information, ideas, images, and much more. We are embedded among billions of people, mostly strangers, yet we need them and they need us: to make a living; to travel; to cope with widespread problems like infectious diseases and terrorism; to assure a clean environment, physical protection, and safe supplies of food and water.

So now we must, of necessity, find decent ways to interact with strangers, move beyond stereotypes, turn strangers into familiar people (to the extent possible), and even turn potential adversaries into friends. We have to learn how to transcend ancient suspicions and biases and learn how to live together with people who are initially strange and perhaps implicitly threatening.[19] In this process, strangeness can be converted to familiarity, suspicion to fascination. How can schools, colleges, and universities respond to this need? Several strategic opportunities have been proposed.

First, we must integrate international and global perspectives into the curriculum in a substantive way. Second, we must encourage learning-by-doing with students engaging with peers from different parts of the world. Third, we must use technology to full advantage to gather international information and encourage contact with people abroad. Fourth, we must respect teachers as central to each of these strategic opportunities, and provide preparation and in-service training. Finally, there is need for international education policies that recognize the importance and provide support for this work. The essential point is the universal widening of educational horizons beyond the parochial focus that currently predominates.

Integrating such information into the regular curriculum is essential because of its importance and because add-ons are too burdensome for most teachers. Support and guidance from educational leaders are vital. Teachers need to become interested, competent, and valued to teach these subjects effectively.

Surprisingly, the work on international education so far makes little connection to the conflict and violence we see around us. In the long run, international education is fundamentally linked to peace education. We must learn how to get along globally through understanding, communication, empathy, respect for other cultures, and ways of dealing fairly with grievances. By teaching our children these lessons, we can make mutual accommodation an attainable goal.

Altogether, these are high aspirations that will require major educational adjustments, public policy changes, and community support. The issues are so important in a rapidly transforming world that these adaptations must be undertaken regardless of the difficulty.

The recent work of the Asia Society of New York provides a valuable example of efforts to expand education's horizons in our increasingly intimate, interdependent world. A major report prepared for the Asia Society gives useful guidance in ways to make education more deeply international. The Society's educational initiatives focus on improving the quality of elementary and secondary education on Asia by providing curricular materials, services, and support for practitioners and schools nationwide. These considerations apply to international education in general—whether the focus is Asia, Africa, Latin America, or Europe.

Education for Peace: The Ultimate Goal

Peace education works toward giving children, adolescents, and young adults clear ideas about how to contribute to the creation of peaceful communities and equitable international relations. The twentieth century has seen an increased interest in peace education, but still it has not entered mainstream education. There has been some over-reliance on good will and exhortation. Useful as these may be, they are only a start. Although many schools have adopted conflict-resolution programs, they usually stop short of addressing the larger issues of war and peace. Yet there is a connection between the two. The challenge is to move beyond a narrow arena (for example, the school) to a broader view—indeed a worldwide outlook.

Essentially, we need to understand ourselves better. Human beings need not be destructive; we can work cooperatively. Modern technology has made warlike behavior suicidal and could lead to the destruction of humanity. In our actual struggle for survival, we must maximize the likelihood that all of humanity will come to be treated as potential allies—if not today, then in due course as we work out problems between us—not as an ideological preference, but as a practical matter of adaptation to the reality of the twenty-first century with all its destructive potential.

The aims of educating for peace should be more positive than the absence of threats, important as that is. We must aspire to a world in which the root causes of civilization's discontents are in fact minimized, basic human needs can be met, and the potential of individuals to live fulfilled lives is an attractive and realistic possibility in light of the profound and pervasive advances in science and technology linked to growing moral concerns.

Many concrete steps that can be taken by governments, intergovernmental organizations, and nongovernmental institutions (NGOs)—especially the pillars of civil society—have been clarified in recent years.[20] Education must encompass the notion that at every level—individual, group, and international—violence is not a satisfactory solution to ubiquitous human conflicts.

International cooperation for democratic development, both political and economic, is central to the vision of world peace with justice. Pluralism is the heart of democracy. Here the attitudes of tolerance, mutual respect, and protection of human rights are valued and perpetuated. The main path for implementation of democratic ideals is through free public education over many years and effective legal protection of human rights. It is fundamentally important to educate specifically for democracy— ranging from the most fundamental principles to operational detail: What are the essentials of democracy and how can they be made to work for all?

Education should be strengthened everywhere to the extent possible to enhance international understanding and cooperation; to value social justice; to diminish prejudices against other groups and nations; and learn how to cope with groups or nations led by fanatical haters—a difficult but not insurmountable problem.[21] Such education should encompass upbringing in the home, day care, schools, universities, adult education, religious institutions, community organizations and the media. All this should include the fundamental challenge of achieving peace in the twenty-first century, before the likelihood of planet-threatening destruction becomes a grim reality.

Education for conflict resolution, violence prevention, and just peace are concepts and strategies leading to a world that eventually transcends war. Historically, as we have noted at the outset, education everywhere has to some degree been ethnocentric and often overtly prejudicial. The time has come for schools and international educational organizations to work together to provide war and peace content based on the best of the world's scholarship, not ethnocentric in intergroup relations or hateful in orientation, nor tending to glorify war. Such content can be adapted for different levels of child and adolescent development in keeping with their age and experience. Strong international organizations such as the United Nations, European Union, Organization for Economic Cooperation and Development, Organization of American States, and African Union should stimulate and challenge their members (and nations that they aid) to put emphasis on education in general and peace education in particular.

Education everywhere should convey an accurate concept of the contemporary human species—a vast, extended, interdependent family sharing fundamental human similarities and a fragile planet. All research-based knowledge of human conflict, the diversity of our species, and the paths to mutual accommodation should be a part of education, conveying both the facts of human diversity and the common humanity we all share. We can convey the fascination of other cultures—making understanding and respect a core attribute of our outlook on the world, including the capacity to interact effectively in the emerging world economy. At the same time, we must take into account the proclivities of each culture to protect human rights and eschew violence.

We emphasize that education for peace is not limited to schools. Religious leaders have the capacity for teaching the ethical and pragmatic basis for tolerance in a pervasive way.[22] Their great investment in education of the young can be directed toward sympathetic understanding of other religions and nonviolent means of problem solving. The historical orientation to peace and good will that religious groups share could serve to enlist them much more actively in preventing the spread of hatred and violence. The general rhetoric of goodwill in many religious schools cries out for translation into social action, including in-depth education on constructive human relations.

Religious leaders can benefit from the inspiring positive results of some religious NGOs and can themselves take on efforts to promote worldwide respect for diversity and nonviolent problem solving. Their focus should include intrafaith and interfaith meetings to examine constructive ways of dealing with intergroup hostility. Leadership is exceedingly important in this entire enterprise. Historically, the worst atrocities have been nurtured or at least triggered by inflammatory political, ethnic, and religious leaders. Religious leaders should condemn hate-promoting coreligionists, and they should advocate international norms of tolerance.

One vital source of leadership in education for peace must come from the world's universities. With virulent prejudice, hatred, and recurrent threats of mass violence looming large in today's world, we are faced with an increasing need to learn how to use the tools of prevention to avoid deadly conflict. There is a serious global concern, especially in light of the proliferation of weapons technologies and the spread of hatred through mass communication. So education is called on to provide information on the profound dangers of deadly conflict and various methods of coping with the contentious issues that lead to violent conflict at every level of social organization.

Considering education for peace, we have touched on numerous substantive problems: causes and consequences of war, concepts and techniques of conflict resolution, and conditions favorable to long-term peaceful relations. Universities must address these fundamental problems in their research and education, including newer concepts such as human security, operational and structural prevention, and changing norms of national sovereignty—and renewed efforts to diminish and control weapons of mass destruction on a universal basis. Not only are universities able to provide undergraduate and graduate courses for their own students, but they are uniquely positioned to train the trainers through teacher education and curriculum development for programs from kindergarten through high school. University scholars who have the most advanced knowledge have shown that they can work collaboratively with teachers, counselors, and others in precollegiate public schools to stimulate students and enrich curricula.

From many conflict dilemmas, guidelines emerge for upgrading preventive capacities. There are specific ways in which the international community can strengthen its capability for promoting democratic governance, productive economic development, and nonviolent problem solving in dangerous situations by setting up mechanisms to address grievances promptly and fairly. There are helpful roles of national governments, intergovernmental organizations, NGOs, and the pivotal institutions of civil society.

International cooperation for democratic development (both political and economic) is a basic pillar of conditions conducive to peaceful living. The essential ingredients of such development center on knowledge, skill, and freedom. Knowledge is mainly generated by research and development; skill is mainly generated by education and training; freedom is mainly generated by democratic institutions. These are vital subjects for the university curriculum and for public understanding.

Universities should play a major role in preventing deadly conflict. To fulfill this promise, they need to give a higher priority to research and teaching in this field; to get more adequate support from governments, foundations, and other donors; to stimulate interdisciplinary and international cooperation in order to get stronger data, deeper insights, and to extend education far beyond any individual campus. In the early part of the twenty-first century, universities and precollegiate students as well as concerned citizens everywhere should have the opportunity to understand how conflicts can be settled promptly and fairly—and how conditions for peaceful living can be developed throughout the world. Technologies (e.g., CD-ROM technology) can help universities cooperate in making valuable information readily available, especially in the educational systems of poor and troubled countries.

Moving beyond the ancient habits of blaming, dehumanizing, repressing, and attacking is very difficult in practice but far from impossible. For millennia, we were utterly convinced that the earth was flat. So, too, we have believed in invidious in-group/out-group distinctions and harsh intergroup relations as a way of life. But science has proven that the earth is not flat. Currently, there is abundant knowledge demonstrating that we are all part of one large human family that now must learn to live together under conditions largely different from those contentious hostilities of the past.

THE GREAT OPPORTUNITIES FOR FUTURE GENERATIONS

Clearly, the human species is capable of remarkable cooperation, mutual ties, loyalty, and compassion as well as hatred, cruelty, violence, and destruction. But whether human groups can ever maintain internal cohesion over long periods without harsh deprecation of other groups is a critical issue. With the vast destructive capabilities of modern weaponry at the disposal of states, groups, and individuals, the human propensity toward violence and intergroup conflict threatens human existence in the twenty-first century.

Deeper understanding is essential to achieve the peaceful, constructive alternative. The scientific and scholarly professions must engage in wide-ranging, careful, systematic research on the conditions under which violent behaviors are likely to occur, the conditions under which human conflict can be effectively resolved, and the conditions under which just peace can be maintained on an enduring basis.

The powerful sectors of society everywhere tend to be complacent about these matters. Violence, including terrorism—whether employed by state, by groups, or by individuals—has often been mistakenly viewed as a faraway problem of someone else. Avoidance and denial substitute for careful scrutiny, authority substitutes for evidence, blaming substitutes for insight, and rigid ideology substitutes for pragmatic problem solving. But this need not be so forever. Indeed, there is an intellectual and moral ferment now to address these critical issues. It is essential to recognize the gravity of the dangers in order to mobilize the positive strengths necessary to overcome them.

The profound transformations in science and technology could mean the virtual elimination of human impoverishment and unprecedented fulfillment of human capacities in this new century. For this to happen, however, human beings will have to come to terms as never before with our own nature, particularly with our tendencies toward prejudice, ethnocentrism, and violent aggression. Those of us with powerful weapons have experienced throughout history an almost irresistible temptation to turn our power against fellow humans who are weak, vulnerable, or perceived to be menacing to us. This remains a serious problem in the contemporary world.

Terrorism is today abetted by an array of technologies that dwarf all previous reality. From the employment of instant worldwide-televised threats to diverse miniaturized weapons of devastation, the old terrorism is rapidly becoming transformed. Terrorism tends to trigger long-term cycles of retaliation and escalation. As we have seen in the Middle East, the Balkans, and Africa, killing can become a way of life and hatred an organizing principle for human groups. Moreover, people in many parts of the world are accustomed to the pervasive violation of human rights involving mental and physical torture, and this in turn foments deep resentment and, ultimately, retaliation. Terrorism thrives on raising children and youth to be hateful.

The modern world—for all its benefits, opportunities, and promises for a better future—leaves many young people feeling uncertain, confused, and largely incompetent. In many countries, there are serious obstacles to the development of youthful self-esteem through socially valued work, initiative taking, and accomplishment, except in violence. The lack of constructive options has predisposed many young people to hostility and the search for a person or groups to blame. Contemporary institutions everywhere—the family, the schools, the media, the religious institutions, the business community, governments, and universities—must search for ways to avert in the young the ravages of hatred and violence and provide instead opportunities for learning, skill development, economic opportunity, and social respect.

We must also find a basis for fundamental human identification across a diversity of cultures. This shared quest for understanding, especially as practiced by the scientific community, knows no national boundaries and no barriers to the free play of information and ideas. Education can help individuals to ask questions of practical importance bearing on fruitful cooperation rather than prejudice, ethnocentrism, and hatred. Individuals can strive, personally and professionally, to enhance understanding of human life as a single, worldwide, interdependent community. How can I work out decent relations with the people in my orbit?

It is certainly not beyond human ingenuity to move this subject higher on the world's agenda. Strong organizations covering wide sectors of science, technology, and education can take an increasingly active role in coping with this critical issue. Hostile attitudes, fanatical beliefs, and rigid ideologies from our past will often hinder such efforts, but human motivation for survival is strong, problem-solving capacities are great, and the time for adaptation is not yet too late.[23]

We have emphasized that personal-development-shaping institutions such as the family, schools, community-based organizations, religious institutions, and the media have the power to mold attitudes and skills that favor decent human relations. They can make constructive use of findings from research on intergroup relations and conflict resolution. We must learn from infancy through the life span how to achieve mutual accommodation among individuals and human groups.

Prejudice and hatred exist all over the world, but there are also touching examples of tolerance, cooperation, and friendship between different groups. What are the conditions under which the outcome can go one way or another? If we could understand such questions better, we could learn to tilt the balance toward peaceful existence. We hope this book is a step in that direction.

Efforts by our key institutions to improve relations among diverse peoples require a solid knowledge base from research. This will shed light on ways in which young people can reduce intergroup tensions and otherwise cope with expressions of ethnic, cultural, or religious intolerance among their peers. Research will find new kinds of interventions to improve the school and community climates for group interaction. We can find out which practices in schools can create an atmosphere of mutual respect and positive relations among peers as well as between students and teachers.

In the twenty-first century, it will be necessary in child and adolescent development to put deliberate, explicit emphasis on developing a prosocial orientation and a sense of worth based not on the deprecation of others but on the constructive attributes of self and others. In counteracting our ancient tendencies toward ethnocentrism and prejudice, we will need to foster reliable human attachments, positive reciprocity, friendly intergroup relations, a mutual-aid ethic, and an awareness of superordinate goals requiring cooperation that include economic well-being, environmental protection, personal security—and indeed human survival. We must seek ways to expand favorable contact between people from different groups and nations. Educational, cultural, and scientific exchanges can be helpful. At a deeper level, joint projects involving sustained cooperation can provide the valuable experience of working together toward a superordinate goal.

As our children and their children learn about the horrifying mass violence that human beings have committed against each other throughout the ages, it is our fervent hope at the beginning of the second millennium that diverse communities of the world will plant seeds of cooperation and reconciliation that will eventually grow into a system in which mass violence becomes increasingly rare or even—dare we say—nonexistent.[24]

It is high time that people everywhere seriously addressed the ubiquity of prejudice, the profound and pervasive impact of ethnocentrism, and the greatly enhanced risks of these ancient orientations in the rapidly changing world of the twenty-first century. Only by so doing can we begin to mobilize the unprecedented strengths needed to foster for the first time a truly common humanity in which decent human relations prevail.

CONCLUSION

The pervasive dangers of the world of the twenty-first century make the subject of this book more than an interesting, well-meaning luxury for education. On the contrary, the urgency and gravity of the problems of deadly conflict, currently evident on every continent, cry out for a fundamental upgrading of education on matters of conflict resolution, prompt and just ways of dealing with grievances, and learning how to construct—for the first time in history—a truly peaceful world.[25]

Toward this difficult but attainable end, the international community (and especially the established democracies) must make every effort to assign and implement a high priority for education in general and four kinds of education in particular: (1) education in mathematics, science, and technology so that every country can have the knowledge and skills to participate in the modern economy; (2) education for health, so that diseases and injuries that now constitute a huge burden of illness and disability can be prevented in the first place; (3) education for conflict resolution, violence prevention, and constructing a peaceful world through specific tools and strategies that enable diverse peoples to live together amicably; and (4) education that is equally available to girls and boys, women and men.

A high priority should be attached to these matters by governments, international organizations (public and private), and NGOs. To help poor countries implement these priorities, education of this sort should be closely linked to development aid, international trade, and direct investment in emerging markets. This would provide powerful economic and psychological incentives to shape behavior in ways that could have a transforming effect throughout the world. If and when this comes to pass, there will be incomparable gains in public health, personal security, economic well-being, and the quality of life altogether. The paths charted in this book make all of this a feasible proposition if only we can mobilize the intellectual and moral strength over sufficient time to bring it about. The needs are worldwide and profound. The responses must be worthy of the ideals.

Epilogue

I am talking about genuine peace, the kind of peace that makes life on earth worth living, the kind that enables men and nations to grow and to hope and to build a better life for their children—not merely peace for Americans but peace for all men and women—not merely peace in our time but peace for all time. . . .

First: Let us examine our attitude toward peace itself. Too many of us think it is impossible. Too many think it unreal. But that is a dangerous, defeatist belief. It leads to the conclusion that war is inevitable—that mankind is doomed—that we are gripped by forces we cannot control. . . . No problem of human destiny is beyond human beings.

Let us focus instead on a more practical, more attainable peace—based not on a sudden revolution in human nature but on a gradual evolution in human institutions—on a series of concrete actions and effective agreements which are in the interest of all concerned. . . .

World peace, like community peace, does not require that each man love his neighbor—it requires only that they live together in mutual tolerance, submitting their disputes to a just and peaceful settlement. And history teaches us that enmities between nations, as between individuals, do not last forever. . . .

So, let us not be blind to our differences—but let us also direct attention to our common interests and to the means by which those differences can be resolved. And if we cannot end now our differences, at least we can help make the world safe for diversity. For, in the final analysis, our most basic common link is that we all inhabit this small planet. We all breathe the same air. We all cherish our children's future. And we are all mortal.

John F. Kennedy, 1963

O, Youth: Do you know that yours is not the first generation to yearn for a life full of beauty and freedom? Do you know that all your ancestors have felt the same as you do—and fell victim to trouble and hatred? Do you know also that your fervent wishes can only find fulfillment if you succeed in attaining a love and an understanding of people, and animals, and plants, and stars, so that every joy becomes your joy and every pain your pain?

Albert Einstein, 1932

To avoid further disasters, we need political restraints on a world scale. But politics is not the whole story. We have experienced the results of technology in the service of the destructive side of human psychology. Something needs to be done about this fatal combination. The means for expressing cruelty and carrying out mass killing have been fully developed. It is too late to stop the technology. It is to the psychology that we should now turn.

Jonathan Glover, 1999

NOTES

CHAPTER 1

1. D. A. Hamburg, "An Evolutionary Perspective on Human Aggression," in *The Development and Integration of Behaviour: Essays in Honour of Robert Hinde*, ed. P. Bateson (Cambridge: Cambridge University Press, 1991), 419–457.

2. R. Levine and D. Campbell, *Ethnocentrism: Theories of Conflict, Ethnic Attitudes, and Group Behavior* (New York: McGraw-Hill, 1972).

3. S. Power, *A Problem from Hell: America and the Age of Genocide* (New York: Basic Books, 2002).

4. D. A. Hamburg, "Human Rights and Warfare: An Ounce of Prevention Is Worth a Pound of Cure," in *Realizing Human Rights: Moving from Inspiration to Impact,* ed. S. Power and G. Allison (New York: St. Martin's Press, 2000).

5. E. Stover and E. O. Nightingale, eds., *Breaking of Bodies and Minds: Torture, Psychiatric Abuse, and the Health Professions* (New York: W. H. Freeman, 1985).

6. D. A. Hamburg, *No More Killing Fields: Preventing Deadly Conflict* (Lanham, Md.: Rowman & Littlefield, 2002), 115–184; D. A. Hamburg, *Prejudice, Ethnocentrism, and Violence in an Age of High Technology* (New York: Annual Report of the Carnegie Corporation of New York, 1984), 8–11.

7. D. A. Hamburg, *Prejudice, Ethnocentrism, and Violence*, 8–11.

8. Constitution of the United Nations Educational, Scientific and Cultural Organization, Preamble and Article 1, adopted November 16, 1945, London.

CHAPTER 2

1. B. B. Smuts et al., eds., *Primate Societies* (Chicago: University of Chicago Press, 1986); W. C. McGrew, L. F. Marchant, and T. Nishida, eds., *Great Ape Societies* (Cambridge: Cambridge University Press, 1996); D. A. Hamburg and E. R. McCown, eds., *The Great Apes* (Menlo Park, Calif.: Benjamin/Cummings Publishing, 1979).

2. S. J. Suomi, "How Gene-Environment Interactions Can Shape the Development of Socioemotional Regulation in Rhesus Monkeys," in *Socioemotional Regulation: Dimensions, Developmental Trends, and Influences*, ed. B. S. Zuckerman and A. F. Lieberman (Skilman, N.J.: Johnson & Johnson Pediatric Institute, Johnson & Johnson Consumer Companies, 2002).

3. Ibid.

4. Smuts et al., *Primate Societies*; McGrew, Marchant, and Nishida, *Great Ape Societies*.

5. Suomi, "How Gene-Environment Interactions Can Shape the Development of Socioemotional Regulation in Rhesus Monkeys."

6. Ibid.

7. D. A. Hamburg and McCown, *Great Apes*.

8. Suomi, "How Gene-Environment Interactions Can Shape the Development of Socioemotional Regulation in Rhesus Monkeys."

9. D. A. Hamburg, "An Evolutionary Perspective on Human Aggression," in *The Development and Integration of Behavior: Essays in Honour of Robert Hinde*, ed. P. Bateson (Cambridge: Cambridge University Press, 1991), 419-457.

10. J. Goodall and D. A. Hamburg, "Chimpanzee Behavior as a Model for the Behavior of Early Man: New Evidence on Possible Origins of Human Behavior," in *American Handbook of Psychiatry*, vol. 6, ed. D. A. Hamburg and H. K. H. Brodie (New York: Basic Books, 1975).

11. D. A. Hamburg, "Psychobiological Studies of Aggressive Behavior," *Nature* 230 (1971): 19-23.

12. R. W. Wrangham, "Sex Differences in Chimpanzee Dispersion," in D. A. Hamburg and McCown, *Great Apes*.

13. A. E. Pusey and C. Packer, "Dispersal and Philopatry," in *Primate Societies*, ed. B. B. Smuts et al. (Chicago: University of Chicago Press, 1986).

14. A. E. Pusey, "Intercommunity Transfer of Chimpanzees in Gombe National Park," in D. A. Hamburg and McCown, *Great Apes*.

15. J. Goodall et al., "Intercommunity Interactions in the Chimpanzee Population of the Gombe National Park," in D. A. Hamburg and McCown, *Great Apes*.

16. J. D. Bygott, "Cannibalism among Wild Chimpanzees," *Nature* 238 (1972): 410-411; Goodall et al., "Intercommunity Interactions in the Chimpanzee Population."

17. J. D. Bygott, "Agonistic Behavior, Dominance, and Social Structure in Wild Chimpanzees of the Gombe National Park," in D. A. Hamburg and McCown, *Great Apes*.

18. T. Nishida, "The Social Structure of Chimpanzees of Mahale Mountains," in D. A. Hamburg and McCown, *Great Apes*; T. Nishida et al., "Group Extinction and Female Transfer in Wild Chimpanzees in the Mahale Mountains," *Zeitschrift für Tierpsychologie* 67 (1985): 284-301.

19. Bygott, "Agonistic Behavior"; R. W. Wrangham, "Evolution of Social Structure," in *Primate Societies*, ed. B. B. Smuts et al. (Chicago: University of Chicago Press, 1986).

20. T. Nishida and M. Hiraiwa-Hasegawa, "Chimpanzees and Bonobos: Cooperative Relationships among Males," in *Primate Societies*, ed. B. B. Smuts et al.

21. R. W. Wrangham, "Evolution of Coalitionary Killing," in *Yearbook of Physical Anthropology* (New York: Wiley-Liss, 1999), 42:1-30.

22. D. A. Hamburg, "Evolutionary Perspective on Human Aggression," 419–457.

23. B. B. Smuts and D. J. Gubernick, "Male-Infant Relationships in Nonhuman Primates: Paternal Investment or Mating Effort?" in *Father-Child Relations: Cultural and Biosocial Contexts*, ed. Barry S. Hewlett (Hawthorne, N.Y.: Aldine de Gruyter, 1992), 1–29.

24. G. Lenski, P. Nolan, and J. Lenski, *Human Societies: An Introduction to Macrosociology,* 7th ed. (New York: McGraw-Hill, 1994).

25. W. Goldschmidt, *Man's Way* (Cleveland, Ohio: World Publishing, 1959).

26. D. A. Hamburg, "Ancient Infants in a High Tech World: Can We Meet the Needs of Very Young Children?" (presented at annual meeting of Zero to Three Society, Washington, D.C., April 24, 1993).

27. P. Dolhinow and N. Bishop, "The Development of Motor Skills and Social Relationships among Primates through Play," in *Primate Patterns*, ed. P. Dolhinow (New York: Holt, Rinehart & Winston, 1972).

28. Carnegie Council on Adolescent Development, *Great Transitions: Preparing Adolescents for a New Century* (New York: Carnegie Corporation of New York, October 1995).

29. Bobbi S. Low, "Behavioral Ecology of Conservation in Traditional Societies," *Human Nature* 7, no. 4 (1996): 353–379.

CHAPTER 3

1. M. Sherif, *Intergroup Conflict and Cooperation: The Robbers Cave Experiment* (Norman: University of Oklahoma Institute of Intergroup Relations, 1961), quoted in E. Aronson, *Nobody Left to Hate: Teaching Compassion after Columbine* (New York: W. H. Freeman, 2000).

2. D. Riesman, *The Lonely Crowd* (New Haven, Conn.: Yale University Press, 1961).

3. D. A. Hamburg, *No More Killing Fields: Preventing Deadly Conflict* (Lanham, Md.: Rowman & Littlefield, 2002), 251–276.

4. B. Lewis, *What Went Wrong? Western Impact and Middle Eastern Response* (New York: Oxford University Press, 2002).

5. S. Talbot and Nayan Chanda, eds., *The Age of Terror: America and the World After September 11* (New York: Basic Books, 2001).

6. M. Glenny, *The Fall of Yugoslavia—The Third Balkan War*, 3rd ed. (New York: Penguin Books, 1996).

7. C. Tilly, *Durable Inequality* (Berkeley: University of California Press, 1998); L. Greenfeld and D. Chirot, *Nationalism and Aggression* (Seattle: University of Washington, 1991).

8. C. Tilly, *Durable Inequality*.

9. Ibid.; Greenfeld and Chirot, *Nationalism and Aggression*.

10. R. S. Wistrich, *Antisemitism: The Longest Hatred* (New York: Pantheon Books, 1991).

11. R. S. Appleby, *The Ambivalence of the Sacred: Religion, Violence, and Reconciliation* (Lanham, Md.: Rowman & Littlefield, 2000).

12. E. Staub, *The Roots of Evil* (New York: Cambridge University Press, 1989).

13. R. Melson, *Revolution and Genocide* (Chicago: University of Chicago Press, 1992).

14. D. A. Hamburg, *No More Killing Fields: Preventing Deadly Conflict* (Lanham, Md.: Rowman & Littlefield, 2002), 17–49.

15. Ibid., 87.

CHAPTER 4

1. K. P. Fischer, *Nazi Germany: A New History* (New York: Continuum, 1995), 345–358.

2. Ibid., 345.

3. Ibid., 346.

4. Ibid.

5. Ibid., 347.

6. Ibid.

7. Ibid.

8. Ibid.

9. G. A. Craig and A. L. George, *Force and Statecraft: Diplomatic Problems of Our Time*, 3rd ed. (New York: Oxford University Press, 1997).

10. Adolph Hitler, *Mein Kampf* (New York: Reynal & Hitchcock, 1941), 625ff., quoted in Fischer, *Nazi Germany*, 348.

11. Fischer, *Nazi Germany*, 352.

12. Ibid., 353.

13. Ibid., 355.

14. Fischer, *Nazi Germany*, 357.

15. M. Ignatieff, *The Warrior's Honor: Ethnic War and the Modern Conscience* (New York: Henry Holt, 1997).

16. Wade Jacoby, *Imitation and Politics: Redesigning Germany* (Ithaca, N.Y.: Cornell University Press, 2000).

17. R. Bragg, "Shaping Young Islamic Hearts and Hatreds," *New York Times*, October 14, 2001, A1.

18. M. B. Olcott and B. Babajanov, "The Terrorist Notebooks," *Foreign Policy* 135, (March/April 2003): 30–40.

19. T. L. Friedman, "In Pakistan, It's Jihad 101," *New York Times*, November 13, 2001, sec. Foreign Affairs.

20. Ibid.

21. D. Jehl, "Pakistan Prepares to Expel Foreign Religious Students," *New York Times*, March 9, 2002, sec. A8.

22. M. Simons, "Trial Examines War Crimes, Free Speech and Journalism," *International Herald Tribune,* March 5, 2002, sec. World News/Focus.

23. Ibid.

24. Ibid.

25. P. Gourevitch, *We Wish to Inform You That Tomorrow We Will Be Killed with Our Families* (New York: Picador USA, 1999), 100.

26. Committee for Accuracy in Middle East Reporting in America, "Memo to the Media: The Root of Palestinian Terrorism Is Hate Education," *New York Times*, May 7, 2002, sec. A31.

27. Ibid.

28. Middle East Media Research Institute, "About Us" (Washington, D.C.: MEMRI, rev. 2003), http://www.memri.org/aboutus.html (accessed July 16, 2003).

29. G. Nordbruch, *Narrating Palestinian Nationalism: An Inquiry into the New Palestinian Textbooks* (Washington, D.C.: MEMRI, December 2, 2001), http://www.memri.org/bin/articles.cgi?Page=archives&Area=sr&ID=SR00601 (accessed July 16, 2003).

30. M. Charfi, "Reaching the Next Muslim Generation," *New York Times*, March 12, 2002, sec. A27.

31. Ibid.

32. United Nations Development Programme, Arab Fund for Economic and Social Development, *Arab Human Development Report 2002: Creating Opportunities for Future Generations* (New York: United Nations Development Programme, 2002), 55.

CHAPTER 5

1. N. Eisenberg and P. H. Mussen, *The Roots of Prosocial Behavior in Children* (Cambridge: Cambridge University Press, 1989), 1–11.

2. E. M. Hetherington and R. D. Parke, *Child Psychology: A Contemporary Viewpoint* 5th ed., rev. R. D. Parke and V. O. Locke (Boston: McGraw-Hill College, 1999), 514–549, 620–663.

3. C. Zahn-Waxler, "The Development of Empathy, Guilt, and Internalization of Distress: Implications for Gender Differences in Internalizing and Externalizing Problems," in *Anxiety, Depression, and Emotion*, ed. R. J. Davidson (New York: Oxford, 2000), 222–265.

4. Ibid.

5. P. D. MacLean, "Brain Evolution Relating to Family, Play, and the Separation Call," *Archives of General Psychiatry* 42 (1985): 405–417, cited in Zahn-Waxler, "Development of Empathy, Guilt, and Internalization of Distress," 222–265.

6. Ibid.

7. W. G. Stephan and K. Finlay, "The Role of Empathy in Improving Intergroup Relations," *Journal of Social Issues* 55 (Winter 1999): 729–743.

8. N. D. Feshbach, "Learning to Care: A Positive Approach to Child Training and Discipline," *Journal of Clinical Child Psychology* 12, no. 3 (1983): 266–271, cited in N. D. Feshbach, "Empathy Training and Prosocial Behavior," in *Aggression and War: Their Biological and Social Bases*, ed. J. Grobel and R. A. Hinde (Cambridge: Cambridge University Press, 1989), 101–111.

9. Ibid.

10. C. D. Batson, *The Altruism Question: Toward a Social Psychological Answer* (Hillsdale, N.J.: Erlbaum, 1991); M. H. Davis, *Empathy: A Social Psychological Approach* (Madison, Wis.: Brown and Benchmark, 1994); and P. A. Oswald, "The Effects of Cognitive and Affective Perspective Taking on Empathic Concern and Altruistic Helping," *Journal of Social Psychology* 136 (1996): 613–623; all cited in Stephan and Finlay, "Role of Empathy," 729–743.

11. C. D. Batson et al., "Is Empathy-Induced Helping Due to Self-Other Merging?" *Journal of Personality and Social Psychology* 73 (1997): 495–509, cited in Stephan and Finlay, "Role of Empathy," 729–743.

12. C. D. Batson et al., "Empathy and Attitudes: Can Feeling for a Member of a Stigmatized Group Improve Feelings toward the Group?" *Journal of Personality and Social Psychology* 72 (1997): 105–118, cited in Stephan and Finlay, "Role of Empathy," 729–743.

13. K. A. Finlay and W. G. Stephan, "Improving Intergroup Relations: The Effects of Empathy on Racial Attitudes," *Journal of Applied Social Psychology* 30 (August 2000): 1720–1737, cited in Stephan and Finlay, "Role of Empathy," 729–743.

14. R. D. Parke and R. G. Slaby, "The Development of Aggression," in *Socialization, Personality, and Social Development*, ed. E. M. Hetherington, vol. 4 of *Handbook of Child Psychology*, ed. P. H. Mussen (New York: Wiley, 1983), 547–641; and G. R. Patterson, *Coercive Family Processes* (Eugene, Oreg.: Castalia, 1982); both cited in Eisenberg and Mussen, *Roots of Prosocial Behavior*, 1–11.

15. D. Bar-Tal, "American Study of Helping Behavior: What? Why? and Where?" in *The Development and Maintenance of Prosocial Behavior: International Perspectives on Positive Morality*, ed. E. Staub et al. (New York: Plenum, 1984), 5–27, cited in Eisenberg and Mussen, *Roots of Prosocial Behavior*, 1–11; R. A. Hinde and J. Groebel, eds., *Cooperation and Prosocial Behaviour* (Cambridge, U.K.: Cambridge University Press, 1991).

16. Bar-Tal, "American Study of Helping Behavior," 5–27.

17. A. Bandura, "Social Cognitive Theory in Cultural Context," *Applied Psychology: An International Review* 51 (April 2002): 269–290.

18. H. L. Rheingold, D. F. Hay, and M. J. West, "Sharing in the Second Year of Life," *Child Development* 47 (1976): 1157, cited in E. Mavis Hetherington and Ross D. Parke, *Child Psychology: A Contemporary Viewpoint*, 5th ed. (Boston: McGraw-Hill College, 1999), 620–663.

19. H. L. Rheingold, "Little Children's Participation in the Work of Adults: A Nascent Prosocial Behavior, *Child Development* 53 (1982): 114–125, cited in Hetherington and Parke, *Child Psychology*, 620–663.

20. N. Eisenberg and R. A. Fabes, "Prosocial Development," in *Social, Emotional, and Personality Development*, ed. N. Eisenberg, vol. 3 of *Handbook of Child Psychology*, ed. W. Damon, 9th ed. (New York: Wiley, 1998), 701–778, cited in Hetherington and Parke, *Child Psychology*, 620–663.

21. D. H. Hamer, "Rethinking Behavior Genetics," *Science* 298 (October 4, 2002): 71–72.

22. D. H. Hamer and P. Copeland, *Living with Our Genes* (New York: Doubleday, 1998).

23. M. H. Davis, C. Luce, and S. J. Kraus, "The Heritability of Characteristics Associated with Dispositional Empathy," *Journal of Personality* 62 (1994): 369–391; and J. P. Ruston et al., "Altruism and Aggression: The Heritability of Individual Differences," *Journal of Personality and Social Psychology* 50 (1986): 1192–1198; both cited in Hetherington and Parke, *Child Psychology*, 620–663.

24. Hamer, "Rethinking Behavior Genetics," 71–72.

25. S. Hearold, "A Synthesis of 1043 Effects of Television on Social Behavior," in *Public Communication and Behavior*, vol. 1, ed. G. Comstock (New York: Academic Press, 1986), 65–133.

26. D. Rosenhaun, "Prosocial Behavior of Children," in *The Young Child*, vol. 2, ed. W. W. Hartup (Washington, D.C.: National Association for the Education of Young Children, 1972), 340–359, cited in Hetherington and Parke, *Child Psychology*, 620–663.

27. M. Dekovic and J. M. Janssens, "Parents' Child-Rearing Style and Child's Sociometric Status, *Developmental Psychology* 28 (1992): 925–932, cited in Hetherington and Parke, *Child Psychology*, 620–663.

28. Rheingold, "Little Children's Participation," 114–125, cited in Hetherington and Parke, *Child Psychology*, 620–663.

29. L. K. Friedrich and A. H. Stein, "Aggressive and Prosocial Television Programs and the Natural Behavior of Preschool Children," *Monographs of the Society for Research in Child Development* 38 (1973, serial no. 151); A. C. Huston et al., *Big World, Small Screen* (Lincoln: University of Nebraska Press, 1992); and A. C. Huston and J. C. Wright, "Mass Media and Children's Development," in *Child Psychology in Practice*, ed. I. E. Sigel and K. A. Renniger, vol. 4 of *Handbook of Child Psychology*, ed. W. Damon (New York: Wiley, 1998), 999–1058; all cited in Hetherington and Parke, *Child Psychology*, 620–663.

30. E. M. Cummings, C. Zahn-Waxler, and M. Radke-Yarrow, "Developmental Changes in Children's Reactions to Anger in the Home," *Journal of Child Psychology and Psychiatry* 25 (January 1984): 163–174.

31. M. Radke-Yarrow and C. Zahn-Waxler, "The Role of Familial Factors in the Development of Prosocial Behavior: Research Findings and Questions," in *Development of Antisocial and Prosocial Behavior*, ed. D. Olweus, J. Block, and M. Radke-Yarrow (Orlando, Fla.: Academic Press, 1986).

32. C. Zahn-Waxler, M. Radke-Yarrow, and R. A. King, "Child Rearing and Children's Prosocial Initiations toward Victims of Distress," *Child Development* 50 (June 1979): 319–330, cited in Davidson, *Anxiety, Depression, and Emotion*, 222–265.

33. Radke-Yarrow and Zahn-Waxler, "Role of Familial Factors."

34. S. Denham et al., "Social Competence in Young Children's Peer Relations: Patterns of De-

velopment and Change," *Child Psychiatry Human Development* 22, no. 1 (1991): 29–44, cited in Davidson, *Anxiety, Depression, and Emotion*, 222–265.

35. Waxler et al., "Child Rearing and Children's Prosocial Initiations toward Victims of Distress," 319–330, cited in Davidson, *Anxiety, Depression, and Emotion*, 222–265.

36. A. Bandura, *Aggression: A Social Learning Analysis* (Englewood Cliffs, N.J.: Prentice Hall, 1973), cited in Eisenberg and Mussen, *Roots of Prosocial Behavior*, 95–107.

37. M. Radke-Yarrow et al., "Caring Behavior of Clinically Depressed and Well Mothers," *Child Development* 65 (October 1994): 1405–1414, cited in Davidson, *Anxiety, Depression, and Emotion*, 222–265.

38. N. Eisenberg and P. H. Mussen, "Socialization by Agents outside the Family," in Eisenberg and Mussen, *Roots of Prosocial Behavior*, 95–107.

39. W. Furman and L. A. Gavin, "Peers' Influence on Adjustment and Development," in *Peer Relationships in Child Development*, ed. T. J. Berndt and G. W. Ladd (New York: Wiley, 1989); W. Furman and J. C. Masters, "Affective Consequences of Social Reinforcement, Punishment, and Neutral Behavior," *Developmental Psychology* 16 (1980): 100–104; and K. H. Rubin, W. M. Bukowski, and J. G. Parker, "Peer Interactions, Relationships, and Groups," in *Social, Emotional, and Personality Development*, ed. N. Eisenberg, vol. 3 of *Handbook of Child Psychology*, 5th ed., ed. W. Damon (New York: Wiley, 1998), 619–700; all cited in Hetherington and Parke, *Child Psychology*, 514–549.

40. R. Charlesworth and W. W. Hartup, "Positive Social Reinforcement in the Nursery School Peer Group," *Child Development* 38 (1967): 993–1002, cited in Hetherington and Parke, *Child Psychology*, 514–549.

41. J. E. Grusec and R. Abramovitch, "Imitation of Peers and Adults in a Natural Setting: A Functional Analysis," *Child Development* 53 (1982): 636–642, cited in Hetherington and Parke, *Child Psychology*, 514–549.

42. A. Bandura, "Social Cognitive Theory," in *Annals of Child Development: Six Theories of Child Development*, vol. 6, ed. R. Vasta (Greenwich, Conn.: JAI Press, 1989); and Rubin et al., "Peer Interactions," 619–700; both cited in Hetherington and Parke, *Child Psychology*, 514–549.

43. Bandura, *Aggression: A Social Learning Analysis*, cited in Eisenberg and Mussen, *Roots of Prosocial Behavior*, 95–107.

44. R. O'Connor, "Modification of Social Withdrawal through Symbolic Modeling," *Journal of Applied Behavior Analysis* 2 (1969): 15–22, cited in Eisenberg and Mussen, *Roots of Prosocial Behavior*, 95–107.

45. A. Bandura, J. E. Grusec, and F. L. Menlove, "Vicarious Extinction of Avoidance Behavior," *Journal of Personality and Social Psychology* 5 (1967): 16–23; Bandura, *Aggression: A Social Learning Analysis*, cited in Eisenberg and Mussen, *Roots of Prosocial Behavior*, 95–107.

46. W. Furman, D. Rahe, and W. W. Hartup, "Social Rehabilitation of Low-Interactive Preschool Children by Peer Intervention," *Child Development* 50 (1979): 915–922, cited in Eisenberg and Mussen, *Roots of Prosocial Behavior*, 95–107.

47. N. Eisenberg et al., "Socialization of Prosocial Behavior in the Preschool Classroom," *Developmental Psychology* 17 (1981): 773–782, cited in Eisenberg and Mussen, *Roots of Prosocial Behavior*, 95–107.

48. M. W. DeVoe, G. F. Render, and J. R. Collins, "Microtechnology Processes and Cooperative Behavior of Third-Grade Children," *Journal of Experimental Education* 47 (1979): 296–301, cited in Eisenberg and Mussen, *Roots of Prosocial Behavior*, 95–107.

49. C. Zahn-Waxler, R. Iannotti, and M. Chapman, "Peers and Prosocial Development," in *Peer Relationships and social Skills in Childhood*, ed. K. H. Rubin and H. S. Ross (New York:

Springer-Verlag, 1982), 133–162, cited in Eisenberg and Mussen, *Roots of Prosocial Behavior*, 95–107.

50. D. Solomon et al., "Cooperative Learning as Part of a Comprehensive Program Designed to Promote Prosocial Development," in *Cooperative Learning: Theory and Research*, ed. S. Sharan (New York: Praeger, 1990), cited (as "*Current Research on Cooperative Learning*, in press") in Eisenberg and Mussen, *Roots of Prosocial Behavior*, 100.

51. K. Lyons-Ruth, L. Alpern, and B. Repacholi, "Disorganized Infant Attachment Classification and Maternal Psychosocial Problems as Predictors of Hostile-Aggressive Behavior in the Preschool Classroom," *Child Development* 64 (1993): 572–585; and K. Lyons-Ruth, M. A. Easterbrooks, and C. Davidson, "Disorganized Attachment Strategies and Mental Lag in Infancy: Prediction of Externalizing Problems at Seven" (paper presented at the biennial meeting of the Society for Research in Child Development, Indianapolis, Ind., April 1995); both cited in Hetherington and Parke, *Child Psychology*, 620–663.

52. A. Raine, P. Brennan, and S. A. Mednick, "Birth Complications Combined with Early Maternal Rejection at Age 1 Year Predispose to Violent Crime at Age 18 Years," *Archives of General Psychiatry* 51 (1994): 984–988, cited in Hetherington and Parke, *Child Psychology*, 620–663; R. Hinde and L. Pulkkinen, "Human Aggressiveness and War," in *Pugwash Occasional Papers* 2 (September 2001): 5–37.

53. P. Cohen and J. S. Brook, "The Reciprocal Influence of Punishment and Child Behavior Disorder," in *Coercion and Punishment in Long-Term Perspectives*, ed. J. McCord (New York: Cambridge University Press, 1995), 154–164; L. D. Eron and L. R. Huesmann, "The Control of Aggressive Behavior by Changes in Attitudes, Values, and the Conditions of Learning," in *Advances in the Study of Aggression*, vol. 2 (New York: Academic Press, 1984); G. R. Patterson, J. B. Reid, and T. J. Dishion, *A Social Learning Approach: Vol. 4. Antisocial Boys* (Eugene, OR: Castalia, 1992); K. Deater-Deckard et al., "Physical Discipline among African American and European American Mothers: Links to Children's Externalizing Behaviors," *Developmental Psychology* 32 (1996): 1065–1072; and K. Deater-Deckard and K. A. Dodge, "Externalizing Behavior Problems and Discipline Revisited: Nonlinear Effects and Variation by Culture, Context, and Gender," *Psychological Inquiry* 8 (1997): 161–175; all cited in Hetherington and Parke, *Child Psychology*, 620–663.

54. Patterson, Reid, and Dishion, *Social Learning Approach*, cited in Hetherington and Parke, *Child Psychology*, 620–663.

55. N. Feshbach and S. Feshbach, "The Relationship Between Empathy and Aggression in Two Age Groups," *Developmental Psychology* 1 (1969): 102–107, cited in N. D. Feshbach, "Empathy Training and Prosocial Behavior," in *Aggression and War: Their Biological and Social Bases*, ed. J. Grobel and R. A. Hinde (Cambridge: Cambridge University Press, 1989), 101–111.

56. Solomon et al., "Cooperative Learning," cited in Eisenberg and Mussen, *Roots of Prosocial Behavior*, 100.

57. Feshbach, "Empathy Training and Prosocial Behavior," 101–111.

58. Ibid.

59. N. D. Feshbach, "The Psychology of Empathy and the Empathy of Psychology" (presidential address at the annual meeting of the Western Psychological Association, Honolulu, HI), 1980, cited in Feshbach, "Empathy Training and Prosocial Behavior," 108.

60. Ibid.

61. D. Bridgeman, "Enhanced Role Taking through cooperative Interdependence: A Field Study," *Child Development* 52 (1981): 1231–1238, cited in Stephan and Finlay, "Role of Empathy," 729–743.

62. E. Aronson et al., *The Jigsaw Classroom* (Beverly Hills, Calif.: Sage, 1978); and E. Aronson

and S. Patnoe, *The Jigsaw Classroom* (New York: Longman, 1997); both cited in Stephan and Finlay, "Role of Empathy in Improving Intergroup Relations," 729–743.

63. J. W. Burton, "The Procedures of Conflict Resolution," in *International Conflict Resolution: Theory and Practice*, ed. E. E. Azar and R. W. Burton (Boulder, Colo.: Lynne Reiner, 1986); J. W. Burton, *Resolving Deep-Rooted Conflict: A Handbook* (Lanham, Md.: University Press of America, 1987); L. W. Doob, "A Cyprus Workshop: An Exercise in intervention Methodology," *Journal of Social Psychology* 84 (1974): 161–178; H. C. Kelman, "Interactive Problem-Solving: A Social Psychological Approach to Conflict Resolution," in *Conflict: Readings in Management and Resolution*, ed. J. Burton and F. Dukes (New York: St. Martin's Press, 1990), 199–215; H. C. Kelman and S. P. Cohen, "Resolution of International Conflict: An Interactional Approach," in *Psychology of Intergroup Relations*, ed. S. Worchel and W. G. Austin (Chicago: Nelson Hall, 1986), 323–432; and N. N. Rouhana and H. C. Kelman, "Promoting Joint Thinking in International Conflicts: An Israeli-Palestinian Continuing Workshop," *Journal of Social Issues* 50 (1994): 157–178; all cited in Stephan and Finlay, "Role of Empathy," 729–743.

64. W. Ury, *Getting to Peace* (New York: Penguin, 1999).

65. J. A. Banks, *Teaching Strategies for Ethnic Studies*, 4th ed. (Boston: Allyn & Bacon, 1987); J. A. Banks, *Multicultural Education*, 2nd ed. (Boston: Allyn & Bacon, 1988); and J. A. Banks, *Educating Citizens in a Multicultural Society* (New York: Teachers College Press, 1997); all cited in Stephan and Finlay, "Role of Empathy," 729–743.

66. Banks, *Teaching Strategies*; C. E. Sleeter and C. A. Grant, "An Analysis of Multicultural Education in the United States," *Harvard Educational Review* 57 (1987): 421–444; and NCSS Task Force, "Curriculum Guidelines for Multicultural Education," *Social Education* (September 1992): 274–294; both cited in Stephan and Finlay, "Role of Empathy," 729–743.

67. J. H. Litcher and D. W. Johnson, "Changes in Attitudes toward Negroes of White Elementary School Students after Use of Multiethnic Readers," *Journal of Educational Psychology* 60 (1969): 148–152; and C. Colca et al., "Combating Racism in the Schools: A Group Work Pilot Project," *Social Work in Education* 5 (1982): 5–18; both cited in Stephan and Finlay, "Role of Empathy," 729–743.

68. C. D. Batson et al., "Empathy and Attitudes: Can Feeling for a Member of a Stigmatized Group Improve Feelings toward the Group?" *Journal of Personality and Social Psychology* 72 (1997): 105–118; A. Barak, "Counselor Training in Empathy by a Game Procedure," *Counselor Education and Supervision* 29 (1990): 170–186; P. I. Erera, "Empathy Training for Helping Professionals: Model and Evaluation," *Journal of Social work Education* 33 (1997): 245–260; and H. A. Pinzone-Glover, C. A. Gidycz, and C. D. Jacobs, "An Acquaintance Rape Prevention Program," *Psychology of Women Quarterly* 22 (1997): 605–621; all cited in Stephan and Finlay, "Role of Empathy," 729–743.

69. Eisenberg and Mussen, *Roots of Prosocial Behavior*, 150–159.

70. R. Hertz-Lazarowitz and S. Sharan, "Enhancing Prosocial Behavior through Cooperative Learning in the Classroom," in *The Development and Maintenance of Prosocial Behavior: International Perspectives on Positive Morality*, ed. E. Staub et al. (New York: Plenum, 1984), 423–443; S. Sharan et al., *Cooperation in Education* (Provo, UT: Brigham Young University Press, 1980); and D. Solomon, E. Schaps, and M. Watson, "Effects of a Comprehensive School-Based Program on Children's Prosocial Behavior" (Paper presented at a meeting of the American Educational Research Association, Washington, D.C., April 1987); all cited in Eisenberg and Mussen, *Roots of Prosocial Behavior*, 150–159.

71. Carnegie Council on Adolescent Development, *Great Transitions: Preparing Adolescents for a New Century* (New York: Carnegie Corporation of New York, October 1995), 115–123.

72. A. Higgins, C. Power, and L. Kohlberg, "The Relationship of Moral Atmosphere to Judgments of Responsibility," in *Morality, Moral Behavior, and Moral Development* (New York: Wiley, 1984), 74–106, cited in Eisenberg and Mussen, *Roots of Prosocial Behavior,* 150–159.

73. E. H. Erikson, *Gandhi's Truth: On the Origins of Militant Nonviolence* (1970; reprint, New York: W. W. Norton & Company, 1993); E. H. Erikson, *Young Man Luther: A Study in Psychoanalysis and History* (1958; reprint, New York: W. W. Norton & Company, 1993).

74. Eisenberg and Mussen, *Roots of Prosocial Behavior,* 150–159.

CHAPTER 6

1. D. A. Hamburg, *Today's Children: Creating a Future for a Generation in Crisis* (New York: Times Books, 1992), 102–103; Carnegie Council on Adolescent Development, *Great Transitions: Preparing Adolescents for a New Century* (New York: Carnegie Corporation of New York, October 1995); Carnegie Council on Adolescent Development, Task Force on Youth Development and Community Programs, *A Matter of Time: Risk and Opportunity in the Nonschool Hours* (New York: Carnegie Corporation of New York, 1992).

2. D. A. Hamburg, *Today's Children,* 51–73.

3. J. P. Shonkoff and D. Phillips, eds., *From Neurons to Neighborhoods: The Science of Early Childhood Development* (Washington, D.C.: National Academy Press, 2000), 299. See also G. G. Fein and K. A. Clarke-Stewart, *Day Care in Context* (New York: Wiley, 1973); M. E. Lamb, "Nonparental Child Care: Context, Quality, Correlates," in *Handbook of Child Psychology,* vol. 4: *Child Psychology in Practice,* 5th ed., ed. W. Damon, I. E. Sigel, and K. A. Renninger (New York: Wiley, 1998), 73–134; and S. Scarr and M. Eisenberg, "Child Care Research: Issues, Perspectives, and Results," *Annual Review of Psychology* 44 (1993): 613–644.

4. Carnegie Task Force on Meeting the Needs of Young Children, *Starting Points: Meeting the Needs of Our Youngest Children* (New York: Carnegie Corporation of New York, 1994).

5. Carnegie Council on Adolescent Development, *Great Transitions.*

6. Boys and Girls Clubs of America, *The Effects of Boys and Girls Clubs on Alcohol and Other Drug Use and Related Problems in Public Housing Projects: A Demonstration Study Sponsored by the Office for Substance Abuse Prevention* (New York: Boys and Girls Clubs of America, March 1991), cited in Carnegie Council on Adolescent Development, *Matter of Time,* 39.

7. H. Ladewig and J. K. Thomas, *Assessing the Impact of 4-H on Former Members* (College Station, TX: Texas A & M University System, 1987), cited in Carnegie Council on Adolescent Development, *Matter of Time,* 38.

8. Girls Incorporated, *Truth, Trust, and Technology: New Research on Preventing Adolescent Pregnancy* (New York: Girls Incorporated, 1991), cited in Carnegie Council on Adolescent Development, *Matter of Time,* 39.

9. J. P. Allen and S. Philliber, *Process Evaluation of the Teen Outreach Program: Characteristics Related to Program Success in Preventing School Dropout and Teen Pregnancy in Year 5, 1988–89 School Year* (New York: Association of Junior Leagues International, 1991), cited in Carnegie Council on Adolescent Development, *Matter of Time,* 39.

10. M. Freedman, C. A. Harvey, and C. Ventura-Merkel, "The Quiet Revolution: Elder Service and Youth Development in an Aging Society" (Washington, D.C.: Carnegie Council on Adolescent Development, Task Force on Youth Development and Community Programs, 1992), cited in Carnegie Council on Adolescent Development, *Matter of Time,* 60. The Freedman, Harvey, and Ventura-Merkel paper lists 24 evaluation studies that have been conducted by the Foster Grandparent program from 1966 through 1988. For a copy of that paper, contact Dr. Ruby Takanishi,

President, Foundation for Child Development, 145 East 32nd Street, New York, NY 10016; www.fcd.org.

11. U.S. Department of the Interior, President's Commission on Outdoors, *National Urban Recreation Study: An Executive Report* (Washington, D.C.: Department of the Interior, 1989). See also J. Littell and J. Wynn, *The Availability and Use of Community Resources for Young Adolescents in an Inner-City and Suburban Community* (Chicago: University of Chicago, Chapin Hall Center for Children, 1989), cited in Carnegie Council on Adolescent Development, *Matter of Time,* 66.

12. Littell and Wynn, *Availability and Use of Community Resources,* ix, cited in Carnegie Council on Adolescent Development, *Matter of Time,* 71.

13. Carnegie Council on Adolescent Development, Task Force on Education of Young Adolescents, *Turning Points: Preparing American Youth for the 21st Century* (New York: Carnegie Corporation of New York, June 1989).

14. B. A. Hamburg, *Life Skills Training: Preventive Intervention for Young Adolescents* (New York: Carnegie Corporation of New York, 1990).

15. D. A. Hamburg, *Today's Children,* 267–271.

16. Carnegie Council on Adolescent Development, *Matter of Time,* 77–97.

17. D. Allensworth et al., *Schools and Health: Our Nation's Investment* (Washington, D.C.: National Academy Press, 1997), 203–204.

18. M. F. Hogan, *Mental Health and School Success: Hearing Summary and Resource Guide* (Columbus, Ohio: Ohio Department of Mental Health, 2001).

19. C. L. Perry et al., "Community-wide Smoking Prevention: Long-term Outcomes of the Minnesota Heart Health Program of the Class of 1989 Study," *American Journal of Public Health* 82 (1992): 1210–1216; S. Sussman et al., "Project towards No Tobacco Use, 1-Year Behavior Outcomes," *American Journal of Public Health* 83, no. 9 (1993): 1245–1250; and S. Tortu and G. J. Botvin, "School-Based Smoking Prevention: The Teacher Training Process," *Preventive Medicine* 18, no. 2 (1989): 280–289; all cited in Allensworth et al., *Schools and Health,* 81–152.

20. L. A. Rohrbach, J. W. Graham, and W. B. Hansen, "Diffusion of a School-Based Substance Abuse Prevention Program: Predictors of Program Implementation," *Preventive Medicine* 22, no. 2 (1993): 237–260, cited in Allensworth et al., *Schools and Health,* 81–152.

21. Ounce of Prevention Fund, *Success for Every Teen: Programs That Help Adolescents Avoid Pregnancy, Gangs, Drug Abuse, and School Drop-Out* (Chicago: Ounce of Prevention Fund, 1990), cited in D. Allensworth et al., *Schools and Health,* 81–152.

22. National Commission on AIDS, *Preventing HIV/AIDS in Adolescents* (Washington, D.C.: National Commission on AIDS, 1993), cited in Allensworth et al., *Schools and Health,* 81–152.

23. B. Starfield, "Preventive Interventions in the Health and Health-Related Sections with Potential Relevance for Youth Suicide," in Alcohol, Drug Abuse, and Mental Health Administration, *Report of the Secretary's Task Force on Youth Suicide: Vols. 1-4,* DHHS Publication No. ADM 89-1624 (Washington, D.C.: Government Printing Office, 1989), cited in Allensworth et al., *Schools and Health,* 81–152.

24. P. Gilder, H. Kressler, and G. McGrew, "Prevention and Early Intervention through Peer Support Retreats," in *Working with Youth in High-Risk Environments: Experiences in Prevention,* ed. C. E. Marcus and J. D. Swisher, OSAP Prevention Monograph 12, DHHS Publication No. ADM 92-1815 (Rockville, Md.: Department of Health and Human Services, 1992), cited in Allensworth et al., *Schools and Health,* 81–152.

25. J. D. Auerbach, C. Wypijewska, and H. K. H. Brodie, eds., *AIDS and Behavior: An Integrated Approach* (Washington, D.C.: National Academy Press, 1994).

26. D. A. Hamburg, G. R. Elliott, and D. L. Parron, eds., *Health and Behavior: Frontiers of Research in Biobehavioral Sciences* (Washington, D.C.: National Academy Press, 1982), 74–87.

27. H. C. Heller and M. L. Kiely, "HUMBIO: Stanford University's Human Biology Curriculum for the Middle Grades," in *Preparing Adolescents for the Twenty-First Century*, ed. R. Takanishi and D. A. Hamburg (Cambridge: Cambridge University Press, 1997).

28. Carnegie Council on Adolescent Development, *Great Transitions*, 92.

29. Ibid., 93.

30. Ibid.

31. D. A. Hamburg, *Today's Children*, 305–306.

32. Carnegie Council on Adolescent Development, *Matter of Time*, 9–15.

33. Ibid., 10–12.

34. Ibid., 12–13.

35. Jane Quinn, "Matter of Time Marching On," *Youth Today* (December 2002/January 2003); 37.

36. Committee on Community-Level Programs for Youth, *Community Programs to Promote Youth Development*, ed. J. Eccles and J. Appleton Gootman (Washington, D.C.: National Academy Press, 2002).

37. Ibid.

38. Ibid., 90–91.

39. Quinn, "Matter of Time Marching On," 37.

CHAPTER 7

1. M. Deutsch and M. E. Collins, *Interracial Housing: A Psychological Evaluation of a Social Experiment*, (Minneapolis: University of Minnesota Press, 1951), cited in E. Aronson, T. D. Wilson, and R. M. Akert, eds., *Social Psychology*, 4th ed. (Upper Saddle River, N.J.: Prentice Hall, 2002), 494.

2. D. G. Myers, *Social Psychology*, 3rd ed. (New York: McGraw-Hill, 1990).

3. M. Sherif and C. W. Sherif, *Groups in Harmony and Tension: An Integration of Studies on Intergroup Relations* (New York: Octagon, 1966), 271–295.

4. Myers, *Social Psychology*.

5. M. B. Brewer, "The Psychology of Prejudice: Ingroup Love or Outgroup Hate," *Journal of Social Issues* 55 (Fall 1999): 429–444.

6. G. W. Allport, "Ingroup Formation," in *The Nature of Prejudice* (Cambridge, Mass.: Addison-Wesley, 1954), cited in Brewer, "Psychology of Prejudice," 429–444.

7. M. B. Brewer and D. T. Campbell, *Ethnocentrism and Intergroup Attitudes: East African Evidence* (Beverly Hills, Calif.: Sage, 1976), cited in Brewer, "Psychology of Prejudice," 429–444.

8. H. Tajfel et al., "Social Categorization and Intergroup Behaviour," *European Journal of Social Psychology* 1 (1971): 149–178, cited in Brewer, "Psychology of Prejudice," 429–444.

9. Allport, *Nature of Prejudice*, 44, cited in Brewer, "Psychology of Prejudice," 434.

10. Brewer, "Psychology of Prejudice," 435.

11. A. Mummendey and H. Schreiber, "Better or Just Different? Positive Social Identity by Discrimination against or by Differentiation from Outgroups," *European Journal of Social Psychology*, 13 (1983): 389–397; and A. Mummendey and B. Simon, "Better or Different? III: The Impact of Importance of Comparison Dimension and Relative Ingroup Size upon intergroup Discrimination," *British Journal of Social Psychology*, 28 (1989): 1–16; both cited in Brewer, "Psychology of Prejudice," 429–444.

12. Similar finding were reported in studies by M. Gluckman, *Custom and Conflict in Africa* (Glencoe, Ill.: Free Press, 1955); R. F. Murphy, "Intergroup Hostility and Social Cohesion," *Amer-*

ican Anthropologist 59 (1957): 1018–1035; sociologists such as L. A. Coser, *The Functions of Social Conflict* (Glencoe, Ill.: Free Press, 1956); and political scientists such as G. A. Almond and S. Verba, *The Civic Culture: Political Attitudes in Five Nations* (Princeton, N.J.: Princeton University Press, 1963); S. M. Lipset, "Some Social Requisites of Democracy, Development, and Politics," *American Political Science Review* 53 (1959): 69–106; S. M. Lipset, *Political Man: The Social Bases of Politics* (Garden City, NY: Doubleday, 1960); all cited in Brewer, "Psychology of Prejudice," 429–444.

13. S. M. Lipset, "Some Social Requisites of Democracy, Development, and Politics," *American Political Science Review*, 53 (1959): 69–106, cited in Brewer, "Psychology of Prejudice," 429–444.

14. Y. Amir, "Contact Hypothesis in Ethnic Relations," *Psychological Bulletin* 71, no. 5 (May 1969): 319–342. We cite the abridged version: Amir, "Contact Hypothesis in Ethnic Relations," in *The Handbook of Interethnic Coexistence*, ed. E. Weiner (New York: Continuum, 1998), 162–181. This handbook is a valuable collection of papers on intergroup relations.

15. M. Sherif and C. W. Sherif, *Groups in Harmony and Tension: An Integration of Studies in Intergroup Relations* (New York: Harper, 1953), cited in Amir, "Contact Hypothesis," 162-181.

16. Allport, *Nature of Prejudice* (Cambridge, Mass.: Addison-Wesley, 1954); G. W. Allport and B. M. Kramer, "Some Roots of Prejudice," *Journal of Psychology*, 22 (1946): 9–39; both cited in Amir, "Contact Hypothesis," 162–181.

17. Allport, *Nature of Prejudice*, 281, cited in Amir, "Contact Hypothesis," 166.

18. Amir, "Contact Hypothesis," 162–181.

19. M. Sherif, *Group Conflict and Cooperation* (London: Routledge & Kegan Paul, 1966), cited in Amir, "Contact Hypothesis," 162–181.

20. Amir, "Contact Hypothesis," 176–178.

21. J. W. Schofield, "Promoting Positive Intergroup Relations in School Settings," in *Toward a Common Destiny: Improving Race and Ethnic Relations in America,* ed. W. D. Hawley and A. W. Jackson (San Francisco: Jossey-Bass, 1995), 257–289.

22. W. G. Stephan and C. W. Stephan, "Intergroup Anxiety," *Journal of Social Issues*, 41, no. 3 (1985): 157–175, cited in Hawley and Jackson, *Toward a Common Destiny*, 257–289.

23. W. D. Hawley et al., "Strategies for Reducing Racial and Ethnic Prejudice: Essential Principles for Program Design," in Hawley and Jackson, *Toward a Common Destiny*, 423–433.

24. Ibid., 425.

25. Ibid.

26. Ibid., 426.

27. Ibid.

28. Ibid., 427.

29. Ibid.

30. Ibid., 428.

31. Ibid., 429.

32. Ibid., 430.

33. Ibid.

34. Ibid., 431.

35. Ibid., 432.

36. Ibid.

CHAPTER 8

1. M. Vernay, "Curriculum and Instruction to Reduce Racial Conflict," *ERIC Clearinghouse on Urban Education Digest* No. 64 (April 1990), ERIC Document Reproduction Service No.

ED322274, cited in R. E. Slavin and R. Cooper, "Improving Intergroup Relations: Lessons Learned from Cooperative Learning Programs," *Journal of Social Issues* 55, no. 4 (Winter 1999): 647–663; also available online at http://eric-web.tc.columbia.edu/digest/pdf/64.pdf (accessed July 16, 2003).

2. R. Hertz-Lazarowitz and S. Sharan, "Enhancing Prosocial Behavior through Cooperative Learning in the Classroom," in *The Development and Maintenance of Prosocial Behavior: International Perspectives on Positive Morality*, ed. E. Staub et al. (New York: Plenum, 1984), 429, cited in N. Eisenberg and P. H. Mussen, *The Roots of Prosocial Behavior in Children* (Cambridge: Cambridge University Press, 1989), 95–107.

3. Ibid., 439, cited in Eisenberg and Mussen, *Roots of Prosocial Behavior,* 95–107.

4. Slavin and Cooper, "Improving Intergroup Relations," 647–663.

5. Ibid.

6. R. E. Slavin, "Synthesis of Research on Cooperative Learning," *Educational Leadership* 48 (1991): 71–82; and R. E. Slavin, "Cooperative Learning and Intergroup Relations," in *Handbook of Research on Multicultural Education*, ed. J. Banks and C. M. Banks (New York: Macmillan, 1995), 628–634; both cited in Slavin and Cooper, "Improving Intergroup Relations," 647–663.

7. R. Crain, R. Mahardand, and R. Narot, *Making Desegregation Work* (Cambridge, Mass.: Ballinger, 1982); and J. Oakes and A. Wells, "Beyond Sorting and Stratification: Creating Alternatives to Tracking in Racially Mixed Secondary Schools" (paper presented at the annual meeting of the American Educational Research Association, San Francisco, Calif., 1995); both cited in Slavin and Cooper, "Improving Intergroup Relations," 647–663.

8. W. Schwartz, "Anti-Bias Conflict Resolution Curricula: Theory and Practice," *ERIC Clearinghouse on Urban Education Digest* No. 97 (May 1994), ERIC Document Reproduction Service No. ED377255, also available online at http://www.ericfacility.net/databases/ERIC_Digests/ed377255.html (accessed July 16, 2003), cited in Slavin and Cooper, "Improving Intergroup Relations," 647–663.

9. R. E. Slavin, *Cooperative Learning: Theory, Research, and Practice*, 2nd ed. (Boston: Allyn & Bacon, 1995), cited in Slavin and Cooper, "Improving Intergroup Relations," 647–663.

10. N. A. Lopez-Reyna, "The Relation of Interactions and Story Quality among Mexican American and Anglo American Students with Learning Disabilities," *Exceptionality* 7 (1997): 245–261; R. E. Slavin, "Are Cooperative Learning and Untracking Harmful to the Gifted?" *Educational Leadership* 48, no. 6 (1991): 68–71; R. E. Slavin, "When and Why Does Cooperative Learning Increase Achievement? Theoretical and Empirical Perspectives," in *Interaction in Cooperative Groups: The Theoretical Anatomy of Group Learning*, ed. R. Hertz-Lazarowitz and N. Miller (New York: Cambridge University Press, 1992), 145–173; and R. E. Slavin, "Cooperative Learning and Intergroup Relations," in *Handbook of Research on Multicultural Education*, ed. J. Banks and C. M. Banks (New York: Macmillan, 1995), 628–634; all cited in Slavin and Cooper, "Improving Intergroup Relations," 647–663.

11. Slavin and Cooper, "Improving Intergroup Relations," 648.

12. E. Aronson et al., *The Jigsaw Classroom* (Beverly Hills, Calif.: Sage, 1978); D. W. Johnson and R. T. Johnson, "Effects of Cooperative and Individualistic Learning Experience on Interethnic Interaction," *Journal of Educational Psychology* 73 (1981): 444–449; and R. E. Slavin, *Cooperative Learning* (New York: Longman, 1983); both cited in Slavin and Cooper, "Improving Intergroup Relations," 647–663.

13. E. G. Cohen, *Designing Groupwork: Strategies for Heterogeneous Classrooms,* 2nd ed. (New York: Teachers College Press, 1994), cited in Slavin and Cooper, "Improving Intergroup Relations," 647–663.

14. D. W. Johnson, R. T. Johnson, and E. J. Holubec, *Circles of Learning: Cooperation in the*

Classroom, 4th ed. (Edina, Minn.: Interaction, 1993), cited in Slavin and Cooper, "Improving Intergroup Relations," 647–663.

15. Slavin, *Cooperative Learning: Theory, Research, and Practice,* cited in Slavin and Cooper, "Improving Intergroup Relations," 647–663.

16. These seven strategies are found in Slavin and Cooper, "Improving Intergroup Relations," 653–657. We follow their excellent description closely.

17. Slavin, *Cooperative Learning: Theory, Research, and Practice,* cited in Slavin and Cooper, "Improving Intergroup Relations," 647–663.

18. R. E. Slavin, "Effects of Biracial Learning Teams on Cross-Racial Friendships," *Journal of Educational Psychology* 71 (1979): 381–387, cited in Slavin and Cooper, "Improving Intergroup Relations," 647–663.

19. R. E. Slavin, *Using Student Team Learning,* 3rd ed. (Baltimore: Johns Hopkins University, Center for Research on Elementary and Middle Schools, 1986), cited in Slavin and Cooper, "Improving Intergroup Relations," 647–663.

20. D. L. DeVries, K. J. Edwards, and R. E. Slavin, "Biracial Learning Teams and Race Relations in the Classroom: Four Field Experiments on Teams-Games-Tournament," *Journal of Educational Psychology* 70 (1978): 356–362, cited in Slavin and Cooper, "Improving Intergroup Relations," 647–663.

21. S. Kagan et al., "Classroom Structural Bias: Impact of Cooperative and Competitive Classroom Structures on Cooperative and Competitive Individuals and Groups, in *Learning to Cooperate, Cooperating to Learn,* ed. R. E. Slavin et al. (New York: Plenum, 1985), 277–312, cited in Slavin and Cooper, "Improving Intergroup Relations," 647–663.

22. R. E. Slavin, M. Leavey, and N. A. Madden, "Combining Cooperative Learning and Individualized Instruction: Effects on Students' Mathematics Achievement, Attitudes, and Behaviors," *Elementary School Journal* 84 (1984): 409–422, cited in Slavin and Cooper, "Improving Intergroup Relations," 647–663.

23. S. Oishi, R. E. Slavin, and N. A. Madden, "Effects of Student Teams and Individualized Instruction on Cross-Race and Cross-Sex Friendships" (paper presented at the annual meeting of the American Educational Research Association, Montreal, Canada, March 1983), cited in Slavin and Cooper, "Improving Intergroup Relations," 647–663.

24. Aronson et al., *Jigsaw Classroom* (1978), cited in Slavin and Cooper, "Improving Intergroup Relations," 647–663.

25. Slavin, *Cooperative Learning: Theory, Research, and Practice,* cited in Slavin and Cooper, "Improving Intergroup Relations," 647–663.

26. S. Ziegler, "The Effectiveness of Cooperative Learning Teams for Increasing Cross-Ethnic Friendship: Additional Evidence," *Human Organization* 40 (1981): 264–268, cited in Slavin and Cooper, "Improving Intergroup Relations," 647–663.

27. D. W. Johnson and R. T. Johnson, *Learning Together and Alone: Cooperative, Competitive, and Individualist Learning,* 4th ed. (Englewood Cliffs, N.J.: Prentice Hall, 1994), cited in Slavin and Cooper, "Improving Intergroup Relations," 647–663.

28. L. Cooper, D. W. Johnson, R. Johnson, and F. Wilderson, "Effects of Cooperative, Competitive, and Individualistic Experiences on Interpersonal Attraction among Heterogeneous Peers," *Journal of Social Psychology* 111 (1980): 243–252, cited in Slavin and Cooper, "Improving Intergroup Relations," 647–663.

29. Y. Sharan and S. Sharan, *Expanding Cooperative Learning through Group Investigation* (New York: Teachers College Press, 1992), cited in Slavin and Cooper, "Improving Intergroup Relations," 647–663.

30. S. Sharan et al., *Cooperative Learning in the Classroom: Research in Desegregated Schools*

(Hillsdale, N.J.: Erlbaum, 1984), cited in Slavin and Cooper, "Improving Intergroup Relations," 647–663.

31. R. H. Weigel, P. L. Wiser, and S. W. Cook, "Impact of Cooperative Learning Experiences on Cross-Ethnic Relations and Attitudes," *Journal of Social Issues* 31 (1975): 219–245, cited in Slavin and Cooper, "Improving Intergroup Relations," 647–663.

32. A. Gonzales, "Classroom Cooperation and Ethnic Balance" (paper presented at the annual convention of the American Psychological Association, New York, August 1979); R. E. Slavin and E. Oickle, "Effects of Cooperative Learning Teams on Student Achievement and Race Relations: Treatment by Race Interactions," *Sociology of Education* 54 (1981): 174–180; and Weigel, Wiser, and Cook, "Impact of Cooperative Learning Experiences on Cross-Ethnic Relations and Attitudes"; all cited in Slavin and Cooper, "Improving Intergroup Relations," 647–663.

33. S. Hansell and R. E. Slavin, "Cooperative Learning and Structure of Interracial Friendships," *Sociology of Education* 54 (1981): 98–106; S. Hansell, "Cooperative Groups, Weak Ties, and the Integration of Peer Friendships," *Social Psychology Quarterly* 47 (1984): 316–328; and R. E. Slavin and N. A. Madden, "School Practices That Improve Race Relations," *American Educational Research Journal* 16 (1979): 169–180; all cited in Slavin and Cooper, "Improving Intergroup Relations," 647–663.

34. R. E. Slavin, "Enhancing Intergroup Relations in Schools: Cooperative Learning and Other Strategies" in *Toward a Common Destiny: Improving Race and Ethnic Relations in America*, ed. W. Hawley and A. Jackson (San Francisco: Jossey-Bass, 1995), 291–314.

CHAPTER 9

1. D. S. Elliot, B. A. Hamburg, and K. R. Williams, "An Integrated Approach to Violence Prevention," in *Violence in American Schools* (Cambridge: Cambridge University Press, 1998), 379–386.

2. U.S. Public Health Service, *Trends in the Well-Being of America's Children and Youth 2000* (Washington, D.C.: U.S. Department of Health and Human Services, 2000), 72, Table ES 3.1A.

3. Ibid., Table HC1.2.

4. Elliot, Hamburg, and Williams, "An Integrated Approach to Violence Prevention," 379–386.

5. National Research Council Institute of Medicine, Forum on Adolescence, Board on Children, Youth, and Families, *Improving Intergroup Relations among Youth* (Washington, D.C.: National Academy Press, 2000), preface and 1–24.

6. M. Deutsch, "A Framework for Thinking about Research on Conflict Resolution Training," in *The Handbook of Conflict Resolution: Theory and Practice*, ed. M. Deutsch and P. T. Coleman (San Francisco: Jossey-Bass, 2000), 571–590.

7. Ibid.

8. P. T. Coleman and M. Deutsch, "The Mediation of Interethnic Conflict in Schools," in *Toward a Common Destiny: Improving Race and Ethnic Relations in America*, ed. W. D. Hawley and A. W. Jackson (San Francisco: Jossey-Bass, 1995), 371–396.

9. M. Van Slyck and M. Stern, "Conflict Resolution in Educational Settings: Assessing the Impact of Peer Mediation Programs," in *Community Mediation: A Handbook for Practitioners and Researchers*, ed. K. G. Duffy, J. W. Grosch, and P. W. Olczak (New York: Guilford Press, 1991), 257–274.

10. M. Van Slyck, M. Stern, and J. Zak-Place, "Promoting Optimal Adolescent Development through Conflict Resolution Education, Training, and Practice: An Innovative Approach for Counseling Psychologists," *Counseling Psychologist* 24 (1996): 433–461.

11. K. S. Shepherd, "Stemming Conflict through Peer Mediation," *School Administrator* 51 (1994): 14–17.

CHAPTER 10

1. G. Repsher, "Strengthening Schools' Anti-Violence Programs," *USA Today*, June 25, 1998.

2. A. Tugend, "Peaceable Playgrounds: Do Conflict Resolution Programs Deliver on Their Promise?" *New York Times*, November 11, 2001, Education Life supplement, sec. 4A, 18.

3. D. S. Elliott, B. A. Hamburg, and K. R. Williams, eds., *Violence in American Schools* (Cambridge: Cambridge University Press, 1998), 236–252.

4. L. D. Eron et al., *Reason to Hope: A Psychosocial Perspective on Violence and Youth* (Washington, D.C.: American Psychological Association, 1994), xii.

5. Ibid.

6. R. A. Feldman, T. E. Caplinger, and J. S. Wodarski, *The St. Louis Conundrum: The Effective Treatment of Antisocial Youths* (Englewood Cliffs, N.J.: Prentice Hall, 1983); J. R. Williams and M. Gold, "From Delinquent Behavior to Official Delinquency," *Social Problems* 20 (1972): 209–229, cited in L. D. Eron et al., *Reason to Hope*, 343.

7. S. L. Jessor and R. Jessor, *Problem Behavior and Psychosocial Development* (New York: Academic Press, 1977), cited in L. D. Eron et al. *Reason to Hope*, 345.

8. U. Bronfenbrenner, *The Ecology of Human Development* (Cambridge, Mass.: Harvard University Press, 1979).

9. R. Hammond and B. Yang, "Psychology's Role in the Public Health Response to Assaultive Behavior among Young African-American Men," *American Psychologist* 48 (1993): 142–154.

10. U.S. Dept. of Health and Human Services, Public Health Service, *Healthy People 2000: National Health Promotion and Disease Prevention Objectives: Full Report, with Commentary* (Washington, D.C.: U.S. Government Printing Office, 1990), 239.

11. Ibid., 240.

12. Federal Bureau of Investigation, *Uniform Crime Reports—1991: Crime in the United States* (Washington, D.C.: U.S. Dept. of Justice, U.S. Government Printing Office, 1992).

13. D. C. Gottfreedson, "School-Based Crime Prevention," in *Preventing Crime: What Works, What Doesn't, What's Promising*, ed. L. W. Sherman et al. (Washington, D.C.: U.S. Dept. of Justice, Office of Justice Programs, 1997), v.

14. Ibid., passim.

15. National Research Council and Institute of Medicine, Committee on Integrating the Science of Early Childhood Development, *From Neurons to Neighborhoods: The Science of Early Childhood Development*, ed. J. P. Shonkoff and D. A. Phillips (Washington, D.C.: National Academy Press, 2000), 5–60.

16. M. W. Lipsey, "Juvenile Delinquency Treatment: A Meta-analytic Inquiry into the Variability of Effects," in *Meta-analysis for Explanation*, ed. T. D. Cook et al. (Beverly Hills, Calif.: Sage, 1992).

17. This figure does not include Byrne Block Grant monies, some of which fund local DARE programs. But even with the Byrne funds, expenditures on school-based prevention are meager.

18. J. Mytton et al., "School-Based Violence Prevention Programs: Systematic Review of Secondary Prevention Trials," *Archives of Pediatrics and Adolescent Medicine* 156 (August 2002): 752–762.

19. E. Aronson, *Nobody Left to Hate: Teaching Compassion after Columbine* (New York: W. H. Freeman, 2000).

20. S. Milgram, "Behavioral Study of Obedience," *Journal of Abnormal and Social Psychology* 67 (1963): 371–378.

21. Aronson, *Nobody Left to Hate*, 4–5.

22. L. Ross, T. M. Amabile, and J. L. Steinmetz, "Social Roles, Social Control, and Biases in Social-Perception Processes," *Journal of Personality and Social Psychology* 35 (1977): 485–494.

23. D. Olweus, "Bully/Victim Problems among Schoolchildren: Basic Facts and Effects of a School-Based Intervention Program," in *The Development and Treatment of Childhood Aggression*, ed. D. Pepler and K. Rubin (Hillsdale, N.J.: Erlbaum, 1991).

24. Aronson, *Nobody Left to Hate*, 135–138.

25. R. J. Bodine and D. K. Crawford, "Research Findings on What Works," in *The Handbook of Conflict Resolution Education: A Guide to Building Quality Programs in Schools* (San Francisco: Jossey-Bass, 1998), 112.

26. D. A. Hamburg, *Today's Children* (New York: Times Books, 1992); Carnegie Task Force on Meeting the Needs of Young Children, *Starting Points: Meeting the Needs of Our Youngest Children* (New York: Carnegie Corporation of New York, 1994); Carnegie Task Force on Learning in the Primary Grades, *Years of Promise: A Comprehensive Learning Strategy for America's Children* (New York: Carnegie Corporation of New York, 1996); Carnegie Council on Adolescent Development, *Great Transitions: Preparing Adolescents for a New Century* (New York: Carnegie Corporation of New York, October 1995).

27. Bodine and Crawford, *Handbook of Conflict Resolution Education*, 113–114.

CHAPTER 11

1. R. J. Bodine and D. K. Crawford, "An Overview of Exemplary Programs," 61–101, and "Research Findings on What Works," 103–114, in *The Handbook of Conflict Resolution Education: A Guide to Building Quality Programs in Schools* (San Francisco: Jossey-Bass, 1998).

2. R. Fisher, W. Ury, and B. Patton, *Getting to Yes: Negotiating Agreement without Giving In* (New York: Penguin, 1991).

3. R. Hall, "Learning Conflict Management through Peer Mediation," in *How Children Understand War and Peace,* ed. A. Raviv, L. Oppenheimer, and D. Bar-Tal (San Francisco: Jossey-Bass, 1999), 281–298.

4. J. Haynes, "Beyond Diversity: Practicing Mediation," in *Proceedings of the Second International Mediation Conference: Mediation and Cultural Diversity,* ed. D. Bagshaw (Adelaide: University of South Australia, Institute of Social Research, 1996), 119–128, cited in Raviv, Oppenheimer, and Bar-Tal, *How Children Understand War and Peace,* 281–298.

5. Hall, "Learning Conflict Management," 281–298.

6. Ibid.

7. A. M. Davis, "Dispute Resolution at an Early Age," *Negotiation Journal* (July 1986): 287–297, cited in Raviv, Oppenheimer, and Bar-Tal, *How Children Understand War and Peace*, 281–298.

8. Ibid.

9. D. W. Johnson, R. T. Johnson, D. Dudley, M. Ward, and D. Magnuson, "Impact of Peer Mediation Training on the Management of School and Home Conflicts," *American Educational Research Journal* 32 (1995): 829–844, cited in Raviv, Oppenheimer, and Bar-Tal, *How Children Understand War and Peace*, 281–298.

10. Hall, "Learning Conflict Management," 281–298.

11. Ibid.

12. R. Fisher and W. Ury, *Getting to Yes: Negotiating Agreement without Giving In* (New York: Penguin, 1983).

13. F. Schrumpf, D. K. Crawford, and R. J. Bodine, *Peer Mediation: Conflict Resolution in Schools: Program Guide* (Champaign, Ill.: Research Press, 1997).

14. R. J. Bodine and D. K. Crawford, *The Peaceable School: A Comprehensive Guide for Teaching Conflict Resolution* (Champaign, Ill.: Research Press, 1994).

15. Bodine and Crawford, *Handbook of Conflict Resolution Education*, 77.

16. Ibid.

17. W. Ury, *Getting to Peace* (New York: Penguin, 1999), 114–139.

18. Bodine and Crawford, *Handbook of Conflict Resolution Education*, 103.

19. Ibid., 61–101, 103–114.

CHAPTER 12

1. D. A. Hamburg, *No More Killing Fields: Preventing Deadly Conflict* (Lanham, Md.: Rowman & Littlefield, 2002), 87–111.

2. Carnegie Council on Adolescent Development, Task Force on Education of Young Adolescents, *Turning Points: Preparing American Youth for the 21st Century* (New York: Carnegie Corporation of New York, June 1989), 45.

3. A. W. Jackson and G. A. Davis, *Turning Points 2000: Educating Adolescents in the 21st Century* (New York: Teachers College Press, Carnegie Council on Adolescent Development, 2000), 211–213.

4. D. A. Hamburg, *Today's Children: Creating a Future for a Generation in Crisis* (New York: Times Books, 1992), 260–262.

5. Carnegie Council on Adolescent Development, *Turning Points: Preparing American Youth*, 70–71.

6. Jackson and Davis, *Turning Points 2000: Educating Adolescents*, 211.

7. Ibid.

8. B. A. Hamburg, "Teaching Life Skills," 260–262.

9. D. A. Hamburg, *Today's Children*, 317–318.

10. Campus Compact, "Structure and Organization" (Providence, R.I.: Campus Compact, rev. 2003), http://www.compact.org/aboutcc/structure.html (accessed July 16, 2003); Campus Compact, "Our Mission" (Providence, R.I.: Campus Compact, rev. 2003), http://www.compact.org/aboutcc/mission.html (accessed July 16, 2003).

11. Campus Compact, "Building the Service Learning Pyramid" (Providence, R.I.: Campus Compact, n.d.), http://www.compact.org/faculty/specialreport.html (accessed July 16, 2003).

12. J. Youniss and M. Yates, *Community Service and Social Responsibility in Youth* (Chicago: University of Chicago Press, 1997), 1–19.

13. V. A. Hodgkinson and M. S. Weitzman, *Volunteering and Giving among American Teenagers 14 to 17 Years of Age* (Washington, D.C.: Independent Sector, 1990), cited in Youniss and Yates, *Community Service*, 18.

14. H. C. Boyte, "Community Service and Service Education," *Phi Delta Kappan* 72 (1991): 765–767; J. Kahne and J. Westheimer, "In the Service of What? The Politics of Service-Learning," *Phi Delta Kappan* 74 (1996): 593–599; and R. D. Logan, "Youth Volunteerism and Instrumentality: A Commentary, Rationale, and Proposal," *Journal of Voluntary Action Research* 14 (1985): 45–50; all cited in Youniss and Yates, *Community Service*, 17.

15. Youniss and Yates, *Community Service*, 135–153.

16. Corporation for National and Community Service, *Principles for High Quality National Service Programs* (Washington, D.C.: Corporation for National and Community Service, 1994); and Alliance for Service Learning in Education Reform, "Standards of Quality for School-Based and Community-Based Service-Learning," *Equity and Excellence in Education* 26 (1993): 71–73; both cited in Youniss and Yates, *Community Service*, 135–136.

17. Youniss and Yates, *Community Service*, 136.

18. Kahne and Westheimer, "In the Service of What?" cited in Youniss and Yates, *Community Service*, 138.

19. K. K. Townsend, "The Most Important Lesson Our Schools Don't Teach," *St. Petersburg Times*, December 27, 1992, p. 1D; and H. Wofford, "Confirmation of Harris Wofford as CEO of the National Corporation for National and Community Service," in *Hearings of the U.S. Senate Labor and Human Resources Committee*, September 7, 1995; both cited in Youniss and Yates, *Community Service*, 139.

20. M. Fine, *Framing Dropouts: Notes on the Politics of an Urban Public High School* (Albany: State University of New York Press, 1991), cited in Youniss and Yates, *Community Service*, 141.

21. D. McAdam, *Freedom Summer* (New York: Oxford University Press, 1988); J. Fendrich, *Ideal Citizens* (Albany: State University of New York Press, 1993); and W. Gamson, *Talking Politics* (Cambridge: Harvard University Press, 1992), cited in Youniss and Yates, *Community Service*, 142.

22. A. J. Kropp, "Kids Need Responsibility," *USA Today*, April 20, 1994, p. 12A, cited in Youniss and Yates, *Community Service*, 142.

23. P. V. Cognetta and N. A. Sprinthall, "Students as Teachers: Role Taking as a Means of Promoting Psychological and Ethical Development During Adolescence," in *Value Development as the Aim of Education*, ed. N. A. Sprinthall and R. L. Mosher (Schenectady, N.Y.: Character Research Press, 1978), 53–68; D. Conrad and D. Hedin, "The Impact of Experiential Education on Adolescent Development," *Child and Youth Services: Youth Participation and Experiential Education* [Special issue] 4 (1982): 57–76; S. Hamilton and M. Fenzel, "The Impact of Volunteer Experience on Adolescent Social Development," *Journal of Adolescent Research* 3 (1988): 65–80; R. A. Rutter and F. M. Newmann, "The Potential of Community Service to Enhance Civic Responsibility," *Social Education* 53 (1989): 371–374; and A. Schlosberg, "Seven-Year Follow-up of an Adolescent Volunteer Program in a Psychiatric Hospital," *Hospital and Community Psychiatry* 42 (1991): 532–533; all cited in Youniss and Yates, *Community Service*, 143.

24. National Commission on Service-Learning, "Executive Summary," in *Learning in Deed: The Power of Service-Learning for American Schools* (Battle Creek, Mich.: W. K. Kellogg Foundation, January 2002), also available online at http://www.learningindeed.org/slcommission/executive_summary.pdf (accessed July 16, 2003).

25. National Commission on Service-Learning, "Service-Learning Satisfies Young People's Desire for Public Service" (Washington, D.C.: National Commission on Service-Learning, January 28, 2002), also available online at http://servicelearningcommission.org/slcommission/press-rel.html (accessed July 16, 2003).

26. National Commission on Service-Learning, "Executive Summary: A Letter from Senator John Glenn" (p. 2 of online version).

27. National Commission on Service-Learning, "Executive Summary," 11.

28. A. Melchior, *Summary Report, National Evaluation of Learn and Serve America* (Waltham, Mass.: Brandeis University, Center for Human Resources, July 1999), also available online at http://heller.brandeis.edu/chr/LSReport.pdf (accessed July 16, 2003), cited in National Commission on Service-Learning, "Full Report," in *Learning in Deed: The Power of Service-Learning for American Schools* (Battle Creek, Mich.: W. K. Kellogg, 2002), p. 29, also available online at http://www.learningindeed.org/slcommission/learningindeed.pdf (accessed July 16, 2003).

29. Learning in Deed, "Service-Learning at a Glance" (New York: National Commission on Service-Learning, n.d.), http://learningindeed.org/tools/glance.html (accessed July 16, 2003).

30. Ibid.

31. National Commission on Service-Learning, "Executive Summary," 5, 16–17.

32. Carnegie Council on Adolescent Development, Task Force on Youth Development and Community Programs, *A Matter of Time: Risk and Opportunity in the Nonschool Hours* (New York: Carnegie Corporation of New York, 1992), 35–37.

33. S. Sagawa, "Ten Years of Youth in Service to America," in *The Forgotten Half Revisited: American Youth and Young Families, 1988–2008*, ed. S. Halperin (Washington, D.C.: American Youth Policy Forum, 1998).

CHAPTER 13

1. E. Hamburg and D. A. Hamburg, "The Powerful Worldwide Reach of Mass Media: Can Media Help to Prevent Deadly Conflict?" (working paper for the Burkle Center for International Relations, University of California, Los Angeles, July 2002).

2. D. Self, writer, *Thirteen Days* (Los Angeles: New Line Cinema with Beacon Pictures), 2001.

3. Hamburg and Hamburg, "Powerful Worldwide Reach of Mass Media."

4. R. M. Liebert, J. M. Neale, and E. S. Davidson, *The Early Window: Effects of Television on Children and Youth* (New York: Pergamon Press, 1973), cited in N. Eisenberg and P. Mussen, *The Roots of Prosocial Behavior in Children* (Cambridge: Cambridge University Press, 1989), 103.

5. L. D. Eron, "The Development of Aggressive Behavior from the Perspective of a Developing Behaviorism," *American Psychologist* 42 (1987): 435–442; L. D. Eron et al., "Does Television Violence Cause Aggression?" *American Psychologist* 27 (1972): 253–263, cited in Eisenberg and Mussen, *Roots of Prosocial Behavior*, 103.

6. J. G. Johnson et al., "Television Viewing and Aggressive Behavior During Adolescence and Adulthood," *Science* 295 (March 29, 2002): 2468–2471.

7. A. C. Huston et al., *Big World, Small Screen: The Role of Television in American Society* (Lincoln: University of Nebraska Press, 1992); Johnson et al., "Television Viewing and Aggressive Behavior," 2468–2471; F. M. Hechinger, *Fateful Choices: Healthy Youth for the 21st Century* (New York: Hill and Wang, 1992).

8. C. A. Anderson and B. J. Bushman, "The Effects of Media Violence on Society," *Science* 295 (March 29, 2002): 2377.

9. Ibid.

10. Ibid., 2377–2379.

11. Ibid.

12. National Institute of Mental Health, "Television and Behavior: Ten Years of Scientific Progress and Implications for the Eighties," Vol. 1: Summary Report (Rockville, Md.: U.S. Department of Health and Human Services, 1982).

13. R. Hobbs, "Teaching Media Literacy—Yo! Are You Hip to This?" *Media Studies Journal* 8, no. 4 (1994), 135–145.

14. G. S. Lesser, "The Role of Television in Moving beyond Hate" (paper presented at conference on Beyond Hate, organized by Elie Wiesel, Boston University, March 19, 1989). Paper available from Prof. G. Lesser at Harvard University.

15. S. E. Mendelson and J. K. Glenn, *Democracy Assistance and NGO Strategies in Post-Communist Societies* (Washington, D.C.: Carnegie Endowment for International Peace, 2000), 25–29.

16. A. C. Huston et al., *Big World, Small Screen*.

17. American Psychological Association, "Violence and Youth," available at http://www.apa.org/pi/pii/violenceandyouth.pdf. (See pp. 32–35.) Accessed August 29, 2003.

18. Johnson et al., "Television Viewing and Aggressive Behavior," 2468–2471.

19. Ibid.

20. Ibid.

21. Ibid.

22. Ibid.

23. Ibid.

24. Anderson and Bushman, "Effects of Media Violence on Society," 2377–2379.

25. L. K. Friedrich and A. H. Stein, "Aggressive and Prosocial Television Programs and the Natural Behavior of Preschool Children," *Monographs of the Society for Research in Child Development* 38, no. 4, serial no. 151, (1973): 1–64, cited in Eisenberg and Mussen, "Socialization by Agents outside the Family," 103.

26. N. Eisenberg and P. Mussen, "Socialization by Agents Outside the Family," in *Roots of Prosocial Behavior*, 103–104.

27. I. M. Ahammer and J. P. Murray, "Kindness in the Kindergarten: "The Relative Influence of Role Playing and Prosocial Television in Facilitating Altruism," *International Journal of Behavioral Development* 2 (1979): 133–157, cited in Eisenberg and Mussen, "Socialization by Agents Outside the Family," 105.

28. J. P. Rushton, "Television as a Socializer," in *Altruism and Helping Behavior*, ed. J. P. Rushton and R. M. Sorrentino (Hillsdale, N.J.: Erlbaum, 1981), 95, cited in Eisenberg and Mussen, "Socialization by Agents Outside the Family," 105.

29. Eisenberg and Mussen, "Socialization by Agents Outside the Family," 106.

30. Lesser, "Role of Television."

31. S. M. Fisch, R. T. Truglio, C. F. Cole, "The Impact of *Sesame Street* on Preschool Children: A Review and Synthesis of 30 Years' Research," *Media Psychology* 1 (1999): 165–190.

32. J. G. Cooney, *The Potential Uses of Television in Preschool Education: A Report to the Carnegie Corporation of New York* (New York: Carnegie Corporation, 1966), cited in Fisch, Truglio, and Cole, "Impact of *Sesame Street*," 167.

33. S. Ball and G. A. Bogatz, *The First Year of Sesame Street: An Evaluation* (Princeton, N.J.: Educational Testing Service, 1970); and G. A. Bogatz and S. Ball, *The Second Year of Sesame Street: A Continuing Evaluation* (Princeton, N.J.: Educational Testing Service, 1971), both cited in Huston et al., *"G" Is for Growing*, 135.

34. T. D. Cook et al., *Sesame Street Revisited* (New York: Russell Sage Foundation, 1975), cited in Fisch, Truglio, and Cole, "Impact of *Sesame Street*," 168.

35. R. A. Reiser, M. A. Tessmer, and P. C. Phelps, "Adult-Child Interaction in Children's Learning from *Sesame Street*," *Educational Communication and Technology Journal* 32 (1984): 217–223; and R. A. Reiser, N. Williamson, and K. Suzuki, "Using *Sesame Street* to Facilitate Children's Recognition of Letters and Numbers," *Educational Communication and Technology Journal* 36 (1988): 15–21; both cited in Fisch, Truglio, and Cole, "Impact of *Sesame Street*," 169.

36. J. C. Wright and A. C. Huston, "Effects of Educational TV Viewing of Lower Income Preschoolers on Academic Skills, School Readiness, and School Adjustment One to Three Years Later: A Report to the Children's Television Workshop" (Lawrence: University of Kansas, Center for Research on the Influences of Television on Children, May 1995), cited in Fisch, Truglio, and Cole, "Impact of *Sesame Street*," 169.

37. Bogatz, and Ball, *Second Year of Sesame Street: A Continuing Evaluation*, cited in Fisch, Truglio, and Cole, "Impact of *Sesame Street*," 169.

38. N. Zill, E. Davies, and M. Daly, "Viewing of *Sesame Street* by Preschool Children and Its Relationship to School Readiness: Report Prepared for the Children's Television Workshop" (Rockville, Md.: Westat, 1994), cited in Fisch, Truglio, and Cole, "Impact of *Sesame Street*," 170.

39. D. N. Anderson et al., "*Sesame Street* and Educational Television for Children," in *A Communications Cornucopia: Markle Foundation Essays on Information Policy*, ed. R. G. Noll and M. E. Price (Washington, D.C.: Brookings Institute, 1998), 279–296, cited in Fisch, Truglio, and Cole, "Impact of *Sesame Street*," 170.

40. G. S. Lesser, *Children and Television: Lessons from Sesame Street* (New York: Vintage/Random House, 1974), cited in Fisch, Truglio, and Cole, "Impact of *Sesame Street*," 171.

41. F. L. Paulson, "Teaching Cooperation on Television: An Evaluation of *Sesame Street* Social Goals Programs," *AV Communication Review* 22 (1974): 229–246, cited in Fisch, Truglio, and Cole, "Impact of *Sesame Street*," 174.

42. C. P. Bankart and C. C. Anderson, "Short-Term Effects of Prosocial Television Viewing on Play of Preschool Boys and Girls," *Psychological Reports* 44 (1979): 935–941; and A. D. Leifer, "How to Encourage Socially-Valued Behavior" (paper presented at the biennial meeting of the Society for Research in Child Development, Denver, Colo., April 1975), ERIC Document Reproduction Service No. ED114175; both cited in Fisch, Truglio, and Cole, "Impact of *Sesame Street*," 174.

43. Bankart and Anderson, "Short-Term Effects of Prosocial Television Viewing," 935–941, cited in Fisch, Truglio, and Cole, "Impact of *Sesame Street*," 174.

44. I. E. Zielinska and B. Chambers, "Using Group Viewing of Television to Teach Preschool Children Social Skills," *Journal of Educational Television* 21 (1995): 85–99, cited in Fisch, Truglio, and Cole, "Impact of *Sesame Street*," 174.

45. Bankart and Anderson, "Short-Term Effects of Prosocial Television Viewing," 935–941, cited in Fisch, Truglio, and Cole, "Impact of *Sesame Street*," 175.

46. Joan Ganz Cooney, founder of Children's Television Workshop and key collaborator in *Sesame Street* from its inception, conversation with author (D. A. Hamburg), May 2002, New York City.

47. G. A. Kohnstam and H. Cammaer, *Sesamstraat: Preliminary Results of a Variety of Studies on the Reception of a 20-Part Series* (Hilversum: Netherlands Broadcasting Foundation, 1976), cited in Fisch, Truglio, and Cole, "Impact of *Sesame Street*," 182.

48. R. Diaz-Guerrero and W. H. Holtzman, "Learning by Televised *Plaza Sésamo* in Mexico," *Journal of Educational Psychology* 66 (1974): 632–643, cited in Fisch, Truglio, and Cole, "Impact of *Sesame Street*," 182.

49. N. Sahin, "Preschoolers' Learning from Educational Television" (paper presented at the 25th International Congress of Psychology, Brussels, Belgium, July 1992); and UNICEF, "Executive Summary: Summary Assessment of *Plaza Sésamo* IV—Mexico" (English translation of unpublished report, Mexico City: UNICEF, 1996), cited in Fisch, Truglio, and Cole, "Impact of *Sesame Street*," 183.

50. "Ulitza Sezam," Department of Research and Content (November 1998), "Preliminary Report of Summative Findings" (oral presentation to Children's Television Workshop, New York City), cited in Fisch, Truglio, and Cole, "Impact of *Sesame Street*," 184.

51. *Early Childhood Matters* [journal of the Bernard van Leer Foundation], no. 90 (October 1998). Available from http://www.bernardvanleer.org/page.asp?pid=26 (accessed July 16, 2003).

52. Epitome Pictures, "Productions" (Toronto, Canada: Epitome Pictures, Inc., rev. 2000), http://www.epitomepictures.com/productions.html (accessed July 16, 2003).

53. "*Degrassi*: The Next Generation" (Toronto, Canada: Epitome Virtual Reality Inc., rev. 2003), http://www.degrassi.ca (accessed July 16, 2003).

54. Carnegie Corporation of New York, Agenda Book, Agenda Item: description of grant made to WGBH Educational Foundation, December 10, 1987, pp. 78–81.

55. Ibid.

CHAPTER 14

1. H. Lebo, *The UCLA Internet Report 2000: Surveying the Digital Future* (Los Angeles: UC Regents, November 2000), 4–5.

2. Lebo, *UCLA Report 2000*, 5.

3. H. Lebo, *The UCLA Internet Report 2001: Surveying the Digital Future, Year Two* (Los Angeles: UC Regents, November 2001), 56–57.

4. E. Boland, "In Modern E-Mail Romances, 'Trash' Is Just a Click Away," *New York Times*, October 19, 1999, sec. G, 8L; K. Hafner, "Did You Get Her E-mail Address?" *New York Times*, January 14, 1999, sec. G, 1L; B. Rothman Morris, "You've Got Romance: Seeking Love Online," *New York Times*, August 26, 1999, sec. G, 1L; D. Schoeneman, "Don't Be Shy, Ladies—Google Him! Check Out His Search Engine First," *New York Observer*, 15 January 2001, 1.

5. *UCLA News*, "Study by UCLA Internet Project Shows E-mail Transformed Personal Communication after Sept. 11 Attacks" (rev. February 6, 2002), available from http://newsroom.ucla.edu/ (accessed July 16, 2003).

6. *Columbia Encyclopedia*, 6th ed. (2001). Available online at www.bartleby.com/65/in/Internet.htm (accessed September 4, 2003).

7. Ibid.

8. Kaiser Family Foundation, *Kids and Media at the New Millennium: A Comprehensive National Analysis of Children's Media Use* (Menlo Park, CA: Kaiser Family Foundation, November 1999), 8, 33.

9. Kaiser, *Kids and Media*, 39, 51.

10. Lebo, *UCLA Report 2001*, 32, 78–79.

11. E. Wartella, B. O'Keefe, and R. Scantlin, *Growing Up with Interactive Media: What We Know and What We Don't about the Impact of New Media on Children* (New York: Markle Foundation, May 2000), 3, 6–8.

12. Wartella, O'Keefe, and Scantlin, *Growing Up with Interactive Media*, 6. The National Alliance has developed and produced video hate games that teach hate and racism. The makers of these violent, vividly real games reportedly wish to produce movies as well.

13. "Geography and the Net: Putting It in Its Place" *The Economist*, August 11, 2001, 18–20.

14. N. Thompson, "Gofer Broke," *Washington Monthly*, November 2001, http://www.washingtonmonthly.com/books/2001/0111.thompson.html (accessed July 16, 2003).

15. Aspen Institute and A. Briggs, "The Public Interest: An International Perspective," in *In Search of the Public Interest in the New Media Environment* (Washington, D.C.: Aspen Institute, 2002), 34–36.

16. Aspen Institute, "Public Interest," 41.

17. B. Gellman, "Cyber-Attacks by Al Qaeda Feared," *Washington Post*, June 27, 2002, http://www.washingtonpost.com/wp-dyn/articles/A50765-2002Jun26.html (accessed July 16, 2003).

18. S. Kalathil and T. C. Boas, *The Internet and State Control in Authoritarian Regimes: China, Cuba, and the Counterrevolution* (Washington, D.C.: Carnegie Endowment, 2001).

19. Aspen Institute, "Public Interest," 32–34.

20. M. Potok, "Internet Hate and the Law," *Southern Poverty Law Center's Intelligence Report*, no. 97 (Winter 2000): 48–49.

21. Southern Poverty Law Center, "The Year in Hate," *Southern Poverty Law Center's Intelligence Report*, no. 105 (Spring 2002), http://www.splcenter.org/intelligenceproject/ip-4u1.html (accessed July 16, 2003).

22. M. A. Lee, "The Swastika & the Crescent," *Southern Poverty Law Center's Intelligence Re-*

port, no. 105 (Spring 2002), http://www.splcenter.org/intelligenceproject/ip-4u3.html (accessed July 16, 2003).

23. Student Press Law Center, "Supreme Court Hears Arguments in Internet Filtering Case" (rev. March 5, 2003), available from http://www.splc.org/newsflash.asp?id=567 (accessed August 9, 2003).

24. Potok, "Internet Hate and the Law," 48–49.

25. Ibid., 49.

26. Ibid.

27. D. E. Kaplan and L. Kim, "Nazism's New Global Threat: The Internet Helps Build a Sophisticated Web of Violent, Well-Funded Racists," *U.S. News and World Report*, 25 (September 2000): 34–35.

28. Kaplan and Kim, "Nazism's New Global Threat," 34.

29. Ibid.

30. Ibid.

31. Conflict Research Consortium, *The Conflict Resolution Information Source* (rev. 2003), http://www.crinfo.org (accessed July 16, 2003).

32. Governor's Advisory Panel on Hate Groups, *Final Report* (January 2000), http://www.governor.ca.gov/govsite/pdf/report3.pdf (July 16, 2003).

33. Office of the Governor, "Governor Davis Signs Civil Rights Legislation" [Press release] (October 1, 2000), available from http://www.governor.ca.gov/ (accessed July 16, 2003).

34. Governor's Advisory Panel on Hate Groups, *Final Report*, 42.

35. Ibid., 41.

36. Anti-Defamation League, Caryl Stern-LaRosa, Ellen Hofheimer Bettmann, *Hate Hurts: How Children Learn and Unlearn Prejudice* (New York: Scholastic, 2000).

37. UNESCO and AED, *Technologies for Education: Potentials, Parameters, and Prospects*, ed. W. D. Haddad and A. Draxler (Paris: UNESCO and AED, 2002), 4. The entire book is available for download from http://www.aed.org/publications/TechEdInfo.html (accessed July 28, 2003).

38. Markle Foundation, "Markle Releases Major Study on Governing the Internet" (July 10, 2001), http://www.markle.org/news/_news_pressrelease_071001.stm (July 16, 2003). The report of the Digital Opportunity Initiative is available from http://www.opt-init.org/framework.html (accessed July 28, 2003).

39. UNESCO and AED, *Technologies for Education*, 4–6.

40. Ibid., 6–9.

41. Ibid., 8.

42. Ibid., 9–16.

43. Accenture, Markle Foundation, and UNDP, *Creating a Development Dynamic: Final Report of the Digital Opportunity Initiative* (New York: Digital Opportunity Initiative, 2001), 10–11.

44. K. Hafner, "Lessons Learned at Dot-Com U.," *New York Times*, Circuits section, May 2, 2002.

45. D. Ekbladh, *Education for Peace in the 21st Century: A Report on the Advisory Meeting on the Academic Program of the University for Peace* (New York: United Nations, University for Peace, March 23–24, 2001), also available online at http://www.upeace.org/documents/news/ny_report.pdf (accessed July 16, 2003).

46. This was a factor in writing this book. Several Web sites that illustrated the positive use of the Web in education folded while we were writing the book. Although all sites that are listed here were up-to-date on the access dates listed, there can be no guarantee of their current addresses, status, or content.

47. United Nations, *Cyberschoolbus* (2003), http://www0.un.org/cyberschoolbus/index.asp (accessed July 16, 2003).

48. Just Kid Inc., *An Environmental Scan of Children's Interactive Media from 2000 to 2002* (New York: Markle Foundation, June 2002).

49. New York State United Teachers, "Honing Classroom Computer Skills," *New York Teacher*, April 21, 1997, http://www.nysut.org/newyorkteacher/backissues/1997-1998/970421computers.html (accessed July 16, 2003); New York State United Teachers, "Getting Wired into High-Tech," *New York Teacher*, October 20, 1997, http://www.nysut.org/newyorkteacher/backissues/1997-1998/971020nywired.html (accessed July 16, 2003).

50. New York State United Teachers, "Teachers Talk About Test Stress," *New York Teacher*, November 8, 2000, 4, also available online at http://www.nysut.org/newyorkteacher/2000-2001/001108testing.html (accessed July 16, 2003).

51. Ibid.

52. Ibid., 5.

53. Luis F. Rivera, "Overcrowded and Overwhelmed," *New York Teacher*, November 8, 2000.

54. J. Seely Brown, "Where Have all the Computers Gone?" *Technology Review*, January/February 2001, http://www.technologyreview.com/articles/brown0101.asp (accessed July 16, 2003).

CHAPTER 15

1. D. A. Hamburg, "Crowding, Stranger Contact, and Aggressive Behavior," in *Society, Stress, and Disease*, vol. 1, ed. L. Levi (New York: Oxford University Press, 1971), 209-218.

2. M. Coeyman, "The Rush to Rewrite History," *Christian Science Monitor*, October 16, 2001, also available online from http://www.csmonitor.com (accessed July 16, 2003).

3. C. M. Barker, *Education for International Understanding and Global Competence* (New York: Carnegie Corporation of New York, 2000), 2.

4. F. M. Hayward and L. M. Siaya, *Public Experience, Attitudes, and Knowledge: A Report on Two National Surveys about International Education* (Washington, D.C.: American Council on Education, 2000), 7-9.

5. F. M. Hayward, *Preliminary Status Report 2000, Internationalization of U.S. Higher Education* (Washington, D.C.: American Council on Education, 2000), 3.

6. H. T. Collins, F. Czarra, and A. F. Smith, "Guidelines for Global and International Studies Education: Challenges, Cultures, and Connections," *Social Education* 62, no. 5 (September 1998): 311-317.

7. Ibid., 313.

8. T. Koh, "The Ignorance on Both Sides Can Cause Trouble," *International Herald Tribune*, July 26, 2001, http://www.iht.com/ihtsearch.php?id=27279&owner=(IHT)&date=20021224041227 (accessed July 16, 2003).

9. N. K. Steinemann, E. B. Fiske, and V. Sackett, *Asia in the Schools: Preparing Young Americans for Today's Interconnected World* (New York: Asia Society, 2001), 65-67.

10. Steinemann, Fiske, and Sackett, "Asia in the Schools," 34.

11. Ibid., 35.

12. Ibid., 38-54.

13. Ibid., 47.

14. Ibid., 48.

15. Asia Society, "The Bill and Melinda Gates Foundation and the Asia Society Announce $7.5 Million Initiative for Urban International Studies Secondary Schools" (press release by New York Asia Society), September 17, 2003.

16. Foreign Policy Association, "Great Decisions Discussion Program" brochure (September 2003). More information on the Great Decisions Discussion Program is available at the Foreign Policy Association's Web site, www.fpa.org.

17. Steinemann, Fiske, and Sackett, *Asia in the Schools*, 56–64.

18. National Coalition on Asia and International Studies in the Schools (meeting in Washington, D.C., at the National Alliance of Business, attended and reported on by research associate for D. A. and B. A. Hamburg), May 29, 2002.

CHAPTER 16

1. A. M. Stomfay-Stitz, *Peace Education in America, 1828–1990: Sourcebook for Education and Research* (Metuchen, N.J.: Scarecrow Press, 1993), 322–347.

2. I. M. Harris, "Types of Peace Education," in *How Children Understand War and Peace*, ed. Amiram Raviv, Louis Oppenheimer, and Daniel Bar-Tal (San Francisco: Jossey-Bass, 1999), 299–317.

3. M. Montessori, *Education for Peace* (1939; reprint, Washington, D.C.: Regnery, 1972).

4. V. Bernat, "Teaching peace," *Young Children* 48, no. 3 (1993): 36–39; and N. Carlsson-Paige and D. Levin, *Helping Young Children Understand Peace, War, and the Nuclear Threat* (Washington, D.C.: National Association for the Education of Young Children, 1985); both cited in *How Children Understand War and Peace*, ed. A. Raviv, L. Oppenheimer, and D. Bar-Tal (San Francisco: Jossey-Bass, 1999), 299–317.

5. R. Feltman, "Change in Peace Attitude: A Controlled Attitude Change Study of Internationalism," *Peace Research* 18, no. 1 (1986): 66–71; P. French, "Preventive Medicine for Nuclear War," *Psychology Today* (September 1984): 70; and J. K. Lyou, "Studying Nuclear Weapons: The Effect on Students," *Peace Research* 19, no. 1 (1987): 11–18; all cited in Raviv, Oppenheimer, and Bar-Tal, *How Children Understand War and Peace*, 299–317.

6. I. M. Harris, "The Challenge of Peace Education: Do Our Efforts Make a Difference?" *Educational Foundations* 6, no. 4 (1992): 75–98, cited in Raviv, Oppenheimer, and Bar-Tal, *How Children Understand War and Peace*, 299–317.

7. D. W. Johnson, R. T. Johnson, and B. Dudley, "Effects of Peer Mediation Training on Elementary Students," *Mediation Quarterly* 10, no. 1 (1992): 89–99, cited in Raviv, Oppenheimer, and Bar-Tal, *How Children Understand War and Peace*, 299–317.

8. L. Lantieri and J. Patti, *Waging Peace in Our Schools* (Boston: Beacon Press, 1996), cited in Raviv, Oppenheimer, and Bar-Tal, *How Children Understand War and Peace*, 299–317.

9. L. Stevahn et al., "The Impact of a Cooperative or Individualistic Context on the Effectiveness of Conflict Resolution Training," *American Education Research Journal* 33, no. 4 (1996): 801–824, cited in Raviv, Oppenheimer, and Bar-Tal, *How Children Understand War and Peace*, 299–317.

10. Metis Associates, *The Resolving Conflict Creatively Program, 1988–1989: A Summary of Recent Findings* (New York: Metis Associates, 1990), cited in Raviv, Oppenheimer, and Bar-Tal, *How Children Understand War and Peace*, 299–317.

11. D. Prothrow-Stith, *Deadly Consequences* (New York: HarperCollins, 1991), cited in Raviv, Oppenheimer, and Bar-Tal, *How Children Understand War and Peace*, 299–317.

12. D. C. Grossman et al., "Effectiveness of Violence Prevention Curriculum among Children in Elementary School: A Randomized Controlled Trial," *Journal of the American Medical Association* 277, no. 20 (May 28, 1997): 1605–1611, cited in Raviv, Oppenheimer, and Bar-Tal, *How Children Understand War and Peace*, 299–317.

13. M. King, *Mahatma Gandhi and Martin Luther King, Jr.: The Power of Nonviolent Action* (Paris: UNESCO, 1999), 419–420.

14. Carnegie Commission on Preventing Deadly Conflict, *Preventing Deadly Conflict* (New York: Carnegie Corporation of New York), 125–127.

15. B. A. Reardon, "Peace Education: A Review and Projection," *Peace Education Reports* 17 (August 1999): 1–48.

16. Ibid., 4.

17. UNESCO, "Declaration and Integrated Framework of Action on Education for Peace, Human Rights, and Democracy," IBE, Geneva, 1994.

18. R. A. Hinde and P. Bateson, "Some Goals in Education for Peace," in *Education for Peace*, ed. R. A. Hinde and D. A. Parry (Nottingham, U.K.: Bertrand Russell House, 1989), 10–17.

19. D. A. Hamburg, *No More Killing Fields: Preventing Deadly Conflict* (Lanham, Md.: Rowman & Littlefield, 2002), 87–113.

20. R. Hinde and L. Pulkkinen, "Human Aggressiveness and War," *Pugwash Occasional Papers* 2 (September 2001): 5–37.

21. *Aggression* is used here to refer to behavior directed toward harming others, and *aggressiveness* refers to the motivation to cause harm to others. Harm may also arise in other ways —for instance, one individual may harm another accidentally or because it is his or her duty to do so.

22. L. Pulkkinen, "Levels of Longitudinal Data Differing in Complexity and the Study of Continuity in Personality Characteristics," in *Methods and Models for Studying the Individual*, ed. R. B. Cairns, L. R. Bergman, and J. Kagan (Beverly Hills, Calif.: Sage, 1998), 161–184, cited in Hinde and Pulkinnen, "Human Aggressiveness and War," 5–37.

23. A. Blumstein, J. Cohen, and D. Farrington, "Criminal Career Research: Its Value for Criminology, *Criminology* 26 (1988): 57–74, cited in Hinde and Pulkinnen, "Human Aggressiveness and War," 5–37.

24. R. Loeb and D. Hay, "Key Issues in the Development of Aggression and Violence from Childhood to Early Adulthood," *Annual Review of Psychology* 48 (1997): 371–410, cited in Hinde and Pulkinnen, "Human Aggressiveness and War," 5–37.

25. J. D. Coie and K. A. Dodge, "Aggression and Anti-Social Behavior," pp. 777–862; J. McCord, "Parental Behavior in the Cycle of Aggression," *Psychiatry* 51 (1988): pp. 14–23; and M. Rothbart and J. Bates, "Temperament," pp. 105–176, in *Handbook of Child Psychology*, vol. 3, ed. W. Damon and N. Eisenberg (1998); also B. Martin, "Parent-Child Relations," in *Review of Child Development Research* 4, ed. F. D. Horowitz (Chicago: Chicago University Press, 1975); all four sources cited in Hinde and Pulkinnen, "Human Aggressiveness and War," 5–37.

26. D. Baumrind, "Current Patterns of Parental Authority," *Developmental Psychology Monographs* 4, no. 1 (1971); R. A. Hinde, A. Tamplin and J. Barrett, "Home Correlates of Aggression in Preschool," *Aggressive Behavior* 19 (1993): 85–105. Both are cited in Hinde and Pulkinnen, "Human Aggressiveness and War," 5–37.

27. D. G. Pruitt, "Aggressive Behavior in Interpersonal and International Relations," in *Perspectives on Deterrence*, ed. P. C. Stern et al. (New York: Oxford University Press, 1989); and D. Archer and R. Gartner, *Violence and Crime in Cross-National Perspective* (New Haven: Yale University Press, 1984); both cited in Hinde and Pulkinnen, "Human Aggressiveness and War," 5–37.

28. L. Pulkkinen, "Children and Violence: A Developmental Perspective," *European Review* 4 (1996): 61–74, cited in Hinde and Pulkinnen, "Human Aggressiveness and War," 5–37.

29. C. Liddell, J. Kemp, and M. Moema, "The Young Lions: South African Children and Youth in Political Struggle," in *The Psychological Effects of War and Violence on Children*, ed. L. A. Leavitt and N. A. Fox (Hillsdale, N.J.: Erlbaum), 199–214, cited in Hinde and Pulkinnen, "Human Aggressiveness and War," 5–37.

30. J. L. Freedman, *Crowding and Behavior* (San Francisco: Freeman, 1975); and P. G. Zim-

bardo, "The Human Choice," in *Nebraska Symposia on Motivation* (Lincoln: University of Nebraska Press, 1969); both cited in Hinde and Pulkinnen, "Human Aggressiveness and War," 5–37.

31. N. K. Humphrey, "The Social Function of Intellect," in *Growing Points in Ethology,* ed. P. P. G. Bateson and R. A. Hinde (Cambridge: Cambridge University Press, 1976), 303–318, cited in Hinde and Pulkinnen, "Human Aggressiveness and War," 5–37.

32. H. Tajfel, *Human Groups and Social Categories* (Cambridge: Cambridge University Press, 1981), cited in Hinde and Pulkinnen, "Human Aggressiveness and War," 5–37.

33. C. de Kock and C. Schutte, "Political Violence with Particular Reference to South Africa," in *Violence in South Africa,* ed. E. Bornman, R. van Eeden, and M. Wentzel (Pretoria, South Africa: Human Sciences Research Council, 1998), 57–84, cited in Hinde and Pulkinnen, "Human Aggressiveness and War," 5–37.

34. S. Brown, *The Causes and Prevention of War* (New York: St. Martin's Press, 1987); J. Haas, *The Anthropology of War,* Cambridge: Cambridge University Press, 1990); and C. McCauley, "Conference Overview," in *The Anthropology of War* (Cambridge: Cambridge University Press, 1990), 1–25; all cited in Hinde and Pulkinnen, "Human Aggressiveness and War," 5–37.

35. R. S. Appleby, *The Ambivalence of the Sacred* (Lanham, Md.: Rowman & Littlefield, 2000), 57–80.

36. Y. Papadakis, "Nationalist Imaginings of War in Cyprus," in *War: A Cruel Necessity?* (London: Tauris, 1995), 54–67; J. Reinharz and G. Mosse, eds., *The Impact of Western Nationalisms* (London: Sage, 1992); both cited in Hinde and Pulkinnen, "Human Aggressiveness and War," 5–37.

37. D. A. Hamburg, *No More Killing Fields,* 87–113.

38. Ibid., 151–185.

39. D. A. Hamburg, "Human Rights and Warfare: An Ounce of Prevention is Worth a Pound of Cure," in *Realizing Human Rights: Moving from Inspiration to Impact,* ed. S. Power and G. Allison (New York: St. Martin's Press, 2000).

40. R. R. LaGamma, "Civic Education and the Seoul Conference of the Community of Democracies" (presentation to the Pocantico Conference on Global Dimensions of Democracy Education by Robert R. LaGamma, Executive Director, Council for a Community of Democracies, June 29, 2002), http://www.ccd21.org/articles/cived_pocantico_june_29.htm (accessed July 16, 2003), section title: "What Is Democracy?" paragraph 1, p. 3 of 6.

41. J. Richardson and R. C. Rowson, "Back Civic Education Worldwide," *International Herald Tribune,* "For Democracy" section, December 6, 2002.

42. LaGamma, "Civic Education."

43. D. A. Hamburg, *No More Killing Fields,* 289–291.

44. LaGamma, "Civic Education," section title: "What Went On in Warsaw?" paragraph 2, pp. 1–2 of 6.

45. Richardson and Rowson, "Back Civic Education Worldwide."

46. Ibid.

47. LaGamma, "Civic Education."

48. United Nations Development Programme, Arab Fund for Economic and Social Development, *Arab Human Development Report 2002: Creating Opportunities for Future Generations* (New York: United Nations Development Programme, 2002), 55.

49. Ibid., 61–62.

50. D. A. Hamburg, *No More Killing Fields,* 187–218.

51. Ibid.

52. D. A. Hamburg and M. B. Trudeau, eds., *Biobehavioral Aspects of Aggression* (New York: Alan R. Liss, 1981).

53. J. T. Dunlop, *Dispute Resolution* (Dover, Mass.: Auburn House Publishing, 1984); H. Raiffa, *The Art and Science of Negotiation* (Cambridge, Mass.: Belknap Press, 1982); J. A. Schellenberg, *The Science of Conflict* (New York: Oxford University Press, 1982); R. Levine and D. Campbell, *Ethnocentrism: Theories of Conflict, Ethnic Attitudes, and Group Behavior* (New York: McGraw-Hill, 1972).

54. R. A. Hinde, "Co-operation and Trust," in Hinde and Parry, *Education for Peace*, 42–51.

55. L. Pulkkinen, "Progress in Education for Peace in Finland," in Hinde and Parry, *Education for Peace*, 88–101.

56. Ibid., 99.

57. Ibid., 95.

58. L. Pulkkinen, letter to author (D. A. Hamburg), January 4, 2001.

59. Kenneth D. Bush and Diana Saltarelli, eds., *The Two Faces of Education in Ethnic Conflict: Towards a Peacebuilding Education for Children* (Florence, Italy: UNICEF Innocenti Research Centre, August 2000), 33–38.

60. J. Carter, *Talking Peace: A Vision for the Next Generation* (New York: Dutton Children's Books, 1993).

CHAPTER 17

1. R. L. Selman, D. Jaquette, and D. R. Lavin, "Interpersonal Awareness in Children: Toward an Integration of Developmental and Clinical Child Psychology," *American Journal of Orthopsychiatry* 47, no. 2 (1977): 264–274, cited in P. G. Avery et al., "Teaching an Understanding of War and Peace through Structured Academic Controversies," in *How Children Understand War and Peace*, ed. A. Raviv, L. Oppenheimer, and D. Bar-Tal (San Francisco: Jossey-Bass Inc., 1999), 260–280.

2. J. Nicholls and J. Nelson, "Students' Conceptions of Controversial Knowledge," *Journal of Educational Psychology* 84, no. 2 (1992): 224–230, cited in Avery et al., "Teaching an Understanding of War and Peace."

3. J. Adelson, "The Political Imagination of the Young Adolescent," *Developmental Psychology* 1 (1971): 1031–1051, cited in Avery et al., "Teaching an Understanding of War and Peace."

4. D. Keating, "Adolescent Thinking," in *At the Threshold: The Developing Adolescent*, ed. S. Feldman and G. Elliott (Cambridge: Harvard University Press, 1990), 54–92, cited in Avery et al., "Teaching an Understanding of War and Peace."

5. Avery et al., "Teaching an Understanding of War and Peace."

6. D. W. Johnson and R. Johnson, *Cooperation and Competition: Theory and Research* (Edina, Minn.: Interaction, 1989); D. W. Johnson and R. Johnson, *Creative Controversy: Intellectual Conflict in the Classroom*, 3rd ed. (Edina, Minn.: Interaction, 1995); D. W. Johnson and R. Johnson, *Teaching Students to Be Peacemakers*, 3rd ed. (Edina, Minn.: Interaction, 1995); and D. W. Johnson, R. Johnson, and E. Holubec, *Cooperation in the Classroom*, 7th ed. (Edina, Minn.: Interaction, 1998); all cited in Avery et al., "Teaching an Understanding of War and Peace."

7. Johnson, Johnson, and Holubec, *Cooperation in the Classroom*, cited in Avery et al., "Teaching an Understanding of War and Peace."

8. D. W. Johnson and R. Johnson, *Creative Controversy*; and D. W. Johnson and R. Johnson, *Teaching Students to Be Peacemakers*; both cited in Avery et al., "Teaching an Understanding of War and Peace."

9. D. W. Johnson and R. Johnson, *Creative Controversy*, cited in Avery et al., "Teaching an Understanding of War and Peace."

10. D. W. Johnson and R. Johnson, "Conflict in the Classroom: Controversy and Learning," *Review of Educational Research* 49, no. 1 (1979): 51–70; D. W. Johnson and R. Johnson, *Coopera-*

tion and Competition; and D. W. Johnson and R. Johnson, *Creative Controversy*; all cited in Avery et al., "Teaching an Understanding of War and Peace."

11. Ibid.

12. Ibid.

13. Ibid.

14. Cited in Avery et al., "Teaching an Understanding of War and Peace," 269.

15. F. M. Newmann, "Qualities of Thoughtful Social Studies Classes: An Empirical Profile," *Journal of Curriculum Studies* 22, no. 3 (1990): 253–275, cited in Avery et al., "Teaching an Understanding of War and Peace."

16. M. Walzer, *Just and Unjust Wars: A Moral Argument with Historical Illustrations*, 3rd ed. (New York: Basic Books, 2000).

17. Carnegie Commission on Preventing Deadly Conflict, *Preventing Deadly Conflict, Final Report* (New York: Carnegie Corporation of New York, December 1997).

18. D. A. Hamburg, *No More Killing Fields: Preventing Deadly Conflict* (Lanham, Md.: Rowman & Littlefield, 2002), 87–111.

19. E. Staub, *The Roots of Evil: The Origins of Genocide and Other Group Violence* (New York: Cambridge University Press, 1989).

20. Carnegie Council on Adolescent Development, *Great Transitions: Preparing Adolescents for a New Century* (New York: Carnegie Corporation of New York, 1995).

21. D. A. Hamburg, *No More Killing Fields*.

22. Ibid., vii.

23. Memorandum from Jeannette L. Aspden, Editor for Special Projects and Consulting Editor, Carnegie Commission on Preventing Deadly Conflict, to Barbara D. Finberg, MEM Associates, New York, N.Y., June 24, 1997.

24. G. Francis, with contributions from Y. Toyama and P. Wichienkuer and in cooperation with the Carnegie Commission on Preventing Deadly Conflict, *Preventing Deadly Conflict: Toward a World without War* (a curriculum module of the Stanford Program on International and Cross-Cultural Education [SPICE] at the Institute for International Studies [IIS], Stanford, CA: Leland Stanford Junior University Board of Trustees, 2000).

25. Monterey Institute of International Studies, Center For Nonproliferation Studies, Critical Issues Forum (rev. January 12, 2003), http://www.cif.miis.edu/cif/about.htm (accessed July 16, 2003).

26. Critical Issues Forum (rev. Jan. 12, 2003), http://www.cif.miis.edu/cif/about.htm (accessed September 25, 2003).

27. Critical Issues Forum (rev. June 17, 2003), http://www.cif.miis.edu/cif/CONF_S03.HTM (accessed September 25, 2003).

28. Monterey Institute of International Studies [press release], "High School Students Study Toxic Terror at the Monterey Institute," April 29, 2001. Contact the Center for Nonproliferation Studies, Monterey Institute of International Studies, 425 Van Buren Street, Monterey, Calif. 93940, phone (831) 647-4154.

29. Compton Foundation, Inc. (n.d.), http://www.comptonfoundation.org/history.html (accessed September 25, 2003), p. 1 of 3.

30. Nuclear Threat Initiative, *About NTI* (n.d.), http://www.nti.org/b_aboutnti/b_index.html (accessed July 16, 2003).

31. Fred W. Wehling, Center for Nonproliferation Studies Education Coordinator and Senior Research Associate, e-mail to D. A. Hamburg, New York, October 31, 2001.

32. W. Potter, Center for Nonproliferation Studies, conversation with D. A. Hamburg, July 24, 2002.

33. Monterey Institute of International Studies, Center For Nonproliferation Studies, *CNS Educational Resources Guide* (2003), http://cnsdl.miis.edu/cnserd/ (accessed September 25, 2003). For more information about the ERG, select "About Guide" on the ERG Web page.

34. Monterey Institute of International Studies, Center For Nonproliferation Studies, *CNS Educational Resources Guide* (2003), http://cnsdl.miis.edu/cnserd/aboutus.htm (accessed September 25, 2003).

35. Monterey Institute of International Studies, Center for Nonproliferation Studies, *Resources for Students and Teachers* (2002), http://cns.miis.edu/cns/edu/wmdt_hs/index.htm (accessed July 16, 2003).

36. Seeds of Peace, "Seeds of Peace International Camp" (New York: Seeds of Peace, n.d.), available from http://www.seedsofpeace.org (accessed July 16, 2003).

37. Seeds of Peace, *About Us: History*, "Seeds of Peace History: A Decade of Peacemaking" (New York: Seeds of Peace, n.d.), available from http://www.seedsofpeace.org (accessed July 16, 2003).

38. Seeds of Peace, "Seeds of Peace International Camp."

39. President William J. Clinton, personal conversation with D. A. Hamburg, New York City, 2002.

40. "Outreach and Development" and "Educational Outreach," Seeds of Peace CD-ROM, available from http://www.seedsofpeace.org (accessed September 25, 2003).

41. Ibid.

42. Seeds of Peace, *Staying Connected* (New York: Seeds of Peace, n.d.), available from http://www.seedsofpeace.org (accessed July 16, 2003).

43. Ibid.

44. Seeds of Peace, *Year-Round Leadership Programs*, "Leadership Conferences" (New York: Seeds of Peace, n.d.), available from http://www.seedsofpeace.org (accessed September 25, 2003).

45. Ibid.

46. Ibid.

47. Ibid.

48. UNHCR The UN Refugee Agency online: type the words "Imagine Coexistence" in search window, then see "Enabling People to Live in Security" (keynote speech by Sadako Ogata at the International Symposium on Human Security (Tokyo, July 28, 2000); available from http://www.unhcr.ch/cgi-bin/texis/vtx/home (accessed September 25, 2003).

49. Carnegie Commission, *Preventing Deadly Conflict*; D. A. Hamburg, *No More Killing Fields*.

50. Ogata, "Enabling People to Live in Security," 3.

51. Ibid., 6.

52. M. Minow, "Education for Co-Existence," *Arizona Law Review* 44, no. 1 (Spring, 2002): 1–29, also available online at http://www.law.arizona.edu/Journals/ALR/ALR2002/vol441/Minow_FINAL.pdf (accessed July 19, 2003).

53. Dennis J. D. Sandole, "Strengthening Transitional Democracies Through Conflict Resolution: Conflict Resolution Education," 552 *Annals* 125 (1997), cited in Minow, "Education for Co-Existence," 5.

54. See W. Paul Vogt, *Tolerance and Education: Learning to Live with Diversity and Difference* (Beverly Hills, Calif.: Sage, 1997), pp. 151–176. The idea of social contact as a basis for positive outcomes began with Gordon Allport's work. See Gordon W. Allport, *The Nature of Prejudice The Nature of Prejudice* (Cambridge, Mass.: Addison-Wesley, 1954), pp. 154; see also *Contact and Conflict in Intergoup Encounters*, edited by M. Hewstone and R. Brown (Oxford, U. K.: Blackstone, 1986), which builds on Allport's work (cited in Minow, "Education for Co-Existence," 10).

55. See Robert Slavin, "Cooperative Learning: Applying Contact Theory in Desegregated Schools," *Journal of Social Issues* 41 (1985): 45, 56, cited in Minow, "Education for Co-Existence," 11.

56. Minow, "Education for Co-Existence," 15.

57. Ibid.

58. Roger J. R. Levesque, *Educating American Youth: Lessons for Children's Human Rights Law*, 27 J.L. & EDUC. 173 (April 1998); *Issues of Democracy*; Human Rights Education Associates Web site (http://hrea.org/); and Human Rights Resource Center, http://www.hrea.org/erc/index.html, all cited in Minow, "Education for Co-Existence," 16.

59. See the Web site of the Office of the United Nations High Commissioner for Human Rights at http://www.unhchr.ch/html/menu6/1/edudec.htm (accessed July 29, 2003).

60. D. A. Hamburg, *No More Killing Fields*.

61. M. S. Strom and W. S. Parsons, *Facing History and Ourselves: Holocaust and Human Behavior* (Watertown, Mass.: Intentional Educations, 1982).

62. J. Carter, "Foreword," in *Religion, The Missing Dimension of Statecraft*, ed. D. Johnston and C. Sampson (New York: Oxford University Press, 1994).

63. Ibid., vii.

64. D. A. Hamburg, *No More Killing Fields*, 87−111.

65. S. Appleby, *The Ambivalence of the Sacred: Religion, Violence, and Reconciliation* (Lanham, Md.: Rowman & Littlefield, 2000), 155−158.

66. Appleby, *Ambivalence of the Sacred*.

67. For a full discussion of this meaning of "tradition," see A. MacIntyre, *After Virtue: A Study in Moral Theory* (Notre Dame, Ind.: University of Notre Dame Press, 1991), 204−205.

68. M. E. Marty and R. S. Appleby, eds., *Fundamentalisms Comprehended* (Chicago: University of Chicago Press, 1995), cited in Appleby, *Ambivalence of the Sacred*, 398.

69. J. Carter, *The Nobel Peace Prize Lecture* (New York: Simon & Schuster, 2002), 16−18.

70. His Holiness the 14th Dalai Lama, *The Dalai Lama's Book of Wisdom* (Hammersmith, U.K.: Thorsons, 1999), 100.

71. Appleby, *Ambivalence of the Sacred*, 73.

72. P. Arthur, interview with R. Scott Appleby, March 2, 1998. On the general theme, see S. Schroeder, "Toward a Higher Identity: An Interview with Mairead Corrigan Maguire," *Christian Century* (April 20, 1994), 414−416, cited in Appleby, *Ambivalence of the Sacred*, 171.

CHAPTER 18

1. D. Ekbladh, *Education for Peace in the 21st Century: A Report on the Advisory Meeting on the Academic Program of the University for Peace* (New York: United Nations, University for Peace, March 23−24, 2001), 37, also available online at http://www.upeace.org/documents/news/ny_report.pdf (accessed July 16, 2003).

2. K. Annan, Speech to the Advisory Meeting, as cited in D. Ekbladh, *Education for Peace in the 21st Century*, 12.

3. K. Egan, agenda item for a meeting at Carnegie Corporation of New York, October 1992.

4. V. Stewart (then chairman of the Education Division of Carnegie Corporation of New York), agenda item for a meeting at Carnegie Corporation of New York, October 1990.

5. Web page of Mary Kiely, Stanford University Center on Adolescence, http://www.stanford.edu/group/adolescent.ctr/Research/kiely.html (accessed July 19, 2003).

6. D. A. Hamburg, *Today's Children: Creating a Future for a Generation in Crisis* (New York: Times Books, 1992), 224−228.

7. *The Harvard Children's Initiative: For Families* (rev. 2003), http://www.gse.harvard.edu/%7ehci/families/families.html (accessed July 19, 2003).

8. Harvard School of Public Health, Division of Public Health Practice: *Violence Prevention Programs* (Cambridge, Mass.: 2001), http://www.hsph.harvard.edu/php/VPP/cvpp.html (accessed July 19, 2003).

9. *Peace by Peace: A Violence Prevention Guide for Communities* can be purchased for $29.95. Those seeking ordering information on the guide may contact the Harvard School for Public Health, Violence Prevention Programs, 1552 Tremont Street, Boston, Mass. 02120, phone (617) 495-7777, e-mail jguzman@hsph.harvard.edu.

10. United Nations Educational, Scientific and Cultural Organization, Division for the Promotion of Quality Education, *Best Practices of Non-Violent Conflict Resolution In and Out-of-School* (Paris: UNESCO, 2002).

11. Harvard Research Programs, Judge Baker Children's Center—Serving At-Risk Children and Families (Boston: 2003), http://www.jbcc.harvard.edu (accessed July 19, 2003).

12. Harvard University Graduate School of Education, *Program in Afterschool Education and Research* (Cambridge, Mass.: 2002), http://www.gse.harvard.edu/~afterschool (accessed July 19, 2003).

13. *The Harvard Children's Initiative: Events* (Cambridge, Mass.: 2003), http://www.gse.harvard.edu/ (accessed July 19, 2003).

14. Agenda items for meetings at Carnegie Corporation of New York, 1985–1990.

15. A. Dunham and K. Egan (then program officers at Carnegie Corporation of New York), agenda items for a meeting at Carnegie Corporation of New York, 1986.

16. K. Egan, agenda items for a meeting at Carnegie Corporation of New York, October 25, 1990.

17. K. Egan and A. Denham, agenda items for a meeting at Carnegie Corporation of New York, 1987.

18. D. A. Hamburg, *Today's Children*, 222.

19. Ibid., 224.

20. G. Francis, with contributions from Y. Toyama and P. Wichienkuer and in cooperation with the Carnegie Commission on Preventing Deadly Conflict, *Preventing Deadly Conflict: Toward a World without War* (a curriculum module of the Stanford Program on International and Cross-Cultural Education (SPICE) at the Institute for International Studies, Stanford University (Stanford, CA: Leland Stanford Junior University Board of Trustees, 2000).

21. Carnegie Commission on Preventing Deadly Conflict, *Preventing Deadly Conflict: Final Report* (Washington, D.C.: Carnegie Commission on Preventing Deadly Conflict, 1997), inside cover.

22. National Center for History in the Schools, *National Standards for United States History: Exploring the American Experience* (Los Angeles, Calif.: UCLA Publication Design Services, 1996), cited in G. Francis et. al., *Preventing Deadly Conflict: Toward a World without War*, 4.

23. G. Francis, *Preventing Deadly Conflict*, 14.

24. Stanford University, Institute for International Studies (Stanford, Calif.: Board of Trustees of Leland Stanford Junior University), http://spice.stanford.edu/about/index.html (accessed July 19, 2003).

25. Monterey Institute of International Studies, Center For Nonproliferation Studies, *About CNS* (Monterey, Calif.: Monterey Institute of International Studies, n.d.), http://www.cns.miis.edu/cns/index.htm (accessed September 26, 2003).

26. W. Potter of the Center for Nonproliferation Studies, conversation with D. A. Hamburg, July 24, 2002.

27. Monterey Institute of International Studies, Center For Nonproliferation Studies, *About*

CNS (Monterey, Calif.: Monterey Institute of International Studies, n.d.), http://www.cns.miis.edu/cns/index.htm (accessed July 19, 2003).

28. Monterey Institute of International Studies, *Research Centers* (Monterey, Calif.: Monterey Institute of International Studies, n.d.), http://www.miis.edu/rcenters-cns.html (accessed July 19, 2003).

29. United Nations, "United Nations Study on Disarmament and Non-Proliferation Education" [Press release] (New York: United Nations, August 10, 2002), http://www.un.org/News/Press/docs/2002/dc2843.doc (accessed July 19, 2003).

30. United Nations General Assembly, "United Nations Study on Disarmament and Non-Proliferation Education," a report of the Secretary-General, August 2002, at the 57th General Assembly session (New York City, August 30, 2002). This report of the UN Secretary-General, Kofi Annan, was submitted upon the conclusion of the work of the Group of Governmental Experts on the subject of disarmament and nonproliferation education in July 2002. For more information see http://disarmament.un.org.education.

31. W. Potter, "Discussion Paper on Disarmament and Nonproliferation Education," prepared for the UN Secretary-General's Board on Disarmament Matters, New York, January 31–February 2, 2000.

32. L. S. Spector, "Nonproliferation Education in the United States—Part I: Undergraduate Education," *The Nonproliferation Review* (Fall/Winter 2002): 9–30.

33. Global Philanthropy, Synergos Institute, *The Harry Frank Guggenheim Foundation,* "Organizational Profile" (New York: Synergos Institute, rev. November 20, 2002), http://www.synergos.org/globalphilanthropy/organizations/hfguggenheim.htm (accessed July 19, 2003).

34. J. M. Hester, "Introduction: Teaching about Violence," *HFG Review* (New York: Harry Frank Guggenheim Foundation, n.d.), http://www.hfg.org/html.pages/mag4/hester.htm (accessed July 19, 2003).

35. R. Jackall, "Violence," *HFG Review* (New York: Harry Frank Guggenheim Foundation, n.d.), http://www.hfg.org/html.pages/mag4/jackall.htm (accessed July 19, 2003).

36. D. A. Hamburg, *No More Killing Fields: Preventing Deadly Conflict* (Lanham, Md.: Rowman & Littlefield, 2002) 1–15.

37. See also H. H. Saunders, "Interactive Conflict Resolution: A View for Policy Makers on Making and Building Peace," in *International Conflict Resolution After the Cold War*, ed. P. C. Stern and D. Druckman (Washington, D.C.: National Academy Press, 2000), 251–293.

38. Lecture given by D. A. Hamburg, 50th Pugwash Conference on Science and World Affairs, Cambridge, U.K., August 6, 2002.

39. Lecture given by D. A. Hamburg, 50th Pugwash Conference.

CHAPTER 19

1. D. A. Hamburg, *No More Killing Fields: Preventing Deadly Conflict* (Lanham, Md.: Rowman & Littlefield, 2002).

2. D. A. Hamburg, *No More Killing Fields*; D. A. Hamburg, *Today's Children: Creating a Future for a Generation in Crisis* (New York: Times Books, 1992).

3. B. B. Smuts et al., eds., *Primate Societies* (Chicago: University of Chicago Press, 1986); W. C. McGrew, L. F. Marchant, and T. Nishida, eds., *Great Ape Societies* (Cambridge: Cambridge University Press, 1996); D. A. Hamburg and E. R. McCown, eds., *The Great Apes* (Menlo Park, Calif.: Benjamin/Cummings Publishing Company, 1979).

4. Smuts et al., *Primate Societies*; McGrew, Marchant, and Nishida, *Great Ape Societies*.

5. M. B. Brewer, "The Psychology of Prejudice: Ingroup Love or Outgroup Hate," *Journal of Social Issues* 55, no. 3, (1999): 429–444.

6. E. Staub, *The Roots of Evil* (New York: Cambridge University Press, 1989).

7. D. A. Hamburg, *No More Killing Fields.*

8. M. Sherif and C. Sherif, *Groups in Harmony and Tension: An Integration of Studies on Intergroup Relations* (New York: Octagon, 1966).

9. D. A. Hamburg, *Today's Children*; Carnegie Council on Adolescent Development, *Great Transitions: Preparing Adolescents for a New Century* (New York: Carnegie Corporation of New York, 1995); Carnegie Council on Adolescent Development, Task Force on Youth Development and Community Programs, *A Matter of Time: Risk and Opportunity in the Nonschool Hours* (Washington, D.C.: Carnegie Council on Adolescent Development, 1992).

10. N. Eisenberg and P. H. Mussen, *The Roots of Prosocial Behavior in Children* (Cambridge: Cambridge University Press, 1989), 1–11.

11. M. Radke-Yarrow and C. Zahn-Waxler, "The Role of Familial Factors in the Development of Prosocial Behavior: Research Findings and Questions," in *Development of Antisocial and Prosocial Behavior*, ed. D. Olweus, J. Block, and M. Radke-Yarrow (Orlando: Academic Press, 1986).

12. Eisenberg and Mussen, *Roots of Prosocial Behavior*, 95–107.

13. R. E. Slavin, "Synthesis of Research on Cooperative Learning," *Educational Leadership* 48 (1991): 71–82; R. E. Slavin, "Cooperative Learning and Intergroup Relations," in *Handbook of Research on Multicultural Education*, ed. J. Banks and C. M. Banks (New York: Macmillan, 1995), 628–634.

14. M. Deutsch, *The Resolution of Conflict* (New Haven, CT: Yale University Press, 1973).

15. M. Van Slyck, M. Stern, and J. Zak-Place, "Promoting Optimal Adolescent Development through Conflict Resolution Education, Training, and Practice: An Innovative Approach for Counseling Psychologists," *Counseling Psychologist* 24 (1996): 433–461.

16. E. Hamburg and D. A. Hamburg, "The Powerful Worldwide Reach of Mass Media: Can Media Help to Prevent Deadly Conflict?" Working Paper No. 30, Center for International Relations (Los Angeles: University of California, Center for International Relations, 2002).

17. Eisenberg and Mussen, *Roots of Prosocial Behavior*, 95–107.

18. J. G. Cooney, "The Potential Uses of Television in Preschool Education: A Report to the Carnegie Corporation of New York" (New York: Carnegie Corporation of New York, 1996).

19. D. A. Hamburg, "Crowding, Stranger Contact, and Aggressive Behavior," in *Society, Stress, and Disease*, vol. 1, ed. L. Levi (New York: Oxford University Press, 1971), 209–218.

20. D. A. Hamburg, *No More Killing Fields*, 87–111.

21. Ibid., 17–49.

22. Ibid., 87–111.

23. D. A. Hamburg, "Prejudice, Ethnocentrism, and Violence in an Age of High Technology," in *Carnegie Corporation of New York Annual Report* (New York: Carnegie Corporation of New York, 1984), 3–15.

24. Ibid.

25. R. J. Fisher, "Conclusion: Paths toward a Peaceful World," in *The Social Psychology of Intergroup and International Conflict Resolution*, ed. R. J. Fisher (New York: Springer-Verlag, 1990).

EPILOGUE

Kennedy, presentation at American University, Washington, D.C., June 10, 1963; this version taken from *"Let the World Go Forth": The Speeches, Statements, and Writings of John F. Kennedy, 1947–1963*, selected and with an introduction by T. C. Sorensen (New York: Dell, 1988), 282–290. Einstein, written into a neighbor's autograph album in Caputh, Germany, 1932; this version taken from Alice Calaprice, *Expanded Quotable Einstein* (Princeton, N.J.: Princeton University Press, 2000), 309. Glover, *Humanity: A Moral History of the Twentieth Century* (London: Jonathan Cape, 1999; New Haven, Conn.: Yale University Press, 2000), 414.

BIBLIOGRAPHY

Adams, Dennis, and Mary Hamm. *Cooperative Learning: Critical Thinking and Collaboration Across the Curriculum.* 2nd ed. Springfield, Ill.: Charles C. Thomas, 1996.

Allensworth, Diane, Elaine Lawson, Lois Nicholson, and James Wyche, eds. *Schools and Health: Our Nation's Investment.* Washington, D.C.: National Academy Press, 1997.

Allport, Gordon. *The Nature of Prejudice.* Cambridge, Mass.: Addison Wesley, 1954.

Anderson, Lisa, ed. *Transitions to Democracy.* New York: Columbia University Press, 1999.

Annan, Kofi. *The Challenge to Preventing Deadly Conflict: Reflections and Recommendations.* New York: Carnegie Commission on Preventing Deadly Conflict, Carnegie Corporation of New York, 1999.

Appleby, R. Scott. *The Ambivalence of the Sacred: Religion, Violence, and Reconciliation.* Lanham, Md.: Rowman & Littlefield, 2000.

Aronson, Elliott. *Nobody Left to Hate: Teaching Compassion after Columbine.* New York: W. H. Freeman, 2000.

Auerbach, Judith D., Christina Wypijewska, and H. Keith H. Brodie, eds. *AIDS and Behavior: An Integrated Approach.* Washington, D.C.: National Academy Press, 1994.

Bandura, Albert. *Aggression: A Social Learning Analysis.* Englewood Cliffs, N.J.: Prentice Hall, 1973.

Barash, David P. *Introduction to Peace Studies.* Belmont, Calif.: Wadsworth, 1991.

Barber, Benjamin R. *Jihad vs. McWorld: How Globalism and Tribalism are Reshaping the World.* New York: Times Books, 1995. Reprint, New York: Ballantine Books, 1996.

Belle, Deborah. *The After-School Lives of Children: Alone and with Others While Parents Work.* Mahwah, N.J.: Erlbaum, 1999.

Bowlby, John. *Attachment.* 2nd ed. New York: Basic Books, 2000.

Brewer, Marilynn B., and Norman Miller. *Intergroup Relations.* Buckingham, U.K.: Open University Press, 1996.

Brewer, Marilynn B., and Roderick M. Kramer. "The Psychology of Intergroup Attitudes and Behavior." *Annual Review of Psychology* 36 (1985): 219–243.

Brown, Michael E., Owen R. Coté, Sean M. Lynn-Jones, and Steven E. Miller. *Nationalism and Ethnic Conflict.* Cambridge: MIT Press, 1997.

Brown, Seyom. *The Causes and Prevention of War.* 2nd ed. New York: St. Martin's Press, 1994.

Canary, Daniel J., William R. Cupach, and Susan J. Messman. *Relationship Conflict: Conflict in Parent-Child, Friendship, and Romantic Relationships.* Thousand Oaks, Calif.: Sage Publications, Inc., 1995.

Carnegie Commission on Preventing Deadly Conflict. *Preventing Deadly Conflict.* New York: Carnegie Corporation of New York, December 1997.

Carnegie Council on Adolescent Development. *Great Transitions: Preparing Adolescents for a New Century.* New York: Carnegie Corporation of New York, 1995.

Carothers, Thomas. *Aiding Democracy Abroad: The Learning Curve.* Washington, D.C.: Carnegie Endowment for International Peace, 1999.

Carter, Jimmy. *Talking Peace: A Vision for the Next Generation.* New York: Dutton Children's Books, 1993.

Chadha, Yogesh. *Gandhi: A Life.* New York: Wiley, 1997.

Chirot, Daniel, and Martin E. P. Seligman, eds. *Ethnopolitical Warfare: Causes, Consequences, and Possible Solutions.* Washington, D.C.: American Psychological Association, 2001.

Cole, Michael, and Sheila R. Cole. *The Development of Children.* 3rd ed. New York: W. H. Freeman, 1996.

Collins, H. Thomas, Frederick R. Czarra, and Andrew F. Smith. "Guidelines for Global and International Studies Education: Challenges, Cultures, and Connection." *Social Education* 62 (1998): 311–317.

Colman, Andrew, ed. *Cooperation and Competition in Humans and Animals.* Berkshire, U.K.: Van Nostrand Reinhold, 1982.

Comer, James P., Michael Ben-Avie, Norris M. Haynes, and Edward T. Joyner, eds. *Child by Child: The Comer Process for Change in Education.* New York: Teachers College Press, 1999.

Commission on Human Security. *Human Security Now.* New York: Commission on Human Security, 2003. [Obtainable through the Ford Foundation.]

Cowie, Helen, Peter Smith, Michael Boulton, and Rema Laver. *Cooperation in the Multi-Ethnic Classroom: The Impact of Cooperative Group Work on Social Relationships in Middle Schools.* London: David Fulton Publishers, 1994.

Craig, Gordon A. *Europe since 1815.* New York: Holt, Rinehart and Winston, 1961.

Craig, Gordon A., and Alexander L. George. *Force and Statecraft: Diplomatic Problems of Our Time.* 3rd ed. New York: Oxford University Press, 1997.

Dahl, Norman C., and Jerome B. Wiesner, eds. *World Change and World Security.* Cambridge: MIT Press, 1978.

de Wit, Jan, and Willard W. Hartup, eds. *Determinants and Origins of Aggressive Behavior.* The Hague, The Netherlands: Mouton, 1974.

Deutsch, Morton. "Constructive Conflict Management for the World Today." *International Journal of Conflict Management* 5, no. 2 (April 1994): 111–129.

———. "A Framework for Thinking about Research on Conflict Resolution Training." In *The Handbook of Conflict Resolution: Theory and Practice,* edited by Morton Deutsch and Peter T. Coleman, 571–590. San Francisco: Jossey-Bass, 2000.

————. *The Resolution of Conflict: Constructive and Destructive Processes.* New Haven, Conn.: Yale University Press, 1973.

Donnerstein, Edward, Ronald G. Slaby, and Leonard D. Eron. "The Mass Media and Youth Aggression." In *Reason to Hope: A Psychosocial Perspective on Violence and Youth*, edited by Leonard D. Eron, Jacquelyn H. Gentry, and Peggy Schlegel, 219–250. Washington, D.C.: American Psychological Association, 1994.

Eccles, Jacquelynne, and Jennifer Appleton Gootman, eds. *Community Programs to Promote Youth Development.* Washington, D.C.: National Academy Press, 2002.

Einstein, Albert. *Ideas and Opinions.* Translated by Sonja Bargmann. New York: Bonanza Books, 1954.

Elliott, Delbert S., Beatrix A. Hamburg, and Kirk R. Williams. *Violence in American Schools.* New York: Cambridge University Press, 1998.

Eron, Leonard D., Jacquelyn H. Gentry, and Peggy Schlegel, eds. *Reason to Hope: A Psychological Perspective on Violence and Youth.* Washington, D.C.: American Psychological Association, 1994.

Evans, Gareth. *Cooperating for Peace: The Global Agenda for the 1990s and Beyond.* St. Leonards, Australia: Allen & Unwin, 1993.

Fisch, Shalom M. and Rosemarie T. Truglio, eds. *"G" is for Growing.* Mahwah, N.J.: Lawrence Erlbaum Associates, 2001.

Fisher, Ronald J., ed. *The Social Psychology of Intergroup and International Conflict Resolution.* New York: Springer-Verlag, 1990.

Ford, Franklin L. *Political Murder: From Tyrannicide to Terrorism.* Cambridge: Harvard University Press, 1985.

Freedman, Lawrence. *War.* New York: Oxford University Press, 1994.

Gellately, Robert, and Ben Kiernan. *The Specter of Genocide: Mass Murder in Historical Perspecive.* Cambridge, U.K.: Cambridge University Press, 2003.

George, Alexander L. *Avoiding War: Problems of Crisis Management.* Boulder, Colo.: Westview Press, 1991.

George, Alexander L., ed. *Avoiding War: Problems of Crisis Management.* Boulder, Colo.: Westview Press, 1991.

Glover, Jonathan. *Humanity: A Moral History of the Twentieth Century.* New Haven, Conn.: Yale University Press, 2000.

Goldschmidt, Walter. *Man's Way: A Preface to the Understanding of Human Society.* Cleveland: World Publishing, 1959.

Goldstein, Arnold P. *The Psychology of Group Aggression.* West Sussex, U.K.: Wiley, 2002.

Goodall, Jane, and David A. Hamburg. "Chimpanzee Behavior as a Model for the Behavior of Early Man: New Evidence on Possible Origins of Human Behavior." In *American Handbook of Psychiatry*, vol. 6, edited by David A. Hamburg and H. Brodie. New York: Basic Books, 1975.

Goodall, Jane. *The Chimpanzees of Gombe: Patterns of Behavior.* Cambridge, Mass.: Belknap Press, 1986.

Goodby, James, Petrus Buwalda, and Dmitri Trenin. *A Strategy for Stable Peace: Toward a Euroatlantic Security Community.* Washington, D.C.: United States Institute of Peace Press, 2002.

Gorbachev, Mikhail. *Gorbachev: On My Country and the World.* Trans. George Shriver. New York: Columbia University Press, 2000.

Greenfeld, L., and Daniel Chirot. *Nationalism and Aggression.* Seattle: University of Washington Press, 1991.

Hamburg, David A. "Emotions in the Perspective of Human Evolution." In *Expression of the Emotions of Man*, edited by Peter H. Knapp, 300–317. New York: International Universities Press, 1963.

———. "An Evolutionary Perspective on Human Aggression." In *Development and Integration of Behavior: Essays in Honour of Robert Hinde*, edited by Patrick Bateson, 419–457. Cambridge: Cambridge University Press, 1991.

———. "Evolution of Emotional Responses: Evidence from Recent Research on Nonhuman Primates." *Science and Psychoanalysis* 12 (1968): 39–52.

———. "Health and Behavior: An Evolutionary Perspective on Contemporary Problems." In *Perspectives on Behavioral Science*, edited by Richard Jessor, 177–200. Boulder, Colo.: Westview Press, 1991.

———. *No More Killing Fields: Preventing Deadly Conflict*. Lanham, Md.: Rowman & Littlefield, 2002.

———. *Today's Children: Creating a Future for a Generation in Crisis*. New York: Times Books, 1992.

Hamburg, David A., Glen R. Elliott, and Dolores L. Parron, eds., *Health and Behavior: Frontiers of Research in Biobehavioral Sciences*. Washington, D.C.: National Academy Press, 1982.

Hamburg, David A., and Jane van Lawick-Goodall. "Factors Facilitating Development of Aggressive Behavior in Chimpanzees and Humans." In *Determinants and Origins of Aggressive Behavior*, edited by W. W. Hartup and J. deWit, 59–85. The Hague, The Netherlands: Mouton, 1974.

Hamburg, David A., and Norman Sartorius, eds. *Health and Behavior: Selected Perspectives*. Cambridge: Cambridge University Press, 1989.

Hamburg, David A., and Michelle B. Trudeau, eds. *Biobehavioral Aspects of Aggression*. New York: Alan R. Liss, 1981.

Hetherington, E. Mavis, and Ross D. Parke. *Child Psychology: A Contemporary Viewpoint*. 5th ed. Boston: McGraw-Hill, 1999.

Hewstone, Miles, Wolfgang Stroebe, and Geoffrey Stephenson, eds. *Introduction to Social Psychology*. 2nd ed. Oxford, U.K.: Blackwell, 1996.

Hinde, Robert A. *Cooperation and Prosocial Behaviour*. Cambridge: Cambridge University Press, 1991.

Hinde, Robert A. *Individuals, Relationships, and Culture: Links Between Ethology and the Social Sciences*. New York: Cambridge University Press, 1988.

Hinde, Robert A., and Donald A. Parry, eds. *Education for Peace*. Nottingham, U.K.: Bertrand Russell House, 1989.

Holsti, Kalevi J. *Peace and War: Armed Conflicts and International Order 1648–1989*. New York: Cambridge University Press, 1991.

Horowitz, Donald L. *Ethnic Groups in Conflict*. Berkeley: University of California Press, 1985.

———. "Making Moderation Pay: The Comparative Politics of Ethnic Conflict Management." In *Conflict and Peacemaking in Multiethnic Societies*, edited by Joseph Montville. New York: Lexington Books, 1990.

Howard, Michael. *The Invention of Peace: Reflections on War and International Order*. New Haven, Conn.: Yale University Press, 2001.

Howard, Ross, Francis Rolt, Hans van de Veen, and Juliet Verhoeven. *The Power of the Media: A Handbook for Peacebuilders*. Utrecht, the Netherlands: Europen Centre for Conflict Prevention in cooperation with the European Centre for Common Ground and the Institute for Media, Policy and Civil Society (IMPACS), 2003.

Institute of Medicine, Committee on Health and Behavior: Research, Practice, and Policy Board on Neuroscience and Behavioral Health. *Health and Behavior: The Interplay of Biological, Behavioral, and Societal Influences.* Washington, D.C.: National Academy Press, 2001.

Iriye, Akira. *Global Community: The Role of International Organizations in the Making of the Contemporary World.* Berkeley: University of California Press, 2002.

James, William. *The Moral Equivalent of War.* Worchester, Mass., 1926.

Johnsson, Berndt. *Preventing Violent Conflict and Building Peace: On Interaction Between State Actors and Voluntary Organizations.* Stockholm: The European Centre for Conflict Prevention and The Swedish Peace Team Forum, 2002.

Johnston, Douglas, and Cynthia Sampson, eds. *Religion, The Missing Dimension of Statecraft.* New York: Oxford University Press, 1994.

Jolly, Alison. *Lucy's Legacy: Sex and Intelligence in Human Evolution.* Cambridge, Mass.: Harvard University Press, 1999.

Keeley, Lawrence H. *War Before Civilization: The Myth of the Peaceful Savage.* New York: Oxford University Press, 1996.

Küng, Hans, ed. *Yes to a Global Ethic.* London: SCM Press Ltd, 1996.

Lee, Phyllis C. "Play as a Means for Developing Relationships." In *Primate Social Relationships: An Integrated Approach,* edited by Robert A. Hinde. Oxford, U.K.: Blackwell Science, 1983.

Lenski, Gerhard, Patrick Nolan, and Jean Lenski. *Human Societies: An Introduction to Macrosociology.* 7th ed. McGraw-Hill, 1994.

Lerner, Richard M. *Adolescence: Development, Diversity, Context, and Application.* Upper Saddle River, N.J.: Prentice Hall, 2001.

Lerner, Richard M., and Celia B. Fisher, eds. *Applied Developmental Science,* vol. 6, no. 4 (2002).

Levine, Robert Alan, and Donald T. Campbell. *Ethnocentrism: Theories of Conflict, Ethnic Attitudes, and Group Behavior.* New York: McGraw Hill, 1972.

Maccoby, Eleanor. *Social Development: Psychological Growth and the Parent-Child Relationship.* San Diego: Harcourt Brace Jovanovich, 1980.

Maeroff, Gene I. *A Classroom of One: How Online Learning Is Changing Our Schools and Colleges.* New York: Palgrave Macmillan, 2003.

Mandelbaum, Michael. *The Ideas That Conquered the World: Peace, Democracy, and Free Markets in the Twenty-first Century.* New York: Public Affairs, 2002.

Marty, Martin E., and R. Scott Appleby, eds. *Accounting for Fundamentalism: The Dynamic Character of Movements.* The Fundamentalism Project Series. Chicago: University of Chicago Press, 1994.

Marty, Martin E., and R. Scott Appleby, eds. *Fundamentalisms Observed.* The Fundamentalism Project Series. Chicago: University of Chicago Press, 1991.

Mathias, Barbara, and Mary Ann French. *40 Ways to Raise a Nonracist Child.* New York: HarperCollins Publishers, 1996.

Mathoma, Pandelani, Greg Mills, and John Stremlau, eds. *Putting People First: African Priorities for the UN Millennium Assembly.* Johannesburg, South Africa: South African Institute of International Affairs, 2000.

McGrew, William C., Linda F. Marchant, and Toshisada Nishida, eds. *Great Ape Societies.* Cambridge: Cambridge University Press, 1996.

McNeill, William H. *The Pursuit of Power.* Chicago: University of Chicago Press, 1982.

Miller, N., and Marilynn B. Brewer, eds. *Groups in Contact: The Psychology of Desegregation.* Orlando, Fla.: Academic Press, 1984.

Millstein, Susan G., Anne C. Petersen, and Elena O. Nightingale, eds. *Promoting the Health of Ado-*

lescents: New Directions for the Twenty-First Century. New York: Oxford University Press, 1993.

Minow, Martha. *Between Vengeance and Forgiveness.* Boston: Beacon Press, 1998.

Montville, Joseph V., ed. *Conflict and Peacemaking in Multiethnic Societies.* New York: Lexington Books, 1990.

Myers, David G. *Social Psychology,* 3rd ed. New York: McGraw-Hill Publishing, 1990.

Naimark, Norman M. *Fires of Hatred: Ethnic Cleansing in Twentieth-Century Europe.* Cambridge, Mass.: Harvard University Press, 2001.

National Research Council, Commission on Behavioral and Social Sciences and Education. "Democratization and Ethnic Conflict." A summary of two meetings hosted by the Panel on Issues in Democratization in Washington, D.C. Washington, D.C.: National Academy Press, 1992.

Nye, Joseph S., Jr. *The Paradox of American Power: Why the World's Only Superpower Can't Go It Alone.* New York: Oxford University Press, 2002.

Nye, Joseph S., Jr., and John D. Donahue, eds. *Governance in a Globalizing World.* Washington, D.C.: Brookings Institution Press, 2000.

Nye, Jr., Joseph S. *Understanding International Conflicts: An Introduction to Theory and History.* 4th ed. New York: Longman, 2003.

Olweus, Dan. "Bullying among Schoolchildren: Intervention and Prevention." In *Aggression and Violence throughout the Life Span,* edited by Ray Dev Peters, Robert J. McMahon, and Vernon L. Quinsey, 100–125. Newbury Park, Calif.: Sage, 1992.

———. *Bullying and School: What We Know and What We Can Do.* Oxford, U.K.: Blackwell, 1993.

Parkes, Colin M., and Joan Stevenson-Hinde, eds. *The Place of Attachment in Human Behavior.* New York: Basic Books, 1982.

Peck, Connie. *Sustainable Peace: The Role of the UN and Regional Organizations in Preventing Deadly Conflict.* Lanham, Md.: Rowman & Littlefield, 1998.

Pereira, Michael, and Lynn Fairbanks, eds. *Juvenile Primates: Life History, Development, and Behavior.* New York: Oxford University Press, 1993.

Power, Samantha, and Graham Allison, eds. *Realizing Human Rights.* New York: St. Martin's Press, 2000.

Pusey, Anne E. "Mother-Offspring Relationships in Chimpanzees after Weaning." *Animal Behavior* 31 (1983): 363–377.

Rees, Martin. *Our Final Hour.* New York: Basic Books. 2003.

Rosenblith, Judy F. *In the Beginning: Development from Conception to Age Two.* 2nd ed. Newbury Park, Calif.: Sage, 1992.

Rubin, Barnett. *Blood on the Doorstep: The Politics of Preventive Action.* New York: Century Foundation/Council on Foreign Relations, 2003.

Ruggiero, Karen M., and Herbert C. Kelman, eds. *Journal of Social Issues, Prejudice, and Intergroup Relations: Papers in Honor of Gordon W. Allport's Centennial* 55, no. 3 (Fall 1999).

Sackett, G. P. "Monkeys Reared in Isolation with Pictures as Visual Input: Evidence for an Innate Releasing Mechanism." *Science* 154 (1966): 1468.

Sagasti, Francisco, and Gonzalo Alcalde. *Development Cooperation in a Fractured Global Order: An Arduous Transition.* Ottawa, Canada: International Development Research Centre, 1999.

Schellenberg, James A. *The Science of Conflict.* New York: Oxford University Press, 1982.

Schine, Joan, ed. *Service Learning: Ninety-sixth Yearbook of the National Society for the Study of Education, Part I.* Chicago: National Society for the Study of Education, 1997.

Selman, Robert L. *The Promotion of Social Awareness.* New York: Russell Sage Foundation, 2003.

Sen, Amartya. *Development as Freedom*. New York: Alfred A. Knopf, 1999.

Sherif, Muzafer, and Carolyn Sherif. *Groups in Harmony and Tension: An Integration of Studies on Intergroup Relations*. New York: Octagon, 1966.

Shirk, Susan L. *How China Opened Its Door: The Political Success of the PRC's Foreign Trade and Investment Reforms*. Washington, D.C.: The Brookings Institution, 1994.

Shonkoff, Jack P., and Deborah A. Phillips, eds. *From Neurons to Neighborhoods: The Science of Early Childhood Development*. Washington, D.C.: National Academy Press, 2000.

Shweder, Richard A., Martha Minow, and Hazel Rose Markus, eds. *Engaging Cultural Differences: The Multicultural Challenge in Liberal Democracies*. New York: Russell Sage Foundation, 2002.

Singer, Peter. *One World: The Ethics of Globalization*. New Haven, Conn.: Yale University Press, 2002.

Slavin, Robert E. "Cooperative Learning and Outcomes Other than Achievement." In *Cooperative Learning: Research, Theory, and Practice*. 2nd ed., 49–54. Boston: Allyn & Bacon, 1995.

Smuts, Barbara B. *Sex and Friendship in Baboons*. 2nd ed. Cambridge: Harvard University Press, 1999.

Smuts, Barbara B., Dorothy L. Cheney, Robert M. Seyfarth, Richard Wrangham, and Thomas T. Struhsaker, eds. *Primate Societies*. Chicago: University of Chicago Press, 1986.

Solomon, Frederick, and Robert Marston, eds. *The Medical Implications of Nuclear War*. Washington, D.C.: National Academies Press, 1986.

Soros, George. *On Globalization*. New York: Public Affairs, 2002.

Staub, Ervin. *The Psychology of Good and Evil: Why Children, Adults, and Groups Help and Harm Others*. Cambridge, U.K.: Cambridge University Press, 2003.

———. *The Roots of Evil*. New York: Cambridge University Press, 1989.

Stedman, Stephen John, Donald Rothchild, and Elizabeth M. Cousens. *Ending Civil Wars: The Implementation of Peace Agreements*. Boulder, Colo.: Lynne Rienner Publishers, Inc., 2002.

Steinbruner, John D. *Principles of Global Security*. Washington, D.C.: Brookings Institution Press, 2000.

Stephan, Walter. *Reducing Prejudice and Stereotyping in Schools*. New York: Teachers College Press, 1999.

Stern, Paul C., and Daniel Druckman. *International Conflict Resolution after the Cold War*. Washington, D.C.: National Academy Press, 2000.

Strasburger, Victor C., and Edward Donnerstein. "Children, Adolescents, and the Media in the 21st Century." *Adolescent Medicine* 11 (2000): 51–68.

Strom, Margot Stern, and William S. Parsons. *Facing History and Ourselves: Holocaust and Human Behavior*. Watertown, Mass.: Intentional Educations, Inc., 1982.

Strum, Shirley C., Donald G. Lindburg, and David A. Hamburg, eds. *The New Physical Anthropology*. Upper Saddle River, N.J.: Prentice Hall, 1999.

Takanishi, Ruby, and David A. Hamburg. *Preparing Adolescents for the Twenty-First Century*. Cambridge: Cambridge University Press, 1997.

Taylor, Donald M., and Fathali Moghaddam. *Theories of Intergroup Relations: International Social Psychological Perspectives*. 2nd ed. Westport, Conn.: Praeger Publishers, 1994.

Tilly, Charles. "States and Nationalism in Europe since 1600." Paper presented at annual meeting of the Social Science History Association, October 1991.

Tutu, Desmond. *The Rainbow People of God: The Making of a Peaceful Revolution*. New York: Doubleday, 1994.

United Nations Educational, Scientific and Cultural Organization, Division for the Promotion of Quality Education. *Best Practices of Non-Violent Conflict Resolution In and Out of School.* Paris: UNESCO, 2002.

Ury, William. *Getting to Peace: Transforming Conflict at Home, at Work, and in the World.* New York: Viking Press, 1999.

Vasquez, John A., and Marie T. Henehan. *The Scientific Study of Peace and War.* New York: Lexington Books, 1992.

Wallach, John. *The Enemy Has a Face: The Seeds of Peace Experience.* Washington, D.C.: United States Institute of Peace Press, 2000.

Wallensteen, Peter. "The New Tribalism." *Dissent* (Spring 1992): 164–171.

———. *Understanding Conflict Resolution: War, Peace, and the Global System.* Thousand Oaks, Calif.: Sage, 2002.

Walzer, Michael. *Just and Unjust Wars: A Moral Argument with Historical Illustrations.* New York: Basic Books, 1977, Preface to 3rd ed., 2000.

Weil, Pierre. *The Art of Living in Peace: Guide to Education for a Culture of Peace.* Paris: United Nations Educational, Scientific and Cultural Organization, 2002.

Weitz, Eric D. *A Century of Genocide: Utopias of Race and Nation.* Princeton: Princeton University Press, 2003.

West, Michael A., Dean Tjosvold, and Ken G. Smith (eds.). *International Handbook of Organizational Teamwork and Cooperative Working.* Chichester, West Sussex; Hoboken, N.J.: Wiley, 2003.

Wiesel, Elie. *And the Sea Is Never Full: Memoirs, 1969–.* New York: Alfred A. Knopf, 1999.

———. *Night.* New York: Bantam Books, 1982.

Wiesel, Elie, and Richard D. Heffner. *Conversations with Elie Wiesel.* Ed. Thomas J. Vinciguerra. New York: Schocken Books, 2001.

Williams, Robin Murphy. *Mutual Accommodation: Ethnic Conflict and Cooperation.* Minneapolis: University of Minnesota Press, 1978.

Wilson, B. J., D. Kunkel, D. Linz, J. Potter, E. Donnerstein, S. L. Smith, E. Blumenthal, and T. Gray. "Violence in Television Programming Overall: University of California, Santa Barbara, Study." In *National Television Violence Study,* vol. 1, edited by M. Seawall, 3–184. Thousand Oaks, Calif.: Sage, 1997.

World Bank. *World Development Report 2003: Sustainable Development in a Dynamic World: Transforming Institutions, Growth, and Quality of Life.* New York: World Bank and Oxford University Press, 2002.

World Health Organization. *Education for Health.* Geneva: World Health Organization, 1988.

Zigler, Edward F., Matia Finn-Stevenson, and Nancy W. Hall. *The First Three Years and Beyond: Brain Development and Social Policy.* New Haven, Conn.: Yale University Press, 2003.

INDEX